Indian Philosophy
(Volume 1)

Tracing the development of Indian philosophy as a single tradition of thought, these two volumes provide a classical exposition of Indian thought. The author showcases ancient philosophical texts and relates them to contemporary issues of philosophy and religion. He presents the essential meaning and significance of individual texts and philosophies and also draws parallels between Indian and western philosophical traditions. The first volume covers the Vedic and Epic periods, including expositions on the hymns of the Rig-Veda, the Upanishads, Jainism, Buddhism, and the theism of the Bhagvadgita. The second investigates the six Brahmanical philosophical systems, the theism of Ramanuja, Saiva ethics, metaphysicas and literature, and the theism of the later Vaishnavas.

This second edition, with a new Introduction by eminent philosopher. J.N. Mohanty, underlines the continuing relevance of the two volumes and the philosophic tradition they represent. Lucidly written, these books will form essential reading for students, teachers, scholars of Indian philosophy as well as general reader interested in the development and growth of Indian thought.

—**J.N. Mohanty** retired as Professor, Department of Philosophy, Temple University, Philadelphia.

'With these two volumes, the whole of Indian thought was skillfully compressed, and distilled, making it possible for an occidental mind and psyche to comprehend and appreciate the convergence and divergence in Indian thought.... Radhakrishnan's broad sweep of Indian philosophy based on a concrete textual foundation provides a splendid over-view.'

—*The Indian Express*

'... [Radhakrishnan] deviates from orthodox position and gives a liberal interpretation ... the two volumes of Indian Philosophy have remained for decades as the standard text books on the subject.'

—*Dharmaprakash Journal*

S. Radhakrishnan (1888–1975)

Indian Philosophy

Second Edition

by

S. Radhakrishnan

VOLUME 1

with a new Introduction
by J.N. Mohanty

Namaskar Goro,

Hopefully you will learn some of this in this life itself.

Happy Birthday.

— Jaideep Prabhu.
Aug. 06, 2009.

OXFORD
UNIVERSITY PRESS

OXFORD
UNIVERSITY PRESS

YMCA Library Building, Jai Singh Road, New Delhi 110001

Oxford University Press is a department of the University of Oxford. It furthers the University's objective of excellence in research, scholarship, and education by publishing worldwide in

Oxford New York
Auckland Cape Town Dar es Salaam Hong Kong Karachi
Kuala Lumpur Madrid Melbourne Mexico City Nairobi
New Delhi Shanghai Taipei Toronto

With offices in
Argentina Austria Brazil Chile Czech Republic France Greece
Guatemala Hungary Italy Japan Poland Portugal Singapore
South Korea Switzerland Thailand Turkey Ukraine Vietnam

Published in India
by Oxford University Press, New Delhi

First published 1923

Revised edition 1929, Indian edition 1940
Published by George Allen & Unwin Ltd
This edition published in India 1989
By arrangement with the original publisher
Oxford India Paperbacks 1996
Second edition 2008
Second impression 2009

ISBN-13: 978-0-19-569841-1
ISBN-10: 0-19-569841-X

Typeset in Goudy 10/12.5
by Eleven Arts, Keshav Puram, Delhi 110 035
Printed by Pauls Press, New Delhi 110 020
Published by Oxford University Press
YMCA Library Building, Jai Singh Road, New Delhi 110 001

Contents

Preface to the Second Edition ix

Preface to the First Edition xi

Introduction by J.N. Mohanty xvii

List of Abbreviations xxi

CHAPTER I: Introduction 1

General characteristics of Indian philosophy—The natural situation of India—The dominance of the intellectual interest—The individuality of Indian philosophy—The influence of the West—The spiritual character of Indian thought—Its close relation to life and religion—The stress on the subjective—Psychological basis of metaphysics—Indian achievements in positive science—Speculative synthesis and scientific analysis—The brooding East—Monistic idealism—Its varieties, non-dualism, pure monism, modified monism and implicit monism—God is all—The intuitional nature of philosophy—Darśana—Śaṁkara's qualifications of a candidate for the study of philosophy—The constructive conservatism of Indian thought—The unity and continuity of Indian thought—Consideration of some charges levelled against Indian philosophy, such as pessimism, dogmatism, indifference to ethics and unprogressive character—The value of the study of Indian philosophy—The justification of the title 'Indian Philosophy'—Historical method—The difficulty of a chronological treatment—The different periods of Indian thought—Vedic, epic, systematic and scholastic—'Indian' histories of Indian philosophy.

PART I: THE VEDIC PERIOD

CHAPTER II: The Hymns of the Ṛg-Veda 39

The four Vedas—The parts of the Veda, the Mantras, the Brāhmaṇas, the Upaniṣads—The importance of the study of the hymns—Date and authorship—Different views of the teaching of the hymns—Their philosophical tendencies—Religion—'Deva'—Naturalism and anthropomorphism—Heaven and Earth—Varuṇa—Ṛta—Sūrya—Uṣas—Soma—Yama—Indra—Minor gods and goddesses—Classification of the Vedic deities—Monotheistic tendencies—The unity of nature—The unifying impulse of the logical mind—The implications of the religious consciousness—Henotheism—Viśvakarman, Bṛhaspati, Prajāpati and Hiraṇyagarbha—The rise of reflection and criticism—The philosophical inadequacy of monotheism—Monism—Philosophy and religion—The cosmological speculations of the Vedic hymns—The Nāsadīya Sūkta—The relation of the world to the Absolute—The Puruṣa Sūkta—Practical religion—Prayer—Sacrifice—The ethical rules—Karma—Asceticism—Caste—Future life—The two paths of the gods and the fathers—Hell—Rebirth—Conclusion.

CHAPTER VII: The Ethical Idealism of Early Buddhism   286

CHAPTER VIII: Epic Philosophy   403

Preface to the Second Edition

It is a pleasure to know that a new edition of this book is called for. It shows that, with all its defects, it has helped to rouse interest in Indian philosophy. I have not made many alterations in the text, but have added explanatory notes intended to clear difficulties, and an Appendix which deals with some of the controversial issues in the field of Indian thought raised by the first volume. My thanks are due to the Editor of *Mind* for his courtesy in permitting me to use in the Appendix the substance of an article which originally appeared in his pages (April 1926).

In preparing this edition, I have been considerably assisted by the suggestions of my friend Professor M. Hiriyanna of Mysore.

May 1929

Preface to the First Edition

Though the world has changed considerably in its outward material aspect, means of communication, scientific inventions, etc., there has not been any great change in its inner spiritual side. The old forces of hunger and love, and the simple joys and fears of the heart, belong to the permanent stuff of human nature. The true interests of humanity, the deep passions of religion, and the great problems of philosophy, have not been superseded as material things have been. Indian thought is a chapter of the history of the human mind, full of vital meaning for us. The ideas of great thinkers are never obsolete. They animate the progress that seems to kill them. The most ancient fancies sometimes startle us by their strikingly modern character, for insight does not depend on modernity.

Ignorance of the subject of Indian thought is profound. To the modern mind Indian philosophy means two or three 'silly' notions about *māyā* , or the delusiveness of the world, *karma*, or belief in fate, and *tyāga*, or the ascetic desire to be rid of the flesh. Even these simple notions, it is said, are wrapped up in barbarous nomenclature and chaotic clouds of vapour and verbiage, looked upon by the 'natives' as wonders of intellect. After a six-months' tour from Calcutta to Cape Comorin, our modern aesthete dismisses the whole of Indian culture and philosophy as 'pantheism,' 'worthless scholasticism,' 'a mere play upon words,' 'at all events nothing similar to Plato or Aristotle, or even Plotinus or Bacon.' The intelligent student interested in philosophy will, however, find in Indian thought an extraordinary mass of material which for detail and variety has hardly any equal in any other part of the world. There is hardly any height of spiritual insight or rational philosophy attained in the world that has not its parallel in the vast stretch that lies between the early Vedic seers and the modern Naiyāyikas. Ancient India, to adapt Professor Gilbert Murray's words in another context, 'has the triumphant, if tragic, distinction of beginning at the very bottom and struggling, however, precariously, to the very summits.'[1] The naive utterances of the Vedic poets, the wondrous suggestiveness of the Upaniṣads, the marvellous psychological analyses of the Buddhists, and the stupendous system of Śaṁkara, are quite as

1. *Four Stages of Greek Religion*, p. 15.

interesting and instructive from the cultural point of view as the systems of Plato and Aristotle, or Kant and Hegel, if only we study them in a true scientific frame of mind, without disrespect for the past or contempt for the alien. The special nomenclature of Indian philosophy which cannot be easily rendered into English accounts for the apparent strangeness of the intellectual landscape. If the outer difficulties are overcome, we feel the kindred throb of the human heart, which because human is neither Indian nor European. Even if Indian thought be not valuable from the cultural point of view, it is yet entitled to consideration, if on no other ground, at least by reason of its contrast to other thought systems and its great influence over the mental life of Asia.

In the absence of accurate chronology, it is a misnomer to call anything a history. Nowhere is the difficulty of getting reliable historical evidence so extreme as in the case of Indian thought. The problem of determining the exact dates of early Indian systems is as fascinating as it is insoluble, and it has furnished a field for the wildest hypotheses, wonderful reconstruction and bold romance. The fragmentary condition of the material from out of which history has to be reconstructed is another obstacle. In these circumstances I must hesitate to call this work a History of Indian Philosophy.

In interpreting the doctrines of particular systems, I have tried to keep in close touch with the documents, give wherever possible a preliminary survey of the conditions that brought them into being, and estimate their indebtedness to the past as well as their contribution to the progress of thought. I have emphasised the essentials so as to prevent the meaning of the whole from being obscured by details, and attempted to avoid starting from any theory. Yet I fear I shall be misunderstood. The task of the historian is hard, especially in philosophy. However much he may try to assume the attitude of a mere chronicler and let the history in some fashion unfold its own inner meaning and continuity, furnish its own criticism of errors and partial insights, still the judgments and sympathies of the writer cannot long be hidden. Besides, Indian philosophy offers another difficulty. We have the commentaries which, being older, come nearer in time to the work commented upon. The presumption is that they will be more enlightening about the meaning of the texts. But when the commentators differ about their interpretations, one cannot stand silently by without offering some judgment on the conflict of views. Such personal expressions of opinion, however dangerous, can hardly be avoided. Effective exposition means criticism and evaluation, and I do not think it is necessary to abstain from criticism in order that I may give a fair and impartial statement. I can only hope that the subject is treated in a calm and dispassionate way, and that whatever the defects of the book, no attempt is made to wrest facts to suit a preconceived opinion. My aim has been not so much to narrate Indian views as to explain them, so as to bring them within the focus of Western traditions of thought. The analogies and parallels suggested between the two thought systems are not to be pressed too far, in view of the obvious fact that the philosophical speculations of India were formulated centuries ago, and had not behind them the brilliant achievements of modern science.

Particular parts of Indian philosophy have been studied with great care and thoroughness by many brilliant scholars in India, Europe and America. Some sections of philosophical literature have also been critically examined, but there has been no attempt to deal with the history of Indian thought as an undivided whole or a continuous development, in the light of which alone different thinkers and views can be fully understood. To set forth the growth of Indian philosophy from the dim dawn of history in its true perspective is an undertaking of the most formidable kind, and it certainly exceeds the single grasp of even the most industrious and learned scholar. Such a standard encyclopaedia of Indian philosophy requires not only special aptitude and absolute devotion, but also wide culture and intelligent co-operation. This book professes to be no more than a general survey of Indian thought, a short outline of a vast subject. Even this is not quite easy. The necessary condensation imposes on the author a burden of responsibility, which is made more onerous by the fact that no one man can attempt to be an authority on all these varied fields of study, and that the writer is compelled to come to decisions on evidence which he himself cannot carefully weigh. In matters of chronology, I have depended almost entirely on the results of research carried on by competent scholars. I am conscious that in surveying this wide field, much of interest is left untouched, and still more only very roughly sketched in. This work has no pretensions to completeness in any sense of the term. It attempts to give such a general statement of the main results as shall serve to introduce the subject to those to whom it may not be known, and awaken if possible in some measure that interest for it to which it is so justly entitled. Even if it proves a failure, it may assist or at least encourage other attempts.

My original plan was to publish the two volumes together. Kind friends like Professor J.S. Mackenzie suggested to me the desirability of bringing out the first volume immediately. Since the preparation of the second volume would take some time and the first is complete in itself, I venture to publish it independently. A characteristic feature of many of the views discussed in this volume is that they are motived, not so much by the logical impulse to account for the riddles of existence, as by the practical need for a support in life. It has been difficult to avoid discussions of, what may appear to the reader, religious rather than philosophical issues, on account of the very close connection between religion and philosophy in early Indian speculation. The second volume, however, will be of a more purely philosophical character, since a predominantly theoretical interest gets the upper hand in the darśanas or systems of philosophy, though the intimate connexion between knowledge and life is not lost sight of.

It is a pleasure to acknowledge my obligations to the many eminent orientalists whose works have been of great help to me in my studies. It is not possible to mention all their names, which will be founding the course of the book. Mention must, however, be made of Max Müller, Deussen, Keith, Jacobi, Garbe, Tilak, Bhandarkar, Rhys Davids and Mrs. Rhys Davids, Oldenberg, Poussin, Suzuki and Sogen.

Several valuable works of recent publication, such as Professor Das Gupta's *History of Indian Philosophy* and Sir Charles Eliot's *Hinduism and Buddhism*, came to hand too late for use, after the manuscript had been completed and sent to the publishers in December 1921. The bibliography given at the end of each chapter is by no means exhaustive. It is intended mainly for the guidance of the English reader.

My thanks are due to Professor J.S. Mackenzie and Mr V. Subrahmanya Aiyar, who were good enough to read considerable parts of the manuscript and the proofs. The book has profited much by their friendly and suggestive counsel. I am much indebted to Professor A. Berriedale Keith for reading the proofs and making many valuable comments. My greatest obligation, however, is to the Editor of the Library of Philosophy, Professor J.H. Muirhead, for his invaluable and most generous help in the preparation of the book for the press and previously. He undertook the laborious task of reading the book in the manuscript, and his suggestions and criticisms have been of the greatest assistance to me. I am also obliged to Sir Asutosh Mookerjee, Kt., C.S.I., for his constant encouragement and the facilities provided for higher work in the Post-Graduate Department of the Calcutta University.

November 1922

Introduction

Sarvepalli Radhakrishnan's *Indian Philosophy,* first published in 1921–3 is a classic which has inspired generations of scholars and intelligentsia alike, in and outside India, to know the vast treasures of Indian philosophical thought. Based on Sanskrit sources and written elegantly, using the diction of his contemporary philosophical style, the two volume work has continued to educate and inform generations of philosophers in India. It is with great enthusiasm and pleasure that I welcome this new edition.

The publication of volume one of *Indian Philosophy* in 1921, in the Muirhead Library of Philosophy series, shot the young scholar to international fame. The same year Sir Asutosh Mukherjee appointed him to the prized King George V Professorship in Philosophy at the University of Calcutta. The Department of Philosophy in Calcutta had such stalwarts as Hiralal Haldar, K.C. Bhattacharya, and S.N. Dasgupta. It created a stir that a young and relatively unknown scholar from the south was placed above them. But soon this young man proved his worth and endeared himself to all by his gentle and courteous manner. A series of publications followed, also invitations to famous lectureships abroad, all crowned by appointment concurrently with his position in Calcutta, to the Spalding Professorship in Eastern Religion and Ethics of at the University of Oxford.

Indian Philosophy followed the footsteps of Mādhava Āchārya's *Sarvadarśanasaṁgraha.* Expositions of the 'six systems' were followed by a chapter in Śaiva, Śākta, and later Vaiṣṇava theistic schools, capped by a brilliantly written concluding chapter. Three chapters were devoted to the Vedānta: one on the Vedāntasūtras, and two others on Advaita Vedānta of Śaṁkara and the theism of Ramanuja respectively. Clearly the author's own preference was the Advaita of Śaṁkara. The entire exposition of the systems was geared towards it as the immanent telos operating through them. As in the case of Mādhava Āchārya's doxography, they all, that is, all the other systems, pointed towards their culmination in Advaita Vedānta.

In order to appreciate Radhakrishnan's interpretive point of view, it is important to bear in mind the general intellectual and spiritual climate in India. 1921, the year of publication of the *Indian Philosophy,* was also the year when Mahatma Gandhi launched his first movement of non-cooperation against the British rule. A few years earlier, Rabindranath

Tagore had won the Nobel Prize for literature. Radhakrishnan had already written a monograph on the philosophy of the Upaniṣads to which Tagore wrote the foreword. *Indian Philosophy* was nurtured by both the rising self-consciousness on the part of India, as well as contributed to it. Besides being an academic philosopher, Radhakrishnan was drawn into the public philosophical discourse in which he excelled. His writings and speeches inspired the intelligentsia of the country.

Philosophically, the dominant ideas during Radhakrishnan's philosophical training in Madras, flowing from the British universities into India, were Hegelian in origin. Hegelianism of various brands obtained in Oxford, and then in Calcutta. An idealistic monism, for which Reality is one and spiritual, manifesting itself in and through the world and history, prevailed. Radhakrishnan was impressed by the close affinity between Hegelian monism and the Advaita, but he was painfully aware of Hegel's misinformed critique of Indian thought as being a product of 'abstract understanding'. Amongst British neo-Hegelians, F.H. Bradley impressed him most and he saw in Bradley's *Appearance and Reality* a close approximation, leaving out Plato and Hegel to Advaita, while he did not fail to note their differences. The University of Calcutta, already full of such neo-Hegelianism (the already mentioned Hiralal Haldar was the author of the first exposition and critique of neo-Hegelianism), was a fertile ground, already ready for Radhakrishnan's ideas.

In this climate, Radhakrishnan's interpretation of Indian thought was characterized by several underlying beliefs. First, he believed in the development of philosophy, in India, following a logical sequence, never at rest, but always on the move. So even in the twentieth century, after thousands of years of movement, it is still not complete, there is room for further development. The beauty of philosophy is in the process. In this, he opposes the conservatives, who look upon the *darśanas* as providing complete systems, each by itself and in totality as well, to which nothing can be added and from which nothing can be taken out. But Radhakrishnan also opposes the liberalism which looks upon the ancient modes of thinking as errors, to be replaced by ideas from the West. His great admiration for the Indian tradition is matched by his recognition that Indian philosophy has to learn from, and profit by, lessons from the West. Furthermore, the history of philosophy in India has been a story not only of progress but also of decline. The most important thing is the future. We need to build upon the achievements of our ancestors.

Perhaps, the most characteristic feature of Radhakrishnan's interpretation is the emphasis on the movement of thought from logical reasoning to spiritual intuition. Logical reasoning marks the progress from consciousness to self-consciousness, but self-consciousness is to be transcended by intuition which he sometimes calls super-consciousness. The contrast between reason and intuition pervades all his writings, and has influenced generations of philosophers in India, but has also been a point for criticism by the younger hard-headed thinkers. There is no doubt that here too he was influenced by Hegel whose *Phenomenology of Spirit* (1807) takes us through the stages, in the development of spirit, of 'consciousness', 'self-consciousness', 'Reason', and 'Spirit'. Thus in Radhakrishnan's view, philosophy has to leave us at a point where religion based, not on fact but on religious experience, takes over. The idea of this higher 'experience' was popularized by him. Modern, rather post-modern, critics have wondered if this is truly Indian, based on Sanskrit sources.

Radhakrishnan is a supreme example of Indian *modernity*. In the age of post-modernism, his thinking has come under attack by the analytic philosophers, by grammarians by Navya Naiyāyikas as well as by a lot of other post-modern thinkers. But none of these critics have risen to that height of nobility and grandeur in writing and in speech which he achieved, which influenced and inspired generations of his countrymen and which in this 'self-contradictory' age of globalization and fragmentation, we may need to revisit.

J.N. Mohanty

Abbreviations

A.V.	Atharva-Veda
B.G.	Bhagavadgītā
E.R.E.	Encyclopaedia of Religion and Ethics
I.A.	Indian Antiquary
J.A.O.S.	Journal of the American Oriental Society
J.R.A.S.	Journal of the Royal Asiatic Society
Milinda	Questions of King Milinda
N.S.	Nyāya Sūtras
O.S.T.	Original Sanskrit Texts
P.	Pañcāstikāyasamayasāra
P.M.	Pūrva-Mīmāṁsā Sūtras
R.B.	Rāmānuja's Bhāṣya on the Vedānta Sūtras
R.B.G.	Rāmānuja's Bhāṣya on the Bhagavadgītā
R.V.	Ṛg-Veda
S.B.	Śaṁkara's Bhāṣya on the Vedānta Sūtras
S.B.E.	Sacred Books of the East
S.B.G.	Śaṁkara's Bhāṣya on the Bhagavadgītā
S.B.H.	Sacred Books of the Hindus
S.D.S.	Sarvadarśanasaṁgraha
S.K.	Śāṁkhya Kārikā
Skt.	Sanskrit
S.S.	Six Systems of Indian Philosophy by Max Müller
S. Sūtras	Sāṁkhya Sūtras
S.S.S.S.	Sarvasiddhāntasārasaṁgraha
Up.	Upaniṣads
U.T.S.	Umāsvāti's Tattvārtha Sūtras
V.S.	Vedānta Sūtras
W.B.T.	Warren: Buddhism in Translations
Y.S.	Yoga Sūtras

CHAPTER I

Introduction

■ General characteristics of Indian philosophy—The natural situation of India—The dominance of the intellectual interest—The individuality of Indian philosophy—The influence of the West—The spiritual character of Indian thought—Its close relation to life and religion—The stress on the subjective—Psychological basis of metaphysics—Indian achievements in positive science—Speculative synthesis and scientific analysis—the brooding East—Monistic idealism—Its varieties, non-dualism, pure monism, modified monism and implicit monism—God is all—The intuitional nature of philosophy—Darśana—Śaṁkara's qualifications of a candidate for the study of philosophy—The constructive conservatism of Indian thought—The unity and continuity of Indian thought—Consideration of some charges levelled against Indian philosophy, such as pessimism, dogmatism, indifference to ethics and unprogressive character—The value of the study of Indian philosophy—The justification of the title 'Indian Philosophy'—Historical method—The difficulty of a chronological treatment—The different periods of Indian thought—Vedic, epic, systematic and scholastic—'Indian' histories of Indian philosophy. ■

I

THE NATURAL SITUATION OF INDIA

For thinking minds to blossom, for arts and sciences to flourish, the first condition necessary is a settled society providing security and leisure. A rich culture is impossible with a community of nomads, where people struggle for life and die of privation. Fate called India to a spot where nature was free with her gifts and every prospect was pleasing. The Himalayas, with their immense range and elevation on one side and the sea on the others, helped to keep India free from invasion for a long time. Bounteous nature yielded abundant food, and man was relieved of the toil and struggle for existence. The Indian never felt that the world was a field of battle where men struggled for power, wealth and domination. When we do not need to waste our energies on problems of life on earth, exploiting nature and controlling the forces of the world, we begin to think of the higher life, how to live more perfectly in the spirit. Perhaps an enervating climate inclined the Indian to rest and retirement. The huge forests with their wide leafy avenues afforded great opportunities for the devout soul to wander peacefully through them, dream strange dreams and burst forth into joyous songs. World-weary men go out on pilgrimages to these scenes of nature, acquire inward peace, listening to the rush of winds and torrents, the music of birds and leaves, and return whole of heart and fresh in spirit. It was in the āśramas and tapovanas or forest hermitages that the thinking men of India meditated on the deeper problems of existence. The security of life, the wealth of natural resources, the freedom from worry, the detachment from the cares of existence, and the absence of a tyrannous practical interest, stimulated the higher life of India, with the result that we find from the beginnings of history an impatience of spirit, a love of wisdom and a passion for the saner pursuits of the mind.

Helped by natural conditions, and provided with the intellectual scope to think out the implications of things, the Indian escaped the doom which Plato pronounced to be the worst of all, viz. the hatred of reason. 'Let us above all things take heed,' says he in the *Phoedo*, 'that one misfortune does not befall us. Let us not become misologues as some people become misanthropes; for no greater evil can befall men than to become haters of reason.' The pleasure of understanding is one of the purest available to man, and the passion of the Indian for it burns in the bright flame of the mind.

In many other countries of the world, reflection on the nature of existence is a luxury of life. The serious moments are given to action, while the pursuit of philosophy comes up as a parenthesis. In ancient India philosophy was not an auxiliary to any other science or art, but always held a prominent position of independence. In the West, even in the heyday of its youth, as in the times of Plato and Aristotle, it leaned for support on some other study, as politics or ethics. It was theology for the Middle Ages, natural science for Bacon and Newton, history, politics and sociology for the nineteenth-century thinkers. In India philosophy stood on its own legs, and all other studies looked to it for inspiration and support. It is the master science guiding other sciences, without which they tend to become empty and foolish. The Muṇḍaka Upaniṣad speaks of *Brahma-vidyā* or the science of the eternal as the basis of all sciences, *sarva-vidyā-pratiṣṭhā*. 'Philosophy,' says Kauṭilya, 'is the lamp of all the sciences, the means of performing all the works, and the support of all the duties.'[1]

Since philosophy is a human effort to comprehend the problem of the universe, it is subject to the influences of race and culture. Each nation has its own characteristic mentality, its particular intellectual bent. In all the fleeting centuries of history, in all the vicissitudes through which India has passed, a certain marked identity is visible. It has held fast to certain psychological traits which constitute its special heritage, and they will be the characteristic marks of the Indian people so long as they are privileged to have a separate existence. Individuality means independence of growth. It is not necessarily unlikeness. There cannot be complete unlikeness, since man the world over is the same, especially so far as the aspects of spirit are concerned. The variations are traceable to distinctions in age, history and temperament. They add to the wealth of the world culture, since there is no royal road to philosophic development any more than to any other result worth having. Before we notice the characteristic features of Indian thought, a few words may be said about the influence of the West on Indian thought.

The question is frequently raised whether and to what extent Indian thought borrowed its ideas from foreign sources, such as Greece. Some of the views put forward by Indian thinkers resemble certain doctrines developed in ancient Greece, so much that anybody interested in discrediting this or that thought system can easily do so.[2] The question of the affiliation of ideas is a useless pursuit. To an unbiased mind, the coincidences will be an evidence of historical parallelism. Similar experiences engender in men's minds similar views. There is no material

1. See I.A., 1918, p. 102. See also B.G., x. 32.

2. Sir William Jones wrote: 'Of the philosophical schools, it will be sufficient here to remark that the first Nyāya seems analogous to the Peripatetic; the second, sometimes called Vaiśeṣika, to the Ionic; the two Mīmāṁsās, of which the second is often distinguished by the name of Vedānta, to the Platonic; the first Sāṁkhya to the Italic; and the second of Patañjali to the Stoic philosophy; so that Gautama corresponds with Aristotle, Kaṇāda with Thales, Jaimini with Socrates, Vyāsa with Plato, Kapila with Pythagoras, and Patañjali with Zeno' (*Works*, i, 360–1. See also Colebrooke, *Miscellaneous Essays*, i. 436 ff.) While the opinion that Greek thought has been influenced by the Indian is frequently held, it is not so often urged that Indian thought owes much to Greek speculation. (See Garbe, *Philosophy of Ancient India*, chap. ii.)

evidence to prove any direct borrowings, at any rate by India, from the West. Our account of Indian thought will show that it is an independent venture of the human mind. Philosophical problems are discussed without any influence from or relation to the West. In spite of occasional intercourse with the West, India had the freedom to develop its own ideal life, philosophy and religion. Whatever be the truth about the original home of the Aryans who came down to the Peninsula, they soon lost touch with their kindred in the West or the North, and developed on lines of their own. It is true that India was again and again invaded by armies pouring into it through the North-Western passes, but none of them, with the exception of Alexander's, did anything to promote spiritual intercourse between the two worlds. Only latterly, when the gateway of the seas was opened, a more intimate intercourse has been fostered, the results of which we cannot forecast, since they are yet in the making. For all practical purposes, then, we may look upon Indian thought as a closed system or an autonomous growth.

II

GENERAL CHARACTERISTICS OF INDIAN THOUGHT

Philosophy in India is essentially spiritual. It is the intense spirituality of India, and not any great political structure or social organisation that it has developed, that has enabled it to resist the ravages of time and the accidents of history. External invasions and internal dissensions came very near crushing its civilisation many times in its history. The Greek and the Scythian, the Persian and the Mogul, the French and the English have by turn attempted to suppress it, and yet it has its head held high. India has not been finally subdued, and its old flame of spirit is still burning. Throughout its life it has been living with one purpose. It has fought for truth and against error. It may have blundered, but it did what it felt able and called upon to do. The history of Indian thought illustrates the endless quest of the mind, ever old, ever new.

The spiritual motive dominates life in India. Indian philosophy has its interest in the haunts of men, and not in supra-lunar solitudes. It takes its origin in life, and enters back into life after passing through the schools. The great works of Indian philosophy do not have that *ex cahtedra* character which is so prominent a feature of the latter criticisms and commentaries. The Gītā and the Upaniṣads are not remote from popular belief. They are the great literature of the country, and at the same time vehicles of the great systems of thought. The Purāṇas contain the truth dressed up in myths and stories, to suit the weak understanding of the majority. The hard task of interesting the multitude in metaphysics is achieved in India.

The founders of philosophy strive for a socio-spiritual reformation of the country. When the Indian civilisation is called a Brāhmanical one, it only means that its main character and dominating motives are shaped by its philosophical thinkers and religious minds, though these are not all of Brāhman birth. The idea of Plato that philosophers must be the rulers and directors of society is practised in India. The ultimate truths are truths of spirit, and in the light of them actual life has to be refined.

Religion in India is not dogmatic. It is a rational synthesis which goes on gathering into itself new conceptions as philosophy progresses. It is experimental and provisional in its nature, attempting to keep pace with the progress of thought. The common criticism that Indian thought, by its emphasis on intellect, puts philosophy in the place of religion, brings out the rational character of religion in India. No religious movement has ever come into existence without developing as its support a philosophic content. Mr Havell observes: 'In India, religion is hardly a dogma, but a working hypothesis of human conduct, adapted to different stages of spiritual development and different conditions of life.'[3] Whenever it tended to crystallise itself in a fixed creed, there were set up spiritual revivals and philosophic reactions which threw beliefs into the crucible of criticism, vindicated the true and combated the false. Again and again, we shall observe, how when traditionally accepted beliefs become inadequate, nay false, on account of changed times, and the age grows out of patience with them, the insight of a new teacher, a Buddha or a Mahāvīra, a Vyāsa or a Śaṁkara supervenes, stirring the depths of spiritual life. These are doubtless great moments in the history of Indian thought, times of inward testing and vision, when at the summons of the spirit's breath, blowing where it listeth and coming whence no one knows, the soul of man makes a fresh start and goes forth on a new venture. It is the intimate relation between the truth of philosophy and the daily life of people that makes religion always alive and real.

3. *Aryan Rule in India,* p. 170. See the article on *The Heart of Hinduism: Hibbert Journal*, October, 1922.

The problems of religion stimulate the philosophic spirit. The Indian mind has been traditionally exercised over the questions of the nature of Godhead, the end of life and the relation of the individual to the universal soul. Though philosophy in India has not as a rule completely freed itself from the fascinations of religious speculation, yet the philosophical discussions have not been hampered by religious forms. The two were not confused. On account of the close connection between theory and practice, doctrine and life, a philosophy which could not stand the test of life, not in the pragmatistic but the larger sense of the term, had no chance of survival. To those who realise the true kinship between life and theory, philosophy becomes a way of life, an approach to spiritual realisation. There has been no teaching, not even the Sāṁkhya, which remained a mere word of mouth or dogma of schools. Every doctrine is turned into a passionate conviction, stirring the heart of man and quickening his breath.

It is untrue to say that philosophy in India never became self-conscious or critical. Even in its early stages rational reflection tended to correct religious belief. Witness the advance of religion implied in the progress from the hymns of the Veda to the Upaniṣads. When we come to Buddhism, the philosophic spirit has already become that confident attitude of mind which in intellectual matters bends to no outside authority and recognises no limit to its enterprise, unless it be as the result of logic, which probes all things, tests all things, and follows fearlessly wherever the argument leads. When we reach the several darśanas or systems of thought, we have mighty and persistent efforts at systematic thinking. How completely free from traditional religion and bias the systems are will be obvious from the fact that the Sāṁkhya is silent about the existence of God, though certain about its theoretical indemonstrability. Vaiśeṣika and Yoga, while they admit a supreme being, do not consider him to be the creator of the universe, and Jaimini refers to God only to deny his providence and moral government of the world. The early Buddhist systems are known to be indifferent to God, and we have also the materialist Cārvākas, who deny God, ridicule the priests, revile the Vedas and seek salvation in pleasure.

The supremacy of religion and of social tradition in life does not hamper the free pursuit of philosophy. It is a strange paradox, and yet noting more than the obvious truth that while the social life of an individual is bound by the rigours of caste, he is free to roam in the matter of opinion. Reason freely questions and criticises the creeds in which men are born. That is why the heretic, the sceptic, the unbeliever, the rationalist and the freethinker, the materialist and the hedonist all flourish in the soil of India. The Mahābhārata says: 'There is no *muni* who has not an opinion of his own.'

All this is evidence of the strong intellectuality of the Indian mind which seeks to know the inner truth and the law of all sides of human activity. This intellectual impulse is not confined to philosophy and theology, but extends over logic and grammar, rhetoric and language, medicine and astronomy, in fact all arts and sciences, from architecture to zoology. Everything useful to life or interesting to mind becomes an object of inquiry and criticism. It will give an idea of the all comprehensive character of intellectual life, to know that even such minutiae as the breeding of horses and the training of elephants had their own śāstras and literature.

The philosophic attempt to determine the nature of reality may start either with the thinking self or the objects of thought. In India the interest of philosophy is in the self of man. Where the vision is turned outward, the rush of fleeting events engages the mind. In India 'Ātmānam viddhi,' know the self, sums up the law and the prophets. Within man is the spirit that is the centre of everything. Psychology and ethics are the basal sciences. The life of mind is depicted in all its mobile variety and subtle play of light and shade. Indian psychology realised the value of concentration and looked upon it as the means for the perception of the truth. It believed that there were no ranges of life or mind which could not be reached by a methodical training of will and knowledge. It recognised the close connexion of mind and body. The psychic experiences, such as telepathy and clairvoyance, were considered to be neither abnormal nor miraculous. They are not the products of diseased minds or inspiration from the gods, but powers which the human mind can exhibit under carefully ascertained conditions. The mind of man has the three aspects of the subconscious, the conscious and the superconscious, and the 'abnormal' psychic phenomena, called by the different names of ecstasy, genius, inspiration, madness, are the workings of the superconscious mind. The Yoga system of philosophy deals specially with these experiences, though the other systems refers to them and utilise them for their purposes.

The metaphysical schemes are based on the data of the psychological science. The criticism that Western metaphysics is one-sided, since its attention is confined to the waking state alone, is not without its force. There are other states of consciousness as much entitled to consideration as the waking. Indian thought takes into account the modes of waking, dreaming and dreamless sleep. If we look upon the waking consciousness as the whole, then we get realistic, dualistic and pluralistic conceptions of metaphysics. Dream consciousness when exclusively studied leads us to subjectivist doctrines. The state of dreamless sleep inclines us to abstract and mystical theories. The whole truth must take all the modes of consciousness into account.

The dominance of interest in the subjective does not mean that in objective sciences India had nothing to say. If we refer to the actual achievements of India in the realm of positive science, we shall see that the opposite is the case. Ancient Indians laid the foundations of mathematical and mechanical knowledge. They measured the land, divided the year, mapped out the heavens, traced the course of the sun and the planets through the zodiacal belt, analysed the constitution of matter, and studied the nature of birds and beasts, plants and seeds.[4] 'Whatever conclusions we may arrive at as to the original source of the first astronomical ideas current in the world, it is probable that to the Hindus is due the invention of algebra and its application to astronomy and geometry. From them also the Arabs received not only their first conceptions of algebraic analysis, but also those invaluable numerical symbols and decimal notation now current everywhere in Europe, which have rendered untold service to the progress of arithmetical science.'[5] 'The motions of the moon and the sun were carefully observed by the Hindus, and with such success that their determination of the moon's synodical revolution is a much more correct one than the Greeks ever achieved. They had a division of the ecliptic into twenty-seven and twenty-eight parts, suggested evidently by the moon's period in days and seemingly their own. They were particularly conversant with the most splendid of the primary planets; the period of Jupiter being introduced by them, in conjunction with those of the sun and the moon into the regulation of

4. We may quote a passage which is certainly not less than 2,000 years before the birth of Copernicus, from the Aitareya Brāhmaṇa: 'The sun never sets nor rises. When people think to themselves the sun is setting, he only changes about after reaching the end of the day, and makes night below and day to what is on the other side. Then when people think he rises in the morning, he only shifts himself about after reaching the end of the night, and makes day below and night to what is on the other side. In fact he never does set at all.' Haug's Edition, iii. 44; Chān. Up., iii. 11. 1–3. Even if this be folklore, it is interesting.

5. Monier Williams, *Indian Wisdom*, p. 184.

their calendar in the form of the cycle of sixty years, common to them and the Chaldeans.'[6] It is now admitted that the Hindus at a very early time conceived and developed the two sciences of logic and grammar.[7] Wilson writes: 'In medicine, as in astronomy and metaphysics, the Hindus once kept pace with the most enlightened nations of the world; and they attained as thorough a proficiency in medicine and surgery as any people whose acquisitions are recorded, and as indeed was practicable, before anatomy was made known to us by the discoveries of modern inquirers.'[8] It is true that they did not invent any great mechanical appliances. For this a kind Heaven, which gave them the great water-courses and abundant supplies of food, is responsible. Let us also remember that these mechanical inventions belong, after all, to the sixteenth century and after, by which time India had lost her independence and become parasitic. The day she lost her freedom and began to flirt with other nations, a curse fell on her and she became petrified. Till then she could hold her own even in arts, crafts and industries, not to speak of mathematics, astronomy, chemistry, medicine, surgery, and those branches of physical knowledge practised in ancient times. She knew how to chisel stone, draw pictures, burnish gold and weave rich fabrics. She developed all arts, fine and industrial, which furnish the conditions of civilised existence. Her ships crossed the oceans and her wealth brimmed over to Judaea, Egypt and Rome. Her conceptions of man and society, morals and religion were remarkable for the time. We cannot reasonably say that the Indian people revelled in poetry and mythology, and spurned science and philosophy, though it is true that they were more intent on seeking the unity of things than emphasising their sharpness and separation.

The speculative mind is more synthetic, while the scientific one is more analytic, if such a distinction be permitted. The former tends to create cosmic philosophies which embrace in one comprehensive vision the origin of all things, the history of ages and the dissolution and decay of the world. The latter is inclined to linger over the dull particulars of the world and miss the sense of oneness and wholeness. Indian thought attempts vast, impersonal views of existence, and makes it easy for the critic to bring the charge of being more idealistic and contemplative,

6. Colebrooke's translation of *Bhaskara's Work of Algebra*, p. xxii.
7. See Max Müller's *Sanskrit Literature*.
8. *Works*, vol. iii. p. 269.

producing dreamy visionaries and strangers in the world, while Western thought is more particularist and pragmatistic. The latter depends on what we call the senses, the former presses the soul sense into the service of speculation. Once again it is the natural conditions of India that account for the contemplative turn of the Indian who had the leisure to enjoy the beautiful things of the world and express his wealth of soul in song and story, music and dance, rites and religions, undisturbed by the passions of the outer world. 'The brooding East,' frequently employed as a term of ridicule, is not altogether without its truth.

It is the synthetic vision of India that has made philosophy comprehend several sciences which have become differentiated in modern times. In the West during the last hundred years or so several branches of knowledge till then included under philosophy, economics, politics, morals, psychology, education have been one by one sheared away from it. Philosophy in the time of Plato meant all those sciences which are bound up with human nature and form other core of man's speculative interests. In the same way in ancient Indian scriptures we possess the full content of the philosophic sphere. Latterly in the West philosophy became synonymous with metaphysics, or the abstruse discussions of knowledge, being and value, and the complaint is heard that metaphysics has become absolutely theoretical, being cut off from the imaginative and the practical sides of human nature.

If we put the subjective interest of the Indian mind along with its tendency to arrive at a synthetic vision, we shall see how monistic idealism becomes the truth of things. To it the whole growth of Vedic thought points; on it are based the Buddhistic and the Brāhmanical religions; it is the highest truth revealed to India. Even systems which announce themselves as dualistic or pluralistic seem to be permeated by a strong monistic character. If we can abstract from the variety of opinion and observe the general spirit of Indian thought, we shall find that it has a disposition to interpret life and nature in the way of monistic idealism, though this tendency is so plastic, living and manifold that it takes many forms and expresses itself in even mutually hostile teachings. We may briefly indicate the main forms which monistic idealism has assumed in Indian thought, leaving aside detailed developments and critical estimates. This will enable us to grasp the nature and function of philosophy as understood in India. For our purposes monistic idealism is of four types:

(1) Non-dualism or Advaitism; (2) Pure monism; (3) Modified monism; and (4) Implicit monism.

Philosophy proceeds on the facts of experience. Logical reflection is necessary to ascertain whether the facts observed by one individual are accepted by all, or are only subjective in their character. Theories are accepted if they account for facts satisfactorily. We have already said that the facts of mind or consciousness were studied by the Indian thinkers with as much care and attention as the facts of the outer world are studied by our modern scientists. The philosophical conclusions of Advaitic monism are based on the data of psychological observation.

The activities of the self are assigned to the three states of waking, dreaming and dreamless sleep. In dream states an actual concrete world is presented to us. We do not call that world real, since on waking we find that the dream world does not fit in with the waking world; yet relatively to the dream state the dream world is real. It is discrepancy from our conventional standards of waking life, and not any absolute knowledge of truth as subsisting by itself, that tells us that dream states are less real than the waking ones. Even waking reality is a relative one. It has no permanent existence, being only a correlate of the waking state. It disappears in dream and sleep. The waking consciousness and the world disclosed to it are related to each other, depend on each other as the dream consciousness and the dream-world are. They are not absolutely real, for in the words of Śaṁkara, while the 'dream-world is daily sublated, the waking world is sublated under exceptional circumstances.' In dreamless sleep we have a cessation of the empirical consciousness. Some Indian thinkers are of opinion that we have in this condition an objectless consciousness. At any rate this is clear, that dreamless sleep is not a complete non-being or negation for such a hypothesis conflicts with the later recollection of the happy repose of sleep. We cannot help conceding that the self continues to exist, though it is bereft of all experience. There is no object felt and there can be none so long as the sleep is sound. The pure self seems to be unaffected by the flotsam and jetsam of ideas which rise and vanish with particular moods. 'What varies not, nor changes in the midst of things that vary and change is different from them.'[9] The self which persists unchanged and is one throughout all the changes is different from them

9. 'Yeṣu vyāvartamāneṣu yad anuvartate tat tebhyo bhinnam' (Bhāmatī).

all. The conditions change, not the self. 'In all the endless months, years and small and great cycles, past and to come, this self-luminous consciousness alone neither rises nor ever sets.'[10] An unconditioned reality where time and space along with all their objects vanish is felt to be real. It is the self which is the unaffected spectator of the whole drama of ideas related to the changing moods of waking, dreaming and sleeping. We are convinced that there is something in us beyond joy and misery, virtue and vice, good and bad. The self 'never dies, is never born—unborn, eternal, everlasting, this ancient one can never be destroyed with the destruction of the body. If the slayer thinks he can slay, or if the slain thinks he is slain, they both do not know the truth, for the self neither slays nor is slain.'[11]

In addition to the ever-identical self, we have also the empirical variety of objects. The former is permanent, immutable, the latter impermanent and ever changing. The former is absolute, being independent of all objects, the latter changes with the moods.

How are we to account for the world? The empirical variety is there bound in space, time and cause. If the self is the one, the universal, the immutable, we find in the world a mass of particulars with opposed characters. We can only call it the not-self, the object of a subject. In no case is it real. The principal categories of the world of experience, time, space and cause are self-contradictory. They are relative terms depending on their constituents. They have no real existence. Yet they are not non-existent. The world is there, and we work in it and through it. We do not and cannot know the why of this world. It is this fact of its inexplicable existence that is signified by the word *māyā*. To ask what is the relation between the absolute self and the empirical flux, to ask why and how it happens, that there are two, is to assume that everything has a why and a how. To say that the infinite becomes the finite or manifests itself as finite is on this view utter nonsense. The limited cannot express or manifest the unlimited. The moment the unlimited manifests itself in the limited, it itself becomes limited. To say that the absolute degenerates or lapses into the empirical is to contradict its absoluteness. No lapse can come to a perfect being. No darkness can dwell in perfect light. We cannot admit that the supreme, which is changeless, becomes limited by changing. To change is to desire or to feel a want, and it shows lack of perfection. The

10. Pañcadaśī, i. 7.
11. Kaṭha Up., ii. 18–19, B.G., ii. 19–20.

absolute can never become an object of knowledge, for what is known is finite and relative. Our limited mind cannot go beyond the bounds of time, space and cause, nor can we explain these, since every attempt to explain them assumes them. Through thought, which is itself a part of the relative world, we cannot know the absolute self. Our relative experience is a waking dream. Science and logic are parts of it and products of it too. This failure of metaphysics is neither to be wept over nor to be laughed over, neither to be praised nor blamed, but understood. With a touching humility born of intellectual strength, a Plato or a Nāgārjuna, a Kant or a Śaṁkara, declares that our thought deals with the relative, and has nothing to do with the absolute.

Though the absolute being is not known in the logical way, it is yet realised by all who strain to know the truth, as the reality in which we live, move and have our being. Only through it can anything else be known. It is the eternal witness of all knowledge. The non-dualist contends that his theory is based on the logic of facts. The self is the inmost and deepest reality, felt by all, since it is the self of all things known and unknown too, and there is no knower to know it except itself. It is the true and the eternal, and there is nought beside it. As for the empirical ramifications which also exist, the non-dualist says, well, they are there, and there is an end of it. We do not know and cannot know why. It is all a contradiction, and yet is actual. Such is the philosophical position of Advaita or non-dualism taken up by Gauḍapāda and Śaṁkara.

There are Advaitins who are dissatisfied with this view, and feel that it is no good covering up our confusion by the use of the word māyā. They attempt to give a more positive account of the relation between the perfect being absolutely devoid of any negativity, the immutable real, felt in the depths of experience and the world of change and becoming. To preserve the perfection of the one reality we are obliged to say that the world of becoming is not due to an addition of any element from outside, since there is nothing outside. It can only be by a diminution. Something negative like Plato's non-being or Aristotle's matter is assumed to account for change. Through the exercise of this negative principle, the immutable seems to be spread out in the moving many. Rays stream out of the sun which nevertheless did not contain them. Māyā is the name of the negative principle which lets loose the universal becoming, thereby creating endless agitation and perpetual disquiet. The flux of the universe is brought about by the apparent degradation of the immutable. The real represents all that is positive in becoming. The things of the world ever struggle to recover their reality, to fill up what is lacking in them, to shake off their individuality and separateness, but are prevented from doing so by their inner void, the negative māyā constituted by the interval between what they are and what they ought to be. If we get rid of māyā, suppress the tendency to duality, abolish the interval, fill up the deficit, and allow the disturbance to relax, space, time and change reach back into pure being. As long as the original insufficiency of māyā prevails, things are condemned to be existent in space—time cause world. Māyā is not a human construction. It is prior to our intellect and independent of it. It is verily the generator of things and intellects, the immense potentiality of the whole world. It is sometimes called the prakṛti. The alternations of generation and decay, the ever-repeated cosmic evolutions, all represent this fundamental deficit in which the world consists. The world of becoming is the interruption of being. Māyā is the reflection of reality. The world-process is not so much a translation of immutable being as its inversion. Yet the world of māyā cannot exist apart from pure being. There can be no movement, if there were not immutability, since movement is only a degradation of the immutable. The truth of the universal mobility is the immobile being.

As becoming is a lapse from being, so is avidyā or ignorance a fall from vidyā or knowledge. To know the truth, to apprehend reality, we have to get rid of avidyā and its intellectual moulds, which all crack the moment we try to force reality into them. This is no excuse for indolence of thought. Philosophy as logic on this view persuades us to give up the employment of the intellectual concepts which are relative to our practical needs and the world of becoming. Philosophy tells us that, so long as we are bound by intellect and are lost in the world of many, we shall seek in vain to get back to the simplicity of the one. If we ask the reason why there is avidyā, or māyā, bringing about a fall from vidyā or from being, the question cannot be answered. Philosophy as logic has here the negative function of exposing the inadequacy of all intellectual categories, pointing out how the objects of the world are relative to the mind that thinks them and possess no independent existence. It cannot tell us anything definite about either the immutable said to exist apart from what is happening in the world, or about māyā, credited with the production of the world. It cannot help us directly to the attainment of reality. It, on the other hand, tells us that to measure reality we have to distort it. It may perhaps serve the interests of truth when once it is independently ascertained. We can think it out, defend it logically and help its propagation. The supporters of pure monism recognise a higher power than abstract intellect which enables us to feel the push of reality. We have to sink ourselves in the universal consciousness and make ourselves co-extensive with all that is. We do not then so much *think* reality as *live* it, do not so much *know* it as *become* it. Such an extreme monism, with its distinctions of logic and intuition, reality and the world of existence, we meet with in some Upaniṣads, Nāgārjuna and Śaṁkara in his ultra-philosophical moods, Śrī Harṣa and the Advaita Vedāntins, and echoes of it are heard in Parmenides and Plato, Spinoza and Plotinus, Bradley and Bergson, not to speak of the mystics, in the West.[12]

Whatever the being, pure and simple, may be to intuition, to intellect it is nothing more or less than an absolute abstraction. It is supposed to continue when every fact and form of existence is abolished. It is the residue left behind when abstractions is made from the whole world. It is a difficult exercise set to the thought of man to think away the sea and the earth, the sun and the stars, space and time, man and God. When an effort is made to abolish the whole universe, sublate all existence, nothing seems to remain for thought. Thought, finite and relational, finds to its utter despair that there is just nothing at all when everything existent is abolished. To the conceptual mind the central proposition of intuition, 'Being only is,' means that there is just nothing at all. Thought, as Hegel said, can only work with determinate realities, concrete things. To it all affirmation implies negation, and vice versa. Every concrete is a becoming, combining being and non-being, positive and negative. So those who are not satisfied with the intuited being, and wish to have a synthesis capable of being attained by thought which has a natural instinct for the concrete, are attracted to a system of objective idealism. The concrete idealists try to put together the two concepts of pure being and apparent becoming in the single synthesis of God. Even extreme monists recognise that becoming depends on being, though not vice versa. We get now a sort of refracted absolute, a God who has in Him the possibility of the world, combines in

12. In the Sāṁkhya philosophy we have practically the same account of the world of experience, which does not in the least stain the purity of the witness self. Only a pluralistic prejudice which has no logical basis asserts itself, and we have a plurality of souls. When the pluralism collapses, as it does at the first touch of logic, the Sāṁkhya theory becomes identical with the pure monism here sketched.

His nature the essence of all being, as well as of becoming, unity as well as plurality, unlimitedness and limitation. The pure being now becomes the subject, transforming itself into object and taking back the object into itself. Position, opposition, and composition, to use Hegelian expressions, go on in an eternal circular process. Hegel rightly perceives that the conditions of a concrete world are a subject and an object. These two opposites are combined in every concrete. The great God Himself has in Him the two antagonistic characters where the one is not only through the other, but is actually the other. When such a dynamic God eternally bound in the rotating wheel is asserted, all the degrees of existence, from the divine perfection up to vile dust, are automatically realised. The affirmation of God is the simultaneous affirmation of all degrees of reality between it and nothing. We have now the universe of thought constructed by thought, answering to thought and sustained by thought, in which subject and object are absorbed as moments. The relations of space, time and cause are not subjective forms, but universal principles of thought. If on the view of pure monism we cannot understand the exact relation between identity and difference, we are here on better ground. The world is identity gone into difference. Neither is isolated from the other. God is the inner ground, the basis of identity; the world is the outer manifestation, the externalisation of self-consciousness.

Such a God, according to the theory of pure monism, is just the lapse from the absolute, with the least conceivable interval separating him from pure being or the absolute. It is the product of avidyā which is separated from vidyā by the least conceivable extent. In other words, this concrete God is *the highest product of our highest intelligence*. The pity is, that it is a *product* after all, and our intelligence, however near it approximates to vidyā, is not yet vidyā. This God has in him the maximum of being and the minimum of defect—still a defect. The first touch of māyā, the slightest diminution of absolute being, is enough to throw it into space and time, though this space and this time will be as near as possible to the absolute unextendedness and eternity. The absolute one is converted into the Creator God existent in some space, moving all things from within without stirring from His place. God is the absolute objectivised as something somewhere, a spirit that pushes itself into everything. He is being-non-being, Brahman-māyā, subject-object, eternal force, the motionless mover of Aristotle, the absolute spirit of Hegel, the (absolute-relative) viśiṣṭādvaita of Rāmānuja, the efficient as well as the final cause of the universe. The world is beginningless and endless, since the energising of God could not have begun and could never come to an end. It is its essential nature to be ever at unrest.

There is no doubt that this is the highest conception which thought can reach. If we follow to the end the natural movement of our intellect which tries to unify the things of the world and synthesise opposites, a principle of explanation which is neither pure being nor pure non-being, but something which combines both, is what we get. This concept is constructed by a compression of all things into the whole. Philosophy on this view is constructive in character, and is therefore positive in its nature and synthetic in its function. Even here logical understanding playing with abstractions shuts us from the concrete in which alone the abstractions live, move and have their being. Thought as reason gets over the difficulties of logical understanding. Starting from the world of experience, we go up to the ultimate principle of God, and from the conception of the whole so gained we descend into details and review the parts. All logical dogmatisms which have confidence in the power of thought end with this conception of the world. The difficulty arises if we doubt the absoluteness of thought. May not our knowledge be relative to the requirements of the mind which unifies and divides? Perhaps for a mind differently shaped, knowledge may be different from what it is. Our present knowledge makes us think that all knowledge will be of this type, but when there are critics who dispute such an assertion, it is difficult to defend the position. Admitting that the conceptual plan of reality revealed to thought is true, still, it is sometimes urged, thought is not identical with reality. By compressing all concepts into one, we do not go beyond concepts. A relation is only a part of the mind that relates. Even an infinitely superior mind is yet a mind and of the same mould as man's. The theory of modified monism is adopted by some Upaniṣads, and the Bhagavadgītā, some followers of Buddhism and Rāmānuja, if not Bādarāyaṇa. In the West Aristotle and Hegel stand out as witnesses to it.

According to the first view perfect being is real; unreal becoming is actual, though, we do not know why. According to the second, the world becoming is a precipitation (apparent) of pure being into space and time by the force of diminution or māyā. According to the third, the highest product we have is a synthesis of pure being and not-being in God. We are immediately under a logical necessity to affirm all intermediate degrees of reality. If pure being is dismissed as a concept useless so far as the world of experience is concerned and we also disregard as illogical the idea of a Creator God, then what exists is nothing more than a mere flux of becoming, ever aspiring to be something else than what it is. The main principle of Buddhism results. In the world of existence, on the hypothesis of modified monism, the specific characters of the degrees of intermediate reality are to be measured by the distance separating them from the integral reality. The common characters of all of them are existence in space and time. Closer attention reveals to us more and more special attributes. Admit the distinction between thinking reals and unthinking objects, and we have the dualistic philosophy of Madhva. Even this is fundamentally a monism so long as the reals are dependent (paratantra) on God, who alone is independent (svatantra). Emphasise the independence of the thinking beings, and we have pluralism according to Sāṁkhya, if only we do not worry about the existence of God which cannot be demonstrated. Add to it the plurality of the objects of the world, we have pluralistic realism, where even God becomes one real, however great or powerful, among others. In the discussions about the intermediate degrees of reality the unit of individuality seems to depend upon the fancy of the philosopher. And whether a system turns out atheistic or theistic is determined by the attention paid to the absolute under the aegis of which the drama of the universe is enacted. It sometimes shines out brilliantly with its light focussed in a God and at other times fades out. These are the different ways in which the mind of man reacts to the problems of the world according to its own peculiar constitution.

There is a cordial harmony between God and man in Indian thought, while the opposition between the two is more marked in the West. The mythologies of the peoples also indicate it. The myth of Prometheus, the representative man, who tries to help mankind by defending them against Zeus who desires to destroy the human race and supplant them with a new and better species, the story of the labours of Hercules who tries to redeem the world, the conception of Christ as the Son of Man, indicate that man is the centre of attention in the West. It is true that Christ is also called the Son of God, the eldest begotten who is to be sacrificed before a just God's anger can be appeased. Our point here is that the *main* tendency of Western culture is an opposition between man and God, where man resists the might of God, steals fire from him in the interests of humanity. In India man is a product of God. The whole world is due to the sacrifice of God. The Puruṣa Sūkta speaks of such an eternal sacrifice which sustains man and the world.[13] In it the whole world is pictured as one single being of incomparable vastness and immensity, animated by one spirit, including within its substance all forms of life.

The dominant character of the Indian mind which has coloured all its culture and moulded all its thoughts is the spiritual tendency. Spiritual experience is the foundation of India's rich cultural history. It is mysticism, not in the sense of involving the exercise of any mysterious power, but only as insisting on a discipline of human nature, leading to a realisation of the spiritual. While the sacred scriptures of the Hebrews and the Christians are more religious and ethical, those of the Hindus are more spiritual and contemplative. The one fact of life in India is the Eternal Being of God.

It is the ultimate presupposition of all philosophy that nothing real can be self-contradictory. In the history of thought it takes some time to realise the importance of this presupposition, and make a conscious application of it. In the Ṛg-Veda there is an unconscious acceptance of the validity of ordinary knowledge. When we reach the stage of the Upaniṣads, dialectical problems emerge and the difficulties of knowledge are felt. In them we find an attempt made to mark the limits of knowledge and provide room for intuition, but all in a semi-philosophical way. When faith in the power of reason was shaken, scepticism supervened, and materialists and nihilists came upon the scene. Admitting the Upaniṣad position that the unseen reality cannot be comprehended by the logical intellect, Buddhism enforced the unsubstantiality of the world. To it, contradiction is of the nature of things, and the world of experience is nothing more than a tension of opposites. We cannot know if there is anything more than the actual, and this cannot be real since it is self-contradictory. Such a conclusion was the end of the Buddhistic development. We have in the theory of Nāgārjuna a philosophically sustained statement of the central position of the Upaniṣads. There is a real, though we cannot know it; and what we know is not real, for every interpretation of the world as an intelligible system breaks down. All this prepared the way for a self-conscious criticism of reason. Thought itself is self-contradictory or inadequate. Differences arise when the question is put, why exactly it is incapable of grasping reality. Is it because it deals with parts and not the whole, or is it because of its structural incapacity or innate self-contradictoriness? As we have

13. R.V., x. 90; see also R.V., x. 81, 3; Śvetāśvatara Up., iii. 3; B.G., xi.

seen, there are those who hold to the rationality of the real with the reservation that reality is not mere reason. So thought is incapable of giving us the whole of reality. The 'that' exceeds the 'what' in Bradley's words. Thought gives us knowledge of reality, but it is only knowledge, and not reality. There are others who feel that the real is self-consistent, and whatever is thought is self-contradictory. Thought works with the opposition of subject and object, and the absolute real is something in which these antitheses are annulled. The most concrete thought, in so far as it tries to combine a many in one, is still abstract, because it is self-contradictory, and if we want to grasp the real, we have to give up thought. On the first hypothesis, what thought reveals is not opposed to reality, but is revelatory of a part of it. Partial views are contradictory only because they are partial. They are true so far as they go, but they are not the whole truth. The second hypothesis tells us that reality can be apprehended by a form of feeling or intuition.[14] The first view also insists on a supplementing of thought by feeling, if reality is to be attained in its fullness. We seem to require another element in addition to thought, and this is suggested by the term 'darśana', which is used to describe a system of philosophy, doctrine of śāstra.

The term 'darśana' comes from the word *dṛś*, to see. This seeing may be either perceptual observation or conceptual knowledge or intuitional experience. It may be inspection of facts, logical inquiry or insight of soul. Generally, 'darśanas' mean critical expositions, logical surveys, or systems. We do not find the word used in this reference in the early stages of philosophical thought, when philosophy was more intuitional. It shows that 'darśana' is not an intuition, however much it may be allied to it. Perhaps the word is advisedly used, to indicate a thought system acquired by intuitive experience and sustained by logical argument. In the systems of extreme monism philosophy prepares the way for intuitional experience by giving us an idea of the impotence of thought. In the systems of moderate monism, where the real is a concrete whole, philosophy succeeds at best in giving an ideal reconstruction of reality. But the real transcends, surrounds and overflows our miserable categories. In extreme monism it is intuitional experience that reveals to us the fullness of reality; in concrete

14. Cf. Bradley, who says that we can reach reality through a kind of feeling, and McTaggart, who looks upon love as the most satisfactory way of characterising the absolute.

monism, it is insight, where knowledge is penetrated by feeling and emotion. Conceptual constructions do not possess the certainty of experienced facts. Again, an opinion or logical view becomes truth only if it stands the test of life.

'Darśana' is a word which is conveniently vague, as it stands for a dialectical defence of extreme monism as well as the intuitional truth on which it is based. Philosophically 'darśana' is putting the intuition to proof and propagating it logically. Even in other systems it applies to the logical exposition of the truth that could be had in conceptual terms with or without the aid of any vivifying intuition. 'Darśana' so applies to all views of reality taken by the mind of man, and if reality is one, the different views attempting to reveal the same must agree with each other. They cannot have anything accidental or contingent, but must reflect the different viewpoints obtained of the one real. By a close consideration of the several views our mind gets by snapshooting reality from different points, we rise to the second stage of a full rendering of reality in logical terms. When we realise the inadequacy of a conceptual account to reality, we try to seize the real by intuition, where the intellectual ideas are swallowed up. It is then that we are said to get the pure 'being' of extreme monism from which we get back to the logical real of thought, which again we begin to spell letter by letter in the different systems themselves. 'Darśana' as applicable to this last means any scientific account of reality. It is the one word that stands for all the complex inspiration of philosophy by its beautiful vagueness.

A 'darśana' is a spiritual perception, a whole view revealed to the soul sense. This soul sight, which is possible only when and where philosophy is lived, is the distinguishing mark of a true philosopher. So the highest triumphs of philosophy are possible only to those who have achieved in themselves a purity of soul. This purity is based upon a profound acceptance of experience, realised only when some point of hidden strength within man, from which he can not only inspect but comprehend life, is found. From this inner source the philosopher reveals to us the truth of life, a truth which mere intellect is unable to discover. The vision is produced almost as naturally as a fruit from a flower out of the mysterious centre where all experience is reconciled.

The seeker after truth must satisfy certain essential conditions before he sets out on his quest. Śaṁkara, in his commentary on the first Sūtra of the Vedānta Sūtras, makes out that four conditions are essential for any student of philosophy. The first condition is a knowledge of the distinction between the eternal and the non-eternal. This does not mean full knowledge, which can come only at the end, but only a metaphysical bent which does not accept all it sees to be absolutely real, a questioning tendency in the inquirer. He must have the inquiring spirit to probe all things, a burning imagination which could extract a truth from a mass of apparently disconnected data, and a habit of meditation which will not allow his mind to dissipate itself. The second condition is the subjugation of the desire for the fruits of action either in the present life or a future one. It demands the renunciation of all petty desire, personal motive and practical interest. Speculation or inquiry to the reflective mind is its own end. The right employment of intellect is understanding the things, good as well as bad. The philosopher is a naturalist who should follow the movement of things without exaggerating the good or belittling the evil on behalf of some prejudice of his. He must stand outside of life and look on it. So it is said that he must have no love of the present or the future. Only then can he stake his all on clear thinking and honest judgment and develop an impersonal cosmic outlook with devotedness to fact. To get this temper he must suffer a change of heart, which is insisted on in the third condition, where the student is enjoined to acquire tranquillity, self-restraint, renunciation, patience, peace of mind and faith. Only a trained mind which utterly controls the body can inquire and meditate endlessly so long as life remains, never for a moment losing sight of the object, never for a moment letting it be obscured by any terrestrial temptation. The seeker after truth must have the necessary courage to lose all for his highest end. So is he required to undergo hard discipline, spurn pleasure, suffer sorrow and contempt. A spiritual discipline which includes pitiless self-examination will enable the seeker to reach his end of freedom. The desire for mokṣa or release is the fourth condition. The metaphysically minded man who has given up all his desires and trained his mind has only one devouring desire to achieve the end or reach the eternal. The people of India have such an immense respect for these philosophers who glory in the might of knowledge and the power of intellect, that they worship them. The prophetic souls who with a noble passion for truth strive hard to understand the mystery of the world and give utterance to it, spending laborious days and sleepless nights, are philosophers in a vital sense of the term. They comprehend experience on behalf of mankind, and so the latter are eternally grateful to them.

Reverence for the past is another national trait. There is a certain doggedness of temperament, a stubborn loyalty to lose nothing in the long march of the ages. When confronted with new cultures or sudden extensions of knowledge, the Indian does not yield to the temptations of the hour, but holds fast to his traditional faith, importing as much as possible of the new into the old. This conservative liberalism is the secret of the success of Indian culture and civilisation. Of the great civilisations of the world, hoary with age, only the Indian still survives. The magnificence of the Egyptian civilisation can be learnt only from the reports of the archaeologists and the readings of the hieroglyphics; the Babylonian Empire, with its marvels of scientific, irrigation and engineering skill, is today nothing more than a heap of ruins; the great Roman culture, with its political institutions and ideals of law and equality, is, to a large extent, a thing of the past. The Indian civilisation, which even at the lowest estimate is 4,000 years old, still survives in its essential features. Her civilisation, dating back to the period of the Vedas, is young and old at the same time. She has been renewing her youth whenever the course of history demanded it. When a change occurs, it is not consciously felt to be a change. It is achieved, and all the time it professes to be only a new name for an old way of thinking. In the Ṛg-Veda we shall see how the religious consciousness of the Aryan invaders takes note of the conceptions of the people of the soil. In the Atharva-Veda we find that the vaguer cosmic deities are added to the gods of the sky and sun, fire and wind worshipped by the Aryan peoples from the Ganges to the Hellespont. The Upaniṣads are regarded as a revival or rather a realisation of something found already in the Vedic hymns. The Bhagavadgītā professes to sum up the teachings of the Upaniṣads. We have in the Epis the meeting-point of the religious conceptions of the highest import with the early nature worship. To respect the spirit of reverence in man for the ancient makes for the success of the new.[15] The old spirit is maintained, though not the old forms. This

15. Cf. 'This claim of a new thing to be old is, in varying degrees, a common characteristic of great movements. The Reformation professed to be a return to the Bible, the Evangelical movement in England a return to the Gospels, the High Church movement a return to the Early Church. A large element even in the French Revolution, the greatest of all breaches with the past, had for its ideal a return to Roman republican virtue or to the simplicity of the natural man' (Gilbert Murray, *Four Stages of Greek Religion*, p. 58).

tendency to preserve the type has led to the fashionable remark that India is immobile. The mind of man never stands still, though it admits of no absolute breach with the past.

This respect for the past has produced a regular continuity in Indian thought, where the ages are bound each to each by natural piety. The Hindu culture is a product of ages of change wrought by hundreds of generations, of which some are long, stale and sad, and others short, quick and joyous, where each has added something of quality to the great rich tradition which is yet alive, though it bears within it the marks of the dead past. The career of Indian philosophy has been compared to the course of a stream which, tumbling joyfully from its source among the northern mountain tops, rushes, through the shadowy valleys and plains, catching the lesser streams in its imperious current, till it sweeps increased to majesty and serene power through the lands and peoples whose fortunes it affects, bearing a thousand ships on its bosom. Who knows whether and when this mighty stream which yet flows on with tumult and rejoicing will pass into the ocean, the father of all streams?

There are not wanting Indian thinkers who look upon the whole of Indian philosophy as one system of continuous revelation. They believe that each civilisation is working out some divine thought which is natural to it.[16] There is an immanent teleology which shapes the life of each human race towards some complete development. The several views set forth in India are considered to be the branches of the self-same tree. The short cuts and blind alleys are somehow reconciled with the main road of advance to the truth. A familiar way in which the six orthodox systems are reconciled is to say that just as a mother in pointing out the moon to the baby speaks of it as the shining circle at the top of the tree, which is quite intelligible to the child, without mentioning the immense distance separating the earth from the moon which would have bewildered it, even so are different views given to suit the varying weakness of human understanding. The Prabodhacandrodaya, a philosophic drama, states that the six systems of Hindu philosophy are not mutually exclusive, but establish from various points of view the glory of the same uncreate God. They together form the living focus of the scattered rays that the many-faceted humanity reflects from the splendid sun. Mādhava's

16. The Greeks call this special quality of each people their 'nature', and the Indians call it their 'dharma'.

Sarvadarśanasaṁgraha (AD 1380) sketches sixteen systems of thought so as to exhibit a gradually ascending series, culminating in the Advaita Vedānta (or non-dualism). In the spirit of Hegel, he looks upon the history of Indian philosophy as a progressive effort towards a fully articulated conception of the world. The truth is unfolded bit by bit in the successive systems, and complete truth is reflected only when the series of philosophies is completed. In the Advaita Vedānta are the many lights brought to a single focus. Vijñānabhikṣu, the sixteenth-century theologian and thinker, holds that all systems are authoritative,[17] and reconciles them by distinguishing practical from metaphysical truth, and looks upon Sāṁkhya as the final expression of truth. Madhusūdana Sarasvatī in his Prasthānabheda writes: 'The ultimate scope of all the munis, authors of these different systems, is to support the theory of māyā, and their only design is to establish the existence of one supreme God, the sole essence, for these munis could not be mistaken, since they were omniscient. But as they saw that men, addicted to the pursuit of external objects, could not all at once penetrate into the highest truths, they held out to them a variety of theories in order that they might not fall into atheism. Misunderstanding the object which the munis thus had in view, and representing that they even designed to propound doctrines contrary to the Vedas, men have come to regard the specific doctrines of these several schools with preference, and thus became adherents of a variety of systems.'[18] This reconciliation of the several systems,[19] is attempted by almost all the critics and commentators. The difference is only about what they regard as the truth. Defenders of Nyāya like Udayana look upon Nyāya, and theists like Rāmānuja consider theism to be the truth. It is in accordance with the spirit of Indian culture to think that the several currents of thought flowing in its soil will discharge their waters into the one river whose flood shall make for the City of God.

From the beginning the Indian felt that truth was many-sided, and different views contained different aspects of truth which no one could fully express. He was therefore tolerant and receptive of other views. He was fearless in accepting even dangerous doctrines so long as they were backed up by logic. He would not allow to die, if he could help it, one jot

17. Sarvāgamaprāmāṇya.
18. See Muir, O.S.T., iv. 1 and 2.
19. Sarvadarśanasāṁarasya.

or tittle of the tradition, but would try to accommodate it all. Several cases of such tolerant treatment we shall meet with in the course of our study. Of course there are dangers incident to such a breadth of view. Often it has led the Indian thinkers into misty vagueness, lazy acceptance and cheap eclecticism.

III

SOME CHARGES AGAINST INDIAN PHILOSOPHY

The main charges against Indian philosophy are those of pessimism, dogmatism, indifference to ethics and unprogressiveness.

Almost every critic of Indian philosophy and culture harps on its pessimism.[20] We cannot, however, understand how the human mind can speculate freely and remodel life when it is filled with weariness and overcome by a feeling of hopelessness. A priori, the scope and freedom of Indian thought are inconsistent with an ultimate pessimism. Indian philosophy is pessimistic if by pessimism is meant a sense of dissatisfaction with what is or exists. In this sense all philosophy is pessimistic. The suffering of the world provokes the problems of philosophy and religion. Systems of religion which emphasise redemption seek for an escape from life as we live it on earth. But reality in its essence is not evil. In Indian philosophy the same word '*sat*' indicates both reality and perfection. Truth and goodness, or more accurately reality and perfection, go together. The real is also the supremely valuable, and this is the basis of all optimism. Professor Bosanquet writes: 'I believe in optimism, but I add that no optimism is worth its salt that does not go all the way with pessimism and arrive at a point beyond it. This, I am convinced, is the true spirit of life; and if any one thinks it dangerous, and an excuse for unjustifiable acquiescence in evil, I reply that all truth which has any touch of thoroughness has its danger for practice.'[21] Indian thinkers are pessimistic in so far as they look upon the world order as an evil and a lie; they are optimistic since they feel that there is a way out of it into the realm of truth, which is also goodness.

20. Chailley, in his *Administrative Problems* (p. 67), asserts that Indian philosophy springs 'from lassitude and a desire for eternal rest.'

21. *Social and International Ideals*, p. 43. Cf. Schopenhauer: 'Optimism, when it is not merely the thoughtless talk of such as harbour nothing but words under their low foreheads, appears not merely as an absurd but also as a really wicked way of thinking, as a bitter mockery of the unspeakable suffering humanity.'

Indian philosophy, it is said, is nothing if not dogmatic, and true philosophy cannot subsist with the acceptance of dogma. The course of our study of Indian thought will be an answer to this charge. Many of the systems of philosophy discuss the problem of knowledge, its origin, and validity as a preliminary to a study of other problems. It is true that the Veda or the śruti is generally considered to be an authoritative source of knowledge. But a philosophy becomes dogmatic only if the assertions of the Veda are looked upon as superior to the evidence of the senses and the conclusions of reason. The Vedic statements are āptavacana, or sayings of the wise, which we are called upon to accept, if we feel convinced that those wise had better means than we have of forming a judgment on the matter in question. Generally, these Vedic truths refer to the experiences of the seers, which any rational rendering of reality must take into account. These intuitional experiences are within the possibility of all men if only they will to have them.[22] The appeal to the Vedas does not involve any reference to an extra-philosophical standard. What is dogma to the ordinary man is experience to the pure in heart. It is true that when we reach the stage of the later commentaries we have a state of philosophical orthodoxy, when speculation becomes an academic defence of accepted dogmas. The earlier systems also call themselves exegetical and profess to be commentaries on the old texts, but they never tended to become scholastic, since the Upaniṣads to which they looked for inspiration were many-sided.[23] After the eighth century philosophical controversy became traditional and scholastic in character, and we miss the freedom of the earlier era. The founders of the schools are canonised, and so questioning their opinions is little short of sacrilege and impiety. The fundamental propositions are settled once for all, and the function of the teacher is only to transmit the beliefs of the school with such changes as his brain can command and the times require. We have fresh arguments for foregone conclusions, new expedients to meet new difficulties and a re-establishment of the old with a little change of front or twist of dialectic. There is less of meditation on the deep problems of life and more of discussion of the artificial ones. The treasure that is the tradition clogs us with its own burdensome wealth, and philosophy ceases to move and sometimes finds it hard to breathe at all. The charge of unprofitableness urged in general against the whole of Indian philosophy may have some point when applied

22. See S.B.V.S., iii. 2. 24.
23. Viśvatomukhāḥ.

to the wordy disquisitions of the commentators who are not the inspired apostles of life and beauty which the older generation of philosophers were, but professional dialecticians conscious of their mission to mankind. Yet even under the inevitable crust of age the soul remains young, and now and then breaks through and sprouts into something green and tender. There arise men like Śaṁkara or Mādhava, who call themselves commentators, and yet perceive the spiritual principle which directs the movements of the world.

It is often urged against Indian philosophy that it is nonethical in character. 'There is practically no ethical philosophy within the frontiers of Hindu thinking.'[24] The charge, however, cannot be sustained. Attempts to fill the whole of life with the power of spirit are common. Next to the category of reality, that of dharma is the most important concept in Indian thought. So far as the actual ethical content is concerned, Buddhism, Jainism and Hinduism are not inferior to others. Ethical perfection is the first step towards divine knowledge.

Philosophy in India, it is said, remains stationary and represents an endless process of threshing old straw. 'The unchanging East' connotes that in India time has ceased to fly and remained motionless for ever. If it means that there is a fundamental identity in the problems, then this sort of unprogressiveness is a feature common to all philosophical developments. The same old problems of God, freedom and immortality and the same old unsatisfactory solutions are repeated throughout the centuries. While the form of the problems is the same, the matter has changed. There is all the difference in the world between the God of the Vedic hymns drinking soma, and the Absolute of Śaṁkara. The situations to which philosophy is a response renew themselves in each generation, and the effort to deal with them needs a corresponding renewal. If the objection means that there is not much fundamental difference between the solutions given in the ancient scriptures of India and Plato's works or Christian writings, it only shows that the same loving universal Spirit has been uttering its message and making its voice heard from time to time. The sacred themes come down to us through the ages variously balanced and coloured by race and tradition. If it means that there is a certain reverence for the past which impels the Indian thinkers to pour new wine

24. Farquhar, *Hibbert Journal*, October 1921, p. 24.

into old bottles, we have already said that this is a characteristic of the Indian mind. The way to grow is to take in all the good that has gone before and add to it something more. It is to inherit the faith of the fathers and modify it by the spirit of the time. If Indian thought is said to be futile because it did not take into account the progress of the sciences, it is the futility which all old things possess in the eyes of the new. The scientific developments have not brought about as great a change in the substance of philosophy as this criticism assumes. The theories so revolutionary in their scientific aspects as the biological evolution and the physical relativity have not upset established philosophies, but only confirmed them from fresh fields.

The charge of unprogressiveness or stationariness holds when we reach the stage after the first great commentators. The hand of the past grew heavy, initiative was curbed, and the work of the scholastics, comparable to that of the medieval Schoolmen, with the same reverence for authority and tradition and the same intrusion of theological prejudice, began. The Indian philosopher could have done better with greater freedom. To continue the living development of philosophy, to keep the current of creative energy flowing, contact with the living movements of the world capable of promoting real freedom of thought is necessary. Perhaps the philosophy of India which lost its strength and vigour when her political fortunes met with defeat may derive fresh inspiration and a new impulse from the era just dawning upon her. If the Indian thinkers combine a love of what is old with a thirst for what is true, Indian philosophy may yet have a future as glorious as its past.

IV

VALUE OF THE STUDY OF INDIAN PHILOSOPHY

It is not merely as a piece of antiquarian investigation that Indian thought deserves study. Speculations of particular thinkers or the ideas of a past age are not without value. Nothing that has ever interested men and women can ever wholly lose its vitality. In the thought of the Vedic Aryans we witness the wrestlings of powerful minds with the highest problems set to thinking man. In the words of Hegel: 'The history of philosophy in its true meaning deals not with the past, but with the eternal and veritable present; and in its results resembles, not a museum of aberrations of the human intellect, but a pantheon of Godlike figures representing various stages of the immanent logic of all human thought.'[25] The history of Indian thought is not what it seems at first sight, a mere succession of ghostly ideas which follow one another in rapid succession.

It is easy to make sport of philosophy, since to those who are content to live among the things of sense and think in a slovenly way, philosophic problems wear a look of unreality, and possess a flavour of absurdity. The hostile critic looks upon the disputes of philosophy as wasteful logic-chopping and intellectual legerdemain concerned with such conundrums as 'Did the hen come first or the egg?'[26] The problems discussed in Indian philosophy have perplexed men from the beginning of time, though they have never been solved to the satisfaction of all. There seems to be an essential human need or longing to know the nature of soul and God. Every thinking man, when he reflects on the fact that he is swept without pause along the great curve of birth to death, the rising flood of life, the ceaseless stream of becoming, which presses ever onward and upward, cannot but ask, What is the purpose of it all, as a whole, apart from the little distracting incidents of the way? Philosophy is no racial idiosyncrasy of India, but a human interest.

If we lay aside professional philosophy, which may well be a futile business, we have in India one of the best logical developments of thought. The labours of the Indian thinkers are so valuable to the advancement of human knowledge that we judge their work to be worthy of study, even if we find manifest errors in it. If the sophisms which ruined the philosophies of the past are any reason for neglecting them, then not only the study of Indian philosophy but of all philosophy should be given up. After all, the residuum of permanent truth which may be acknowledged as the effective contribution to human thought even with regard to the most illustrious thinkers of the West, like Plato and Aristotle, is not very great. It is easy to smile at the exquisite rhapsodies of Plato or the dull dogmatism of Descartes or the arid empiricism of Hume or the bewildering paradoxes of Hegel, and yet withal there is no doubt that we profit by the study of their works. Even so, though only a few of the vital truths of Indian thinkers have moulded the history of the human mind, yet there are general

25. *Logic*, p. 137. Wallace's translation.

26. After all, this question is not so trite or innocent as it appears to be. See Samuel Butler's *Luck or Cunning*.

syntheses, systematic conceptions put forward by a Bādarāyaṇa or a Śaṁkara which will remain landmarks of human thought and monuments of human genius.[27]

To the Indian student a study of Indian philosophy alone can give a right perspective about the past of India. At the present day the average Hindu looks upon his past systems, Buddhism, Advaitism, Dvaitism, as all equally worthy and acceptable to reason. The authors of the systems are worshipped as divine. A study of Indian philosophy will conduce to the clearing up of the situation, the adopting of a more balanced outlook and the freeing of the mind from the oppressing sense of the perfection of everything that is ancient. This freedom from bondage to authority is an ideal worth striving at. For when the enslaved intellect is freed, original thinking and creative effort might again be possible. It may be a melancholy satisfaction to the present day Indian to know some details of his country's early history. Old men console themselves with the stories of their youth, and the way to forget the bad present is to read about the good past.

V

PERIODS OF INDIAN THOUGHT

It is necessary to give some justification for the title 'Indian Philosophy,' when we are discussing the philosophy of the Hindus as distinct from that of the other communities which have also their place in India. The

27. Many scholars of the West recognise the value of Indian philosophy. 'On the other hand, when we read with attention the poetical and philosophical movements of the East, above all those of India, which are beginning to spread in Europe, we discover there so many truths, and truths so profound, and which make such a contrast with the meanness of the results at which the European genius has sometimes stopped, that we are constrained to bend the knee before that of the East, and to see in this cradle of the human race the native land of the highest philosophy' (Victor Cousin). 'If I were to ask myself from what literature, we here in Europe, we who have been nurtured almost exclusively on the thoughts of Greeks and Romans, and of one Semitic race, the Jewish, may draw that corrective which is most wanted, in order to make our inner life more perfect, more comprehensive, more universal, in fact more truly human, a life, not for this life only, but a transfigured and eternal life—again, I should point to India' (Max Müller). 'Among nations possessing indigenous philosophy and metaphysics, together with an innate relish for these pursuits, such as at present characterises Germany, and in olden times was the proud distinction of Greece, Hindustan holds the first rank in point of time' (Ibid.).

most obvious reason is that of common usage. India even today is mainly Hindu. And we are concerned here with the history of Indian thought up till AD 1000 or a little after, when the fortunes of the Hindus became more and more linked with those of the non-Hindus.

To the continuous development of Indian thought different peoples at different ages have brought their gifts, yet the force of the Indian spirit had its own shaping influence on them. It is not possible for us to be sure of the exact chronological development, though we shall try to view Indian thought from the historical point of view. The doctrines of particular schools are relative to their environment and have to be viewed together. Otherwise, they will cease to have any living interest for us and become dead traditions. Each system of philosophy is an answer to a positive question which its age has put to itself, and when viewed from its own angle of vision will be seen to contain some truth. The philosophies are not sets of propositions conclusive or mistaken, but the expression and evolution of a mind with which and in which we must live if we wish to know how the systems shaped themselves. We must recognise the solidarity of philosophy with history, of intellectual life with the social conditions.[28] The historical method requires us not to take sides in the controversy of schools, but follow the development with strict indifference.

While we are keenly alive to the immense importance of historical perspective, we regret that on account of the almost entire neglect of the chronological sequences of the writings it is not possible for us to determine exactly the relative dates of the systems. So unhistorical, or perhaps so ultra-philosophical, was the nature of the ancient Indian, that we know more about the philosophies than about the philosophers. From the time of the birth of Buddha Indian chronology is on a better foundation. The rise of Buddhism was contemporaneous with the extension of the Persian power to the Indus under the dynasty of Achaemenidae in Persia. It is said to be the source of the earliest knowledge of India in the West obtained by Hecateus and Herodotus.

28. In the image of Walter Pater. 'As the strangely twisted pine-tree, which would be a freak of nature on an English lawn, is seen, if we replace it in thought, amid the contending forces of the Alpine torrent that actually shaped its growth, to have been the creature of necessity, of the logic of certain facts, even so the most fantastic beliefs will assume their natural propriety when they are duly correlated with the conditions round them of which they are in truth a part' (*Plato and Platonism*, p. 10).

The following are the broad divisions of Indian philosophy: (I) The Vedic Period (1500 BC–600 BC) covers the age of the settlement of the Aryans and the gradual expansion and spread of the Aryan culture and civilisation. It was the time which witnessed the rise of the forest universities, where were evolved the beginnings of the sublime idealism of India. We discern in it successive strata of thought, signified by the Mantras or the hymns, the Brāhmaṇas, and the Upaniṣads. The views put forward in this age are not philosophical in the technical sense of the term. It is the age of groping, where superstition and thought are yet in conflict. Yet to give order and continuity to the subject, it is necessary for us to begin with an account of the outlook of the hymns of the Ṛg-Veda and discuss the views of the Upaniṣads.

(2) The Epic Period (600 BC to AD 200) extends over the development between the early Upaniṣads and the darśanas or the systems of philosophy. The epics of the Rāmāyaṇa and the Mahābhārata serve as the vehicles through which was conveyed the new message of the heroic and the godly in human relations. In this period we have also the great democratisation of the Upaniṣad ideas in Buddhism and the Bhagavadgītā. The religious systems of Buddhism, Jainism, Śaivism, Vaiṣṇavism belong to this age. The development of abstract thought which culminated in the schools of Indian philosophy, the darśanas, belongs to this period. Most of the systems had their early beginnings about the period of the rise of Buddhism, and they developed side by side through many centuries; yet the systematic works of the schools belong to a later age.

(3) The Sūtra Period (from AD 200) comes next. The mass of material grew so unwieldy that it was found necessary to devise a shorthand scheme of philosophy. This reduction and summarisation occurred in the form of Sūtras. These Sūtras are unintelligible without commentaries, so much so that the latter have become more important than the Sūtras themselves. Here we have the critical attitude in philosophy developed. In the preceding periods we have philosophical discussions, no doubt, where the mind did not passively receive whatever it was told, but played round the subject, raising objections and answering them. By happy intuition the thinkers pitch upon some general principles which seem to them to explain all aspects of the universe. The philosophical syntheses, however profound and acute they may be, suffered throughout from the defect of being pre-critical, in the Kantian sense of the term. Without a previous criticism of the human capacity to solve philosophical problems, the mind looked at

the world and reached its conclusions. The earlier efforts to understand and interpret the world were not strictly philosophical attempts, since they were not troubled by any scruples about the competence of the human mind or the efficiency of the instruments and the criteria employed. As Caird puts it, mind was 'too busy with the object to attend to itself.'[29] So when we come to the Sūtras we have thought and reflection become self-conscious, and not merely constructive imagination and religious freedom. Among the systems themselves, we cannot say definitely which are earlier and which later. There are cross-references throughout. The Yoga accepts the Sāṁkhya, the Vaiśeṣika recognises both the Nyāya and the Sāṁkhya. Nyāya refers to the Vedānta and the Sāṁkhya. Mīmāṁsā directly or indirectly recognises the pre-existence of all others. So does the Vedānta. Professor Garbe holds that the Sāṁkhya is the oldest school. Next came Yoga, next Mīmāṁsā and Vedānta, and last of all Vaiśeṣika and Nyāya. The Sūtra period cannot be sharply distinguished from the scholastic period of the commentators. The two between them extend up till the present day.

(4) The Scholastic Period also dates from the second century AD. It is not possible for us to draw a hard and fast line between this and the previous one. Yet it is to this that the great names of Kumārila, Śaṁkara, Śrīdhara, Rāmānuja, Madhva, Vācaspati, Udayana, Bhāskara, Jayanta, Vijñānabhikṣu and Raghunātha belong. The literature soon becomes grossly polemical. We find a brood of schoolmen, noisy controversialists indulging in over-subtle theories and fine-spun arguments, who fought fiercely over the nature of logical universals. Many Indian scholars dread opening their tomes which more often confuse than enlighten us. None would deny their acuteness and enthusiasm. Instead of thought we find words, instead of philosophy logic-chopping. Obscurity of thought, subtlety of logic, intolerance of disposition, mark the worst type of the commentators. The better type, of course, are quite as valuable as the ancient thinkers themselves. Commentators like Śaṁkara and Rāmānuja re-state the old doctrine, and their restatement is just as valuable as a spiritual discovery.

There are some histories of Indian philosophy written by Indian thinkers. Almost all later commentators from their own points of view discuss other doctrines. In that way every commentator happens to give an idea of the other views. Sometimes conscious attempts are made to

29. *Critical Philosophy of Kant*, vol. i, p. 2.

deal with the several systems in a continuous manner. Some of the chief of these 'historical' accounts may here be mentioned. Ṣaḍdarśanasamuccaya, or the epitome of the six systems, is the name of a work by Haribhadra.[30] Samantabhadra, a Digambara Jain of the sixth century, is said to have written a work called Āptamīmāṁsā, containing a review of the various philosophical schools.[31] A Mādhyamika Buddhist, by name Bhāvaviveka, is reputed to be the author of a work called Tarkajvāla, a criticism of the Mīmāṁsā, Sāṁkhya, Vaiśeṣika and Vedānta schools. A Digambara Jain, by name Vidyānanda, in his Aṣṭasāhasrī, and another Digambara, by name Merutuṅga, in his work on Ṣaḍdarśanavicāra (AD 1300) are said to have criticised the Hindu systems. The most popular account of Indian philosophy is the Sarvadarśanasaṁgraha, by the well-known Vedāntin Mādhavācārya, who lived in the fourteenth century in South India. The Sarvasiddhāntasārasaṁgraha assigned to Śaṁkara,[32] and the Prasthānanabheda by Madhusūdana Sarasvatī,[33] contain useful accounts of the different philosophies.

30. Mr Barth says: 'Haribhadra, who according to tradition died in AD 529, but by more exact testimony lived in the ninth century, and who had several homonyms, was a Brāhmin converted to Jainism. He is famous still as the author of Fourteen Hundred Prabandhas (chapters of works), and seems to have been one of the first to introduce the Sanskrit language into the scholastic literature of the Śvetāmbara Jains. By the six systems the Brāhmins understand the two Mīmāṁsās, the Sāṁkhya and the Yoga, the Nyāya and the Vaiśeṣika. Haribhadra, on the other hand, expounds under this title very curtly in eighty-seven slokas, but quite impartially, the essential principles of the Buddhists, the Jainas, the followers of the Nyāya, the Sāṁkhya, the Vaiśeṣika and the Mīmāṁsā. He thus selects his own school and those with whom the Jainas had the closest affinities, and puts them in between the schools of their greatest enemies, the Buddhists and the ritualists of the school of Jaimini. These last he couples with the Lokāyatikas, the atheistic materialists, not simply from sectarian fanaticism and on his own judgment, but following an opinion that was then prevalent even among the Brāhmins' (*Indian Antiquary*, p. 66, 1895).

31. Vidyabhushan, *Mediaeval Systems of Indian Logic*, p. 23.

32. The ascription seems to be incorrect. See Keith: *Indian Logic*, p. 242, n. 3.

33. See Max Müller, *Six Systems*, pp. 75–84.

PART I

The Vedic Period

CHAPTER II

The Hymns of the Ṛg-Veda

■ The four Vedas—The parts of the Veda, the Mantras, the Brāhmaṇas, the Upaniṣads—The importance of the study of the hymns—Date and authorship—Different views of the teaching of the hymns—Their philosophical tendencies—Religion—'Deva'—Naturalism and anthropomorphism—Heaven and Earth—Varuṇa—Ṛta—Sūrya—Uṣas—Soma—Yama—Indra—Minor gods and goddesses—Classification of the Vedic deities—Monotheistic tendencies—The unity of nature—The unifying impulse of the logical mind—The implications of the religious consciousness—Henotheism—Viśvakarman, Bṛhaspati, Prajāpati and Hiraṇyagarbha—The rise of reflection and criticism—The philosophical inadequacy of monotheism—Monism—Philosophy and religion—The cosmological speculations of the Vedic hymns—The Nāsadīya Sūkta—The relation of the world to the Absolute—The Puruṣa Sūkta—Practical religion—Prayer—Sacrifice—The ethical rules—Karma—Asceticism—Caste—Future life—The two paths of the gods and the fathers—Hell—Rebirth—Conclusion. ■

I

THE VEDAS

The Vedas are the earliest documents of the human mind that we possess. Wilson writes: 'When the texts of the Ṛg and Yajur Vedas are completed, we shall be in the possession of materials sufficient for the safe appreciation of the results to be derived from them, and of the actual condition of the Hindus, both political and religious, at a date co-eval with that of the yet earliest known records of social organisation—long anterior to the dawn of Grecian civilisation—prior to the oldest vestiges of the Assyrian Empire yet discovered—contemporary probably with the oldest Hebrew writings, and posterior only to the Egyptian dynasties, of which, however, we yet know little except barren names; the Vedas give us abundant information respecting all that is most interesting in the contemplation of antiquity.'[1] There are four Vedas: Ṛg, Yajur, Sāma and Atharva. The first three agree

1. J.R.A.S., vol. 13, 1852, p. 206.

not only in their name, form and language, but in their contents also. Of them all the Ṛg-Veda is the chief. The inspired songs which the Aryans brought with them from their earlier home into India as their most precious possession were collected, it is generally held, in response to a prompting to treasure them up which arose when the Aryans met with large numbers of the worshippers of other gods in their new country. The Ṛg-Veda is that collection. The Sāma-Veda is a purely liturgical collection. Much of it is found in the Ṛg-Veda, and even those hymns peculiar to it have no distinctive lessons of their own. They are all arranged for being sung at sacrifices. The Yajur-Veda, like the Sāma, also serves a liturgical purpose. This collection was made to meet the demands of a ceremonial religion. Whitney writes: 'In the early Vedic times the sacrifice was still, in the main, an unfettered act of devotion, not committed to the charge of a body of privileged priests, not regulated in its minor details, but left to the free impulses of him who offered it, accompanied with Ṛg and Sāma hymns and chants, that the mouth of the offerer might not be silent while his hands were presenting to the divinity the gift which his heart prompted.... As in process of time, however, the ritual assumed a more and more formal character, becoming finally a strictly and minutely regulated succession of single actions, not only were the verses fixed which were to be quoted during the ceremony, but there established themselves likewise a body of utterances, formulas of words, intended to accompany each individual action of the whole work to explain, excuse, bless, give it a symbolical significance or the like.... These sacrificial formulas received the name of Yajus, from the root Yaj, to sacrifice.... The Yajur-Veda is made up of these formulas, partly in prose and partly in verse, arranged in the order in which they were to be made use of at the sacrifice.'[2] The collections of the Sāma and the Yajur Vedas must have been made in the interval between the Ṛg-Vedic collection and the Brāhmanical period, when the ritualistic religion was well established. The Atharva-Veda for a long time was without the prestige of a Veda, though for our purposes it is next in importance only to the Ṛg-Veda, for, like it, it is a historical collection of independent contents. A different spirit pervades this Veda, which is the production of a later era of thought. It shows the result of the compromising spirit adopted by the Vedic Aryans in view of the new gods

2. J.A.O.S. Proceedings, vol. iii. p. 304.

and goblins worshipped by the original peoples of the country whom they were slowly subduing.

Each Veda consists of three parts known as *Mantras*, *Brāhmaṇas* and *Upaniṣads*. The collection of the mantras or the hymns is called the Saṁhitā. The Brāhmaṇas include the precepts and religious duties. The Upaniṣads and the Āraṇyakas are the concluding portions of the Brāhmaṇas which discuss philosophical problems. The Upaniṣads contain the mental background of the whole of the subsequent thought of the country. Of the early Upaniṣads Aitareya and Kauṣītaki belong to the Ṛg, Kena and Chāndogya to the Sāma, Īśā and Tittirīya and the Bṛhadāraṇyaka to the Yajur, and Praśna and Muṇḍaka to the Atharva-Veda. The Āraṇyakas come between the Brāhmaṇas and the Upaniṣads, and, as their name implies, are intended to serve as objects of meditation for those who live in forests. The Brāhmaṇas discuss the ritual to be observed by the householder, but when in his old age he resorts to the forests, some substitute for ritual is needed, and that is supplied in the Āraṇyakas. The symbolic and spiritual aspects of the sacrificial cult are meditated upon, and this meditation takes the place of the performance of the sacrifice. The Āraṇyakas form the transition link between the ritual of the Brāhmaṇas and the philosophy of the Upaniṣads. While the hymns are the creation of the poets,[3] the Brāhmaṇas are the work of the priests, and the Upaniṣads the meditations of the philosophers. The religion of nature of hymns, the religion of law of the Brāhmaṇas and the religion of spirit of the Upaniṣads, correspond in a very close way to the three great divisions in the hegelian conception of the development of religion. Though at a later stage the three have existed side by side, there is no doubt that they were originally developed in successive periods. The Upaniṣads, while in one sense a continuation of the Vedic worship, are in another a protest against the religion of the Brāhmaṇas.

II

IMPORTANCE OF THE STUDY OF THE VEDIC HYMNS

A study of the hymns of the Ṛg-Veda is indispensable for any adequate account of Indian thought. Whatever we may think them, half-formed

3. R.V., i. 164. 6.; x. 129. 4.

myths or crude allegories, obscure gropings or immature compositions, still they are the source of the later practices and philosophies of the Indo-Aryans, and a study of them is necessary for a proper understanding of subsequent thought. We find a freshness and simplicity and an inexplicable charm as of the breath of the spring or the flower of the morning about these first efforts of the human mind to comprehend and express the mystery of the world.

The text of the Veda which we possess has come to us from that period of intellectual activity when the Aryans found their way into India from their original home. They brought with them certain notions and beliefs which were developed and continued on the Indian soil. A long interval must have elapsed between the composition and the compilation of these hymns. Max Müller divides the Saṁhitā period into the two called the Chandas and the Mantra periods.[4] In the former the hymns were composed. It was the creative epoch characterised by real poetry, when men's emotions poured themselves out in songs; we have then no traces of sacrifices. Prayer was the only offering made to the gods. The second is the period of collection or systematic grouping. It was then that the hymns were arranged in practically the same form in which we have them at present. In this period sacrificial ideas slowly developed. When exactly the hymns were composed and collected is a matter of conjecture. We are sure that they were current some fifteen centuries before Christ. Buddhism, which began to spread in India about 500 BC, presupposes not only the existence of the Vedic hymns but the whole Vedic literature, including the Brāhmaṇas and the Upaniṣads. For the sacrificial system of the Brāhmaṇas to become well established, for the philosophy of the Upaniṣads to be fully developed, it would require a long period.[5] The development of thought apparent in this vast literature requires at least a millennium. This is not too long a period if we remember the variety and growth which the literature displays. Some Indian scholars assign the Vedic hymns to 3000 BC, others to 6000 BC. The late Mr Tilak dates the hymns about 4500 BC, the Brāhmaṇas 2500 BC,

4. Attempts are sometimes made to assign the hymns to five different periods marked by differences of religious belief and social custom. See Arnold: *Vedic Metre.*

5. From them many of the technical terms of later philosophies, such as Brahman, Ātman, Yoga, Mīmāṁsā, are derived.

the early Upaniṣads 1600 BC. Jacobi puts the hymns at 4500 BC. We assign them to the fifteenth century BC and trust that our date will not be challenged as being too early.

The Ṛg-Veda Saṁhitā or collection consists of 1,017 hymns or sūktas, covering a total of about 10,600 stanzas. It is divided into eight aṣṭakas,[6] each having eight adhyāyas, or chapters, which are further subdivided into vargas or groups. It is sometimes divided into ten maṇḍalas or circles. The latter is the more popular division. The first maṇḍala contains 191 hymns, and is ascribed roughly to fifteen different authors or Ṛṣis (seers or sages) such as Gautama, Kaṇva, etc. In the arrangement of the hymns there is a principle involved. Those addressed to Agni come first, those to Indra second, and then the rest. Each of the next six maṇḍalas is ascribed to a single family of poets, and has the same arrangement. In the eighth we have no definite order. It is ascribed like the first to a number of different authors. Maṇḍala nine consists of hymns addressed to Soma. Many of the hymns of the eighth and ninth Maṇḍalas are found in the Sāma-Veda also. Maṇḍala ten seems to be a later appendage. At any rate, it contains views current at the last period of the development of the Vedic hymns. Here the native hue of the earlier devotional poetry is sicklied over with the pale cast of philosophic thought. Speculative hymns about the origin of creation, etc., are to be met with. Together with these abstract theorisings are also found in it the superstitious charms and exorcisings belonging to the Atharva-Veda period. While the speculative parts indicate the maturing of the mind which first revealed itself in the lyrical hymns, this feature shows that by that time the Vedic Aryans must have grown familiar with the doctrines and practices of the native Indians, and both these are clear indications of the late origin of the tenth book.

III

THE TEACHING OF THE VEDAS

Different views of the spirit of the Vedic hymns are held by competent scholars who have made these ancient scriptures their life study. Pfleiderer speaks of the 'primaeval child-like naïve prayer of Ṛg-Veda.' Pictet maintains that the Aryans of the Ṛg-Veda possessed a monotheism,

6. An eighth portion is an aṣṭaka.

however vague and primitive it might be. Roth and Dayānanda Sarasvatī, the founder of the Arya Samaj, agree with this view. Ram Mohan Roy considers the Vedic gods to be 'the allegorical representations of the attributes of the supreme Deity.' According to others, Bloomfield among them, the hymns of the Ṛg-Veda are sacrificial compositions of a primitive race which attached great importance to ceremonial rites. Bergaigne holds that they were all allegorical. Sāyaṇa, the famous Indian commentator, adopts the naturalistic interpretation of the gods of the hymns, which is supported by modern European scholarship. Sāyaṇa sometimes interprets the hymns in the spirit of the later Brāhmanic religion. These varying opinions need not be looked upon as antagonistic to one another, for they only point to the heterogeneous nature of the Ṛg-Veda collection. It is a work representing the thought of successive generations of thinkers, and so contains within it different strata of thought. In the main, we may say that the Ṛg-Veda represents the religion of an unsophisticated age. The great mass of the hymns are simple and naïve, expressing the religious consciousness of a mind yet free from the later sophistication. There are also hymns which belong to the later formal and conventional age of the Brāhmaṇas. There are some, especially in the last book, which embody the mature results of conscious reflection on the meaning of the world and man's place in it. Monotheism characterises some of the hymns of the Ṛg-Veda. There is no doubt that sometimes the several gods were looked upon as the different names and expressions of the Universal Being.[7] But this monotheism is not as yet the trenchant clear-cut monotheism of the modern world.

Mr Aurobindo Ghosh, the great Indian scholar-mystic, is of opinion that the Vedas are replete with suggestions of secret doctrines and mystic philosophies. He looks upon the gods of the hymns as symbols of the psychological functions. Sūrya signifies intelligence, Agni will, and Soma feeling. The Veda to him is a mystery religion corresponding to the Orphic and Eleusinian creeds of ancient Greece. 'The hypothesis I propose is that the Ṛg-Veda is itself the one considerable document that remains to us from the early period of human thought of which the historical Eleusinian and Orphic mysteries were the failing remnants, when the spiritual and psychological knowledge of the race was concealed for reasons now

7. See R.V., i. 164–46 and 170–71.

difficult to determine, in a veil of concrete and material figures and symbols which protected the sense from the profane and revealed it to the initiated. One of the leading principles of the mystics was the sacredness and secrecy of self-knowledge and the true knowledge of the gods. This wisdom was, they thought, unfit for, perhaps even dangerous, to the ordinary human mind, or in any case liable to perversion and misuse and loss of virtue if revealed to vulgar and unpurified spirits. Hence they favoured the existence of an outer worship effective but imperfect for the profane, and an inner discipline for the initiate, and clothed their language in words and images which had equally a spiritual sense for the elect and a concrete sense for the mass of ordinary worshippers. The Vedic hymns were conceived and constructed on these principles.'[8] When we find that this view is opposed not only to the modern views of European scholars but also to the traditional interpretations of Sāyaṇa and the system of Pūrva-Mīmāṁsā, the authority on Vedic interpretation, we must hesitate to follow the lead of Mr Aurobindo Ghosh, however ingenious his point of view may be. It is not likely that the whole progress of Indian thought has been a steady falling away from the highest spiritual truths of the Vedic hymns. It is more in accordance with what is known of the general nature of human development, and easier to concede that the later religions and philosophies arose out of the crude suggestions and elementary moral ideas and spiritual aspirations of the early mind, than that they were a degradation of an original perfection.

In interpreting the spirit of the Vedic hymns we propose to adopt the view of them accepted by the Brāhmaṇas and the Upaniṣads, which came immediately after. These later works are a continuation and a development of the views of the hymns. While we find the progress from the worship of outward nature powers to the spiritual religion of the Upaniṣads easily intelligible according to the law of normal religious growth—man everywhere on earth starts with the external and proceeds to the internal—the Upaniṣads do not care for the early nature worship, but only develop the suggestions of the highest religion contained in the Vedas. This interpretation is in entire harmony with the modern historical method and the scientific theory of early human culture, and accords well with the classic Indian view as put forth by Sāyaṇa.

8. Ārya, vol. i, p. 60.

IV

PHILOSOPHICAL TENDENCIES

In the Ṛg-Veda we have the impassioned utterances of primitive but poetic souls which seek some refuge from the obstinate questionings of sense and outward things. The hymns are philosophical to the extent that they attempt to explain the mysteries of the world not by means of any superhuman insight or extraordinary revelation, but by the light of unaided reason. The mind revealed in the Vedic hymns is not of any one type. There were poetic souls who simply contemplated the beauties of the sky and the wonders of the earth, and eased their musical souls of their burden by composing hymns. The Indo-Iranian gods of Dyaus, Varuṇa, Uṣas, Mitra, etc., were the productions of this poetic consciousness. Others of a more active temperament tried to adjust the world to their own purposes. Knowledge of the world was useful to them as the guide of life. And in the period of conquest and battle, such useful utilitarian deities as Indra were conceived. The genuine philosophical impulse, the desire to know and understand the world for its own sake, showed itself only at the end of this period of storm and stress. It was then that men sat down to doubt the gods they ignorantly worshipped and reflected on the mysteries of life. It is at this period that questions were put to which the mind of man could not give adequate answers. The Vedic poet exclaims: 'I do not know what kind of thing I am; mysterious, bound, my mind wanders.' Even though germs of true philosophy appear at a late stage, still the view of life reflected in the poetry and practice of the Vedic hymns is instructive. As legendary history precedes archaeology, alchemy chemistry, and astrology astronomy, even so mythology and poetry precede philosophy and science. The impulse of philosophy finds its first expression in mythology and religion. In them we find the answers to the questions of ultimate existence, believed by the people in general. These happen to be products of imagination, where mythical causes are assumed to account for the actual world. As reason slowly gains ascendancy over fancy, an attempt is made to distinguish the permanent stuff from out of which the actual things of the world are made. Cosmological speculations take the place of mythical assumptions. The permanent elements of the world are deified, and thus cosmology becomes confused with religion. In the early stages of reflection as we have them in the Ṛg-Veda, mythology, cosmology and religion are found intermixed. It will be of interest to describe briefly the views of the hymns under the four heads of theology, cosmology, ethics and eschatology.

V

THEOLOGY

A religious growth of many centuries cannot be a simple and transparent creed admitting of easy definition and classification. A striking aspect of the hymns is their polytheistic character. A great many gods are named and worshipped. Yet some of the hymns shock us by their highly abstract philosophising, and from primitive polytheism to systematic philosophy it is a long, long way. Three strata of thought can be discerned in the religion of the hymns of the Ṛg-Veda, which are naturalistic polytheism, monotheism and monism.

An important point to be borne in mind in this discussion is that the word 'deva' is so very elusive in its nature and is used to indicate many different things.[9] 'Deva is one who *gives* to man.'[10] God is deva because He gives the whole world. The learned man who imparts knowledge to fellow man is also a deva.[11] The sun, the moon and the sky are devas because they give light to all creation. Father and mother and spiritual guides are also devas.[12] Even a guest is a deva. We have to take into account only that notion of deva which answers at least roughly to the modern conception of God. It then means bright.

The process of god-making in the factory of man's mind cannot be seen so clearly anywhere else as in the Ṛg-Veda. We have in it the freshness and splendour of the morning of man's mind still undulled by past custom or fixed routine. There is no such thin as a beginning in the history of ideas, and we have to start somewhere. We may begin with the identification of the Vedic gods in some of their aspects with certain forces of nature, and point out how they were gradually raised to moral and superhuman beings. The earliest seers of the Vedic hymns delighted in sights of nature in their

9. The Nirukta says: 'Devo dānād vā dīpanād vā dyotanād vā dyusthāno vā bhavati.' vii. 15.

10. We may compare this with the English word 'lady,' which seems to have meant originally the kneader of the loaf. Lord has a somewhat similar origin—the guardian of the loaf.

11. Vidvāṁso hi devāḥ.

12. Mātṛdevo bhava, pitṛdevo bhava, ācāryadevo bhava.

own simple unconscious way. Being essentially of a poetic temperament, they saw the things of nature with such intensity of feeling and force of imagination that the things became suffused with souls. They knew what it was to love nature, and be lost in the wonders of dawn and sunrise, those mysterious processes which effect a meeting of the soul and nature. To them nature was a living presence with which they could hold communion. Some glorious aspects of nature became the windows of heaven, through which the divine looked down upon the godless earth. The moon and the stars, the sea and the sky, the dawn and the nightfall were regarded as divine. This worship of nature as such as the earliest form of Vedic religion.

Soon cold reflection sets in. An unconscious effort to penetrate into the inner nature of things results. Man is busy making gods in his own image. The religion of the undeveloped man, the world over, has been a kind of anthropomorphism. We cannot acquiesce in the chaos of the physical world. We try to understand it in some way and arrive at some theory of life with the conviction that some hypothesis is better than none. Naturally we project our own volitional agency and explain phenomena by their spiritual causes.[13] We interpret all things on the analogy of our own nature and posit wills behind physical phenomena. The theory is not to be confused with animism, for it does not hold to a universal animation of nature. It is a sort of polytheism where striking phenomena of nature, of which India is so full, are deified. The religious instinct reveals itself in this way. In moments of deep religious feelings, when man is delivered from some imminent peril, or realises his utter dependence on the mighty forces of nature, he feels the reality of the presence of God. He hears the voice of God in the tempest and sees his hand in the stilling of the wave. So late as the period of the Stoics we meet with similar conceptions. 'The Sun, Moon and Stars and Law and Men who have turned into Gods.'[14] It is a good thing that the

13. As Taylor puts it: 'The operations of the world seemed to be carried on by other spirits, just as the human body was held to live and act by virtue of its own inhabiting spirit-soul' (*Primitive Culture*). In his *Natural History of Religions*, Hume wrote: 'There is a universal tendency among mankind to conceive all beings like themselves.... The unknown causes which continually employ their thoughts appearing always in the same aspect, are all apprehended to be of the same kind or species. Nor is it long before we ascribe to them thought and reason and passion and sometimes even the limbs and figures of men.'

14. Chrysippus. See Gilbert Murray's *Four Stages of Greek Religion*, p. 17.

Vedic Aryan had faith in the reality of an unseen world. He had no doubt about it. Gods are. Naturalism and anthropomorphism seem to be the first stages of the Vedic religion.

It is now a commonplace of history that the Vedic Aryans and the Iranians descended from the same stock and exhibit great affinities and resemblance. They came down from their common home into India and the Iran of the Zoroastrians, and in that central home they dwelt as one undivided race till the necessities of life, want of room, the spirit of adventure, obliged them to leave their motherland and wander in quest of new fields in different directions.[15] That is why we find so many affinities in the ancient religions and philosophical ideas of India and Persia. Dr Mills says: 'The Avesta is nearer the Veda than the Veda is to its own epic Sanskrit.' There is an underlying continuity of language. When the Aryans came to India through the Punjab they found the natives of India whom they called Dasyus opposing their free advance.[16] These Dasyus were of a dark complexion, eating beef and indulging in goblin worship. When the Aryans met them they desired to keep themselves aloof from them. It is this spirit of exclusiveness born of pride of race and superiority of culture

15. Indians and the Iranians are said to belong to the larger family of Indo-Europeans, with their subdivisions of Teutonic, Celtic, Slavonic, Italic, Hellenic, Armenian races. From a comparison of the beliefs and practices of these people scholars infer a sort of Indo-European religion. Animism and magic, ancestor worship and belief in immortality are said to be the main elements of the Indo-European religion. Recent ethnologists, such as Ripley, seem to adopt a somewhat different classification of races. Some identify the Aryan race with the Teutonic or the Nordic. We have nothing to do with these here. The history of Indian thought commences only when the Aryans of Central Asia separated themselves into two groups, the one making through Afghanistan to India and the other spreading over the territory called the Iran.

16. The details of the wanderings of those who first called themselves Aryans cannot be decided with any definiteness from the now available data. The Vedic hymns reveal a later stage of social life when Sanskrit was a spoken language and the Aryan race was split up into many branches. Nor are we prepared to admit that the Dravidians were the aborigines of India. The Dravidians seem to have come to India at a much earlier date than the Aryans, and had their civilisation well established in India before the coming of the Aryans. The Dravidians, it is true, adopted the Aryan forms of life, but in their turn they influenced the Aryan civilisation. The numerous tribes who still inhabit mountainous regions difficult to access were perhaps the original inhabitants of India.

that developed into the later caste spirit. The anxiety to keep their religion pure from contamination led the Aryans to collect together their own sacred literature. The word saṁhitā, which means 'collection', suggests that the hymns of the Ṛg-Veda were collected at the period when the Aryans and the non-Aryans met on the soil of India. We shall begin our sketch of the Vedic gods with those Indo-Iranian ones held in common by the two sister races before their separation.

The feeling of the incompleteness of this world, the weakness of man, the need felt for a higher spirit, a guide, a friend, a support on which man could rest, to whom he could appeal in distress, is natural to the sick heart of man. At that early age nothing could answer to this feeling for the infinite so well as the boundless and brilliant firmament of heaven. The sun and the moon and the stars may change, storms break and clouds roll away, but the sky abides for ever. Dyaus[17] is not merely an Indo-Iranian deity, but an Indo-European one. It survives in Greece as Zeus, in Italy as Jupiter (Heavenly Father), and among the Teutonic tribes as Tyr and Tyi. Deva meant originally bright, and later was applied to all the bright ones, the sun, the sky, the stars, the dawn, the day, etc. It became a general term connoting the common features of all shining ones. The earth also was soon deified. Heaven and Earth at the beginning had perhaps only the physical aspects of vastness, breadth, productiveness.[18] The attributes ascribed to the Earth are such as 'yielding honey', 'full of milk'. But very early Heaven and Earth became endowed with human qualities such as 'not decaying,' 'father' and 'mother.' Moral attributes such as beneficence, omniscience and righteousness were also added.[19] It may be that there has been steady advance from the physical to the personal and from the personal to the divine. Earth and Heaven, the first objects of worship the world over, though probably in the beginning they were looked upon as independent beings, soon entered into a marriage alliance. The Earth was looked upon as the fruitful mother, impregnated by Heaven. In the Homeric hymns the Earth is addressed as 'Mother of Gods, the wife of the starry Heaven.'[20] Earth and Heaven are the universal parents who give life to all creatures and grant them the means of subsistence. In the Ṛg-Veda they are generally addressed in the dual number a two beings forming but one concept, for all between, the sun, the dawn, the fire, the wind and

17. *Div*, to shine.
18. i. 160. 2; i. 187. 5; iv. 56. 3; vi. 70. 1–2.
19. i. 159. 1; i. 160. 1; iv. 56. 2; vi. 70. 6.
20. See Max Müller, *India: What can it teach us?* p. 156.

the rain were their offspring. They are the parents of men and gods.[21] As the number of gods increased the question arose as to who made Heaven and Earth. 'He was indeed among the gods the cleverest workman, who produced the brilliant ones (Heaven and Earth) that gladden all things; he who measures the two bright ones by his wisdom and establishes them on everlasting supports.'[22] This creative power is assigned to Agni,[23] Indra,[24] or Soma.[25] Other gods also come in for this honour.[26]

Varuṇa is the god of the sky. The name is derived from the root '*var*', to 'cover' or 'compass'. He is identical with the Greek Ouranos and the Ahuramazda of the Avesta. His physical origin is manifest. He is the coverer or the enfolder. He covers the whole starry expanse of heaven 'as with a robe, with all the creatures thereof and their dwellings.'[27] Mitra is his constant companion. Varuṇa and Mitra, when used together, express night and day, darkness and light. Varuṇa's figure is steadily transformed and idealised till he becomes the most moral god of the Vedas. He watches over the world, punishes the evildoers and forgives the sins of those who implore his pardon. The sun is his eye, the sky is his garment and the storm is his breath.[28] Rivers flow by his command;[29] the sun shines, the star and the moon are in their courses for fear of him.[30] By his law heaven and earth are held apart. He upholds the physical and the moral order. He is no capricious god, but a 'dhṛtavrata,' one of fixed resolve. Other gods obey his orders. He is omniscient, and as such knows the flight of the birds in the sky, the path of the ships on the ocean and the course of the wind. Not a sparrow can fall without his knowledge. He is the supreme God, the God of gods, harsh to the guilty and gracious to the penitent. He conforms to the eternal law of the moral world which he has established. Yet in his mercy he is willing to forgive those who offend against him. 'He is merciful even to him who has committed sin.'[31] In almost all the hymns to Varuṇa

21. i. 185. 4; i. 159. 1–2; i. 106. 3; iii. 3. 11; iv. 56. 2; vi. 17. 7; vii 53. 1–2; ix. 85, 12; x. 1. 7; x. 35. 3; x. 64. 14; x. 65. 8; x. 11. 9.
22. R.V., i. 160. 4; see also iv. 56. 3.
23. i. 67. 3.
24. x. 89. 4.
25. ix. 101. 15.
26. iii. 31. 12.
27. viii. 41.
28. vii. 87. 2.
29. i. 24. 8; ii. 28. 4; vii. 87. 5.
30. i. 24. 10; i. 25. 6; i. 44. 14; ii. 14; ii. 28. 8; iii. 54. 18; viii. 25. 2.
31. vii. 87. 7.

we find prayers for the forgiveness of sin, filled with confessions of guilt and repentance,[32] which show that the Aryan poets had a sense of the burden of sin and prayer.

The theism of the Vaiṣṇavas and the Bhāgavatas, with its emphasis on bhakti, is to be traced to the Vedic worship of Varuṇa, with its consciousness of sin and trust in divine forgiveness. Professor Macdonell says that 'Varuṇa's character resembles that of the divine ruler in a monotheistic belief of an exalted type.'[33]

32. The following hymn to Varuṇa translated by Muir into verse, vol. v. O.S.T., p. 64, though from the Atharva-Veda (iv. 16. 1–5), brings out the high conception of God cherished by the Vedic Aryans:

'The mighty Lord on high, our deeds, as if at hand espies:
The gods know all men do, though men would fain their deeds disguise.
Whoever stands, whoever moves, or steals from place to place,
Or hides him in his secret cell—the gods his movements trace.
Wherever two together plot, and deem they are alone,
King Varuṇa is there, a third, and all their schemes are known.
This earth is his, to him belong those vast and boundless skies;
Both seas within him rest, and yet in that small pool he lies.
Whoever far beyond the sky should think his way to wing.
He could not there elude the grasp of Varuṇa the king.
His spies descending from the skies glide all this world around,
Their thousand eyes all-scanning sweep to earth's remotest bound.
Whate'er exists in heaven and earth, whate'er beyond the skies,
Before the eyes of Varuṇa, the king, unfolded lies.
The ceaseless winkings all he counts of every mortal's eyes:
He wields this universal frame, as gamester throws his dice.
Those knotted nooses which thou fling'st, O God, the bad to snare,—
All liars let them overtake, but all the truthful spare.'

Again: 'How can I get near to Varuṇa? will he accept my offering without displeasure? When shall I, with a quiet mind see him propitiated?'

'I ask, O Varuṇa, wishing to know this my sin; I go to ask the wise, the sages, all tell me the same: Varuṇa it is who is angry with thee.'

'Was it for an old sin, O Varuṇa, that thou wishest to destroy thy friend who always praises thee? Tell me, thou unconquerable Lord and I will quickly turn to thee with praise, freed from sin.'

'Absolve us from the sins of our fathers, and from those which we committed with our own bodies.'

'It is not our own doing, Varuṇa, it was a slip; an intoxicating draught, passion, dice, thoughtlessness.'

33. *Vedic Mythology*, p. 3

The law of which Varuṇa is the custodian is called the Ṛta. Ṛta literally means 'the course of things'. It stands for law in general and the immanence of justice. This conception must have been originally suggested by the regularity of the movements of sun, moon and stars, the alternations of day and of night, and of the seasons. Ṛta denotes the order of the world. Everything that is ordered in the universe has Ṛta for its principle. It corresponds to the universals of Plato.[34] The world of experience is a shadow of reflection of the Ṛta, the permanent reality which remains unchanged in all the welter of mutation. The universal is prior to the particular, and so the Vedic seer thinks that Ṛta exists before the manifestation of all phenomena. The shifting series of the world are the varying expressions of the constant Ṛta. So Ṛta is called the father of all. 'The Maruts come from afar from the seat of the Ṛta.'[35] Viṣṇu is the embryo of the Ṛta.[36] Heaven and earth are what they are by reason of the Ṛta.[37] The tendency towards the mystic conception of an unchanging reality shows its first signs here. The real is the unchanging law. What is, is an unstable show, an imperfect copy. The real is one without parts and changes, while the many shift and pass. Soon this cosmic order becomes the settled will of a supreme god, the law of morality and righteousness as well. Even the gods cannot transgress it. We see in the conception of Ṛta a development from the physical to the divine. Ṛta originally meant the 'established route of the world, of the sun, moon and stars, morning and evening, day and night.' Gradually it became the path of morality to be followed by man and the law of righteousness observed even by gods. 'The dawn follows the path of Ṛta, the right path; as if she knew them before. She never oversteps the regions. The sun follows the path of Ṛta.'[38] The whole universe is founded on Ṛta and moves in it.[39] This conception of Ṛta reminds us of Wordsworth's invocation to duty.

34. Hegel characterises the categories or universals of logic as 'God before the creation of the world or any planet.' I owe this reference to Professor J.S. Mackenzie. The Chinese sage Lao Tsū recognises a cosmic order or the *Tao*, which serves as the foundation for his ethics, philosophy and religion.

35. iv. 21. 3.

36. i. 156. 3.

37. x. 121. 1.

38. i. 24. 8, Heraclitus says 'Helios (the sun) will not overstep the bounds.'

39. iv. 23. 9.

Thou dost preserve the stars from wrong;
And the most ancient heavens, through thee, are fresh and strong.

What law is in the physical world, that virtue is in the moral world. The Greek conception of the moral life as a harmony or an ordered whole is suggested here. Varuṇa, who was first the keeper of the physical order, becomes the custodian of the moral order, *Ṛtasya gopa* and the punisher of sin. The prayer to the gods is in many cases for keeping us in the right path. 'O Indra, lead us on the path of Ṛta, on the right path over all evils.'[40]

So soon as the conception of Ṛta was recognised there was a change in the nature of gods. The world is no more a chaos representing the blind fury of chance elements, but is the working of a harmonious purpose. This faith gives us solace and security whenever unbelief tempts us and confidence in ourselves is shattered. Whatever might happen, we feel that there is a law of righteousness in the moral world answering to the beautiful order of nature. As sure as the sun rises tomorrow virtue will triumph. Ṛta can be trusted.

Mitra is the companion of Varuṇa and is generally invoked along with him. He represents sometimes the sun and sometimes the light. He is also an all-seeing, truth-loving god. Mitra and Varuṇa are joint-keepers of the Ṛta and forgivers of sin. Gradually, Mitra comes to be associated with the morning light and Varuṇa with the night-sky. Varuṇa and Mitra are called the Ādityas, or the sons of Aditi, along with Aryaman and Bhaga.

Sūrya is the sun. He has some ten hymns addressed to him. The worship of the sun is natural to the human mind. It is an essential part of the Greek religion. Plato idealised sun-worship in the *Republic.* To him the sun was the symbol of the Good. In Persia we have sun-worship. The sun, the author of all light and life in the world, has supernatural powers assigned to him. He is the life of 'all that moveth and standeth.' He is all seeing, the spy of the world. He rouses men to perform their activities, dispels darkness and gives light. 'Sūrya is rising, to pace both worlds, looking down on men, protector of all that travel or stay, beholding right and wrong among men.'[41] Sūrya becomes the creator of the world and its governor.

Savitṛ, celebrated in eleven entire hymns, is also a solar deity. He is described as golden-eyed, golden-handed and golden-tongued. He is

40. x. 133. 6.
41. R.V., vii. 60.

sometimes distinguished from the Sun,[42] though often identified with him. Savitṛ represents not only the bright sun of the golden day, but also the invisible sun of night. He has a lofty moral side, being implored by the repentant sinner for the forgiveness of sin: 'Whatever offence we may have committed against the heavenly host, through feebleness of understanding, or through weakness or through pride or through human nature, O Savitṛ, take from us this sin.'[43] The Gāyatrī hymn is addressed to Sūrya in the form of Savitṛ: 'Let us meditate on that adorable splendour of Savitṛ; may he enlighten our minds.' The oft-quoted hymn from the Yajur-Veda, 'O God Savitṛ, the Creator of All, remove the obstructions and grant the blessings,' is addressed to Savitṛ.

Sūrya in the form of Viṣṇu supports all the worlds.[44] Viṣṇu is the god of three strides. He covers the earth, heaven and the highest worlds visible to mortals. None can reach the limits of his greatness. 'We can from the earth know two of thy spaces, thou alone, O Viṣṇu, knowest thine own highest abode.'[45] Viṣṇu holds a subordinate position in the Ṛg-Veda, though he has a great future before him. The basis of Vaiṣṇavism is, however, found in the Ṛg-Veda, where Viṣṇu is described as *bṛhatśarīrah*, great in body, or having the world for his body, *pratyety āhavam*, he who comes in response to the invitation of the devotees.[46] He is said to have traversed thrice the earth spaces for the sake of man in distress.[47]

Pūṣan is another solar god. He is evidently a friend of man, being a pastoral god and the guardian of cattle. He is the god of wayfarers and husbandmen.

Ruskin says: 'There is no solemnity so deep to a rightly thinking creature as that of the dawn.' The boundless dawn from which flash forth every morning light and life becomes the goddess Uṣas, the Greek Eos, the brilliant maid of morning loved by the Aśvins, and the sun, but vanishing before the latter as he tries to embrace her with his golden rays.

The Aśvins are invoked in about fifty hymns and in parts of many others.[48] They are inseparable twins, the bright lords of brilliance and

42. R.V., vii. 63.
43. iv. 54. 3.
44. i. 21. 154.
45. i. 22. 18; vii. 59. 1–2.
46. i. 155. 6.
47. *Mānave bādhitāya*, iv. 6.
48. Aśvins are literally horsemen.

lustre, strong and agile and fleet as eagles. They are the children of Heaven, and the Dawn is their sister. It is supposed that the phenomenon of twilight is their material basis. That is why we have two Aśvins corresponding to the dawn and the dusk. They gradually become the physicians of gods and men, wonder-workers, protectors of conjugal love and life and the deliverers of the oppressed from all kinds of suffering.

We have already mentioned Aditi from whom the several gods called Ādityas are born. Aditi literally means 'unbound or unlimited.' It seems to be a name for the invisible, the infinite which surrounds us on all sides, and also stands for the endless expanse beyond the earth, the clouds and the sky. It is the immense substratum of all that is here and also beyond. 'Aditi is the sky, Aditi is the intermediate region, Aditi is father and mother and son, Aditi is all the gods and the five tribes, Aditi is whatever has been born, Aditi is whatever shall be born.'[49] Here we have the anticipation of a universal all-embracing, all-producing nature itself, the immense potentiality or the prakṛti of the Sāṁkhya philosophy. It corresponds to Anaximander's Infinite.

An important phenomenon of nature raised to a deity is Fire. Agni[50] is second in importance only to Indra, being addressed in at least 200 hymns. The idea of Agni arose from the scorching sun, which by its heat kindled inflammable stuff. It came from the clouds as lightning. It has also its origin in flintstone.[51] It comes from fire sticks.[52] Mātariśvan, like Prometheus, is supposed to have brought fire back from the sky and entrusted it to the keeping of the Bhṛgus.[53] The physical aspects are evident in the descriptions of Agni as possessing a tawny beard, sharp jaws and burning teeth. Wood or ghee is his food. He shines like the sun dispelling the darkness of night. His path is black when he invades the forests and his voice is like the thunder of heaven. He is dhūmaketu, having smoke for his banner. 'O Agni, accept this log which I offer to thee, blaze up brightly and send up thy sacred smoke, touch the topmost heavens with thy mane and mix with the beams of the sun.'[54] Fire is thus seen to dwell not only on earth in the hearth and the altar but also in the sky and the

49. R.V., i. 89.
50. Latin Ignis.
51. ii. 12. 3.
52. Sanskrit araṇis.
53. The name of a clan.
54. R.V., ii. 6.

atmosphere, as the sun and the dawn and as lightning in the clouds. He soon becomes a supreme god, stretching out heaven and earth. As the concept grew more and more abstract it also became more and more sublime. He becomes the mediator between gods and men, the helper of all. 'O Agni, bring hither Varuṇa to our offering. Bring Indra from the skies, the Maruts from the air.'[55] 'I hold Agni to be my father. I hold him to be my kinsman, my brother and also my friend.'[56]

Soma, the god of inspiration, the giver of immortal life, is analogous to the Haoma of the Avesta and Dionysos of Greece, the god of the wine and the grape. All these are the cults of the intoxicants. Miserable man requires something or other to drown his sorrows in. When he takes hold of an intoxicating drink for the first time, a thrill of delight possesses him. He is mad, no doubt, but he thinks it is a divine madness. What we call spiritual vision, sudden illumination, deeper insight, larger charity and wider understanding—all these are the accompaniments of an inspired state of the soul. No wonder the drink that elevates the spirit becomes divine. Whitney observes: 'The simple-minded Aryan people, whose whole religion was a worship of the wonderful powers and phenomena of nature, had no sooner perceived that the liquid had power to elevate the spirits and produce a temporary frenzy under the influence of which the individual was prompted to and capable of deeds beyond his natural powers, than they found in it something divine; it was to their apprehension a god, endowing those into whom it entered with god-like powers; the plant which afforded it became to them the king of plants, the process of preparing was a holy sacrifice; the instruments used therefore were sacred. The high antiquity of this cultus is attested by the references to it found occurring in the Persian Avesta; it seems, however, to have received a new impulse on Indian territory.'[57] Soma is not completely personalised. The plant and the juice are so vividly present to the poet's mind that he cannot easily deify them. The hymns addressed to Soma were intended to be sung while the juice was being pressed out of the plant. 'O Soma, poured out for Indra to drink, flow on purely in a most sweet and exhilarating current.'[58] In viii. 48. 3 the worshipper exclaims: 'We have drunk the Soma, we have become immortal, we have entered into light, we have known the gods.'

55. R.V., x. 70. 11.
56. R.V., x. 7. 3.
57. J.A.O.S., iii. 292.
58. ix. 1.

This confusion of spiritual ecstasy with physical intoxication is not peculiar to the Vedic age. William James tells us that the drunken consciousness is a bit of the mystic consciousness. It is believed that we can attain the divine through physical intoxication. Soma gradually acquires medicinal powers, helping the blind to see and the lame to walk.[59] The following beautiful hymn to Soma points out how important a place he occupies in the affections of the Vedic Aryans.

> Where there is eternal light, in the world, where the sun is placed, in that immortal, imperishable world, place me, O Soma.
> Where the son of Vivasvat reigns as King, where the secret place of heaven is, where these mighty waters are, make me immortal.
> Where life is free, in the third heaven of heavens, where the worlds are radiant, there make me immortal.
> Where wishes and desires are, where the bowl of the bright Soma is, where there is food and rejoicing, there make me immortal.
> Where there is happiness and delight, where joy and pleasure reside, where the desires of our desire are attained, there make me immortal.[60]

In the hymn to Soma just quoted there is a reference to the son of Vivasvat, who is the Yama of the Ṛg-Veda answering to the Yima, the son of Vivanhvant of the Avesta. There are three hymns addressed to Yama. He is the chief of the dead, not so much a god as a ruler of the dead. He was the first of mortals to die and find his way to the other world, the first to tread the path of the fathers.[61] Later he acts as the host receiving new-comers. He is the king of that kingdom, for he has the longest experience of it. He is sometimes invoked as the god of the setting sun.[62] In the Brāhmaṇas Yama becomes the judge and chastiser of men. But in the Ṛg-Veda he is yet only their king. Yama illustrates the truth of the remark which Lucian puts into the mouth of Heraclitus: 'What are men? Mortal gods. What are gods? Immortal men.'

59. vii. 68. 2, and x. 25. 11.

60. S.B.E., Vedic Hymns, part i. See Gilbert Murray's translation of the *Bacchae of Euripides*, p. 20.

61. Pitṛyāna, x. 2. 7.

62. x. 14.

Parjanya was the Aryan sky god. He seems to have become Indra after the Aryans entered India, for Indra is unknown to the other members of the Aryan family. In the Vedas Parjanya is another name for the sky. 'The Earth is the mother and I am the son of the Earth, Parjanya is the father. May he help us.'[63] In the Atharva-Veda Earth is called the wife of Parjanya.[64] Parjanya is the god of cloud and rain.[65] He rules as god over the whole world; all creatures rest in him; he is the life of all that moves and rests.[66] There are also passages where the word Parjanya is used for cloud or rain.[67] Max Müller is of opinion that Parjanya is identical with the Lithuanian god of thunder called Perkunas.[68]

Of all the phenomena of nature which arouse the feeling of awe and terror, nothing can challenge comparison with thunder storms. 'Yes, when I send thunder and lightning,' says Indra, 'then you believe in me.' Judging from the hymns addressed to him, Indra is the most popular god of the Vedas. When the Aryans entered India they found that, as at present, their prosperity was a mere gamble in rain. The rain god naturally becomes the national god of the Indo-Aryans. Indra is the god of the atmospheric phenomena, of the blue sky. He is the Indian Zeus. His naturalistic origin is clear. He is born of waters and the cloud. He wields the thunder-bolt, and conquers darkness. He brings us light and life, gives us vigour and freshness. Heaven bows before him and the earth trembles at his approach. Gradually, Indra's connexion with the sky and the thunder-storms is forgotten. He becomes the divine spirit, the ruler of all the world and all the creatures, who sees and hears everything, and inspires men with their best thoughts and impulses.[69] The god of the thunder-storm vanquishing the demons of drought, and darkness becomes the victorious god of battles of the Aryans in their struggles with the natives. The times were of great activity, and the people were engaged in an adventure of conquest and domination. He will have nothing to do with the native peoples of alien

63. A.V., xii. 1. 12.
64. xii. 1. 42.
65. R.V., v. 83.
66. R.V., vii. 101. 6.
67. See R.V., i. 164. 5; vii. 61.
68. *India: What can it teach us?* Lect. VI.
69. viii. 37. 3; viii. 78. 5.

faiths. 'The hero-god who as soon as born shielded the gods, before whose might the two worlds shook—that, ye people, is Indra; who made fast the earth and the heaving mountains, measured the space of air, upheld the heaven—that, ye people, is Indra; who slew the serpent and freed the seven streams, rescued the cows, the pounder in battle—that, ye people, is Indra; the dread god of whom ye doubting ask, where is he, and sneer, he is not, he who sweeps away the enemies' possessions, have faith in him—that, ye people, is Indra; in whose might stand horses, cattle and armed hosts, to whom both lines of battle call—that, ye people, is Indra; without whose aid men never conquer, whose arrow little thought of slays the wicked—that, ye people, is Indra.'[70] This champion-god acquires the highest divine attributes, rules over the sky, the earth, the waters and the mountains,[71] and gradually displaces Varuṇa from his supreme position in the Vedic pantheon. Varuṇa, the majestic, the just and the serene, the constant in purpose, he is not fit for the struggling, conquering, active times on which the Aryans have entered. So we hear the echo of this great revolution in the Vedic world in some hymns.[72]

Indra had also to battle with other gods worshipped by the different tribes settled in India. There were worshippers of waters,[73] the Aśvattha

70. R.V., ii. 12.

71. x. 89. 10.

72. (Varuṇa speaks): 'I am the king; mine is the lordship. All the gods are subject to me, the universal life-giver, and follow Varuṇa's ordinances. I rule in men's highest sanctuary—I am king Varuṇa—I, O Indra, am Varuṇa, and mine are the two wide, deep, blessed worlds. A wise maker, I created all the beings; Heaven and earth are by me preserved. I made the flowing waters to swell. I established in their sacred seat the heavens. I, the holy Āditya, spread out the tripartite universe' (heaven, earth and atmosphere).

(Indra speaks): 'I am invoked by the steed-possessing men when pressed hard in battle; I am the mighty one who stirs up the fight and whirls up the dust, in my overwhelming strength. All that have I done, nor can the might of all the gods restrain me, the unconquered; when I am exhilarated by libations and prayers, then quake both boundless worlds.'

The Ṛṣi speaks: 'That thou didst all these things, all beings know; and now thou hast proclaimed it to Varuṇa, O Ruler! Thee Indra men praise as the slayer of Vṛtra; it was thou who didst let loose the imprisoned waters' (iv. 42).

'I now say farewell, to the father, the Asura; I go from him to whom no sacrifices are offered, to him to whom men sacrifice—in choosing Indra, I give up the father though I have lived with him many years in friendship. Agni, Varuṇa and Soma must give way; the power goes to another. I see it come' (x. 124).

73. x. 9. 1–3.

tree.[74] Many of the demons with whom Indra fought were the tribal gods such as Vṛtra, the serpent.[75] Another foe of Indra, in the period of the Ṛg-Veda, was Kṛṣṇa, the deified hero of a tribe called the Kṛṣṇas. The verse reads: 'The fleet Kṛṣṇa lived on the banks of the Aṁśumatī (Jumna) river with ten thousand troops. Indra of his own wisdom became cognisant of this loud-yelling chief. He destroyed the marauding host for our benefit.'[76] This is the interpretation suggested by Sāyaṇa, and the story has some interest in connection with the Kṛṣṇa cult. The later Purāṇas speak of the opposition between Indra and Kṛṣṇa. It may be that Kṛṣṇa is the god of the pastoral tribe which was conquered by Indra in the Ṛg-Veda period, though at the time of the Bhagavadgītā he recovered much lost ground and got reinforced by becoming identified with the Vāsudeva of the Bhāgavatas and the Viṣṇu of the Vaiṣṇavas. It is this miscellaneous origin and history that make him the author of the Bhagavadgītā, the personation of the Absolute, as well as the cowherd playing the flute on the banks of the Jumna.[77]

By the side of Indra are several minor deities representing other atmospheric phenomena, Vāta or Vāyu, the wind, the Maruts, the terrible storm-gods, and Rudra the howler. Of wind a poet says: 'Where was he born and whence did he spring, the life of the gods and the germ of the world? That god moves about, where he listeth, his voices are heard, but he is not to be seen.'[78] Vāta is an Indo-Iranian god. The Maruts are the deifications of the great storms so common in India, 'when the air is darkened by dust and clouds, when in a moment the trees are stripped of their foliage, their branches shivered, their stems snapped, when the earth seems to reel and the mountains shake and the rivers are lashed into foam and fury.'[79] Maruts are powerful and destructive usually, but sometimes

74. R.V., i. 135. 8.

75. R.V., vi. 33. 2; vi. 29. 6.

76. viii. 85. 13–15.

77. Later on, the Kṛṣṇa cult became superior to the lower forms of worship of snakes and serpents and to the Vedic worship of Indra. Sister Nivedita writes: 'Kṛṣṇa conquers the snake Kālīya and leaves his own footprint on his head. Here is the same struggle that we can trace in the personality of Śiva as Nāgesvara, between the new devotional faith and the old traditional worship of snakes and serpents. He persuades the shepherds to abandon the sacrifice to Indra. Here he directly overrides the older Vedic gods, who, as in some parts of the Himalayas today, seem to know nothing of the interposition of Brahmā' (*Footfalls of Indian History*, p. 212).

78. x. 168. 34.

79. Max Müller, *India; What can it teach us*? p. 180.

they are also kind and beneficent. They lash the world from end to end, or clear the air and bring the rain.[80] They are the comrades of Indra and sons of Dyaus. Indra is sometimes called the eldest of the Maruts. On account of their fierce aspects they are considered to be the sons of Rudra the militant God.[81] Rudra has a very subordinate position in the Ṛg-Veda, being celebrated only in three entire hymns. He holds a thunder-bolt in his arms and discharges lightning shafts from the skies. Later he becomes Śiva the benignant, with a whole tradition developed round him.[82]

We also come across certain goddesses similarly developed. Uṣas and Aditi are goddesses. The river Sindhu is celebrated as a goddess in one hymn,[83] and Sarasvatī, first the name of a river, gradually becomes the goddess of learning.[84] Vāk is the goddess of speech. Araṇyānī is the goddess of the forest.[85] The later Śākta systems utilise the goddesses of the Ṛg-Veda. The Vedic Aryan prayed to the Śakti or the energy of God, as he meditated on the adorable divine light that burnt up all dross: 'Come thou, O goddess, that granteth our prayers, Thou art the unperishing, the equal of Brahman.'[86]

When thought advanced from the material to the spiritual, from the physical to the personal, it was easy to conceive of abstract deities. Most of such deities occur in the last book of the Ṛg-Veda, thus indicating their relatively late origin. We have Manyu,[87] Śraddhā,[88] etc. Certain qualities associated with the true conception of god are deified. Tvaṣṭṛ, sometimes identified with Savitṛ,[89] is 'the maker' or the constructor of the world. He forged Indra's thunder-bolt, sharpened the axe of Brahmaṇaspati, made the cups out of which the gods drink Soma, and gave shape to all living things. Brahmaṇaspati is a very late god, belonging to the period when sacrifices began to come into vogue. Originally the lord of prayer, he soon

80. R.V., i. 37. 11; i. 64. 6; i. 86. 10; ii. 34. 12.
81. i. 64. 2.
82. R.V., vii. 46. 3; i. 114. 10; i. 114. 1.
83. x. 75. 2, 4, 6.
84. vi. 61.
85. x. 146.
86. Āyātu varadā devī, akṣaram brahmasammitam. Tait. Ār., x. 34. 52.
87. Wrath, x. 83. 4.
88. Faith, x. 151.
89. iii. 55. 19.

became the god of sacrifices. We see in him the transition between the spirit of the pure Vedic religion and the later Brāhmanism.[90]

VI

MONOTHEISTIC TENDENCIES

As we shall see in our discussion of the Atharva-Veda, mythical conceptions from beyond the limits of the Aryan world belonging to a different order of thought entered into the Vedic pantheon. All this crowding of gods and goddesses proved a weariness to the intellect. So a tendency showed itself very early to identify one god with another or throw all the gods together. The attempts at classification reduced the gods to the three spheres of the earth, the air and the sky. Sometimes these gods are said to be 333, or other combinations of three in number.[91] The gods are also invoked in pairs when they fulfil identical functions. They are sometimes thrown together in one large concept of a Viśve devāḥ, or pantheon. This tendency at systematisation had its natural end in monotheism, which is simpler and more logical than the anarchy of a crowd of gods and goddesses thwarting each other.

Monotheism is inevitable with any true conception of God. The Supreme can only be one. We cannot have two supreme and unlimited beings. Everywhere the question was asked whether a god was himself the creation of another. A created god is no God at all. With the growing insight into the workings of the world and the nature of godhead the many gods tended to melt into one. The perception of unity realised in the idea of Ṛta worked in support of monotheism. If the varied phenomena of nature demand many gods, should not the unity of nature require a single god who embraces all things that are? Trust in natural law means faith in one God. The advance of this conception implies the paralysis of superstition. An olderly system of nature has no room for miraculous interferences in which alone superstition and confused thought find the signs of polytheism. In the worship of Varuṇa we have the nearest approach to monotheism.

90. Roth remarks: 'All the gods whose names are compounded with pati (lord of) must be reckoned among the more recent. They were the products of reflection.' This is, however, incorrect as a general statement. Cf. Vāstoṣpati. I owe this information to Professor Keith.

91. See R.V., iii. 9. 9.

Attributes moral and spiritual, such as justice, beneficence, righteousness, and even pity were ascribed to him. There has been a growing emphasis on the higher and more idealistic side to the suppression or comparative neglect of the gross or material side. Varuṇa is the god to whom man and nature, this world and the other all belong. He cares not only for external conduct but also for inner purity of life. The implicit demand of the religious consciousness for one supreme God made itself manifest in what is characterised as the henotheism of the Vedas. It is, according to Max Müller, who coined the term, the worshipping of each divinity in turn, as if it were the greatest and even the only god. But the whole position is a logical contradiction, where the heart showed the right path of progress and belief contradicted it. We cannot have a plurality of gods, for religious consciousness is against it. Henotheism is an unconscious groping towards monotheism. The weak mind of man is yet seeking for its object. The Vedic Aryan felt keenly the mystery of the ultimate and the inadequacy of the prevailing conceptions. The gods worshipped as supreme stand side by side, though for the moment only one holds the highest position. The one god is not the denial of the other gods. Even minor gods sometimes assume the highest rank. It all depends upon the devotion of the poet and the special object he has in view. 'Varuṇa is the heaven, Varuṇa the earth, Varuṇa the air, Varuṇa is the universe and all besides.' Sometimes Agni is all the gods. Sometimes Indra is greater than all gods. For the moment each god seems to become a composite photograph of all others. Self-surrender of man to God, the central fact of religious experience, is possible only with one God. Thus henotheism seems to be the result of the logic of religion. It is not, as Bloomfield suggests, 'polytheism grown cold in service, and unnice in its distinctions, leading to an opportunist monotheism, in which every god takes hold of the sceptre and none keeps it.'[92]

When each god is looked upon as the creator and granted the attributes of Viśvakarman, maker of the world, Prajāpati, lord of creatures, it is easy to drop the personal peculiarities and make a god of the common functions, especially when the several gods are only cloudy and confused concepts and not real persons.

The gradual idealisation of the conception of God as revealed in the cult of Varuṇa, the logic of religion which tended to make the gods flow into one another, the henotheism which had its face set in the direction

92. *The Religion of the Veda*, p. 199.

of monotheism, the conception of Ṛta or the unity of nature, and the systematising impulse of the human mind—all helped towards the displacement of a polytheistic anthropomorphism by a spiritual monotheism. The Vedic seers at this period were interested in discovering a single creative cause of the universe, itself uncreated and imperishable. The only logical way of establishing such a monotheism was by subordinating the gods under one higher being, or controlling spirit, which could regulate the workings of the lower gods. This process satisfied the craving for one god and yet allowed them to keep up the continuity with the past. Indian thought, however daring and sincere, was never hard and rude. It did not usually care to become unpopular, and so generally made compromises; but pitiless logic, which is such a jealous master, had its vengeance, with the result that to-day Hinduism, on account of its accommodating spirit, has come to mean a heterogeneous mass of philosophies, religions, mythologies and magics. The many gods were looked upon as the different embodiments of the universal spirit. They were ruling in their own respective spheres under the suzerainty of the supreme. Their powers were delegated and their lordship was only a viceroyalty, but not a sovereignty. The capricious gods of a confused nature-worship became the cosmic energies whose actions were regulated in a harmonious system. Even Indra and Varuṇa become departmental deities. The highest position in the later part of the Ṛg-Veda is granted to Viśvakarman.[93] He is the all-seeing god who has on every side eyes, faces, arms, feet, who produces heaven and earth through the exercise of his arms and wings, who knows all the worlds, but is beyond the comprehension of mortals. Bṛhaspati has also his claims for the supreme rank.[94] In many places it is prajāpati, the lord of creatures.[95] Hiraṇyagarbha, the golden god, occurs as the name of the Supreme, described as the one Lord of all that exists.[96]

VII

MONOTHEISM *VERSUS* MONISM

That even in the days of the Vedic hymns we have not merely wild imagination and fancy but also earnest thought, and inquiry, comes out

93. See x. 81. 82.
94. See x. 72.
95. See x. 85. 43; x. 189. 4; x. 184. 4; Śatapatha Brāh., vi. 6. 8. 1–14; x. 1. 3. 1.
96. x. 121.

from the fact that we find the questioning mood asserting itself very often. The necessity to postulate a number of gods is due to the impulse of mind which seeks to understand things instead of accepting facts as they are given to it. 'Where is the sun by night?' 'Where go the stars by day?' 'Why does the sun not fall down?' 'Of the two, night and day, which is the earlier, which the later?' 'Whence comes the wind, and whither goes it?'[97] Such are the questions and the feelings of awe and wonder which constitute the birthplace of all science and philosophy. We have seen also the instinctive groping for knowledge revealing itself in all forms and fancies. Many gods were asserted. The longing of the human heart could not be satisfied with a pluralistic pantheon. The doubt arose as to which god was the real one. Kasmai devāya haviṣā vidhema, 'to what god shall we offer our oblation?[98] The humble origin of the gods was quite patent. The new gods grew on Indian soil, and some were borrowed from the native races. A prayer to make us faithful[99] is not possible in a time of unshaken faith. Scepticism was in the air. Indra's existence and supremacy were questioned.[100] The nāstika or the denying spirit was busy at work dismissing the whole as a tissue of falsehood. Hymns were addressed to unknown gods. We reach the 'twilight of the gods.' In which they are slowly passing away. In the Upaniṣads the twilight changed into night and the very gods disappeared but for the dreamers of the past. Even the single great Being of the monotheistic period did not escape criticism. The mind of man is not satisfied with an anthropomorphic deity. If we say there is one great god under whom the others are, the question is not left unasked. 'Who has seen the firstborn, when he that had no bones bore him that has bones? Where is the life, the blood, the self of the universe? Who went to ask of any who knew?'[101] It is the fundamental problem of philosophy. What is the life or essence of the universe? Mere dogma will not do. We must feel or experience the spiritual reality. The question therefore is, 'Who has seen the firstborn?'[102] The seeking minds did not so much care for personal comfort and happiness as for absolute truth. Whether you look upon God with the savage as an angry and offended man or with the civilised as a

97. R.V., i. 24. 185.
98. x. 121.
99. x. 151.
100. x. 86. 1; vii. 100–3; ii. 12. 5.
101. R.V., i. 4. 164.
102. Ko dadarśa prathamā jāyamānam?

merciful and compassionate being, the judge of all the earth, the author and controller of the world, it is a weak conception that cannot endure criticism. The anthropomorphic ideas must vanish. They give us substitutes for God, but not the true living God. We must believe in God, the centre of life, and not His shadow as reflected in men's minds. God is the inexhaustible light surrounding us on all sides. Prāṇo Virāṭ ('Life is immense'). It includes thoughts no less than things. The same reveals itself under different aspects. It is one, uniform, eternal, necessary, infinite and all-powerful. From it all flows out. To it all returns. Whatever the emotional value of a personal God may be, truth sets up a different standard and requires a different object of worship. However cold and remote, awful and displeasing it may seem to be, it does not cease to be the truth. Monotheism, to which a large part of humanity even to-day clings, failed to satisfy the later Vedic thinkers.

They applied to the central principle the neuter term Sat, to show that it is above sex. They were convinced that there was something real of which Agni, Indra, Varuṇa, etc., were only the forms or names. That something was, not many, but one, impersonal, ruling 'over all that is unmoving and that moves, that walks or flies, being differently born.'[103] 'The real is one, the learned call it by various names, Agni, Yama and Mātariśvan.'[104]

The starry heavens and the broad earth, the sea and the everlasting hills,

> Were all the workings of one mind, the features
> Of the same face, blossoms upon one tree;
> Characters of the great apocalypse,
> The types and symbols of eternity,
> The first and the last and midst and without end.[105]

This one is the soul of the world, the reason immanent in the universe, the source of all nature, the eternal energy. It is neither the heaven nor the earth, neither sunshine nor storm, but another essence, perhaps the Ṛta substantiated, the Aditi spiritualised, the one breathing breathless.[106] We cannot see it, we cannot adequately describe it. With a touching sincerity

103. iii. 54. 8.
104. Ekaṁ sad viprā bahudhā vadanti
Agniṁ yamam mātariśvānam āhuḥ (i. 164. 46).
105. Wordsworth, Prelude 6.
106. x. 129. 2.

the poet concludes: 'We never will behold him who gave birth to these things.' 'As a fool, ignorant in my own mind, I ask for the hidden places of the gods—not having discovered I ask the sages who may have discovered, not knowing in order to know.'[107] It is the supreme reality which lives in all things and moves them all, the real one that blushes in the rose, breaks into beauty in the clouds, shows its strength in the storms and sets the stars in the sky. Here then we have the intuition of the true God, who of all the gods is the only God, wonderful any day, but surpassingly wonderful because it was at such an early hour in the morning of mind's history that the true vision was seen. In the presence of this one reality, the distinction between the Aryan and the Dravidian, the Jew and the heathen, the Hindu and the Muslim, the pagan and the Christian, all fade away. We have here a momentary vision of an ideal where of all earthly religions are but shadows pointing to the perfect day. The one is called by many names. 'Priests and poets with words make into many the hidden reality which is but one.'[108] Man is bound to form very imperfect ideas of this vast reality. The desires of his soul seem to be well satisfied with inadequate ideas, 'the idols which we here adore.' No two idols can be exactly the same, since no two men have exactly the same ideas. It is stupidity to quarrel about the symbols by which we attempt to express the real. The one God is called differently according to the different spheres in which he works or the tastes of the seeking souls. This is not to be viewed as any narrow accommodation to popular religion. It is a revelation of a profound philosophic truth. To Israel the same revelation came: 'The Lord, thy God, is one.' Plutarch says: 'There is One Sun and One sky over all nations and one Deity under many names.'

> O! God, most glorious, called by many a name,
> Nature's Great King, through endless years the same;
> Omnipotence, who by thy just decree
> Controllest all, hail, Zeus, for unto thee
> Behoves thy creatures in all lands to call.[109]

Of this monistic theory of the Ṛg-Veda Deussen writes: 'The Hindus arrive at this monism by a method essentially different from that of other

107. R.V., x. 121; x. 82. 7; i. 167. 5–6.
108. x. 114; see also the Yajur-Veda, xxx. 2. 4. See Yāska's *Nirukta*, vii. 5.
109. The Hymn of Cleanthes.

countries. Monotheism was attained in Egypt by a mechanical identification of the various local gods, in Palestine by proscription of other gods and violent persecution of their worshippers for the benefit of their national god Jehovah. In India they reached monism, though not monotheism on a more philosophical path, seeing through the veil of the manifold the unity which underlies it.'[110] Max Müller says: 'Whatever is the age when the collection of our Ṛg-Veda Saṁhitā was finished, it was before that age that the conviction had been formed that there is but One, One Being, neither male nor female, a Being raised high above all the conditions and limitations of personality and of human nature, and nevertheless the Being that was really meant by all such names as Indra, Agni, Mātariśvan, nay, even by the name of Prajāpati, Lord of creatures. In fact, the Vedic poets had arrived at a conception of the godhead which was reached once more by some of the Christian philosophers at Alexandria, but which even at present is beyond the reach of many who call themselves Christians.'[111]

In some of the advanced hymns of the Ṛg-Veda the Supreme is indifferently called He or It. The apparent vacillation between monotheism and monism, a striking feature of Eastern as well of Western philosophy, revealed itself here for the first time in the history of thought. The same formless, impersonal, pure and passionless being of philosophy is worshipped by the warm full-blooded heart of the emotional man as a tender and benevolent deity. This is inevitable. Religious consciousness generally takes the form of a dialogue, a communion of two wills, finite and infinite. There is a tendency to make of God an infinite person over against the finite man. But this conception of God as one among many is not the highest truth of philosophy. Except for a few excessively logical people who wish to push their principles to their extreme conclusions, there cannot be religion without a personal God. Even the philosopher when asked to define the highest reality cannot but employ terms which reduce it to the lower level. Man knows that his limited powers cannot compass the transcendent vastness of the Universal Spirit. Yet he is obliged to describe the Eternal in his own small way. Bound down by his limitations he necessarily frames inadequate pictures of the vast, sublime, inscrutable source and energy of all things. He creates idols for his own satisfaction. Personality is a limitation, and yet only a personal God can be worshipped. Personality implies the distinction of self and not-self, and hence is

110. *Outlines of Indian Philosophy*, p. 13.
111. S.S., pp. 51, 52.

inapplicable to the Being who includes and embraces all that is. The personal God is a symbol, though the highest symbol of the true living God. The formless is given a form, the impersonal is made personal; the omnipresent is fixed to a local habitation; the eternal is given a temporal setting. The moment we reduce the Absolute to an object of worship, it becomes something less than the Absolute. To have a practical relationship with finite will, God must be less than the Absolute, but if He is less than the Absolute, then He cannot be the object of worship in any effective religion. If God is perfect, religion is impossible; if God is imperfect, religion is ineffective. We cannot have with a finite limited God the joy of peace, the assurance of victory and the confidence in the ultimate destiny of the universe. True religion requires the Absolute. Hence to meet the demands of both popular religion and philosophy, the Absolute Spirit is indiscriminately called He or It. It is so in the Upaniṣads. It is so in the Bhagavadgītā and the Vedānta Sūtras. We need not put this down to a conscious compromise of theistic and monistic elements or any elusiveness of thought. The monistic conception is also capable of developing the highest religious spirit. Only prayer to God is replaced by contemplation of the Supreme Spirit that rules the world, the love that thrills it in an unerring but yet lavish way. The sympathy between the mind of the part and that of the whole is productive of the highest religious emotion. Such an ideal love of God and meditation on the plenitude of beauty and goodness flood the mind with the cosmic emotion. It is true that such a religion seems to the man who has not reached it and felt its power too cold or too intellectual, yet no other religion can be philosophically justified.

All forms of religion which have appeared on earth assume the fundamental need of the human heart. Man longs for a power above him on which he could depend, One that is greater than himself whom he could worship. The gods of the several stages of the Vedic religion are the reflections of the growing wants and needs, the mental gropings and the heart-searchings of man. Sometimes he would want gods who would hear his prayers and accept his sacrifices, and we have gods answering to this prescription. We have naturalistic gods, anthropomorphic gods, but none of them answered to the highest conception, however much one might try to justify them to the mind of man by saying that they were the varying expressions of the one Supreme. The scattered rays dispersed among the crowd of deities are collected together in the intolerable splendour of the One nameless God who alone could satisfy the restless craving of the human heart and the sceptic mind. The Vedic progress did not stop until it reached this ultimate reality. The growth of religious thought as embodied in the hymns may be brought out by the mention of the typical gods: (1) Dyaus, indicative of the first state of nature worship; (2) Varuṇa, the highly moral god of a later day; (3) Indra, the selfish god of the age of conquest and domination; (4) Prajāpati, the god of the monotheists; and (5) Brahman, the perfection of all these four lower stages. This progression is as much chronological as logical. Only in the Vedic hymns we find them all set down side by side without any conception of logical arrangement or chronological succession. Sometimes the same hymn has suggestions of them all. It only shows that when the text of the Ṛg-Veda came to be written all these stages of thought had already been passed, and people were clinging to some or all of them without any consciousness of their contradiction.

VIII

COSMOLOGY

The Vedic thinkers were not unmindful of the philosophical problems of the origin and nature of the world. In their search for the first ground of all changing things, they, like the ancient Greeks, looked upon water, air, etc., as the ultimate elements out of which the variety of the world is composed. Water is said to develop into the world through the force of time, saṁvatsara or year, desire or kāma, intelligence or puruṣa, warmth or tapas.[112] Sometimes water itself is derived from night or chaos, tamas, or air.[113] In x. 72 the world ground is said to be the asat, or the non-existent, with which is identified Aditi, the infinite. All that exists is diti, or bounded, while the a-diti, the infinite, is non-existent. From the infinite, cosmic force arises, though the latter is sometimes said to be the source of the infinite itself.[114] These theories, however, soon related themselves to the non-physical, and physics by alliance with religion became metaphysics.

In the pluralistic stage the several gods, Varuṇa, Indra, Agni, Viśvakarman, were looked upon as the authors of the universe.[115] The method of creation is differently conceived. Some gods are supposed to build the world as he carpenter builds a house. The question is raised as

112. x. 190.
113. x. 168.
114. x. 72. 3.
115. vii. 86; iii. 32. 80; x. 81. 2.; x. 72. 2; x. 121. 1.

to how the tree or the wood out of which the work was built was obtained.[116] At a later stage the answer is given that Brahman is the tree and the wood out of which heaven and earth are made.[117] The conception of organic growth or development is also now and then suggested.[118] Sometimes the gods are said to create the world by the power of sacrifice. This perhaps belongs to a later stage of Vedic thought.

When we get to the monotheistic level the question arises as to whether God created the world out of His own nature without any pre-existent matter or through His power acting on eternally pre-existent matter. The former view takes us to the higher monistic conception, while the latter remains at the lower monotheistic level, and we have both views in the Vedic hymns. In x. 121 we have an account of the creation of the world by an Omnipotent God out of pre-existent matter. Hiraṇyagarbha arose in the beginning from the great water which pervaded the universe. He evolved the beautiful world from the shapeless chaos which was all that existed.[119] But how did it happen, it is asked, that the chaos produced Hiraṇyagarbha? What is that unknown force or law of development which led to his rise? Who is the author of the primeval waters? According to Manu, Harivaṁśa and the Purāṇas, God was the author of chaos. He created it by His Will, and deposited a seed in it which became the golden germ in which He Himself was born as the Brahmā or the Creator God. 'I am Hiraṇyagarbha, the Supreme Spirit Himself become manifested in the form of Hiraṇyagarbha.'[120] Thus the two eternally co-existent substances seem to be the evolution of the one ultimate substratum.

This is exactly the theory of a later hymn called the Nāsadīya hymn, which is translated by Max Müller.

> There was then neither what is nor what is not, there was no sky, nor the heaven which is beyond. What covered? Where was it, and in whose shelter? Was the water the deep abyss (in which it lay)?
>
> There was no death, hence was there nothing immortal. There was no light (distinction) between night and day. That One breathed by itself without breath, other than it there has been nothing.

116. x. 31. 7; cf. x. 81. 4.
117. See Tait. Brāh.
118. x. 123. 1.
119. Cf. Manu, i. 5. 8; Maitrī Up., 5. 2.
120. Manu, v. 9.

Darkness there was, in the beginning all this was a sea without light; the germ
that lay covered by the husk, that One was born by the power of heat (tapas).
Love overcame it in the beginning, which was the seed springing from mind,
poets having searched in their heart found by wisdom the bond of what is
in what is not.

Ray which was stretched across, was it below or was it above? There
were seed-bearers, there were powers, self-power below, and will above.
Who then knows, who has declared it here, from whence was born this creation?
The gods came later than this creation, who then knows whence it arose?
He from whom this creation arose, whether he made it or did not make it, the
highest seer in the highest heaven, he forsooth knows, or does even he not
know?[121]

We find in this hymn a representation of the most advanced theory of creation. First of all there was no existent or non-existent. The existent in its manifested aspect was not then. We cannot on that account call it the non-existent, for it is positive being from which the whole existence arrives. The first line brings out the inadequacy of our categories. The absolute reality which is at the back of the whole world cannot be characterised by us as either existent or non-existent. The one breathed breathless by its own power.[122] Other than that there was not anything beyond. First cause of all it is older than the whole world, with the sun, moon, sky and stars. It is beyond time, beyond space, beyond age, beyond death and beyond immortality. We cannot express what it is except that it is. Such is the primal unconditioned groundwork of all being. Within that Absolute Consciousness there is first the fact of affirmation or positing of the primal 'I.' This corresponds to the logical law of identity, A is A, the validity of which presupposes the original self-positing. Immediately there must be also a non-ego as the correlate of the ego. The I confronts the not-I, which answers to 'A is not B.' The 'I' will be a bare affirmation, a mere abstraction, unless there is *another* of which it is conscious. If there is no other, there is no ego. The ego implies non-ego as its condition. This opposition of ego and non-ego is the primary antithesis, and the development of this implication from the Absolute is said to be by tapas. Tapas is just the 'rushing forth,' the spontaneous 'out-growth,' the projection of being into existence, the energising impulse, the innate spiritual fervour of the

121. x. 129; see also S.S., pp. 65. 65. See Śat. Brāh., x. 5. 3. 1.
122. Cf. Aristotle's unmoved mover.

Absolute. Through this tapas we get being and non-being, the I and the not-I, the active Puruṣa and the passive prakṛti, the formative principle and the chaotic matter. The rest of the evolution follows from the interaction of these two opposed principles. According to the hymn, desire constitutes the secret of the being of the world. Desire or kāma is the sign of self-consciousness, the germ of the mind, *manaso retaḥ*. It is the ground of all advance, the spur of progress. The self-conscious ego has desires developed in it by the presence of the non-ego. Desire[123] is more than thought. It denotes intellectual stir, the sense of deficiency as well as active effort. It is the bond binding the existent to the non-existent. The unborn, the one, the eternal breaks forth into a self-conscious Brahmā with matter, darkness, non-being, zero, chaos opposed to it. Desire is the essential feature of this self-conscious Puruṣa. The last phrase, 'ko veda?' ('who knows?') brings out the mystery of creation which has led later thinkers to call it māyā.

There are hymns which stop with the two principles of Puruṣa and prakṛti. In x. 82. 5–6, of the hymn to Viśvakarman, we find it said that the waters of the sea contained the first or primordial germ. This first germ is the world egg floating on the primeval waters of chaos, the principle of the universe of life. From it arises Viśvakarman, the firstborn of the universe, the creator and maker of the world. The waters are the chaos of the Greeks, the 'without-form and void' of Genesis, with the infinite will reposing on it.[124] Desire, will, self-consciousness, mind, vāk, or the word, all these are the qualities of the infinite intelligence, the personal God brooding over the waters, the Nārāyaṇa resting on the eternal Ananta. It is the god of Genesis who says, 'Let there be, and there was.' 'He thought, I will create the worlds, then He created these various worlds, water, light, etc.' The Nāsadīya hymn, however, overcomes the dualistic metaphysics in a higher monism. It makes nature and spirit both aspects of the one Absolute. The Absolute itself is neither the self nor the other, is neither

123. Greek mythology, it is interesting to notice, connects Eros, the god of love, corresponding to Kāma, with the creation of the universe. Plato says in his Symposium: 'Eros neither had any parents nor is he said by any unlearned men or by any poet to have had any ...' According to Aristotle, God moves as the object of desire.

124. Cf. it with the account of the Genesis: 'And darkness was on the face of the deep and the spirit of God was moving on the face of the waters' (Gen. i. 2); see also R.V., x. 121; x. 72.

self-consciousness of the type of I, nor unconsciousness of the type of not-I. It is a higher than both these. It is a transcending consciousness. The opposition is developed within itself. According to this account the steps of creation, when translated into modern terms, are: (1) the Highest Absolute; (2) the bare self-consciousness, I am I; (3) the limit of self-consciousness in the form of another. This does not mean that there is a particular point at which the Absolute moves out. The stages are only logically but not chronologically successive. The ego implies the non-ego, and therefore cannot precede it. Nor can the non-ego precede the ego. Nor can the Absolute be ever without doing tapas. The timeless whole is ever breaking out in a series of becomings, and the process will go on till the self reaffirms itself absolutely in the varied content of experience which is never going to be. So the world is always restless. The hymn tells us the how of creation, not the whence. It is an explanation of the fact of creation.[125]

We see clearly that there is no basis for any conception of the unreality of the world in the hymns of the Ṛg-Veda. The world is not a purposeless phantasm, but is just the evolution of God. Wherever the word māyā occurs, it is used only to signify the might or the power: 'Indra takes many shapes quickly by his māyā.'[126] Yet sometimes māyā and its derivatives, māyin, māyāvant, are employed to signify the will of the demons,[127] and we also find the word used in the sense of illusion or show.[128] The main tendency of the Ṛg-Veda is a naïve realism. Later Indian thinkers distinguish five elements, ether or ākāśa, air, fire, water and earth. But the Ṛg-Veda postulates only one, water. It is the primeval matter from which others slowly develop.

It is obviously wrong to think that according to the hymn we discussed there was originally non-being from out of which being grew. The first condition is not absolute non-existence, for the hymn admits the reality of the one breathing breathless by itself. It is their way of describing the absolute reality, the logical ground of the whole universe. Being and non-being, which are correlative terms, cannot be applied to the One which is beyond all opposition. Non-being only means whatever now visibly exists

125. Cf. with this the conception of a Demiurge, as used by Plato in the *Timaeus*. The conception of creative imagination, set forth by E. Douglas Fawcett in his two books, *The World as Imagination* and *Divine Imagining*, may also be compared.

126. vi. 47. 18.

127. v. 2. 9; vi. 61. 3; i. 32. 4; vii. 49. 4; vii. 98. 5.

128. x. 54. 2.

had then no distinct existence. In x. 72. 1, it is said, 'the existent sprang from the non-existent.' Even here it does not mean being comes from non-being but only that distinct being comes from non-distinct being. So we do not agree with the view that the hymn is 'the starting-point of the natural philosophy which developed into the Sāṁkhya system.'[129]

The creation of the world is sometimes traced to an original material as it were; in the Puruṣa Sūkta[130] we find that the gods are the agents of creation, while the material out of which the world is made is the body of the great Puruṣa. The act of creation is treated as a sacrifice in which Puruṣa is the victim. 'Puruṣa is all this world, what has been and shall be.'[131] Anthropomorphism when once it is afoot cannot be kept within bounds, and the imagination of the Indian brings out the greatness of his God by giving him huge dimensions. The poetic mind conjures up a vast composition pointing out the oneness of the whole, world and God. This hymn is not, however, inconsistent with the theory of creation from the One Absolute described above. The whole world even according to it is due to the self-diremption of the Absolute into subject and object, Puruṣa and Prakṛti. Only the idea is rather crudely allegorised. The supreme reality becomes the active Puruṣa, for it is said: 'From the Puruṣa Virāt was born, and from Virāt again Puruṣa.' Puruṣa is thus the begetter as well as the begotten. He is the Absolute as well as the self-conscious I.

IX

RELIGION

We have seen how physical phenomena first came to attract attention and were assigned personalities. The deification of natural phenomena has a mischievous influence on religious thought and practice. The world becomes peopled with gods possessed of the human sense of justice and capable of being influenced by the human qualities of hate and love. Many of the gods are not even sufficiently humanised and easily lapse into their

129. See Macdonell, *Vedic Reader*, p. 207. There are vedic thinkers who postulate being or non-being as the first principle (x. 129. 1; x. 72. 2) so far as the world of experience is concerned, and these perhaps gave rise to the later logical theories of satkāryavāda, the existence of the effect in the cause, and asatkāryavāda, the non-existence of the effect in the cause.

130. x. 90.

131. x. 90. 2.

past naturalistic condition. Indra, for example, born of waters and cloud, sometimes crashes down from heaven in thunder. Vedic gods, as Bloomfield says, represent 'arrested personification.' But even the humanised gods are only crudely personal. They have hands and feet like men. They are given the actual bodily shape, the warring passions of the human breast, the outer polish of a fair skin, and the dignity of a long beard. They fight and feast, drink and dance, eat and rejoice. Some of them are described to be priests in function such as Agni and Bṛhaspati; others are warriors, like Indra and the Maruts. Their food is just the favourite food of man, milk and butter, ghee and grain; their favourite drink is the Soma juice. They have their share of human weakness and are easily pleased by flattery. Sometimes they are so stupidly self-centred that they begin to discuss what they should give. 'This is what I will do—not that, I will give him a cow or shall it be a horse? I wonder if I have really had Soma from him.'[132] In their eyes a rich offering is much more efficacious than a sincere prayer. It is a very simple law of give and take that binds gods and men, though the perfect reciprocity governing their relations in the later Brāhmaṇas is yet remote.

'To make the elements of a nature religion human is inevitably to make them vicious. There is no great moral harm in worshipping a thunderstorm even though the lightning strikes the good and the evil quite recklessly. There is no need to pretend that the lightning is exercising a wise and righteous choice, but when once you worship an imaginary quasi-human being who throws the lightning you are in a dilemma. Either you have to admit that you are worshipping and flattering a being with no moral sense, because he happens to be dangerous, or else you have to invent reasons for his wrath against the people who happen to be struck. And they are pretty sure to be bad reasons. The God if personal becomes capricious and cruel.'[133] True to this view, the Vedic worship of the natural powers is not quite sincere, but utilitarian. We fear the gods whose effects are dangerous to us, and love those that help us in our daily pursuits. We pray to Indra to send down rain, and yet beg him not to send the storm. The sun is implored to impart a gentle warmth, and not force the world into drought and famine by scorching heat. The gods become the sources of material prosperity, and prayers for the goods of the world are very common. And since there is a division of functions and attributes, we

132. Oldenberg, *Ancient India*, p. 71.
133. Gilbert Murray: *Four Stages of Greek Religion*, p. 88.

pray to particular deities for specific things.[134] The invocations to the gods are monotonously simple.[135] The gods were conceived as strong rather than good, powerful rather than moral. Such a religion is not capable of satisfying men's ethical aspirations. It shows the strong moral sense of the Vedic Aryan, that in spite of the prevalent tendency of utilitarian worship he yet regards the gods as being in general moral as inclined to help the good and punish the wicked. The highest religious aspiration of man to unite himself with the Supreme is recognised.[136] The many gods are helpful only as enabling their devotees to reach the Supreme.[137]

It was inevitable that sacrifices should come. For the depth of one's affection for God consists in the surrender of one's property and possessions to Him. We pray and offer. Even when sacrificial offerings came into fashion, the spirit was considered more important and the real nature of the sacrifice was insisted on. 'Utter a powerful speech to Indra which is sweeter than butter on honey.'[138] Śraddhā or faith in all ceremonies is necessary.[139] Varuṇa is a god who looks into the secret recesses of the human heart to find out the deep-lying motive. Gradually having conceived the gods as human, much too human, they thought that a full meal was the best way to the heart of God.[140]

The question of human sacrifice is much debated. The case of Śunaśśepa[141] does not indicate that human sacrifices are either allowed or encouraged in the Vedas. We hear of horse sacrifices.[142] But against all such there were protests heard even then. Sāma-Veda says: 'O, Ye Gods! We use no sacrificial stake. We slay no victim. We worship entirely by the

134. x. 47. 1; iv. 32. 4; ii. 1; ii. 6; vii. 59; vii. 24. 6; vii. 67. 16.

135. x. 42. 4.

136. R.V., x. 88. 15; i. 125. 5; x. 107. 2.

137. i. 24. 1.

138. ii. 24. 20; vi. 15. 47.

139. i. 55. 5; i. 133. 5; i. 104. 6.

140. 'Ritual in Homer is simple and uniform. It consists of prayer accompanied by the sprinkling of the grain, followed by animal burnt offering. Part of the flesh is tasted by the worshippers and then made over by burning to the gods. The rest is eaten as a banquet with abundance of wine' (Harrison, *Stages of Grecian Life*, pp. 87–88). Agni is pre-eminently the god of sacrifices in India. It is so even in ancient Greece. Fire carries the offerings from earth to heavenly gods. In all these things there is nothing specially Indian.

141. R.V., i. 6. 24.

142. R.V., ii., iii. vi., vii.

repetition of the sacred verses.'[143] This cry of revolt is taken up by the Upaniṣads and carried on by the Buddhist and the Jaina schools.

Sacrifices represent the second stage of the Vedic religion. In the first it was simple prayer. According to Pārāśarasmṛti we have 'meditation in the Kṛtayuga, sacrifices in the Treata, worship in the Dvāpara, praises and prayers in Kali.' This view accords well with what the Viṣṇupurāṇa says that the rules of sacrifices were formulated in the tretāyuga.[144] We may not agree with the division into yugas, but the logic of the growth of religious practice from meditation to sacrifice, from sacrifice to worship, from worship to praise and prayer, seems to be founded on fact.

The Vedic religion does not seem to be an idolatrous one. There were then no temples for gods. Men had direct communion with gods without any mediation. Gods were looked upon as friends of their worshippers. 'Father Heaven', 'Mother Earth', 'Brother Agni'—these are no idle phrases. There was a very intimate personal relationship between men and gods. Religion seems to have dominated the whole life. The dependence on God was complete. The people prayed of even the ordinary necessities of life. 'Give us this day our daily bread' was true to the spirit of the Vedic Aryan. It is the sign of a truly devout nature to depend on God for even the creature comforts of existence. As we have already said, we have the essentials of the highest theism in the worship of Varuṇa. If bhakti means faith in a personal God, love for Him, dedication of everything to His service and the attainment of mokṣa or freedom by personal devotion, surely we have all these elements in Varuṇa worship.

In x. 15 and x. 54 we have two hymns addressed to the pitaras or fathers, the blessed dead who dwell in heaven. In the Vedic hymns they are invoked together with the devas.[145] They are supposed to come in the form of invisible spirits to receive the prayers and offerings at sacrifices. The social tradition is revered perhaps in the worship of the fathers. There are, however, some students of the Vedas who believe that the hymns of the Ṛg-Veda do not know of any obsequial offerings to ancestral manes.[146]

A criticism that is generally urged against the Vedic religion is that the consciousness of sin is absent in the Veda. This is an erroneous view. Sin,

143. i., ii. 9. 2.
144. vi. 2; See the story of Purūravas.
145. x. 15.
146. Behari Lal, *The Vedas*, p. 101.

in the Vedas, is alienation from God.[147] The Vedic conception of sin is analogous to the Hebrew theory. The will of God is the standard of morality. Human guilt it short-coming. We sin when we transgress the commands of God. The gods are the upholders of the Ṛta, the moral order of the world. They protect the good and punish the wicked. Sin is not merely the omission of the external duties. There are moral sins as well as ritual sins.[148] It is a consciousness of sin that calls for propitiatory sacrifices. Especially in the conception of Varuṇa we have the sense of sin and forgiveness which reminds us of modern Christian doctrines.

While as a rule the gods of the Ṛg-Veda are regarded as the guardians of morality, some of them still retain their egoistic passions, being only magnified men, nor are there poets wanting who are able to see the hollowness of all this. One hymn[149] points out how all gods and men are dominated by self-interest. The decay of the old Vedic worship is traceable to this low conception of many gods. Otherwise we cannot understand the beautiful hymn,[150] which recommends the duty of benevolence without any reference to gods. The gods seem to have become too weak to support a pure morality. The idea of an ethics independent of religion popularised in Buddhism is suggested here.

X

ETHICS

Turning to the ethics of the Ṛg-Veda, we find that the conception of Ṛta is of great significance. It is the anticipation of the law of karma, one of the distinguishing characteristics of Indian thought. It is the law which pervades the whole world, which all gods and men must obey. If there is law in the world, it must work itself out. If by any chance its effects are not revealed here on earth, they must be brought to fruition elsewhere. Where law is, disorder and injustice are only provisional and partial. The triumph of the wicked is not absolute. The shipwreck of the good need not cause despair.

Ṛta furnishes us with a standard of morality. It is the universal essence of things. It is the satya or the truth of things. Disorder or An-Ṛta is

147. vii. 86. 6; see also vii. 88, 5, 6.
148. i. 23. 22; i. 85.
149. ix. 115.
150. x. 117.

falsehood, the opposite of truth.[151] The good are those who follow the path of Ṛta, the true and the ordered. Ordered conduct is called a true vrata. Vratāni are the ways of life of good men who follow the path of Ṛta.[152] Consistency is the central feature of a good life. The good man of the Vedas does not alter his ways. Varuṇa, the perfect example of the follower of Ṛta, is a dhṛtavrata, of unalterable ways. When ritual grew in importance, Ṛta became a synonym for yajña or sacrificial ceremony.

After giving us a general account of the ideal life, the hymns detail the specific contents of the moral life. Prayers are to be offered to the gods. Rites are to be performed.[153] The Vedas assume a very close and intimate relationship between men and gods. The life of man has to be led under the very eye of God. Apart from the duties owed to gods there are also duties to man.[154] Kindness to all is enjoined; hospitality is reckoned a great virtue. 'The riches of one who gives do not diminish.... He who possessed of food hardens his heart against the feeble man craving nourishment, against the sufferer coming to him (for help) and pursues (his own enjoyment even) before him, that man finds no consoler.'[155] Sorcery, witchcraft, seduction and adultery are condemned as vicious.[156] Gambling is denounced. Virtue is conformity to the law of God, which includes the love of man. Vice is disobedience to this law. 'If we have sinned against the man who loves us, have ever wronged friend or comrade, have ever done an injury to a neighbour who ever dwelt with us or even to a stranger, O Lord! free us from the guilt of this trespass.'[157] Some of the gods cannot be persuaded or diverted from the paths of righteousness by any amount of offerings. 'In them is to be discerned neither right nor left, neither before nor behind. They neither wink nor sleep, they penetrate all things; they see through both evil and good; everything, even the most distant, is near to them; they abhor and punish death; sustain and support all that lives.

There are also indications of an ascetic tendency. Indra is said to have conquered heaven by asceticism.[158] But the dominant note is not one of

151. See R.V., vii. 56. 12; ix. 115. 4; ii. 6. 10; iv. 5. 5; viii. 6. 2; 12; vii. 47. 3.
152. ix. 121. 1; x. 37. 5.
153. R.V., i. 104. 6; i. 108. 6; ii. 26. 3; x. 151.
154. R.V., x. 117.
155. viii. 6. 5; i. 2. 6.
156. vii. 104. 8 ff; iv. 5. 5.
157. R.V., v. 85. 7.
158. x. 127.

asceticism. In the hymns we find a keen delight in the beauties of nature, its greatness, its splendour and its pathos. The motive of the sacrifices is love of the good things of the world. We have yet the deep joy in life and the world untainted by any melancholy gloom. Ascetic practices were, however, known. Fasting and abstinence were regarded as means of attaining various supernatural powers. In ecstatic moods it is said that the gods have entered into men.[159] The earliest reference to the ecstatic condition of ascetic sages is in Ṛg-Veda, x. 136.[160]

The Puruṣa Sūkta has the first reference to the division of Hindu society into the four classes. To understand the natural way in which this institution arose, we must remember that the Aryan conquerors were divided by differences of blood and racial ancestry from the conquered tribes of India. The original Aryans all belonged to one class, every one being priest and soldier, trader and tiller of the soil. There was no privileged order of priests. The complexity of life led to a division of classes among the Aryans. Though to start with each man could offer sacrifices to gods without anybody's mediation, priesthood and aristocracy separated themselves from the proletariat. Originally the term Vaiśya referred to the whole people. As we shall see, when sacrifices assume an important rôle, when the increasing complexity of life rendered necessary division of life, certain families, distinguished for learning, wisdom, poetic and speculative gifts, became representatives in worship under the title of Purohita, or one set in front. When the vedic religion developed into a regulated ceremonialism, these families formed themselves into a class. In view of their great function of conserving the tradition of the Aryans, this class was freed from the necessity of the struggle for existence. For those engaged in the feverish ardour of life cannot afford the freedom and the leisure necessary for thought and reflection. Thus one class concerned with the things of spirit came into existence. The Brāhmins are not a priesthood pledged to support fixed doctrines, but an intellectual aristocracy charged with the moulding of the higher life of the people. The kings who became the patrons of the learned Brāhmins were the Kṣatriyas or the princes who had borne rule in those days. The word Kṣatriya comes from Kṣatra, 'rule, dominion'. It has the same meaning in the Veda, the Avesta and the Persian inscriptions. The rest were classed as the people or the Vaiśyas.

159. x. 86. 2.
160. See also vii. 59. 6; x. 114. 2; x. 167. 1; x. 109. 4.

Originally occupational, the division soon became hereditary. In the period of the hymns, professions were not restricted to particular castes. Referring to the diversity of men's tastes, one verse says: 'I am a poet, my father is a doctor, my mother a grinder of corn.'[161] There are also passages indicative of the rising power of the Brāhmin. 'In his own house he dwells in peace and comfort, to him for ever holy food flows richly, to him the people with free will pay homage—the king with whom the Brāhmin has precedence.'[162] Those who followed the learned professions, those who fought, those who traded all belonged to one whole, which was divided by a wider gulf from the conquered races, who were grouped into two broad divisions of (*a*) the Draviḍians, forming the fourth estate, and (*b*) the aboriginal tribes. The division into Aryans and Dasyus is a racial one, being based on blood and descent. It is sometimes said that the aborigines converted and accepted by the Aryans are the Śūdras, while those excluded by them are the Panchamas.[163] It is maintained by others that the Aryans had in their own communities Śūdras even before they came to the southern part of India. It is not easy to decide between these rival hypotheses.

The system of caste is in reality neither Aryan nor Draviḍian, but was introduced to meet the needs of the time when the different racial types had to live together in amity. It was then the salvation of the country, whatever its present tendency may be. The only way of conserving the culture of a race which ran the great risk of being absorbed by the superstitions of the large numbers of native inhabitants, was to pin down rigidly by iron bonds the existing differences of culture and race. Unfortunately this device to prevent the social organisation from decay and death ultimately prevented it even from growing.[164] The barriers did not show any signs of weakening when the tide of progress demanded it. While they contributed to the

161. ix. 112. 3.

162. iv. 50. 8.

163. See Farquhar: *Outline of the Religious Literature of India*, p. 6.

164. Referring to the hardening of classes into castes, Rhys Davids writes: 'It is most probable that this momentous step followed upon and was chiefly due to the previous establishment of a similar hard and fast line preventing any one belonging to the non-Aryan tribes from inter-marrying with an Aryan family or being incorporated into the Aryan race. It was the hereditary disability the Aryans had succeeded in imposing upon races they despised, which, reacting within their own circle and strengthened by the very intolerance that gave it birth, has borne such better fruit through so many centuries' (*Hibbert Lectures*, p. 23).

preservation of the social order they did not help the advancement of the nation as a whole. But this gives us no right to condemn the institution of caste as it was originally introduced. Only caste made it possible for a number of races to live together side by side without fighting each other. India solved peaceably the inter-racial problem which other people did by a decree of death. When European races conquered others, they took care to efface their human dignity and annihilate their self-respect. Caste enabled the Vedic Indian to preserve the integrity and independence of the conquering as well as the conquered races and promote mutual confidence and harmony.

XI

ESCHATOLOGY

The Vedic Aryans entered India in the pride of strength and joy of conquest. They loved life in its fullness. They therefore showed no great interest in the future of the soul. Life to them was bright and joyous, free from all the vexations of a fretful spirit. They were not enamoured of death. They wished for themselves and their posterity a life of a hundred autumns.[165] They had no special doctrines about life after death, though some vague conceptions about heaven and hell could not be avoided by reflective minds. Rebirth is still at a distance. The Vedic Aryans were convinced that death was not the end of things. After night, the day; after death, life. Beings who once had been, could never cease to be. They must exist somewhere, perhaps in the realm of the setting sun where Yama rules. The imagination of man with his shuddering fear of death had not yet made Yama into a terrible lord of vengeance. Yama and Yamī are the first mortals who entered the other world to lord over it. When a man dies he is supposed to reach Yama's kingdom. Yama had found for us a place, a home which is not to be taken from us. When the body is thrown off, the soul becomes endowed with a shining spiritual form and goes to the abode of goods where Yama and the fathers live immortal. The dead are supposed to get to this paradise by passing over water and a bridge.[166] A reference to the paths of the fathers and the gods is found in x. 88. 15. This might be, as has been suggested, due to the distinction of the ways in which the smoke ascends in cremation and sacrifice. The distinction is yet in an undeveloped form.

165. R.V., x. 18.
166. x. 6. 10; ix. 41. 2.

The departed souls dwell in heaven revelling with Yama. They there live an existence like ours. The joys of heaven are those of earth perfected and heightened. 'These bright things are the portion of those who bestow largesses; there are suns for them in heaven; they attain immortality; they prolong their lives.'[167] Stress is sometimes laid on the sensuous character in the Vedic picture of future life. But as Deussen observes: 'Even Jesus represents the kingdom of heaven as a festal gathering where they sit down to table[168] and drink wine,[169] and even a Dante or a Milton could not choose but borrow all the colours for their pictures from this world of earth.'[170] The gods are supposed to become immortal through the power of the Soma. To become like gods is the goal of our endeavour. For the gods live in a spiritual paradise enjoying a kind of unalloyed bliss. They neither hunger nor thirst, neither marry nor are given in marriage. In their ideal descriptions of the other world, the contrast between the life on earth and the life hereafter arises. The blessed gods live for ever. We are children of a day. The gods have happiness in heaven above where Yama rules; we have misery for our lot on earth. What should we do to gain immortality? We have to offer sacrifices to gods, since immortality is a free gift from heaven to the god-fearing. The good man who worships the gods becomes immortal. 'Sage Agni! The mortal who propitiates thee becomes a moon in heaven.'[171] Already the difficulty is felt. Does he become the moon or does he become like the moon? Sāyaṇa explains it as: 'He becomes like the moon, the rejoicer of all';[172] others contend that he *becomes* the moon.[173] There are indications that the Vedic Aryan believed in the possibility of meeting his ancestors after his death.[174]

The question arises what happens to us if we do not worship the gods. Is there a hell corresponding to a heaven, a separate place for the morally guilty, the heretics, who do not believe in gods? If the heaven is only for the pious and the good, then the evil-minded cannot be extinguished at death nor can they reach heaven. So a hell is necessary. We hear of Varuṇa

167. i. 25. 6.
168. Matt. vii. 11.
169. Matt. xxvi. 9.
170. *The Philosophy of the Upaniṣads*, p. 320.
171. ii. 2; x. 1. 3.
172. Āhlādaka sarveṣām.
173. Candra eva bhavati.
174. i. 24. 1; vii. 56. 24.

thrusting the evil-doer down into the dark abyss from which he never returns. Indra is prayed to consign to the lower darkness the man who injures his worshipper.[175] It seems to be the destiny of the wicked to fall into this dark depth and disappear. We do not as yet get the grotesque mythology of hell and its horrors of the later purāṇas. Heaven for the righteous and hell for the wicked is the rule. Reward follows righteousness, and punishment misconduct. I do not think that the joyless regions veiled in blind darkness into which the ignorant pass after death are only the world in which we live, though that is Deussen's view. We have no inklings as yet of saṁsāra or even gradations of happiness. There is a passage in the Ṛg-Veda[176] which reads: 'After he has completed what he has to do and has become old he departs hence; departing hence he is once more born; this is the third birth.' This has reference to the Vedic theory that every man has three births: the first as a child, the second by spiritual education, and the third after death. We meet with the belief in the soul as a moving life principle.[177] In x. 58, the soul of an apparently unconscious man is invited to come back to him from the trees, the sky and the sun. Evidently it was thought that the soul could be separated from the body in certain abnormal conditions. All this, however does not imply that the Vedic Aryans were familiar with the conception of rebirth.

XII

CONCLUSION

The hymns form the foundation of subsequent Indian thought. While the Brāhmaṇas emphasise the sacrificial ritual shadowed forth in the hymns, the Upaniṣads carry out their philosophical suggestions. The theism of the Bhagavadgītā is only an idealisation of Varuṇa-worship. The great doctrine of karma is yet in its infancy as Ṛta. The dualistic metaphysics of the Sāṁkhya is the logical development of the conception of Hirānyagarbha floating on the waters. The descriptions of the ecstatic conditions caused by the performance of sacrifice or the singing of hymns or the effects of the Soma juice when we see the glories of the heavenly world remind us of the yogic states of divine blessedness where voices are heard and visions seen.

175. x. 132. 4; iv. 5. 5: ix. 73. 8; x. 152. 4.
176. iv. 27. 1.
177. i. 164. 30.

REFERENCES

MAX MÜLLER AND OLDENBERG, The Vedic Hymns; S.B.E., vols. xxxii and xlvi.
MUIR, Original Sanskrit Texts, vol. v.
RAGOZIN, Vedic India.
MAX MÜLLER, Six Systems of Indian Philosophy, chap. ii.
KAEGI, The Ṛg-Veda (Eng. Trans.).
GHATE, Lectures on the Ṛg-Veda.
MACDONELL, Vedic Mythology; Vedic Reader.
BARUA, Pre-Buddhistic Indian Philosophy, pp. 1–38.
BLOOMFIELD, The Religion of the Veda.

CHAPTER III

Transition to the Upaniṣads

■ The general character of the Atharva-Veda—Conflict of cultures—The primitive religion of the Atharva-Veda—Magic and mysticism—The Yajur-Veda—The Brāhmaṇas—Their religion of sacrifice and prayer—The dominance of the priest—The authoritativeness of the Veda—Cosmology—Ethics—Caste—Future life. ■

I

THE ATHARVA-VEDA

'The hymns of the Ṛg-Veda inextricably confused; the deities of an earlier era confounded; and again merged together in a pantheon now complete; the introduction of strange gods; recognition of a hell of torture; instead of many divinities, the one that represents all the gods and nature as well; incantations for evil purposes and charms for a worthy purpose; formulae of malediction to be directed against those "whom I hate and who hate me"; magical verses to obtain children, to prolong life, to dispel evil magic, to guard against poison and other ills; the paralysing extreme of ritualistic reverence indicated by the exaltation to godhead of the "remnant" of sacrifice; hymns to snakes, to diseases, to sleep, time, and the stars; curses on the "priest plaguer"—such in general outline is the impression produced by a perusal of the Atharvan after that of the Ṛg-Veda.'[1] In the Ṛg-Veda we come across strange utterances of incantations and spells, charms and witchcrafts, hymns to inanimate things, devils and demons, etc. We have the charms of the robbers to lull the dwellers in a house to sleep,[2] spells to prevent evil spirits causing women to miscarry,[3] and charms to expel diseases.[4] Though sorcery and magic prevailed in the times of the Ṛg-Veda, the Vedic seers did not encourage or recognise them. The stray references have the appearance of an external addition, while in the Atharva-Veda they are the main theme.

1. Hopkins, *The Religions of India*, p. 151.
2. R.V., vii. 55.
3. R.V., x. 122.
4. R.V., x. 163.

The weird religion that the Atharva-Veda represents is doubtless older than that of the Ṛg-Veda, though the Atharva-Veda collection is a later one. The Vedic Aryans as they advanced into India came across uncivilised tribes, wild and barbarous, and worshipping snakes and serpents, stocks and stones. No society can hope to continue in a state of progressive civilisation in the midst of uncivilised and half-civilised tribes, if it does not meet and overcome the new situation by either completely conquering them or imparting to them elements of its own culture. The alternatives before us are either to destroy the barbarian neighbours or absorb them, thus raising them to a higher level, or allow ourselves to be overwhelmed and swamped by them. The first course was impossible on account of the paucity of numbers. The pride of race and culture worked against the third. The second was the only alternative left open, and it was adopted. While the Ṛg-Veda describes the period of conflict between the fair-skinned Aryans and the dark Dasyus, which Indian mythology makes into a strife of Devas and Rakṣasas, the Atharva-Veda speaks to us of the period when the conflict is settled and the two are trying to live in harmony by mutual give and take. The spirit of accommodation naturally elevated the religion of the primitive tribes but degraded the Vedic religion by introducing into it sorcery and witchcraft. The worship of spirits and stars, trees and mountains and other superstitions of jungle tribes crept into the Vedic religion. The effort of the Vedic Aryan to educate the uncivilised resulted in the corruption of the ideal which he tried to spread. In his Introduction to the translation of the selections from the Atharva-Veda, Bloomfield remarks: 'Even witchcraft is part of the Hindu's religion; it had penetrated and become intimately blended with the holiest Vedic rites; the broad current of popular religion and superstition has infiltrated itself through numberless channels into the higher religion that is presented by the Brāhmin priests, and it may be presumed that the priests were neither able to cleanse their own religious beliefs from the mass of folk belief with which it was surrounded, nor is it at all likely that they found it in their interest to do so.'[5] Such are the revenges which the weak of the world have on the strong. The explanation of the miscellaneous character of the Hindu religion, which embraces all the intermediate regions of thought and belief from the wandering fancies of savage superstitions to the highest insight of daring thought, is here. From the

5. S.B.E., vol. xliii.

beginning the Aryan religion was expansive, self-developing and tolerant. It went on accommodating itself to the new forces it met with in its growth. In this can be discerned a refined sense of true humility and sympathetic understanding. The Indian refused to ignore the lower religions and fight them out of existence. He did not possess the pride of the fanatic that his was the one true religion. If a god satisfies the human mind in its own way, it is a form of truth. None can lay hold upon the whole of truth. It can be won only by degrees, partially and provisionally. But they forgot that intolerance was sometimes a virtue. There is such a thing as Gresham's law in religious matters also. When the Aryan and the non-Aryan religions, one refined and the other vulgar, the one good and the other base, met, there was the tendency for the bad to beat the good out of circulation.

II

THEOLOGY

The religion of the Atharva-Veda is that of the primitive man, to whom the world is full of shapeless ghosts and spirits of death. When he realises his helplessness against the natural forces, the precariousness of his own existence so constantly subject to death, he makes death and disease, failure of monsoon and earthquake, the playground of his fancy. The world becomes crowded with goblins and gods, and the catastrophes of the world are traced to dissatisfied spirits. When a man falls ill, the magician and not the physician is sent for, and he employs spells to entice the spirit away from the patient.[6] The terrific powers could only be appeased by bloody sacrifices, human and animal. The fear of death gave a loose rein to superstition. Madame Ragozin writes: 'We have here, as though in opposition to the bright, cheerful pantheon of beneficent deities, so trustingly and gratefully addressed by the Ṛṣis of the Ṛg-Veda, a weird repulsive world of darkly scowling demons, inspiring abject fear such as never sprang from Aryan fancy.'[7] The religion of the Atharva-Veda is an amalgam of Aryan and non-Aryan ideals. The distinction between the spirit of the Ṛg-Veda and that of the Atharva-Veda is thus described by Whitney: 'In

6. If such a view persisted, it was because it had an element of truth. Modern psychology has come to recognise the power of suggestion as a remedy for the ills of the flesh, specially nervous disorders.

7. *Vedic India*, pp. 117–18.

the Ṛg-Veda the gods are approached with reverential awe, indeed, but with love and confidence also; a worship is paid them which exalts the offerer of it; the demons embraced under the general name Rakṣas are objects of horror, whom the gods ward off and destroy; the divinities of the Atharva are regarded rather with a kind of cringing fear, as powers whose wrath is to be deprecated and whose favour curried; it knows a whole host of imps and hobgoblins, in ranks and classes, and addresses itself to them directly, offering them homage to induce them to abstain from doing harm. The mantra, prayer, which in the older veda is the instrument of devotion, is here rather the tool of superstition; it wrings from the unwilling hands of the gods the favours which of old their goodwill to men induced them to grant, or by simple magical power obtains the fulfilment of the utterer's wishes. The most prominent feature of the Atharva is the multitude of incantations which it contains. These are pronounced either by the person who is himself to be benefited or more often by the sorcerer for him, and are directed to the procuring of the greatest variety of desirable ends.... There are hymns, too, in which a single rite or ceremony is taken up and exalted, somewhat in the same strain as the Soma in the Pāvamāna hymns of the Ṛg; others of a speculative mystical character are not wanting; yet their number is not so great as might naturally be expected, considering the development which the Hindu religion received in the periods following after that of the primitive Veda. It seems in the main that the Atharva is a popular rather than a priestly religion; that, in making the transition from the Vedic to modern times, it forms an intermediate step, rather to the gross idolatries and superstitions of the ignorant mass than to the sublimated pantheism of the Brāhmins.'[8] A religion of magic, with its childish reliance on sorcery and witchcraft, takes the place of the purer Vedic religion; the medicine man who knows how to scatter the spirits and control them holds the supreme position. We hear of great ascetics who obtain the mastery of nature by tapas. They reduce the elemental forces to their control by their asceticism. It was then well known that ecstatic conditions could be induced by the mortification of the body. Man can participate in divine power by the hidden force of magic. The professors of magic and witchcraft were accepted by the Vedic seers, and their calling was dignified, with the

8. P.A.O.S., iii. pp. 307–8.

result that magic and mysticism soon became confused. We find people sitting in the midst of five fires, standing on one leg, holding an arm above the head, all for the purpose of commanding the forces of nature and subduing the gods to their will.

While the Atharva-Veda gives us an idea of demonology prevalent among the superstitious tribes of India, it is more advanced in some parts than the Ṛg-Veda, and has certain elements in common with the Upaniṣads and the Brāhmaṇas. We have the worship of Kāla, time; Kāma, or love; Skambha, or support. The greatest of them all is Skambha. He is the ultimate principle, called indiscriminately Prajāpati, Puruṣa and Brahman. He includes all space and time, gods and Vedas and the moral powers.[9] Rudra is the lord of animals, and forms the point of linkage between the Vedic religion and the later Śiva worship. Śiva in the Ṛg-Veda means only auspicious, but is not the name of a god; the Rudra in the Ṛg-Veda is a malignant cattle-destroying deity.[10] Here he is the lord of all cattle, Paśupati. Prāṇa is hailed as a life-giving principle of nature.[11] The doctrine of vital forces which figures so much in later Indian metaphysics is first mentioned here, and may possibly be a development of the principle of air of the Ṛg-Veda. While the deities of the Ṛg-Veda were of both sexes, the males were more prominent. In the Atharva-Veda the emphasis is shifted. No wonder in Tāntric philosophies sex becomes the basis. The sacredness of the cow is recognised, and Brahma-loka is mentioned in the Atharva-Veda.[12] Hell is known by its proper name. Naraka, with all its horror and tortures,[13] is fairly familiar.

Even the magical portion of the Atharva-Veda shows Aryan influence. If magic has to be accepted, the next best thing is to refine it. Bad magic is condemned and good magic encouraged. Many charms make for harmony in family and village life. The barbarous and bloody sacrifices which still persist in unaryanised parts of India are condemned. The old title of the Atharva-Veda, 'Atharvāṅgirasaḥ', shows that there were two different strata in it, one of Atharvan and the other of Aṅgiras. The former refers to auspicious practices used for healing purposes.[14] The hostile practices belong to the Aṅgirases. The first is medicine and the second is witchcraft, and the two are mixed up.

9. See x. 7.7.13, 17.
10. R.V., iv. 3. 6; i. 114. 10.
11. A.V., x. 7.
12. xix. 71. 1.
13. xii. 4. 36.
14. Bheṣajani, A.V., xi. 6. 14.

The Atharva-Veda, the result of so much compromise, seemed to have had a good deal of trouble in obtaining recognition as a Veda.[15] It was regarded with contempt, since its central feature was sorcery. It contributed to the growth of a pessimistic outlook in India. Men cannot believe in the devil and the tempter and yet retain joy in life. To see demons close at hand is to shudder at life. In fairness to the Atharva-Veda, it must be recognised that it helped to prepare the way for the scientific development in India.

III

THE YAJUR-VEDA AND THE BRĀHMAṆAS

In the history of thought creative and critical epochs succeed each other. Periods of rich and glowing faith are followed by those of aridity and artificiality. When we pass from the Ṛg-Veda to the Yajur- and the Sāma-Vedas and the Brāhmaṇas, we feel a change in the atmosphere. The freshness and simplicity of the former give place to the coldness and artificiality of the latter. The spirit of religion is in the background, while its forms assume great importance. The need for prayer-books is felt. Liturgy is developed. The hymns are taken out of the Ṛg-Veda and arranged to suit sacrificial necessities. The priest becomes the lord. The Yajur-Veda gives the special formulas to be uttered when the altar is to be erected, etc., and the Sāman describes the songs to be chanted at the sacrifice. These Vedas may be discussed along with the Brāhmaṇas, since they all describe the sacrificial liturgy. The religion of the Yajur-Veda is a mechanical sacerdotalism. A crowd of priests conducts a vast and complicated system of external ceremonies to which symbolical significance is attached and to the smallest minutiae of which the greatest weight is given. The truly religious spirit could not survive in the stifling atmosphere of ritual and sacrifice. The religious feeling of the adoration of the ideal and the consciousness of guilt is lacking. Every prayer is coupled with a particular rite and aims at securing some material advantage. The formulas of the Yajur-Veda are full of dreary repetitions of petty requests for the goods of life. We cannot draw a sharp distinction between the age of the hymns of the Ṛg-Veda and the other Vedas and the Brāhmaṇas, since the tendencies which became predominant in the latter

15. In many of the early scriptures we have only the three Vedas mentioned, R.V., x. 90. 9; v. 7. 1; Tait. Up., ii. 2–3. The canonical works of the Buddhists do not mention the Atharva-Veda. At a later date the Atharva-Veda also acquired the status of a Veda.

were also found in the hymns of the Ṛg-Veda. We can say with some degree of certainty that the mass of the hymns of the Ṛg-Veda belongs to an age earlier than that of the Brāhmaṇas.

IV

THEOLOGY

The Brāhmaṇas, which form the second part of the Vedas, are the ritual textbooks intended to guide the priests through the complicated details of sacrificial rites. The chief of them are the Aitareya and the Śatapatha. Differences of detail in interpretation led to the formation of several schools of the Brāhmaṇas. The period is marked by important changes in the religious evolution, which have permanently affected its future history. The emphasis on sacrifice, the observance of caste and the āśramas, the eternity of the Veda, the supremacy of the priest, all belong to this age.

We may begin by noting the additions made to the Vedic pantheon during the period. Viṣṇu rose in importance in the Yajur-Veda. The Śatapatha Brāhmaṇa makes him the personification of sacrifice.[16] The name Nārāyaṇa also occurs in it, though it is only in the Taittirīya Āraṇyaka that the two Nārāyaṇa and Viṣṇu are brought into relation. Śiva makes his appearance, and is referred to under different names in the Kauśītaki Brāhmaṇa.[17] Rudra has now a benignant form and is called Giriśa.[18] The Prajāpati of the Ṛg-Veda becomes the chief god and the creator of the world. Viśvakarman is identified with him.[19] Monotheism is inculcated. Agni is very important. Brahmaṇaspati, the lord of prayer, becomes the leader of hymns and the organiser of rites. Brahman in the Ṛg-Veda means a hymn or a prayer addressed to God. From the subjective force which helped the seer to compose a prayer, it came to mean the object prayed for. From being the cause of prayer, we may say it came to mean the power of sacrifice; and since in the Brāhmaṇas the whole universe is regarded as produced from sacrifice, Brahman came to signify the creative principle of the world.[20]

16. v. 2. 3. 6; v. 4. 5. 1; xii. 4. 1. 4; xiv. 1. 1. 6. and 15.
17. vi. 1–9.
18. See Tait. Saṁhita, iv. 5. 1; Vājasaneyi Saṁhitā, ix.
19. Śat. Brāh., viii. 2. 1. 10; viii. 2. 3. 13.
20. There are several passages where Brahman is used in this sense. 'Verily in the beginning this universe was the Brahman; it created the gods' (Śat. Brāh., xi. 2. 3. 1. See also x. 6. 3, and Chān. Up., iii. 14. 1).

The religion of the Brāhmaṇas was purely formal. The poetic fire and the heartiness of the Vedic hymns are no more. Prayer comes to mean the muttering of mantras, or the utterance of sacred formulas. Loud petitions were thought necessary to rouse God to action. The words became artificial sounds with occult powers. Nobody could understand the mystery of it all, except the priest who claimed for himself the dignity of a god on earth. The one ambition was to become immortal like the gods, who attained that status by performing sacrifices.[21] All are subject to the influence of sacrifices. Without them, the sun would not rise. We can depose Indra from his throne in heaven if we perform a hundred horse-sacrifices. The sacrifices please the gods and profit men. Through them the gods become the friends of men. The sacrifices were made as a rule for gaining earthly profits and not heavenly bliss. A rigid soul-deadening, commercialist creed based on a contractual motive took the place of the simple devout religion of the Vedas.[22] The sacrifices of the Vedic hymns were a superfluous appendage of prayers indicative of true religion but now they occupy the central place. Every act done, every syllable uttered at the ceremony is important. The religion of the Brāhmaṇas became loaded with symbolic subtleties, and was ultimately lost in a soulless mechanism of idle rites and pedantries of formalism.

The increasing dominance of the idea of sacrifice helped to exalt the position of the priests. The ṛṣi of the Vedic hymns, the inspired singer of truth, becomes now the possessor of a revealed scripture, the repeater of a magical formula. The simple occupational division of the Aryans into the three classes assumes during the period an hereditary character. The highly elaborate nature of the sacrificial ceremonial demands special training for the priestly office. The patriarchal head of the family could no more conduct the complex and minute system of the sacrificial ceremony. Priesthood became a profession and a hereditary one. The priests who possessed the Vedic lore became the accredited intermediaries between gods and men and the dispensers of the divine grace. The yajamāṇa, or the man for whom the rite is performed, stands aside. He is a passive agent supplying men, money and munitions; the priest does the rest for him. Selfishness, with its longing for power, prestige and enjoyment, pressed its way in and dimmed the lustre of the original ideal. Attempts were

21. Śat, Brāh., iii. 1. 4. 3; Aitareya Brāh., ii. 1. 1.

22. 'He offers a sacrifice to the gods with the text: "Do thou give to me and I will give to thee; do thou bestow on me and I will bestow on there"' (Vājasaneyi Saṁhitā, iii. 50. See also Śat. Brāh., ii. 5. 3. 19).

made to mislead the people about the value of the offerings. A monopoly of functions and offices was secured. The ground was consolidated by the development of an extravagant symbolism. Language was used as if it was given to us to hide our thoughts. Only the priests could know the hidden meaning of things. No wonder the priest claimed for himself a divine dignity. 'Verily there are two kinds of gods; for the gods themselves assuredly are gods, and then the priests who have studied and teach Vedic lore are the human gods.'[23]

We have here and there priests who seriously declare that they can bring about the death of him who actively employs them, though they have the moral sense to know that such an act is forbidden.[24] Another circumstance which further strengthened the priestly class was the necessity for the preservation of the Vedas which the Aryans brought with them, and round which, as we shall see in the sequel, a halo of sanctity grew. The Brāhmin class was entrusted with their preservation. If the Vedas are to survive, the Brāhmin must be true to his vocation. He imposed on himself accordingly severe conditions. 'A Brāhmin unlearned in holy writ is extinguished in an instant like dry grass on fire.'[25] A Brāhmin should shun worldly honour as he should shun poison. As a brahmacārin or student, he must control his passions, wait on his preceptor and beg for his food; as a householder he must avoid wealth, speak the truth, lead a virtuous life, and keep himself pure in mind and body. The Brāhmins felt that they should be faithful to the charge committed to their keeping. We need not speak of the wonderful way in which they have preserved the Vedic tradition against all the dangerous accidents of history. Even to-day we can meet in the streets of Indian cities these walking treasure-houses of Vedic learning. The rigid barriers of the later age are to be traced to historical accidents. In the age of the Brāhmaṇas there was not much material distinction among the twice-born Aryans. They could all be educated in Vedic knowledge.[26] 'The sacrifice is like a ship sailing heavenward; if there be a sinful priest in it that one priest would make it

23. Śat. Brāh., ii. 2. 2. 6; ii. 4. 3. 14.

24. Tait. Saṁhitā, i. 6. 10. 4, and Ait. Brāh., ii. 21. 2.

25. Manu.

26. Manu says: 'A twice-born man, a Brāhmin, Kṣatriya or Vaiśya, unlearned in the Vedas, soon falls, even while living, to a condition of Śūdra.' In the Mahābhārata we read: 'The order of Vānaprasthas, of sages who dwell in forests and live on fruits, roots and air, is prescribed for the three twice-born classes, the order of householders is prescribed for all.'

sink.'[27] So morality was not dismissed at altogether irrelevant. The Brāhmin priests were neither wicked nor stupid. They had their own ideas of duty and righteousness which they tried to preach to others. They were honest, upright men, who obeyed the rules, observed ceremonies and defended dogmas to the best of their ability. They had a sense of their calling and fulfilled it with zest and reverence. They framed elaborate codes of laws expressing their great love of learning and humanity. If they erred, it was because they were themselves fettered by a tradition. They were sincere souls whatever their hallucinations. They felt no shadow of doubt about the truth of their own orthodoxy. Their thought was paralysed by the conventions of the times. Yet no one would say that their pride in their own culture and civilisation was illegitimate at a time when the world around was steeped in barbarism and a thousand rude and tyrannous elements provoked them into this feeling.

In the nature of things, a professional priesthood is always demoralising. But there is no reason to think that the Brāhmin of India was more pompous and hypocritical than any other. As against the possible degeneration, protests were uttered by the true Brāhmins, filled with the serene calm and the simple grandeur of the prophet soul even in that age. They raised a revolt against the ostentation and hypocrisy of the selfish priest and blushed at the corruption of a great ideal. In any estimate of the priesthood it is to be remembered that the Brāhmins take into account the duties to be performed by the householder. There were other stages of the Vānaprastha and the Sannyāsa where ritual is not binding at all. The Brāhmanical rule would not have lasted if it had been felt as tyrannical or coercive. It commanded the confidence of the thinking, since it only insisted that everybody should fulfil his social duties.

In later philosophy we hear much of what is called the authoritativeness of the Vedas or Śabdapramāṇa. The darśanas or systems of philosophy are distinguished into orthodox or heterodox according as they accept or repudiate the authority of the Veda. The Veda is looked upon as a divine revelation. Though the Hindu apologists of later day offer ingenious interpretations in support of Vedic authority, still, so far as the Vedic seers are concerned, they mean by it the highest truth revealed to a pure mind. 'Blessed are the pure in heart for they shall see God.' The ṛṣi of the Vedic hymns calls himself not so much the composer of the hymns as the seer of them.[28] It is seeing

27. Śat. Brāh., iv. 2. 5. 10.

28. The world 'Veda' is derived from the Aryan root 'vid', which means 'seeing'. Cf. Vision (from Latin video); Ideas (from Greek eidos), wit.

with the mind's eye or intuitive seeing. The ṛṣi has his eyes unblinded by the fumes of passion, and so can see the truth which is not evident to the senses. He only transmits the truth which he sees but does not make.[29] The Veda is called 'Śruti,' or the rhythm of the infinite heard by the soul. The words dṛṣṭi and śruti, which are the Vedic expressions, point out how the Vedic knowledge is not a matter of logical demonstration, but an intuitive insight. The poet's soul hears or has revealed to it the truth in its inspired condition, when the mind is lifted above the narrow plane of the discursive consciousness. According to the Vedic seers the contents of the hymns are inspired and revelatory only in this sense. It is not their intention to suggest anything miraculous or supernatural. They even speak of the hymns as their own compositions or creations. They compare their work as poets with that of the carpenter, the weaver, the rower,[30] and give natural explanations of it. The hymns are shaped by the feelings of the human heart.[31] Sometimes they say they found the hymns.[32] They also attribute them to the exaltation consequent on the drink of Soma.[33] In a very humble spirit they hold the hymns to be God-given.[34] The idea of inspiration is not yet transformed into that of an infallible revelation. When we come to the Brāhmaṇas we reach an age when the divine authority of the Vedas is accepted as a fact.[35] The claim to divine revelation, and therefore eternal validity, is set up in this period. Its origin is easily intelligible. Writing was then unknown. There were neither printers nor publishers. The contents of the Vedas were transmitted by oral repetition through a succession of teachers. To ensure respect, some sanctity was attached to

29. 'All artistic creation', says Beethoven, 'comes from God, and relates to man only in so far as it witnesses to the action of the divine within him.'

30. See Muir, Sanskrit Texts, vol. iii.

31. R.V., i. 117. 2; ii. 35. 2.

32. x. 67. 1.

33. vi. 47. 3.

34. i. 37. 4; iii. 18. 3. In the second chapter of Muir's *Sanskrit Texts* (vol. iii. pp. 217–86) we have a collection of passages which clearly show that 'though some at least of the ṛṣis appear to have imagined themselves to be inspired by the gods in the expression of their religious emotion and ideas, they at the same time regarded the hymns as their own compositions, or as (presumably) the compositions of their forefathers, distinguishing between them as new and old and describing their own authorship in terms which could only have been dictated by a consciousness of its reality.'

35. See Aitareya Brāhmaṇa, vii. 9.

the Vedas. In the Ṛg-Veda Vāk, or speech, was a goddess. And now they said from Vāk the Vedas issued forth. Vāk is the mother of the Vedas.[36] In the Atharva-Veda the mantra is said to possess magical power. 'The Vedas issued like breath from the self-existent.[37] The Vedas came to be regarded as divine revelation, communicated to the ṛṣis, who were inspired men. Śabda, articulate sound, is considered eternal. The obvious effect of this view of the Vedas is that philosophy becomes scholastic. When the spoken word, real and alive, gets fixed in a rigid formula, its spirit expires. The authoritativeness of the Veda formulated so early in the history of Indian thought has affected the whole course of subsequent evolution. In later philosophy the tendency developed to interpret the unsystematic and not always consistent texts of the earlier age in line with set opinions. When once the tradition is regarded as sacred and infallible it must be represented as expressing or implying what is considered to be the truth. This accounts for the fact that the same texts are adduced in support of varying tenets and principles, mutually contradictory and inconsistent. If fidelity to dogma and diversity of view should live together, it is possible only through absolute freedom of interpretation, and it is here that the Indian philosophers show their ingenuity. It is surprising that, in spite of the tradition, Indian thought kept itself singularly free for a long time from dogmatic philosophising. The Indian thinkers first arrive at a system of consistent doctrine and then look about for texts of an earlier age to support their position. They either force them into such support or ingeniously explain them away. There has been one good effect of this Vedic tradition. It has helped to keep philosophy real and living. Instead of indulging in empty disputations and talking metaphysics which has no bearing on life, the Indian thinkers had a fixed foundation to go upon the religious insight of the highest seers as expressed in the Vedas. It gave them a hold on the central facts of life, and no philosophy could afford to discard it.

V

THEORIES OF CREATION

With regard to the theories of creation, though the lead of the Ṛg-Veda is generally followed, there are some fanciful accounts also mentioned. After

36. Vedānām mātā. Tait. Brāh., ii. 8. 8. 5. Compare the opening of St. John's Gospel: 'In the beginning was the Word.'

37. Śat. Brāh., xi. 5. 81 ff., and also the Puruṣa Sūkta.

the Ṛg-Veda, the Taittirīya Brāhmaṇa says, 'formerly nothing existed, neither heaven nor atmosphere nor earth.' Desire is the seed of existence. Prajāpati desires offspring and creates. 'Verily in the beginning Prajāpati alone existed here. He thought with himself, how can I be propagated? He toiled and practised austerities. He created living beings.'[38]

VI

ETHICS

In fairness to the religion of the Brāhmaṇas, it is to be said that we find frequent traces in them of high moral sense and exalted sentiment. The conception of man's duty first arises here. Man is aid to owe some debts or duties to gods, men and animals. The duties are distinguished into (1) those to the gods, (3) those to seers, (3) those to manes, (4) those to men, (5) and those to the lower creation. He who discharges them all is the good man. No man can touch his daily meal without offering parts of it to gods, fathers, men and animals, and saying his daily prayers. This is the way to live in harmony with the world around him. Life is a round of duties and responsibilities. The conception is certainly high and noble whatever the actual filling of the ideal may be. Unselfishness can be practised in all our acts. In the Śatapatha Brāhmaṇa, the sacrifice of all things, *sarvamedha*, is taught as a means to the attainment of spiritual freedom.[39] Godliness is of course the first duty. It does not consist in the mechanical performance of fixed ritual. It consists in praise and good works. Godliness means trying to be divine as much as possible. Truth-speaking is an essential part of godliness. It is a religious and moral duty. Agni is the lord of vows and Vāk the lord of speech. Both will be displeased if truthfulness is not observed.[40] We notice already the symbolical interpretation of sacrifices. There are passages which point to the essential futility of works. 'Yonder world cannot be obtained by sacrificial gifts or by asceticism by the man who does not know this. That state belongs only to him who has this knowledge.'[41] Adultery is condemned as a sin against the gods, especially Varuṇa. In all

38. Śat. Brāh., ii. 5. 1. 1–3.

39. xiii. 7. 1. 1.

40. 'One law the gods observe—Truth.' Śat. Brāh., i. 1. 1. 4.; see also i. 1. 1. 5; iii. 3. 2. 2, and iii. 4. 2. 8, and ii. 2. 2. 19.

41. Śat. Brāh., x. 5. 4. 15.

cases of evil-doing, confession is supposed to make the guilt less.[42] Asceticism is also held up as a worthy ideal, for the gods are supposed to have obtained divine rank by austerity.[43]

The āśrama dharma was introduced or more correctly formulated in this age.[44] The Vedic Aryan's life has the four stages or āśramas, as they are called, of (1) Brahmacārin or student, when he is expected to study one or more Vedas; (2) the Gṛhastha or the householder, when he has to fulfil the duties mentioned in the scriptures, social and sacrificial; (3) the Vānaprastha or the hermit, when the devotee spends his time in fasting and penance; and (4) the Sannyāsin or the ascetic, who has no fixed abode. He is without any possessions or property and longs for union with God. The four parts of the Veda, the hymns, the Brāhmaṇas, the Āraṇyakas and the Upaniṣads answer to the four stages of the Vedic Aryan's life.[45] Beneath the formalism of ceremonial worship there was at work a spirit of true religion and morality, from which the heart of man obtained satisfaction. It is this ethical basis which has helped the Brāhmanical religion with all its weaknesses to endure so long. Side by side with its insistence on the outer, there was also the emphasis on inner purity. Truth, godliness, honour to parents, kindness to animals, love of man, abstinence from theft, murder and adultery, were inculcated as the essentials of a good life.

The institution of caste is not the invention of an unscrupulous priesthood, but a natural evolution conditioned by the times. It was consolidated in the period of the Brāhmaṇas. The Puruṣa Sūkta, though a part of the Ṛg-Veda, really belongs to the age of the Brāhmaṇas. It is clear that there were then inter-marriages between the Aryans and the Dasyus.[46] To avoid too much confusion of blood, an appeal was made to the pride of the Aryans. What was originally a social institution became a religious one. A divine sanction was given to it, and the laws of caste became immutable. The flexibility of the original class system gave way to the

42. Śat. Brāh., ii. 5. 2. 20.

43. Tait. Brāh., iii. 12. 3.

44. The word āśrama, derived from a root meaning 'to toil,' shows that the Indians realised that suffering was incidental to all progress.

45. The account of these stages varies with the authorities. See Bṛh., Up., iii. 5. 1; Āpastamba Sūtras, ii. 9. 21. 1; Gautama Sūtras, iii. 2; Bodhāyana, ii. 6. 11. 12; Manu., v. 137, vi. 87; Vasiṣṭha, vii. 2.

46. A.V., v. 17. 8.

rigidity of the caste. In the early Vedic period the priests formed a separate profession, but not a separate caste. Any Aryan could become a priest, and the priestly class was not necessarily superior to the warrior or the trading classes. Sometimes they were even treated with contempt.[47] But now the exclusiveness born of pride becomes the basis of caste. It tended to suppress free thought and retarded the progress of speculation. The moral standard sank. The individual who transgressed the rules of caste was a rebel and an outcaste. The Śūdras were excluded from the highest religion. Mutual contempt increased. 'These are the words of Kṣatriya,' is a typical Brāhmin way of characterising the words of an opponent.[48]

VII

ESCHATOLOGY

In the Brāhmaṇas we do not find any one view about the future life. The distinction between the path of the fathers and that of the devas is given.[49] Rebirth on earth is sometimes looked upon as a blessing and not an evil to be escaped from. It is promised as a reward for knowing some divine mystery.[50] But the most dominant view is that of immortality in heaven, the abode of the gods. 'He who sacrifices thus obtains perpetual prosperity and renown and conquers for himself a union with the two gods Āditya and Agni and an abode in the same sphere.'[51] Particular sacrifices enable us to reach the spheres of particular gods.[52] Even the stars are regarded as the abode of the dead. It is individual existence, though in a better world, that is the aim still. 'In the Brāhmaṇas immortality, or at least longevity, is promised to those who rightly understand and practise the rites of sacrifice, while those who are deficient in this respect depart before time to the next world where they are weighed in a balance,[53] and receive good and evil according to their deeds. The more sacrifices any one has offered, the more ethereal is the body he obtains, or as the Brāhmaṇa expresses it,[54] the

47. See R.V., vii. 103. 1. 7 and 8; x. 88. 19.
48. Śat. Brāh., viii. 1. 4. 10.
49. Ibid., vi. 6. 2. 4.
50. Ibid., i. 5. 3. 1. 4.
51. Ibid., xi. 6. 2. 5.
52. Ibid., ii. 6. 4. 8.
53. xi. 2. 7. 33.
54. x. 1. 5. 4.

more rarely does he need to eat. In other texts, on the contrary,[55] it is promised as the highest reward that the pious man shall be born in the next world, with his entire body, sarva tanūh.'[56] Thus far the difference between the Vedic and the Brāhmanical views is that while according to the Ṛg-Veda the sinner is reduced to nothing while the virtuous obtain immortality, in the Brāhmaṇas both are born again to undergo the results of their actions. As Weber puts it: 'Whereas in the oldest times immortality in the abodes of the blessed, where milk and honey flow, is regarded as the reward of virtue or wisdom, whilst the sinner or the fool is, after a short life, doomed to the annihilation of the personal existence, the doctrine of the Brāhmaṇas is that after death all are born again, in the next world, where they are recompensed according to their deeds, the good being rewarded and the wicked punished.'[57] The suggestion is that there is only one life after this, and its nature is determined by our conduct here. 'A man is born into the world which he has made.'[58] 'Whatever food a man eats in this world by that food he is eaten in the next world.'[59] Good and evil deeds find their corresponding rewards and punishments in a future life. Again: 'Thus have they done to us in yonder world, and so we do to them again in this world.'[60] Gradually the idea of an equalising justice developed. The world of the fathers, as in the Ṛg-Veda, was one of the ways, but the distinction arose between the Vedic gods and their world and the way of the fathers and their world of retributive justice. We have not yet the idea of a recurrence of births in the other world and expiations for actions done on earth. But the question cannot be avoided whether the wicked suffer eternal punishment and the good enjoy eternal bliss. 'To men of the mild disposition and reflective spirit of the Indians it would not appear that reward and punishment could be eternal. They would conceive that it must be possible by atonement and purification to become absolved from the punishment of the sins committed in this short life. And in the same way they could not imagine that the reward of virtues practised during the same brief period could continue for ever.' When we

55. iv. 6. 1. 1; xi. 1. 8. 6.; xii. 8. 3. 31.
56. Weber quoted in J.R.A.S., i. 1865, 306 ff.
57. Ibid.
58. Śat. Brāh., vi. 2. 2. 27. Kṛtaṁ lokaṁ puruṣo'bhiyāyate.
59. Śat. Brāh., xii. 9. 11.
60. Śat. Brāh., ii. 6.

finish experiencing our rewards and punishments, it is suggested that we die to that life and are reborn on earth. The natural rhythm by which life gives birth to death and death to life leads us to the conception of a beginningless and endless circuit.[61] The true ideal becomes redemption from the bondage of life and death or release from saṁsāra. 'He who sacrifices to the gods does not gain so great a world as he who sacrifices to the Ātman.'[62] 'He who reads the Vedas is freed from dying again and attains to a sameness of nature with Brahman.'[63] Death with birth for its cause seems to have become a thing to be avoided. Later we find the conception that those who merely perform rites without knowledge are born again and repeatedly become the food of death.[64] In another passage[65] there is suggested the Upaniṣad conception of a higher state than that of desire and its fulfilment, the condition of true immortality. 'This soul is the end of all this. It abides in the midst of all the waters; it is supplied with all objects of desire; it is free from desire, and possesses all objects of desire, for it desires nothing.' 'By knowledge men ascend to that condition in which desires have passed away. Thither gifts do not reach nor austere devotees who are destitute of knowledge. For one who does not possess this knowledge does not attain that world by gifts or by rigorous abstention. It pertains only to those who have such knowledge.'[66] The Brāhmaṇas contain all the suggestions necessary for the development of the doctrine of rebirth. They are, however, only suggestions, while individual immortality is the main tendency. It is left for the Upaniṣads to systematise these suggestions into the doctrine of rebirth. While the conceptions of karma and rebirth are unquestionably the work of the Aryan mind, it need not be denied that the suggestions may have come from the aborigines, who believed that after death their souls lived in animal bodies.

In spite of suggestions of a higher ethics and religion, it must be said that the age was, on the whole, one of Pharisaism, in which people were more anxious about the completion of their sacrifices than the perfection of their souls. There was need for a restatement of the spiritual experience,

61. See Aitareya Brāh., iii. 44.
62. xi. 2. 6.
63. x. 5. 6. 9.
64. Śat. Brāh., x. 4. 3. 10. See also x. 1. 4. 14; x. 2. 6. 19; x. 5. 1. 4; xi. 4. 3. 20.
65. x. 5. 4. 15.
66. Śaṁkara refers to this passage in his Commentary on the *Vedānta Sūtras* to show how near to his own view this position is.

the central meaning of which was obscured by a legalistic code and conventional piety. This the Upaniṣads undertake.

REFERENCES

BLOOMFIELD, The Atharva-Veda, S.B.E., vol. xliii.
EGGELING, Śatapatha Brāhmaṇa, S.B.E., vol. xii. Introduction.
HOPKINS, The Religions of India, chap. ix.

CHAPTER IV

The Philosophy of the Upaniṣads

■ Introduction—The fluid and indefinite character of the teaching of the Upaniṣads—Western students of the Upaniṣads—Date—Early Upaniṣads—The great thinkers of the age—The hymns of the Ṛg-Veda and the doctrine of the Upaniṣads compared—Emphasis on the monistic side of the hymns—The shifting of the centre from the object to the subject—The pessimism of the Upaniṣads—The pessimistic implications of the conception of saṁsāra—Protest against the externalism of the Vedic religion—Subordination of the Vedic knowledge—The central problems of the Upaniṣads—Ultimate reality—The nature of Ātman distinguished from body, dream consciousness and empirical self—The different modes of consciousness, waking, dreaming, dreamless sleep and ecstasy—The influence of the Upaniṣads analysis of self on subsequent thought—The approach to reality from the object side—Matter, life, consciousness, intelligence and ānanda—Śaṁkara and Rāmānuja on the status of ānanda—Brahman and Ātman—Tat tvam asi—The positive character of Brahman—Intellect and intuition—Brahman and the world—Creation—The doctrine of māyā—Deussen's view examined—Degrees of reality—Are the Upaniṣads pantheistic?—The finite self—The ethics of the Upaniṣads—The nature of the ideal—The metaphysical warrant for an ethical theory—Moral life—Its general features—Asceticism—Intellectualism—Jñāna, Karma and Upāsana—Morality and religion—Beyond good and evil—The religion of the Upaniṣads—Different forms—The highest state of freedom—The ambiguous accounts of it in the Upaniṣads—Evil—Suffering—Karma—Its value—The problem of freedom—Future life and immortality—Psychology of the Upaniṣads—Non-Vedāntic tendencies in the Upaniṣads—Sāṁkhya—Yoga—Nyāya—General estimate of the thought of the Upaniṣads—Transition to the epic period. ■

I

THE UPANIṢADS

The Upaniṣads[1] form the concluding portions of the Veda, and are therefore called the Veda-anta, or the end of the Veda, a denomination

1. The word Upaniṣad from *upa ni sad*, 'sitting down near'. It means 'sitting

which suggests that they contain the essence of the Vedic teaching. They are the foundations on which most of the later philosophies and religions of India rest. 'There is no important form of Hindu thought, heterodox Buddhism included, which is not rooted in the Upaniṣads.'[2] Later systems of philosophy display an almost pathetic anxiety to accommodate their doctrines to the views of the Upaniṣads, even if they cannot father them all on them. Every revival of idealism in India has traced its ancestry to the teaching of the Upaniṣads. Their poetry and lofty idealism have not as yet lost their power to move the minds and sway the hearts of men. They contain the earliest records of Indian speculation. The hymns and the liturgical books of the Veda are concerned more with the religion and practice than with the thought of the Aryans. We find in the Upaniṣads an advance on the Saṁhita mythology, Brāhmaṇa hair-splitting, and even Āraṇyaka theology, though all these stages are to be met with. The authors of the Upaniṣads transform the past they handle, and the changes they effect in the Vedic religion indicate the boldness of the heart that beats only for freedom. The aim of the Upaniṣads is not so much to reach philosophical truth as to bring peace and freedom to the anxious human spirit. Tentative solutions of metaphysical questions are put forth in the form of dialogues and disputations, though the Upaniṣads are essentially the outpourings or deliverances of philosophically tempered minds in the face of the facts of life. They express the restlessness and striving of the human mind to grasp the true nature of reality. Not being systematic philosophy, or the production of a single author, or even of the same age, they contain much that is inconsistent and unscientific; but if that were all, we cannot justify the study of the Upaniṣads. They set forth fundamental conceptions which are sound and satisfactory, and these constitute the means by which their own innocent errors, which through exclusive emphasis have been exaggerated into fallacious philosophies, can be corrected. Notwithstanding the variety of authorship and the period of

---

down near' the teacher to receive instruction. It gradually came to mean what we receive from the teacher, a sort of secret doctrine or *rahasyam*. Sometimes it is made to mean what enables us to destroy error, and approach truth. Śaṁkara, in his introduction to the Taittirīya Upaniṣad, says: 'Knowledge of Brahman is called Upaniṣad because in the case of those who devote themselves to it, the bonds of conception, birth, decay, etc., become *unloosed*, or because it *destroys* them altogether, or because it leads the pupil very near to Brahman, or because therein the highest God is seated.' See Pandit, March, 1872, p. 254.

2. Bloomfield, *The Religion of the Veda*, p. 51.

time covered by the composition of these half-poetical and half-philosophical treatises, there is a unity of purpose, a vivid sense of spiritual reality in them all, which become clear and distinct as we descend the stream of time. They reveal to us the wealth of the reflective religious mind of the times. In the domain of intuitive philosophy their achievement is a considerable one. Nothing that went before them for compass and power, for suggestiveness and satisfaction, can stand comparison with them. Their philosophy and religion have satisfied some of the greatest thinkers and intensely spiritual souls. We do not agree with Gough's estimate that 'there is little that is spiritual in all this,' or that 'this empty intellectual conception, void of spirituality, is the highest form that the Indian mind is capable of.' Professor J.S. Mackenzie, with truer insight, says that 'the earliest attempt at a constructive theory of the cosmos, and certainly one of the most interesting and remarkable, is that which is set forth in the Upaniṣads'.[3]

II

THE TEACHING OF THE UPANIṢADS

It is not easy to decide what the Upaniṣads teach. Modern students of the Upaniṣads read them in the light of this or that preconceived theory. Men are so little accustomed to trust their own judgment that they take refuge in authority and tradition. Though these are safe enough guides for conduct and life, truth requires insight and judgment as well. A large mass of opinion inclines today to the view of Śaṁkara, who in his commentaries on the Upaniṣads, the Bhagavadgītā and the Vedānta Sūtras, has elaborated a highly subtle system of non-dualistic metaphysics. Another is equally vehement that Śaṁkara has not said the last word on the subject, and that a philosophy of love and devotion is the logical outcome of the teaching of the Upaniṣads. Different commentators, starting with particular beliefs, force their views into the Upaniṣads and strain their language so as to make it consistent with their own special doctrines. When disputes arise, all schools turn to the Upaniṣads. Thanks to the obscurity as well as the richness, the mystic haze as well as the suggestive quality of the Upaniṣads, the interpreters have been able to use them in the interests of their own religion and philosophy. The Upaniṣads had no set theory of philosophy or dogmatic scheme of theology to propound. They hint at the truth in life, but not as

3. E.R.E., vol. viii, p. 597; see also Hume, *The Thirteen Principal Upaniṣads*, p. 2.

yet in science or philosophy. So numerous are their suggestions of truth, so various are their guesses at God, that almost anybody may seek in them what he wants and find what he seeks, and every school of dogmatics may congratulate itself on finding its own doctrine in the sayings of the Upaniṣads. In the history of thought it has often happened that a philosophy has been victimised by a traditional interpretation that became established at an early date, and has thereafter prevented critics and commentators from placing it in its proper perspective. The system of the Upaniṣads has not escaped this fate. The Western interpreters have followed this or that commentator. Gough follows Śaṁkara's interpretation. In his Preface to the *Philosophy of the Upaniṣads* he writes: 'The greatest expositor of the philosophy of the Upaniṣads is Śaṁkara of Śaṁkarācārya. The teaching of Śaṁkara himself is the natural and the legitimate interpretation of the philosophy of the Upaniṣads.'[4] Max Müller adopts the same standpoint. 'We must remember that the orthodox view of the Vedānta is not what we should call evolution, but illusion. Evolution of the Brahman or pariṇāma is heterodox, illusion or vivarta is orthodox Vedānta.... To put it metaphorically, the world according to the orthodox Vedāntin does not proceed from Brahman as a tree from a germ, but as a mirage from the rays of the sun.'[5] Deussen accepts the same view. We shall try to ascertain the meaning which the authors of the Upaniṣads intended, and not what later commentators attributed to them. The latter give us an approximately close idea of how the Upaniṣads were interpreted in later times, but not necessarily a true insight into the philosophic synthesis which the ancient seekers had. But the problem is, do the thoughts of the Upaniṣads hang together? Could all of them be traced to certain commonly acknowledged principles about the general make-up of the world? We are not so bold as to answer this question in the affirmative. These writings contain too many hidden ideas, too many possible meanings, too rich a mine of fancies and conjectures, that we can easily understand how different systems can draw their inspiration from the same sources. The Upaniṣads do not contain any philosophic synthesis as such, of the type of the system of Aristotle or of Kant or of Śaṁkara. They have the consistency of intuition rather than of logic, and there are certain fundamental ideas which, so to say, form the first sketch of a philosophic system. Out of these ideas a coherent and consistent doctrine might be developed. It is, however, difficult to be

4. P. xi–xii.
5. S.B.E., vol. xv, p. xxvii.

confident that one's working up of elements which knew neither method nor arrangement is the correct one, on account of the obscurity of many passages. Yet with the higher ideals of philosophic exposition in view, we shall consider the Upaniṣad ideas of the universe and of man's place in it.

III

NUMBER AND DATE OF THE UPANIṢADS

The Upaniṣads are generally accounted to be 108 in number, of which about ten are the chief, on which Śaṁkara has commented. These are the oldest and the most authoritative. We cannot assign any exact date to them. The earliest of them are certainly pre-Buddhistic, a few of them are after Buddha. It is likely that they were composed between the completion of the Vedic hymns and the rise of Buddhism (that is the sixth century BC) The accepted dates for the early Upaniṣads are 1000 BC to 300 BC. Some of the later Upaniṣads on which Śaṁkara has commented are post-Buddhistic, and belong to about 400 or 300 BC. The oldest Upaniṣads are those in prose. These are non-sectarian. The Aitareya, the Kauṣītaki, the Taittirīya, the Chāndogya, the Bṛhadāraṇyaka, and parts of the Kena are the early ones, while verses 1–13 of the Kena, and iv. 8–21 of the Bṛhadāraṇyaka, form the transition to the metrical Upaniṣads, and may be put down as later additions. The Kaṭhopaniṣad is later still. We find in it elements of the Sāṁkhya and the Yoga systems.[6] It also quotes freely from the other Upaniṣads and the Bhagavadgītā.[7] The Māṇḍūkya is the latest of the pre-sectarian Upaniṣads. The Atharva-Veda Upaniṣads are also of later growth. Maitrāyaṇī Upaniṣads has elements in it of both the Sāṁkhya and the Yoga systems. The Śvetāśvatara was composed at the period when the several philosophical theories were fermenting. It shows in many passages an acquaintance with the technical terms of the orthodox systems and mentions many of their prominent doctrines. It seems to be interested in presenting a theistic syncretism of the Vedānta, the Sāṁkhya and the Yoga. There is more of pure speculation present in the early prose Upaniṣads,

6. See ii. 18–19; ii. 6. 10 and 11.

7. See i. 2. 5; and Muṇḍaka, ii. 8; i. 2–7, and Gītā, ii. 29; ii. 18–19, and ii. 19–20 and ii. 23, and Muṇḍaka, iii. 2–3, Gītā, i. 53. Some scholars are inclined to the view that the Kaṭha Upaniṣad is older than the Muṇḍaka and the Gītā.

while in the later ones there is more of religious worship and devotion.[8] In presenting the philosophy of the Upaniṣads, we shall take our stand mainly on the pre-Buddhistic ones, and strengthen our views as derived from them by those of the post-Buddhistic ones. The main Upaniṣads for our purposes are the Chāndogya and the Bṛhadāraṇyaka, the Taittirīya and the Aitareya, the Kauśītaki and the Kena; the Īśā and the Māṇḍūkya come next.

IV

THE THINKERS OF THE UPANIṢADS

Unfortunately, we know very little of the lives of the great thinkers whose reflections are embodied in the Upaniṣads. So careless were they of personal fame and so anxious for the spread of truth, that they fathered their views on the honoured deities and heroes of the Vedic period. Prajāpati and Indra, Nārada and Sanatkumāra figure as dialecticians. When the history of the great thinkers of the Upaniṣad period with their distinctive contributions comes to be written, the following names, if we leave aside the mythical ones, will stand out: Mahidāsa Aitareya, Raikva, Śāṇḍilya, Satyakāma Jābāla, Jaivali, Uddālaka, Śvetaketu, Bhāradvāja, Gārgyāyana, Pratardana, Bālāki, Ajātaśatru, Varuṇa, Yājñavalkya, Gārgī and Maitreyī.[9]

8. Deussen arranges the Upaniṣads in the following order:—

1. Ancient prose Upaniṣads: Bṛhadāraṇyaka, Chāndogya, Taittirīya, Aitareya Kauṣītaki, Kena (partly in prose).
2. Verse Upaniṣads: Īśā, Kaṭha, Muṇḍaka and Śvetāśvatara.
3. Later prose: Praśna and Maitrāyaṇī.

All these, excepting the Maitrāyaṇī, are called the classical Upaniṣads.

About the Maitrāyaṇī, Professor Macdonell writes: 'Its many quotations from the other Upaniṣads, the occurrence of several later words, the developed Sāṁkhya doctrine presupposed by it, distinct references to the anti-Vedic heretical schools, all combine to render the late character of this work undoubted. It is, in fact, a summing up of the old upaniṣadic doctrines with an admixture of ideas derived from the Sāṁkhya system and from Buddhism' (*Sanskrit Literature*, p. 230).

Nṛsiṁhottaratāpanīya is one of the twelve Upaniṣads explained by Vidyāraṇya in his 'Sarvopaniṣadarthānubhūtiprakāśa'.

9. The interested reader will find a lucid account of these thinkers and their views in the excellent work of my friend and colleague, Dr Barua, *Pre-Buddhistic Indian Philosophy*.

V

THE HYMNS OF THE ṚG-VEDA AND THE UPANIṢADS

In view of the distinctive character of their contents, the Upaniṣads are regarded as a class of literature independent of the Vedic hymns and the Brāhmaṇas. The simple faith in gods of the hymns was, as we saw, displaced by the mechanical sacerdotalism of the Brāhmaṇas. The Upaniṣads feel that the faith that ends in a church is not enough. They attempt to moralise the religion of the Vedas without disturbing its form. The advance of the Upaniṣads on the Vedas consists in an increased emphasis on the monistic suggestions of the Vedic hymns, a shifting of the centre from the outer to the inner world, a protest against the externalism of the Vedic practices and an indifference to the sacredness of the Veda.

Amid all the confused ferment of Vedic devotions a certain principle of unity and comprehension was asserting itself. In some hymns the conception of a single central power was actually formulated. The Upaniṣads carry out this tendency. They recognise only one spirit—almighty, infinite, eternal, incomprehensible, self-existent, the creator, preserver and destroyer of the world. He is the light, lord and life of the universe, one without a second, and the sole object of worship and adoration. The half-gods of the Veda die and the true God arrives. 'How many gods are there really, O Yajñavalkya?' 'One', he said.[10] 'Now answer us a further question: Agni, Vāyu, Āditya, Kāla (time), which is breath (Prāṇa), Anna (food), Brahmā, Rudra, Viṣṇu. Thus do some meditate on him, some on another. Say which of these is the best for us?' And he said to them: 'These are but the chief manifestations of the highest, the immortal, the incorporeal Brahman.... Brahman, indeed, is all this, and a man may meditate on, worship or discard also those which are its manifestations.'[11] The visible infinite (objective) and the invisible infinite (subjective) are taken up into the spiritual whole.

The polytheistic conceptions were too deeply rooted in the Indian consciousness to be easily overthrown. The many gods were subordinated to the One. Without Brahman, Agni cannot burn a blade of grass, Vāyu cannot blow a whisp of straw. 'For fear of him, fire burns, for fear of him, the sun shines, and for fear of him the winds, the clouds and death perform

10. Bṛh. Up., iii. 9. 1.

11. Maitrāyaṇī Upaniṣad, iv. 5–6; see also Muṇḍaka, i. 1. 1; Taittirīya, i. 5; Bṛh., i. 4. 6; see also i. 4. 7; i. 4. 10.

their office'.[12] Sometimes the many gods are made parts of one whole. The five householders led by Uddālaka approach king Aśvapati, who asked each of them, Whom do you meditate on as the Self? The first answered heaven; the second, the sun; the third, air; the fourth, ether; the fifth, water; and the king replies that each of them worshipped only a part of the truth. Heaven is the head, the sun the eye, the air the breath, the ether the trunk, the water the bladder, and the earth the feet of the central reality, which is pictured as the world-soul. Compromise between the philosophic faith of the few and the fancied superstition of the crowds is the only possible reconciliation; we cannot abolish the old forms, for that would be to ignore the fundamental nature of humanity, as well as the patent differences, in the moral and intellectual states of believers who were not capable of acquiring at once the highest wisdom. Another factor also determined the attitude of the Upaniṣads. Their aim was not science or philosophy, but right living. They wished to liberate the spirit from the trammels of the flesh, that it might enjoy communion with God. Intellectual discipline was subsidiary to holiness of life. Besides, there was the feeling of reverence for the past. The Vedic seers were the ancients of blessed memory, whose doctrines is was impious to attack. In this way the Upaniṣads sought to square a growing idealistic philosophy with the dogmas of a settled theology.

The sources of man's spiritual insight are two-fold: objective and subjective—the wonders of the world without and the stress of the human soul. In the Vedas the vast order and movement of nature engages attention. Their gods represent cosmic forces. In the Upaniṣads we return to explore the depths of the inner world. 'The self-existent pierced the openings of the senses so that they turn outwards; therefore man looks outward, not inward into himself; some wise man, however, with his eyes closed and wishing for immortality, saw the self behind.'[13] From the outward physical fact, attention shifts to the inner immortal self situated at the back of the mind, as it were. We need not look to the sky for the bright light; the glorious fire is within the soul. The soul of man is the keyhole to the landscape of the whole universe, the Ākāśa within the heart, the limpid lake which mirrors the truth. The altered outlook brought about a consequential change. Not the so-called gods, but the true living God, the Ātman has to be worshipped. God's dwelling-place is the heart of man. 'Brahmaṇaḥ

12. Tait. Up.
13. Kaṭha Up., iv 1.

kośo'si',[14] Thou art the sheath of Brahman. 'Whosoever worships another deity, in such a manner as he is another, another "I am", does not know.'[15] The inner immortal self and the great cosmic power are one and the same. Brahman is the Ātman and the Ātman is the Brahman. The one supreme power through which all things have been brought into being is one with the inmost self in each man's heart.[16] The Upaniṣads do not uphold the theory of grace in the same spirit as the Vedas do. We do not have appeals to the Vedic gods, who were the sources of material prosperity for increase of happiness, but only prayers for deliverance from sorrow.

The emphasis on sorrow is sometimes interpreted as indicating an extravagant pessimism on the part of the Indian ṛṣis. It is not so. The religion of the Vedas certainly was more joyous, but it was a lower form of religion, where thought never penetrated beneath the husk of things. It was a religion expressing the delight of man at being in a world full of pleasures. The gods were feared and also trusted. Life on earth was simple and sweet innocence. The spiritual longing of the soul rebukes light-hearted joyousness and provokes reflection on the purpose of man's existence. Discontent with the actual is the necessary precondition of every moral change and spiritual rebirth. The pessimism of the Upaniṣads is the condition of all philosophy. Discontent prevails to enable man to effect an escape from it. If there is no way of escape, if no deliverance is sought after, then dissatisfaction is mischievous. The pessimism of the Upaniṣads has not developed to such an extent as to suppress all endeavour and generate inertia. There was enough faith in life to support all genuine search for truth. In the words of Barth: 'The Upaniṣads are much more instinct with the spirit of speculative daring than the sense of suffering and weariness.'[17]

14. Tait. Up.

15. Bṛh. Up., i. 4, 10.

16. See Chāndogya, iii. 14. Cf. Augustine: 'I asked the earth for God, and it answered me, "I am not He"; I asked the sea and the depths and the creeping things, and they answered, "We are not the God, seek thou above us." I asked the breezy gales, and the airy universe, and all its denizens replied, "Anaximenes is mistaken, I am not God"; I asked the heaven, sun, moon, stars, "Neither are we," say they, "the God whom thou seekest"; and I asked unto all things which stand about the gateways of my flesh (the senses), "Ye have told me of my God, that ye are not He; tell me something of Him", and they cried with a loud voice, "He made us"'. The search goes on until the inward self is questioned, when the answer is: 'Thy God is unto thee, even the life of thy life' (*Confessions*, x. chap. 6).

17. *Religions of India*, p. 84.

'Within the limits of the Upaniṣads there are indeed few explicit references to the misery of the life caught in the ceaseless cycle of death and birth. And its authors are saved from pessimism by the joy they feel at the message of redemption they proclaim.'[18] The formulation of the theory of saṁsāra or rebirth is no proof that the Upaniṣads are pessimistic. Life on earth is the means of self-perfection. We have to undergo the discipline of saṁsāra in our efforts towards the higher joy and the complete possession of spiritual truth. That which gives zest to life is the supreme motive of the joy of self-conquest. Saṁsāra is only a succession of spiritual opportunities. Life is a stage in spiritual perfection, a step in the passage to the infinite. It is the time for preparing the soul for eternity. Life is no empty dream and the world no delirium of spirit. In the later versions of rebirth in Indian thought we miss this ennobling ideal, and birth becomes the result of an error of the soul and saṁsāra a dragging chain.

At the stage of life represented by the Brāhmaṇas, the simple religion of the Vedic hymns was one of sacrifices. Men's relations with the gods were mechanical, a question of give and take, profit and loss. The revival of spirituality was the need of the age immersed in formalism. In the Upaniṣads we find a return to the fresh springs of spiritual life. They declare that the soul will not obtain salvation by the performance of sacrifices. It can be obtained only by the truly religious life, based on an insight into the heart of the universe. Perfection is inward and spiritual, not outward and mechanical. We cannot make a man clean by washing his shirt. A consciousness of the identity of one's own soul with the great All-soul is the essence of a truly spiritual life. The uselessness of ritual, the futility of sacrifices as means to salvation are brought out. God is to be honoured by spiritual worship and not external ceremony. We cannot save ourselves by praising God. We cannot impress Him by sacrifices. The authors of the Upaniṣads had a sufficient sense of the historic to know that their protest would become ineffective if it should demand a revolution in things. They therefore ask only for a change in the spirit. They reinterpret sacrifices and allegorise them. In some passages[19] we are asked to meditate on the horse-sacrifice.[20] This meditative effort helps us to realise the meaning of the sacrifice, and it is said to be quite as valuable as making a sacrifice. By

18. Cave, *Redemption, Hindu and Christian*, p. 64.
19. Bṛh. Up., i. 1, 2.
20. Aśvamedha.

giving detailed descriptions of the kind of plank, the nature of the wood, etc., they show that they are not indifferent to the sacrificial religion. While adhering to the forms they try to refine them. They say that all sacrifices are for the sake of realising the self of man. Life itself is a sacrifice. 'The true sacrifice is man; his first twenty-four years are his morning libation ... in hunger, in thirst, in abstinence from pleasure standeth his consecration.... In his eating and drinking and in his pleasures he keeps a holy festival, and in his laughter and feasting and marrying he sings hymns of praise. Self-discipline, generosity, straightforwardness, ahiṁsā,[21] and truth in speech, these are his payments, and the bath of purification when the sacrifice is over is death.'[22] We are told how the divine nature every day sacrifices itself; by its sacrifice do we live. Sacrifice is made to mean not feasting but renunciation. Make every action, every feeling and every thought an offering to God. Let your life be one sacrament or yajña. Sometimes we are told that the sacrifices are necessary as preparations for the higher path. Nobody can tread the higher road without fulfilling the requirements of the lower. Sacrifices are necessary for the unenlightened, though they alone will not do. They give us admission to the world of the fathers, which after a temporary sojourn in the moon leads back to a new earthly existence. Ceremonialism is contrasted with spiritual worship.[23] There are occasions when the sacrificial and priestly religion strikes them as superficial, and then they give vent to all their irony. They describe a procession of dogs to march like a procession of the priests, each holding the tail of the other in front and saying, 'Om! Let us eat. Om, let us drink ... etc.'[24] Thus the rigid ritual of the Brāhmaṇas, which gave little comfort to the weak heart of man, was held in check in the Upaniṣads.

The attitude of the Upaniṣads is not favourable to the sacredness of the Vedas. Like the rationalistic thinkers of a later day, they adopt a double attitude towards Vedic authority. They consider the Veda to be of supernatural

21. Innocence.

22. Chān. Up., iii. Cf. Isaiah lviii. 6–7: 'Is not this the fast that I have chosen? To loose the bonds of wickedness, to undo the heavy burdens, and to let the oppressed go free, and that ye break every yoke? Is it not to deal thy bread to the hungry, and that thou bring the poor that are cast out to thy house? When thou sest the naked, that thou cover him, and that thou hide not thyself from thine own flesh?' See Plato, *Euthyphron*. 14. E; *Laws*, 906, D. Jowett's Edition.

23. See also Chān. Up., i. 1. 10.

24. Ibid., i. 12, 4. 5.

origin, as when they say, 'Just as when a fire is laid with damp wood, clouds of smoke spread all around, so in truth from this great being, has been breathed forth the Ṛg-Veda, the Yajur-Veda, the Sāma-Veda, the hymns of the Atharvas and the Aṅgirasas, the narratives, the histories, the sciences, the mystical problems, the poems, the proverbs, and the expositions—all these have been breathed forth from Him.'[25] It is also recognised that the Vedic knowledge is much inferior to the true divine insight,[26] and will not liberate us. Nārada said: 'I know the Ṛg-Veda, Sir, the Yajur, the Sāma-Veda, with all these I know only the Mantras and the sacred books, I do not know the Self.'[27] The Muṇḍaka Upaniṣad says: 'Two kinds of knowledge must be known, the higher and the lower. The lower knowledge is that which the Ṛg, Sāma, Atharva-Veda, Ceremonial, Grammar give ... but the higher knowledge is that by which the indestructible Brahman is apprehended'.[28]

VI

THE PROBLEMS DISCUSSED IN THE UPANIṢADS

The central theme of the Upaniṣads is the problem of philosophy. It is the search for what is true. Dissatisfaction with things and second causes suggests the questions, which we read at the beginning of the Śvetāśvatara: 'Whence are we born, where do we live, and whither do we go? O, ye who know Brahman, tell us at whose command we abide here whether in pain or in pleasure. Should time or nature, or necessity or chance, or the elements be considered to be the cause, or he who is called Puruśa, the man that is the Supreme spirit?' In the Kena Upaniṣads the pupil asks, 'At whose wish does the mind sent forth proceed on its errand? At whose command does the first breath go forth, at whose wish do we utter this speech? What god directs the eye or the ear?'[29] The thinkers did not take experience to be an inexplicable datum, as common sense does. They wondered whether the report of the senses could be taken as final. Are the mental faculties by which we acquire experience self-existent, or are they themselves effects

25. Bṛh. Up., ii. 4. 10.

26. See Chāndogya. v. 3. 10. Bṛh., 3. 5. 1; iv. 4. 21; vi. 2. 1. Kauṣītaki, i.; Tait., ii. 4; Kaṭha, ii. 23.

27. Chān. Up., vii. 2.

28. Muṇḍaka, i. 1. 4–5; Maitrāyana, vi. 21.

29. i. 1.

of something mightier still, which lies behind them? How can we consider physical objects, effects and products as they are, to be quite as real as their causes? There must be something ultimate at the back of it all, a self-existent, in which alone the mind can rest. Knowledge, mind, the senses and their objects are all finite and conditioned. In the field of morals we find that we cannot get true happiness from the finite. The pleasures of the world are transient, being cut off by old age and death. Only the infinite gives durable happiness. In religion we cry for eternal life. All these force upon us the conviction of a timeless being, a spiritual reality, the object of philosophical quest, the fulfilment of our desires, and the goal of religion. The seers of the Upaniṣads try to lead us to this central reality which is infinite existence (sat), absolute truth (cit), and pure delight (ānanda). The prayer of every human heart is 'Lead me from the unreal to the real, lead me from darkness to light, lead me from death to immortality.'[30]

We shall deal with the philosophy of the Upaniṣads under the two heads of metaphysics and ethics. We shall present their views of ultimate reality, the nature of the world, and the problem of creation under metaphysics, and their analysis of the individual, his destiny, his ideal, the relation of karma to freedom, the highest conception of mukti or release, and the doctrine of rebirth under ethics.

VII

THE NATURE OF REALITY

In solving the question of the nature of ultimate reality, the Upaniṣad thinkers seek to supplement the objective vision of the Vedic seers by a subjective one. The highest conception reached in the Vedic hymns was that of the one reality (Ekaṁ Sat), which realises itself in all the variety of existence. This conclusion is strengthened in the Upaniṣads, where the problem is sometimes approached by way of a philosophical analysis of the nature of the self which they call the Ātman. The etymology of this word is obscure. In the Ṛg-Veda x. 16. 3 it means breath or the vital essence. Gradually it acquired the meaning of soul or self. The theory of the true self or Ātman is not set out with any clearness or fullness of detail, nor are isolated statements connected into a coherent system. In a dialogue between the teacher Prajāpati and the pupil Indra, narrated in the Chāndogya

30. Asato mā sad gamaya, tamaso mā jyotir gamaya, mṛtyor mā amṛtaṁgamaya. Bṛh. Up., i. 3. 27.

Upaniṣad,[31] we find a progressive development in the definition of self through the four stages of (1) the bodily self, (2) the empirical self, (3) the transcendental self, and (4) the absolute self. The question discussed is not so much psychological as metaphysical. What is the nature of the self of man, his central being? Prajāpati opens the discussion by giving certain general characteristics which the true self should possess. 'The self which is free from sin, free from old age, from death and grief, from hunger and thirst, which desires nothing but what it ought to desire and imagines nothing but what it ought to imagine, *that* it is which we must try to understand'.[32] It is the subject which persists throughout the changes, the common factor in the states of waking, dream, sleep, death, rebirth and final deliverance.[33] It is the simple truth that nothing can destroy. Death does not touch it nor vice dissolve it. Permanence, continuity, unity, eternal activity are its characteristics. It is a world self-complete. There is nothing outside of it to set against it. Modern criticism will object to the whole procedure as a case of *petitio principīi*. By the characteristics of self-containedness and self-completeness being assumed, the solution is taken for granted. But as we shall see, this line of procedure has its own meaning. Prajāpati makes it clear that the self of man consists in the truly subjective, which can never become an object. It is the person that sees, not the object seen.[34] It is not the bundle of qualities called the 'me', but the I which remains beyond and behind inspecting all these qualities. It is the subject in the truest sense, and it can never become the object. Much of the content of the self as ordinarily used can become an object. The argument assumes that whatever becomes an object belongs to the not-self. We must strip away everything of our actual self alien to or different from the self. The first answer given is that the body which is born, grows up and decays and dies, is the true self. The self, according to Prajāpati, is indeed he who is seen when you look into another's eye or a pail of water or a mirror. It is suggested that we observe a picture even to the very hairs and nails. To indicate that it is not the self, Prajāpati asks Indra to adorn himself, put on the best clothes and look again into the water and the mirror, and he sees his likeness well adorned with best clothes and clean. A doubt occurs

31. viii. 3–12.
32. vii. 7. 1.
33. See Bṛh. Up., iv. 4. 3.
34. viii. 7. 3.

to Indra. 'As this self in the shadow or the water is well adorned when the body is well adorned, well dressed when the body is well dressed, well cleaned when the body is well cleaned, that self will also be blind if the body is blind, lame if the body is lame, crippled if the body is crippled, and perish, in fact, as soon as the body perishes. I see no good in this.'[35] Indra approaches his teacher Prajāpati, and after another long interval is told that 'he who moves about happy in dreams is the self.' The true self is not the body which is exposed to all suffering and imperfections, which is a material phenomenon. The body is only an instrument used by consciousness, while consciousness is not the product of the body. And now Indra is told that the dreaming subject is the self, but he feels another difficulty. 'Though it is true that that self is not rendered faulty by faults of body, nor struck when it is struck, nor lamed when it is lamed, yet it is as if they struck him in dreams, as if they chased him. He becomes even conscious as it were of pain and sheds tears, therefore I see no good in this'.[36] Prajāpati took the dream states instead of other mental experiences, because dreams being more independent of body are crucial in their nature. The self is supposed to roam untrammelled in dreams. In them the mind is said to float free of the accidents of body. This view equates the self with the ever-growing and changing mental experiences. This is the empirical self, and Indra rightly recognises that this empirical self is subject to the accidents of experience. It cannot be the subject, for every moment it is changing. Though it is independent of body, dream states do not seem to be self-existent, which the true self of Ātman must be. The ego dependent on the limitations of time and birth cannot be said to be eternal. The self tethered to a local and temporal environment is a creature of time. It is the wanderer in the world of saṁsāra. It constructs for itself an imperfect world out of imperfect data. It is not indestructible, nor has it boundless freedom. We seem to require a subject as the ground and sustainer of all experience, a vaster reality of which the dream states as well as waking experience are only imperfect revelations. A mere flux of states cannot be sustained by itself. The empirical self is not eternal in its own right. Indra again approaches Prajāpati, explains to him his position, and after a long time is taught. 'When a man being asleep, reposing and at perfect rest, sees no dreams,

35. vii. 9. 1.
36. viii. 10. 2. 3.

that is the self.'[37] Prajāpati understands Indra's difficulty. The self could not be reduced to a series of states, for that would be to explain away the reality of a permanent ego, and make Ātman subject to the vicissitudes of our chance experiences. Indra has to be taught that the objects of experience require a permanent subject by which they could be experienced. Prajāpati intended to bring out how, while a grin required a cat, everywhere except in Alice's wonderland, a cat need not always have a grin. The object depends upon the subject, but not the subject on the object in the same sense. Without the self there can be no knowledge, no art, no morality. Objects out of relation to a self are non-existent. From the subject are all objects and the subject itself is not a thing among other things. To enable Indra to realise that the self is the subject of all experiences, Prajāpati employs the method of abstraction which has its own disadvantages. Our life is ordinarily busy with things. The world is too much with us. Our self is lost in feelings, desires and imaginations, and does not know what it really is. Leading the life of mere objectivity, absorbed in the things of nature, ever busy with the active pursuits of the world, we do not want to waste a moment's thought on the first principle of all things—the self of man. Knowledge is taken for granted. To reflect on it, to understand its implications, means mental strain. In the history of European thought the question of the possibility of knowledge is a late one, but when it was put, it was realised that knowledge was impossible without what Kant called the transcendental unity of apperception, what Plotinus referred to as the 'accompaniment' by the soul of its own mental activities. The most elementary presentation requires the reality of self. In the most apparently passive perceptions we realise the activity of the self. All changes, all experiences, assume a central self. The changes themselves are recognised as changes within a whole, which we are trying to actualise. Prajāpati wishes to bring out the necessity of this self by urging that the self continuously exists, even when the waking or the dreaming experience is suspended. In sleep, deep and dreamless, we have no felt objects of experience, but we cannot on that account say there is no self. Prajāpati assumes that Indra will admit the reality of a self in sleep, for the continuity of consciousness, despite the temporal gaps, cannot otherwise be accounted for. Devadatta, after good sleep, continues to be Devadatta, since his experiences unite

37. viii. 11. 1.

themselves to the system which existed at the time when he went to sleep. They link themselves to his thoughts and do not fly to any other's. This continuity of experience requires us to admit a permanent self underlying all contents of consciousness. That which exists in sleep without any objects to contemplate is the self. The mirror is not shattered simply because nothing is seen in it. Prajāpati tries to bring out the absolute supremacy of the subject over the object, the truth of Yajñavalkya's statement that even when all objects are extinguished, the subject persists in its own light. 'When the sun has set, when the moon has set, and when the fire is put out, the self alone is his light'.[38] But Indra was too much of a psychologist for Prajāpati. He felt that this self, freed from all bodily experience, from the shapeless mass of dreams, etc., this objectless self, is a barren fiction. If the self is not what it knows, feels and reacts upon, if it is divorced from it and thus emptied of its content, what remains? 'Nothing', said Indra. 'To be free from everything is to be nothing'.[39] Gautama, the Buddha, takes up the analogy of a tree and asks what is that tree which is supposed to remain, after we tear away its leaves, hew down its branches, strip off its bark, etc.? Peel off layer after layer of an onion, and what remains? Nothing. Bradley points out: 'The ego that pretends to be anything either before or beyond its concrete psychical filling is a gross fiction and a mere monster, and for no purpose admissible'.[40] On this view in dreamless sleep there is no self at all. Locke declares that every drowsy nod explodes the self theory. 'In sleep and trances the mind *exists not*—there is no time, no succession of ideas. To say the mind exists without thinking is a contradiction nonsense, nothing'.[41] Indra seems to have been an empiricist ages before Locke and Berkeley. 'If the soul in a perfectly dreamless sleep thinks, feels, and wills nothing, is the soul then at all, and if it is, how is it?' asks Lotze. 'How often has the answer been given, that if this could happen, the soul would have no being. Why have we not the courage to say that as often as this happenes the soul is not?'[42] Indra has the courage to declare it.[43] 'It is indeed destroyed'. This has an important lesson which is again and again

38. Bṛh. Up., iv. 3. 6.
39. Bradley, *Ethical Studies*, p. 52.
40. *Appearance and Reality*, p. 89.
41. Berkeley's *Works*, vol. i. p. 34.
42. *Metaphysics*, Eng. Translation, vol. ii., p. 317.
43. Vināśamevāpīto bhavati, Chān. Up., viii. 11. 1–2.

forgotten in Indian thought. To deny the life without is to destroy the god within. Those who think that we reach the highest point attainable, in pure subjectivity must turn to the dialogue of Indra and Prajāpati. The condition freed from the limits imposed by the organism, from time and space, from the existence of objects, is simple annihilation, according to Indra. This contentless ego, this abstract *cogito* of Descartes, this formal unity of Kant, this objectless subject supposed to stand behind, unrelated to all empirical consciousness, is an impossibility. Philosophical reflection as well as psychological analysis leads to this result. But Prajāpati was trying to emphasise the identity of the self which is unaffected by the changes of experience. He was anxious to point out that while the self was not exclusive of conscious states, it was not the conscious states. Dr McTaggart puts the whole point thus: 'What does the self include? Everything of which it is conscious. What does it exclude? Equally-Everything of which it is conscious. What can it say is not inside it? Nothing. What can it say is not outside it. A single abstraction. And any attempt to remove the paradox destroys the self. For the two sides are inevitably connected. If we try to make it a distinct individual by separating it from all other things, it loses all content, of which it can be conscious, and so loses the very individuality which we started by trying to preserve. If, on the other hand, we try to save its content, by emphasising the inclusion at the expense of the exclusion, then the consciousness vanishes; and since the self has no contents, but the objects of which it is conscious, the contents vanish also'.[44] Indra shows the risks in conceiving the self as a transcendental one. The self must be shown to be the true life of the whole, and not a mere abstraction. Hence the next step, when Indra explains to Prajāpati his difficulty in the words, 'in truth that dreamless sleeping subject does not know himself that he is, nor does he know anything that exists. He is gone to utter annihilation, I see no good in this'.[45] Prajāpati points out how it is an identity, running in and through differences. The whole world is the one process of the self-realisation of the absolute thought. 'Maghavan![46] This body is mortal and all is subject to death. It is the abode of the self, which is immortal and without body. He is the person of the eye, the eye itself is the instrument of seeing. He who knows, let me

44. *Hegelian Cosmology*, sec. 27.
45. viii. 11. 1.
46. Another name for Indra.

smell this, he is the self, the nose is the instrument of smelling, etc.'[47] The self is shown to be not an abstract formal principle, but an active universal consciousness, existing, to adopt Hegel's phraseology, both in itself and for itself. It is simple self-sameness as well as varied distinctions. It is both subject and object. The objects we know in experience are based on it. The true infinite self is not the self which is simply not finite. It is none of the limited things, but yet the basis of all of them. It is the universal self, which is immanent as well as transcendent. The whole universe lives and breathes in it. 'The moon and the sun are its eyes, the four quarters of the sky its ears, the wind its breath'.[48] It is the blazing light that burns in the deeps of personality, the universal ākāśa from which all creatures proceed,[49] the vital principle of creation,[50] the subject in which the entire world moves trembling.[51] There is nothing outside it. It contains all consciousness of objects implicitly. There is nothing in the universe which is not involved in the infinite self in us. This self which embraces all is the sole reality containing within itself all the facts of nature and all the histories of experience. Our small selves are included in it and transcended by it. This is the subject which is more than the flux of presentations, which are only imperfect revelations of it. All our states of consciousness revolve round this central light. Abolish it, they vanish. Without a subject there will be no flux, no order of sensations in space or sequences in time. It renders possible memory and introspection, knowledge and morality. The Upaniṣads contend that this subject is the universal ground which is in all individuals. It is hidden in all things and pervades all creation. 'There is no second outside it, no other distinct term.'[52] 'As breathing he is named breath, as speaking speech, as seeing eye, as hearing ear, as understanding mind, all these are but names for his operations'.[53] It is only the self thus

47. viii. 12. Cf. Plato, who distinguishes in the *Timæus*, two souls, one immortal and the other mortal. The mortal soul consists of passions and affections. It is the empirical ego which identifies itself with the perishing world of change and death. The immortal soul is the intelligent principle common to man and the world, the divine spark enclosed in human personality (*Timæus* and *Phædo*). We have also the same distinction in Aristotle's *intellectus agens* as opposed to perishing mind and memory.

48. Mundaka, i. 1; Chān., iii. 13. 7.

49. Chān., i. 91.

50. Chān., i. 11. 5.

51. Kaṭha, vi. 1.

52. Bṛh., iv. 3. 23; Chān., viii. 1. 3.

53. Bṛh., i. 4. 7; Kauṣītaki, iii.

understood that can be looked upon as the permanent subject persisting in waking and dreaming, death and sleep, bondage and liberation. It is present throughout, surveying all the worlds. It is the universal subject and yet the universal object. It sees and yet sees not. As the Upaniṣad has it, 'When then he sees not, yet is he seeing, although he sees not; since for the seer there is no interruption of seeing because he is imperishable; but there is no second beside him, no other distinct from him, for him to see'.[54] The self is the whole. 'I indeed am this whole universe.'[55]

This universal self by its very nature cannot be perceived. As Śaṁkara puts it, 'The witness self illumines consciousness, but never itself is in consciousness'. It is not a datum of experience, not an object, though all objects are for it. It is not a thought, but all thoughts are for it. It is not a thing seen, but is the principle of all seeing. As Kant would say, the condition of the empirically known is not the known itself. 'What I must presuppose in order to know an object', says Kant, 'I cannot know as an object.' The subject of all experience cannot itself be an experience. If it is experience, the question arises, by whom is it known? Knowledge always works dually. This self, therefore, is indefinable. Like all ultimate principles, it has only to be accepted. It is the explanation of all else, though it itself remains unexplained. The old difficulty of Comte that the subject cannot turn round and catch itself is not altogether imaginary. 'The soul which is not this or that, nor aught else, is intangible, for it cannot be laid hold of.'[56] The Upaniṣads refuse to identify the self with the body, or the series of mental states or the presentation continuum or the stream of consciousness. The self cannot be a relation which requires a ground of relations, nor a connexion of contents, which is unintelligible without an agent who connects. We are obliged to accept the reality of a universal consciousness which ever accompanies the contents of consciousness and persists even when there are no contents. This fundamental identity, which is the presupposition of both self and not-self, is called the Ātman. None can doubt its reality.[57]

The Māṇḍūka Upaniṣad gives us an analysis of consciousness leading to the same conclusion. We shall start with a free rendering of what it says on this point.[58] The soul has three conditions which are all included in a

54. Bṛh., iv. 3. 23.
55. Aham eva idam sarvo'smi.
56. Bṛh., iii. 7. 3; iv. 4. 22.
57. Na hi kaścit sandigdhe ahaṁ vā nāhaṁ veti. Bhāmatī.
58. i. 2. 7.

fourth. They are waking, dreaming, sleeping, and what is called turīya. The first condition is that of wakefulness, where the self is conscious of the common world of external objects. It enjoys the gross things. Here the dependence on the body is predominant. The second condition is that of dreaming, where the self enjoys subtle things,[59] fashions for itself a new world of forms with the materials of its waking experience. The spirit is said to roam freely unfettered by the bonds of the body. The third is the condition of sound sleep, where we have neither dreams nor desires. It is called suṣupti. The soul is said to become temporarily one with Brahman and enjoy bliss. In deep sleep we are lifted above all desires and freed from the vexations of spirit. The oppositions are, so to say, lost in this pure-objectless-knowing subject condition.[60] Śaṁkara observes that the phenomena of duality caused by the action of the mind are present in the other two conditions, but absent here. In several passages we are told that we taste the nature of absolute bliss in dreamless sleep, where a man is cut off from the distracting world. The soul is divine in origin, though clogged with the flesh. In sleep it is said to be released from the shackles of the body and to gain back its own nature. We read in an Aristotelian fragment, 'whenever the soul is alone and by itself in sleep, it recovers by its proper nature.'[61] The natural divinity of the soul reasserts itself when freed from the tyranny of the flesh. 'He giveth his beloved truth in sleep.' The analogy of eternal dreamless sleep is used to bring out how all outer activities are then suppressed. But there was the likelihood of its being confused with sheer unconsciousness. So the Māṇḍūkya Upaniṣad points out that the highest is not this dreamless sleep, but another, a fourth state of the soul, a pure intuitional consciousness, where there is no knowledge of objects internal or external. In deep sleep the spirit dwells in a region far above the changeful life of sense in absolute union with Brahman. The turīya condition brings out the positive aspect of the negative emphasised in the condition of deep sleep. 'The fourth is not that which is conscious of the subjective, nor that which is conscious of the objective, nor that which is conscious of both, nor that which is simple consciousness, nor that which is an all-sentient mass, nor that which is all darkness. It is unseen, transcendent, inapprehensible, uninferrable, unthinkable,

59. See Bṛh., iv. 3. 9. 14.
60. See Bṛh., ii. 1 Kauṣītaki, iv.; Chān., vi. 8. 1; Praśna., iv. 4; iv. 3. 7.
61. Fragment 2.

indescribable, the sole essence of the consciousness of self, the completion of the world, the ever peaceful, all blissful, the one unit, this indeed is the Ātman'.[62] It is symbolised by the Aumkara, with its parts of A-U-M, the waking, the dreaming and the sleeping states. It is not an exclusive self, but the common ground of all, their basis of identity.[63] In deep sleep we may be said to reach an eternal unity in which all distinctions vanish and the entire universe is obliterated. But since this cannot be considered the highest state, a higher positive is suggested. To the empirical individual, if the not-self goes, his individuality also vanishes. So there is a suspicion that the abolition of the objects would reduce the self into a thin abstraction, but in the highest universal self the reality of all objects is included. Objects of the world are known and loved by us only in so far as they enter our self, which comprehends in itself all objects of the universe and has nothing outside. It is the unchanged and persistent identity which continues in the midst of all change. The moods pass and vary but the self remains the same. It has no beginning, no end, though the objects of which it is conscious have a beginning and an end. 'Never has the cessation of consciousness been experienced, or witnessed directly; or if it has been, then the witness, the experiencer, himself still remains behind as the continued embodiment of that same consciousness'.[64] It is the foundation of all existence, the one witness to and the only possible support of all we know, though the nature of the dependence of the objects of knowledge on the subject so insistently repeated is not very clear. The three conditions of the self, waking, dreaming, sleeping, together with that which comprehends them all, are called respectively the Viśva, the Taijasa, the Prājña and the Turīya states.[65]

From this analysis of the three states of dreaming, waking and sleeping, it follows that all of them are unreal, though not non-existent. 'What is naught at the beginning and naught at the end must surely be naught in the middle'.[66] Judged by it, waking experience is not real. If it is said that the dream states are unreal since they do not cohere with the rest of our experience, may it not be urged that the waking experience does not cohere

62. i. 7.

63. Triṣu dhāmasu yat tulyam sāmānyam—Gauḍapāda's Kārikās, i. 22.

64. See Devī Bhāgavata, iii. 32. 15–16.

65. The Buddhist discrimination of the four planes of kāma, rūpa, arūpa and lokottara, answers to this division.

66. Gauḍapāda's Kārikā, i. 6.

with dreams? Dreams may be coherent within themselves, even as waking experience is within its own bounds. The worlds seem to be real only in relation to the particular moods of the self. It is not right to apply the standard of waking experience to the dream world and condemn it. Dreaming and waking experiences are both unreal though in different degrees. The condition of dreamless sleep is one in which we have no distinct cognitions of anything internal or external. It is a distinctionless mass under the pall of darknees, comparable to Hegel's night, in which all cows are black. We have here the negative condition of the highest state, freedom from sorrow. But Ātman is not this absence of unhappiness. It is positive bliss. It is neither waking nor dreaming nor sleep, but the fourth witnessing to as well as transcending the three. The negative descriptions given indicate that we as finite cannot know the positive nature of it. The fourth is realised, not so much by negating the three as by transcending them all. It is impossible for us finite beings to define the character of the ideal reality, though the Upaniṣads are quite emphatic that it is not a blank. Yet to refute false ideas of the highest and to point the truth that it is no abstraction, they indulge in inadequate concepts. Strictly speaking we cannot say anything of it. Yet for purposes of discussion, we are obliged to use intellectual concepts with their limited validity.

The problem of the self is one of the most important discussed in the Upaniṣads. It occurs again as the Adhyātma Vidyā in the Bhagavadgītā and the Vedānta Sūtras. The analysis of the nature of self is the legacy of the Upaniṣads bequeathed to the subsequent systems of thought. It has given rise to many misconceptions. Contradictory doctrines of the nature of self are held by Buddha and Śaṁkara, Kapila and Patañjali, whose views can be traced to the Upaniṣads. It was not the intention of the Upaniṣads to make of the deeper self an abstract nothingness. It is the fullest reality, the completest consciousness, and not a mere negative calm, untroubled by any unrest and unpolluted by any blot or blemish. The logic of thought has in it a negative movement, where it rises by the repudiation of the finite, but this is only a stage in the onward march. By the negative process the self has to recognise that its essence is not in its finitude or self-sufficiency. By the positive method it finds its true self in the life and being of all. All things exist within this true self. Some Buddhists make of the self mere emptiness, and on this assumption rightly dismiss it as an abstraction of the metaphysician. We cannot find this self in any corner of the field of consciousness. Not finding it there, we rush to the conclusion that it is nothing. The Sāṁkhya takes it to be a simple and pure, though passive, spirit, which in spite of its apparent simplicity has some character and uniqueness, and so we get the doctrine of the boundless plurality of souls. Some Vedāntins adopt the view that the true self or Brahman is pure, calm, peaceful and untroubled, and hold that there is only one self. By throwing the emphasis on the passive side they run the risk of reducing it to mere emptiness. There are Buddhistic sects which reduce the self to mere intelligence, which can somehow think without any contents.

VIII

BRAHMAN

We may now proceed to define the ultimate reality from the objective side, when it is called Brahman.[67] In the Ṛg-Veda we have seen that the monistic idea was arrived at. The Upaniṣads undertake the task of a more logical definition of the Eternal Spirit ever acting and ever resting. In another place we have traced the progress from the lower imperfect conceptions to the more adequate ones as formulated in the Taittirīya Upaniṣad.[68] In chapter iii the son approaches the father with the request to teach him the nature of reality from which all things flow and to which all return. The

67. The question how Brahman came to denote the supreme reality of the Upaniṣads has been answered in different ways by different scholars. Haug holds that Brahman means prayer, being derived from the root Bṛh, to swell or to grow. It is that which swells or grows. Sacred prayers cause the growth, and then it came to mean the force of nature, and later the supreme reality. According to Roth, Brahman is first the force of will directed to the gods, then it came to mean a sacred formula, and then the Absolute. Oldenberg thinks that in the Vedic times, when the world was peopled with many gods and mysterious forces capable of producing happiness and misery, the most powerful man was the medicine man, who wielded the magic spell and produced whatever effect was desired. Then Brahman meant a magic spell. During the time of the Brāhmaṇas it referred to the sacred hymns used in the sacrifices. Perhaps some of these hymns were used as spells for producing magical effects. The word was slowly transferred to the central energy which produces the world. Deussen holds that Brahman is prayer, which elevates the soul, when we perceive the truth, and the truth came to be denoted by the word. Max Müller traces it to 'word,' as is evident from the name Bṛhaspati or Vācaspati, lord of speech. That which utters is Brahman (S.S., pp. 52, 70). We need not trouble ourselves about the etymology of the word. To us, it is clear, Brahman means reality, which grows, breathes or swells.

68. See *Reign of Religion*, chap. xiii.

son is given the general features of Brahman, and is asked to discover the content which satisfies these requirements. 'That from which these beings are born, that in which when born they live, and that into which they enter at their death, that is Brahman'.[69] Things of the world are ever changing their forms, and they cannot be considered to be real in an ultimate sense. Is there anything unalterably fixed underlying the universe of changing things, nāmarūpa, name and form, as the Upaniṣads call them? The son considers matter to be the ultimate reality. It is the most prominent aspects of the outer world. This view is held by the lokāyatas, or the materialists. The son soon discovers that matter cannot account for the life phenomena. Vegetable growth requires a different explanation. He hits upon prāṇa or life as the ultimate principle.[70] Matter does not hold the secret of life, though life cannot exist without matter. There is something in life which enables it to absorb and transmute the inorganic elements. This something is the vital principle which in man helps to change the vegetable product into blood, bone and muscle. It is the principle which pervades the universe and binds human beings with the rest of creation.[71] The son is sure that life belongs to a different order from matter though prāṇa is the essence of the body.[72] Again he is dissatisfied with the solution of prāṇa as the ultimate reality, for conscious phenomena which we come across in the animal world are not explicable by the principle of life. Manas, or perceptual consciousness, is a product distinct from life and matter. It seems to be the crown of the vital process. So the son believes that manas is Brahman. Even this will not suffice, for there are intellectual facts which mere perceptual consciousness does not take into account. Vijñāna or intelligence is Brahman.[73] Some schools of Buddhism adopt this view. The son realises that even intellectual self-consciousness is incomplete, being subject to discord and imperfection. It is the aim of the Upaniṣads to point out that elements of duality and externality persist at the intellectual level, however much we may try to overcome them. In knowledge and morality we have the subject-object relation. There must be something higher than mere intellect, where existence is no longer formulated in terms of knowledge. The unity of existence requires that

69. iii. 1.
70. Prāṇa means breath. See R.V., i. 66. 1; iii. 53. 21; x. 59. 6.
71. See Praśna, ii.
72. Bṛh., i. 3. 90. See Chān., vi. 2. 4.
73. See Ait., iii. 3; Tait., iii. 5.

we must transcend the intellectual level. Thought, as ordinarily understood, deals with objects viewed as beyond or other than the process of thinking. It reaches outwards to a somewhat other than and contrasted with itself. Reality is different from thought, and can be reached in the turīya state of highest immediacy, which transcends thought and its distinctions, where the individual coincides with the central reality. Ānanda or delight is the highest fruition, where the knower, the known and the knowledge become one. Here the philosophical quest terminates, the suggestion being that there is nothing higher than ānanda. This ānanda is active enjoyment or unimpeded exercise of capacity. It is not sinking into nothingness, but the perfection of being.[74] 'The discerning see by their superior knowledge the Ātman which shines all bliss and immortality'.[75] Strictly speaking, we cannot give any account of the highest reality of ānanda. Even the question whether it is abstract or concrete is illogical. Intellectual necessities require us to give some description. It is truer to consider it concrete than abstract. Each higher principle is more concrete and inclusive than the lower one, and therefore ānanda, which is Brahman, is the most inclusive of all. From it all things flow. By it all things are sustained, and into it all things are dissolved. The different parts, the mineral world, the plant life, the animal kingdom, and the human society, are not related to the highest in any abstract or mechanical way. They are one in and through that which is universal about them. All parts in the universe share in the light of this universal spirit and possess specific features on account of the special functions which they have to perform. The parts are not self-subsistent factors, but are dependent aspects of the one. 'Sir, on what does the infinite rest? On its own greatness or not even on greatness'. Everything else hangs on it and it hangs on nothing. The organic and living nature of the relation of the parts to the whole is brought out in many passages. 'As all spokes are contained in the axle, and in the felly of a wheel, thus also, all beings and all gods, all worlds and all organs, also are contained in that self'.[76] 'There is that ancient tree whose roots grow upward and whose branches go downward. That is the bright, Brahman, the immortal, all worlds are contained in it and no one goes beyond it'.[77]

74. See Muṇḍaka Up.
75. Muṇḍaka, ii. 8.
76. Bṛh., ii. 5. 15.
77. Kaṭha, ii. 6. 1. See also Tait., i. 10; B.G., xv. i.

We have defined reality as ānanda, and thus contradicted the statement frequently made that the ultimate is indefinable. Constructive attempts at obtaining a comprehensive reality generally end in a concrete whole. If, however, we try to reconcile the defined reality with the undefined one, which also the Upaniṣads support, then we shall have to say that ānanda in the present context is not the ultimate reality, but only the highest conceivable by the thought of man. It is not the absolute or the eternal being which ever exists in its own essentiality. To the logical mind, the whole is real, and within it falls the diversity of the world. The concrete ānanda is the prāmāṇika sattā, or the real revealed to thought, and answers to the highest Brahman accepted by Rāmānuja. The pure Brahman free from all the predicates is the nirupādhika satta, or the Nirguṇa Brahman accepted by Śaṁkara. The former is an organised whole; the latter is an indefinable real. Yet even according to Śaṁkara it is the latter that shows itself as the former. The one of intuition appears as the whole of knowledge.[78]

This difference of view has resulted in a good deal of discussion about the interpretation of ānanda in the Upaniṣads. Śaṁkara squarely says that ānandamaya, by its suffix maya, indicates that it is only a phenomenal effect. Unless it were different from Ātman, there can be no talk of reasoning about it. If it were pure Brahman, it will be inappropriate to give it form and attribute to it head, limbs, as the Taittirīya Upaniṣad does. If ānanda were Brahman there would be no separate mention of Brahman as the supporting tail of ānanda.[79] So Śaṁkara concludes, 'Ānandamaya Ātman is an effect, and not the unconditioned Ātman'. Rāmānuja, on the other hand, argues that this ānanda is Brahman. The suffix of maya indicates only

78. The Upaniṣads are definite about the fact that the supreme is indefinable, though they give intellectual accounts of it which are not absolutely true. If any logical description be true at all, it is Rāmānuja's way of putting it. Śaṁkara, in the true spirit of the Upaniṣads, contends that there is a higher than the logical highest, which is Rāmānuja's. In discussing the philosophy of Śaṁkara, we shall see how he establishes the inadequacy of the highest categories to the reality intended by them. He contends that we cannot say whether the absolute is finite or infinite, or both or neither. It is the same with all relations like whole and part, substance and quality, cause and effect. A rational demonstration of the limits of thought such as the one we have in Śaṁkara is rendered possible only by the intervening of the great Buddhist tradition between the Upaniṣads and Śaṁkara.

79. Brahma puccham pratiṣṭhā.

fullness or prācurya. Though with regard to matter, life, etc., it is clearly stated that there is some other inside, anyo'ntara Ātmā, no such inner reality is asserted for ānanda. Ascribing limbs, etc., is nothing more than kalpana or imagination. Puccham Brahma need not be taken as implying any difference between ānanda and Brahman. The two may be related as whole and part,[80] which is sometimes the significance of the accusative usage. Immediately after the reference to ānandamaya, it is said in the Upaniṣad 'sokāmayata,' 'he desired,' and this masculine gender can only refer to ānandamaya, and not to puccham Brahma, which is neuter. Other forms of bliss, like priya, moda, are included within the whole of ānanda, and the disciple reaches his final resting-place when he gets to ānanda. We have many cases in the same Upaniṣad where the word ānanda is used as a synonym for final reality.

It is obvious that the whole controversy is due to the doubt whether ānanda is to be looked upon as the logical highest or the ultimate being. The Upaniṣads did not draw any hard and fast line of distinction between the simple one of intuition supported by Śaṁkara and the concrete whole of Rāmānuja. If we separate the two, it will become impossible for us to admit any distinction or value in the world of concrete existence. The Upaniṣads imply that the Īśvara is practically one with Brahman. Very strict usage and meticulous philosophic accuracy require us to say that there is the slightest conceivable diminution from the absolute when we come to the self-conscious, I am I.[81] This quasinought is quite enough for Śaṁkara to precipitate pure being, the basal thought and fact of all, into the world of space, time and cause. The Upaniṣads by implication admit that the moment we think the pure being, we make nothing the principle of distinction and difference, equally basal. The self-conscious God, who later develops into the organised whole of existence, is the maximum of being and the minimum of non-being. He is least penetrated with objectivity and touched by externality. The One is revealed in the existences of the world, and that is why we are able to ascertain the degrees of reality possessed by the objects of the world by measuring the distance separating them from the One. Each lower degree consists in a diminution of the higher, though throughout the scale of existences from the highest to the lowest we have the revelation of Brahman as well as the common characters

80. Samudāyasamudāyībhāva.
81. Bṛh., i. 4, 10.

of space, time and cause. The lower things are far away from the simple being than the higher ones, so much so that the ānandamaya of the Upaniṣads, the concrete Brahman of Rāmānuja, the Īśvara of Śaṁkara, is the nearest to it. Nothing nearer can be thought. The supreme Brahman or ānanda at the level of vijñāna or self-consciousness becomes the personal Īśvara with a voluntary limitation. God or self is the ground of unity, and matter or not-self becomes the principle of plurality.[82]

IX

BRAHMAN AND ĀTMAN

The two, the objective and the subjective, the Brahman and the Ātman, the cosmic and the psychical principles, are looked upon as identical. Brahman is Ātman.[83] 'He who is this Brahman in man, and who is that in the sun, those are one'.[84] The transcendent conception of God held in the Ṛg-Veda is here transformer into an immanent one. The infinite is not beyond the finite but in the finite. The subjective character of the Upaniṣad teaching is responsible for this change. The identity between the subject and the object was realised in India before Plato was born. Deussen speaks of it thus: 'If we strip this thought of the various forms, figurative to the highest degree and not seldom extravagant, under which it appears in the Vedānta texts, and fix our attention upon it solely in its philosophical simplicity as the identity of God and the soul, the Brahman and the Ātman, it will be found to possess a significance reaching far beyond the Upaniṣads, their time and country; nay, we claim for it an inestimable value for the whole race of mankind. We are unable to look into the future, we do not know what revelations and discoveries are in store for the restlessly inquiring human spirit; but one thing we may assert with confidence—whatever new and unwonted paths the philosophy of the future may strike out, this principle will remain permanently unshaken, and from it no deviation can possibly take place. If ever a general solution is reached of the great riddle, which presents itself to the philosopher in the nature of things, all the more clearly the further our knowledge extends, the key can only be found where alone the secret of nature lies open to us from within, that is to say, in our innermost self. It was here that for the

82. See Tait., i. 5; S.B. and R.B. on V.S., i. 1. 6.
83. Tait., i. 5.
84. ii. 8. See also iii. 10; Chān., iii. 13. 7; iii. 14.2.4; Bṛh., v. 5.2; Muṇḍaka, ii. 1. 10.

first time the original thinkers of the Upaniṣads, to their immortal honour, found it when they recognised our Ātman, our inmost individual being, as the Brahman, the inmost being of universal nature and of all her phenomena'.[85] This identity of subject and object is not a vague hypothesis, but the necessary implication of all relevant thinking, feeling and willing. The human self cannot think, conquer and love nature, were it unthinkable, unconquerable and unlovable. Nature is the object of a subject, quite rational and thoroughly intelligible, capable of control and worthy of love. It exists for man. The stars serve as lamps for his feet, and the darkness to lull him into slumber. Nature summons us to the spiritual reality of life and answers the needs of the soul. It is formed, vitalised and directed by the spirit. From the beginning of reflection this oneness of subject and object, the existence of one central reality, pervading and embracing all, has been the doctrine of the devout. Religious mysticism and deep piety witness to the truth of the great saying, 'That art thou', 'Tat tvam asi'. We may not understand it, but that does not give us a sufficient right to deny it.

The different conceptions of Brahman correspond to the different ideas of the Ātman, and vice versa. The stages of waking, dreaming, sleeping, and the conception of ecstasy of the self, are clearly discriminated in the later Vedānta writings and answer to the different conceptions of Brahman. The highest Brahman which is ānanda is just Ātman, as realised in the fourth or the turīya state. There the object and the subject are one. The seer, the seeing eye and the object seen merge together in one whole. When we identify the Ātman with the self-conscious individual, Brahman is viewed as the self-conscious Īśvara with a force opposed to him. As the self-conscious individual will be a mere abstraction apart from some content or object from which he derives his being, even so the Īśvara requires an element opposing him. The conception of Īśvara is the highest object of the religious consciousness. When the Ātman is identified with the mental and vital self of man (manas and prāṇa), Brahman is reduced to the Hiraṇyagarba or the cosmic soul, which comes between the Īśvara and the soul of man. This Hiraṇyagarbha is looked upon as related to the universe in the same way as the individual soul is related to its body. We see here the influence of the Ṛg-Veda. The world is supposed to have a consciousness and a will. Mind always goes with body, vaster orders of mind accompanying vaster orders of body. The world in which we live has

85. *Philosophy of the Upaniṣads*, pp. 39–40.

its own mind, and this mind is Hiraṇyagarbha. This conception of world soul appears in the Upaniṣads under various names and forms. It is called Kārya Brahmā, or the effect God, the Brahmā of *Natura Naturata*, as distinguished from the Kāraṇa Brahmā or the Causal God of Īśvara, or the *natura naturans*. This effect God is the totality of created existences of which all finite objects are parts. The conscious totality of all effects is Brahmā or Hiraṇyagarbha. It is not radically different from the Brahman. Brahman is the simple, individual, absolutely self-identical, One, without a second. Once He is looked at as the creator of Īśvara, again as the Created or Hiraṇyagarbha. Even this Brahmā comes from the Brahman[86]—'He is the source of Brahmā'; the entire objective universe is sustained by this knowing subject. While the individual subjects pass away, he lives contemplating the world. When we identify the Ātman with our body, Brahman becomes the Cosmos or the Virāṭ. Virāṭ is the all, the hypostasisation of the conception of the world as a whole. It is the totality of things, the sum of all existence. 'This is he, the internal Ātman of all created things whose head is Agni, whose eyes are the sun and the moon, whose ears are the four directions, whose speech is the Vedas which have emanated from Him, whose breath is Vāyu, whose heart is all the universe, and from whose feet the earth proceeded.'[87] The body of the Virāṭ is made of the material objects in their aggregate. He is the manifested God whose senses are the directions, whose body is the five elements, and whose consciousness glows with the feeling 'I am all.' Prior to the evolution of the Virāṭ must have occurred the evolution of the Sūtrātman, the cosmic intelligence or Hiraṇyagarbha, having for his vehicle the totality of subtle bodies. Virāṭ comes into being after Hiraṇyagarbha. In the form of Virāṭ, Hiraṇyagarbha becomes visible. Till the effect is evolved, this Sūtrātman is consciousness associated with the subtle body (sūkṣma śarīra). He abides as a mere potentiality of intelligence and motion (Vijñāna and Kriyā) in the first cause. The Virāṭ is the universal self manifested in the gross physical matter of the world, Brahmā is the same manifested in the subtle matter of the universe. The Sūtrātman is Hiraṇyagarbha. The supreme self beyond cause and effect is the Brahman, but when it becomes self-conscious with a non-ego opposed to it we have the Īśvara.[88] The following table suggests the scheme:—

86. Muṇḍaka, iii. 13. 1.

87. Muṇḍaka, iv. 4. 11.

88. In the suṣupti condition we have the subject self with the object world suppressed, though not abolished.

Subject (ātman).	*Object (Brahman)*
1. The bodily self (Viśva)	1. Cosmos (Virāt or Vaiśvānara).
2. The Vital self (Taijasa).	2. The soul of the world (Hiraṇyagarbha).
3. The intellectual self (Prājña).	3. Self-consciousness (Īśvara).
4. The intuitive self (Turīya)	4. Ānanda (Brahman).

If a logical account is permitted, then we may say that the Brahman of the Upaniṣads is no metaphysical abstraction, no indeterminate identity, no void of silence. It is the fullest and the most real being. It is a living dynamic spirit, the source and container of the infinitely varied forms of reality. The distinctions, instead of being dissolved away as illusory, are transfigured in the highest reality. The syllable 'AUM', generally employed to represent the nature of Brahman, brings out its concrete character.[89] It is the symbol of the supreme spirit, the 'emblem of the most high.'[90] 'Aum' is the symbol of concreteness as well as completeness. It stands for the three principal qualities of the supreme spirit personified as Brahmā, Viṣṇu and Śiva in later literature. 'A' is Brahmā the creator, 'U' is Viṣṇu the preserver, and 'M' is Śiva the destroyer.[91] The Īśā Upaniṣad asks us to worship Brahman both in its manifested and unmanifested conditions.[92] It is not an abstract monism that the Upaniṣads offer us. There is difference but also identity. Brahman is infinite not in the sense that it excludes the finite, but in the sense that it is the ground of all finites. It is eternal not in the sense that it is something back beyond all time, as though there were two states temporal and eternal, one of which superseded the other, but that it is the timeless reality of all things in time. The absolute is neither the infinite nor the finite, the self or its realisation, the one life or its varied expressions, but is the real including and transcending the self and its realisation, life and its expression. It is the spiritual spring which breaks, blossoms and differentiates itself into numberless finite centres. The word Brahman means growth, and is suggestive of life, motion and progress, and not death, stillness or stagnation. The ultimate reality is described as sat, cit and ānanda—existence, consciousness, and bliss. 'Knowledge, power and action are of its nature'. It is self-caused.[93] Taittirīya says Brahman is

89. Aum is only the sign of the Eternal spirit, the thing signified even as an idol signifies Viṣṇu ' 'pratimeva Viṣṇoḥ' (Śaṁkara Comm., Tait., i. 6).

90. Manu., ii. 83; see also Tait., i. 7; Kaṭha, i. 2. 15–16.

91. See Chān., i. 3. 6–7. Bṛh. Up., ii. 3. 1. and viii. 3, 4–5.

92. Ubhayam saha, both together.

93. Svayam-bhū Īśa, vii.

existence, consciousness and infinity. It is a positive reality, 'Full is that, full is this'.[94] It is obvious that the ultimate reality is not thought, or force, or being exclusively, but the living unity of essence and existence, of the ideal and real, of knowledge, love and beauty. But as we have already said, it can only be described negatively by us, though it is not a negative indeterminate principle.

X

INTELLECT AND INTUITION

The ideal of intellect is to discover the unity which comprehends both the subject and the object. That there is such a unity is the working principle of logic and life. To find out its contents is the aim of philosophic endeavour. But the enterprise is doomed to disappointment on account of the inherent incapacity of intellect to grasp the whole. Intellect, with its symbols and shibboleths, creeds and conventions, is not by itself adequate to the grasp of the real, 'from which all speech with the mind turns away unable to reach it'.[95] 'The eye does not go thither, nor speech nor mind. We do not know. We do not understand how any one can teach it'.[96] The ultimate reality cannot be made into an objective representation which the intellect can grasp. 'How should he know him by whom he knows all this? How, O Beloved, should he know himself the knower'.[97] Objective knowledge of the subject is impossible. It is 'unseen but seeing, unheard but hearing, unperceived but perceiving, unknown but knowing'.[98] Ātman is not non-existent, simply because it cannot be objectively represented. Though man's intellectual capacities are not adequate for its comprehension, still they will have no existence but for it.[99] 'That which one cannot think with the mind, but that by which they say the mind is made to think, know that alone to be the Brahman'.[100] Intellect works with the categories of space, time, cause and force, which involve us in deadlocks and antinomies. Either we must postulate a first cause, in which case causality ceases to be a universal

94. Bṛh., v. 1. i. 1.
95. Taittirīya, ii. 4.
96. Kena, ii. 3; Muṇḍaka, ii. 1; see Kaṭha, i. 3. 10.
97. Bṛh., ii. 4. 13; see also iii. 4. 2.
98. Bṛh., iii. 7. 23; see iii. 8. 11.
99. See Bṛh., iii. 8. 11; ii. 4, 14; iv. 5. 15.
100. Kena.

maxim, or we have an endless regress. The puzzle cannot be solved by intellect, pure and simple. It must confess itself to be bankrupt when ultimate questions arise. 'The gods are in Indra; Indra is in the Father God, the Father God is in Brahmā, but in what is Brahmā?' and Yājñavalkya answers: 'Ask not too much.'[101] Our intellectual categories can give descriptions of the empirical universe under the forms of space, time and cause, but the real is beyond these. While containing space, it is not spatial; while including time, it transcends time; while it has a causally bound system of nature within it, it is not subject to the law of cause. The self-existent Brahman is independent of time, space and cause. The space independence is brought out crudely in the Upaniṣads. Brahman is said to be omnipresent, all-pervading, infinitely great and infinitely small. 'That which is above the heaven, O Gārgī, and that which is beneath the earth, that which men call the past, present and future, all that is woven within and throughout in space. But wherein then is space woven within and without? In truth, in this imperishable one, is space woven within and throughout, O Gārgī'.[102] Brahman is described as being free from the limitations of time. It is viewed as an eternity without beginning and end, or as an instantaneous duration occupying no definite time interval. He is independent of past and future,[103] and lord of all,[104] at whose feet time rolls along.[105] In emphasising the independence of causal relations Brahman is represented to be an absolutely static being, free from all the laws of becoming of which the universal rule is causality. This way of establishing Brahman's independence of causal relations countenances the conception of Brahman as absolute self-existence and unchanging endurance, and leads to misconceptions. Causality is the rule of all changes in the world. But Brahman is free from subjection to causality. There is no change in Brahman though all change is based on it. There is no second outside it, no other distinct from it. We have to sink all plurality in Brahman. All proximity in space, succession in time, interdependence of relations rest on it. The comprehension of this profound philosophic synthesis cannot be obtained so long as we remain at the level of intellect. The Upaniṣads assert sometimes that thought gives

101. Bṛh., iii. 6. 1.
102. Bṛh., iii. 8. 7; see also iv. 2. 4; Chān., iii. 14. 3, and viii. 24. 7.
103. Kaṭha, ii. 14.
104. Bṛh., iv. 4. 15.
105. iv. 4. 16. 17.

us imperfect, partial pictures of reality, and at other times that it is organically incapable of reaching reality. It deals with relations and cannot grasp the relationless absolute. But there is nothing on earth existing in space or time which is not an appearance of the absolute. No knowledge is entirely false, though none is entirely true. The nearest approach to truth is the conception of an organised whole, though it is not completely true on account of the relational character which, however near to cancellation it may have come, is never absolutely abolished. It is the highest form of the absolute the mind of man can hit upon. Intellect, in the sense of mere understanding, working with the limited categories of time, space and cause, is inadequate. Reason also fails, though it takes us beyond understanding. It does not help us to attain reality, which is not merely an idea but a spirit. An idea of reason is an imperfect fragment of reality which is more than idea. The real is neither true nor false. Our judgments about the real may be true or false, since they imply the dualism between idea and reality. We have to pass beyond thought, beyond the clash of oppositions, beyond the antinomies that confront us when we work with the limited categories of abstract thinking, if we are to reach the real where man's existence and divine being coincide. It is when thought becomes perfected in intuition that we catch the vision of the real. The mystics the world over have emphasised this fact. Pascal dwells on the incomprehensibility of God, and Bossuet bids us not to be dismayed by the divergencies, but regard them all trustfully as the golden chains that meet beyond mortal sight at the throne of God.

According to the Upaniṣads there is a higher power which enables us to grasp this central spiritual reality. Spiritual things require to be spiritually discerned. The Yoga method is a practical discipline pointing out the road to this realisation. Man has the faculty of divine insight or mystic intuition, by which he transcends the distinctions of intellect and solves the riddles of reason. The chosen spirits scale the highest peak of thought and intuit the reality. By this intuitive realisation 'the unheard becomes heard, the unperceived becomes perceived, and the unknown becomes known.'[106] The problems raised by intellect solve themselves the moment we transcend reasoning and start to live the religious life.[107] The Upaniṣads ask us therefore to lay aside our pride of intellect and self-consciousness, and approach

106. Chāndogya, vi. 13; see also Bṛh. ii. 4. 5.
107. Muṇḍaka, iii. 1. 8.

facts with the fresh outlook of a child. 'Let a Brāhmin renounce learning and become as a child'.[108] No man shall enter into the kingdom of God except he first become as a little child. The highest truths are to be felt by the simple and pure-minded, and not proved to the sophisticated intellect. 'Let him not seek after many words, for that is mere weariness of tongue'.[109] 'Not by learning is the Ātman attained, not by genius and much knowledge of books'.[110] It is attained by the mystics in their moments of illumination. It is direct knowledge or immediate insight. In the mystic experience the soul finds itself in the presence of the highest. It is lost in awareness, contemplation and enjoyment of the ultimate Reality. It does not know what it is when it reaches it. There is nothing higher than it. Other things are all in it. It then fears no evil, no untruth, but is completely blessed. This spiritual vision relieves us from all passion and suffering. The soul in its exaltation feels itself to be at one with what it sees. Plotinus says: 'In the vision of God, that which sees is not reason, but something greater than and prior to reason, something presupposed by reason, as is the object of vision. He who then sees himself, when he sees, will see himself as a simple being, will be united to himself as such, will feel himself become such. We ought not even to say that he will see, but he will be that which he sees, if indeed it is possible any longer to distinguish seer and seen, and not boldly to affirm that the two are one. He belongs to God and is one with Him, like two concentric circles; they are one when they coincide and two only when they are separated'.[111] All the aspirations of the human mind, its intellectual demands, its emotional desires, and its volitional ideals are there realised. It is the supreme end of man's effort, the termination of personal life. 'This is the supreme end of that, this is the supreme treasure of that, this is the supreme dwelling of that, this is the supreme joy of that.'[112] It is on a level with perceptual experience, but, unlike the latter, it is not objective and verifiable by others. It cannot, like

108. Bṛh., iii. 5. 1. This translation is adopted by Deussen and Gough, though Max Müller translates thus: 'Let a Brāhmin after he has done with learning wish to stand by real strength.' This rests on the inferior reading of *balyena* in lieu of *bālyena*; 'tasmād brāhmaṇaḥ pāṇḍityaṁ nirvidya bālyena tiṣṭhāset.'

109. Bṛh., iv. 4. 21.

110. Kaṭha, ii. 23.

111. Inge, *Plotinus*, vol. ii, p. 140.

112. Eṣāsya paramā gatiḥ, eṣāsya paramā sampat, Eṣo'sya paramo lokaḥ, eṣo'sya parama ānandaḥ. (Bṛh., iv. 3. 32.)

inferential knowledge, be communicated to others. It is impossible to give a formal exposition of it. The mystic insight is inarticulate. As to a man born blind we cannot explain the beauty of a rainbow or the glory of a sunset, even so to the non-mystic the vision of the mystic cannot be described. 'God put it into my head, and I cannot put it into yours', is the last word of the mystic experience. Simply because it is incommunicable, it does not become less valid than other forms of knowledge. We can describe this experience only by metaphors. For the light blinds us and makes us dumb. We cannot render a full report of the ineffable. Bāhva, when asked by king Vāśkali to explain the nature of Brahman, kept silent, and when the king repeated his request, the sage broke out into the answer: 'I tell it to you, but you do not understand it, Śānto 'yam ātmā: this Ātman is peaceful, quiet'.[113] To any suggested definitions of intellect we can only answer, it is not this, it is not this.[114] The negative definitions point out how the positive attributes known to us are inadequate to the highest. 'There is no measure of him whose glory verily is great'.[115] Contradictory predicates are attached to Brahman to indicate that we are obliged to use negative conceptions so long as we employ the dialectics of intellect, though positive features are revealed when Brahman is intuited. 'It is subtler than the subtle, greater than the great'.[116] 'It moves, it does not move; it is far and it is near; it is within all this and without all this'.[117] These seemingly inconsistent accounts are not the sign of any confusion of thought.

The absolute is implied in all experience, for every object of the world is based on the absolute, though none of them expresses it completely. So those who imagine they do not know the absolute, do know it, though imperfectly; and those who think they know the absolute really do not know it completely. It is a state of half-knowledge and half-ignorance. The Kena Upaniṣad says: 'It is unknown to those who know and known to those who do not know'.[118] The Upaniṣads do not maintain that intellect is a useless guide. The account of reality given by it is not false. It fails only when it attempts to grasp the reality in its fullness. Everywhere else it

113. S.B. iii. 2. 17.

114. See Bṛh., iii. 9. 26; iv. 2. 4.; iv. 4. 22.; iv. 5. 15; ii. 3. 6. Kaṭha, iii. 15; Praśna, iv. 10; Chāndogya, vii. 24. 1; Muṇḍaka, i. 1. 7; ii. 1. 2; iii. 1. 7–8.

115. Yajur-Veda.

116. Śvetaśvatara, iii. 20; Kena, i. 3.

117. Īśā, v.

118. ii. 3.

succeeds. What the intellect investigates is not the unreal, though it is not the absolutely real. The antinomies of cause and effect, substance and attribute, good and evil, truth and error, subject and object, are due to the tendency of man to separate terms which are related. Fichte's puzzle of self and not-self, Kant's antinomies, Hume's opposition of facts and laws, Bradley's contradictions, can all be got over, if we recognise that the opposing factors are mutually complementary elements based on one identity. Intellect need not be negated, but has only to be supplemented. A philosophy based on intuition is not necessarily opposed to reason and understanding. Intuition can throw light on the dark places which intellect is not able to penetrate. The results of mystic intuition require to be subjected to logical analysis. And it is only by this process of mutual correction and supplementation that each can live a sober life. The results of intellect will be dull and empty, unfinished and fragmentary, without the help of intuition, while intuitional insights will be blind and dumb, dark and strange, without intellectual confirmation. The ideal of intellect is realised in the intuitive experience, for in the supreme are all contraries reconciled. Only by the comradeship of scientific knowledge and intuitive experience can we grow into true insight. Mere reasoning will not help us to it.[119] If we content ourselves with the verdict of intellect, then we shall have to look upon the plurality and independence of individuals as the final word of philosophy. Competition and struggle will be the end of the universe. Abstract intellect will lead us to false philosophy and bad morals. Brahman is concealed by such knowledge.[120] The unreflecting attitude is perhaps better than this kind of intellectualism. 'All who worship what is not knowledge enter into blind darkness; those who delight in knowledge enter, as it were, into greater darkness'.[121] An intellectual knowledge of diversity without the intuitive realisation is worse than the blind ignorance of faith, bad as it is. The contradictions of life and logic have to be reconciled in the spirit of Emerson's Brahmā.

> They reckon ill who leave me out;
>   When me they fly I am the wings;
> I am the doubter and the doubt.

119. Kaṭha, ii. 9.
120. Medhayā pihitaḥ. Tait. Up.
121. Bṛh., iv. 4–10; see Īśā, ix.

The one eternal spirit expresses, embraces, unifies and enjoys the varied wealth of the world with all its passions and paradoxes, loyalties and devotions, truths and contradictions. Weak souls, unaware of this all-embracing reality, grow weary of the fight, intellectual, aesthetic and moral. But they have to draw courage from the fact that the joy of harmony has to be derived from the struggle of discordant elements. The seeming contradictions belong to the life of spirit. The one spirit shows its being in all the oppositions of life and thought, the puzzles of Hume, the problems of Kant, the conflicts of empiricism and the dogmas of speculation.

By insisting on intuition more than on thought, on ānanda more than on vijñāna, the Upaniṣads seem to support the non-dualism referred to in the Introduction. So long as we skim on the surface of reality with the notions of thought, we do not get at the deeper spirit. In ānanda man is most and deepest in reality. In the unexplored depths of individual experience, the inner ānandamaya, lies the stuff of reality. Intellectual systems disdain to descend into the rich mine of life. Whatever is reduced to vijñāna has become unreal, though it tends to become universal and objective. What is not conceptualised or categorised is the truly subjective. The organised whole of vijñāna gives a logical impress to identity. The intuition shows up the fact of identity. In trying to know the identity we superficialise it by breaking it into differences and try to get them back to the identity by constructing a system. But the fact once broken into the relations can never through mere logic have its oneness restored. As we have more than once observed, the first touch of logic is responsible for the transformation of the One into a system.

XI

CREATION

It is clear from our account of the nature of Brahman that the Upaniṣads are dissatisfied with the materialist and vitalist theories of evolution. Matter cannot develop life or consciousness unless it had the potentialities of them in its nature. No amount of shocks from the external environment can extort life out of mere matter. Ānanda cannot be the end of evolution unless it was also the beginning of it. The end is present throughout, though in a suppressed form. The individual things of the world possess the features of their ultimate source and end. 'Whatever there is belonging to the son belongs to the father; whatever there is belonging to the father belongs to the son'.[122] Everything in the world, not merely the human individual, is in essence the ultimate reality itself. Development means the manifestation of the potentialities of things by the removal of the obstructing energies. From the scientific point of view, we notice the different degrees of development in the things of the world. The philosopher is interested in the common ground of unity. The multiplicity of the world is based on the one spirit. 'Who indeed could live, who breathe, should not this ānanda be in ākāśa?'[123] The sun rises punctually, the stars run in their courses, and all things stand in their order and faint not in their watches because of the eternal spirit which slumbers not nor sleeps. 'All shine after Him who shines. By His radiance is all this illumined'.[124] Ānanda is the beginning and the end of the world, the cause as well as the effect, the root as well as the shoot of the universe.[125] The efficient and the final causes are one. The matter with which the process of evolution starts is not an independent entity. It has hidden in it the highest ānanda. The course of development is a transition from the potential to the actual. Matter has more potential in it than life. In the graduated scale of the types of existence, the later is the more evolved or the formed, and the earlier is the more potential or the unformed. To use the words of Aristotle, the earlier is the matter and the later is the form. Matter is the passive principle which requires to be energised or informed. We have in the logical accounts a god overlooking matter, stirring it up into motion. This god is prajñāna, or the eternally active self-conscious reason.[126] He is responsible for the whole realm of change. The Upaniṣads fight shy of the conception of an omnipotent mechanic fashioning pre-existing matter into the universe. If God excludes matter, even though the latter is reduced to a mere potentiality, we cannot escape dualism, since God would remain opposed to matter. Such a dualism is the characteristic feature of the system of Aristotle with its distinction of the first mover and the first matter. For the Upaniṣads, both form and matter, the ever active consciousness and the passive non-consciousness, are aspects of a single reality. Matter itself is a god.[127] Its first forms of fire, water, and earth are looked upon as divine,

122. Aitareya Āraṇyaka, ii. 1. 8. 1.
123. Tait., ii.
124. Muṇḍaka, ii. 2. 10.
125. Mūla and tūla, Aitareya Āraṇyaka, ii. 1. 8. 1.
126. Aitareya Āraṇyaka, i. 3. 3. 6.
127. Chān., vi. 8. 4–6.

since they are all informed by the one spirit. The Sāṁkhya dualism is repugnant to the Upaniṣads. The transcendent reality is the ground or explanation of the struggle between spirit and matter.[128] The whole world is conceived as possessing an identity of purpose as well as a common substratum of change. The Upaniṣads bring out in several fanciful and mythological accounts of creation the great truth of the oneness of the world. Brahman is the sole and the whole explanation of the world, its material and efficient cause. The entities of the world are knots in the rope of development, which begins with matter and ends in ānanda.

'That created itself by itself'.[129] 'He creates the world and then enters it'.[130] A personal god, Prajāpati, tired of solitude, draws forth from himself everything that exists, or produces the world after having divided himself into two, one half male and the other half female.[131] Sometimes the personal or created being is represented as himself proceeding from a material substratum. On other occasions the primary substance of things is represented as manifesting itself in the created existence.[132] The Ātman pervades things as the salt which has dissolved in water pervades the water; from the Ātman things spring as the sparks fly out from the fire, as threads from the spider, or sound from the flute.[133] The theory of emanation where the bringing of a product into existence does not affect the source of the product is also suggested. The light coming from the sun leaves the sun unchanged. This seems to be the justification for the later theory that the individual is a mere ābhāsa or appearance of Brahman. The metaphors of the spinning of the web by the spider, the bearing of the child by the mother, the production of notes from musical instruments, attempt to bring out the intimate relationship between the cause and the effect. It is the tādātmya or oneness between Brahman and the world that is conveyed in all this wealth of symbol

128. Praśna, i. 3.

129. Tait. Up., See also Bṛh., ii. 1. 20; Muṇḍaka, i. 1. 7; ii. 1. 1.

130. Bṛh., iv. 7.

131. Bṛh., 1. 2. 14. We have something similar to this in the Chinese doctrine of Yang and Yin. The primeval chaos is said to have been broken up by the antagonism of these two principles of expansion and contraction. The Yang is the male force in all creatures and the Yin is the female. Compare also the view of Empedocles.

132. Chān., iii. 39.

133. Chān., vii. 21. 2; vi. 2. 1; Bṛh., iv. 5; Muṇḍaka, ii.

and image. The external world is not something separate, existing side by side with the Ātman. The ultimate ground of being, Brahman, and the empirical state of being, the world are not different. The world of plurality can be reduced without residuum into the everlasting one, Brahman. The Upaniṣads are decisive about the principle that Brahman is the sole source of life in all that lives, the single thread binding the whole plurality into a single unity. When the problem of the co-existence of the plurality and unity is taken up, the Upaniṣads speak in the language of similes and symbols, but do not give any definite answer. We cannot in the absence of knowledge of Brahman dogmatise about the relation of the empirical world to Brahman. The two cannot be unrelated, for all that is, is one, and yet we do not know how precisely they are one. The former aspect is brought out in the argument that Brahman is the material as well as the efficient cause of the world; the latter when it is said that we do not know anything of it at all. It is māyā, or mysterious, or anirvacanīya (inexplicable), as Śaṁkara puts it. We cannot ask how the relationless Brahman is related to the world. The presumption is that the world of relations does not in any way affect the nature of Brahman. The destruction of the world of experience does not in the least take away from the being of Brahman. Brahman can exist and does exist apart from the world of relations. The world is not an essential factor in the existence of Brahman. A reciprocal dependence of the world on Brahman and vice versa would be to reduce Brahman to the level of the world and subject it to the categories of time and purpose. The incapacity to define the relaton of the absolute to the world is not to be construed as a repudiation of the world as a screen imagined by the finite man, which hides the absolute. For it is declared that world of space, time and cause has its reality in Brahman. The absolute is so far present in this world of relations as to enable us to measure the distance of the things of the world from the absolute and evaluate their grades of reality. Brahman is in the world, though not as the world. The Upaniṣads do not face the question directly. The only way to reconcile the several accounts is by taking our stand on the absolute self-sufficiency of Brahman. The perfection of Brahman implies that all the worlds, states and aspects, and all the manifestations, past, present and future, are realised in it in such wise that they are nothing without it, though it is independent of all other existence. If without conforming to the strict philosophical position, that we do not know the precise relation between the Brahman and the world, we proceed to characterise it, it is truer to say that the world is the self-limitation of the supreme than that it is a creation of it. For the creation of the world by God would imply that God was alone once upon a time, and at a certain point in His history He created the world. It is not right to look upon God as cause antecedent in time to the world as effect. It is better to make the world the expression of God. As a matter of fact, in many passages the Upaniṣads declare that the world is only a development of the absolute spirit. Nature is a system of spontaneity or self-evolving autonomy, since it is the energising of the absolute. In this development, the first stage is represented by the rise of the two factors of a self-conscious God and the passive potentiality of matter. The ultimate fact is the self-sufficiency of Brahman, and we cannot say how the world is related to it. If we insist on some explanation, the most satisfactory one is to make the absolute a unity with a difference or a concrete dynamic spirit. We then reach the self and the not-self, which interact and develop the whole universe.[134] Self-expression becomes the essence of the absolute. Activity

134. An attempt is made by Babu Bhagavan Das, in his translation of a work called Praṇavavāda, attributed to Gārgyāyana, to interpret a great saying of the Upaniṣads, *aham etat na*, 'I not this', into a highly philosophical doctrine. Aham or self is the self-conscious Īsvara. Etat is nature or not-self. The relation between the two is signified by *na*, a negation. 'The self is not the not-self'. In the syllable *AUM*, 'A' represents the self, 'U' the not-self, and 'M' the negation of the two, but all these three are rolled into the 'AUM,' the Praṇava. The world is interpreted to be a negative reflection of the Aham. It is affirmed by the self for its own realisation. Etat is the unreal shadow, while Aham is the reality. The interpretation is ingenious; but we have to remember that what is denied is not the Etat (not-self) as the reflexion of Aham (self) but only the Etat (not-self) as cut off from Aham (self). The many as separate and apart from the One is denied. Brahman the reality causes, if such a term is legitimate, all difference. In Indian thought this symbol AUM stands for many things. Every kind of trinity is represented by AUM. Being, non-being and becoming; birth, life and death; Prakṛti, Jīvātman and Paramātman; Sattva, Rajas and Tamas; past, present and future; Brahmā, Viṣṇu and Śiva. The conception of Brahmā, Viṣṇu and Śiva emphasises the different aspects of the one Supreme, which contains the three conditions. God by a free act of His will creates, or more philosophically posits, an eternal universe. This positing God is Brahmā. He views it, contemplates it, sustains it, enjoys it as being distinct from himself. This God is Viṣṇu. He receives it back into his own unity as an indissoluble element of his being, then he is Śiva. Those who imagine that the three states are exclusive postulate three personal agencies embodying the three different functions.

is the law of life. Force is inherent in existence. Māyā, in the sense of energy, is potentially eternal in being.

There is hardly any suggestion in the Upaniṣads that the entire universe of change is a baseless fabric of fancy, a mere phenomenal show or a world of shadows. The artistic and poet souls of the Upaniṣads lived always in the world of nature and never cared to fly out of it. The Upaniṣads do not teach that life is a nightmare and the world a barren nothing. Rather is it pulsing and throbbing with the rhythm of the world harmony. The world is God's revelation of Himself. His joy assumes all these forms.[135] But there is a popular view which identifies the Upaniṣad doctrine with an abstract monism, which reduces the rich life of this world into an empty dream. If we start with the facts of everyday experience and try to account for them, we are reduced to the two factors of a self-conscious Īśvara and indeterminate matter. Intellectually we are convinced of the oneness of these two. Our difficulty is the reconciliation between the two: subject and object on the one hand, and the Brahman explicitly asserted by the Upaniṣads on the other. The real is one, yet we have the two. It is from this duality that the difference of the world arises. We are confronted with a blank wall. If philosophy is bold and sincere, it must say that the relation cannot be explained. The one somehow becomes two. This seems to be the most logical view in the circumstances: 'The immanence of the absolute in finite centres and of finite centres in the absolute, I have always set down as inexplicable ... to comprehend it is beyond us and even beyond all intelligence'.[136] The inexplicability of the relation between the two is assumed by the Upaniṣads, and the later Vedānta gives to it the name of māyā.

The difficulty of giving a satisfactory explanation is traced to the imperfection of the human mind, which employs inadequate categories of space, time and cause, which are self-contradictory. The aspects of the world known to them are fragmentary and are not genuinely real. They are appearances somehow in and of, but not for reality. Everything we come across in our finite experience breaks down somewhere or other

135. Ānandarūpam amṛtam yad vibhāti.

136. Bradley, *Mind*, No. 74, p. 154. Cf. Green: 'The old question, why God made the world, has never been answered, nor will be. We know not why the world should be; we only know that there it is'. *Prolegomena to Ethics*, Sec. 100.

and becomes contradictory. While all finite experiences are limited and incomplete, they are so in different degrees, and it is not right to put them all on a general level or give to them all equal reality or, more accurately, equal unreality. The doctrine of māyā gives abstract expression to this general feature of all experience of the finite that it falls short of the absolute.

While intellectual modesty born of the consciousness of human imperfection compelled the thinkers of the Upaniṣads to rest in negative statements of the supreme reality, the false imitators of the Upaniṣad ideal, with an extreme of arrogant audacity, declare that Brahman is an absolutely homogeneous impersonal intelligence—a most dogmatic declaration alien to the true spirit of the Upaniṣads. Such a positive characterisation of the nature of Brahman is illogical—for even Śaṁkara says that the real is non-dual, advaita, and nothing positive.

There are passages, according to Thibaut, 'whose decided tendency it is to represent Brahman as transcending all qualities, as one undifferentiated mass of impersonal intelligence'.[137] 'And as the fact of the appearance of the manifold world cannot be denied, the only way open to thoroughly consistent speculation was to deny at any rate its reality, and to call it a mere illusion due to an unreal principle, with which Brahman is indeed associated, but which is unable to break the unity of Brahman's nature just on account of its own unreality'.[138] Māyā, according to Thibaut, reconciles the appearance of diversity with the reality of the One, but unfortunately the conception of an abstract intelligence is a meaningless notion, which is disallowed by the anti-dogmatist attitude of the Upaniṣad theory. The Upaniṣads do not support an abstract conception of the ultimate reality. Their philosophy is not so much a monism as an advaitism (not twoness). The distinction of subject and object is not absolute, though it is real in the world. We cannot split the world into two halves of subject and object, for Brahman underlies both. While it denies duality, it does not affirm that all things could be dissolved into one except in a figurative sense.[139]

137. Introduction to V.S., p. cxxlii.

138. Ibid., cxxv.

139. We find that the passages which employ the illustration of clay (copper, etc.) to explain the oneness of Brahman and the world, use the words 'vācārambhaṇaṁ vikāro nāmadheyam mṛttikety eva satyam'. Its meaning seems to be that all are modifications of the one substance, marked by different names. Śaṁkara interprets this to mean that 'the modification (vikāra) originates and exists merely in speech; in reality there is no such thing as effect. It is merely a

Other friendly interpreters of the Upaniṣads also contend that the Upaniṣads support the doctrine of māyā in the sense of the illusoriness of the world. Let us inquire into the value of their contention. Deussen, who has done much to popularise Vedāntic lore in Europe, points out that four different theories of creation occur in the Upaniṣads. They are—(1) that matter exists from eternity independently of God, which He fashions, but does not create; (2) that God creates the universe out of nothing, and the latter is independent of God, although it is His creation; (3) that God creates the universe by transforming Himself into it; (4) that God alone is real, and there is no creation at all. The last, according to him, is the fundamental view of the Upaniṣads. The world in space and time is an appearance, an illusion, a shadow of God. To know God we must reject the world of appearance. What inclines Deussen to this view is his own belief that the essence of every true religion is the repudiation of the reality of the world. Having come to that conclusion on independent grounds, he is anxious to find support for his doctrine in the philosophic systems of ancient

---

name, and therefore unreal'. It is vyāvahārikam or empirical, but it does not follow that it is mithyā or falsehood. It has also to be noted that the statement is made by Uddālaka, who held a theory of matter which admitted only changes of form. The material, according to him, is one continuous whole, in which qualitatively distinct particles of matter are mixed together. The passage says that the development is noticed by the giving of a different name. Name and form are used in the Upaniṣads to indicate individuality. See Bṛh., i. 4. 7. Development of the one into the many is the rise of name and form out of the primary principle. There is no suggestion that the modifications denoted by name and form are unreal. They have, of course, no reality apart from Brahman. Nāmarūpa is not what the English words name and form indicate. They correspond to the form and matter of Aristotle. The two together constitute the individuals of the world. In Buddhism rūpa stands for the gross body and nāma for the subtle mind. In the Upaniṣads the development of name and form means the individualisation of the One. The individualisation is the principle of creation, the central feature of the cosmic process. Things and persons are ultimately only modes of the existence of God. They are not real on their own account. Only Brahman is so real. Their separateness is superficial. Salvation in the Upaniṣads is the cessation of the sense of separateness of nāmarūpa. The Muṇḍaka Upaniṣad says: 'He who has attained the highest wisdom unites with the universal spirit, delivered from nāmarūpa as the flowing streams enter into rest in the sea, leaving nāmarūpa behind'. Again, the cause is more real than the effect. God is the cause of all persons and things. As gold is the essence of gold ornaments, Brahman is the reality of the world, its sattāsāmānya or common substratum.

India, the Upaniṣads and Śaṁkara, ancient Greece, Parmenides and Plato, and modern Germany, Kant and Schopenhauer. In his eagerness to find support for his position he is not very careful about the facts. He admits that the prevailing doctrine of the Upaniṣads is the pantheistic one, while the 'fundamental' doctrine is the illusion hypothesis. That the pantheistic view is the 'prevailing' one, Deussen is obliged to concede by the mere pressure of facts. That the illusion view is the 'fundamental' one is his own reading of the facts. Between the two, the fact of pantheism and the reading of illusionism, a compromise has to be effected. Deussen achieves it by holding that it is a concession to clamour and the empirical demands of the unregenerate man. 'For the fundamental thought, that is held fast at least as a principle at all stages, even at the lowest, which maintains the independent existence of matter, is the conviction of the sole reality of the Ātman; only that side by side with and in spite of this conviction, more or less far reaching concessions were made to the empirical consciousness of the reality of the universe, that could never be entirely cast off'.[140] The first argument urged in support of the 'illusion' hypothesis is that the Upaniṣads assert the sole reality of Brahman. It follows that the world is unreal. We agree that Ātman is the sole reality. If we know it, all else is known. That there is no plurality, no change outside it, is admissible. But that there is no change at all and no plurality at all, either in or out, such an unqualified proposition is hard to understand. 'Nature,' says Deussen, 'which presents the appearance of plurality and change is a mere illusion.'[141] In the same strain Mr Fraser argues: 'This doctrine of the illusion of all appearances of reality follows naturally and logically from the repeated teachings in the Upaniṣads regarding the non-duality of the self of Ātman or Brahman as the sole reality of the universe'.[142] In these arguments the infinite is taken in a false sense. It is equated with the not-finite; the eternal is made the not-temporal. When the eternal becomes a timeless abstraction, the life of the world in time becomes unreal. The opposition between the world in space and time and the world absolute and eternal is ultimate. But the Upaniṣads nowhere say that the infinite excludes the finite. Wherever they assert that Brahman is the sole reality they are careful enough to add that the world is rooted in Brahman, and as such has a share of

140. *The Philosophy of the Upaniṣads*, pp. 161–2.
141. Pp. 193–94.
142. *Indian Thought*, p. 68.

reality. 'The finite is in the infinite. This Ātman is the entire universe'.[143] It is prāṇa. It is speech. It is mind. It is everything in the universe. God is present in the vile dust and the small mote.[144] The affirmation of the real involves the affirmation of all that is based on it. From the doctrine of the sole reality of Brahman follows the relative reality of what is included in or based on it.

Deussen urges that 'the passages which declare that with the knowledge of the Ātman all is known, 'deny' the universe of plurality.' We do not admit this contention. If the Ātman is the universal self embracing within it all thinking things and the objects of all thought, if there is nothing outside it, then it follows that if it is known all else is known. The true knowledge which leads us to liberation helps us to realise the one indwelling spirit. There is no suggestion that the Ātman and the world exclude each other; in that case what Indra said to Prajāpati would be true, and Ātman which excludes everything definite and distinct, would be the barest abstraction. If we ignore differences, we reduce the absolute to a non-entity. We do not improve the case of the absolute by repudiating the relative. The eternal need not give away the temporal as null and void. Loyalty to the highest experience of man, religious and moral, philosophic and aesthetic, requires us to recognise the reality of the temporal as rooted in the eternal, of the finite as subsisting in the infinite, of man as born from God. To deny the contingent and the individual is to falsify the necessary and the universal. The many passages which declare the world to be rooted in Brahman are explained away by Deussen as a concession to empirical consciousness. The Upaniṣads would not have seriously put forth doctrines about the relativity of the world if it was their view that the world was a mere illusion. An unworkable interpretation is adopted by Deussen, and arbitrary arguments are employed to support what is fundamentally unsound. Deussen himself, in attempting to give the credit for the 'illusion' hypothesis to the great German philosopher Kant, admits that the hypothesis was not really, or perhaps explicitly, held by the Upaniṣad thinkers. For he writes: 'There is still always a broad distinction between the one Brahman and the multiplicity of his appearances, nor were ancient thinkers, or indeed any thinkers before Kant, able to rise to the conception

143. Chāndogya, ii. 4. 26.

144. Muṇḍaka, ii. 2. 11; Kaṭha, ii. 5. 2; Tait., iii. 1; Chān., iii. 14. 1. ii. 14. 2–4; vi. 9. 1; Bṛh., ii. 4. 6; iv. 5. 7; ii. 5. 2; v. 3. 1.; i. 4. 16; ii. 5. 15; iii. 7. 15; iv. 4. 23.

that the entire unfolding in space and time was a merely subjective phenomenon'.[145] Deussen correctly suggests that the Upaniṣads could not have held the view of the subjectivity of the world. The different theories of creation are enunciated just to point out that there is essential dependence between Brahman and the world. There are passages, we admit, which declare that the variegated universe is due to the development of name and form from out of the one absolute. These indicate only that the fundamental essence of all things is the one reality, and if we are lost in the name and form world, we run the risk of missing the deep-lying essence which gives rise to all the variety. This name and form-world hides, so to say, the immortal essence.[146] We have to pierce behind the veil which surrounds all mortal things. The objects in space and time conceal the essence of things. The passing semblance of life is in no wise its immortal truth. The real being is above these things. He manifests himself through the world. The manifestation is at the same time a concealment. The more complete is the manifestation, the more is the reality concealed. God hides Himself and manifests Himself by drawing a veil over His face. The hidden meaning of things is opposed to the testimony of the senses. The world, while it manifests His glory, conceals His pure absolute nature. The truth, the unique substance, the absolute void of phenomena and rid of limitations,

145. P. 103. Deussen seems to interpret Kant in the light of the Upaniṣads and the Upaniṣads in the light of Kant, with the result that he has practically misconstrued both. Kant is anxious that his idealism should not be confused with Berkeleyan subjectivism quite as much as Śaṁkara is anxious that his idealism should not be identified with Buddhistic subjectivism. Perhaps with Schopenhauer Deussen thinks that Kant's refutation of idealism is a stupid after-thought and a great blunder. It is doubtful whether students of Kant would agree with Deussen's view. 'The well-known argument of Kant also, which bases immortality on the realisation of the moral law implanted in us, a result only attainable by an infinite process of approximation, tells not for immortality in the usual sense, but for transmigration' (p. 314).

146. Bṛh., i. 6. 3. Amṛtaṁ satyena cchannam. The ambiguity of the word 'sat' is responsible for much of the confusion of the Upaniṣad view of reality. Sat in one sense means all that exists. The world of change and growth is 'sat' in this sense. Sat also stands for the reality that persists in the midst of all change, the immortal or the amṛtam. The Taittirīya calls the former sat and the latter tyat. Since tyat is opposed to the existent sat, it is sometimes called asat or anṛtam (Tait., ii. 6). Usually, the permanent reality or Brahman is called sat and the world of change asat (Chān., vi. 2. 1: iii. 19. 1).

is covered by the multiplicity and plurality of the created universe. The objects of the world, including the finite selves, imagine that they are separate and self-existent, and seem to be engaged in the work of self-maintenance. They forget that they all spring from an identical source, from which they derive sustenance. This belief is due to māyā or delusion. 'Each little leaf on a tree may very naturally have sufficient consciousness to believe that it is an entirely separate being, maintaining itself in the sunlight and the air, withering away and dying when the winter comes on—and there is an end of it. It probably does not realise that all the time it is being supported by the sap which flows from the trunk of the tree, and that in its turn it is feeding the tree too—that its self is the self of the whole tree. If the leaf could really understand itself, it would see that its self was deeply, intimately connected, practically one with the life of the whole tree'.[147] Below the separate wave crests of consciousness there is the unfathomed common depth of life, from which all spirits draw the springs of their being. If we look upon the objects as separate and self-existent, we erect a screen which shuts us from the truth. The falsely imagined self-subsistence of finite objects clouds the glow of heaven. When we penetrate beneath the second causes to the essence of all things, the veils fall apart and we see that the principle underlying them is the same as that which dwells in us. It is this need to go behind second causes to realise the truth of the oneness of things that is brought out in the dialogue between the father and the son in the Chāndogya Upaniṣads (vi. 10 ff.).

> 'Fetch me from thence a fruit of the Nyagrodha tree.' 'Here is one, Sir.' 'Break it.' 'It is broken, Sir.' 'What do you see there?' 'These seeds, almost infinitesimal.' 'Break one of them.' 'It is broken, Sir.' 'What do you see there?' 'Not anything, Sir.'
>
> The father said: 'My son, that subtle essence which you do not perceive there, of that very essence this great Nyagrodha tree exists. Believe it, my son, That which is the subtle essence, in it all that exists has its self. It is the True. It is the self, and thou, O Śvetaketu, art it'.

The father points out to the son some typical objects of nature in succession and exhorts him to realise the philosophical truth of the unity of life and the continuity of man's life with that of the universe. We cannot easily conceive this one reality which is concealed by the many

147. Edward Carpenter, *Pagan and Christian Creeds*, p. 301.

objects. We are too worldly, too experienced, too serious about ourselves for that realisation. We live on the surface, cling to forms, worship appearance.

Deussen ignores the central truth of the Upaniṣad philosophy when he holds that according to it 'the whole universe, all children, possessions and wisdom,' must 'vanish into the nothingness, which they really are.'[148] On this hypothesis it is necessary to explain away all those passages which declare Brahman, the sustainer of the universe, to be one with the psychical principle of the individual self, on the principle of accommodation. 'The same spirit of accommodation lies at the basis of the form assumed by the doctrine of Brahman as a psychical principle.'[149] 'The Upaniṣads find a peculiar pleasure in identifying the Ātman as the infinitely small within us with the Ātman as the infinitely great outside us.'[150] When we are in trouble, we have no more to bring in God, but only make concession to weak human nature.

'Metaphysical knowledge impugns the existence of any reality outside of the Ātman, that is the consciousness. The empirical view, on the contrary, teaches that a manifold universe exists externally. From a combination of these antagonistic propositions originated the doctrine that the universe is real, and yet the Ātman remains the sole reality, for the Ātman is the universe.'[151] It is not easy to understand how the two propositions are antagonistic and the conclusion an irreconcilable compromise. When it is said that there is no reality outside Ātman, it is meant that the Ātman is the universal spirit or consciousness, including all else. When it is said that 'a manifold universe exists external to us,' the 'us' refers to the empirical individuals who are limited by mind and body, possessing local habitations and temporal settings. Surely to such beings the world is real, being set over against them. The Ātman we are in search of is not the object of knowledge but the basis of all knowledge. It is the presupposition of material and spiritual worlds alike. The thinking beings of jīvas, the psychological selves, are part of the world of nature. In that world they externally act on other beings and are acted on by them. But logically Ātman is the condition of there being a world of related objects at all. All existence is existence for self. The world is beyond us as psychological selves. It is there within the universal self. The conclusion

148. P. 33.
149. Pp. 135–36.
150. Pp. 193–94.
151. Pp. 341–42.

states, the universe is real to us, for we are not yet perfect selves. Ātman is the sole reality, and it includes the universe also. Any other position would be illogical. As empirical selves we are opposed by the world, limited by the objects. As our life, which is first opposed to matter, gradually absorbs and remoulds into itself the mechanical side of things, even so the subject has to transfigure the object. Then what was at the start external and objective becomes only a condition of the subject's activity. This process goes on steadily till the subject completely dominates the object and becomes all in all. Then there would be no obstacle outside the subject, but till then the goal is not reached. The annulling of the opposition is the sign of spirit's growth. The conclusion that the world is a mere appearance would follow if the individual subject, this particular link in the chain of evolution, bound by space and time, be looked upon as the absolute reality. If we, as we are, were Brahman, if we were the sole reality, then the world opposed to us would be a mere magic show. But the self asserted to be the sole reality is the perfect self, which we have yet to become. To that perfect self, which includes all that is within and without us, there is nothing opposed. It is a confusion between the finite self of man, with all its discord and contradiction, and the ultimate self of Brahman, that suggests to Deussen an imaginary antagonism which he tries to overcome by an artificial device.

There are some passages which say that we ought not to see plurality (nānā) in Brahman.[152] These passages try to indicate the oneness of the world. The emphasis is on the one infinite and not the many finites. In our waking life we imagine the opposition between the subject and the object to be real. Sober reflection tells us that the opposition is not ultimate. Duality of subject and object is not the ultimate truth. When it is said that duality is not all, that duality is not final, it does not mean that there is no duality at all, that there is no distinction or variety. It is this false view of one school of Buddhism that Śaṁkara protests against. So long as we imagine the world to be due to something else than the absolute we are lost. It is the existence of a factor separate from Ātman that the Upaniṣads protest against. Arguing from the similes of salt and water, fire and sparks, spider and threads, flute and sound, employed by the Upaniṣads to represent the relation of Brahman to the world, Oldenberg says: 'We can detect behind these similitudes by which men strove to bring the living power of the Ātman in the universe near to their understanding, a

152. See Bṛh., iv. 4. 19.

conviction, though at the same time but a half-conscious conviction, of the existence of an element in things separate from the Ātman. The Ātman, says the Indian, pervades the universe, as the salt the water in which it has dissolved, but we may easily go on to add, as a complement to this, that although no drop of the salt water is without salt, the water continues, notwithstanding, to be something separately constituted from the salt. And thus we may infer the Ātman is to the Indian certainly the sole actuality, light diffusing, the only significant reality in things, but there is a remainder left in things which he is not.' It is against such a view that the repudiations of dualism are intended. The Upaniṣads make it clear that they do not mean to make the world of creation stand separate from the Ātman. They seem to be clamourously insisting on the adequacy of the Ātman to all experience. Unlike abstract idealism, the Upaniṣad doctrine is distinguished by its resolute devotedness to fact. Its highest principle or God is the eternal spirit,[153] which transcends and includes the objective world[154] and the subjective man.[155] In the highest state there is only one Brahman. 'We see nothing else, hear nothing else, know nothing else.'[156] In the supreme illumination of the soul[157] we feel the oneness of subject and object, the relativity of the world, the non-ultimate nature of the oppositions. 'There is neither day nor night remaining any more, no existence, no non-existence—only God alone.'[158] St Paul says: 'When that which is perfect is come, then that which is in part shall be done away.' Similarly Ruysbroeck: 'The fourth mode is a state of emptiness made one with God in bare love and in divine light.... So that a man forgetteth himself and knoweth neither himself nor God, nor any creature, nor aught else but love alone.' It is this integral oneness of intuitive experience that is indicated by all those passages which ask us to see no distinction in the highest.

We admit that according to the Upaniṣads, plurality, succession in time, co-existence in space, relations of cause and effect, oppositions of subject and object, are not the highest reality. But this is not saying that they are non-existent. The Upaniṣads support the doctrine of māyā only in the sense that there is an underlying reality containing all elements from the personal God to the telegraph post. Śaṁkara says: 'That Ātman is in the

153. Adhidaivam.
154. Adhibhūtam.
155. Adhyātman. See Tait., i. 7.
156. Chān., vii. 23.
157. Ātmabuddhiprakāśa.
158. Śvetāśvatara, iv. 18.

hearts of all living creatures, from Brahmā to a reed.' The different grades of individuality are all broken lights of the one absolute. Māyā represents at the conceptual level the self-distinction residing in the very heart of reality, propelling it to develop itself. The particular things are and are not. They have an intermediate existence. Measured by the perfection of the absolute, the unlimited fullness of the one reality, the world of plurality, with all its pain and disruption, is less real. Compared with the ideal of the supreme one, it is wanting in reality. Even if we look upon the persons and things of the world as shadows of a substance, still, so long as the substance is real, the shadows also have relative reality. Though the things of the world are imperfect representations of the real, they are not illusory semblances of it. The oppositions and conflicts which are in the foreground are relative modes of the absolute unity, which is in the background. Duality and manyness are not the reality.[159]

The unreflecting consciousness hastily assumes that the finite world is absolutely real. This is not so. The forms and energies of the world are not final and ultimate. They themselves need explanation. They are not self-originated or self-maintained. There is something behind and beyond them. We must sink the universe in God, the finite in the infinite, the real of uncritical perception in the Brahman of intuition. There is no suggestion in the Upaniṣads that the objects which lie around us on every side in infinite space, to which by virtue of our bodily frames we all belong, are only apparitions.

There has been much criticism of the theory of the Upaniṣads under the false impression that it supports the illusory nature of the world. It is contended that progress is unreal because progress is change, and change is unreal since time in which change occurs is unreal. But the whole charge is due to a misconception. It is true that the absolute is not in time, while time is in the absolute. Within the absolute we have real growth, creative evolution. The temporal process is an actual process, for reality manifests itself in and through and by means of the temporal changes. If we seek the real in some eternal and timeless void, we do not find it. All that the Upaniṣads urge is that the process of time finds its basis and significance in an absolute which is essentially timeless. For real progress this conception of the absolute is necessary. Without this all-comprehending absolute we cannot be certain that the flux of the universe is an evolution,

159. That is why the word 'iva' is used in some of the Upaniṣads. See Bṛh., ii. 4. 14; iv. 3. 7; iv. 4. 19.

that change is progress, and that the end of the world is the triumph of the good. The absolute guarantees that the process of the world is not chaotic but ordered; that the development is not haphazard or the result of chance variations. Reality is not a series of disconnected states. Were it so, were there not an absolute, we should be landed in an endless process, which would have no plan or purpose underlying it. The unity of the absolute functions throughout the process of the evolution of the world. We are not impotently struggling to realise something which is not yet and can never be. In a sense the real is expressed at every moment of its history. Being and becoming, that which is and that which is to be, are identical. With such a view, the teaching of the Upaniṣads is in essential harmony. They do not support the doctrine of the world illusion. Hopkins says: 'Is there anything in the early Upaniṣads to show that the authors believed in the objective world being an illusion? Nothing at all.'[160]

XII

DEGREES OF REALITY

So far as the absolute is concerned, there are no degrees at all. The conception of degrees has meaning only for the finite intelligence which distinguishes things. It has no ultimate value. When the manyness of the world is taken over into the one, the conception of degrees is transcended. In the metaphysical reality of the Upaniṣads we have no scale of reals. Yet it has significance in the world of experience. All progress in the world involves it. Any demand for advance and alteration in existence presupposes it. The approximation to the character of the real in the relative world of things is the test of the more or less of reality. We know enough of the ultimate to make use of it in this world. This view of the Upaniṣads is defended by Śaṁkara. In reply to the dilemma, Is Brahman known or is it not known?, if known, we need not inquire into its nature; if not known, it will not be worth our while to inquire, Śaṁkara says that reality as self is indubitably known. It posits itself in such sayings as 'I question,' or 'I doubt.' That something is real is a self-evident truth, and it is its nature

160. J.A.O.S., xxii., p. 385. Sir R.G. Bhandarkar holds that 'the opinion expressed by some eminent scholars that the burden of the Upaniṣad teaching is the illusive character of the world and the reality of one soul only is manifestly wrong, and I may even say is indicative of an uncritical judgment' (*Vaiṣṇavism*, p. 2, *f.n.*).

that we have to understand. This reality which we realise serves as the criterion to distinguish degrees in existence. The theory of the world illusion is inconsistent with the conception of degrees of reality. The Upaniṣads give us a hierarchy of different grades of reality down from the all-embracing absolute, which is the primary source as well as the final consummation of the world process. The different kinds of being are higher and lower manifestations of the one absolute spirit. For nothing on earth stands alone, however relatively complete and self-subsisting it may appear. Every finite object holds within itself distinctions which point beyond. While the absolute is in all finite things and permeates them, the things differ in the degree of their permeability, in the fullness of the reflections they give forth.

Not all parts like, but all alike informed
With radiant light....

There is a richer revelation of reality in organised life than in brute matter, more in human society than in organised life. The rank of the categories as higher and lower is determined by the adequacy of their expression of reality. Life is a higher category than matter. Self-conscious thought is more concrete than mere consciousness. 'He who knows the gradual development of the self in him obtains himself more development. There are herbs and trees and all that is animal, and he knows the self gradually developing in them. For in herbs and trees sap only is seen, but citta or consciousness in animated being. Among animated beings, again, the self develops gradually, for in some sap is seen (as well as consciousness), but in others consciousness is not seen, and in man, again, the self develops gradually, for he is most endowed with knowledge. He says what he has known, he sees what he has known. He knows what is to happen to-morrow, he knows the visible and the invisible worlds. By means of the mortal he desires the immortal—thus is he endowed. With regard to other animals, hunger and thirst are a kind of understanding. But they do not say what they have known, nor do they see what they have known. They do not know what is to happen to-morrow, nor the visible and the invisible worlds. They go so far and no farther.'[161] We see that though the same reality is seen 'in the star, in the stone, in the flesh, in the soul and the clod,' still it is

161. Aitareya Āraṇyaka, ii. 3. 1–5.

seen more fully in living beings than in dead matter, in developing man than in the satisfied beast, in the spiritual life than in the intellectual.[162] In this process of self-realisation of self-fulfilment the lowest is the earth. The Upaniṣad thinkers have advanced on the Vedic conception of a single element-water. Sometimes three elements of fire, water and earth are admitted.[163] The five elements of ether, air, fire, water and earth, are distinguished, 'From that self (Brahman) sprang forth ether (ākāśa); from ether air, from air fire, from fire water, from water earth. From earth herbs, from herbs food, from food seed, from seed man. Man thus consists of the essence of food.'[164] In discussing the physical basis of life the author gives an account of the evolution of matter. The higher possesses the properties of the lower. Ether comes first, with the single property of sound. It is that through which we hear. From ether we proceed to air, which has the property of ether, and in addition that of tangibility. It is that through which we hear and feel. From air comes fire. It is that by which we hear, feel and see. From fire we get to water. We can taste it also. From water comes earth, that by which we hear, feel, see, taste and smell. Though the science presupposed might appear to be fanciful at the present day, still there was a principle involved in the account. It is in the Upaniṣads that we have for the first time the doctrine of the five elements. The distinction of the elemental essence or the tanmātra and the gross embodiment or substance is suggested.[165] The Chāndogya Upaniṣad sometimes suggests that the things of the world are qualitatively distinct from one another, and may be divided into infinite parts. Uddālaka propounds the theory that matter is infinitely divisible and qualitatively distinct. There is no

162. The Aitareya Upaniṣad alludes to the fourfold classification of jīvas into those born of uterus, jarāyuja, like men and the higher animals; those born of egg, aṇḍaja, like crows and ducks; those born of moisture, svedaja, like worms and insects; and those born of earth, udbhijja, like plants (iii. 3). The classification proceeds on the mode of appearance of the different beings on earth. See also Manu, i. 43–46. Aristotle speaks of vegetable, animal and human souls. Leibniz classifies living beings into plants, animals and men.

163. By the combination of these three, all other bodies are formed. See Chāndogya Up., vi. 2. 3–4. Possibly this view is the origin of the Sāṁkhya doctrine of tanmātras or subtle essences, giving rise to gross substances. See also Praśna Up., iv. 8.

164. Tait., ii. 1.

165. See Praśna, iv. 8; Aitareya, ii. 3; Kaṭha, ii. 15; Praśna, vi. 4.

such thing as the transformation of things into one another. When we get butter from churning curds, curds do not get transformed into butter, but the particles of butter are already in the curds, and the process of churning enables them to rise upwards.[166] The position of Anaxagoras, that different kinds of matter interpenetrate each other, is similar to this: 'If then an empirical fact, such as the assimilation of nutriment, appears to show us the conversion (say) of corn into flesh and bone, we must interpret this as meaning that the corn contains in itself, in such minute quantities as to be imperceptible, just that into which it is transformed. It veritably consists of particles of flesh and blood, and marrow and bone.'[167] The atomic theory of Kaṇāda is also suggested in the view that the particles only combine and separate. Matter is represented as a chaotic mass, like the juices of various trees blended together in honey.[168] It is not impossible to see in this the germs of the Sāṁkhya theory. The development of matter is accounted for by either the entry of the jīvātman into matter or the animation of matter by spirit in varying degrees. Sometimes the principle of motion is located within matter itself. Prāṇa or life, though it arises out of matter, is not fully explicable by matter. Similarly, consciousness, though it arises from life, is not intelligible on the hypothesis of prāṇa or vitalism. When we get to man we have self-conscious thought. Man is higher than stones and stars, beasts and birds, since he can enter into the fellowship of reason and will, affection and conscience, yet he is not the highest, since he feels the pain of contradiction.

Before we pass from this section let us consider whether the Upaniṣad doctrine is rightly regarded as pantheistic. Pantheism is the view which identifies God with the sum of things and denies transcendence. If the nature of the absolute is exhausted completely by the course of the world, if the two become one, then we have pantheism. In the Upaniṣads we come across passages which declare that the nature of reality is not exhausted by the world process. The existence of the world does not take away from the perfection of the absolute. In a beautiful image it is said: 'That is full and this is full. From that full rises this full. Taking away this full from that, what remains is yet full.' Even God in transforming Himself into the world has forfeited nothing of His nature. As early as the Ṛg-Veda it is

166. Chān., vi. 6. 1.
167. Adamson, *The Development of Greek Philosophy*, p. 50.
168. Chān., vi. 9. 1–2.

said that all beings are only a fourth of the Puruṣa, while the three other fourths remain immortal in the shining regions.[169] According to the Bṛhadāraṇyaka (v. 14), one foot of Brahman consists of the three worlds, the second of the triple knowledge of the Veda, the third of the three vital breaths, while the fourth, exalted above the dust of earth, shines as the sun.[170] The Upaniṣads declare that the universe is in God. But they never hold that the universe is God. God is greater than the universe, which is His work. He is as much and more beyond this, as the human personality is beyond the body, which is the instrument of its life here. They refuse to imprison God in the world. From this it does not follow that God is the external Creator existing separate from the world. God expresses Himself in the world, and the world is the expression of His life. God in the infinite fullness of His being transcends His actual manifestations in the universe of finite, physical and psychical entities which He has called into existence. God is transcendent as well as immanent. The Upaniṣads are not pantheistic in the bad sense of the term. Things are not thrown together into a heap called God, without unity, purpose or distinction of values. The philosophy of the Upaniṣads revolts against the deistic conception of God. It does not say that God is outside the world, and now and again makes His presence felt by supernatural revelation or miraculous interference. It is pantheism, if it is pantheism to say that God is the fundamental reality of our lives, and we cannot live without Him. Everything on earth is finite and infinite, perfect and imperfect. Everything seeks a good beyond itself, tries to rid itself of its finiteness and become perfect. The finite seeks self-transcendence. This clearly establishes that the Infinite Spirit is working in the finite. The real is the basis of the unreal. If the doctrine of the indwelling of the divine is enough justification for condemning a system as pantheism, the philosophy of the Upaniṣads is a pantheism. But pantheism in this sense is an essential feature of all true religion.

XIV

THE INDIVIDUAL SELF

The Upaniṣads make out that of finite objects the individual self has the highest reality. It comes nearest to the nature of the absolute, though it is not the absolute itself. There are passages where the finite self is looked

169. x. 90. 3. See also Chāndogya Up., iii. 12. 6.
170. iv. 3. 32.

upon as a reflection of the universe. The whole world is the process of the finite striving to become infinite, and this tension is found in the individual self. According to the Taittirīya the several elements of the cosmos are found in the nature of the individual. In the Chāndogya Upaniṣad (vi. 11. 3 and 4) fire, water and earth are said to constitute the jīvātman or the individual soul, together with the principle of the infinite.[171]

Man is the meeting-point of the various stages of reality. Prāṇa corresponds to Vāyu, the breath of the body to the wind of the world, manas to ākāśa, the mind of man to the ether of the universe, the gross body to the physical elements. The human soul has affinities with every grade of existence from top to bottom. There is in it the divine element which we call the beatific consciousness, the ānanda state, by which at rare moments it enters into immediate relations with the absolute. The finite self or the embodied soul is the Ātman coupled with the senses and mind.[172]

The different elements are in unstable harmony. 'Two birds, akin and friends, cling to the self-same tree. One of them eats the sweet berry, but the other gazes upon him without eating. In the same tree—the world tree—man dwells along with God. With troubles overwhelmed, he faints and grieves at his own helplessness. But when he sees the other, the Lord in whom he delights—ah, what glory is his, his troubles pass away.'[173] The natural and the divine have not as yet attained a stable harmony. The being of the individual is a continual becoming, a striving after that which it is not. The infinite in man summons the individual to bring about a

171. Since God collected and resumed in man
The firmaments, the strata and the lights,
Fish, fowl, and beast and insect—
Of various life caught back upon His arm all their trains,
Reorganised and constituted man,
The microcosm, the adding up of works.

Browning.

See also Aitareya, iii. 3; Śvetāśvatara, ii. 12. 6; Praśna, vi. 11. The individual subject is the world in miniature, and the world is the individual writ large. Plato in his *Timæus* institutes an analogy between the macrocosm and the microcosm, the universe and man. The soul of the world is said to be compounded by God Himself out of the changeless and the changeful and inserted in the midst of the universe (34. B). The universe, according to him, is a magnified man. See Tait., i. 3, and Ānandagiri's commentary on it.

172. Chān., viii. 12. 3.

173. Muṇḍaka, iii. 1. 2. See R.V., i. 164. 20.

unity out of the multiplicity with which he is confronted. This tension between the finite and the infinite which is present throughout the world-process comes to a head in the human consciousness. In every aspect of his life, intellectual, emotional and moral, this struggle is felt. He can gain admission into the kingdom of God, where the eternal verities of absolute love and absolute freedom dwell only by sinking his individuality and transforming the whole of the finiteness into infiniteness, humanity into divinity. But as finite and human, he cannot reach the fruition or attain the final achievement. The being in which the struggle is witnessed points beyond itself, and so man has to be surpassed. The finite self is not a self-subsisting reality. Be he so, then God becomes only another independent individual, limited by the finite self. The reality of the self is the infinite; the unreality which is to be got rid of is the finite. The finite individual loses whatever reality he possesses if the indwelling spirit is removed. It is the presence of the infinite that confers dignity on the self of man. The individual self derives its being and draws its sustenance from the universal life. *Sub specie æeternitatis*, the self is perfect.[174] There is a psychological side on which the selves repel each other and exclude one another. From this apparent fact of exclusiveness we should not infer real isolation of selves. The exclusiveness is the appearance of distinction. It ought to be referred to the identity, otherwise it becomes a mere abstraction of our minds. The hypothesis of exclusive selves leaves no room for the ideals of truth, goodness and love. These presuppose that man is not perfect as he is, that there is something higher than the actual self which he has to attain to secure peace of mind. 'And the independent reality of the individual, when we examine it, is in truth mere illusion. Apart from the community, what are separate men? It is the common mind within him which gives reality to the human being, and taken by himself, whatever else he is, he is not human.... If this is true of the social consciousness in its various forms, it is true certainly no less of that common mind which is more than social. The finite minds that in and for religion form one spiritual whole have indeed in the end no visible embodiment, and yet, except as members in an invisible community, they are nothing real. For religion, in short, if the one indwelling spirit is removed, there are no spirits left.'[175]

174. See Śaṁkara; Introduction to V.S.
175. Bradley, *Truth and Reality*, p. 435.

Though the individual soul fighting with the lower nature is the highest in the world, it is not the highest realisable. The striving discordant soul of man should attain to the freedom of spirit, the delight of harmony and the joy of the absolute. Only when the God in him realises itself, only when the ideal reaches its fruition is the destiny of man fulfilled. The struggles, the contradictions and the paradoxes of life are the signs of imperfect evolution, while the harmony, the delight and the peace, mark the perfection of the process of evolution. The individual is the battlefield in which the fight occurs. The battle must be over and the pain of contradiction transcended for the ideal to be realised. The tendency to God which begins in completed man will become then a perfect fruition. Man is higher than all other aspects of the universe, and his destiny is realised when he becomes one with the infinite. Nature has life concealed in it, and when life develops, nature's destiny is fulfilled. Life has consciousness concealed in it, and when it liberates consciousness, its end is reached. The destiny of consciousness is fulfilled when intellect becomes manifest. But the truth of the intellect is reached when it is absorbed in the higher intuition, which is neither thought nor will nor feeling, but yet the goal of thought, the end of will and the perfection of feeling. When the finite self attains the supreme, the godhead from which it descended, the end of spiritual life is reached. 'When to a man who understands, the self has become all things, what sorrow, what trouble, can there be to him, who has once beheld that unity?'

XV

THE ETHICS OF THE UPANIṢADS

In estimating the value of the ethics of the Upaniṣads we have to consider the logical implications of the ideal set forth, and develop the suggestions made in the texts. From our previous discussion, it is obvious that the Upaniṣads have for their ideal the becoming one with God. The world is not for itself. It issues from God, and must therefore seek its rest in God. Throughout the process of the world we witness this infinitisation of the finite. Like the rest of the world, man, feeling the pressure of the infinite in him, reaches out his hands to clasp the highest. 'All birds go towards the tree intended for their abode, so all this goes to the supreme self.'[176] 'May I enter Thee, such as Thou art, O, Lord; may Thou, O Lord, enter me....

176. Praśna, iv. 7.

May I become well cleansed, O Lord.'[177] 'Thou art my resting-place.'[178] The realisation of the oneness with God is the ideal of man. The difference between human consciousness and all else is that while all seek the infinite, man alone has an idea of the end. After ages of development man has become conscious of the great scheme of the universe. He alone feels the summons of the infinite, and consciously grows towards the heavenly stature awaiting him. The absolute is the deliberate goal of the finite self.

That it is the highest perfection, the most desirable ideal, is brought out in many ways. It is a state 'far above hunger and thirst, above sorrow and confusion, above old age and death.' 'As the sun, the eye of the universe, remains far off and unaffected by all sickness that meets the eye, so also the One, the Ātman, who dwells in all creatures, dwells afar and untouched by the sorrows of the world.' To live in the world of plurality, staking all on the small self, subject to disease and suffering, is indeed a misfortune. The undoing of the causes which lead to finite existence is the proper aim of man. A return from the plurality into the One is the ideal goal, the most ultimate value. It gives satisfaction to the whole being of man. It is, according to the Taittirīya Upaniṣad, 'Prāṇārāmam mana-ānandam, śāntisamṛddham amṛtam,' 'the delight of life and mind, the fullness of peace and eternity.' Lower goals which we crave after may satisfy the vital organism or the mental desires, but this includes them and transcends them. We have different kinds of pleasures answering to the different levels of our existence, the vital pleasure, the sensuous, the mental and the intellectual, but the highest is ānanda.

Whatever ethics we have in the Upaniṣads is subsidiary to this goal. Duty is a means to the end of the highest perfection. Nothing can be satisfying short of this highest condition. Morality is valuable only as leading to it. It is the expression of the spiritual impulse to perfection implanted in the heart of man, the instinct of the individual soul. It is obedience to the Eternal Reality which constrains our conscious self. This is the meaning of the expression that duty is 'the stern daughter of the voice of God.' The perfect ideal of our life is found only in the Eternal Reality. The law of morality is an invitation to become perfect, 'even as your heavenly Father is perfect.'

Before we take up the discussion of the ethical life, we may consider the objections urged generally against the possibility of ethics in the

177. Tait., i. 4.
178. Tait., i. 4; see Bṛh., iv. 3. 32.

philosophical system of the Upaniṣads. If all is one, it is asked, how can we have moral relations? If the absolute is perfection, where is there any need for the effort to realise what is already accomplished? But monism does not mean an obliteration of the distinction of good and evil. The sense of otherness and multiplicity essential to ethical life is allowed for by the Upaniṣads. They point out that there is no meaning in asking us to love our neighbour or achieve the unity of the world in love, if exclusiveness and difference are fundamental in the lives of men. If men were really external to each other, as the Leibnizean monads, without the corrective of the pre-established harmony, then the ethical ideal is impossible of realisation. If we are called upon to love our neighbour, it is because all are one in reality. My neighbour and myself are one in our inmost self, if the superficial and ephemeral distinctions are transcended. The true self, absolutely and eternally valid, is beyond the fluctuating particulars of time and space and all that finds its place in them. It is no mere empty phrase to be told to transcend our exclusiveness. Mokṣa literally means release, release from the bondage to the sensuous and the individual, the narrow and the finite. It is the result of self-enlargement and freedom. To live in perfect goodness is to realise one's life in all. This ideal for which the moral nature of man cries can be attained only if the finite self transcends its narrow individuality and identifies itself with the whole. The path of deliverance is the path of soul growth. The reality in which we are to abide by transcending our individuality is the highest, and that is the reality asserted by the Upaniṣads.

It is urged that there is no room for any ethical endeavour on the hypothesis that man is divine in nature. Simply because it is said that God is in man, it does not follow that with it there is an end of all endeavour. God is not in man in such an obvious fashion that he can possess Him absentmindedly and without effort or struggle. God is present as a potentia or a possibility. It is man's duty to lay hold of Him by force and action. If he does not do it, he fails in his duty as man. The God in man is a task as well as a fact, a problem as well as a possession. Man in his ignorance identifies himself with the external wrappings, the physical and mental envelopments. Desire for the absolute conflicts with his finitude or his limitation. 'Though the individual is lit with the divine spark, he is not wholly divine. His divinity is not an actuality, but a part of God aspiring to be the whole. As he is, he is dust and deity, God and brute crossed. It is the task of the moral life to eliminate the non-divine element, not by destroying it, but by suffusing it with the divine spirit.'[179] Man is a contradiction between the finite heritage of nature and the infinite ideals of spirit, and by a gradual submission of the chaotic principles of nature to the divine spirit he has to work up to his destiny. It is his aim to break the shell of his own little being and blend in love and perfect union with the divine principle. The problem of morality has a significance for man whose life is a struggle or a warfare between the finite and the infinite, the demoniac and the divine elements. Man is born for the struggle, and does not find his self until he feels the opposition.

From the references in the Upaniṣads to the different ways of attaining the highest, Rāthītara's truth, Pauruśiṣṭi's austerity and Maudgalya's learning,[180] it is clear that the thinkers of the period reflected a good deal on the problems of ethics. Without attempting to elaborate the views of the different thinkers, we may describe certain general propositions accepted by them all.

The ideal of ethics is self-realisation. Moral conduct is self-realised conduct, if by the self we mean not the empirical self, with all its weakness and vulgarity, selfishness and smallness, but the deeper nature of man, free from all fetters of selfish individuality. The lusts and passions of the animal self, the desires and ambitions of egoism, restrict the vital energies to the plane of the lower self and contract the life of the soul, and they are to be held in check. For the growth of the soul, or the realisation of the highest, the obstacles and influences must be subdued. The moral life is one of understanding and reason, and not of mere sense and instinct. 'Know the self or Ātman as the Lord who sits in the chariot called the body, buddhi or intelligence is the charioteer, mind is the reins, the senses are the horses, and the objects are the roads. The self, the senses and the mind combined, the intelligent call the enjoyer. But he who has no understanding, but is weak in mind, his senses run riot like the vicious horses of a charioteer. He who has understanding, and is strong-minded, his senses are well controlled, like the good horses of a charioteer. He who is without understanding, who is thoughtless and impure, never reaches the immortal, immaterial state, but enters into the round of birth. But he who has understanding, and he who is thoughtful and pure, reaches the state from which there is no return.'[181] The drive of desire has to be checked. When desire seizes the

179. *International Journal of Ethics*, 1914, p. 169.
180. Tait., i. 9.
181. Kaṭha Upaniṣad.

helm the soul suffers shipwreck, since it is not the law of man's being. If we do not recognise the ideal prescribed by reason, and do not accept a higher moral law, our life will be one of animal existence, without end or aim, where we are randomly busy, loving and hating, caressing and killing without purpose or reason. The presence of reason reminds us of something higher than mere nature, and requires us to transform our natural existence into a human one, with meaning and purpose. If, in spite of indications to the contrary, we make pleasure the end of our pursuits, our life is one of moral evil, unworthy of man. 'Man is not in the least elevated above mere animalism by the possession of reason, if his reason is only employed in the same fashion as that in which animals use their instincts.'[182] Only the wicked make gods of the things of the world and worship them. 'Now Virocana, satisfied in his thought, went to the asuras and preached to them the doctrine that the bodily self alone is to be worshipped, that it alone is to be served, and he who worships body and serves it gains both worlds—this and the next. Therefore they call even now a man who does not give alms here, who has not faith, and offers no sacrifices, an asura, for this is the doctrine of the asuras.'[183] Our life, when thus guided, will be at the mercy of vain hopes and fears. 'The rational life will be marked by unity and consistency. The different parts of human life will be in order and make manifest the one supreme ideal. If, instead of reason, our senses guide us, our life will be a mirror of passing passions and temporary inclinations. He who leads such a life will have to be written down, like Dogberry, an ass. His life, which will be a series of disconnected and scattered episodes, will have no purpose to take, no work to carry out, no end to realise. In a rational life, every course of action, before it is adopted, is brought before the bar of reason, and its capacity to serve the highest end is tested, and if found suitable adopted by the individual.'[184]

A life of reason is a life of unselfish devotion to the world. Reason tells us that the individual has no interests of his own apart from the whole, of which he is a part. He will be delivered from the bondage to fortune and caprice only if he gives up his ideas of separate sensuous existence. He is a good man who in his life subordinates personal to social ends, and he is a bad man who does the opposite. The soul in committing a selfish deed

182. Kānt, *Critique of Pure Reason.*
183. Chāndogya, viii. 8. 4–5.
184. *International Journal of Ethics*, 1914, pp. 171–2.

imposes fetters on itself, which can be broken only by the reassertion of the life universal. This way of sympathy is open to all and leads to the expansion of the soul. If we want to escape from sin, we must escape from selfishness. We must put down the vain conceits and foolish lies about the supremacy of the small self. Each of us conceives himself to be an exclusive unit, an ego sharply marked off from whatever lies outside his physical body and mental history. From this egoism springs all that is morally bad. We should realise in our life and conduct that all things are in God and of God. The man who knows this truth will long to lose his life, will hate all selfish goods and sell all that he has, would wish even to be despised and rejected of the world, if so he can come into accord with the universal life of God. In one sense the Upaniṣad morality is individualistic, for its aim is self-realisation; but 'individualistic' ceases here to have any exclusive meaning. To realise oneself is to identify oneself with a good that is not his alone. Moral life is a God-centred life, a life of passionate love and enthusiasm for humanity, of seeking the infinite through the finite, and not a mere selfish adventure for small ends.[185]

Finite objects cannot give us the satisfaction for which our soul hungers. As in the field of intellect we miss the ultimate reality in the objects of the empirical world, even so the absolute good we seek for in morality is not to be found in finite satisfactions. 'The infinite is bliss, there is no bliss in things finite.'[186] Yājñavalkya, leaving for the forest, proposed to divide his property between his two wives, Maitreyī and Kātyāyanī. Maitreyī did not know what to do; sitting among her household possessions, rather sadly she was looking outwards towards the forest. That day she administered a rebuke to the petty man who pursues worthless aims in such breathless haste. Finite things produce the opposite of what we aim at through them. The spirit in us craves for true satisfaction, and nothing less than the infinite can give us that. We seek finite objects, we get them, but there is no satisfaction in them. We may conquer the whole world, and yet we sigh that there are no more worlds to conquer. 'Whatever he reaches he wishes to go beyond. If he reaches the sky, he wishes to go beyond.'[187] Most of us are on 'the road that leads to wealth in which many men perish.'[188] By

185. Īśā Upaniṣad, 1.
186. Chān., vii. i. 24.
187. Aitareya Āraṇyaka, ii. 3.3. 1.
188. Kaṭha, ii. 2–3.

becoming slaves to things, by swathing ourselves in external possessions, we miss the true self. 'No man can be made happy by wealth.' 'The hereafter never rises before the eyes of the careless youth, befooled by the delusion of wealth. 'This is the world,' he thinks; 'there is no other.' Thus he falls again and again into the power of death.'[189] 'Wise men, knowing the nature of what is immortal, do not look for anything stable here among things unstable.'[190] Man is in anguish when he is separated from God, and nothing else than union with God can satisfy his heart's hunger.[191] The unbounded aspirations of the soul for the ideally beautiful, the specklessly pure, are not answered by the objects limited in space, time and the shackles of sense. Many men there are who wish to realise the ideal of an absolutely worthy existence in love of another being. So long as that being is another human self, localised in space and time, the ideal is never attained. It is self-deception to seek the fullness of love and beauty in another human being, man or woman. The perfect realisation can only be in the Eternal. Detachment from the world and its possessions is necessary for this. From the beginning there were people who sought deliverance from sorrow in retirement from the world. Many there were who left wife and child, goods and chattels, and went out as mendicants, seeking the salvation of the souls in poverty and purity of life. These groups of ascetics, who burst the bonds that bound them to a home life, prepared the way for the monasticism of the Buddhists. A life of holy renunciation has been recognised to be the chief path to deliverance.

It follows that the Upaniṣads insist on the inwardness of morality and attach great importance to the motive in conduct. Inner purity is more important than outer conformity. Not only do the Upaniṣads say 'do not steal', 'do not murder', but they also declare 'do not covet', or 'do not hate or yield to anger, malice and greed'. The mind will have to be purified, for it is no use cutting the branches if one leaves the roots intact. Conduct is judged by its subjective worth or the degree of sacrifice involved.

The Upaniṣads require us to look upon the whole world as born of God as the self of man is. If insistence on this doctrine is interpreted as reducing all love finally to a well-directed egoism, the Upaniṣads admit that morality and love are forms of the highest self-realisation, but only

189. Kaṭha, i. 2. 6.

190. Kaṭha, ii. 4. 2.

191. 'Miserable comforters are ye all, O that I knew where I might find Him' (Job).

object to the word 'egoism' with all its associations. Yājñavalkya maintains that self-love lies at the foundation of all other kinds of love. Love of wealth and property, clan and country are special forms of self-love. The love of the finite has only instrumental value, while love of the eternal has intrinsic worth. 'The son is dear for the sake of the eternal in him.' Finite objects help us to realise the self. Only the love of the Eternal is supreme love, which is its own reward, for God is love.[192] To love God is bliss; not to love Him is misery. To love God is to possess knowledge and immortality; not to love Him is to be lost in doubt and delusion, sorrow and death.[193] In all true religion it is the same dominating motive that we have. 'He that sinneth against me wrongeth his own soul. All they that hate me love death.'[194] The sinners are the slayers of their souls, according to the Upaniṣads 'ātmahano janāḥ'.

The Upaniṣads ask us to renounce selfish endeavours, but not all interests. Detachment from self and attachment to God are what the Upaniṣads demand. The ideal sage has desires, though they are not selfish desires. 'He who has no desires, who is beyond desires, whose desires are satisfied, whose desire is the soul, being even Brahman obtains Brahman.'[195] Kāma, which we are asked to renounce, is not desire as such, but only the animal desire, lust, the impulsive craving of the brute man. Freedom from kāma is enjoined, but this is not blank passivity. We are asked to free ourselves from the tyranny of lust and greed, from the fascination of outward things, from the fulfilment of instinctive cravings.[196] Desire as such is not forbidden. It all depends upon the object. If a man's desire is the flesh, he becomes an adulterer; if things of beauty, an artist; if God, a saint. The desires for salvation and knowledge are highly commended. A distinction is drawn between true desires and false ones,[197] and we are asked to share in the true ones. The filial piety and affection of a Naciketas, the intense love and devotion of a Sāvitrī are not faults. The Lord of all creation has kāma in the sense of desire. 'He desired (akāmayata), let me become many.' If the Lord has desires, why should not we? We do not find in the

192. Kāmāyatana. Bṛh., iii. 9. 11.

193. Bṛh., iv. 4. 5.

194. Prov., viii. 36. See Īśā. Up.

195. Bṛh., iv. 4. 6.

196. The true saint is described as śānta, śrānta, dānta, uparata, samāhit. These all imply the conquest of passion.

197. Chāndogya, vii. 1. 3.

Upaniṣads any sweeping condemnation of affections. We are asked to root out pride, resentment, lust, etc., and not the tender feelings of love, compassion and sympathy. It is true that here and there the Upaniṣads speak of tapas a means of spiritual realisation. But tapas only means the development of soul force, the freeing of the soul from slavery to body, severe thinking or energising of mind, 'whose tapas consists of thought itself.'[198] Life is a great festival to which we are invited, that we might show tapas or self-renunciation, dāna or liberality, ārjavam or right dealing, ahiṁsā or non-injury to life, and satyavacanam or truthfulness.[199] It is the spirit of distinterestedness that is conveyed by tapas or tyāga. 'Not by karma, not by offspring, not by wealth, but by renunciation can immortality be gained.'[200] The Chāndogya Upaniṣad says 'śraddhā tapaḥ.'[201] Faith is asceticism. To realise freedom from the bondage of outward things one need not go to the solitude of the forest and increase his privations and penances that so the last remnants of earthly dependence might be thrown away. 'By renunciation thou shouldst enjoy,' says the Īśā Upaniṣad. We can enjoy the world if we are not burdened by the bane of worldly possessions; we are princes in the world if we do not harbour any thought of covetousness. Our enjoyment of the world is in direct proportion to our poverty. A call to renunciation in the sense of killing out the sense of separateness and developing disinterested love is the essence of all true religion.[202]

There was a change in Indian thought after the Vedic period.[203] Due to the asceticism of the Atharva-Veda, the mystic tendency increased. During the period of the hymns of the Ṛg-Veda there was a sort of selfish abandonment to pleasure. The spiritual instinct of the human soul asserted itself, and in the period of the Upaniṣads the protest against the tyranny of the senses was heard in clear tones. No more is the spirit to follow helpless and miserable the flesh that rages and riots. But this spirit of renunciation did not degenerate in the Upaniṣads into the insane asceticism of a later day, which revelled in the burning of bodies and such other practices. In the manner of Buddha, Bhāradvāja protests against

198. Muṇḍaka, i. 1. 9.
199. Chān., iii. 16; Tait., i. 9.
200. Nārāyaṇīya, iv. 21.
201. v. 10.
202. 'Thou fool, that which thou sowest is not quickened except it die' (1 Cor. xv. 36).
203. See Rhys Davids, *Buddhism, Hibbert Lectures*, pp. 21–22.

both worldly life and asceticism.[204] We may even say that this measureless and fanatical asceticism is not indicative of a true renunciation, but is only another form of selfishness. Attempts to gain solitary salvation embodying the view that one's soul is more precious than all the world's souls put together are not the expression of any genuine modesty of spirit. The Upaniṣads require us to work but disinterestedly. The righteous man is not he who leaves the world and retires to a cloister, but he who lives in the world and loves the objects of the world, not for their own sake, but for the sake of the infinite they contain, the universal they conceal. To him God has unconditional value, and all objects possess derived values as vehicles of the whole or as the ways to God. Every common duty fulfilled, every individual sacrifice made, helps the realisation of the self. We may be fathers, for that is a way of transcending our narrow individuality and identifying ourselves with the larger purposes. Human love is a shadow of the divine love. We may love our wives for the sake of the joy that burns at the heart of things. 'In truth, not for the husband's sake is the husband dear, but for the sake of the Ātman is the husband dear,' says the Upaniṣad. The same is asserted with constant repetition of wife, sons, kingdoms, the Brāhmin and the warrior castes, world regions, gods, living creations and the universe. They are all here, not on their own account, but for the sake of the Eternal.[205] The objects of the world are represented not as lures to sin, but as pathways to the divine bliss. When once we have the right vision, we may have wealth, etc.[206] 'Tato me śriyam āvaha.' 'After that bring me wealth.' And Śaṁkara points out that wealth is an evil to the unregenerate, but not to the man of wisdom. Things of the world seemingly undivine are a perpetual challenge to the spiritual soul. He has to combat their independence and turn them into expressions of the divine. He does all work in this spirit of detachment. 'To be detached is to be loosened from every tie which binds a soul to the earth, to be dependent on nothing sublunary, to lean on nothing temporal. It is to care nothing what other men choose to say or think of us or do; to go about our work as soldiers go to battle, without a care for the consequences, to account credit, honour, name, easy circumstances, comfort, human affection, just nothing at all when any religious obligation requires sacrifice of them.'[207] The Upaniṣads

204. See Muṇḍaka Up.
205. Bṛh., ii. 4. 5.
206. Tait., i. 4.
207. Newman, *University Sketches*, p. 127.

demand a sort of physical preparation for the spiritual fight. Cleansing, fasting, continence, solitude, etc., as purificatory of the body, are enjoined. 'May my body become fit, may my tongue become extremely sweet, may I hear much in my ears.'[208] This is not to despise the body as a clog and an encumbrance to the human soul. Nor has this purifying of the body, freeing of the senses, development of the mind, anything in common with self-torture.[209] Again, in the Chāndogya Upaniṣad[210] we are told that the world of Brahman belongs to those who find it by brahmacarya. Brahmacarya is the discipline a student has to undergo when studying under a guru. It is not an ascetic withdrawal from the world, for the same Upaniṣad in viii. 5 makes brahmacarya equivalent to the performing of sacrifices. It looks as if these were meant as a warning against the false interpretation of brahmacarya as aloofness from the world. The body is the servant of the soul and not its prison. There is no indication in the Upaniṣads that we must give up life, mind, consciousness, intelligence, etc. On the other hand, the doctrine of divine immanence leads to an opposite conclusion.

'The Indian sages, as the Upaniṣads speak of them,' according to Gough, 'seek for participation in divine life, not by pure feeling, high thought, and strenuous endeavour, not by unceasing effort to learn the true and do the right, but by the crushing out of every feeling and every thought by vacuity, apathy, inertion and ecstasy.'[211] The aim of the Upaniṣads, according to Eucken, is 'not so much a penetration and overcoming of the world as a separation and liberation from it; not an enhancement of life in order to maintain it even in face of the hardest resistance, but an abatement, a softening of all hardness, a dissolution, a fading away, a profound contemplation.'[212] The view here stated that the Upaniṣads demand a release from the conditions which constitute human life is a complete misconception. The Upaniṣads do not ask us to rencounce life, do not taboo desires as such. The essence of ethical life is not the sublation of the will. The false asceticism which regards life as a dream and the world as an illusion, which has obsessed some thinkers in India as well as in Europe,

208. Tait., i. 4.

209. Gough makes a mistake by translating tapas into self-torture. In Tait. i. 4. the injunctions are to the effect that the body must be rendered fit for the habitation of God.

210. viii. 4. 3.

211. *Philosophy of the Upaniṣads*, pp. 266–267.

212. *Main Currents*, p. 13.

is foreign to the prevailing tone of the Upaniṣads. A healthy joy in the life of the world pervades the atmosphere. To retire from the world is to despair of humanity and confess the discomfiture of God. 'Only performing works one should desire to live a hundred years.'[213] There is no call to forsake the world, but only to give up the dream of its separate reality. We are asked to pierce behind the veil, realise the presence of God in the world of nature and society. We are to renounce the world in its immediacy, break with its outward appearance, but redeem it for God and make it express the divinity within us and within it. The Upaniṣad conception of the world is a direct challenge to the spiritual activity of man. A philosophy of resignation, an ascetic code of ethics, and a temper of languid world-weariness are an insult to the Creator of the universe, a sin against ourselves and the world which has a claim on us. The Upaniṣads believe in God, and so believe in the world as well.

The Upaniṣads do not content themselves with merely emphasising the spirit of true religion. They also give us a code of duties, without which the moral ideal will be an uncertain guide. All forms of conduct where passion is controlled and reason reigns supreme, where there is self-transcendence in the sense of freedom from the narrowness of selfish individuality, where we work because we are all co-operators in the divine scheme, are virtuous, and their opposites vicious. Restraint, liberality and mercy are virtues.[214] The principle that the left hand should not know what the right hand does is expressed in the following words: 'Give with faith, give not without faith, give in plenty, give with bashfulness, give with fear, give with sympathy.'[215] In Chāndogya (iii. 17) meditation, charity right dealing, non-injury to life and truthfulness are laid down as right forms of conduct.[216] To shrink from torturing the brute creation, to be sorry for a hunted hare, may be, according to our modern notions, silly sentimentalism fit only for squeamish women. But in the Upaniṣads love of brute creation is considered to be a great virtue. Kindness and compassion for all that has life on earth is a general feature of Indian ethics. It is a crime to kill a deer for sport or worry a rat for amusement. To attain conquest over passions, a discipline is sometimes enjoined. The Indian thinkers believe

213. Īśā Upaniṣad, ii.
214. Bṛh., v. 2.
215. Tait., i. 11.
216. See also i. 9. 12.

in the dependence of mind on body, and so prescribe purity of food as necessary for the purity of mind.[217] Control over the passions must be spontaneous, and when that is not possible forcible restraint is sometimes adopted. A distinction is made between tapas, or forcible constraint of passions, and nyāsa, or spiritual renunciation. Tapas is for the vānaprastha who is in the lower stage, while nyāsa is for the sannyāsin. The yogic practices of concentration, contemplation, etc., are to be met with. 'The wise should sink speech in the mind and the mind into buddhi.'[218] Meditation and concentration as means of cleansing the mind are also enjoined. The individual is asked to turn all his thoughts inward and think only of God, not with an eye to obtaining favours, but to becoming one with Him. But even this exaltation of contemplative life is not necessarily an escape from reality. It is only the means by which we can see the ultimate truth of things. 'With sharp and subtle mind is He beheld.'[219] The four āśramas of the brahmacārin or student, gṛhastha or householder, vānaprastha or anchorite, and sannyāsi or wandering mendicant, are mentioned as representing the different steps by which man gradually purifies himself from all earthly taint and becomes fit for his spiritual home.

Retirement from the world is enjoined for every Aryan when once his duties to society are fulfilled. It comes at the end of a man's career. The ascetic wanderer, whose life is love and conduct righteousness, turns his eyes towards heaven and keeps himself free from the temptations of the world. The simple but devout minds of India were haunted by dreams of imperishable beauty and echoes of unceasing music. They live so intimately with the ideal that they are persuaded of its reality. To us it may be a dream, yet it is a dream in which they live, and it is therefore more real than the reality they ignore. A severe training of body and soul is prescribed for the ascetic, who alone can live such an ideal life. His life must be governed by the strictest purity and poverty. He is required to wear the yellow garments, shave his head and beg for his food in the streets. These are the means to help the soul to humility. The soul can mount to everlasting bliss by means of carefully regulated prayers and fastings. What makes an ascetic great is his holiness and humility. It is not the capacity to do clever conjurer's tricks or dream hysteric dreams, but it is to remain pure from

217. Āhāraśuddhau satvaśuddhiḥ.
218. Kaṭha, i. 3. 10.
219. Ibid., iii. 12.

lust and resentment, passion and desire. This living martyrdom is ever so much more difficult than killing oneself. Death is easy. It is life that is taxing. A true ascetic is not one who gives up home and society to escape the social bonds; he is not one who becomes a sannyāsin because he suffers shipwreck in life. It is these latter that draw disgrace on the whole institution. The true sannyāsin is he who, with self-control and spiritual vision, suffers for mankind. The labour of life is laid upon us to purify us from egoism, and social institutions are devices to help the growth of the soul. So after the gṛhasthāśrama, or the stage of the householder, comes that of the recluse. The Upaniṣads declare that the knowers of Ātman relinquish all selfish interests and become mendicants. 'Knowing Him, the Ātman, Brāhmins relinquish the desire for posterity, the desire for possessions, the desire for worldly prosperity, and go forth as mendicants.'[220] In Ancient India, though the sannyāsin is poor and penniless, lives on daily charity, and has no power or authority of any kind, he is still held in such high esteem that the emperors of the world bow to him. Such is the reverence for holy life.

The āśramadharma, one of the central features of the Hindu religion, attempts to fill the whole of life with the power of spirit. It insists that a life of rigorous chastity is the proper preparation for married life. To the thinkers of the Upaniṣads, marriage is a religious sacrament, a form of divine service.[221] The home is sacred, and no religious ceremony is complete without the wife taking part in it. After the individual realises to the full the warmth and glow of human love and family affection, through marriage and parenthood, he is called upon to free himself slowly from attachment to home and family in order that he might realise his dignity as a citizen of the universe. If Buddhism failed to secure a permanent hold on the mind of India, it was because it exalted the ideal of celibacy over that of marriage and allowed all to enter the highest order of sannyāsins, regardless of their previous preparation for it. The sannyāsins are a spiritual brotherhood

220. According to Oldenberg, this is the earliest trace of Indian monasticism. 'From these Brāhmins, who knowing the Ātman renounce all that is earthly, and become beggars, the historical development progresses in a regular line up to Buddha, who leaves kith and kin, and goods and chattels, to seek deliverance, wandering homeless in the yellow garb of monk. The appearance of the doctrine of the Eternal One and the origin of monastic life in India are simultaneous; they are the two issues of the same important occurrence' (Oldenberg: *Buddha*, p. 32).

221. See Tait., Up., i.

without possessions, without caste and nationality, enjoined to preach in the spirit of joy the gospel of love and service. They are the ambassadors of God on earth, witnessing to the beauty of holiness, the power of humility, the joy of poverty and the freedom of service.

The rules of caste prescribe the duties to society. Man has to fulfil his duties whatever his lot may be. The functions depend on the capacities. Brāhminhood does not depend on birth, but on character. The following story reveals this truth:

Satyakāma, the son of Jabālā, addressed his mother and said: 'I wish to become a brahmacārin, mother. Of what family am I?'

She said to him: 'I do not know, my child, of what family thou art. In my youth, when I had to move about much as a servant, I conceived thee. So I do not know of what family thou art. I am Jabālā by name. Thou art Satyakāma. Say that thou art Satyakāma Jābāla.'

He going to Gautama, the son of Haridrumat, said to him: 'I wish to become a brahmacārin with thee, Sire. May I come to you?'

He said to him: 'Of what family art thou, my friend?'

He replied: 'I do not know, Sire, of what family I am. I asked my mother, and she answered: 'In my youth, when I had to move about much as a servant, I conceived thee. I do not know of what family thou art. I am Jabālā by name, thou art Satyakāma.' I am therefore Satyakāma Jābāla, Sire'.

He said to him: 'No one but a true Brāhmin would thus speak out. Go and fetch fuel, I shall initiate thee. Thou hast not swerved from the truth.'[222]

The whole philosophy of the Upaniṣads tends towards the softening of the divisions and the undermining of class hatreds and antipathies. God is the inner soul of all alike. So all must be capable of responding to the truth and therefore possess a right to be taught the truth. Sanatkumāra, the representative of the Kṣatriyas, instructs the Brāhmin Nārada about the ultimate mystery of things. Higher philosophy and religion were by no means confined to the Brāhmin class. We read of kings instructing the famous teachers of the time about the deep problems of spirit. Janaka and Ajātaśatru are Kṣatriya kings who held religious congresses where philosophical disputations were conducted. It was a period of keen intellectual

222. Chāndogya, iv. 4. 1. 4.

life. Even ordinary people were interested in the problems of philosophy. Wise men are found wandering up and down the country eager to debate. The Brāhmin editors of the Upaniṣads had so sincere a regard for truth that they were ready to admit that Kṣatriyas took an important part in these investigations.[223] Women, though they were much sheltered so far as the struggle for life was concerned, had equal rights with men in the spiritual struggle for salvation. Maitreyī, Gārgī discuss the deep problems of spirit and enter into philosophic tournaments.[224]

It is true that the Upaniṣads lay stress on knowledge as the means to salvation. 'Tarati śokam ātmavit,' the knower of Ātman, crosses all sorrow. 'Brahmavid Brahmaiva bhavati,' the knower of Brahman, becomes indeed Brahman. Because the Upaniṣads lay stress on jñāna, and look upon all morality as a preliminary to it, there are critics who contend that the Upaniṣads in their enthusiasm for jñāna relegate the will to a subordinate place. Deussen, after urging that morality has no meaning for the enlightened, says that it is not necessary even for the unenlightened. 'Moral conduct cannot contribute directly but only indirectly to the attainment of the knowledge that brings emancipation. For this knowledge is not a becoming something which had no previous existence and might be brought about by appropriate means, but it is the perception of that which previously existed from all eternity.'[225] But the Upaniṣads do not advocate knowledge in the narrow sense of the term as the sole means to salvation. 'That self cannot be gained by the knowledge of the Veda or by understanding or by much learning.'[226] Right living is also insisted on. Knowledge should be accompanied by virtue. If the candidate for theology does not possess moral and spiritual attainments, he is not admitted, whatever be his zeal and inquisitiveness.[227] Jñāna, we must make it clear, is not mere intellectual ability. It is the soul-sense. The mind of the applicant must not be too restless or too much taken up with the world to fix itself on the Highest. His heart must be purified and warmed by devotion to God. We hear in the Upaniṣads of people who are required to go through a long course of moral and spiritual discipline before they are taken up as students by those ṛṣis, the specialists in the science of God. In the Praśna

223. See Kauṣītaki Up., i. 4. 2; Bṛh., iii. 7; Chān. v. 3. 7.
224. Bṛh., ii. 4.
225. *Philosophy of the Upaniṣads*, p. 362.
226. Muṇḍaka, iii. 2. 3. See also iii. 1. 8.
227. See Kaṭha, i. 2. 24–25.

Upaniṣad, Pippalāda sends away six inquirers after God for another year of discipline. In the Chāndogya Upaniṣad, Satyakāma Jābāla is sent to the wilds of the forests to tend the teacher's cattle, that thereby he might cultivate habits of solitary reflection and come into contact with nature. The jñāna which the Upaniṣads emphasise is the faith which becomes the living law of the soul's energy. As the tree bears fruit, knowledge must realise itself in work. When we have jñāna we are said to possess truth, make it our own and be transformed by it. This is not possible for 'one who has not ceased from wicked conduct, who is not calm, who is not collected and in whose heart there is not peace.' Rāmānuja therefore interprets knowledge to be dhyāna, meditation, or upāsana, worship. There does not seem to be any justification for the interpretation that excludes moral life from knowledge. It is true that the Upaniṣads urge that mere works will not do, unless these express the feeling of unity with the self. 'Nay, even if one who does not know that self should perform here some great holy work, it will perish for him in the end. If the man worships the self only as his true spirit, his work does not perish. For whatever he desires, that he obtains from this self.'[228] This passage insists that works must be performed with knowledge. Without faith in the transcendent mere works languish.[229] The real end of man cannot be reached by mere mechanical goodness. In all works, in offering sacrifices, in observing ritual, there is self-transcendence, but not necessarily identification with the infinite. All works, must be done with the definite motive of promoting the interest of the real self. Without God our life has no aim, no existence and no support. The Upaniṣads condemn the rites and sacrifices performed with the sole idea of bringing about large returns of outward good either in this world or in the next. We should not do our duty with the motive of purchasing shares in the other world or opening a bank account with God. In protesting against such a mechanical conception of duty in the Brāhmaṇas, the Upaniṣads lay stress on a necessary truth. But they lend no support to the view that works and knowledge are exclusive of each other, and that knowledge alone leads to salvation. The Upaniṣads insist on a life of spirit which combines both jñāna and karma.

Just as the ideal of the intellect cannot be realised so long as we remain at the intellectual level, but can be found when we transcend that level,

228. Bṛh., i. 4. 15.
229. See Bṛh., iii. 8. 10.

and rise to intuition, even so the ideal of morality cannot be reached so long as we remain at the moral level, but can be reached when we rise to religion. At the moral level the two sides of our nature, the finite and the infinite, are in conflict. The finite breathes egoism or ahaṁkāra, and gives the individual a sense of his separateness from the universal. The infinite in him rushes forth to realise itself in the world. The self-fulfilment of spirit is opposed by the tendency to the disintegration of spirit. We attempt to hold the lower nature in check through the practice of morality, but until the lower is completely spiritualised the ideal is not attained. It is when we destroy the exclusiveness of our individuality and therewith the sense of separateness that we enter the joy of religion and realise the full freedom of the spirit.

The possibility of this religious realisation is the presupposition of all morality. Without it we cannot be sure that the aspirations of morality will be realised. In the face of disasters and dreads, death and disease, the conviction that in spite of the apparent discord and contradiction all things work together for good, cheers us. Morality requires the postulate of religion. God gives us the security that all is well with the world and man is bound to win. 'When a man finds his peace and resting-place in that invisible, intangible, inexpressible, unfathomable, then has he attained to peace. If, however, a man admits therein an interval, a separation, then his unrest continues; it is, moreover, the unrest of one who imagines himself wise.'[230] With this religious guarantee the pressure of circumstance or the persecution of man fails to disquiet us. No rivalry provokes us to anger or bitterness. Religion is the inspiration of morality. Without religion morality becomes an eternal striving, a perpetual progress, an endless aspiration towards something we do not have. In religion all this is turned into realisation, enjoyment and fruition. Then is the weakness of finite endowment overcome, and the finite self becomes endowed with a meaning and a mission. When once this consciousness is reached the continuance or the cessation of bodily existence becomes a matter of indifference.[231] Man is consumed with the fire of the love of God and the service of humanity. He does not care whether the path he has to traverse is smooth

230. Bṛh., iv. 2. 4.

231. 'I have seen the wicked in great power, and spreading himself like a green bay tree. Yet he passed away, and lo, he was not: yea, I sought him, but he could not be found. Mark the perfect man, and behold the upright: for the end of that man is peace' (Psa. xxxvii. 35–37).

or rough. When a man realises the truth, evil turns away from him and is itself destroyed, just as a ball of earth hitting against a solid stone.[232]

As the intuitional level goes beyond the categories of intellect, even so does the religious level pass beyond the distinctions of good and evil. He who reaches the highest is above all laws.[233] 'Him does not afflict the thought, why have I not done what is good, why have I committed sin?'[234] He fears nothing and does not trouble himself about his deeds and misdeeds in the past. 'He the immortal is beyond both, beyond good and evil; what is done and what is left undone cause him no pain, his domain is affected by no action.' This admits the possibility of blotting out the effects of a sinful life by a sincere change of heart. On this principle is based the Christian doctrine that no amount of sin is a bar to salvation, provided an act of sure repentance has been performed. When once the soul attains the real, 'in whom to dwell is happiness imperishable', the human body is suffused with the splendour of divinity in which all that is mean and vile shrivels and dies. The question of morality has no significance. For it is no more the individual that *does* anything. His will is God's will and his life God's life. He has joined the whole, and thus become the whole. All action flows from the spring in God. There is no more the distinction between God and the individual. Dr Bosanquet, in his excellent little book on *What Religion Is*, brings out this fundamental oneness of the highest condition. 'In the purity of love and will with the supreme good, you are not only 'saved,' but you are 'free' and 'strong'.... You will not be helped by trying to divide up the unity and tell how much comes from 'you' and how much from 'God.' You have got to deepen yourself in it, or let it deepen itself in you, whatever phrase expresses the fact best to your mind'.[235]

232. Chāndogya, i. 2. 7.
233. Kauṣītaki, ii. 8; Bṛh., iv. 4. 22.
234. Tait., ii. 9.
235. Pp. 20–21. 'As a drop of water is diffused in a jar of wine, taking its taste and colour, and as molten iron becomes like to fire and casts off its form, and as the air transfused with sunlight is transformed into that same light, so that it seems not illumined but itself the light, thus in the saints every human affection must in ineffable mode be liquefied of itself and transfused into the Will of God. How could God be all, if in man anything of man remained? A certain substance will remain, but in another form, another glory, another power' (St. Bernard, quoted in *Mind*, 1913, p. 329).

Unfortunately, this central truth of religious life is not sufficiently understood by even some good students of Indian thought. The latest critic of the Upaniṣads, Dr Hume, observes: 'There is a wide difference between the Upaniṣadic theory and the theory of the Greek sages, that the man who has knowledge should thereby become virtuous in character, or that the result of teaching should be a virtuous life. Here the possession of some metaphysical knowledge actually cancels all past sins and even permits the knower unblushingly to continue in "what seems to be much evil" with perfect impunity, although such acts are heinous crimes and are disastrous in their effect for others who lack that kind of knowledge.'[236] We have already said that the knowledge of the Upaniṣads is not metaphysical acumen or dialectical subtlety, but the realisation of the highest as the supreme power at the heart of the universe. This spiritual perception is possible only with a thorough transformation of human nature in its theoretical and practical aspects. What Dr Hume calls 'the possession of some metaphysical knowledge' is possible only for the pure in heart. They have perfect freedom. 'In that highest state a thief is not a thief, a murderer not a murderer. He is not followed by good, nor followed by evil, for he then overcomes all the sorrows of the heart.'[237] The free can do what they choose with perfect impunity, but this freedom is not 'the madness of license.'[238] The mystic becomes a law unto himself and the lord of himself and of the world in which he lives. Laws and regulations are necessary for those men who do not naturally conform to the dictates of conscience. But for those who have risen above their selfish egos, morality becomes the very condition of their being, and law is fulfilled in love. There is no possibility of evil-doing in them. Pressure from without is converted into an inward acceptance. Till the spiritual life is won, the law of morality appears to be an external command which man has to obey with effort and pain. But when the light is obtained it becomes the internal life of the spirit, working itself out unconsciously and spontaneously. The saint's action is an absolute surrender to the spontaneity of spirit, and is not an unwilling obedience to externally imposed laws. We have the free outpouring of an unselfish spirit which does not calculate the rewards of action or the penalties of omission. The conventional standards, the

236. Introduction to *The Thirteen Principal Upaniṣads*, p. 60.
237. Bṛh., iv.
238. Rabindranath Tagore, *Sadhana*, p. 18.

external duties and the ethical rules become meaningless to him. The soul delights in that supreme blessedness, perceives the unity of all, and loves the world as we love our separate selves. 'A perfectly good will would therefore be equally subject to objective laws (viz. laws of good), but could not be conceived as *obliged* thereby to act lawfully, because of itself from its subjective constitution it can only be determined by the conception of good. Therefore no *imperatives* hold for the Divine will or in general for a holy will; *ought* is here out of place, because volition is already of itself necessarily in unison with the law.'[239] The moral laws are its expression, and therefore do not bind it. Such a supreme soul is the creator of values and svarāṭ,[240] a law to himself. In the scheme of the world we have three classes of beings: (1) Those who strive after self-assertion and gratification of appetites, the bad men who, if ever they practise virtue, do so for selfish reasons, such as hope of heaven or fear of hell; (2) men who know the law and try to conform to it with great effort and trouble, since their selves are subject to discord; and (3) the saviours of the world, who have overcome the conflict of life and attained peace. They know the purpose of life and live up to it unconsciously and automatically. The Upaniṣad asks us in cases of doubt and difficulty to conduct ourselves in the manner in which the knowers of Brahman devoted to duty would do.[241] These great men go on doing their daily work, diffusing virtue as the star diffuses light and the flower perfume, without even being aware of it. Every man can realise such a condition. The possibility of becoming one with God can be established only by the actuality of it. The fact of realisation is the only proof of the possibility of the identification of man with the all-powerful spirit. According to Christian thinkers, one such complete manifestation of God in man is in the personality of Jesus. The Upaniṣads declare that all men have in them the possibility of rising to their full divine stature, and can realise it if they strive for it.

Since morality has a meaning only in the imperfect world where man is struggling to realise his highest nature, it is sometimes said that in the metaphysical system of the Upaniṣads morality does not find a worthy place. Deussen observes that when 'the knowledge of the Ātman has been gained, every action and therefore every moral action also has been

239. Kant's *Metaphysics of Morals*, p. 31 (Abbot's edition).
240. Svayam eva rājaḥ.
241. Tait. i. 11.

deprived of meaning.'[242] All through we have been indicating the basis of such complaints. Moral activity is not an end in itself. It is to be taken over into the perfect life. Only this has transcendental worth. The liberated in the fine phrase of the Talmud share with the Almighty in the work of creation. Here we have morality as obedience to a law displaced by the true idea of free service of an end, spontaneous devotion to the whole. In this state the individual being is absorbed in the Supreme. This alone has transcendental worth, but the moral struggle as preparing the way for it is not useless.

XVI

THE RELIGIOUS CONSCIOUSNESS

Religion is essentially a matter of life and experience. The Upaniṣads prescribe three stages in the growth of the religious consciousness, viz. sravaṇa, which literally means listening, manana or reflection, and nididhyāsana or contemplative meditation.[243] The first stage points to the place of tradition in religious life. For the initiation of faith in the living God, some kind of traditional revelation is necessary. 'Blessed are they that have not seen and yet have believed'. The bulk of men rest with tradition and symbol. Religion, according to the Upaniṣads, is not, however, to be confused with traditionalism. By strenuous intellectual effort, we should try to understand the essential meaning of or the truth contained in the tradition. The need for rational thought is brought out in the second stage. The mere assumption of the first stage becomes now a logical conclusion. The understanding of truth, however, is not the attainment of reality. To the highest religious consciousness, the real is not something inferred, but given. This experience of reality, this consciousness of the infinite, requires the development of a mode of apprehension distinct from that of mere reason. Nididhyāsana, or contemplative meditation, helps us to transform the logical idea into a spiritual perception, or darśana, which is another name for the effective realisation of truth already admitted. It is to stand alone, and like Whitman, after a logical study of astronomy, 'to gaze in perfect silence at the stars'. It is to hold before the mind's eye the object we seek to know. Meditation is not advised as a means to trance

242. *Philosophy of the Upaniṣads*, p. 362.

243. Bṛh., Up., ii. 4. 5; iv. 5. 6. Udayana in his *Kusumāñjali*, 1. 3. quotes a verse which mentions āgama or scripture, anumāna or inference, and dhyāna or meditation.

and catalepsy, which are most emphatically denounced, but only as a help for the mind to rest on the object. By suppressing all fluctuations of thought and the distractions of desire, we allow the mind to settle on the object, penetrate it and become one with it. The worship of God, the practice of goodness and the pursuit of truth are aids to the building up of the life of truth in the soul. While the speculative mind contemplates the being of God, the emotional nature in its passionate devotion for God loses itself in Him. The object is no more outside us as in ordinary experience. There is an intense realisation, which pulses through the whole being, a becoming one with God as it were. The worshipper grows akin to that which he worships. The object becomes not only the content of but the consciousness itself of the contemplator. The transformation of mind is in a sense the transformation of existence itself. The Upaniṣads speak to us of the intuition of minor deities as well as the ecstatic intuition of Brahman. So long as the objects intuited have limitations or traces of individuality, the ultimate goal is not reached. We must intuit Brahman to become Brahman.

It is clear that the religion of the Upaniṣads insists on a transformation of the whole nature of man. It is not a mere formal cult or an ethical discipline or a dogmatic creed. It is untrue to say that the Upaniṣads do not care for the non-intellectual sides of human nature. They provide room for an emotional as well as a speculative religion. The Upaniṣads are aware of the contradictions which ordinary religious consciousness is apt to exhibit. If God is perfect goodness, then morality is already realised, for everything that is must be the expression of a perfect will. If God is the Creator of the world, then He must bring something into existence which limits His nature. Either the world created is distinct from God the Creator, in which case He is limited by His creation, or the two are identical, a possibility which is repugnant to all religion and morality. In religion we have the will of man set over against the will of God. If the two are one, then there is no morality, for there is no independent reality of the human will. If the two are different, then God becomes limited and finite, and a finite God cannot inspire confidence in us. Again, if we attribute to God a free will, then He can overrule karma, and caprice will become the central fact; if on the other hand He is subject to laws and treats us according to our karma, then His freedom is restricted. These contradictions may lead us to think that the highest conception of God we can possibly have is not the highest reality. Religion may lag behind and have to be content with a finite God, however contradictory such a conception may be. This may be justified on the ground that it is not its main business to discover the highest truth, and that philosophically we may have to admit that all conceptions of God, however lofty they may be, are only relative.[244] While this may be the implication of the Upaniṣad theory, it becomes an explicit doctrine only when the intuitive vision of the Upaniṣads is converted into a scientific system of thought. The Upaniṣads, indeed, recognise higher and lower forms of religion.

We have to remember that the highest religion of the Upaniṣads, which insists on meditation and morality and worship of God in spirit and in truth, is not encumbered by such traditional dogmas and miracles as still hang upon the skirts of other religions. Its central principle that there is one supreme reality that manifests itself in the universe is not asserted as a dogma. It is the ultimate truth at which it is possible for human understanding to arrive. The progress of science and philosophy does not conflict with it but only confirms it. The Upaniṣads religion is the feeling of reverence and love for the great spirit. Such meditation is spiritualised bhakti. It recognises also that the distinction between subject and object melts away in the heart of religious fervour. The oneness and wholeness of the world is the supreme fact of the Upaniṣad religion. This may not satisfy the ordinary religious consciousness. Man as finite self is incapable of grasping the absolute reality. He makes an object of it set over against himself. The Absolute becomes a personal God. Though it is not the final truth, ordinary religious consciousness requires it. God is the friend and helper, the father and creator, the governor of the universe. He is said to be the supreme person (Puruṣottama), but He does not rule the world from without. In that case there would be no organic connection between Him and the world. He is the inner guide or the antaryāmi. Though a person, he is said to be above all, in all, and through all. All things are of Him, in Him and unto Him. But as Jacobi would put it, an understood God is no God at all. To imagine God is what we think is nothing less than blasphemy. Though the God of religion is a limited expression of the absolute, it is not a mere imaginative presentation. In the development of the absolute into the universe conceived by the finite mind, the first existent being is the God or the universal soul possessing self-consciousness. He is the absolute personified. The Upaniṣads do not care to identify Him with

244. See Kena, i. 5. 8.

the ideal tendency of things opposing and struggling through the non-ideal; in that case He would be reduced to the level of the finite. According to the Upaniṣads, the Absolute and God are one; we call it the supreme Brahman to emphasise its transcendence of the finite, its unknowability, its all-comprehensiveness; we call it Īśvara to emphasise the personal aspect so necessary for religious devotion. The relation between the two, the absolute Brahman and the personal Īśvara, may be like that of the true Lord to the idol.[245] Yet the two are one. The absolute is both personal and impersonal.[246] Meditation on the supreme becomes the passionate devotion to the Lord of the universe. The individual looks upon God as something transcendent, and feels acutely the need of grace. Devaprasāda, or grace of God, is the condition of the deliverance of man from bondage. 'This Ātman cannot be attained through study or intelligence or much learning—whom he wishes to attain by him it can be attained. To him the Ātman reveals its true nature.'[247] Sometimes the religious passion grows so fervent that the devotee exclaims: 'It is He who inspires to do good works the man whom He will lead on high, and it is He who inspires to do evil works the man whom He will lead downwards.'[248] The oneness of God and man is realised only after a good deal of discipline and exercise. When the ideal of religion is reached, the personal conception is transcended. The higher we go in religious experience, the more we perceive the identity between the object of worship and the worshipper, till at last the two become one. Then there is no worship in the traditional sense of the term. The absolute is felt as a boundless spirit pervading the whole universe and flooding the soul of man. Our limits fall away and the defects incident to man's imperfection dissolve. The end of religion is the transcendence of religion. Ideal religion overcomes the duality with which it starts. Religious worship starts with fear, passes through reverence, love and communion with the eternal, and culminates in the ecstatic life, where God and the soul melt into each other. Religious worship has to be accepted until the perfect condition is reached.

Imperfect forms of worship are admitted as preparatory to the perfect. The Upaniṣads are led into inconsistent notions when they try to do too much justice to the conflicting creeds which prevailed among the peoples of the time. Some believed in magic; some tried to subdue the powers of

245. Śaṁkara's Commentary on Tait., i. 6. 'Śālagrama iva viṣṇoḥ.'
246. Mūrtāmūrtam. Śaṁkara's Commentary on Tait., i. 6.
247. Muṇḍaka, iii. 2. 3; Kaṭha, ii. 23.
248. Kauṣītaki, iii. 8.

nature by concentration and other ascetic practices; some were lost in a futile formalism; some worshipped the Vedic gods; some tried to effect an escape from this world of change by means of spiritual insight. The Upaniṣad thinkers, conscious of the weakness of human understanding which has to limit the God present in all things, at all times, and in all places to some special place, time and thing, recognise that if lower forms of worship are dismissed, there is the risk of banishing God altogether out of life. Some worship is better than none, and so it is said that we become whatever form we worship. 'Let him worship the Brahman as support, and he becomes supported. Let him worship Brahman as greatness, and he becomes great. Let him worship Brahman as mind, he becomes endowed with mind. And let him worship Brahman as Brahman, and he will become possessed of Brahman.'[249] God reveals Himself in different ways to different men. This is not to be confused with the doctrine of incarnations, which is unknown to the Upaniṣads. The Upaniṣads consider the highest form of religion to be spiritual meditation on the absolute; next in rank is the passionate devotion to the one immanent Lord; lowest of all is the worship of the Vedic devas and other deities.

It is frequently urged that the Upaniṣads do not admit of any religious worship. Dr Urquhart writes: 'However clearly the attitude of true worship may seem to be indicated, there is a constant refrain sometimes even in the same verse to the effect that the self who is to be worshipped is the self of the worshipper, and that consequently there is no such distinction between the two (God and man), as is demanded by the fully theistic relation.'[250] The Upaniṣads are emphatic about the oneness of God and man. The relative difference we recognise between the two is taken over in a higher unity. 'If a man worships another divinity with the idea that he and the God are different, he does not know.'[251] The unity of spirit is the first principle of the Upaniṣad doctrine. Divine immanence is its central fact. If that is inconsistent with religious worship, it means only that theism has no place for true religion, since a true theism must accept divine immanence. All true religion declares that finite things are not self-sustained, are not self-evolved, but that God is over all, through all, in all, the ground of existence, the source of life and the goal of desire. 'If I ascend up into

249. Tait., iii. 10; see also Chān., i. 3. 12; Bṛh., i. 2. 13.
250. *The Upaniṣads and Life*, p. 60.
251. Bṛh., i. 4. 10.

heaven, thou art there: if I make my bed in hell, behold, Thou art there. If I take the wings of the morning, and dwell in the uttermost parts of the sea; even there shall Thy hand lead me.'[252] 'Am I a God, at hand, saith the Lord and not a God afar off? Can any hide himself in secret places that I shall not see him? saith the Lord; Do not I fill Heaven and earth?' 'In God, we live and move and have our being,'[253] and 'He who dwelleth in love, dwelleth in God, and God in him.'[254] All true religion recognises the immanence of God and is highly mystic.

XVII

MOKṢA OR RELEASE

Is the highest state of religious realisation, the atonement with the supreme godhead, a mere vanishing into nothingness? The Upaniṣad view is that there is in the highest condition a disintegration of individuality, a giving up of selfish isolation, but it is not a mere nothing or death. 'As the flowing rivers disappear in the sea, losing their name and form, thus a wise man, freed from name and form, goes to the divine person who is beyond all.'[255] The Upaniṣads do not recognise the ultimate reality of the narrow individual self. Those who pray for personal immortality take their stand on the ultimateness of the individual, and urge its maintenance beyond the world. The real in finite life, what is best in the individual's nature, is the infinite, and that persists beyond the limits of physical existence. Nothing of value is lost. Whatever spiritual values we seek after on earth and find imperfectly, we possess in the highest condition absolutely. As human beings we reach our ideals imperfectly, in flashes and moments of insight. In the highest condition we attain to them perfectly, completely and absolutely. The Taittirīya Upaniṣad points out how the bliss we have in the world is only a shadow of the divine bliss, a feeble apology for it.[256] After all our troubles in the sea of life we do not reach a desert shore where we are obliged to die of hunger. The liberated condition must be looked upon as the fullest expression of the self. The ascent to God will be a lapse into the void or the abyss, if the ultimate Brahman is itself looked upon as an

252. Psalm cxxxix.
253. St Paul.
254. St John.
255. Muṇḍaka, iii. 2. 8. See also Praśna, vi. 5.
256. See ii. 8; Kauṣītaki, i. 3. 5; Bṛh., iv. 3. 33.

abstraction. Then the goal of man is annihilation. The Upaniṣads dispute such a conclusion. The highest is a state of rapture and ecstasy, a condition of ānanda, where the creature as creature is abolished, but becomes one with the Creator, or more accurately realises his oneness with Him. We cannot describe this perfection adequately. We use symbols. The nature of eternal life is a condition of ānanda or freedom, a state of joyous expansion of the soul, where heaven and earth are felt to flow together.

Its nature cannot be characterised except through image and metaphor. We have some states in this life which may be taken as illustrations of eternal or timeless existence. Baron Von Hügel speaks to us of trance conditions which 'appear to the experiencing soul, in proportion to their concentration, as timeless, i.e. as non-successive, simultaneous, hence as *eternal*.... The eternity of the soul is not here a conclusion drawn from the apparent God-likeness in other respects, of the soul when in this condition, but the eternity, on the contrary, is the very centre of the experience itself, and is the chief inducement to the soul for holding itself to be divine. The soul's immortality cannot be experienced in advance of death, whilst its eternity, in the sense indicated, is or seems to be directly experienced in such 'this-life' states. Hence the belief in immortality is here derivative, that in eternity is primary.'[257] In the enjoyment of a melody, the contemplation of a work of art, in grasping an argument as a whole, we have the mystical condition, the sight of God, the experience of eternity.[258]

257. *Eternal Life*, p. 27.

258. St Augustine in his *Confessions*, says: 'Suppose all the tumult of the flesh in us were hushed for ever, and all sensible images of earth and sea and air were put to silence; suppose the heavens were still and even the soul spoke no words to itself, but passed beyond all thought of itself; suppose all dreams and revelations of imagination were hushed with every word and sign and everything that belongs to this transitory world; suppose they were all silenced—though, if they speak to one who hears, what they say is, 'we made not ourselves, but He made us who abides for ever'—yet suppose they only uttered this and then were silent, when they had turned the ears of the hearer to Him who made them, leaving Him to speak alone, not through them but through Himself, so that we could hear His words, not through any tongue of flesh nor by the voice of an angel, nor in thunder, nor in any likeness that hides what it reveals; suppose then that the God whom through such manifestations we have learnt to love were to be revealed to us directly without any such mediation—just as, but now, we reached out of ourselves and touched by a flash of insight the eternal wisdom that abides above all; suppose, lastly, that this vision of God were to be prolonged for ever, and all other inferior modes of

The temporal happenings become eternal when viewed in relation to the absolute, and thus assigned their true worth.

Since from our human point of view it is not possible to describe the fullness of the absolute reality, the Upaniṣads do not describe precisely the condition of ultimate freedom. There are two conflicting accounts running throughout: that it is a state of likeness to God, and that it is a state of oneness with God.

There are passages where the individual is said to become one with the highest. 'The praṇava is the bow, the Ātman is the arrow, and the Brahman is said to be its mark. It should be hit by one who is self-collected, and that which hits becomes like the arrow, one with the mark, that is Brahman'.[259] The Ātman becomes one with Brahman.[260] Here absolute identity between the soul and Brahman is asserted. Again, 'All these become one in the highest imperishable Brahman.'[261] 'He becomes merged in the supreme undecaying Ātman.'[262] 'He becomes omniscient and becomes all'.[263] 'He enters into all.'[264] The redeemed soul enters into all things and becomes all things in spirit. 'Having attained him, the seers content with their knowledge, their purpose accomplished, free from all desire, and with full composure, having attained the all-pervading Ātman on all sides, ever concentrating their minds, enter into everything.'[265] They who see the whole universe held firm in the one all-enfolding presence cannot have any sorrow or torment. 'Having without doubt well ascertained the significance of the knowledge of the Vedānta, the seekers, their minds purified by dint of renunciation attain the worlds of that Brahman, and when their body falls, their Ātman being one with the highest immortal Brahman, are absolved all round.'[266] The liberated soul feels his oneness with God so

vision were to be taken away, so that this alone should ravish and absorb the beholder and entrance him in mystic joy, and our very life for ever like the moment of clear insight and inspiration to which we rose—is not this just what is meant by the words "Enter thou into the joy of thy Lord"?'

259. Muṇḍaka, ii. 2. 2. See also Kaṭha, ii. 15.

260. Śaravat tanmayo bhavet.

261. Muṇḍaka, iii. 2. 7. Sarva ekībhavanti.

262. Praśna, iv. 9.

263. iv. 10. Sa sarvajñaḥ sarvo bhavati.

264. i. vii. Sarvam evāviśanti.

265. Muṇḍaka, iii. 2. 5.

266. iii. 2. 6.

intensely that he calls himself the creator of the world. 'I am the food, I am the food-eater. I am the subject, I am the object, I am the two together. I am the firstborn, the destroyer of the world also. I am the sunlike light. I am the centre of the world, of immortal gods.'[267] These passages seem to imply that there is no sense of individuality, and therefore no possibility of action in the highest state. It seems to be a survival without consciousness, where body is dissolved and mind extinguished and all is lost in a boundless darkness. If we please, we may call it the sleep without dreams, or the peace without understanding. When Yājñavalkya explains it to Maitreyī in the words: 'As a lump of salt which is thrown into the water dissolves and cannot be gathered up again, but wherever water is drawn, it is salty, so truly is it with this great being, the endless, the unlimited, the fullness of knowledge, from these beings it came into view and with them it vanishes. There is no consciousness after death,' Maitreyī observes; 'This speech of thine, that there is no consciousness after death perplexes me.' Yājñavalkya replies: 'I tell thee nothing perplexing, it is quite comprehensible. Where there is a duality of existences, one can see the other, one can smell the other, one can speak to the other, one can hear the other, one can think of the other, one can apprehend the other. But where everything has turned into his Ātman, by whom and whom shall he see, by whom and whom shall he smell, by whom and to whom shall he speak, by whom and whom shall he hear, think and apprehend? By whom shall he apprehend him through whom he apprehends this universe? Through whom shall he apprehend him the apprehender?' From this it is clear that in some way hard for our intellect to grasp the soul attains liberation devoid of any activity, perception, thought or consciousness, which are all symptomatic of a dualistic vision. These activities rest on the opposition of subject and object, and are possible only in the world of relativity. In the absolute world, all plurality is said to disappear with the resulting activities of perception and action. It is then the everlasting, unchangeable itself, in whose perfection all movement is stilled, all colours pale and all sounds pass away. This is the negative side of freedom, which is all that is open to finite intelligence. There is also the positive side. Simply because we as finite cannot describe the fullness of the absolute state, it does not become a negative blank. Negatively, the soul seems to lose all distinction and become something

267. Tait., iii.

which is neither this nor that, but some vague indeterminate somewhat. Those careless beings who make a show of sleeping through it all may really be very active. When the positive aspect is emphasised, the liberated soul is looked upon as a perfected individual with a status of absolute equality with the supreme soul.[268] The passages which declare that the liberated soul traverses the worlds, obtaining all its wishes, indicate that the freed soul has yet an active existence. 'Traversing these worlds, having the food he likes, taking the form he likes, he sits singing songs.'[269] And yet he has the feeling that he is one with God. According to the Chāndogya, immortality is lifting oneself up to the region of the deity.[270] Muṇḍaka holds it to be the companionship with God.[271] Absolute likeness with God is also suggested.[272] To make room for such individual action it is said that the individual becomes like God. Whatever differences there might be about the exact nature of the highest condition, one thing is clear, that it is a state of activity, full of freedom and perfection. Strictly speaking, we cannot describe that state, but if a description is wanted, it is best to consider it to be a state of divine life. The self is not annihilated any more than the ray of the sun is lost in the sun, the wave of the sea in the ocean, the notes of music in the one harmony. The song of the individual is not lost in the music of the world march. It is the same for ever and yet not the same. It is said that the liberated soul becomes one with all and lives a life in unity with God. The positive description seems to suggest a sense of individuality which helps him to act in this world, though this individuality is not based on any self-feeling. This individualisation of life seems to be necessary for the fulfilment of the joy of the one supreme. Even though for purposes of self-expression there is this possession of a centre of individuality, we are told that the soul is conscious of its glory and the greatness of immortality. It feels that God is at work in the cosmic drama, where the divine consciousness plays and acts. The liberated individual also plays in the same drama with full possession of the truth. There is nothing which does not bend to his purposes. 'He maketh the winds His angels, and the flaming fires His ministers.'

268. Paramaṁ sāmyam upaiti. Muṇḍaka, iii. 1. 3.
269. Tait., iii. 10. 8.
270. ii. 22.
271. iii. 2. 6.
272. iii. 1. 3.

The philosophical reconciliation of the varying descriptions had to wait till a later day. It is possible to eliminate the sense of egoism even in this life, and he who achieves perfection in this life is called a jīvanmukta. His joy of immortality realises itself in the freedom of movement.

The vagueness of the Upaniṣad doctrines led to the development of different theories from the same texts. Some Buddhists interpret the Upaniṣad idea to be an entire loss, some Vedāntins as the self-immersion of the individual soul in the supreme. Others hold that it is an eternal existence absorbed in the thought, love and enjoyment of the supreme, and not an annihilation. The cry of the devotee poet, 'I want to eat sugar, and do not want to become sugar,' expresses this view. The religious philosophers of Vaiṣṇavism and Śaivism adopt this standpoint. But almost all Indian thinkers are agreed that mokṣa is release from birth and death. Union with God is another name for becoming eternal. When 'eternity' is translated into the terms of the phenomenal world, it becomes birthlessness and deathlessness.

XVIII

EVIL AND SUFFERING

The problem of evil is a stumbling-block to all monistic systems. The metaphysical problem of the rise of the finite has already been dealt with. We are now concerned with the question of moral evil. In the Vedic hymns, virtue is conformity with the Vedic precepts and vice non-conformity. In the Upaniṣads knowledge of life eternal is virtue and ignorance vice. Conduct expressive of this false vision and consequent isolation of self is evil conduct. All objects of the world, according to the Upaniṣads, are to be sought after as gateways to God. If we look upon them as solid and secluded, and regard ourselves as separate units, then we sin morally. Error is the denial by the ego of the supremacy of the whole, or its own assertion of self-sufficiency. Evil is the denial in conduct by the ego of the supremacy of the whole. Sin is the product of the shallow insight, breeding selfish egoism, that hugs its own narrowness and shrinks from all sacrifice. The Upaniṣads do not say that evil is illusion or that evil is permanent. In either case it will be the duty of man to bow submissively to it. Evil is unreal in the sense that it is bound to be transmuted into good. It is real to the extent that it requires effort to transform its nature.

Sin is making self higher than God, while holiness is displacing self-consciousness by God-consciousness. Man can never cling to evil for all time. It is in a state of unstable equilibrium, being opposed to the nature of things. Morality, according to the Upaniṣads, expresses the true nature of things. Only the good can ultimately prevail. 'The true prevails, not the untrue.'[273] Evil is something negative, self-contradictory, a principle of death; good, positive and real, a principle of life. That evil cannot be all satisfying is plain from the pathetic unrest of the present day world, with all its wealth and luxury and control over mechanism.

There are many passages which emphasise the difficulty of attaining Brahman. 'He of whom many are not even able to hear, whom many, even when they hear of Him, do not comprehend; wonderful is a man when found who is able to teach Him the self, wonderful is he who comprehends Him.'[274] The path that leads to salvation is like 'the sharp edge of a razor, difficult to cross and hard to tread.'[275] The realisation of spirit is not a smooth development or uninterrupted advance. The progress to perfection is through pain and suffering. The hard flints must come into violent conflict before they can produce the sparks of fire. The chick has to undergo the pain of separation from the shell before it can reach the intangible light and air. Moral conduct seems to go against the grain of things. The good and the pleasant are not always conjoined. 'The good is one thing, the pleasant another. These two have different objects and chain a man. It is well with him who chooses the good. He who chooses the pleasant misses his end.'[276] Pleasure seems to lie in the satisfaction of the natural impulse, and the good requires the taming of the forces of nature. Man in the moral scheme seems to be seeking the true self which he has somehow missed. But until the true self is realised, the moral law assumes the form of an external compulsion. The good does not seem to be the pleasant. Morality implies a wrestling with the lower tendency, the pursuit of which appears pleasant. When man struggles to free himself from his natural entanglements, life becomes intense with strife. Suffering is the condition of progress. Struggle is the law of existence and sacrifice the principle of evolution. The more the struggle and sacrifice, the greater are the joy and the freedom. All progress has this destructive side. Every gain in spirit involves a loss in nature. But the loss is not a real loss. Were it real and absolute, then the loss would be a dead loss and we could not afford it. Suffering is

273. Muṇḍaka, iii. 1. 6.
274. Kaṭha, i. 2. 7; B.G., ii. 29.
275. Ibid., i. 3. 14.
276. Ibid., i. 2. 1. 2.

the ransom the son of man has to pay if he would attain his crown. It reveals to us the incomplete nature of the self and world. 'It is good for me that I have been afflicted,' says the Psalmist: for suffering is the messenger of God revealing to us the imperfection of the world, the episodic nature of earthly life. The discipline of suffering has also its use in the education of the spirit. Resistance drives the soul to put forth its whole strength, and thus compels it to grow. The darker the sky the brighter will the stars shine. Suffering cannot be abolished so long as spiritual life has to be lived under human conditions. Until the whole being is made an offering to God, the process of gradual rise through suffering cannot cease. 'Man verily is the sacrifice,' says the Upaniṣad.[277] Life is a perpetual dying till we are face to face with God. Life is a place of torment, where the human spirit writhes to possess the eternal. Veil after veil is to be withdrawn. The illusions of life are to be torn away and our cherished dreams dispersed before the life divine can be reached.

XIX

KARMA

The law of karma is the counter-part in the moral world of the physical law of uniformity. It is the law of the conservation of moral energy. The vision of law and order is revealed in the Ṛta or the Ṛg-Veda. According to the principle of karma there is nothing uncertain or capricious in the moral world.[278] We reap what we sow. The good seed brings a harvest of good, the evil of evil. Every little action has its effect on character. Man knows that some of the tendencies to action which now exist in him are the result of conscious or intelligent choice on his part. Conscious actions tend to become unconscious habits, and not unnaturally the unconscious tendencies we find in ourselves were regarded as the result of past conscious actions. We cannot arrest the process of moral evolution any more than we can stay the sweep of the tides or the course of the stars. The attempt to overleap the law of karma is as futile as the attempt to leap over one's shadow. It is the

277. Chān., iii. 16. 1.

278. Carlyle puts this principle thus: 'Fool! thinkest thou that because no Boswell is there to note thy jargon, it therefore dies and is buried? Nothing dies, nothing can die. The idlest word thou speakest is a seed cast into time, which brings forth fruit to all eternity.' 'Be not deceived; God is not mocked: for whatsoever a man soweth, that shall he also reap' (Gal. vi. 7).

psychological principle that our life carries with it a record that time cannot blur or death erase. To remedy the defects of the old Vedic idea, that redemption from sin could be had by sacrifices to gods, great emphasis is laid on the law of karma. It proclaims the awful doom, the soul that sinneth, it shall die. Not through sacrifices, but through good deeds does a man become good. 'A man becomes good by good deeds and bad by bad deeds.'[279] Again, 'Man is a creature of will. According as he believes in this world, so will he be when he is departed.'[280] So we are asked to will the good and do the good. 'Whatever world he covets by his mind, and whatever objects he wishes, for the man of pure mind, he gains those worlds and those objects; therefore let him who longs for bhūti, manifested power, worship him who knows the Ātman.'[281] The requital of action makes saṁsāra with birth and death, beginningless and endless. The karma theory embraces in its sweep men and gods, animals and plants.

Since the sense of individual responsibility is emphasised, there are critics who think that the karma doctrine is inconsistent with social service. It is said that there is no emphasis on the bearing of one another's burdens. As a matter of fact, the Upaniṣads hold that we can be free from karma only by social service. So long as we perform selfish work we are subject to the law of bondage. When we perform disinterested work we reach freedom. 'While thus you live there is no way by which karma clings to you.'[282] What binds us to the chain of birth and death is not action as such but selfish action. In an age when the individual was ever ready to shirk responsibility for what he did by throwing the burden on providence or stars or some other being than his own self, the doctrine of karma urged that a man 'fetters himself by himself, like a bird by its nest.'[283] What looms over us is no dark fate but our own past. We are not the victims of a driving doom. Suffering is the wages of sin. There is no question that such an idea is a great incentive to good conduct. It only says that there are some limiting conditions of human action. We did not make ourselves. When we come up against the impossible, we realise that we cannot do anything we please. Karma rightly understood does not discourage moral effort, does not fetter the mind or chain the will. It only says that every act is the inevitable outcome of the

279. Bṛh., iii. 2. 13.
280. Chān., iii. 14. 1. See also Bṛh., iv. 4. 5.
281. Chān., iii. 1. 10.
282. Īśā, ii.
283. Maitrāyaṇī Up., iii. 2.

preceding conditions. There is a tendency of the cause to pass into the effect. If the spirit, which is on a higher plane than nature, does not assert its freedom, past conduct and present environment will account completely for the actions of man. Man is not a mere product of nature. He is mightier than his karma. If the law is all, then there is no real freedom possible. Man's life is not the working of merely mechanical relations. There are different levels—the mechanical, the vital, the sentient, the intellectual and the spiritual—these currents cross and recross and inter-penetrate each other. The law of karma, which rules the lower nature of man, has nothing to do with the spiritual in him. The infinite in man helps him to transcend the limitations of the finite. The essence of spirit is freedom. By its exercise man can check and control his natural impulses. That is why his life is something more than a succession of mechanically determined states. His acts to be free must not be expressive of the mere force of habit or shock of circumstance, but of the freedom of the inner soul. The spiritual nature is the basis of his initiative and endeavour. The mechanical part is under constraint. Were man merely the sum of natural conditions, he would be completely subject to the law of karma. But there is a soul in him which is the master. Nothing external can compel it. We are sure that the material forces of the world must bend to the spiritual rule, and so can the law of karma be subjected to the freedom of spirit. Man can have the highest freedom only when he becomes one with God. 'He who departs from this world, without having known the soul or those true desires, his part in all worlds is a life of constraint. But he who departs from this world after having known the soul and those true desires, his part in all worlds is a life of freedom.'[284] Becoming one with God is the attainment of the highest freedom. The more we live in the presence of God, the more we assert the rights of spirit, the more free we are; the more we lose our grip on the whole to which we belong, the more selfish we are, the more is our bondage to karma. Man oscillates between nature and spirit, and so is subject to both freedom and necessity.

Karma has a cosmic as well as a psychological aspect. Every deed must produce its natural effect in the world; at the same time it leaves an impression on or forms a tendency in the mind of man. It is this tendency or saṁskāra or vāsana that inclines us to repeat the deed we have once done. So all deeds have their fruits in the world and effects on the mind.

284. Chān., viii. 1. 6.

So far as the former are concerned, we cannot escape them, however much we may try. But in regard to mental tendencies we can control them. Our future conduct holds all possibilities. By self-discipline we can strengthen the good impulses and weaken the bad ones.

The actions of men are capable of prediction and pre-calculation. If rational, they will show certain properties: we shall detect in them an inward coherence, an unselfish purpose, and so on. But from that we cannot assume that the acts are determined in any mechanical sense. Every living soul is potentially free. His acts are not a mere unwinding of the thread from a reel. Man possesses freedom as the focus of spiritual life. God has not granted him freedom from outside. He possesses freedom because he is rooted in God. The more he realises his true divine nature, the more free is he.

It is sometimes argued that the law of karma is inconsistent with theism.[285] Karma is a blind unconscious principle governing the whole universe. It is not subject to the control even of God. We do not require a judge to administer a mechanical law. The principle of karma is not inconsistent with the reality of the absolute Brahman. The moral law of karma is the expression of the nature of the absolute. Anthropomorphically we can say a divine power controls the process. Ṛta is the law in the Vedas. Varuṇa is the lord of Ṛta. Karma refers to the unchanging action of the gods.[286] It is an expression of the nature of reality. It renders impossible any arbitrary interference with moral evolution. The same conclusion is arrived at by modern theories of scientific law and habit, which are irreconcilable with capricious interference. If miracles are necessary to prove God, then science has killed God for all time. Divine interference is regulated by laws. God does not act by private volitions, as Malebranche would say. Only the karma theory can give us a just conception of the spiritual universe. It brings out the living rational nature of the whole. It is the mechanism by which spirit works. The freedom of the spiritual world is expressed in the world of nature by the iron law of mechanical necessity.[287] Freedom

285. See MacNicol, *Indian Theism*, p. 225.

286. Devānāṁ dhruvāṇi vratāni.

287. We need not oppose the law of karma to the will of God as conceived in the Upaniṣads. The two are not exclusive of each other. Should there be many gods as in the Vedic theory, the gods themselves will be subject to karma. 'The Gods cannot save even a man whom they love when the dread fate of death lays hold upon him. Zeus himself laments that it is "fate" that his son Sarpedon, dearest to him of all men, must die at the hands of Patroclus. He "does not venture to undo what

and karma are the two aspects of the same reality. If God is immanent in the cosmos, then His spirit resides in the machine. The divine expresses itself in law, but law is not God. The Greek fate, the Stoic reason, and the Chinese Tao, are different names for the primary necessity of law.

There is no doctrine that is so valuable in life and conduct as the karma theory. Whatever happens to us in this life we have to submit in meek resignation, for it is the result of our past doings. Yet the future is in our power, and we can work with hope and confidence. Karma inspires hope for the future and resignation to the past. It makes men feel that the things of the world, its fortunes and failures, do not touch the dignity of the soul. Virtue alone is good, not rank or riches, not race or nationality. Nothing but goodness is good.

XX

FUTURE LIFE

In the Upaniṣads we find an advance on the Vedic and the Brāhmanical conceptions of future life, though there is not yet any consistent theory about it. It is the idea of rebirth that is the prominent one in the Upaniṣads. The earliest form of this idea occurs in the Śatapatha Brāhmaṇa, where the notion of being born again after death and dying repeatedly is coupled with that of retribution. It is said that those who have right knowledge and perform their duties are born again after death for immortality, while those who do not have such knowledge and neglect their duties are reborn again and again, becoming the prey of death.[288] The Brāhmaṇa assumes births and deaths only in the next world. In the Upaniṣads the belief is transformed into the doctrine of rebirth in the world. We cannot say that the two have been reconciled. Sometimes we find them together. Good and evil actions experience a twofold retribution, once in the other world and again by a renewed life on earth. It is said that the soul, after it has journeyed to heaven in radiant form on the burning of the corpse, returns thence immediately through the three regions to a new existence.[289] There are evidences that the belief in rebirth was only being matured in the

---

fate decrees." It is impossible even for a God to avoid the fate that is ordained. "What is ordained," says Athena in Euripides, using Anaximander's word, "is master of the Gods and thee."' Cornford: *From Religion to Philosophy*, pp. 12, 13.

288. Cf. The conception of punarmṛtyu. Kauṣītaki Brāhmaṇa, xxv. 1.

289. Bṛh., vi. 2. 14.

time of the Upaniṣads, since some passages of the Upaniṣads are not familiar with it.[290] The earliest passages incorporating the belief of rebirth are Chāndogya, v. 3. 10, and Bṛhadāraṇyaka, vi. 2.

That the highest kind of immortality is becoming one with Brahman is clearly enunciated in the Upaniṣads. When Gods were the supreme realities, freedom lay in union with them. Now Brahman is the first principle of things and the ultimate basis of the world. So life eternal is union with Brahman. When we fall short of our highest freedom, we are bound down in the sphere of time and are hurried from one state of being into another. The undelivered soul is subject to the law of birth and death, and has to work out its destiny by lives on earth. While true immortality is for the liberated, survival in time is for the bound. We hear the prayer, 'May I never go to the white, toothless, devouring abode.'[291] The kind of birth depends on the nature of the work done. It is called heaven when the individual lifts himself up to a higher life, and hell when he throws himself down into a lower one. This existence in saṁsāra is not the true existence of the soul. We have to bear the servitude of saṁsāra so long as the finite elements cling to us. With the finite we can never reach the absolute, however near we may come to it. Progress is a ceaseless growth or perpetual approximation. When the finite element is completely given up, then oneness with God is realised, and there is no return to saṁsāra.[292] Saṁsāra is intended to discipline the spirit.

The world of nature reveals to us how all things on earth are impermanent and unreal. We find in it recurrent death and rebirth of all things. 'Like corn decays the mortal, like corn is he born again.'[293] In destruction we find only the precursor of renewed existence. Death is only the gate of life. Though the law of karma is not yet committed to any precise equivalence between merit and experience, still it is asserted that the nature of the birth depends on the conduct of man. 'Those whose conduct has been good will quickly attain some good birth, the birth of a Brāhmin, a Kṣatriya or a Vaiśya. But those whose conduct is evil will quickly attain an evil birth the birth of a hog, or dog, or a caṇḍāla.'[294]

290. Bṛh., i. 5. 16.
291. Chān., viii. 14. 1.
292. Chān., iv. 16. 6.
293. Kaṭha, i. 8.
294. Chān., v. 10. 7.

Between one life and another there is a persisting identity, though our consciousness may not testify to it. This is not a great weakness, since large portions of human life tend sometimes to be forgotten. The theory is concerned more with the conservation of values than with the continuance of consciousness. Since the Brahman which is the universal soul is not subject to bondage, that which persists from birth to birth is said to be what a man does or his karma. 'Does the soul survive bodily death? Yājñavalkya, if after the death of the man his spirit goes into fire, his breath into wind, his eyes into the sun, his mind into the moon, his ear into the directions of space, his body into the earth, his self into the ether, the hair of his body into plants, the hair of his head into trees, the blood and semen into water—what then becomes of the man?' is the question put by Ārtabhāga to Yājñavalkya. They arrive at the conclusion, 'verily one becomes good through good deeds, evil through evil deeds.'[295] The reality of life is character, not body or mind. It survives the disruption of death. The Upaniṣads hold that while karma changes, the universal self endures. If with some Buddhists we dismiss Brahman as useless, we shall have to say that only karma persists.

There is no mention of animals in the teaching of Yājñavalkya, which ends with the fourth book of the Bṛhadāraṇyaka Upaniṣad, though in some later passages of the same Upaniṣad,[296] as well as in the Chāndogya, Kauṣītaki, etc., the migration into animal bodies is also mentioned. The idea may have been derived from the beliefs of the aboriginal tribes. In almost all regions of the world the untutored savage thought that human souls could pass into animal bodies. The Aryan invaders, in their commerce with the original inhabitants of India, came across the notion that animals and plants possessed souls, and human souls sometimes took their dwelling in them. The holiness of life in all things, the equality of origin in the flower, the insect, the animal and the man were the fundamental ideas of the Upaniṣads, which betrayed them into an acceptance of this position. It has also great practical value. The tenderness shown to animals in the āśramas of the forests favoured the doctrine. Proud man was required to get rid of his snobbery and exclusiveness, and admit with the humility of a St Francis that the black beetle was his brother. This is not strange when

295. Bṛh., iii. 2. 13.
296. vi. 3. 16.

we think of the modern theories of evolution and their emphasis on the close affinity between men and animals.

No philosophy could discard its past. The Upaniṣad theory of future life had to reckon with the old Vedic doctrine of rewards and punishments in another world. The conservative spirit of man tried to combine the new idea of rebirth with the earlier eschatology, which spoke of the joyous world of the spirits of the dead where Yama presided and the joyless regions of darkness. This led to a complication of the Upaniṣad theory, which had to distinguish three ways after death. 'For we have heard even the saying of a ṛṣi, "I heard of two paths for men, one leading to the fathers, the other leading to the devas. On those paths all that lives, moves on, whatever there is between father Sky and mother Earth."'[297] The Upaniṣads mention the two paths by which a departed soul proceeds to enjoy the fruits of its karma done in its life-time on earth. One is called the devayāna or the arcirmārga, the path of light, and the other pitṛyāna or the dhūmamārga, the path of darkness. The former leads to the plane of Brahmā or satyaloka, through the different spheres of Agni, etc. From this there is no return. Devayāna had a meaning so long as Brahmā was looked upon as an objective being, seated on a high throne in his own palace, to which the good went. But when the identity of self and Brahman is reached, the throne of Brahmā totters and devayāna becomes the pathway to the oneness with the highest. The pitṛyāna takes to candraloka or the region of the moon through the different spheres of smoke, night, etc. He who goes to the devayāna does not come back to this world, but he who goes to the pitṛyāna, after enjoying the fruits of his good acts, comes back to the earth. There are many differences in detail. According to the Kauṣītaki, all go to the moon after death, though from the moon a few go by the path of the fathers to Brahmā, while others return to the various forms of existence, ranging from man to worm, according to the quality of their work and degree of knowledge.[298] The devayāna and pitṛyāna correspond to the kingdom of light and the kingdom of darkness or ajñāna, which involves us in saṁsāra. A third path leading to the joyless regions enveloped in darkness is also mentioned.[299] 'Those who make a gift of barren cows, which have drunk

297. Bṛh., vi. 2. 2.
298. i. 2. 3.
299. Bṛh., iv. 11.

water and eaten hay and given their milk, themselves go to the joyless regions.'[300] This is the third road on which creatures which live and die, worms, insects, creeping things crawl.[301] The freed man who realises his identity with Brahman need not go anywhere for his salvation.[302] Even where he is, he enjoys Brahman. 'His prāṇas do not go anywhere. Being Brahman he is merged in Brahman.'[303] Those who realise freedom do not go through any path, but those who have to reach it by an ascent go through the devayāna. Since a gradual ascent is described, it is said to be the path of kramamukti.

The mechanism of rebirth is explained in different ways. 'Then his knowledge and his works and his previous experience take him by the hand. As a caterpillar which has wriggled to the top of a blade of grass draws itself over to a new blade, so does the man after he has put aside his body draw himself over to a new existence.'[304] Again: 'As a goldsmith taking a piece of gold forms another shape with it, more new and agreeable, so throwing off this body and obtaining that state of knowledge, the soul forms a shape which is more new and agreeable, suited to the world.' 'As the sculptor takes the material from a statue and chisels therefrom another, newer, fairer form, so this soul also, after it has taken off the body and rid itself of ignorance, creates for itself another, newer, fairer form, whether of the fathers, of the Gandharvas, or the gods, or Prajāpati, or Brahmā, or other beings.'[305] It is sometimes said that the soul at death gathers into itself the vital spirits and departs, taking them all to another body, exalted or not according to the deeds done in the body it has left.[306] This view is developed in the later doctrines into the conception of a liṅga śarīra, made familiar to western readers by theosophists as the astral body. This subtle body serves as the vehicle of mind and character, and is not disintegrated with the death of the physical body. It forms the basis of a new physical body which it moulds upon itself, effecting as it were a materialisation maintained

300. Kaṭha, i. 3.

301. Bṛh., vi. 2. 16. We meet with similar traditions in the Gnostic writings as well as in St Paul. See Harrison *Prolegomena to Greek Religion*, and Gardner, *The Religious Experiences of St. Paul.*

302. Kaṭha, vi. 14.

303. Bṛh., 4. 4. 6.

304. Bṛh., iv. 4. 3.

305. Bṛh., iv. 4. 4. See also Chān., v. 10. 2; Kauṣītaki, i. 2; Bṛh. i. 5. 16.

306. See Bṛh., iv. 3. 38; iv. 4. 5. Praśna, iii. 10; Kauṣītaki, iv. 3.

throughout the next life. It is also said that the creatures emerge into individual life from the one true being and merge into it again.[307]

The thinkers of the Upaniṣads do not support the materialistic view that the soul is annihilated at death. They have a strong conviction of the continuity of life, and maintain that there is something which survives bodily death. The sexual act creates the conditions in which a new life appears, but it is, on no account, an adequate explanation of the new life itself. The birth of consciousness cannot be explained by the development of a cell. The theological hypothesis that God creates a new soul every time a child is born does not seem to be more satisfactory than the Upaniṣad theory that the individual jīva is manifesting itself in the germ and assuming the shape that it is obliged to take.

The theory of rebirth is quite as logical as any other hypothesis that is in the field, and is certainly more satisfactory than the theories of absolute annihilation or eternal retribution. It accounts for the apparent moral disorder and chaos of suffering. The unfair distribution of pain seems to contradict the rationality of the universe. As irregularities of the empirical world are a challenge to the logical faith, so moral disorder is a challenge to the belief in the goodness of the principle at work. If our faith is rational, there cannot be any intellectual or moral confusion. If moral chaos is ultimate, then moral paralysis would be the result. We have to reconcile the strangely chaotic appearances of the moral world with the faith in a good and great God. We should not be content with thinking that the world is organised in a haphazard manner. The hypothesis which traces the disorder and the suffering of the moral world to the freedom of man cannot account for the inequalities with which men are thrust into the world. These differences in the initial equipment contradict the idea of a divinely ordered universe. This hypothesis of rebirth gives us some explanation of the original difference. It makes us feel that the joy and suffering of the world are there for the progressive education of character. Punishment is not only vindictive but also remedial. We are punished for our sins, and are at the same time purified by punishment. It is good that we suffer.

The question of the origin of the hypothesis of rebirth we have answered by anticipation. We have seen how it arises naturally from the mass of thought by which the Upaniṣad thinkers were surrounded. The Vedas speak to us of the two ways of the gods and the fathers. The original

307. Chān., vi. 9. 2; vi. 10. 1. 2.

inhabitants of India supply us with the idea of the migration of human souls into trees and animals. The need for recompense is urged in the Brāhmaṇas. With these ready to hand, the Upaniṣads had only to round them off into the doctrine of saṁsāra. We are not therefore obliged to seek for it any independent source. If in ancient Greece we find doctrines similar to it, they may have had independent origin and growth, though modern scholarship is against such a view. On this question we may quote two authorities on Indian and Greek thought. Macdonell observes that the 'dependence of Pythagoras on Indian philosophy and science certainly seems to have a high degree of probability. The doctrine of metempsychosis in the case of Pythagoras appears without any connection or explanatory background, and was regarded by the Greeks as of foreign origin. He could not have derived it from Egypt as it was not known to the ancient Egyptians.'[308] Gomperz writes: 'There is a far closer agreement between Pythagorism and the Indian doctrine, not merely in their general features, but even in certain details such as vegetarianism; and it may be added that the formulae which summarise the whole creed of the circle and the wheel of births are likewise the same in both. It is almost impossible for us to refer this identity to mere chance.... It is not too much to assume that the curious Greek who was the contemporary of Buddha, and it may have been of Zarathustra too, would have acquired a more or less exact knowledge of the religious speculations of the East, in that age of intellectual fermentation, through the medium of Persia.'[309] One thing is clear that the Indians did not borrow it from outside.

XXI

THE PSYCHOLOGY OF THE UPANIṢADS

Though there is no systematic psychological analysis in the Upaniṣads, we can gather from them the ideas which they adopted. In the Praśna Upaniṣad,[310] the ten indriyas, the five organs of action and the five senses of knowledge, the motor and the sensory apparatus are mentioned. These indriyas work under the control of manas, the central organ whose chief functions are perception and action. Without mind the senses are

308. *History of Sanskrit Literature*, p. 122.

309. *Greek Thinkers*, vol. i., p. 127. For a different view, see Keith on *Pythagoras and Transmigration*, *J.R.A.S.*, 1909.

310. iv. 2.

useless.[311] That is why the mind is called the chief of the senses. Without mind or prajñā, speech does not make known anything. 'My mind was absent,' he says. 'I did not perceive that world; without prajñā the eye does not make known any form.'[312] 'I was absent in mind, I did not see; I was absent in mind, I did not hear; in this manner it is evident that a person sees with the mind, hears with the mind.'[313] The mind was looked upon as material in nature.[314] For sense perception, therefore, the Upaniṣads make out that what is necessary is neither the mere sense nor its mere functioning, but a self which perceives through the sense, a seeing eye. Perception is said to be due to the proximity of the senses to their objects.[315] One can do only one mental act at a time.[316] Buddhi or intelligence is higher than manas. The functions of buddhi are found in the Aitareya. 'Sensation, perception, ideation, conception, understanding, insight, resolution, opinion, imagination, feeling, memory, volition, conation, the will to live, desire and self-control, all these are different names of intellection.'[317] This analysis cannot stand criticism, but is important, since it indicates that even so early as the period of the Upaniṣads there were psychological discussions. The highest of all is the soul which is the eye of the eye, the ear of the ear. It controls buddhi, manas, the indiryas, the prāṇas, etc.[318] It is known to be all-pervasive and absolute.[319] There are passages where the soul is given physical properties and said to dwell in the cavity of the heart.[320] It is also said to be of the size of a grain of barley or rice,[321] of the measure of a span,[322] or the thumb.[323] If we remember that Aristotle in his *De Anima*

311. Bṛh., i. 5. 3.
312. Kauṣītaki.
313. Bṛh., iii. 1. 4.
314. Professor Alexander reduces mind to a particular reality as material in structure as the electron of the physicist.
315. Compare the views of Empedocles and Democritus on the point.
316. Kauṣītaki, iii. 2.
317. iii. 2.
318. Bṛh., iv. 4. 5; i. 4. 17; v. 6; ii. 1. 17; iii. 7. 22; iv. 3. 7; iv. 5. 13.
319. Kaṭha, i. 2. 21; Muṇḍaka, i. 1. 6.
320. Bṛh., iv. 3. 17; v. 6; Chān., viii. 3. 3; v. i. 6; Kaṭha, ii. 20; iii. 1; iv. 6; vi. 18; and Śvetāśvatara, iii. 11. 20. Hṛdaya or hṛtpadma is a subtle centre of the spinal cord.
321. Bṛh., v. 6. 1; Chān., iii. 14. 3.
322. Chān., v. 18. 1.
323. Kaṭha, vi. 17; ii. 21; Śvet., iii. 13.

located the soul in the heart and Galen in the brain, and Descartes imagined the seat of the soul to be the pineal gland, and Lotze the brain, it is not surprising that the psychologists of the Upaniṣads located it in the region of the heart.

The mind is wider than consciousness. That consciousness is only one aspect of mental life, a state of our spiritual world, and not that world itself, is a profound truth, which western thought is slowly coming to recognise. Since the time of Leibniz consciousness is admitted to be only an accident of mental representation, and not its necessary and essential attribute. His contention that 'our inner world is richer, ampler and more concealed,' was well known to the writers of the Upaniṣads.

The Māṇḍūkya Upaniṣad mentions the different conditions of the soul, waking, dreaming, sleep and the intuitive turīya. In the waking condition the manas and the sense organs are all active. In dream states the senses are said to be quiescent and lost in the manas, a proposition which modern psychology disputes. But according to the Upaniṣads, so long as our sense organs are active, we are only dozing, but not dreaming. We are in a half-waking condition. In authentic dream states the mind alone operates in a free and unfettered manner. The difference between the waking and the dream states consists in this, that in the waking condition the mind depends on the outward impressions, while in dreaming it creates its impressions and enjoys them. It may, of course, use the materials of the waking hours. Suṣupti, or deep sleep, is also a normal occurrence of man's life. In it the mind and the senses are both said to be inactive. There is a cessation of the empirical consciousness with its distinction of object and subject. It is said that in this state we have an objectless consciousness when the self attains to a temporary union with the absolute. Be that as it may, it is clear that it is not complete non-being or negation. It is difficult to concede that the self continues to exist in deep sleep, enjoying bliss though it is bereft of all experience. As a matter of fact, the Upaniṣads themselves account for the physiological and unconscious activities by the principle of life, 'prāṇa,' which is said to govern the processes of breathing, circulation, etc. Perhaps organic memory may be the explanation of the continuity of consciousness. Notwithstanding the absence of cognition, it is open to question whether the self in the condition of sleep experiences positive bliss. Turīya is the consciousness of unity, though not the empirical apprehension thereof. It is the mystic realisation of the oneness of all, which is the crown of spiritual life.

Before we take up the question of the non-Vedāntic tendencies of the Upaniṣads, it may be well to sum up the general metaphysical standpoint of the Upaniṣads. At the very start we said that there was considerable ambiguity in the position of the Upaniṣads, making it liable to different interpretations. It is difficult to decide whether it is the Advaita (or non-dualism) of Śaṁkara, or the modified position of Rāmānuja that is the final teaching of the parent gospel. Tendencies which could be completed in either direction are to be met with. The Upaniṣads are not conscious of any contradiction between them. The advaitic (non-dual) Brahman reached by intuition and the concretely defined reality are not really distinct, since they are only two different ways of representing the same. They are the intuitional and the intellectual ways of apprehending the same reality. On the former view the world is an appearance of the absolute; to the latter it is an expression of God. In neither case is the world to be dismissed as altogether unreal or illusory, since on such a view we cannot admit of any distinctions of value in the world of experience. Through the influence of Buddhism and its schools, the non-dual nature of reality and the phenomenal nature of the world came to be emphasised in the systems of Gauḍapāda and Śaṁkara. As a matter of fact, such an advaitic philosophy seems to be only a revised version of the Mādhyamika metaphysics in vedic terminology. The religious reconstruction of the epics and the Bhagavadgītā and the theistic emphasis in the Nyāya, led to the development of the Viśiṣṭādvaita, or modified monism of Rāmānuja. As a matter of fact, the non-dualists or Advaitins are called Pariśuddha Saugatas, or purified Buddhists, and the Viśiṣṭādvaitins Pariśuddha. Naiyāyikas, or purified Nyāya followers.

XXII

ELEMENTS OF SĀṀKHYA AND YOGA IN THE UPANIṢADS

There are germs of non-Vedāntic philosophies such as Sāṁkhya and yoga in the Upaniṣads. The Sāṁkhay philosophy establishes a dualism between puruṣa and prakṛti, where prakṛti is the source of all existence and puruṣa the disinterested spectator of the evolution of prakṛti. It also holds to the plurality of puruṣas or knowing subjects.[324] The Upaniṣads do not support

324. The idea of an avyakta or prakṛti, the source of all differentiation, is distinctly suggested in the Upaniṣads. 'Beyond the senses are the rudiments of its objects; beyond these rudiments is the mind; beyond the mind is Ātman known as mahat

the theory of a plurality of puruṣas, though a natural process of criticism and development of one side of the doctrine leads to it. We have seen how the monism of the Upaniṣads becomes a monotheism so far as the purposes of religion are concerned. A monotheism implies the separate existence of the individual soul over against the supreme soul. The result is a plurality of individual souls. But the Sāṁkhya theorists had the insight to perceive that the independence of the supreme and the individual souls is hard to maintain. One is subversive of the other. One of them, either the supreme or the individual souls, had to be cancelled. When the function of productivity was assigned to prakṛti, God became superfluous. The Upaniṣads protest against the transfer of creative functions to mere matter divorced from God. Their main tendency is to support the hypothesis of an absolute spirit on the background of which subject and object arise.[325]

The beginnings of the Yoga system are to be found in the Upaniṣads. It is the conviction of the Upaniṣad writers that reality is not rightly perceived by our imperfect understandings. The mind of man is compared by them to a mirror in which reality is reflected. The extent to which we know reality depends on the state of our mind, whether it can respond to the full wealth of reality or not. Colours are not revealed to the blind nor music to the deaf, nor philosophic truth to the feeble-minded. The process of knowing is not so much a creation as a discovery, not so much a production as a revelation. It follows that the revelation will be imperfect or distorted, if there is any taint or imperfection clinging to the instrument. The selfish desires and passions get between the instrument of mind and

---

(great), beyond the mahat is avyakta, the unmanifested; beyond the avyakta is the puruṣa, beyond the puruṣa there is nothing.' (Kaṭha, iii. 10. 11; see also vi. 7. 8.) Beyond the indeterminate whence all creation issues there is only God. 'By tapas Brahman increases in size and from it food is produced; from food life, mind, the elements, the worlds, karma, and with it its fruits.' (Muṇḍaka, i. 1.) Food or annam in this passage is interpreted by Śaṁkara as the unmanifested (avyākṛtam). In the Praśna Upaniṣad, iv., we have an account of how all things are resolved into the imperishable in the order of the five elements with the corresponding mātras or subtle elements. See Praśna, iv. 8. In the Upaniṣads prakṛti is said to be derived from god. The word 'Puruṣa' means the supreme Ātman. The Sāṁkhya theory of puruṣa as a passive witness may have been suggested by the famous passage about the two birds, 'where the one feeds on the delicious fruit and the other, not tasting it, looks on.' (Muṇḍaka, iii. 1. 1).

325. See Aitareya, i. 1. 2.; Bṛh., i. 4. 3; Chān., vi. 2. 6; Tait., ii. 1.

the reality to be revealed. When the personality of the subject affects the nature of the instrument, the reflection becomes blurred. The ignorance of the observer clouds the object with his fancies. His prevailing prejudices are cast over the truth of things. Error is just the intrusion into the reality of the defects of the instrument. An impartial and impersonal attitude is necessary for the discovery of truth, and all that is merely personal impedes this process. We must be saved from the malformation and the miscarriage of our minds. The clamant energies of the mind must be bent to become the passive channels for the transmission of truth. The *Yoga* method gives directions how to refine the mind and improve the mirror, keep it clean by keeping out what is peculiar to the individual. It is only through this discipline that we can rise to that height of strenuous impersonality from which the gifted souls of the world see distant visions. This method is in consonance with the Upaniṣad theory of the self. Our ordinary consciousness turns its back on the eternal world and is lost in the perishing unreal world cast by the mind out of sense impressions. When we rise above the empirical self we get not a negation but an intensification of self. When the self is bound down to its empirical accidents, its activities are not fully exercised. When the limitations of empirical existence are transcended, the universal life is intensified, and we have an enrichment of self or enhancement of personality. Then it draws all experience into it. In the lower stages, when the self is identified with any definite centre generated by the accidents of time and space, the world of experience is not made its own. The adherence to a narrow circle of experience must be overcome before we can gather into ourselves the world of experience, whose centre as well as circumference is God and man. Then we rise to a condition in which, in the words of the Upaniṣads, 'there is no difference between what is within and what is without.' The Yoga method insists that the false outward outlook must be checked before the true inward ideal is given a chance of life and expression. We must cease to live in the world of shadows before we can lay hold of the eternal life.

The Yoga system requires us to go through a course of mental and spiritual discipline. The Upaniṣads also emphasise the practice of austere virtues before the end can be reached. In the Praśna Upaniṣad Pippalāda sends away six inquirers after God for another year of discipline with the command, 'Go ye and spend another year in leading the life of celibacy (brahmacarya), in practising asceticism, in cherishing reverential faith (śraddhā).' The life of celibacy, where the student will have no family attachment to perturb his mind, would enable him to give whole-hearted attention to his work. The penances will give him mental quiet and remove the restlessness of mind which is such a great obstacle to knowledge. Śraddhā or faith is necessary for all work. The essence of Yoga philosophy, as of all mystic teaching, is the insistence on the possibility of coming into direct contact with the divine consciousness by raising the human to a plane above its normal level.

We must control the mind which binds us to outer things and makes slaves of us, to realise freedom. Being the victims of outer objects and circumstances, we do not reach satisfaction. 'As rain water that has fallen on a mountain ridge runs down on all sides, thus does he who sees a difference between qualities run after them on all sides. As pure water poured into pure water remains the same, thus, O Gautama, is the self of a thinker who knows.'[326] The mind of a man who does not know his own self goes hither and thither like the water pouring down the crags in every direction. But when his mind is purified, he becomes one with the great ocean of life which dwells behind all mortal forms. The outward mind, if allowed free scope, gets dispersed in the desert sands. The seeker must draw it inward, hold it still to obtain the treasure within. We have to force utterance into feeling, feeling into thought, and thought into universal consciousness; only then do we become conscious of the deep peace of the eternal.[327] Only when 'the five sources of knowledge are at rest along with the mind and the intellect is inactive' do we reach the highest.[328] 'Having taken the bow furnished by the Upaniṣads, the great weapon, and fixed in it the arrow rendered pointed by constant meditation, and having drawn it with the mind, fixed on the Brahman, aim happy youth at that mark, the immortal Brahman.'[329] The Kauṣītaki Upaniṣad speaks of Pratardana as the founder of a new system of self-control or saṁyamana, which is known by the name of the Inner sacrifice.[330] He insists that the individual should exercise perfect

326. Kaṭha Up., ii. 15.

327. Kaṭha, ii. 13. Cf. 'Thought is best when the mind is gathered into herself, and none of these things trouble her—neither sounds nor sights nor pain, nor any pleasure—when she has as little as possible to do with the body and has no bodily sense or feeling, but is aspiring after being' Plato's *Phædo*.

328. Kaṭha, ii. 12.

329. Muṇḍaka, ii. 2. 2.

330. Antaram agnihotram, ii. 5.

control over his passions and emotions. The Upaniṣads sometimes suggest that we can induce the trance condition by control of breath,[331] though more often they speak to us of the method of concentration.[332] Mystic words such as Aum, Tadvanam,[333] Tajjalān,[334] are the symbols on which we are asked to fix attention. The way to reach steadiness of mind is by concentration or fixing the thought for a time on one particular object by effacing all others. Only practice helps us to grow perfect in this art.

The only indication of the later Nyāya logic occurs in Muṇḍaka.[335] 'This Ātman cannot be attained by one devoid of strength, or by excitement, or by tapas, or by liṅga.' Liṅga, as we shall see, is a technical term of Nyāya logic, the binding link, the middle term of inference.[336] The empirical theory of knowledge, that the nature of reality is to be known by way of induction, is brought out in some passages. 'By one clod of clay all that is made of clay is known ... by one nugget of gold all that is made of gold is known.'[337] Pratardana insists that knowledge is possible only through a subject-object relation.

XXIII

PHILOSOPHICAL ANTICIPATIONS

The Upaniṣads determine the main issues of philosophical inquiry and mark out the lines of subsequent philosophical discussion. Apart from suggestions of other theories, we have seen that the Upaniṣads contain the elements of a genuine philosophical idealism, insisting on the relative reality of the world, the oneness and wholeness of spirit, and the need of an ethical and religious life. Though the philosophical synthesis presented in the Upaniṣads, with its fundamental idea of the unity of the consciousness of self, with the principle which binds all things, constitutes the strength of the Upaniṣad thought, its weakness lies in the fact that this synthesis is achieved not so much by explicit reason as by intuition. It does not offer a logical reconciliation of the different elements which it brings together, though it has a firm hold on the central idea of all true philosophy.

331. Bṛh., i. 5. 23.
332. Praśna, v. 1.
333. Kena, iv. 6.
334. Chān., iii. 14. 1.
335. iii. 2. 4. Deussen and Hume give to the text a different sense.
336. Liṅga—link. See also Chān., vi. 8. 4.
337. Chān., vi. 1. 4–6.

The beliefs of the Vedic religion weighed upon the Upaniṣad thinkers. Though they did not scruple to criticise them, they were still hampered by the legacy of the past. They tried to be champions of future progress as well as devotees of ancient greatness. This was obviously a hard task judged from the results. The Upaniṣad religion, while it preached a pure and spiritual doctrine, which had no specified forms of worship, which did not demand a priestly hierarchy, yet tolerated these things, nay, even recognised them. 'The various karmas which seers found in the mantras are true, and were much practised in the Treta age; practise them always with true desires; it is your way to the attainment of the fruits of karma.'[338] The vedic gods had their own place in the sun. None asked the people to forsake the gods they were wont to worship. Ingenious explanations, suggestions and symbolism helped to interpret the old superstition in consistency with the new idealism. While the hour demanded fidelity to the spiritual ideal, we find the Upaniṣads a good deal of temporising. They began as a movement towards the liberation of the individual from the shackles of external authority and excessive conventionalism. They ended in rivetting the old chains. Instead of establishing new values for life, they tended to propagate the traditional ones. To preach a spiritual democracy is a very different thing from establishing it. The Upaniṣads endeavoured laudably to combine a lofty mysticism with the ancestral faith. But the age never felt even a living option between the new spiritual ideal and the mythologies of the past. The lofty idealism of the Upaniṣads did not realise itself as a popular movement. It never influenced society as a whole. The sacrificial religion was still the dominating force; the Upaniṣads only added respectability to it. The old faith was inspired with a new vitality derived from the breath of a spirit from another sphere. If the idealism of the Upaniṣaḍs had permeated the masses, there would have been a great remodelling of the racial character and a regeneration of social institutions. But neither of these things happened. The lower religion with much of superstition prevailed. The priesthood became powerful. The conservatism of the religious institutions and contempt for the masses lived side by side with a higher spirit adopted by a few votaries of the perfect life. It was an age of spiritual contradiction and chaos. The teaching of the Upaniṣads became so flexible as to embrace within it the most diverse forms of doctrine

338. Muṇḍaka, i. 2. 1.

from a refined idealism to a crude idolatry. The result was that the higher religion was swamped by the lower.

Everywhere we had contradictory notions. In religion, there was Vedic polytheism and sacrifices tempered by Upaniṣad monism and spiritual life. In social matters, there was caste, the rigours of which were mitigated by the catholic spirit of universalism. In eschatology, there was the conception of rebirth mixed up with ideas of hell. But the true was overwhelmed by the false, and the chaos of the Brāhmanical religion, with all its conflicting theories, soon reached a climax in the post-Upaniṣad or the pre-Buddhist period. This period was one of spiritual dryness, where truth hardened into tradition, and morality stiffened into routine. Life became a series of observances. The mind of man moved within the iron circle of prescribed formulas and duties. The atmosphere was choked with ceremonialism. One could not wake up or rise from his bed, bathe or shave, wash his face, or eat a mouthful, without muttering some formula or observing some rite. It was an age when a petty and barren creed set too much store by mere trifles and hollow superstitions. An arid and heartless philosophy, backed by a dry and dogmatic religion, full of affectation and exaggeration, could not satisfy the thinking few for any time, or the masses for a long time. A period of disintegration followed when attempts were made to carry out the Upaniṣad revolt in a more systematic manner. The illogical combination of the Upaniṣad monism and the Vedic polytheism, the Upaniṣad spiritual life and the Vedic sacrificial routine, the Upaniṣad mokṣa and saṁsāra and the Vedic hell and heaven, the Upaniṣad universalism and the popular caste, could no longer live together. Reconstruction was the greatest need of the hour. A deeper and more spiritual religion which could come down to the common life of man was what the times were waiting for. Before a true synthesis could be obtained, the elements artificially combined required to be torn away from the connection into which they have been brought and set in abstract opposition to each other. The Buddhists, the Jainas, and the Cārvākas or materialists pointed to the artificial condition of the prevailing religion. The first two attempted a reconstruction, emphasising the ethical needs of the spirit. But their attempts were on revolutionary lines. While they tried to carry out the ethical universalism of the Upaniṣad teaching, they imagined that they completely broke off from the authority of the Brāhmanical caste, the sacrificial system and the prevailing religion. The

Bhagavadgītā and the later Upaniṣads tried to reckon with the past and bring about a synthesis of the illogical elements in a more conservative spirit. It may be that these radical and conservative protests against the religion as it prevailed in the post-Upaniṣad period were formulated in different parts of the country, Buddhism and Jainism in the east and Bhagavadgītā in the west, the ancient stronghold of the Vedic religion. It is to this period of intellectual ferment, revolt and reconstruction that we now pass.

REFERENCES

MAX MÜLLER, The Upaniṣads (S.B.E. Vols I. and XV.).
DEUSSEN, The Philosophy of the Upaniṣads.
GOUGH, The Philosophy of the Upaniṣads.
BARUA, Pre-Buddhistic Indian Philosophy.
MAHADEVA SASTRI, The Taittirīya Upaniṣad.
RANADE, The Psychology of the Upaniṣads (Indian Philosophical Review), 1918–1919.
HUME, The Thirteen Principal Upaniṣads.

PART II

The Epic Period

CHAPTER V

Materialism

■ The epic period, 600 BC to AD 200-Intellectual stir—Freedom of thought—The influence of the Upaniṣads—The political conditions of the time—The many-sided philosophic activity of the epic period—The three chief tendencies of ethical revolt, religious reconstruction and systematic philosophy—Common ideas of the age—Materialism—Its antecedents—Lokāyata—Theory of knowledge—Matter the only reality—Body and mind—No future life—No God—Hedonistic ethics—The repudiation of the authority of the Vedas—The effects of the theory—Later criticism of materialism. ■

I

THE EPIC PERIOD

While the events related in the two epics of the Rāmāyaṇa and the Mahābhārata mostly occurred in the Vedic period, when the early Aryans poured in large numbers into the Gangetic valley and settled down, the Kurus round Delhi, the Pāñcālas near Kanouj the Kosalas near Oudh, and the Kāśis in Benares, we have no evidence to show that the epics were compiled earlier than the sixth century BC. The Vedas themselves were arranged and systematised in the period of the Aryan expansion in the Gangetic valley. Perhaps it was in the same period that the great war between the Kurus and the Pāṇḍavas, the subject of the great epic, Mahābhārata, was fought. According to both the Indian tradition and the information of the epic, Vyāsa, the compiler of the Vedas, was a contemporary of the war. The Rāmāyaṇa deals with the wars of the Aryans with the then natives of India, who adopted the Aryan civilisation. The Mahābhārata belongs to a period when the Vedic hymns had lost their original force and meaning, and when ceremonial religion appealed to the people and caste grew into prominence. We may therefore put the beginning of the epic period somewhere in the sixth century before Christ, though changes were introduced into the epics to suit the conditions till the second century AD, when they assumed their final form.

There are many indications to show that it was an age keenly alive to intellectual interest, a period of immense philosophic activity and many-sided development. We cannot adequately describe the complex inspiration of the times. The people were labouring with the contradictions felt in the things without and the mind within. It was an age full of strange anomalies and contrasts. With the intellectual fervour and moral seriousness were also found united a lack of mental balance and restraint of passion. It was the era of the Cārvākas as well as of the Buddhists. Sorcery and science, scepticism and faith, license and asceticism were found commingled. When the surging energies of life assert their rights, it is not unnatural that many yield to unbridled imagination. Despite all this, the very complexity of thought and tendency helped to enlarge life. By its emphasis on the right of free inquiry the intellectual stir of the age weakened the power of traditional authority and promoted the cause of truth. Doubt was no longer looked upon as dangerous.

Intuition was giving place to inquiry, religion to philosophy. The marvellous uncertainty and ambiguity of existence, the discordant attempts to systematise the world, the bewildering chaos of arbitrary by-ways, side-streets and resting-places of thought invented by suffering humanity trembling in fear and delighting in the new and the untried, the desert of unbelief, exhaustion and frigidity in the midst of energy, youth and enterprise, make the epic period an eventful era in the history of Indian thought. The sickly minded and the suffering of reduced vitality and weak nerves the world over try to heal their sickness by either seeking repose and calm, deliverance and nirvāṇa through art, knowledge, morality, or else intoxication, ecstasy, bewilderment and madness. So in this age of experiments in philosophy ever so many new systems were put forward. Opinion was set against opinion, ideal against ideal. Change in the habits of thought is created not by one single influence, but by a combination of several. In the Ṛg-Veda the germs of free speculation and suggestions of scepticism were present.[1] With the excessive devotion to the externals of worship there was noticeable even in the Brāhmaṇas an intrepid longing for philosophical discussion. When attempts are made to smother the intellectual curiosity of people, the mind of man rebels against it, and the inevitable reaction shows itself in an impatience of all formal authority and a wild outbreak of the emotional life long repressed by the discipline of the ceremonial religion. The Upaniṣadas developed the spirit of inquiry, however much they professed to rest on the old Vedic faith. When once

1. R.V., vii. 89. 3–4.

we allow thought to assert its rights it cannot be confined within limits. By introducing new modes of inquiry, by moulding a new cast and tone of mind, the thinkers of the Upaniṣads helped more than any others to set the current of the age. By their philosophical tournaments they inaugurated a change, the full meaning and direction of which were hidden even from them. It is to be noted that while the Upaniṣad thought developed in the western part of the Gangetic tract, the east was not so much assimilating it as acquiring it. The western speculations were not admitted in the eastern valley without debate and discussion.

There were also political crises which unsettled men's minds. Among the small states which were being then established there were petty dissensions. Outside invaders disturbed the peace of the country. Loud complaints were heard about the degeneracy of the age, the lust of princes and the greed of men. 'I behold the rich in this world,' says a Buddhist Sutta. 'Of the goods which they have acquired in their folly, they give nothing to others; they eagerly heap riches together, and farther and still farther they go in their pursuit of enjoyment. The king, although he may have conquered the kingdoms of the earth, although he may be ruler of all land this side the sea up to the ocean's shore, would still insatiate, covet that which is beyond the sea. The king and many other men with desires unsatisfied fall a prey to death ... neither relatives nor friends nor acquaintances save the dying man; the heirs take his property, but he receives the reward of his deeds; no treasures accompany him who dies, nor wives, nor child, nor property, nor kingdom.'[2] The sense of failure, the failure of state and society, the loss of hope in the world, the diffidence of humanity threw the individual back on his soul and his emotions. Others there were who were prepared to pursure holiness and neglect the imperfect and transitory life, to reach some dream world far off which shall subsist without sin or corruption, the same yesterday, to-day and for ever. Almost all turned away from life in weariness, disgust and despair. The allurement of the present yielded to the attractions of the beyond. People were casting covetous eyes on short-cuts to salvation. A deep consciousness of worldly defeat was the inspiration of the times. The conception of a good God naturally goes with the moral government of the world. When suspicion of the nature of life on earth arises, the belief in God is weakened. When everybody thinks that life is suffering, at least a doubtful blessing, it is not

2. Oldenberg, *Buddha*, p. 65.

easy to continue in the old faith. The faith of centuries was dissolving like a dream. The hold of authority was loosened and traditional bonds weakened. In the tumult of thought consequent on the disintegration of faith and the declaration of the independence of man, ever so many metaphysical fancies and futile speculations were put forward. An age stricken with a growing sense of moral weakness is eager to clutch at any spiritual stay. We have the materialists with their insistence on the world of sense, the Buddhists with their valuable psychological teaching and high ethics. While there were some who clung to the Vedas with the desperation of the drowning man, the reformers gave themselves over to the moral task of living clean lives and doing good work, deliberately refusing to speculate about the possibility of the beyond. Ascetics, Tīrthaṅkaras or ford-makers claimed to be founders of new paths. Gautama and Vardhamāna were the most prominent reformers. Buddhist books mention other heretical teachers: Sañjaya the sceptic, who repudiated all knowledge of self and limited his inquiries to the question of the attainment of peace; Ajita Keśakambaḷin the materialist, who rejected all knowledge by insight and resolved man into the four elements which dispersed at death; Pūraṇa Kāśyapa the indifferentist, who refused to acknowledge moral distinctions and adopted the view of non-causation or fortuitous origin[3] and passivity of soul; Maskarin Gosāla the fatalist, who held that man had no power over life or death, and who believed that all things were living jīvas in process of constant change determined by their immanent energy till they attained perfection;[4] and Kakuḍa Kātyāyana, who maintained the qualitative distinctness of the elements of being, earth, water, fire, air, space and soul, with pleasure and pain as principles of change, making and unmaking individuals.[5] Numberless teachers rose in different parts of the country announcing the good news of the secret of deliverance.

It is possible to trace to the early epic period the beginnings of many of the reconstructing movements of thought which have enriched a later age. Though they existed even in this period, they did not attain their full strength till we reach the end of the epic era. In the divine economy of life the disease and the remedy appear simultaneously, and wherever the poisonous streams of error flow there too springs up the tree of life whose

3. Ahetuvāda, Sāmaññaphalasutta. Dīgha Nikāya.i.

4. Majjhima Nikāya, I. See also Sūtrakṛtāṅga.

5. Cf. With this the philosophy of Empedocles with its four elements and two principles of change, love which combines and hatred which separates.

leaves are for the healing of the nations. The teaching of the Vedic seers and the Upaniṣads were condensed into Sūtras. Coldly logical and highly devotional systems of thought were promulgated. The Cārvākas, the Buddhists and the Jainas appeared first. Immediately, as a sort of reaction, attempts were made to emphasise the theistic side of the Upaniṣad teaching. Buddhism and Jainism, with their emphasis on the ethical, failed to supply any nutriment to the deeper spiritual wants and emotions. When the spiritual sense of the masses could not be satisfied by the thin abstractions of the Upaniṣads or the brilliant pantheon of the Vedas, much less the vague idealisings of the moral principle of the jainas and the Buddhists, there were reconstructions providing a religion less formal, less cold and more satisfying than the Upaniṣad cult as then understood, systems which gave a living, personal God instead of a vague, arid absolute. The Bhagavadgīitā, where Kṛṣṇa is represented as an incarnation of Viṣṇu as well as the Eternal Brahman of the Upaniṣads, the Pāñcarātra system, the Śaivism of the Śvetāśvatara and other later Upaniṣads, and the Mahāyāna form of Buddhism, where Buddha becomes an eternal God, belong to this religious reaction. In this period some speculative souls were eagerly pressing forward towards new light along philosophic lines. The germs of systematic philosophy were found sprouting up. The Sāṁkhya and the Yoga systems in their early forms, the Nyāya and the Vaiśeṣika developed on independent lines, though they attempted to fortify their positions by appealing to the Vedas. The two Mīmāṁsās were more directly derived from the exegesis of the Vedic texts. All those systems were promulgated definitely towards the end of the epic period. The contradictions of the time appeared in conflicting systems, each of them representing one phase of the spirit of the age. It is necessary for us to distinguish in this period three different strata of thought, which are both chronologically and logically successive: (1) The systems of revolt, such as the Cārvāka theory, Jainism and Buddhism (600 BC); (2) the theistic reconstruction of the Bhagavadgītā and the later Upaniṣads (500 BC); and (3) the speculative development of the six systems (300 BC), which attained definiteness about the end of AD 200 or so.

II

COMMON IDEAS OF THE AGE

Before we take up the three systems of the materialists, the Jainas and the Buddhists, we may shortly notice the ideas which were common to the age. Rebirth and the suffering of life embodying the idea of impermanence were current. That life is suffering and the objects of the world only lures and torments, seemed to be the heritage from the Upaniṣads. Witness the question of Naciketas to Yama: 'Shall we be happy with maidens, horses, wealth, royalty, when we see thee, O Death?'[6] The wheel of rebirth is an elaboration of the doctrine of suffering. The conception of an endless migration from birth to birth, life to life seemed to be a dull fancy, depriving existence of its meaning and life of its joy. 'The spirit can bear the thought of a decision of its destiny once for all, the torment of all eternity; but the endless migration from world to world, from existence to existence, the endlessness of the struggle against the pallid power of that ever-recurring destruction—a thought like this might well chill the heart even of the brave with a shudder at the resultlessness of all this unending course of things.'[7] All schools of thought which arose in this age adopt this conception of impermanence. Different names are given to it, such as Jagadvyāpāra, Saṁsāra, Vyavahāra, Prapañca. The law of karma is its necessary corollary. The question is inevitable whether there is any way out of this wheel, any deliverance from death. In the hermitages, the austerities mentioned in the Atharva-Veda were practised for the winning of supernatural power. Faith in the purifying power of tapas or asceticism was strong. Tapas, as austere asceticism, displaced the processes of meditation and contemplation suggested in the Upaniṣads. To apprehend God in mystic vision, the soul is to be disciplined into stillness. The ascetic groups were found scattered throughout, practising self-torture. Caste was growing more and more into recognition.

III

MATERIALISM

Materialism is as old as philosophy, and the theory is to be met within the pre-Buddhistic period also. Germs of it are found in the hymns of the Ṛg-Veda. 'Several vestiges show that even in the pre-Buddhistic India proclaimers of purely materialistic doctrines appeared; and there is no doubt that those doctrines had ever afterwards, as they have today, numerous secret followers.'[8] In the early Buddhist scriptures there are references to this doctrine. 'Man is composed of four elements. When man dies, the earthly element returns and relapses into the earth; the watery element returns

6. Katha Up.
7. Oldenberg, *Buddha*, p. 45.
8. Garbe, *The Philosophy of Ancient India*, p. 25.

into the water, the fiery element returns into the fire, the airy element returns into the air; the senses pass into space. Wise and fool alike, when the body dissolves, are cut off, perish, do not exist any longer.'[9] The materialists must have preceded Buddhism, since the oldest Buddhist books mention them.[10] There are references to this doctrine in the epics.[11] Manu refers to nāstikas (nihilists) and paṣaṇḍas (heretics).[12] The classic authority on the materialist theory is said to be the sūtras of Bṛhaspati, which have perished. Our chief sources are the polemical works of other schools. The Sarvadarśanasaṁgraha gives a summary of the teaching of the school in its first chapter.

IV

DOCTRINES

In their zeal to break down the ecclesiastical monopoly and proclaim absolute freedom of religious belief, the materialists went to the other extreme. We learn from their views where uncontrolled thought breaking loose from all restrictions lands us. The substance of this doctrine is summed up by a character in the allegorical play of Prabodhacandrodaya. 'Lokāyata is always the only śāstra; in it only perceptual evidence is authority; the elements are earth, water, fire and air; wealth and enjoyment are the objects of human existence. Matter can think. There is no other world, Death is the end of all.'[13] The śāstra is called Lokāyata,[14] for it holds that only this world or loka is. The materialists are called Lokāyatikas. They are also called Cārvākas, after the name of the founder.

What is arrived at by means of direct perception is the truth. That alone exists. What is not perceivable is non-existent, for the simple reason that it is not perceived. There is no inference at all. When we see smoke, we are reminded of fire, through association or memory of past perceptions. This is why inference is sometimes true and sometimes false. Materialists of a later day assigned causes for their view of inference. We cannot have

9. Rhys Davids, *Dialogues of Buddha*, ii, p. 46.

10. Rhys Davids, *American Lectures*, p. 24.

11. See Śāntiparva, verses 1414 and 1430–1442; and Śalyaparva, 3619; and see also Viṣṇu Purāṇa, iii. 18. 14–26.

12. Institutes of Manu, ii. 11; iii. 150, 161. iv. 30, 61, 163; v. 89; viii. 22. 309; ix. 65. 66; xii. 33. 95. 96.

13. Act ii.

14. Lokāyata, directed to the world of sense, is the Sanskrit word for materialism.

inferences unless we have knowledge of universal connexions. Perception does not give us a universal relation nor can it be due to inference, for such an inference would require another, and so on. Testimony of others is of no value. Analogy cannot account for inference, and so inference is invalid. It is only a subjective association which may be justified, if at all, by accident.

Since sense perception is the only form of knowledge, matter becomes the only reality. It alone is cognizable by the senses. What is material is real. The ultimate principles are the four elements: earth, water, fire and air. These are eternal, and can explain the development of the world from the protozoon to the philosopher. Intelligence is the modification of the four elements, and it is destroyed when the elements from which it arises are dissolved. 'That intelligence which is found to be embodied in modified forms of the non-intelligent elements is produced in the same way in which the red colour is produced from the combination of betel, areca nut and lime.[15] As the inebriating power is developed from the mixing of certain ingredients, so is consciousness produced out of the mixture of the four elements. Given the four elements, the self-conscious life mysteriously springs forth, just as the genius makes its appearance when Aladdin rubs his lamp. Thought is a function of matter. To use the famous saying of Cabanis, the brain secretes thought as the liver secretes bile. There is no need for us to look upon the soul as distinct from the body. It is only the body qualified by intelligence. The Ātman is the body itself, which is characterised by such attributes as are implied in the expressions, 'I am stout,' 'I am young,' 'I am old,' 'I am an adult,' etc.'[16] We have no evidence of the separate existence of soul and body. We do not see the self without a body. 'Who has seen the soul existing in a state separate from the body? Does not life result from the ultimate configuration of matter?'[17] Consciousness is invariably found in connexion with the body. Therefore it is the body. Man is what he eats. Sadānanda speaks of four different materialistic schools. The chief point of dispute is about the conception of the soul. One school regards the soul as identical with the gross body, another with the senses, a third with breath, and a fourth with the organ of thought.[18] On any view the soul is only a natural phenomenon. In defence of this position the

15. S.S.S.S., ii. 7.
16. S.S.S.S., ii. 6.
17. Prabodhacandrodaya, ii.
18. Ved āntasāra.

materialists quote scripture, as when they refer us to the Upaniṣad saying: 'Springing forth from these elements, it is destroyed. When they are destroyed—after death no intelligence remains.'[19] From this it follows that it is foolish to think that the soul is going to reap the rewards of its acts in a future state. It is an error of judgment that leads to the assumption of another world. There is no world other than this, neither heaven nor hell. These are the inventions of impostors. Religion is a foolish aberration, a mental disease. A god is not necessary to account for the world. Under the dominance of religious prejudices men are accustomed to the idea of another world and of God, and when the religious illusion is destroyed, they feel a sense of loss and have an uncomfortable void and privation. Nature is absolutely dead to all human values. It is indifferent to good and bad. The sun shines equally on the good and the evil. If nature has any quality, it is that of transcendent immorality. The majority of men, thanks to their weakness, believe that there are deities, protectors of innocence and avengers of crime, who are open to persuasion and flattery. All this is due to lack of thinking. We do not see anywhere in the course of the world interposition of superior beings. We falsely interpret natural phenomena when we trace them to gods and demons. It was impossible for those denying spirits to look upon nature as if it were a proof of a good God, to interpret history as if it were a revelation of a divine reason, to explain personal experiences as if they were the intimations of Providence. To treat history as God's witness to justice, or the events of the world as things planned by Providence for the salvation of the soul, is nothing short of hypocrisy. Nature does things herself without any meddling by the gods. The variety of the world is born of itself. Fire is hot and water cold because it is all in the nature of things. 'Who colours wonderfully the peacocks, or who makes the cuckoos coo so well? There is, in respet of these, no cause other than nature.'[20] With an audacious dogmatism the philosophy swept the world clean of all its values,[21] and put down belief in God and the other world as a sign of mendaciousness, feminism, weakness, cowardice, or dishonesty.

19. Brh. Up., ii. 4. 12.

20. S.S.S.S., ii.5.

21. The Nyāya and the Vaiśeṣika, Mr Banerjee thinks, were originally atheistic though their modern adherents have made of them theistic creeds. According to Kumārila, atheistic sentiments were common among the adherents of the Pūrvamīmāṁsā school.

On this theory pleasure and pain are the central facts of life. An unqualified hedonism is the ethical ideal of the materialist school. Eat, drink and be merry, for death comes to all, closing our lives.

While life is yours, live joyously;
None can escape Death's searching eye;
When once this frame of ours they burn,
How shall it e'er again return?[22]

Virtue is a delusion and enjoyment is the only reality. Life is the end of life. There was a distrust of everything good, high, pure and compassionate. The theory stands for sensualism and selfishness and the gross affirmation of the loud will. There is no need to control passion and instinct, since they are nature's legacy to men. While the Upaniṣads prescribe resignation and severity of life and development of universal benevolence and love, the materialists proclaim the doctrine of uncontrolled energy, self-assertion and reckless disregard of all authority. It is not fair that one man should rule and another obey, since all men are made of the same stuff. Moral rules are conventions of men. We forget the essential aim of life, pleasure, when we adopt the negative methods of fasting and penance. 'Those who inquire whether slaying animals, indulgence in pleasures of sense, or taking what belongs to another be lawful or unlawful, do not act conformably to the principal end of life.'[23] To the Buddhist theory that pleasures are mixed with pain the materialist replies: 'They conceive that you ought to throw away the pleasures of life because they are mixed with pain, but what prudent man will throw away unpeeled rice which encloses excellent grain because it is covered with the husk'?[24] 'Nor may you say that sensual pleasures are not the end of man because they are always mixed with some kind of pain. It is the part of wisdom to enjoy the pure pleasure as far as we can, and leave aside the pain which inevitably accompanies it. It is not therefore for us, through a fear of pain, to reject the pleasures which our nature instinctively recognises as congenial.[25]

22. S.D.S., p. 2
23. Prabodhacandrodya, ii.
24. Ibid.
25. S.D.S., p. 4.

The authority of the Vedas was denounced in the most bitter terms. The Vedic texts are tainted by the three faults of untruth, self-contradiction and tautology.

> There is no heaven, no final liberation, nor any soul in another world,
> Nor do the actions of the four castes, orders, etc., produce any real effect.
> The Agnihotra, the three Vedas, the ascetic's three staves, and smearing one's self with ashes,
> Were made by Nature as the livelihood of those destitute of knowledge and manliness.
> If a beast slain in the Jyotiṣṭoma rite will itself go to heaven,
> Why then does not the sacrificer forthwith offer his own father?
> If the Śrāddha produces gratification to beings who are dead,
> Then here, too, in the case of travellers when they start, it is needles
> to give provisions for the journey.
> If beings in heaven are gratified by our offering the Śrāddha here,
> Then why not give the food down below to those who are standing on the house- top?
> While life remains let a man live happily, let him feed on ghee even
> though he runs in debt,
> When once the body becomes ashes, how can it ever return again?
> If he who departs from the body goes to another world,
> How is it that he comes not back again, restless for love of his kindred?
> Hence it is only as a means of livelihood that Brāhmins have established here.
> All these ceremonies for the dead—there is no other fruit anywhere,
> The three authors of the Vedas were buffoons, knaves and demons.
> All the well-known formulae of the pandits, jarphari, turphari, etc.
> And all the obscene rites for the queen commanded in the Aśvamedha,
> These were invented by buffoons, and so all the various kinds of presents to the priests,
> While the eating of flesh was similarly commanded by night-prowling demons. (S.D.S. i.)

Obviously this account has an element of caricature of the Cārvāka position. A philosophy professed seriously for centuries could not have been of the coarse kind that it is here reported to be.[26]

26. See Rhys David, *Dialogues of Buddha*, i. pp. 166–172.

V

GENERAL REFLECTIONS

The materialist theory had a good deal to do with the repudiation of the old religion of custom and magic. Liberal efforts at improving existing institutions sanctioned by time and embodied in the habits of people will remain ineffectual if the indifference and superstition of centuries are not shaken up by an explosive force like the Cārvāka creed. Materialism signifies the declaration of the spiritual independence of the individual and the rejection of the principle of authority. Nothing need be accepted by the individual which does not find its evidence in the movement of reason. It is a return of man's spirit to itself and a rejection of all that is merely external and foreign . The Cārvāka philosophy is a fanatical effort made to rid the age of the weight of the past that was oppressing it. The removal of dogmatism which it helped to effect was necessary to make room for the great constructive efforts of speculation.

In later Indian thought materialism naturally has come in for a good deal of severe and contemptuous treatment. The classic argument that it is impossible to evolve a subject from an object, since there is no object without a pre-existing subject, has been often repeated. Consciousness cannot be the result of natural forces. The theory that there is no self apart from body is criticised on the following grounds: (1) Our inability to realise consciousness apart from the body does not imply that consciousness is a property of the body, for the body may only be an auxiliary to the realisation of consciousness. Perception of light is not possible without light. But from this it does not follow that perception is light or a property thereof. (2) If consciousness were a property of the body, then there could be no consciousness of the body, for consciousness cannot be the property of that of which one is conscious, but that which is conscious. In other words, the subject cannot be reduced to the object or its property. (3) If consciousness were a property of the body, then it must be capable of being perceived by others than the owner of the body, for we know that properties of material things could be perceived by others. But the consciousness of one person is his private property, and cannot be known by others in the same way as by the self. (4) Even the body which is of the nature of a contrivance implies some one who controls it. Consciousness belongs to that controller. The materialist position is found to be self-destructive. If man is a product of mere nature, it is inconceivable how he should come to form moral ideals of any kind. The theory that perception is the only source of knowledge is criticised by many schools of thought. We may give one example here from the *Sāmkhyatattvakaumudī*. 'When the materialist affirms that inference is not a means of knowledge, how is it that he can know that a man is ignorant or in doubt or in error? For ignorance, doubt and error cannot possibly be discovered in other men by sense perception. Accordingly, even by the materialist, ignorance, etc., in other men must be inferred from conduct and from speech, and therefore inference is recognised as a means of knowledge even against his will.' Nihilism and scepticism are the results of a consistent adoption of the perceptual theory of knowledge. Ideas which move the world cease to be real on this theory, because they cannot be measured by the tape. In spite of all these defects, which are too much on the surface, this school exercised a profound influence on the current beliefs and broke the fascination of the past. It applied to the main questions of philosophy a judgment free from the fancies of theology and the dictates of authority. When people begin to reflect with freedom from presuppositions and religious superstition they easily tend to the materialist belief, though deeper reflection takes them away from it. Materialism is the first answer to the question of how far our unassisted reason helps us in the difficulties of philosophy.

REFERENCES

Sarvadarśanasaṁgraha, translated by Cowell and Gough, chap. i.

Sarvasiddhāntasārasaṁgraha ascribed to Śaṁkarācārya, translated by M. Raṅgācārya, chap. ii.

Prabodhacandrodaya, Act ii.

COLEBROOKE, Miscellaneous Essays, i., pp. 402 ff.

MUIR, J.R.A.S., 1862, vol. 19, pp. 299 ff.

CHAPTER VI

The Pluralistic Realism of the Jainas

■ Jainism—Life of Vardhamāna—Division into Śvetāmbaras and Digambaras—Literature—Relation to Buddhism—The Sāṁkhya philosophy and the Upaniṣads—Jaina logic—Five kinds of knowledge—The Nayas and their divisions—Saptabhaṅgī—Criticism of the Jaina theory of knowledge—Its monistic implications—The psychological views of the Jainas—Soul—Body and mind—Jaina metaphysics—Substance and quality—Jīva and ajīva—Ākāśa, Dharma and Adharma—Time—Matter—The atomic theory—karma—Leśyās—Jīvas and their kinds—Jaina ethics—Human freedom—Ethics of Jainism and of Buddhism compared—Caste—Saṅgha—Attitude to God—Religion—Nirvāṇa—A critical estimate of the Jaina philosophy. ■

I

JAINISM

As the Buddhists are the followers of Buddha, the awakened, the Jainas are the followers of Jina, the victor, a title applied to Vardhamāna, the last prophet of the Jainas. It is applicable also to those men and women who have conquered their lower nature and realised the highest. The name Jainism indicates the predominantly ethical character of the system.

II

VARDHAMĀNA

Vardhamāna, the elder contemporary of Buddha, was the second son of a Kṣatriya chieftain in Magadha, the modern Behar. According to the tradition, he was born in 599 BC and he died in 527 BC. 'Vardhamāna was like his father, a Kāśyapa. He seems to have lived in the house of his parents till they died, and his elder brother, Nandivardhana, succeeded to what principality they had. Then, at the age of twenty-eight, he, with the consent of those in power, entered the spiritual career, which in India, just as the Church in Western countries, seems to have offered a field for the ambition of younger sons. For twelve years he led a life of austerities, visiting even the wild tribes of the country, called Rādha. After the first year he went about naked. From the end of these twelve years of preparatory self-mortification dates Vardhamāna's Kevaliship. Thereafter he was recognised as omniscient, as a prophet of the Jainas or a Tīrthaṅkara (the founder of the path), and had the titles Jina (spiritual conqueror), Mahāvīra (great hero), etc., which were also given to Śākyamuni. The last thirty years of his life he passed in teaching his religious system, and organising his order of ascetics, which, as we have seen above, was patronised, or at least countenanced, chiefly by those princes with whom he was related through his mother.'[1] Vardhamāna called himself the expounder of tenets held by a succession of twenty-three earlier sages or tīrthaṅkaras, whose history is more or less legendary. He was not so much the founder of a new faith as the reformer of the previously existing creed of Pārśvanātha, who is said to have died in 776 BC. Jaina tradition ascribes the origin of the system to Ṛṣabha, who lived many centuries back. There is evidence to show that so far back as the first century BC there were people who were worshipping Ṛṣabhadeva, the first tīrthaṅkara. There is no doubt that Jainism prevailed even before Vardhamāna or Pārśvanātha. The Yajur-Veda mentions the names of three Tīrthaṅkaras-Ṛṣabha, Ajitanātha and Ariṣṭanemi. The Bhāgavata Purāṇa endoreses the view that Ṛṣabha was the founder of Jainism. Whatever be the truth of it all, the Jains believe that their system had previously been proclaimed through countless ages by each one of a succession of great teachers.

Vardhamāna's followers were drawn chiefly from the Kṣatriya aristocracy, and he organised them into a regular community, with lay and monastic members of both sexes. We have reason to believe that under the influence of Vardhamāna followers of two different creeds had joined the order, those who agreed with him that complete abandonment of possessions involved the giving up of all clothing, and those of the order of Pārśvanātha, who stopped short of this extreme measure of renunciation and looked upon clothing as a necessity. Perhaps this fact is referred to in the Uttarādhyayana[2] account of the union of the two churches of Keśi and Gautama. This question of clothes *versus* no clothes led to the great schism and division of the Jainas into the Śvetāmbara (white robed) and the Digambara (skyclad or nude) sects, which took place in AD 79 or 82.

These two sects are distinguished not so much by their philosophical views as by their ethical tenets. The Digambaras hold that Kevalins or

1. Jacobi, Introduction, p. xv., S.B.E., vol. xxii; see also pp. 217 ff.
2. Lecture XXIII.

perfect saints live without food, that a monk who owns any property such as wearing clothes cannot reach nirvāṇa, and that no woman can attain liberation. They represent the Tīrthaṅkara as nude, unadorned and with downcast eyes, and think that Vardhamāna never married. They disown the canonical books of the Śvetāmbaras and themselves possess none.

III

LITERATURE

The faith was preserved in men's minds, as usual. The knowledge of the scriptures was slowly decaying, till in the fourth century BC the need for fixing the cannon was keenly felt. A council met for the purpose at Pāṭaliputra near the end of the fourth century, BC, though the final form of the canon is due to the Council at Valabhī, presided over by Devarddhi some 800 years later, about AD 454. Eighty-four works are recognised as belonging to the canonical literature. Among them are forty-one Sūtras, a number of Prakīrṇakas or unclassified works, twelve Niryuktis or commentaries, one Mahābhāṣya or the great commentary. The forty-one Sūtras include the eleven Aṅgas, the twelve Upāṅgas, the five Chedas, the five Mūlas and eight miscellaneous works, such as Bhadrabāhu's Kalpasūtra.[3] These were in Ardha-Māgadhi, but Sanskrit became a favourite language of Jainism after the Christian era. According to the Digambaras, it was in AD 57 that the sacred lore was reduced to writing, when those learned in it were not available, and the only sources of information were what people remembered about the sayings of Vardhamāna and the Kevalins. The scriptures relating to the seven tattvas, the nine padārthas, the six dravyas and the five astikāyas,[4] were formed on their basis.[5]

3. Translated by Jacobi in S.B.E., vol. xxii.

4. See Jaini, *Outlines of Jainism*, appendix v.

5. Among the extra-canonical works of the Śvetāmbaras, the following are of philosophical interest: (1) Umāsvāti's Tattvārthādhigama Sūtra (after 3rd century AD). It has ten chapters and has been commented upon by many writers. It is a very popular book. (2) Siddhasena Divākara's Nyāyāvatāra (5th century AD). (3) Haribhadra's Ṣaḍdarśanasamuccaya (9th century AD). (4) Merutuṅga's (14th century AD) Ṣaḍdarśanavicāra. Navatattva belongs to this period, though its author is unknown. Among the chief philosophical works of the Digambaras may be mentioned: (1) Kundakundācārya Pañcāstikāyasāra (50 BC). It is said that Kundākundācārya is the Elacārya, the author of Tirukkural, while Tiruvaḷḷuvar was only its publisher. (2) Vidyānanda's Jainaślokavārtika (8th century AD).

IV

RELATION TO OTHER SYSTEMS

Buddhism and Jainism deny the existence of an intelligent first cause, adore deified saints, possess clergy practising celibacy, and think it sinful to take the life of any animal for any cause. Their founders are men who made themselves perfect, though they were not always so. Both the systems are indifferent, if not opposed, to the authority of the Vedas. From the striking similarities in the lives and teachings of Buddha and Vardhamāna, it is sometimes argued that the two systems of Buddhism and Jainism are one, and that Jainism is only an offshoot of Buddhism. Barth writes: 'The legend of Vardhamāna, or to apply to him the name which is most in use, Mahāvīra, the great hero, the Jina of the present age presents so many and so peculiar points of contact with that of Gautama Buddha, that we are instinctively led to conclude that one and the same person is the subject of both. Both are of royal birth; the same names recur among their relations and disciples. They were born and they died in the same country and at the same period of time. According to the accepted reports, the nirvāṇa of the Jina took place in 526 BC, that of Buddha in 543 BC; and if we make allowances for the uncertainty inherent in these data, the two dates may be considered to be identical. Coincidences quite similar occur in the course of the two traditions. Like the Buddhists, the Jainas claim to have been patronised by the Maurya princes. A district which is a holy land for the one is almost always a holy land for the other, and their sacred places adjoin each other in Behar, in the peninsula of Guzerat, on mount Abu in Rājasthān,

---

(3) Guṇabhadra's Ātmānuśāsana (9th century). (4) Amitacandra's Tattvārthasāra, and (5) Puruṣārthasiddhyupāya (9th century). (6) Nemicandra's Dravyasaṁgraha (10th century), which treats of dravyas or substances. (7) Gommaṭasāra, which discusses the five subjects of bandha or bondage, badhyamāna or what is bound, bandhasvāmin or that which binds, bandhahetu or the cause of bondage, and bandhabheda or the ways of breaking the bondage. (8) Labdhisāra, which treats of labdhi or attainment. (9) Kṣapaṇasāra, which discusses the ways and means by which Kaṣāyas (passions) may be removed; and (10) Trilokasāra, which contains a description of the three lokas or regions of the universe; and (11) Sakalakīrti's Tattvārthasāradīpikā (AD 1464). Malliṣeṇa's Syādvādamañjari (13th century AD) and Devasūri's Pramāṇanayatattvālokālaṁkāra (11th century AD) are other works of considerable importance. Several of these works are translated into English in the series of the *Sacred Books of the Jains*.

as well as elsewhere. If we collate together all these correspondences in doctrine, organisation, religious observances and traditions, the inference seems inevitable that one of the two religions is a sect, and in some degree the copy of the other. When in addition to this we think of the manifold relations which there are between the legend of Buddha and the Brāhmanical traditions, relations which are wanting in the legend of Mahāvīra; when we reflect, moreover, that Buddhism has on its behalf the testimony of the edicts of Aśoka, and that from that time, the third century before our era, it was in possession of a literature, some of the titles of which have been transmitted to us, while the most ancient testimonies of an unquestionable nature in favour of Jainism do not go farther back than the fifth century after Christ; when we reflect further that the chief sacred language of the Buddhists, the Pāli, is almost as ancient as these edicts, while that of the Jainas, the Ardha-Māgadhi, is a prākrit dialect obviously more recent; when we add to all these the conclusions, very uncertain it is true in the present state of our knowledge, which are furnished by the internal characteristics of Jainism, such as its more mature systematisation, its tendency to expatiate, and the pains it is always taking to demonstrate its antiquity, we shall feel no hesitation in admitting that of the two, Buddhism is the one which is best entitled to the claim of originality.'[6] Colebrooke, however, contends that Jainism is older than Buddhism, since it adopts the animistic belief that nearly everything is possessed of a soul.[7] Either view goes against the Indian tradition which looks upon Jainism and Buddhism as two distinct faiths. The Hindu śāstras never confuse them, and their testimony is confirmed by the researches of Guérinot, Jacobi and Bühler, among others. It is now conclusively established that Vardhamāna was an historical person distinct from Gautama Buddha and Jainism a system quite independent of Buddhism. Guérinot has emphasised five great points of difference between Vardhamāna and Gautama Buddha relating to their birth, the deaths of their mothers, their renunciation, illumination and death. Vardhamāna was born at Vaiśālī about 599 BC, while Gautama was born at Kapilavastu about 567 BC. Vardhamāna's parents lived up to a good old age, while Gautama's mother died soon after giving birth to him. Vardhamāna assumed the ascetic life with the consent of his relatives, while Gautama made himself a monk against the wishes of his

6. Barth, *The Religions of India*, pp. 148–150.
7. Colebrooke, *Miscellaneous Essays*, ii, p. 276.

father. Vardhamāna had twelve years of ascetic preparation, while Gautama obtained illumination at the end of six years. Vardhamāna died at Pawa in 527 BC, while Gautama died at Kusinagar about 488 BC. Jacobi attempts to prove the priority and independence of Jainism to Buddhism by several distinct lines of evidence which we shall briefly indicate here, referring the interested reader to this learned discussions.[8] The Nigganṭhas (those who have no bonds) of the Buddhist books are the followers of Vardhamāna, and must be at least as old as the fourth century BC, if not older. The *Nātaputta* of Pāli Buddhist literature is Vardhamāna. A reference to the doctrine of the Nigganṭhas, as given in Buddhist canonical literature, confirms the identity of the Nigganṭhas and the Jains. 'The Nigganṭha Nātaputta ... knows and sees all things, claims perfect knowledge and faith; teaches the annihilation by austerities of the old karma and prevention by inactivity of new karma. When karma ceases, misery ceases.'[9] Aśoka's edicts refer to the sect of the Jains.[10] The Buddhist books themselves refer to the Jainas as the rivals of Buddhism. Internal evidence confirms the view of independence. The Jaina theory of the soul and knowledge are so distinctive of Jainism and dissimilar to those of Buddhism that one cannot be a borrowed product of the other. The similarities in doctrine between the two on the questions of karma and rebirth prove nothing, since these are the common features of all Indian systems. For these reasons we look upon Jainism as an earlier creed than Buddhism. M. Poussin is of opinion that the Jains were 'a powerful mendicant order which originated or was reorganised a few years before Śākyamuni.'[11]

According to Colebrooke, Jainism and Sāṁkhya philosophy have some points in common. They both believe in the eternity a matter and the perpetuity of the world. The dualism of the one is not unlike that of the other. Only while the Sāṁkhya derives the development of the material world and living beings from the principles of puruṣa and prakṛti, the

8. See Introduction to vols. xxii and xlv., S.B.E.

9. S.B.E., vol. xxii., pp. xv ff. Buddhaghoṣa's Commentary on Brahmajālasutta of the Dīghanikāya refers to the view of cold water possessing life, as also the Jaina denial of the ājīvaka doctrine that the soul has colour. Sāmaññaphalasutta refers possibly to the four vows of Pārśvanātha. In Majjhima Nikāya (56) and Mahāvagga (vi. 31), we have accounts of the conversion by Buddha of the lay disciples of Vardhamāna.

10. See Vincent Smith, *Aśoka*, pp. 192–193.

11. *The Way to Nirvāṇa*, p. 67.

Jains trace them all to primeval nature.[12] The similarity is only apparent. The Jaina conception of the activity of the soul has more in common with the Nyāya-Vaiśeṣika theory than with the Sāṁkhya view of the unaffected and inactive nature of the soul; nor do we find much agreement between the two in any essential doctrine such as causation.

Attempts are sometimes made by students of Jainism to represent it as a revolt of the critical fair-minded Kṣatriya, against the clever unscrupulous Brāhmin, who disallowed to all others the privilege of entering on the fourth order of the sannyāsins, and claimed exclusive control of the sacrifices. Such a theory cannot be sustained when we realise that the Brāhmin made no such claim as regards the order of the sannyāsin, for all the upper classes were allowed to pass through the āśramas. Were the exclusiveness of the Brāhmin the cause of revolt, it should have been led not by the Kṣatriyas, who were as good or as bad as the Brāhmins in this respect, but by the other classes. We have no reason to believe that the suffering of the common people led to the rise of Jainism. It is an expression of the general ferment of thought which prevailed at the beginning of the epic period, and we need not invent any anti-Brāhmin prejudice for an explanation of its rise. When different views of life and doctrine professed by different peoples come into touch with each other, there is bound to be an interpenetration of thought, giving rise to an extraordinary development of feeling and belief, and Jainism is one manifestation of this mental unrest.

The doctrine of rebirth enunciated in the Upaniṣads, sometimes in an extravagant form, led to the idea that all things in the world possessed souls. Naturally the Jaina believed that every material thing, fire, wind and plant, also had a spirit in it. On such a view the simple joy of the earlier peoples in sacrifices could not last. The times were ripe for revolt. The belief that all things, animals and insects, plants and leaves, were possessed of souls, when coupled with the idea of rebirth, led to a horror of taking life in any form. Vardhamāna insisted that we should not injure life whether in sport or in sacrifice. To strengthen the position of protest, the Jains denied God for whose propitiation the sacrifices were being offered. God cannot be held responsible for the sorrows of life. Jainism seeks to show a way out of the misery of life by austerity, inward and outward. When we become perfect, we do not escape into a nirvāṇa of nothingness, but enter into a

12. Tattvārthādhigama Sūtra, Commentary on, iii. 6.

state of being without qualities and relations, and removed from all chances of rebirth.

The Jaina system is looked upon as unorthodox (avaidika), since it does not accept the authority of the Veda. It is not therefore possible for it to look upon its own system of thought as a mere revelation by the Jina. Its claim to acceptance is its accordance with reality. Its scheme of the universe is said to be based on logic and experience. In their metaphysics, the Jainas accept the Vedic realism, though they do not systematise it in the spirit of the Upaniṣads. Prakṛti is analysed and given an atomic constitution. The puruṣas cease to be passive spectators, but become active agents. The central features of Jaina philosophy are its realistic classification of being, its theory of knowledge, with its famous doctrines of Syādvāda and Saptabhangi, or seven-fold mode of predication and its ascetic ethics. Here, as in the other systems of Indian thought, practical ethics is wedded to philosophical speculation. The realistic metaphysics and ascetic ethics may have come down to Vardhamāna from his predecessors, but the theory of knowledge is probably due to him, and is not without its interest to the modern student of the history of philosophy.

V

THEORY OF KNOWLEDGE

The Jains admit five kinds of knowledge: mati, śruti, avadhi, manaḥparyāya and kevala.[13] (1) Mati is ordinary cognition, obtained by normal means of sense perception. It includes smṛti or remembrance and saṁjñā or pratyabhijñā or recognition; curita or tarka, or induction based on observation; abhinibodha or anumāna, or deductive reasoning.[14] Matijñāna is sometimes distinguished into three kinds, viz. upalabdhi or perception, bhāvanā or memory, and upayoga or understanding.[15] Matijñāna is knowledge by means of the indriyas or the senses and mind, which is called anindriya, to distinguish it from senses. We always have sense presentation or darṣana prior to the rise of matijñāna. (2) Sruti or testimony is knowledge derived through signs, symbols or words. While

13. U.T.S., i. 9, and D.S. 5.

14. Pp. 18–19. For the Jaina view of the syllogism, see the chapter on the Nyāya in vol. ii.

15. Pp. 19–20.

matijñāna gives us knowledge by acquaintance, this gives only knowledge by description. Śrutajñāna is of four kinds, namely, labdhi or association, bhāvanā or attention, upayoga or understanding, and naya or aspects of the meaning of things.[16] Naya is noticed here since the different interpretations of the scriptural texts come up for discussion. (3) Avadhi is direct knowledge of things even at a distance of time or space. It is knowledge by clairvoyance. (4) Manaḥparyāya is direct knowledge of the thoughts of others, as in telepathic knowledge of others' minds. (5) Kevala or perfect knowledge comprehends all substances and their modfications.[17] It is omniscience unlimited by space, time or object. To the perfect consciousness the whole reality is obvious. This knowledge, which is independent of the senses, which can only be felt and not described, is possible only for purified souls free from bondage.

The first three kinds of knowledge are liable to error, while the last two cannot be wrong.[18] The validity of knowledge consists in its practical efficiency, in its enabling us to get what is good and avoid what is evil. Valid knowledge is a faithful representation of objects, and is therefore practically useful. Invalid knowledge represents things in relations in which they do not exist. When we mistake a rope for a snake, our error consists in seeing a snake where it is not. Invalid knowledge is subject to contradiction, while valid knowledge is not so. Erroneous knowledge is what is characterised by samśaya or doubt (affecting mati and śruti), viparyaya or mistake, or the opposite of truth (which may be found in avadhi), and anadhyavasāya or wrong knowledge caused by carelessness or indifference. We have eight kinds of knowledge, the five right and the three wrong ones. Only one kind of knowledge is active at a time.[19]

Knowledge is pratyakṣa or direct, when it is immediate and parokṣa or indirect when it is mediated by some other kind of knowledge. Of the five kinds of knowledge, mati and śruti are parokṣa and the rest pratyakṣa.[20] Mati or ordinary cognition which we obtain by the senses and mind is parokṣa, since there is dependence on the senses.[21] There are some, however, who view sense knowledge as pratyakṣa or direct. 'Perception or darśana

16. Pp. 20.
17. U.T.S., i. 29.
18. U.T.S., i. 31. p. 42.
19. U.T.S., i. 30.
20. U.T.S., i. 11 and 12.
21. U.T.S., i. 14.

is of four kinds, perception through visual sensations, perception through non-visual senses, again that through the faculty of avadhi or clairvoyance, and lastly through kevala or infinite perception, which is unlimited and apprehends all reality.'[22]

Caitanya or consciousness is the essence of jīva, and the two manifestations of caitanya are perception (darśana) and intelligence (jñāna).[23] In darśana the details are not perceived, while in jñāna they are. The former is simple apprehension, the latter conceptual knowledge. 'That perception of the generalities (sāmānya) of things without particularities (viśeṣa) in which there is no grasping of details is called darśana.[24] It involves several stages, which are: (1) Vyañjanāvagraha, where the stimulus acts on the peripheral ends of the sense organs and brings the subject into a certain relation with the object; (2) Arthāvagraha, where consciousness is excited and a sensation felt, where the person is barely conscious of the object; (3) Īhā, where the mind desires to know the details of the object, its resemblances to and differences from others; (4) Avāya, where takes place the reintegration of the present and the past, and the recognition of the object as this and not that; and (5) Dhāraṇā, where we recognise that sensations reveal qualities of things. An impression[25] results by which we are able to

22. Pp. 24–25. See also Siddhasena Divākara, Nyāyāvatāra, 4. Sometimes pratyakṣa is said to be of two kinds, saṁvyavahārika and pāramārthika. The latter includes avadhi, manaḥparyāya and kevala, and the former both what is caused by the senses (indriyanibandhana) and what is not caused by them (anīndriyanibandhana). The Sāṁvyavahārika pratyakṣa is what we have in everyday life, and on it perception and memory depend. It is defined by the Pramāṇamīmāṁsāvṛtti as the act of satisfying a desire to cognise. (Samīcīnaḥ pravṛttinivṛttirūpo vyavahāraḥ saṁvyavahāraḥ. Pratyakṣa is entire or sakala in the case of kevalin's knowledge and vikala, or deficient in other cases.) Parokṣa is divided into five kinds: of (1) smṛta or memory of what is already experienced, as when we remember a man whom we saw before; (2) pratyabhijñā, or knowledge derived from resemblances of things, as when we identify a new object with something about which we read before; (3) tarka, or reasoning from universals; (4) anumāna or knowledge by means of the middle term; and (5) āgama or verbal testimony of an ancient being. In the *Pramāṇanayatattvālokālaṁkāra*, the distinction between direct (pratyakṣa) and indirect (parokṣa) knowledge is said to be one of degree of clearness. See II and III. It is, because, according to the Jains, the outer sense activity is only an indirect help to the rise of perceptual knowledge.

23. D.S., 4.

24. D.S., 43.

25. Saṁskāra.

remember the object later. This analysis reveals the mediate character of perception, and also tells us that things are extra-mental realities. The existence of an objective reality beyond and beside consciousness, apprehended by perception and understood by intelligence, is asserted by the Jainas The attributes and relations of things are directly given in experience and are not products of thought or imagination. The process of knowing does not modify the object of knowledge. The relation between knowledge and its object is an external one with regard to physical objects, though it is different in the case of self-consciousness. The consciousness of the jīva is ever active, and this activity reveals its own nature as well as that of the object. Jñeya or object of knowledge includes self and not-self. As light reveals itself and other objects, even so does jñāna reveal itself and others. The Nyāya-Vaiśeṣika theory, that knowledge reveals only external relations but not itself, is rejected by the Jainas. In knowing any object, the self knows itself simultaneously. If it did not know its own existence, none else could impart this knowledge to it. Every act of perception and knowledge implies the statement 'I know it thus and thus.' Knowledge is always appropriated by the self. The question, how consciousness can reveal the nature of unconscious objects, is dismissed as absurd, since it is the nature of knowledge to reveal objects.

In the case of self-consciousness, the relation between knowledge (jñāna) and the object of knowledge (jñeya) is very intimate. Jñānin and Jñāna, the subject of knowledge and knowledge are also inseparable, though distinguishable. In self-consciousness, the subject of knowledge, the object of knowledge, and knowledge itself are different aspects of a single concrete unity. There are no jīvas without jñāna, since that would take away the cetana or conscious character of the jīvas and reduce them to the level of ajīva dravyas, and there can be no jñāna without selves, for that would make jñāna foundationless.

In its perfect condition the soul is pure jñāna and darśana (knowledge and intuition),[26] which arise simultaneously, or are together. In the mundane jīvas, jñāna is preceded by darśana.[27] Perfect knowledge is free from doubt (saṁśaya), perversity (vimoha) and indefiniteness (vibhrama).[28] The karmas which obscure the different varieties of darśana are called

26. D.S., 6.
27. D.S., 44.
28. D.S., 42.

the Darśanāvaraṇīya karmas, and those which obscure the different kinds of jñāna are called the jñāna-varaṇīya karmas.[29] All knowledge is in the soul, though it manifests itself when the disturbing media are removed. The impediments are passions and emotions, which cause the inflow of matter and prevent the soul from exercising its natural function in full measure, and interests in the physical concerns of life which confine our knowledge to the immediately useful. So aspects of reality in which we are not interested are shut off by selective attention. When the soul is unimpeded by the influences of matter which obscure knowledge, and freely functions, it is capable of omniscience, or knowledge of all things, past, present and future. In our empirical lives, the purity of the soul is defiled by the absorption of the unconscious substance, matter. By tearing it asunder, by destroying its energies, we tend to increase our knowledge. When the opposing energies are completely overthrown, the soul vibrates at its natural rhythm and exercises its function of unlimited knowing. Souls are substances characterised by intelligence, and their differences are due to the degrees of their connexions with matter.

Knowledge is of two forms, *pramāṇa*, or knowledge of a thing as it is in itself, and *naya*, or knowledge of a thing in its relation. The doctrine of nayas or standpoints is a peculiar feature of the Jaina logic. A naya is a standpoint from which we make a statement about a thing. We define and separate our standpoints by abstraction. The conceptions that belong to them, or partial views, are the outcome of purposes that we pursue. The result of this abstraction and concentration on particular ends is the relativity of knowledge. To occupy one particular standpoint is not to deny the others. For certain purposes the view that the sun goes round the earth is quite as effective as the other, that the earth goes round the sun. Even in the Upaniṣads we have glimpses of how reality reveals itself in different ways at different stages of our knowledge. Much of the confusion of Buddhism is due to its false exaggeration of the relative principle of flow into the absolute truth. What is true from one standpoint may not be true from another. Particular aspects are never adequate to the whole reality. The relative solutions are abstractions under which reality may be regarded, but do not give us a full and sufficient account of it. Jainism makes basic and fundamental the principle that truth is relative to our standpoints. The general character of reality is given in several partial views.

29. For a classification of these, see Jaini, *Outlines of Jainism*, pp. 30–31.

There are many ways in which nayas are divided, and we shall notice the chief of them here. According to one scheme, there are seven nayas, of which four refer to objects or meanings, and three to words, and all these lead to fallacies (ābhāsas) when taken as absolute and entire. The *artha* (object or meaning) nayas are the following:

(1) *Naigamanaya*. There are two ways in which it is interpreted. It is said that it relates to the purpose or end of a course of activity which is present throughout. When we see a man carrying water, fire, utensils, etc., and we ask him, 'What are you doing?' he says, 'I am cooking food,' we have an illustration of Naigamanaya. It tells us of the general purpose which controls the series of acts and emphasises the teleological character of life.[30] This view is adopted by Pūjyapāda. Siddhasena adopts a different view. We have naigamanaya when we comprehend a thing as having both generic and specific qualities and we do not distinguish between them. (2) *Saṁgrahanaya* emphasises the common features. It is the class point of view. Though it is true that the class is not real apart from individuals, it is sometimes useful to notice the general features. This Saṁgrahanaya is of two kinds, Parasaṁgraha or the ultimate class view, which takes into account the fact that all things partake of the nature of reality. Aparasaṁgraha is the inferior class view. The abstract absolutist position is regarded as the ābhāsa of the Saṁgrahanaya. Jainism admits the distinction between sāmānya or universal and viśeṣa or particular features, though it regards it as a relative one. Sāṁkhya and Advaita Vedānta deny viśeṣas, while Buddhism denies sāmānya. Nyāya-Vaiśeṣika accepts both, and looks upon the concrete thing as a complex made up of the universal and the particular. But Jainism considers the distinction to be a relative one, while Nyāya-Vaiśeṣika looks upon it as absolute. (3) *Vyavahāranaya* is the popular conventional point of view based on empirical knowledge. We know things in their entirety and emphasise their striking individualities. The specific features arrest attention. The hypothesis of materialism, and we may add pluralism, are the ābhāsas of this naya. (4) *Ṛjusūtranaya* is narrower than the Vyavahāranaya. It takes into account the state of a thing at a particular point or time. It overlooks all continuity and identity. To it the real is the momentary. A thing is what it is at the present moment. The Jains look upon it as the presupposition of the Buddhist philosophy. While this naya is useful to expose the hollowness of an abstract philosophy of 'being,' it

30. See commentary on T.S., 1. 33.

is useless as an ultimate account of truth. The remaining three are Śabdanayas. (5) *Śabdanaya* is based on the fact that a name has the function of calling up to our mind the particular object referred to or implied by the name, whatever it be, an individual thing, attribute, relation or action. Each name has its own meaning, and different words may also refer to the same object. The relation between terms and their meanings is a relative one, and if we forget this, fallacies arise. (6) *Samābhirūḍhanaya* distinguishes terms according to their roots. It is an application of the Śabdanaya. (7) *Evambhūtanaya* is a specialised form of the sixth kind. Of the various aspects and gradations in the manifestation of a thing, only one is contemplated by the root of a term, and it is this aspect that is the legitimate meaning of a term in its current usage. The same thing in a different attitude must be designated by a different term altogether. Each of these seven nayas has a larger extent than that which follows it. Naigama has the largest extent and Evambhuta the least. Each naya or point of view represents one of the many ways from which a thing can be looked at. If any one point of view is mistaken for the whole we have a *nayābhāsa*. According to the Jains, the Nyāya-Vyśeṣika, the Sāṁkhya, the Advaita Vedānta, and the Buddhist systems adopt the first four nayas respectively and mistake them for the whole truth.

The nayas are also distinguished into (1) dravyārthika, from the point of view of substance, and (2) paryāyārthika, from the point of view of modification or condition. Each of them has several subdivisions. The dravyārthika nayas consider the permanent nature of things, while the paryāyārthika ones relate to their perishable aspects.

Since all these standpoints are relative, we have also what is called the Nayaniścaya, or the true and complete point of view. The Niścayanaya is of two kinds, Śuddhaniścaya and Aśuddhaniścaya. The former deals with the pure unconditioned reality, while the latter contemplates conditioned existence.

To those familiar with the conception of philosophy as a criticism of categories, we need not say that this doctrine of nayas or standpoints is a logical one. The Jains are fond of quoting the old story of the six blind men, who each laid hands on a different part of the elephant and tried to describe the whole animal. The man who caught the ear thought that the creature resembled a winnowing fan, the holder of the leg imagined that he was clinging to a big round pillar, etc. It was he who saw the whole that perceived that each had only a portion of the truth. Almost all philosophical disputes arise out of a confusion of standpoints. The question is often asked, whether the effect is the same as its material cause or different from it. That it pre-exists in the cause and is made manifest by the operation which that cause undergoes is the view of satkāryavāda, adopted by the Vedānta and the Sāṁkhya philosophies. The asatkāryavāda of the Vaiśeṣikas urges that the effect is something new and did not exist before. Jainism decides the dispute by a reference to the different standpoints implied in the two. If we consider the effect such as a gold necklace to be a mere substance, it is the same as the gold of which it is made; but if we look at the necklace as a modification, it is new, and did not exist in the mere substance of gold. The contributions which each standpoint makes are always partial views reached by processes of abstraction.

The most important use of these standpoints is of course the Syādvāda or the Saptabhaṅgī. It is the use in seven different ways of judgments which affirm and negate, severally and jointly, without self-contradiction, thus discriminating the several qualities of a thing. The difficulty of predication is got over on the Jaina theory, since it holds that subject and predicate are identical from the point of view of substance and different from the point of view of modification.

The view is called Syādvāda, since it holds all knowledge to be only probable. Every proposition gives us only a perhaps, a may be or a syād. We cannot affirm or deny anything absolutely of any object. There is nothing certain on account of the endless complexity of things. It emphasises the extremely complex nature of reality and its indefiniteness. It does not deny the possibility of predication, though it disallows absolute or categorical predication. The dynamic character of reality can consist only with relative or conditional predication. Every proposition is true, but only under certain conditions, i.e. hypothetically.

It holds that there are seven different ways of speaking of a thing or its attributes, according to the point of view. There is a point of view from which substance or attribute (1) is, (2) is not, (3) is and is not, (4) is unpredicable, (5) is and is unpredicable, (6) is not and is unpredicable, and (7) is, is not and is unpredicable.

1. *Syād asti.* From the point of view of its own material, place, time and nature, a thing is, i.e. exists as itself. The jar exists as made of clay, in my room at the present moment, of such and such a shape and size.

2. *Syād nāsti.* From the point of view of the material, place, time and nature of another thing, a thing is not, i.e. it is not no-thing. The jar does

not exist as made of metal, at a different place or time or of a different shape and size.

3. *Syād asti nāsti.* From the point of view of the same quaternary, relating to itself and another thing, it may be said that a thing is and is not. In a certain sense the jar exists and in a certain sense it does not. We say here what a thing is as well as what it is not.

4. *Syād avaktavya.* While in three we make statements that a thing is in its own self and is not, as another successively, it becomes impossible to make these statements at once. In this sense a thing is unpredicable. Though the presence of its own nature and the absence of other-nature are both together in the jar, still we cannot express them.

5. *Syād asti avaktavya.* From the point of view of its own quaternary and at the same time from the joint quaternary of itself and no-thing, a thing is and is unpredicable. We note here both the existence of a thing and its indescribability.

6. *Syād nāsti avaktavya.* From the point of view of the quaternary of the no-thing and at the same time from the joint quaternary of itself and no-thing, a thing is not and is also unpredicable. We note here what a thing is not as well as its indescribability.

7. *Syād asti nāsti avaktavya.* From the point of view of its own quaternary as well as that of no-thing and at the same time from the joint quaternary of itself and no-thing, a thing is, is not and is indescribable. We bring out the inexpressibility of a thing as well as what it is and what it is not.[31]

Of these seven possible ways of speaking about a thing or its attributes, the first two are the chief, the simple affirmative that a thing is in its svarūpa (own form), svadravya (own matter), svakṣetra (own place), and svakāla (own time), and the simple negative that a thing is not in its pararūpa (other form), paradravya (other matter), parakṣetra (other place), and parakāla (other time.) The latter is the negative fact. This doctrine insists on the correlativity of affirmation and negation. All judgments are double-edged in their character. All things are existent as well as non-existent (sadasadātmakam).[32] A thing is what it is and is not what it is not. According to this view, all negation has a positive basis. Even imaginary concepts like skyflower possess a positive basis in the two reals sky and flower,

31. T.S., p. 14; P. 16.
32. Svarūpeṇa sattvāt, pararūpeṇa ca asattvāt.

though their combination is unreal. It emphasises the fundamental truth that distinction is necessary for thought. A thing which has nothing from which it can be distinguished is unthinkable. The absolute devoid of distinctions within as well as without is truly unthinkable. For all things which are objects of thought *are* in one sense and *are not* in another.

Śaṁkara and Rāmānuja[33] criticise the Saptabhaṅgī view on the ground of the impossibility of contradictory attributes co-existing in the same thing. Rāmānuja writes; 'Contradictory attributes such as existence and non-existence cannot at the same time belong to one thing, any more than light and darkness.' The Jains admit that a thing cannot have self-contradictory attributes at the same time and in the same sense. All that they say is that everything is of a complex nature, an identity in difference. The real comprehends and reconciles differences in itself. Attributes which are contradictory in the abstract coexist in life and experience. The tree is moving in that its branches are moving, and it is not moving since it is fixed to its place in the ground. It is necessary for us to know a thing clearly and distinctly, in its self-existence as well as in its relations to other objects. The second point urged by the Vedāntins that the Saptabhaṅgī doctrine is of no practical utility is an expression of personal opinion over which we need not linger. Nor can it be contended that the Saptabhaṅgī doctrine is inconsistent with the other views of the Jaina philosophy. It is a logical corollary of the *anekāntavāda*, the doctrine of the manyness of reality. Since reality is multiform and ever changing, nothing can be considered to be existing everywhere and at all times and in all ways and places, and it is impossible to pledge ourselves to an inflexible creed.

VI

VALUE OF JAINA LOGIC

Before we pass on to the next section, it may be useful to bring together at this point a few critical reflections suggested by the Jaina logic. We have incidentally mentioned the strong points of the theory of knowledge of the Jainas and defended it against the attacks of the Vedāntins. Yet in our opinion the Jaina logic leads us to a monistic idealism, and so far as the Jainas shrink from it they are untrue to their own logic. We shall enforce

33. S.B., ii. 2. 33; R.B., ii. 2. 31.

this criticism from the metaphysical side at a later stage of our discussion. Let us here understand the implications of the Jaina logic.

The theory of relativity cannot be logically sustained without the hypothesis of an absolute. It is true that the law of contradiction on which Jaina logic takes its stand involves that distinction is necessary for thought, but a thing which is absolutely distinct from others is as unreal to thought as a thing which is absolutely one with others. Thought is not mere distinction, but it is also relation. Everything is possible only in relation to and as distinct from others. The law of contradiction is the negative aspect of the law of identity. All distinction presupposes unity. Since for the Jainas thought furnishes the clue to reality, the final expression of reality must be a concrete monism that accounts for all existence. It is not a one excluding the many, or a many excluding order or unity. The Jaina logic revolts against all abstractions, and will not commit itself to any false distinction of either-or, one or many. The Jainas admit that things are one in their universal aspect (jāti or kāraṇa) and many in their particular aspect (vyakti or kārya). Both these, according to them, are partial point of view. A plurality of reals is admittedly a relative truth. We must rise to the complete point of view and look at the whole with all the wealth of its attributes. If Jainism stops short with plurality, which is at best a relative and partial truth, and does not ask whether there is any higher truth pointing to a one which particularises itself in the object of the world, connected with one another vitally, essentially and immanently, it throws overboard its own logic and exalts a relative truth into an absolute one.

Only such a theory of monism is consistent with the Jaina theory of relations which are not independent of and external to what they relate. Meaning enters into reality, and between subject and object there is an intimate relation. The dualism of mind and external world, whatever truth it may have at the psychological level, is overcome when we rise to the standpoint of logic as theory of knowledge. If the two, subject and object, the individual mind and the independent reality, are separate, then there can be no knowledge at all. Either knowledge is arbitrary and groundless or the dualism is wrong. Subject and object are not separate existences held together by an external bond. They are a unity in duality, a duality in unity. If we suppress either term, the whole is dissolved. The distinction of subject and object is not a relation between two independent entities, but a distinction made by knowledge itself within its own field. If Jaina logic does not recognise the need for this principle, which includes within it the distinction of subject and object, it is because it takes a partial view for the whole truth.

If we are to accept the above interpretation of its principle of relativity, the self which takes up the different points of view cannot be the particular empirical self, but something deeper. Knowledge is not merely individual. If the analysis of reality is to be more than subjective, we must admit the activity of one self in the many individuals home we know empirically as objects of knowledge. Before any question of knowledge arises, this one self must be presupposed as the ultimate and final fact within which fall all distinctions of subject and object. And this self is not a passing feeling or a transient phase of consciousness.

The fact that we are conscious of our relativity means that we have to reach out to a fuller conception. It is from that higher absolute point of view that the lower relative ones can be explained. All true explanation is from above downwards.

It is only in the light of this absolute principle that we shall be able to apply a scale of values to the relative conceptions and estimate their worth. All truth is relative when compared with the absolute truth. All knowledge transcends the given and points beyond itself. With a continuous advance towards fuller and fuller truth, the object itself loses its apparently given character. When we reach absolute knowledge the distinction between subject and object is overcome. Only in the light of such an absolute standard could we correct the abstractions of the lower. Then shall we see that the several relatives are only stages in a continuous process which has the realisation of the soul's freedom for its determining end. The recognition of every form of knowledge as relative, something bound to pass over into something else, requires us to assume a larger reality, an absolute in which all the relatives fall.

But is there any way of comprehending the nature of this absolute? We cannot get an idea of the positive full-orbed reality by putting together our partial views. A mere pooling of the contributions of the different standpoints will not lead us to the truth in itself. If we follow the spirit of Jaina logic, thought is bound up with the relative and cannot give us a knowledge of the absolute. If thought cannot grasp reality, is there any other power that can? The question is not explicitly raised, but the answer is implicitly given in the affirmative. A careful consideration of *Kevalajñāna*, or the knowledge possessed by the free, will tell us that the Jaina theory by implication accepts the method of intuition and the philosophy of absolutism.

According to the Jaina theory, the highest kind of knowledge which combines all the characters manifested in experience is that possessed by the Kevalin or the liberated. It is full or perfect knowledge which is the soul's characteristic in its pure and undefiled condition. This perfect knowledge which is the essence of the soul, manifests itself in different degrees in different kinds of beings on account of the influence of the external force of matter whose association or union has the effect of suppressing the clear knowledge of the soul. This unconscious matter, when it joins the soul substance, cripples its powers according to the type of bondage or fusion of soul and matter. The different types of consciousness depend on the operation of the opposing forces of matter, ranging from that in which these forces are actually in full play, in which case the knowing power of the soul can manifest itself only through the one sense of touch, as in metals and the like, to that in which all of them are removed, when the full blaze of omniscience is reached. The intermediate types between these two limits are determined by the destruction, entire or partial, of the energies obstructing knowledge. Knowledge which is of the essence of the soul, is hidden or revealed according to the pressure of matter upon it. Everything lies latent in the self, and only wants removal of the causes which prevent the manifestation of knowledge. When the impediments are removed, the soul becomes all comprehensive knowledge, unlimited by time or space. There are no emotions to disturb or interests to obscure the full splendour of that soul whose essence is consciousness. Nor can we say that there are differentiating marks in this perfect condition. The object of knowledge is the whole of reality, and the subject has become pure intelligence, wherein no limits or distinctions are possible. The unreal distinctions of the empirical world are no longer present in it. In short, the distinctions are due to an element which does not persist, and what persists is the soul whose nature is consciousness. The Jainas cannot logically support a theory of pluralism.

VII

PSYCHOLOGY

Before we take up the metaphysical views of the 'Jainas, we may notice their psychological opinions. They admit a dualism between mind and body. The five senses or indriyas are distinguished into dravya-indriyas or physical sense organs and bhāva-indriyas or their psychical counterparts.[34] The common element between the eye which is the enjoyer of form and its object is colour. The eye is adapted to respond to colour, which is a property of matter. Since the sense organs are only the exteriorised powers or instruments of the jīva, the elements which render the enjoyment of all objects possible exist in the constitution of the soul itself. The senses are the capacities for enjoyment, and the sensible qualities which exist outside are the objects of enjoyment. A good deal of psychological analysis is discernible in the divisions of touch into eight kinds: hot and cold, rough and smooth, soft and hard, light and heavy; of taste into five: pungent, acid, bitter, sweet and astringent; of smell into two: good and bad; of colour into five: black, blue, yellow, white and pink; and sound into seven: ṣaḍja, ṛṣabha, gāndhāra, madhyama, pañcama, daivata, niṣāda, i.e. do, re, me, fa, sol, la, si. Sense perception is the result of the contact between the sense organ and the object. This mechanical contact is not the complete explanation of the psychical perception. It only helps to remove the veil which hides the knowledge of the soul. The subject is a jñānin, a bhoktṛ as well as a kartṛ, a knower, an enjoyer and a doer. Three forms of consciousness are recognised; knowing, feeling, or the experiencing of the fruits of karma[35] and willing.[36] Conation and feeling are closely allied. As a rule, we have first feeling, then conation, and lastly knowledge.[37] The relation between jīva and pudgala is that of subject to object. The force which brings about their union is not knowledge, for we may know a thing and yet not be compelled to act on it. The omniscience of the Siddhātman involves the reflection of the universe in consciousness, though the soul is not necessarily in bondage. Interaction depends on the desires of the jīva. This subjection to desire and consequently to bondage is not essential for the jīva, since it is possible to be saved from desire.

34. T.S., ii. 19. Similarly, manas has the two aspects of physical and psychical. When the soul is said to occupy the whole body, it means that soul and body are the psychical and physical counterparts of one entity. It is an empty device to account for the psychical perception of physical objects. We do not solve the problem of the relation of soul and body by repeating the properties of both in every sense or indriya.

35. Karmaphalacetana.

36. P. 38.

37. P. 39.

Every jīva is a composite of body and soul, of which the soul is the active partner, while the body is the inactive passive one. Jainism avoids the defects of both mentalism and materialism by recognising the correlativity of mind and matter. But Jainism does not see that the distinction of self and not-self is the outcome of the essential character of mind. It accepts the two substance theory in all its nakedness, looking upon knowledge as something apart a process taking place between them. Nor is Jainism aware of the conception of development according to which the body in its higher phases assumes new properties. It is obliged to rest content with a dualism of mind and body and stop at the psychological point of view. It cannot adopt the theory of interaction, but has to accept the view of parallelism with all its difficulties. 'Karmic matter itself through its own essential nature brings about its own changes. Jīva, too, in the same way, through its own impure states of thought that are conditioned by karma, brings about its own thought changes.'[38] The two form two independent series, self-sufficient and complete. To the question, as to why the jīva should suffer the fruits of karma, if the two are independent, a sort of pre-established harmony is suggested.[39] In the world we have material bodies large and small, of which some are karmic matter, with a tendency to be attracted by the jīvas. By their coexistence, jīva and karmic material molecules are brought together. The settling of karmic matter in jīva is due to this contiguous coexistence. It cannot be said that the mind exerts an active influence. The commentator on Pañcāstikāyasamayasāra explains the relation by the analogy of the casket which becomes black by contact with collyrium powder. The two self-determining agencies somehow get harmoniously blended. Since direct causal relation between the two series is rejected, no better explanation than a mysterious harmony is possible.

On this view knowledge becomes a mystery. It ceases to be the ultimate fact behind which we cannot go. We adopt a deliberately restricted outlook and, imagining an opposition between subject and object, look upon mind as one thing confronted by another thing called the environment. We do not perceive things that are external, but have only images and pictures of them which are supposed to represent the external world. There cannot be any agreement between idea and reality unless there is a common factor between them. But in that case the theory of a mind which looks out of its own chamber into an alien universe falls to the ground.

38. Pp. 43–44.
39. Pp. 45–52.

The soul is said to have dimensions, and be capable of expansion and contraction. The soul cannot be smaller than the physical body, for then it will not be able to feel the bodily affections as its own. It is of a very small size when it starts in the womb, but goes on gradually expanding with the body, till it attains to its full proportions. At the end of each earthly life it contracts again into the seed of the next birth which it has to undergo. The diffusion of the soul in the body is not like any other diffusion in nature, since the soul is simple and devoid of parts. 'Just as the lotus hued ruby, when placed in a cup of milk imparts its lustre to the milk, so the jīva residing in its own body imparts its lustre or intelligence to the whole body.'[40] The souls which are infinite in number and of medium size occupy innumerable points of space in lokākāśa or the mundane world.[41] According to Śaṁkara,[42] the hypothesis of the soul having the same size as its body is untenable, for, from its being limited by the body, it would follow that the soul, like the body, is also impermanent, and if impermanent, it would have no final release. Further, a soul which leaves a particular body will get into difficulties when, in the course of rebirth, it has to inhabit a larger body. We may grossly conceive the soul as capable of becoming bigger or smaller by addition or subtraction of parts. New particles will be constantly carried in and old particles will be getting out, so that we can never be sure that the same soul continues for any length of time. If it is said that certain essential particles remain unchanged, there does not seem to be any way of distinguishing between the essential and the accidental. The Jainas answer these objections by citing analogies. As a lamp whether placed in a small pot or a large room illumines the whole space, even so does the jīva contract and expand according to the dimensions of the different bodies.

VIII

METAPHYSICS

In metaphysics Jainism is opposed to all theories which do not emphasise ethical responsibility. The ethical interest in human freedom is the

40. Pp. 11–12. 'The soul is present,' says Maher in his *Psychology*, 'though in a non-qualitative manner, throughout the whole body; moreover, it is so present everywhere in the entirety of its essence, although it may not be capable of ubiquitously therein exercising all its faculties.'

41. Madhyamaparimāṇa, i.e., neither all pervading nor atomic.

42. S.B., II. 2. 33–36.

determining consideration. The theories of the creation of the world by God, or its development out of prakṛti or its unreality, are criticised on the ground that they cannot account for either the origin or the cessation of suffering.[43] To regard the intelligent subject as the product of the five elements is as fruitless from the ethical point of view as to make out that the variety of the world is a manifold presentation of the one intelligent principle.[44] Moral distinctions lose their value on the hypothesis of the passivity of the soul.[45] To say that the soul is safe in its eternity and the events of the world are the results of the mechanical combination and separation of the elements of existence would take away the initiative from the soul and make moral responsibility meaningless.[46] The fatalist theory that all things are fixed by nature obviously leaves no room for individual effort.[47] Ethical values require that the individual can make or unmake himself in the world, and that the soul has a self-identity which it preserves even in the ultimate condition.[48] This metaphysical theory of reality may be approached by a preliminary discussion of the nature of substance or dravya, and mode or paryāya.

The Jainas do not hold that being is permanent, without becoming, change and end. Everything is produced, continues and is again destroyed. The definition of substance depends on our standpoint. It is that which always exists, as the universe, which has no beginning or end. It is the subject of qualities and modifications. Anything which has origin, existence and destruction is a substance. It is again that which performs some functions. Generally, existing things are considered to be permanent as regards their substance and accidental as regards their changeable aspects. Material things continue to exist as matter; as particular things they change. Being is not unalterable in its nature. The Jainas do not concern themselves about transcendental being, but only of being as found in experience. The things of the world undergo change, gaining new qualities and losing old ones. The possession of certain qualities in common makes us say that the new and the old are forms of one substance. Reality to them is a unity in difference and nothing beyond. They adopt a theory of bhedābheda or

43. Sūtrakṛtāṅga, 1. i. 3. 5–9.
44. Ibid., 1. i. 1. 7–10. 11–12; 11. i. 16. 17.
45. Ibid., 1. i. 1. 13.
46. Ibid., 1. i. 1. 15; 11. i. 22–24.
47. Ibid., 1. i. 2. 1–5; 1. i. 4. 8–9; 11. i. 32.
48. Ibid., 1. i. 3. 11.

difference in identity. Substance is that which persists in and through its own qualities and modifications. Substance and quality are inseparable. A thing is defined as that which has many qualities.[49] It is a dynamic reality, an identity which changes.[50] 'Substance is one, the inherent essence of all things, manifests itself through diverse forms, has the three characteristics of creation, destruction and staying, and may be described by opposites.'[51]

Qualities or guṇas inhere in substances as materiality in atoms, and they cannot exist by themselves. The chief qualities are: (1) Existence, (2) Enjoyability, (3) Substantiveness, (4) Knowability, (5) Specific character or identity or essence, (6) the quality of possessing some kind of form. These general qualities are common to dravyas, and each of the latter has also its own specific features. We should not abstract any of these qualities and exalt it to a substantive level. Yet 'there is neither quality without substance nor substance without quality.'[52] The Nyāya theory of the absolute distinction of substance and quality is refuted. A thing exists in and through the qualities and the qualities constitute the thing. The difference is one of reference and not existence. 'If the substance is entirely separate and distinct from its qualities, then it may change into infinite other substances, or again, if the qualities can exist separate from their substance, there will be no necessity for a substance at all.'[53] The Nirguṇa Brahman theory as well as the Kṣaṇikavāda are implicitly refuted.[54] Substance and qualities may be externally related as in 'Devadatta's cow,' or internally as in the 'tall cow.' 'Just as dhana and jñāna (wealth and wisdom) make the owners dhani and jñāni (rich and wise), though expressing two ways of relationship, unity and diversity, even so the relation between substance and qualities implies two aspects of identity and difference.'[55] 'The relation between substance and quality is one of coeval

49. P. xi; see also xii and xiii–xiv.

50. P. ix.

51. 'Anantadharmātmakam vastu'; Haribhadra's Ṣaḍdarśanasamuccaya, 57.

52. P. v.

53. Pp. 26–27.

54. There is no sāmānya without viśeṣa and no viśeṣa without sāmānya. Maṇibhadra in his Vṛtti on Haribhadra's Ṣaḍdarśanasamuccaya, 46, quotes a verse: 'Dravyam paryāyaviyutam, paryāyā dravyavarjitāḥ kva kadā kena kim rupā dṛṣta mānena kena ceti.'

55. P. 29.

identity, unity, inseparability and essential simplicity; the unity of substance and qualities is not the result of union or combinaiton.'[56]

The dravya with the qualities must exist in some form or state. This mode of existence is paryāya and is subject to change. The substance gold with its qualities of malleability and yellowness is not subject to change. The guṇas or qualities continue while the paryāyas or forms change. There are two kinds of paryāyas or modifications (1) Modifications of the essential qualities of a thing or substance. The colour of water may change, though colour is a constant property.[57] (2) Modifications of the accidental qualities such as muddiness. Water need not always be muddy.[58]

The whole universe of being is traced to the two everlasting uncreated coexisting but independent categories of jīva and ajīva. The jīva is the enjoyer and the ajīva or the jaḍa is the enjoyed. That which has consciousness is jīva, that which has not consciousness, but can be touched, tasted, seen and smelt, is ajīva. The latter is devoid of the three kinds of consciousness. It is the object.[59] 'What knows and perceives the various objects, desires pleasure and dreads pain, acts beneficially or harmfully, and experiences the fruit thereof, that is jīva.'[60] Jīva and ajīva do not correspond to I and not-I. It is an objective classification of things in the universe that underlies the distinction of jīva and ajīva. Animate beings are composed of soul and body, and their souls being distinct from matter are eternal. Ajīva is divided into two main classes, those without form (arūpa), as dharma, adharma, space, time, and those with form (rūpa), as pudgala or matter.

The first ajīva dravya or inanimate substance is ākāśa or space. It is divided into (1) the part occupied by the world of things, lokākāśa, and (2) the space beyond it, the alokākāśa, which is absolutely void and empty, an abyss of nothing.[61] Of a point of space or pradeśa, the following definition is given: 'Know that something to be pradeśa, which is obstructed by one indivisible atom of pudgala, and which can give space to all particles.'[62] In such a pradeśa one element of dharma, one of adharma, one particle

56. Pp. 31–32.
57. Sahabhāvin paryāya. It co-exists with the substance and its qualities.
58. Kramabhāvin paryāya. It succeeds another modification.
59. P. 101.
60. Pp. 98–99.
61. Pp. 69–70; see also D.S., 19–20.
62. D.S., 27.

of kāla or time, and many atoms of matter in a subtle state may exist. Space by itself is not a condition of motion and of rest.[63] Things left together hanging in space would lead to chaos. To produce a cosmos they must be bound by laws of movement and rest. Dharma is the principle of motion. 'Dharma is devoid of qualities of taste, colour, smell, sound and contact. It pervades the whole world, and is continuous because of inseparability; has extension because of coextensiveness with space. Though in reality of ekapradeśa, yet in vyavahāra is of many pradeśas.'[64] It is amūrta or non-corporeal, and is continuous and non-composite. 'Because it has the infinite manifestations of the incorporeal nature, agurulaghu, and because of its dialectic nature of persistence through appearance and disappearance, it is a real existence. Itself being unaffected by movement, it conditions the motion of those things that can move, matter and life,'[65] 'even as water itself, being indifferent or neutral, is the condition of the movement of fish.'[66] Dharma has none of the specific properties of matter, and yet it is a self-subsisting reality devoid of all sensible qualities. It is the medium of movement though not its cause. Adharma is the principle of rest. It is also devoid of sense qualities, is non-corporeal and coextensive with lokākāśa.[67] The two principles are non-active, non-physical, non-atomic and non-discrete in structure. Dharma and adharma are neutral conditions, udāsīnahetu, of movement and rest. Efficient causes are different. Otherwise objects would be always moving or resting. They are not merely the accompanying conditions of movement and rest, but appear to be the cosmic principles forming the background of all the moving and the resting things of the world. They are the connecting media binding together the chaotic crowd of isolated fragments into an ordered whole. It is to be carefully noted that dharma and adharma in Jaina philosophy do not stand for merit and demerit, for which it has other terms, puṇya and pāpa. They are the forces that cause movement and rest. Space with dharma and adharma forms the condition for the subsistence of all things, souls and matter. Space gives room to subsist, dharma makes it possible for things to move or be moved and adharma to rest. These three functions

63. Pp. 71 and 72.
64. P. 63.
65. P. 64.
66. Pp. 58–59; Pp. 67–68; see also D.S., 17, and Vardhamāna Purāṇa, xvi. 29.
67. Pp. 66–67.

of subsistence, motion and rest are assigned to space in modern philosophy. The three are mutually interpenetrating. From the point of view of locality, they are of the same size and form, an inseparable unity. They are distinguished because of the difference of functions.

Time or kāla is sometimes recognised as a quasi-substance. It is an all-pervading form of the universe on which are strung the successive movements of the world. It is not a summation of a series of discontinuous changes, but a process of persistence, an enduring from the past into the present.

Time has astitva or existence, but no kāyatva or magnitude. It has no extension, being unilateral.[68] A distinction is made between eternal time, without form, beginning or end, and relative time, with beginning and end and variations of hour, minute, etc. The former is called kāla and the latter samaya. Kāla is the substantial cause of samaya. Vartana or continuity of changes is inferred from pariṇāma or modification.[69] 'Relative time is determined by changes or motion in things. These changes themselves are the effects of absolute time.'[70] Time is called a cakra, a wheel. Since in course of time all things are liable to dissolution of form, time is also called the destroyer.[71]

Matter or pudgala is the next category to be considered. 'Whatever is perceived by the senses, the sense organs, the various kinds of śarīras (or bodies of jīvas), the physical mind, the karmas, etc., are mūrta, or figured objects. These are all pudgala.'[72] 'Sound, union, fineness, grossness, shape, division, darkness, and image, with lustre and heat, are modifications of the substance known as pudgala.'[73] Matter is an eternal substance undetermined with regard to quantity and quality. It may increase or diminish in volume without any addition or loss of particles. It may assume any form and develop various qualities. It is the vehicle of energy which is

68. See D.S. 25. If we say that even an atom of pudgala has one pradeśa and cannot be called kāya it is replied: 'An atom, though having one pradeśa becomes of many pradeśas through being pradeśa in many skandhas. For this reason, from the ordinary point of view the omniscient call it kāya.' (D.S., 26.)

69. Pp. 2–6.

70. Pp. 78–79.

71. Compare 'Kalo'smi,' B.G., xi. 32.

72. Pp. 62–63.

73. D.S., 16.

essentially kinetic or of the nature of motion. This motion belongs to the substance pudgala, and is of two kinds, simple motion, or parispanda, and evolution, or pariṇāma. Pudgala is the physical basis of the world. Matter itself is said to exist in six different forms of different degrees of fineness and visibility. The qualities of touch, taste, smell, colour and sound are associated with pudgala. The Jains argue that everything in the world except souls and space is produced from matter. Things which we perceive consist of gross matter. There is also subtile matter beyond the reach of our senses, and this is transformed into the different degrees of karma.

The Jaina physics has for its chief principle the atomic structure of the universe. The physical objects apprehended by senses consist of atoms or paramāṇus. An absolutely homogeneous mass of pudgalas which by differentiation breaks up into several kinds of atoms qualitatively determined is assumed. An atom (aṇu) has no points, beginning, middle or end. It is infinitesimal, eternal and ultimate. It is neither created nor destroyed. It is amūrta (formless), though the basis of all mūrta (form). Sometimes it is said to have form in the sense that it can be perceived by the kevali or the omniscient. The atoms are said to possess weight. The heavier move downwards and the lighter upwards. Each atom occupies one point of space or pradeśa.[74] When in the subtle state, innumerable atoms occupy the space of one gross atom. Each atom has a kind of taste, colour, smell and contact.[75] These qualities are not permanent and fixed. Material things are produced by the combination of atoms which are subject to mutual attraction. Two atoms form a compound, when one is viscous and the other dry, or when both are of different degrees of viscousness and dryness. Atomic linking takes place only when the atoms are of unlike natures. The attraction and repulsion of atoms are admitted by the Jains. The movement of atoms is brought about by means of space, dharma and adharma. The compounds, or skandhas combine with others and so on. Pudgala therefore exists in the two forms of aṇu, or atom, and skandha, or aggregate. The skandhas vary from binary aggregates to infinite compounds. Every perceivable object is a skandha, and the physical world as a whole is a mahāskandha, or the great aggregate. The changes of the physical universe are traced to atomic disintegration or aggregation.[76] We have already said

74. Pp. 57–58.
75. P. 57.
76. Pp. 54–57.

that the atoms are not constant in their nature, but are subject to change or development (pariṇāma), which consists in their assuming new qualities. It also follows that there are not different kinds of atoms answering to the different elements of earth, water, fire and air. The atoms by developing the characteristic qualities of the elements become differentiated and form the elements. The Nyāya-Vaiśeṣika theory holds that there are as many kinds of atoms as there are elements, while the Jainas think that the homogeneous atoms produce different elements by varying combinations. The qualitative differences of primary atoms are denied.[77] In this matter the Jainas agree with Leucippus and Democritus. The figures formed by the arrangement of the atoms into groups are manifold. It is said that the atom may develop a motion of its own so swift that it traverses in one moment the whole universe from one end to the other.

Karma according to the Jains is of material nature (paudgalika). Only thus can the Jains conceive that thoughts and ideas affect our character and create or modify the tendencies of our souls. Karma is a substantive force, matter in a subtle form. The kind of matter fit to manifest karma fills all cosmic space. It has the peculiar property of developing the effects of merit and demerit. The soul by its commerce with the outer world becomes literally penetrated with the particles of subtle matter. These become karma and build up a special body called kārmaṇaśarīra, which does not leave the soul till its final emancipation. This karmic matter retards the radiance of the soul. Bhāvakarma is immediate to the jīvas, while dravyakarma belongs to the body. The two are associated together, though they are distinct and separate as the conscious and the non-conscious cetana and acetana). Karma works in such a way that every change which takes place leaves a mark which is retained and built into the organism to serve as the foundation for future action. It is there actual and acting in the nature of the jīvas. Five classes of karmic conditions are mentioned. Each of these determines its corresponding bhāva or mental state. 'On account of the rise, suppression, annihilation, mixed suppression or unconditioned thought, the jīva has five bhāvas or thought conditions.'[78] The last is unconditioned by karma, while the four others are conditioned by changes on the physical side. In the usual course of things karma takes effect and produces its proper results. The soul is said to be in the Audayika state. By

77. Pp. 58–59.
78. P. 39, udaya, upaśama, kṣaya, kṣayopaśama, pariṇāma.

proper effort karma may be prevented from taking effect for some time. Though it is neutralised, it is still present, like fire covered by ashes. The soul is then said to be in the Aupaśamika state. When karma is not only prevented from working, but is annihilated altogether, then the soul is in the Kṣāyika state which leads to mokṣa. There is a fourth state of the soul, Kṣāyopaśamika, which partakes of the nature of all the preceding ones. In this condition some karma is annihilated some neutralised and some active. It is the state of those whom we call, good, while the Kṣāyika and Aupaśamika states belong to holy men.[79]

The ajīva thus consists of five entities, of which four are immaterial, amūrta, viz. space, time, dharma and adharma, and the fifth pudgala is material, or mūrta, or figured. These five categories constitute the world or loka, and beyond is the immeasurable infinite called aloka.[80]

Different from matter and material things are souls, jīvas (literally lives). In the Jaina writings the word jīva is variously used, and denotes life, vitality, soul and consciousness. Jīva is living experience, which is so utterly unlike the physical things of the outer world. The jīvas are infinite in number and are of different kinds. (1) Nityasiddha, or the ever perfect; (2) Mukta, or the liberated; and (3) the Baddha, or the bound. The second

79. When karma penetrates the soul it is transformed into eight kinds of prakṛti which make up the kārmaṇa śarīra. These eight kinds of karma include the Jñānāvaraṇīya, or that which obscures the inborn knowledge of the soul, producing different degrees of knowledge or ignorance, and Darśanāvaraṇīya, or that which obscures right intutions; Vedanīya, or that which obscures the blissful nature of the soul and produces pleasure, pain, and Mohanīya, or that which disturbs the right attitude of the soul with regard to faith, conduct, passions and emotions, and produces doubt, error and other mental disturbances. The other four deal with the status of an individual being: Āyuṣka, or that which determines the length of life in one birth; Nāma, or that which produces the various circumstances or elements which collectively make up an individual existence, the body with its general and specific qualities; Gotra, or that which determines the nationality, caste, family and social standing of an individual; and Antarāya, or that which obstructs the inborn energy of the soul and prevents the doing of good even when there is a desire for it.

Connected with the karma theory is the doctrine of leśyās, of which there are six. The totality of karmas taken up by a soul induce in it a transcendental colour or complexion which cannot be perceived by the naked eye. These have a moral bearing. The state of a soul is produced by its inborn nature and the karma with which it is associated. Each kind of karma has its predestined limits within which it must be purged off.

80. P. 3.

class of jīvas will not become embodied. They have achieved their purity and dwell in a state of supramundane perfection unconcerned with worldly affairs. The mundane jīvas are a prey to illusion, and are condemned to submit to the yoke of matter through an infinite succession of lives. The freed souls are absolutely pure and free from any taint of matter. In them the partnership between soul and matter is dissolved. They are the nirupādhi jīvas, which lead a life of pure existence and infinite consciousness, and possess infinite knowledge (anantajñāna), infinite perception (anantadarśana), infinite power (anantavīrya) and infinite bliss (anantasukha). The sopādhijīvas, which are wandering in the circle of existence, are pursued by the cruel parasite matter. Through ignorance the jīva identifies itself with matter. It is clear that jīva in the sense of the freed indicates the pure subject, which is simple and incorruptible. It answers to the Upaniṣad Ātman, the logical, self-existing, unchangeable subject precedent to all cognition, feeling and will. As applied to the impure saṁsārin, jīva is an empirical category determined by life. This ambiguous usage is responsible for a good deal of confusion in the Jaina metaphysics. Except in final release the soul is always in connection with matter, the link between the two being karma. The soul persists throughout all changes and is not a product of the body. The Jains admit that there is no creation of a new substance or destruction of the old. It is only a fusion of elements in a few form. The jīvas are many, but are alike eternal. Their characteristic essence is consciousness or cetana, which is never destroyed, however much it is obscured by external causes. They are regarded as possessing size which is varying in different cases. They contract and expand according to the dimensions of the body with which they are incorporated for the time being. The question of the different kinds of jīvas is important for the Jainas, in view of their insistence on ahiṁsā, or the inviolability of life. Jīvas are divided according to the number of sense organs they possess. The highest are those which have five senses: touch, taste, smell, sight and hearing (pañcendriya). The lowest have one sense, touch (ekendriya). Between the two come those with two, three and four senses. The higher animals, men and gods, possess a sixth internal organ (manas), and are said to be rational.[81] The senses and bodies do not constitute the essence of the soul, which lies in the consciousness underlying them all.[82] The

81. See Pp. 88–96.
82. Pp. 97–98.

soul is not distinct from its attribute of jñāna or knowledge, and since the ways of knowledge are diverse, the world of reality is also said to be multiverse by the wise.[83] Self and its knowledge are inseparable. In unredeemed souls knowledge and joy are contracted. Everything from the solar system to the dewdrop has a soul, and not merely men and animals. There are elemental souls, e.g. earth souls, fire souls, which live and die and are born again in the same or other elemental bodies. These are either gross or subtle. In the latter case they are invisible. Plants are the jīvas of one sense. Each plant may be the body of one soul, or may possess a multitude of embodied souls. Though some other Indian philosophers also admit that plants possess souls, the Jaina thinkers have developed this theory in a remarkable way. Plants in which only one soul is embodied are always gross, and exist in the habitable part of the world only. But those plants of which each is a colony of plant lives may be subtle, and therefore invisible, and be distributed all over the world. These subtle plants are called nigoda. They are composed of an infinite number of souls, forming a very small cluster, with respiration and nutrition in common. Innumerable nigodas form a globule, and the world is packed with them. These nigodas supply souls in the vacancies caused by those who have attained nirvāṇa. It is said that an infinitesimally small fraction of one single nigoda has furnished souls in place of those liberated from the beginningless past down to the present. We cannot therefore hope that the world will at any time be empty of living beings.[84] A peculiar feature of the Jaina theory is its doctrine that there are souls even in inorganic objects, like metals and stones.

The condition of a soul depends on the condition of its body. In an inorganic body the soul's consciousness is dormant, while it just stirs in the organic body. Consciousness is active in human beings. Compare the saying: 'All flesh is not the same flesh: but there is one kind of flesh of men, another flesh of beasts, another of fishes, and another of birds.'

The jīva is characterised by knowledge, and though it has no form, is yet an agent enjoying the fruits of karma and possessing the same extent as the body.[85] It undergoes real changes, otherwise it cannot be a causal agent.[86] It is the upādānakartṛ or the material cause of bhāvas, or thoughts,

83. Pp. 25–26; see also pp 33–34.
84. See Lokaprakāśa, vi. 31 ff.
85. D.S., 2.
86. Pp. 40–41.

while karmic matter is the nimitta, or the determining cause.[87] The potter has the idea (bhāva), and the pot exists in his consciousness, and there arises the actual pot with the material clay. Yet throughout its infinite forms the soul maintains its nature or identity. Birth and death are only paryāyas, or modifications of the soul. The freed soul is one with the soul in saṁsāra.[88] It is not necessary for the soul to be always entangled in the meshes of the dialectic process of evolution. In other words, it can maintain its existence independent of the body. Consciousness is a reality independent of matter and in no sense its product. It is eternal, with neither beginning nor end. Only compounds break up and are annihilated.

We have now described briefly the five ajīva dravyas and the sixth jīva. Of these six all else, excepting time, are astikāyas,[89] or spatial existences, and have the possibility of spatial relations. Time is real, but is non-spatial. It is therefore a dravya, or substance possessing independent existence, but not an astikāya, or an extensive magnitude. The several dravyas can move in the same place and interpenetrate without losing their essential nature. The six dravyas of the Jainas are different from the nine elements of the Vaiśeṣika theory: earth, air, light, water, ākāśa or ether, kāla or time, dik or direction, manas and souls. The first four are brought under matter by the Jainas. They are the common properties of matter corresponding to the different senses. On account of the transmutability and the liability of different particles to fuse, matter is considered a unit. The Vaiśeṣikas look upon ākāśa as the source of sound, while the Jainas consider sound to be produced by the vibrations of material particles.[90]

The two jīva and ajīva are exhaustive categories of the universe. Of the six dravyas, jīva and pudgala form the chief. The others are the principle of their action or the results of their interaction. Saṁsāra is nothing but the entanglement of jīva in matter. Jīva and pudgala are the sakriya dravyas, or efficient causes, which move from place to place. Dharma and adharma condition movements, but are neither direct causes nor indirect conditions of change, and are therefore called sakriyāniṣkriya dravyas. The link of union between jīva and ajīva is karma. The production, fruition and destruction of karma, together with jīva and ajīva, are the principles or

87. Pp. 39–40.
88. P. 1.
89. Asti, exists; kāya, occupying space.
90. P. xi.

tattvas of Jainism.[91] Jīva and ajīva are the main principles, which are generally united. The absolute liberation of jīva from ajīva is mokṣa. It is the goal of all endeavour. This ideal can be realised only by the stoppage and shedding of karma. Saṁvara is that which stops. By it we block the channels through which karma finds entrance into the soul. Nirjarā is that which utterly and entirely wears away all sins previously committed. The need for these two arises on account of āsrava, or inflow, and bandha, or bondage. Āsrava is the influex of alien matter into the soul. Bandha is what binds the soul to the body. It is caused by wrong belief (mithyādarśana), non-renunciation (avirati), carelessness (pramāda), passions (kaṣāya), and vibrations set up in the soul through mind, body and speech (yoga).[92] Mithyātva is simply taking a thing for what it is not.[93] While inflow and bondage are the results of wrong karma, stoppage and shedding result from right conduct. Throughout we have the distinction of bhāva (mental) and dravya (physical) changes. The thoughts determine karma.[94]

The cause of the soul's embodiment is the presence in it of karmic matter. It is this that spoils the natural qualities of the soul, knowledge and intuition. The soul is never completely separated from matter until its final release. The defilement of the soul happens thus. Subtle matter ready to be transformed into karma pours into the soul. As each particular karma is caused by some act, good, bad or indifferent, so it in its turn produces certain painful or pleasant consequences. When a particular karma produces its effect it is purged from the soul, and if this process of discharge should take place uninterruptedly, all taint of matter will be abolished. But, unfortunately, purging and binding go on together, and the soul continues to move in the circle of saṁsāra. At death the soul, with its kārmaṇa-śarīra, goes in a few moments to the place of its new birth, and there assumes a fresh body, expanding or contracting according to the dimensions of the latter. The mundane souls are divided into four classes according to the

91. The seven tattvas are jīva, ajīva, āsrava, bandha, saṁvara, nirjarā and mokṣa (T.S., 4). Sometimes pāpa, sin, and puṇya, merit, are also added, when we get nine padārthas (P. 116; D.S., 28).

92. U.T.S., vii., 1.

93. Asatī satbuddhi. The Advaita theory of āvaraṇa and vikṣepa has some resemblance to this doctrine of the Jainas.

94. See D.S., 29 ff.

place of their birth: (1) those born in hell, (2) those in the animal world, (3) those in human society, and (4) those in the divine kingdom.[95]

IX

ETHICS

If deliverance is to be achieved, the lower matter is to be subdued by the higher spirit. When the soul is free from the weight which keeps it down, it rises up to the top of the universe where the liberated dwell. The radical conversion of the inner man is the way to freedom. The apparatus of morality is necessary to bring about the reformation of man's nature and prevent the formation of new karma. The way to nirvāṇa lies through the three jewels (triratna) of faith in Jina, knowledge of his doctrine and perfect conduct. 'Belief in real existence or tattvas is right faith; knowledge of real nature without doubt or error is right knowledge. An attitude of neutrality without desire or aversion towards the objects of the external world is right conduct.'[96] The three together form one path, and are to be simultaneously pursued. Virtue consists in the fivefold conduct of one who has knowledge and faith. (1) Innocence, or ahiṁsā, which is not mere negative abstention, but positive kindness to all creation; (2) charity and truth speaking; (3) honourable conduct such as not stealing; (4) chastity in word, thought and deed; and (5) renunciation of all worldly interests mark the good man. The last rule is sometimes interpreted in an extreme way that good men should go naked. It only signifies that so long as we are conscious of distinctions and open to a sense of shame, salvation is distant from us. The Jaina ethics lay stress on both faith and works. A distinction is drawn between the code for laymen and that for ascetics.[97] All those actions which lead to peace of mind are puṇya. There are nine ways of obtaining puṇya or merit such as giving food to the deserving, water to the thirsty, clothes to the poor, shelter to monks, etc. Hiṁsā, or infliction of suffering, is the great sin or pāpa. Other sins are untruthfulness, dishonesty, unchastity, covetousness. Anger, conceit, deceit, avarice tie us down to the world, and their opposites of patience, humility, simplicity

95. P. vi.
96. Pp. 85–86; see also T.S., i. 1.
97. T.S., vii. 20 ff.

and contentment further the growth of the spiritual instincts. Other sins, such as hatred, quarrelsomeness, slander, defamation, abuse of others, lack of self-control, hypocrisy and false faith are also mentioned. Sin is no offence against God, but only against man.

> He prayeth well, who loveth well
> Both man and bird and beast.
> He prayeth best who loveth best
> All things both great and small.
>
> COLERIDGE

The ethical system of the Jainas is more rigorous than that of the Buddhists. It looks upon patience as the highest good and pleasure as a source of sin.[98] Man should attempt to be indifferent to pleasure and pain. True freedom consists in an independence of all outer things. 'That jīva, which through desire for outer things experiences pleasurable or painful states, loses his hold on self and gets bewildered, and led by outer things. He becomes determined by the other.'[99] 'That jīva, which being free from relations to others and from alien thoughts through its own intrinsic nature of perception and understanding perceives and knows its own eternal nature to be such, is said to have conduct that is absolutely self-determined.'[100] 'Man! Thou art thine own friend; why wishest thou for a friend beyond thyself?'[101] We do not have absolute fatalism, for though karma decides all, our present life, which is in our power, can modify the effects of the past. It is possible for us to evade the effects of karma by extraordinary exertions. Nor is there any interference by god. The austere heroes are blessed not because of the uncertain whims of a capricious God, but by the order of the universe of which they themselves are a part. Meditation is enjoined, since it enables us to acquire strength for fulfilling the vows.[102] The rigorous character of the discipline may be inferred from the eleven stages of a householder's life and the fourteen stages of the

98. Ācārāṅgasūtra, S.B.E., xxii. p. 48; see also pp. 50–51.
99. Pp. 128–29.
100. Pp. 130–31.
101. S.B.E., xxii. p. 33.
102. T.S., vii. 4–10.

evolution of the soul. This grim ideal of asceticism has been practised in India by many great devotees who did themselves to death.

The chief feature of Jainism is ahiṁsā, or respect for and abstinence from everything that has life. The scrupulous enforcement of this rule has led to many practices which come in for cheap sneering at the hands of unsympathetic students. Lest any life be destroyed, some Jains sweep the ground as they go, walk veiled for fear of inhaling a living organism, strain water and reject even honey. It is true that ahiṁsā in the strict sense cannot be practised. The Mahābhārata says: 'The world is filled with creatures which cannot be seen by the eye, though inferred by logic. When we move our eyelids, their limbs break and fall.'[103] The Bhāgavatapurāṇa declares that 'life is the life of life.'[104] When these simple truths are forgotten, life becomes well-nigh impossible. A morbid fear of injuring perchance any life anywhere governs the conduct of the orthodox Jains.

While Buddhism repudiates suicide, Jainism holds that it 'increaseth life.' If asceticism is hard to practise, if we cannot resist our passions and endure austerities, suicide is permitted. It is sometimes argued that after twelve years of ascetic preparation one can kill himself, since nirvāṇa is assured. As usual with the systems of the time, women are looked upon as objects of temptation.[105] In common with other systems of Indian thought and belief, Jainism believes in the possibility of non-Jainas reaching the goal if only they follow the ethical rules laid down. Ratnaśekhara in the opening lines of his Sambodhasattari says: 'No matter whether he is a Ṣvetāmbara or a Digambara, a Buddhist or a follower of any other creed, one who has realised the self-sameness of the soul, i.e. looks on all creatures as his own self, attains salvation.'

The Jainas are not opposed to the caste system, which they try to relate to character. 'By one's actions one becomes a Brāhmin, or a Kṣatriya, or a Vaiśya, or a Śūdra.... Him who is exempt from all karmas we call a Brāhmin.'[106] 'The Jains and the Buddhists use the word Brāhmin as an honorific title, applying it even to persons who did not belong to the caste

103. Śāṅtiparva, 15. 26.
104. i. 13. 46. Jīvo jīvasya jīvanam.
105. S.B.E., xxii. p. 48.
106. S.B.E., xlv. p. 140.

of Brāhmins.'[107] The exclusiveness and pride born of caste are condemned by the Jainas. The Sūtrakṛtāṅga denounces the pride of birth as one of the eight kinds of pride by which man commits sin.[108]

The Jain saṅgha, or community, is fourfold, containing monks and nuns, lay-brothers and lay-sisters. With the Buddhists the lay-members were not organically connected with the clergy. With a smaller constituency than that of Buddhism, with no missionary zeal, Jainism has survived in India, while Buddhism has passed away. Mrs Stevenson offers an explanation for this fact. 'The character of Jainism was such as to enable it to throw out tentacles to help it in its hour of need. It had never, like Buddhism, cut itself off from the faith that surrounded it, for it had always employed Brāhmins as its domestic chaplains, who presided at its birth rites, and often acted as officiants at its death and marriage ceremonies and temple worship. Then, too, amongst its chief heroes it had found niches for some of the favourites of the Hindu pantheon, Rāma, Kṛṣṇa and the like. Mahāvīra's genius for organisation also stood Jainism in good stead now, for he had made the laity an integral part of the community, whereas in Buddhism they had no part nor lot in the order. So, when storms of persecution swept over the land, Jainism simply took refuge in Hinduism, which opened its capacious bosom to receive it; and to the conquerors it seemed an indistinguishable part of that great system.'[109]

The materialistic view of karma leads the Jains to attribute more importance than the Buddhists, to the outer act in contrast to the inner motive. Both Buddhism and Jainism admit the ideal of negation of life and personality. To both life is a calamity to be avoided at all costs. They require us to free ourselves from all the ties that bind us to nature and bring us sorrow. They glorify poverty and purity, peace and patient suffering. Hopkins caricatures the Jaina system when he calls it, 'a religion in which the chief points insisted upon are that one should deny God, worship man and nourish vermin.'[110] The remarkable resemblance between Jainism and Buddhism, in their ethical aspects, is due to the fact that they both

107. S.B.E., xxii., p. xxx.

108. Yet the Jains recruit their clergy from certain families in preference to others. They observe caste within the community.

109. *The Heart of Jainism*, pp. 18–19.

110. *The Religions of India*, p. 297.

borrow from the same Brāhmanical sources. 'The Brāhmin ascetic was the model from which they borrowed many important practices and institutions of ascetic life.'[111]

X

ATTITUDE TO THEISM

The development of the world is rendered possible by the doctrine of the indefiniteness of being and interaction of substances. There is no god necessary for creation or destruction. 'There can be no destruction of things that do exist, nor can there be creation of things out of nothing. Coming into existence and ceasing to exist, things have, because of their attributes and modes.'[112] The substances by their interaction produce new sets of qualities. The Jains repudiate the theory of the creation of the world out of nothing or a series of accidents. The systematic working of the laws of nature cannot be a product of luck or accident. There is no need to assume with the theologian any first cause of the universe. We cannot conceive how a non-creative God suddenly becomes creative. On such a hypothesis the question of the material out of which the world is created is difficult to answer. Did it or did it not exist in some form prior to the making of the world? If it is said that it all depends on the inscrutable will of God, we should put an end to all science and philosophy. If things can function only in obedience to the will of God, there is no reason why they should be endowed with distinct attributes. Different substances need not have specific functions which cannot be exchanged. Water can burn and fire cool if that be the will of God. As a matter of fact, however, we find that different substances have their own specific functions belonging to their own nature, and the substances themselves would be destroyed if their functions were annihilated. If it is argued that everything that exists must have a maker, then that maker himself would stand in need of another maker, and we should be landed in an infinite regress. The way of escape from this circle is to assume the reality of a self-subsisting maker, who is the author of everything else. The Jaina thinker asks, If it be possible for one being to be self-subsistent and eternal, is it not possible for more things and beings to be uncreated and substantive? He puts forth the

111. S.B.E., xxii., p. xxiv.
112. P. vii.

hypothesis of a number of substances, and the world is explained on the theory of the necessity of the substances to manifest themselves. The whole universe of being consisting of mental and material factors has existed from all eternity, undergoing an infinite number of revolutions produced by the powers of nature without the intervention of any eternal deity. The diversities of the world are traced to the five co-operating conditions of time (kāla), nature (svabhāva), necessity (niyati), activity (karma), and desire to be and act (udyama). The seed may be instinct with powers, but before it grows into a tree it must have the help of the time or season, natural environment and the act of its being placed in the soil. Its own nature determines the kind of tree into which it grows.

Though there is no such being distinct from the world called God, yet certain of the elements of the world when properly developed obtain deification. These are the arhats, the supreme lords, the omniscient souls who have overcome all faults. Though there is no divine creative spirit, still every soul when it reaches its highest perfection becomes a Paramātman or supreme soul.[113] God is only the highest, noblest and fullest manifestation of the powers which lie latent in the soul of man. All perfect men are divine, and there is no rank among them, since all are equal.

Strictly speaking, there is no room for devotion or bhakti in the Jaina system. All attachment according to it should cease. Personal live is to be burnt up in the glow of asceticism. But weak man is obliged to develop a sort of devotion towards the great tīrthaṅkaras, however much strict logic may prohibit it. The lay members demanded a creed and a cult suited to their moral and religious condition. When Jainism began to spread beyond the place of its origin, the necessity to satisfy the religious aspirations of the normal man became urgent. Otherwise, worshippers of other gods could not be converted into Jainism. When followers of the Kṛṣṇa cult came into the fold of Jainism, a relationship was established between the 22nd Tīrthaṅkara (Ariṣṭanemi) and Kṛṣṇa. Many Hindu gods crept in, so that to-day we find divisions of Jainas into the Vaiṣṇavas and the non-Vaiṣṇavas.

The life of a god in heaven is one of the forms that a soul might assume by the accumulation of merit. When the merit is exhausted, that life passes away. Gods are only embodied souls like men and animals, different from them in degree, but not in kind. The greater power and perfection

113. Compare Professor Alexander's theory of angels. *Space, Time and Deity*, vol. ii. pp. 346, 365.

belonging to the divine body and organism are the rewards of the good deeds of a former life. The liberated souls are above the gods. They are never born again. They have no longer any connexion with the world and exert no influence on it. They do not look to the steep ascent leading to the goal or offer a helping hand to those struggling on the upward path. When prayers are addressed to the famous Jinas who have reached perfection and passed out of the world of change and woe, they cannot and do not return answers to the prayers, since they are utterly indifferent to all that happens in the world and are entirely free from all emotion. But there are the gods who watch and control true discipline.[114] They hear the prayers and bestow favours. So far as the Jinas are concerned, the best mode of worshipping them is to adopt their advice. Realisation of one's true self and not devotion to Tīrthaṅkaras is the way to freedom.[115] Meditation or adoration of the Jina sanctifies the soul. Since the severely simple religion of the Jainas did not admit grace or forgiveness, it could not appeal to the masses, and so halting compromises were made.

XI

NIRVĀṆA

Nirvāṇa or deliverance is not annihilation of the soul, but its entry into a blessedness that has no end. It is an escape from the body, though not from existence. We have already said that the liberated being by avoiding all emotions becomes characterless, with no interest in the lives of its fellows or inclination to help them. 'The liberated is not long nor small ... nor black, nor blue, nor bitter, nor pungent: neither cold nor hot.... Without body, without rebirth ... he perceives, he knows, but there is no analogy, (whereby we can know the nature of the liberated soul); its essence is without form; there is no condition of the unconditioned.'[116] The siddha state is not the cause or the effect of the saṁsāra series. It is absolutely unconditioned.[117] Causality has no hold on the redeemed soul. 'Know that from the ordinary point of view, perfect faith, knowledge and conduct are the causes of liberation, while in reality one's own soul consisting of these

114. Śāsanādhiṣṭhāya devatāḥ.
115. P. 140 ff.
116. S.B.E., xxii. p. 52.
117. P. 14.

three (is the cause of liberation).'[118] We cannot say anything positive about the freed soul, nor can we strictly speaking know that there is a plurality of liberated souls. The state of perfection is passively described as freedom from action and desire, a state of utter and absolute quiescence, a rest that knows no change or ending, a passionless and ineffable peace. The energy of past karma is extinguished, and the spirit, though still existent, has no chance of re-embodiment. Though not quite consistently, positive descriptions are given of the freed soul as that it has infinite consciousness, pure understanding, absolute freedom and eternal bliss.[119] It can perceive and know, since perception and knowledge are functions of the soul and not of the sense organs. The freed soul has a beginning but no end, while a bound soul has no beginning but has an end. These freed souls enjoy a kind of interpenetrating existence on account of their oneness of status. Their soul substance has a special power by which an infinity of souls could exist without mutual exclusion. The identity of the saved is determined by the living rhythm retaining the form of the last physical life and by the knowledge of the past. This ideal of freedom is manifested in the most perfect degree in the lives of the twenty-four Jain tīrthaṅkaras.

The loka, or the universe, is held in the middle of the aloka, in the form of the trunk of the man, with siddhaśīla at the top, the place where the head should be. This siddhaśīla is the abode of the omniscient souls, and may be called the spiritual eye of the universe. So mokṣa is said to be eternal upward movement.[120] On liberation the soul goes upward, because of the momentum due to its previous activity,[121] the non-existence of the relation to the elements which kept it down,[122] breaking of the bondage,[123] and its natural tendency to go upwards.[124]

118. D.S., 39; see also 40.

119. P. 7.

120. Nityordhvagamanam mukti.

121. Pūrvaprayogāt.

122. Asaṅgatvāt.

123. Bandhacchēdāt.

124. Tathāgatipariṇāmāt. See U.T.S., x. 8. The siddha souls are of five kinds: (1) The tīrthaṅkaras, or the liberated who preached Jainism in the embodied condition; (2) the arhats, or the perfect souls who await the attainment of nirvāṇa after shedding the kārmaṇaśarīra; (3) the ācāryas, or heads of ascetic groups; (4) the upādhyāyās, or teaching saints; and (5) sādhus, a class which includes the rest (D.S., 50–54).

XII

CONCLUSION

Jainism offers us an empirical classification of things in the universe, and so argues for a plurality of spirits. In logic, as we have seen, it takes its stand on the relativity of knowledge, the obvious fact that the relations of objects within the world are not fixed or independent, but are the results of interpretation. Moreover, the theory that reality and meaning are inseparable makes for monism in metaphysics and not pluralism. As a matter of fact, the pluralistic universe in Jainism is only a relative point of view, and not an ultimate truth.

Jainism looks upon the universe as filled with jīvas, even as Leibniz thought that the world was filled with monads. 'In the smallest particle of matter there is a world of living creatures, entelechies or souls. Each portion of matter may be conceived as like a garden full of plants, or like a pond full of fishes. But each branch of every plant, each member of any animal, each drop of its liquid parts, is also some such garden or pond. And though the earth and the air which are between the plants of the garden, or the water which is between the fish of the pond, be neither plant nor fish, yet they also contain plants and fishes, but mostly so minute as to be imperceptible to us. Thus there is nothing fallow, nothing sterile, nothing dead in the universe, no chaos, no confusion save in appearance, somewhat as it might appear to be in a pond at a distance, in which one would see a confused movement and, as it were, a swarming of fish in the pond without separately distinguishing the fish themselves.' We shall see that the metaphysical scheme of the Jainas has affinities with Leibniz's monadism and Bergson's creative evolutionism.[125]

A jīva is whatever is living, whatever is not mechanical. It answers to the life element of Bergson. It is also a subject of experience, and corresponds to the monad of Leibniz. It is anything for which the mechanical explanation is inadequate. Since Jainism is the product of an age of immature philosophising, we find that it is not clearly aware of the exact distinctions between jīva and Ātman, ajīva and matter. A jīva is a particular kind of

125. Though in its origin the Jaina view might have been a rather crude form of physical science, later Jaina thinkers developed definite philosophical grounds capable of being clearly stated and defended.

existent thing. The liberated jīva freed from matter is called the Ātman. The Ātman is pure consciousness untainted by matter. It excludes all space and externality. It is the jīva purified and raised to its highest spiritual status, which is mere formless consciousness. Pudgala is not pure matter untouched by consciousness. It already bears the impress of spirit. Ātman is spirit or being, and matter is the negative principle of non-being. The latter corresponds to the space of Bergson or the materia prima of Leibniz. The bare materiality of pudgala is the direct opposite of spirit. It is mere difference, and therefore according to Jaina logic unreal. A jīva is a combination of the two. It is material—spiritual.[126] It is the soul loaded with matter, involved in bondage. All jīvas in saṁsāra are associated with this negative material element. Jainism believes that these three, Ātman or the pure spirit, pure matter, and jīva, which is a combination of the two, are existent, though the first two are imperceptible to us. The pudgala skandha, which we see, has also an element of consciousness, and is as much as jīva as anything else so far as its essence is concerned. The jīva and the ajīva of the Jainas are not the empirical abstractions of Ātman or consciousness and matter or non-consciousness, but the products of an interaction between the two. The pudgala bears on it the impress of self, and the jīva is already penetrated by matter. It is an inaccurate usage that makes us confuse jīva and ajīva with being and non-being. Strictly speaking, Ātman and non-Ātman are the primary elements, the two irreconcilable and antagonistic principles. Jīva possesses more of self, ajīva more of not-self. They represent two orders of arrangement in the whole.

To the empirical vision the jīvas constitute the universe, and every jīva is a concrete unity, a compound substance. It is a one in many, or a many in one. The relation between the two is beginningless. In the world of saṁsāra the two are never separated. The goal of all jīvas towards which they ought to strive is the shedding off of all matter. All centres of living activity are jīvas.

In the universe, we are told, the two Ātman and matter, subject and object, are always found together. Throughout experience we have the strife between the two, where the one tries to dominate the other. It is interesting to know that the spiritual element of the jīva is said to possess an upward tendency, while the material element has a downward tendency.

126. See *Outlines of Jainism*, p. 77.

A jīva inhabiting the body of a human being may become so weighted with matter that it passes into an earthly life.

We have gradations of jīvas according as they exhibit more or less of the dominance of self over not-self. In the highest stages of divine existence, the level of gods to be distinguished from that of pure souls or siddhātmans, who have no taint of matter, we have the largest amount of the domination of self and the not-self is at its lowest conceivable point. In the lowest stages we have the pure externality of things to things where the not-self is at its highest. As we rise to plants and animals, we have more of self and less of not-self. They have a unity and a simplicity which constitute their individuality. They carry their past in their present activity. When we attain to the status of gods, the not-self is at its lowest point. The joy of life rises to the god-rhythm of the universe. In things between the metals and the gods, self and not-self are at strife. In pure soul and in bare matter we have exclusively the spiritual and the non-spiritual; only they are not the reals of experience.

Can we say that the plurality of jīvas on this hypothesis is the ultimate truth of metaphysics? We are told that in jīvas there are two separate tendencies at work. The world open to us has this duality of self and not-self, sat and asat. The *sat* is real, the soul with its omniscience; the *asat* is the element which obscures this fact of omniscience and makes the jīva a limited one. In its innate nature, in its omniscient overflow, the soul is said to fill the whole universe, but the jīva becomes reduced to a single point in which the universe is reflected as into a centre. It is *asat* that is the basis of individuality. It is the negative principle that makes the jīva a separate centre of interests, a limited expression of the omniscient soul, an existence in the psychological order. The body constitutes the degree of imperfection and gives a standpoint to the soul. The different kinds of jīvas, metals, plants, animals, men and gods, are distinct, because their bodies are distinct. It follows that, though the soul which dwells in them all is the same, the negative principle of matter creates the empirical distinctness of individuals. 'The separateness and individuality of a jīva is only from the point of view of vyavahāra, or experience. Truly speaking, the essence of all jīvas is consciousness.'[127] Plurality of souls is a relative conception which reality presents when we lay stress on sensation, feeling

127. D.S., 3. 7 and 8.

and bondage, as if they were the only true moments of the real. We were obliged to transcend the conception of an empirical centre and rise to a logical subject in the Jaina theory of knowledge. The subject is such a persistent fact that the whole world is only for it.[128] When reflection by imperfect abstraction reduces the subject to a finite mind conditioned by an organism, with a particular location in space and time, we get the idea of the independence of the jīvas. In other words, to use Śaṁkara's famous expressions, we have the doctrine of the plurality of jīvas only so long as we treat the subject as an object which can be scrutinised. If we follow the implications of thought and disentangle the subject from embodiment in sensation and feeling, free it from all contact with the object, we shall see that there is only one subject in reality. Jainism did not choose to realise this height or look towards this ideal, and it is true that this exercise of thought is difficult at our level. For human thought a barrier is fixed between the ideal and the actual. We are compelled by our finiteness to start with particulars from which we cannot shake ourselves free.

Jainism even considers the theory of the oneness of the absolute and argues against it. 'If there were but one soul common to all beings, they could not be known from one another nor could they experience different lots; there would not be Brāhmins, Kṣatriyas, Vaiśyas and Śūdras, insects, birds and snakes; all would be men and gods. We make equal both those who lead a blameable life and those who in this world practise right conduct.'[129] There is no need to deny the plurality at the psychological or the empirical level, where only the question of the enjoyment of the fruits of karma arises. Where the mind is bound by organic conditions the doctrine of plurality has meaning, but our question is, can we consider this limited jīva to be the ultimate truth? If this limitation be an essential condition of the soul which it can never shake off, then the plurality of jīvas is real, but the Jainas believe that the limitations are accidental in the sense that they do not pertain to the essence of the soul, and in the state of freedom the soul is utterly freed from them. In that case we shall be illogical if we consider

128. Compare Bosanquet: 'It is freely admitted that in cognition the self is universal. It goes out into a world which is beyond its own given being, and what it meets there it holds in common with other selves, and in holding it ceases to be a self-contained and repellent unit.' (*Gifford Lectures*, Second Series, chap. ii.)

129. Sūtrakṛtāṅga, ii. 7. 48 and 51; see also i. 1. 1.

the accidental plurality of souls to be the final expression of truth. It is an accepted canon of metaphysical criticism that what is not at the beginning or end cannot be said to be really in its present process.[130] Plurality may be actual or existent, but it is not real.

It is not possible for us to support the doctrine of the plurality of souls when we have no means of finding out whether in the ultimate condition there is any basis of distinction. Salvation is inconsistent with a separate personality that is throughout hampered by what is external and contingent and is bound up with the bodily organism and nature itself. The particularity of self opens the way to error and sin, and salvation means the abolition of this particularity.

Metaphysically, the question of monism or dualism is determined by the relation of the two tendencies at work in the world. The Jainas do not take up the question of origins. We have no attempt at deducing the categories or supplying a rigid proof of their ultimateness. They repudiate the theory of an extra-cosmic deity conceived of as a whimsical despot. We do not misrepresent the Jaina theory if we say that it looks upon God, nature and soul as aspects of the same. There is no God except the soul in its ideal integrity. To conceive of God in any other way is to make him finite. The mind of man excludes itself from others and is of a limited nature, but if we get a mind which is not restricted by limitations, but can present itself to itself in its completeness, then the limitations that characterise human experience pass away. The eternal consciousness is within the human experience. It is the power that directs us to get beyond all finite forms. In knowledge with the unity of content it establishes for all minds, we are lifted above the psychological self, which is exclusive of others. From the mind conditioned by space and time we reach a mind through which alone space and time relations arise. The infinite is inherent in the finite. That is why the finite is ever struggling to break down its finiteness and reach out to the fullest freedom, and when the freedom of spirit is reached all is overcome. There cannot be any system of jīvas apart from such a spirit.

What is the relation between the spiritual and the material tendencies which are struggling in the world of experience? Are they differences within a whole? They seem to be well adapted to each other and to promote the

130. Ādāv ante ca yan nāsti vartamāne pi tat tathā.

progress of the whole. While they are opposed to each other, they do not seem to be opposed to the unity which is a synthesis of opposites. By emphasising such facts the Jaina theory would be led to the hypothesis of a concrete universal, a reality at once divided and united. To such a view there would be nothing purely spiritual or purely material. Both these are abstractions of logic. The real is a concrete whole of which pure being and pure matter are abstractions. They are moments of the one universal, antagonistic, but inseparable elements of one whole. The universal is manifesting itself in the life of the world. The struggle of opposites is present in all degrees of reality, though their opposition is overcome in the harmony of the absolute. If Jaina logic looks upon thought as the ultimate category and regards the central nature of reality as what is revealed by thought, then a concrete monism will be the result. A pure spirit, an abstract absolute, with nothing to struggle against, an actionless spiritual energy, a motionless being is mere nothing. Yet inconsistently Jainism asserts a condition of soul completely severed from matter, an upward movement without the potentiality of the downward in it. Kumārila urges that the reality of siddhātmans cannot be established by logical proof. 'No omniscient being is perceived by us here. Nor can his reality be established by inference.[131] The Jainas take their stand on the innate nature of the soul, which can be manifested when the hindrances are removed. Even Kumārila agrees that the soul has a natural capacity for grasping all things, and there are ways and means by which we can develop this capacity. If we emphasise this aspect of Jaina philosophy and remember that there is intuitional knowledge of the kevalin, which is higher than thought, we are led to a monism absolute and unlimited, which would require us to look upon the striving world, where all things roam about midway between reality and nothingness, as unreal. We can look upon the world as real only when we shut out of view the highest aspect of pure spirit. If we recognise it, then the not-self is merely the other of self, some reflection thereof not quite as real as the self, something which is ultimately to be sublated. The world becomes then an appearance created by the force of the not-self. In this way we are led to a severe monism of the type advanced by Śaṁkara. One thing, however, is clear, that it is only by stopping short at a half-way house that Jainism is able to set forth a pluralistic realism.

131. S.D.S., chap. iii.

REFERENCES

S.B.E., vols. xxii and xlv.
JACOBI, Articles on Jainism and the Jaina Atomic Theory in E.R.E., vol. vii.
UMĀSVĀTI, Tattvārtha Sūtra. (Sacred Books of the Jains.)
NEMICANDRA, Dravyasaṁgraha. (Sacred Books of the Jains.)
KUNDAKUNDĀCĀRYA, Pañcāstikāyasamayasāra. (Sacred Books of the Jains.)
JAINI, Outlines of Jainism.
MRS STEVENSON, The Heart of Jainism.
BARODIA, History and Literature of Jainism.

CHAPTER VII

The Ethical Idealism of Early Buddhism

■ Introduction—The evolution of Buddhist thought—Literature of early Buddhism—The Three Piṭakas—Questions of King Milinda—Visuddhimagga—Life and personality of Buddha—Conditions of the time—The world of thought—The futility of metaphysics—The state of religion—Moral life—Ethics independent of metaphysics and theology—The positivist method of Buddha—His rationalism—Religion within the bounds of reason—Buddhism and the Upaniṣads—The four truths—The first truth of suffering—Is Buddhism pessimistic?—The second truth of the causes of suffering—Impermanence of things—Ignorance—The dynamic conception of reality—Bergson—Identity of objects and continuity of process—Causation—Impermanence and momentariness—The world order Being and becoming in the Upaniṣads and early Buddhism—Aristotle, Kant and Bergson—Śaṁkara on the kṣaṇikavāda—The nature of becoming—Is it objective or only subjective?—External reality—Body and mind—The empirical individual—Nairātmyavāda—Nature of the Ātman—Nāgasena's theory of the soul—Its resemblance to Hume's—The nature of the subject—Śaṁkara and Kant—Buddhist psychology—Its relation to modern psychology—Sense perception—Affection, will and knowledge—Association—Duration of mental states—Subconsciousness—Rebirth—Pratītyasamutpāda—Nidānas—Avidyā and the other links in the chain—The place of avidyā in Buddha's metaphysics—The ethics of Buddhism—Its psychological basis—Analysis of the act—Good and evil—The middle path—The eightfold way—Buddhist Dhyāna and the Yoga philosophy—The ten fetters—The Arhat—Virtues and vices—The motive of moral life—The inwardness of Buddhist morality—The charge of intellectualism—The complaint of asceticism—The order of mendicants—Saṅgha—Buddha's attitude of caste and social reform—The authority of the Vedas—The ethical significance of Karma—Karma and freedom—Rebirth—Its mechanism—Nirvāṇa—Its nature and varieties—The Nirvāṇa of Buddhism and the Mokṣa of the Upaniṣads—God in early Buddhism—The criticism of the traditional proofs for the existence of God—The absolutist implications of Buddhist metaphysics—The deification of Buddha—Compromises with popular religion—Buddhist theory of knowledge—Buddha's pragmatic agnosticism—Buddha's silence on metaphysical problems—Kant and Buddha—The inevitability of metaphysics—The unity of thought between Buddhism and the Upaniṣads—Buddhism and the Sāṁkhya theory—Success of Buddhism. ■

I

EARLY BUDDHISM

There is no question that the system of early Buddhism is one of the most original which the history of philosophy presents. In its fundamental ideas and essential spirit it approximates remarkably to the advanced scientific thought of the nineteenth century. The modern pessimistic philosophy of Germany, that of Schopenhauer and Hartmann, is only a revised version of ancient Buddhism. It is sometimes said to be 'little more than Buddhism vulgarised.' As far as the dynamic conception of reality is concerned, Buddhism is a splendid prophecy of the creative evolutionism of Bergson. Early Buddhism suggests the outline of a philosophy suited to the practical wants to the present day and helpful in reconciling the conflict between faith and science. This will be clearly seen if we confine our attention to the leading principles of early Buddhism and do not emphasise the varying phases of its growth and the mythical legends which have crystallised round the primitive teaching and the founder, Buddha himself.

II

EVOLUTION OF BUDDHIST THOUGHT

Buddhist thought even in India has an evolution of over a thousand years to show. As Rhys Davids observes: 'Buddhism varies, through slight degrees, as the centuries pass by in almost every book.' In the second century after Buddha's death, no less than eighteen varieties of Buddhistic doctrine can be traced.[1] In the realm of ideas, life means change. It is not possible for us to thrust the whole development into this era. While early Buddhism and the Hīnayāna and the Mahāyāna forms of it belong to this

1. Rhys Davids, J.R.A.S., 1891, 'The Sects of the Buddhists'.

period, the four schools of Buddhistic thought take us beyond it. We propose, however, to refer to the Buddhistic schools in treating of this period, since towards the end of it they were fairly well developed.

III

LITERATURE

For an account of early Buddhism we have to depend on the *Piṭakas*, or the Baskets of the Law. The views set forth in them, if not the actual doctrine taught by Buddha himself, are yet the nearest approximation to it we possess. They represent what early Indian Buddhists believed to be the sayings and doings of their master. We have in them an account of the beliefs about Buddha and his teaching prevalent at the time when the piṭakas were compiled and written down. They were probably compiled and completed before 241 BC, when the third Council was held. They are undoubtedly the earliest and most authoritative account of Buddha's teaching now in existence.

According to the late traditions of Buddhism, a short time after Gautama's death, or after 'the lamp of wisdom had been blown out by the wind of impermanence,' disputes arose among the followers of Buddha about certain matters of doctrine. To settle them a council was called together at Rājagṛha, near Magadha. When the whole order was assembled, *Kāśyapa*, the most learned of Buddha's disciples was asked to recite the metaphysical views set forth in the *Abhidhammapiṭaka*. *Upāli*, the oldest disciple of Buddha then living, was called upon to repeat the laws and rules of discipline which are found in the *Vinayapiṭ*aka. Lastly, *Ānanda*, Buddha's favourite disciple, was asked to repeat the *Suttapiṭaka*, containing the stories and parables told by Buddha during his preaching tour. For a long time the teaching of Buddha was transmitted through the regular succession of teachers and disciples, and was reduced to writing only in 80 BC, in the reign of King Vattagāmani, in Ceylon. 'The text of the three piṭakas and the commentary thereon did the most wise bhikṣus hand down in former times orally, but since they saw that the people were falling away (from the orthodox teaching) the bhikṣus met together, and in order that the true doctrines might endure, they wrote them down in books.'[2] The Pāli canon has the three divisions of (1) Sutta or tales, (2) Vinaya or discipline, (3)

2. Mahāvaṁśa, chap. xxxiii.

Abhidhamma or doctrine. The first *Sutta piṭaka* has five divisions, called Nikāyas. The first four of these consists of Suttas or lectures mainly by Buddha in the form of speeches or dialogues. There is no difference in the doctrines they inculcate[3]. About this basket of discourses or Sutta piṭaka as a whole, Rhys Davids says: 'In depth of philosophic insight, in the method of Socratic questioning often adopted, in the earnest and elevated tone of the whole, in the evidence they afford of the most cultured thought of the day, these discourses constantly remind the reader of the dialogues of Plato.... It is quite inevitable that as soon as it is properly translated and understood, this collection of the dialogues of Gautama will come to be placed, in our schools of philosophy and history, on a level with the dialogues of Plato.'

3. The five divisions are the following:

(a) Dīgha Nikāya is the collection of long lectures containing thirty-four suttas, each dealing with one or more points of Buddhistic doctrine. The first of them is *Brahmajāla suta*, the second *Sāmaññaphala sutta* (on the reward of asceticism). *Ambaṭṭha sutta* speaks of Buddha's attitude to caste. *Kūṭadanta sutta* speaks of the relation of Brāhmanism and Buddhism. *Tevijja sutta* contrasts the Brahmin culture with Buddhist ideals. *Mahānidāna sutta* speaks of causation. *Sigālovāda sutta* speaks of the duties of the Buddhist layman. *Mahāparinibbāna sutta* gives an account of the last days of Buddha.

(b) The *Majjhima Nikāya* is the collection of lectures of middle length, about 152 sermons and dialogues dealing with all points of Buddhist religion.

(c) *Saṁyutta Nikāya* is the collection of combined lecutres. It contains the famous *Dhammachakkapavattana sutta*, 'lecture on setting in motion the wheel of the law.' It is usually called the sermon of Benares, and is also found in the Vinayapiṭaka.

(d) *Aṅguttara Nikāya* has over 2,300 suttas in eleven sections, so arranged that in the first are treated objects of one kind, in the second those of which there are two kinds, and so on.

(e) *Khuddaka Nikāya* is the collection of small pieces. It has fifteen divisions: (1) *Khuddakapāṭha* (2) *Dhammapada* (3) *Udāna*, (4) *Itivuttaka* (5) *Suttanipāta* (6) *Vimānavatthu* (7) *Petavatthu* (8) *Theragāthā* (9) *Therīgāthā* (10) *Jātaka* (11) *Niddesa* (12) *Paṭisambhidāmagga* (13) *Apadāna* (14) *Buddhavaṁsa* (15) *Cariyā piṭaka*. The Theragāthā and Therīgāthā are of great poetic merit and human interest. Their songs of deliverance and joy are ascribed to members of the Saṅgha who have attained to *arhattā*, the perfect peace and delight beyond words, in the lifetime of Gautama. The Jātakas relate the legendary histories of the previous births of Gautama, and are very valuable to the student of folklore. Dhammapada (S.B.E., vol. x) contains the gist of the essential principles of Buddha's doctrine. Those who have not the patience and the ability to master the three piṭakas resort to this summary of Buddhist ethics.

The *Vinayapiṭaka*, which deals with ecclesiastical discipline and prescribes rules and regulations to govern the lives of monks, has three main divisions, two of which are subdivided: (1) *Suttavibhaṅga*, divided into (a) *Pārājika* (b) *Pācittiya* (2) *Khandaka* divided into (a) *Mahāvagga*, (b) *Cullavagga* (3) *Parivāra*, the third *Abhidhammapiṭaka*[4] deals with psychological ethics and, incidentally, metaphysics and philosophy, and has seven sub-divisions: (1) Dhamma Saṅgaṇi, ascribed to the first half or the middle of the fourth century BC; (2) Vibhaṅga; (3) Kathāvattu; (4) Puggalapaññatti; (5) Dhātu; (6) Yamaka; and (7) Paṭṭhāna. This is the Pāli canon, setting forth the doctrines known as the Theravāda, since they were collected at the first Council by the Theras or the Elders.[5]

Sometimes Milinda Pañha, or *Questions of King Milinda*,[6] a dialogue between the Buddhist teacher and acute dialectician Nāgasena and the Greek king Menander, who ruled over the Indus territory and the valley of the Ganges from about 125 to 95 BC, is also included in the Pāli canon, as in Siam. This work is in great use in Ceylon, where it is the standard authority. It was written sometime about or after the beginning of the Christian era. We need not consider this book to be the epitome of the teaching of Buddha. The discussion seems to have taken place some 400 years after Buddha's death, and represents to us a form of Buddhism which came into vogue much later than the age of Buddha. The *Questions of King Milinda*, according to Rhys Davids, is 'the masterpiece of Indian prose, and indeed the best book of its class, from a literary point of view, that had been produced in any country.' Buddhaghoṣa considers it to be the most authoritative work after the Pāli piṭakas.[7] While the Pāli piṭakas may be substantially identical with the teaching of Buddha, in the *Questions of Milinda* we seem to get a more negative interpretation of the Buddhist teaching. Nāgasena seems to commit Buddha to a negative dogmatism which denies soul, God and a future for the liberated. He is a thoroughgoing rationalist, who adopted the scientific method rigorously and tore off the screen of make-believe which pious hands had woven round the image of truth to disguise its uglier aspects. Realising that the seeker of truth must at least be truthful, he held that the make-believe of religion was no escape

4. Abhidhamma is generally translated 'metaphysics'; Doctrine brings out the Pāli sense better.

5. See Oldenberg, *Dīpavaṁśa*, p. 37.

6. S.B.E., vols. xxxv. and xxxvi.

7. S.B.E., xxxv., p. xvi.

for the sufferings of mankind. On obviously incomplete data Buddha might have withheld judgment. Nāgasena doubted the caution of Buddha and became actively negative. To him lack of evidence for an opinion was a sufficient reason for disbelieving it. For believing on incomplete evidence is not only a blunder but a crime. Suspended judgment was Buddha's attitude; reckless repudiation was Nāgasena's amendment. In working out with remorseless logic the consequences of Buddha's ideas, he has unwittingly revealed their inadequacy.

Buddhaghoṣa's Visuddhimagga is a later work (AD 400) composed by a Brāhmin convert to Buddhism. It sets forth the Hīnayāna arhat ideal and develops the old doctrine. Buddhaghoṣa is the first Buddhist commentator. His Atthasālinī is a valuable commentary on Dhammasaṅgaṇi. The Theravāda did not develop much after Buddhaghoṣa's time. Other Pāli works of great historical, though not of philosophical, importance are the Dīpavaṁśa (fourth century AD) and the Mahāvaṁśa (fifth century AD). Our account of early Buddhism in this chapter will be confined mainly to the piṭakas and the orthodox commentaries. The *Questions of King Milinda* will also be used, but with reservation. Even when later works are made use of, we shall take care that no idea is introduced which is not contained in the earlier texts.

IV

BUDDHA'S LIFE AND PERSONALITY

When we pass from the Upaniṣads to early Buddhism, we pass from a work of many minds to the considered creed of a single individual. In the Upaniṣads we have an amazing study of an atmosphere, in Buddhism the concrete embodiment of thought in the life of a man . This unity of thought and life worked wonderfully on the world of the time. The singular personality and life of Buddha had much to do with the success of early Buddhism.

Any man with imagination will be struck with amazement when he finds that six centuries before Christ there lived in India a prince second to none before him or after in spiritual detachment, lofty idealism, nobility of life and love for humanity. The name of 'Buddha,' the knower, the enlightened, is that by which Gautama, the wandering preacher, is known to his disciples and through them to the world.[8] He was born *circa* 567 BC.

8. Buddha means the enlightener, and is a common name applied to many in India. It is a term like Christ which means the anointed.

His own name is Siddhārtha, or he who has accomplished his aim; his family name Gautama, his father's name Śuddhodana, and mother's Māyā. He was the heir to the Śākya kingdom, and was brought up in Kapilavastu, the capital of the Śākyas, by the second wife of Śuddhodana, Mahayāpatī, Gautama's mother having died seven days after his birth. It is said that he married his cousin Yaśodharā, and had a son, by name Rāhula, who became later his disciple. Early enough the burden and mystery of this unintelligible world pressed upon him with great force. He was much disturbed by the transience and uncertainty of life, and became keenly conscious of the black depths in which multitudes of human beings perish in darkness and sin. The story of the four signs which Gautama met on the road of Kapilavastu, the aged man bowed down by years, the sick man scorched by fever, the corpse followed by mourners weeping and tearing their hair and the mendicant friar, points the moral that the misery of the world left a sting on his sensitive nature.[9] The sights of suffering were enough to awaken in him a consciousness of the age-long burden that bears hardest on the innocent and threatens with shipwreck even the best endeavours of man. Individual instances of suffering to Buddha were illustrations of a universal problem. All that was fixed in him was shaken and he trembled at life.

Impressed by the emptiness of the things of sense, he renounced the ease, power and wealth of the palace to meditate on the eternal, and open for his fellowmen an escape from the meanness of life and the illusions of the flesh. In those days seekers after truth, haunted and obsessed by mental unrest, used to become wandering hermits. The seeker for light must begin his search by a repudiation of the good things of the world. In conformity with the ancient custom Buddha left his home and adopted the ascetic's life. He cast off his dignity, put on the yellow robe and begged for his bread, wandering up and down the streets of the world seeking for light and peace.

9. The force of fatality in a similar manner stirred George Sand to reflect on the sorrow of the world. 'When the sadness, the want, the hopelessness, the vice of which human society is full, rose up before me, when my reflections were no longer bent upon my proper destiny, but upon that of the world of which I was but an atom, my personal despair extended itself to all creation, and the law of fatality arose before me in such appalling aspect that my reason was shaken by it.' Quoted by W.S. Lilly, *Many Mansions*. See also Mahāpadānasuttanta; Rhys Davids, *Dialogues of Buddha*, vol. ii.

He made this great renunciation at the age of twenty-nine.[10] He tried to find spiritual rest by philosophic thought, and spent some time voyaging through strange seas of thought alone, but not with much success. Subtle dialectics are no cure for mental unrest. The other means of escape was through bodily austerities. Gautama went with five faithful friends to a solitary spot in the jungles of Uruvelā and there gave himself up to fasting and other bodily mortifications of the most severe type, seeking peace of soul through the fervour of asceticism. He could not gain any solace from it, for the truth was as far off as ever. He was growing desperate, and one night came very near dying, having fainted from fatigue and sheer starvation. Truth was yet a problem and life an interrogation.

After full six years of intense ascetic discipline Buddha became convinced of the futility of the method. The emptiness of wealth, the wisdom of the schools and the austerity of asceticism were all weighed in the balance and found wanting. With a body purified by abstinence, a mind refined by humility and a heart attuned by solitude, he sought wisdom in the wilderness. He turned to God's creation in the world if hapily he could learn the truth from the beauty of the dawn, the glory of the sun and the wealth of nature and life. He took to meditation and prayer. Legendary accounts speak of the doings of Māra to distract Buddha's attention and turn him from his purpose, now by violent assaults, now by tempting allurements. Māra did not succeed. Seated under the 'botree' on a bed of grass, Gautama remained facing the east, steadfast and immovable, with his mind fixed to a purpose—'Never from this seat will I stir until I have attained the supreme and absolute wisdom.' He spent seven weeks under the tree. 'When the mind grapples with a great and intricate problem, it makes its advances, it secures its positions step by step, with but little realisation of the gains it has made, until suddenly with an effect of abrupt illumination, it realises its victory. So it would seem it happened to Gautama.'[11] In one of his deeply meditative moods, while resting under the tree, to which his devoted followers gave the name of Bodhinanda, or

10. The popular story describes the act with great force. It is said that he arose at midnight, went to the door of his wife's chamber, and saw her sleeping, resting one hand on her baby's head. He had wished to take his son in his arms for a last embrace, but the fear of waking the young mother withheld him. He turned away and fled into the night in search for light.

11. Wells, *The Outline of History*, p. 207.

seat of intelligence, a new light broke upon his mind. The object of his quest was in his possession.

When he found enlightenment after years of steady search and meditation, he felt charged with the mission to announce to the doomed multitudes the way to everlasting felicity. He preached the gospel of the four Aryan truths and the eightfold path to the distracted world. Without troubling himself with the subtleties of metaphysics, he preached the ethical way, that he might save the masses of men living in sin and infamy. The serenity and gentleness of his face, the beauty and dignity of his life, the earnestness and enthusiasm of his love, the wisdom and the eloquence of his message won the hearts of men and women alike. For his first pupils he selected the five ascetic friends of his. To them he uttered his first sermon on 'Dharmacakrapravartana,' or 'Setting in motion the Wheel of the Law.' They accepted his teaching and were duly ordained the first members of the Buddhist order or Saṅgha. The number of disciples gradually increased. Missionaries were sent in all directions to teach the new dharma. The earliest converts and the most renowned were Sāriputta and Mogallāna, ascetics of Rājagṛha, who received the truth from Assaji, one of the five original disciples. Buddha personally admitted them into the order. Other famous disciples who fill a large place in the early chronicles of Buddhism were Upāli, who recited the text of the Vinaya at the first council after the death of Buddha; Kāśyapa, the president of the Council, an important Buddhist of the times, since it is said for his coming the cremation of Buddha's body was delayed; and Ānanda, Buddha's cousin and favourite pupil, who watched Buddha with tender feeling and great care and was nearest to him when he died. Thousands enrolled themselves among his adherents. A number of Brāhmin teachers became converts to Buddhism. When Buddha visited his father's court twelve years after he left it, it was only to welcome his father and mother, wife and son to his fold. Many became lay disciples, and a few women were also permitted to form themselves into an order of Buddhist nuns.

When he realised after a missionary life of nearly forty years that the time drew near for him to give up his body and attain parinirvāṇa,[12] he spent his last hours in giving counsels and directions to Ānanda and the

12. While nirvāṇa is attained and enjoyed during life, parinirvāṇa could be realised only at death, with the dissolution of the bodily life. See Parinibbāna Sutta, S.B.E., xi.

assembled monks. Subhadra, a wandering ascetic, listened to his teaching in the last moments, and was the last disciple converted by Buddha himself. Buddha asked his disciples to state their doubts and difficulties that he might remove them. They kept silent. Then the Blessed One addressed his brethren: 'And now, brethren, I take my leave of you: all the constituents of being are transitory: work out your salvation with diligence.'[13] He is said to have died at the age of eighty. The great Buddha typifies for all time the soul of the East with its intense repose, dreamy gentleness, tender calm and deep love. He is known by several names: Śākyamuṇi, the sage of Śākyas; Thatāgata, he who has arrived at the truth.

The facts here mentioned may be accepted as authentic. There are other incidents mentioned in Lalitavistara[14] and the Jātaka tales, more or less legendary.[15] When we remember that the Buddhist works which give an account of the life of Buddha are 200 years later than the events to which they relate, it will not be a surprise that they contain much that is legendary, interwoven with much that is authentic.[16] The teeming imagination of his followers embellished the story of his life with countless legends. The latter do not describe so much the real life of the teacher as the way he strikes their heart and imagination.[17]

13. Mahāparinibbānasutta, vi. 1. Philosophy, according to Plato's *Phædo* is the meditation of death. Compare Marcus Aurelius: 'All comes to stench and refuse at last.... All things are alike—familiar, fleeting, foul.... Anon earth will cover us all; then earth in its turn will change; then the resultant of the change; then the resultant of the resultant, and so *ad infinitum*. The billows of change and variation roll apace, and he who ponders them will feel contempt for all things mortal.' Quoted in Edwyn Bevan's *Hellenism and Christianity*, p. 185.

14. Edwin Arnold's *Light of Asia*.

15. Nidānakatha, vol. i of the Jātakas and Buddhacarita by Aśvaghoṣa.

16. The earliest account of the life of Buddha is contained in the Mahāpadānasuttanta, Discourse No. 14 of Dīghanikāya. It is said to contain an autobiography of Buddha.

17. While we are willing to admit that much of the popular account of Buddha is legendary, we are not so ready to accept the recent view that it is all a legend. We refer to the theory started by M. Senart and developed by a few others that the whole story of Buddha is a mere myth, added at a later date to a religion which had a natural growth. M. Senart maintains that we have in the story of Buddha a sun myth mixed with many other heterogeneous tendencies. We are not prepared to admit this hypothesis. The incidents related in the story of Buddha are natural and belong to a real tradition. We have evidence of the early existence of the books. The religion of Buddha cannot be understood unless it is viewed as the work of a

V

THE CONDITIONS OF THE TIME

Every system of thought embodies and reflects the tendencies of the time, and cannot be understood unless we realise the point of view from which it looked at the world, and the habit of thought which made it possible. From the unwritten literature later reduced to writing, it is possible to infer the condition of the times in which Buddha was born. There was not one vast Indian empire, but only princes of particular tribes and clans who were trying to form small states. Several dialects were in use, though Sanskrit was the one sacred language. The Vedas had already gained a mysterious sanctity. The customs and rules codified later in the laws of manu were in force, though they had not the rigidity which they acquired at a later day. The six philosophical schools were not developed, though the spirit of speculation which made them possible was at work. Moral life suffered, since metaphysical subtleties and theological discussions absorbed the energies of people.

A congeries of conflicting theories and guesses, accepted by some and denied by others, changing with men, reflecting the individual characters, emotions and wishes of their authors, filled the air. There were no admitted facts or principles which all recognised, but only dissolving views and intuitions. Discussions were ripe about the finiteness or infiniteness, or neither or both, of the world and the self, and the distinction of truth and appearance, the reality of a world beyond, the continuance of the soul after death and the freedom of the will. Some thinkers identified mind and soul, others distinguished them from each other. Some held to the supremacy of God, others to that of man. Some argued that we know nothing about it; others flattered their audiences with mighty hopes and confident assurances. Some were busy building elaborate metaphysical theories; others were equally busy demolishing them. Many theories independent of the Vedic tradition arose. There were the Nigganṭhas, or fetter-freed; the Samanas, or the ascetics who did not belong to the Brāhmanical order; those who sought peace of soul in the renunciation of the world; those who practised self-mortification denying themselves

---

real genius of commanding spiritual fervour. Even M. Senant recognises Buddha as a teacher, but thinks a sun myth is woven into his life. The central incidents of Buddha's life, however, cannot be mythical.

nourishment for long periods; those who tried spiritual abstraction, the dialecticians, the controversialists, the materialists and the sceptics, and those who are wise in their own conceit, like Saccaka, who had the audacity to say, 'I know no Samana, no Brāhmaṇa, no teacher, no master, no head of a school, even though he calls himself the holy supreme Buddha, who, if he face me in debate, would not totter, tremble, quake, and from whom the sweat would not exude. And if I attacked a lifeless pillar with my language, it would totter, tremble, quake; how much more a human being!'[18] It was an age of speculative chaos, full of inconsistent theologies and vague wranglings.[19]

The exuberant fancy of the metaphysically minded thus sported with time, space and eternity, and vulgarised the noble art of philosophy. Great truths were hidden away in the fogs of misty metaphysics. It is those who do not see the truth that strike out in the paths of fiction. Buddha was struck by the clashing enthusiasms, the discordant systems, the ebb and flow of belief, and drew from it all his own lesson of the futility of metaphysical thinking. The salvation of the soul does not depend on minute distinctions of metaphysical conceits, or the habit of restless questioning, or the refinement of reason by the subtle disputes of sects. The indecision of thought, though it may not be taxing to the intellect of man, was injurious to his ethical interests. Anarchy in thought was leading to anarchy in morals. Therefore Buddha wished to steer clear of profitless metaphysical discussions. Whatever metaphysics we have in Buddhism is not the original Dhamma but added to it (abhidhamma).[20] Buddhism is essentially psychology, logic and ethics, and not metaphysics.

In the vast continent of India, man's marvellous capacity for creating gods, the stubborn impulse to polytheism had free scope. Gods and ghosts, with powers to injure and annoy, as well as to bless and glorify, governed the life of the peoples. The multitude esteemed highly the Vedic religion, with its creeds and rituals, rites and ceremonies. Like the pagans of Europe, who vowed to Mercury the tenth part of their goods to be enriched, or a cock to Aesculapius in order to be healed, they were busy pleasing the gods. Even the one Almighty God of the monotheists was a very human

18. Oldenberg, *Buddha*, p. 70.

19. The sixty-two theories prevalent at the time of Gautama Buddha, mentioned in the Brahmajālasutta, are analysed by Rhys Davids in his American lectures on Buddhism.

20. Abhi, beyond: dhamma, physics. Medhamnas are further analysed in Abhidhamna. Cf. Aristotle. See Atthasālinī, Introductory Discourse.

sort of god, though of a heroic mould, kindly when allowed his own way, angry when thwarted, and merciful when his rage had spent itself. The relation between the one God and his worshippers was that of master and slave. He is a revengeful war-lord, entitled to deal with us as He will and bid us stand against the foe in battle line. He interfered rather too much with the world. Comets were signs of His anger sent to warn a sinful world. If the warning is neglected, He may send a pestilence to decimate innocent people. Miracles were the order of the day. The universal prevalence of law, though conceived by the Upaniṣads, was not yet a living belief. Stern monotheism, moreover, resulted in a shifting of responsibility to God's shoulders. If we are bad, He is responsible; if good even He. Either from pure caprice or from the desire to avenge the slight offered to Him by the sinful act of some remote ancestor, He has doomed the majority of mankind to disappointment and suffering.

Every sin is a violation of God's law, and the only way to please Him is by repentance and rolling in the dust Sin is an offence against God, who alone has to be satisfied. People were indifferent to the natural consequences of sin, though lip allegiance was paid to the law of karma. Over all men's activities there hung the thundercloud of an angry God. The result was that religion was distinguished from life, and God and the world were opposed.

The cruel rites with which worship was accompanied shocked the conscience of Buddha. There is much damage done to the moral nature of man by a superstitious belief in God. Many good men do devil's work in the belief that it has divine sanction. It is difficult to overestimate the amount of evil which has resulted in the world from a confusion of morality and religion. Abraham is commanded by God to sacrifice his son, and Saul is called upon to massacre his captives in cold blood. The views which under the name of religion crept into life and had so far prevailed as almost to extinguish any spark of spiritual vigour cut Buddha to the quick.

The sceptics on this theory need not be moral. So long as morality is based on a divine command miraculously conveyed, every discovery of science and development of thought would impair the basis of morals. The feeble in faith may reject the sanctions of morality.

Buddha, like Lucretius, felt that the world would be better for the triumph of natural law over supernaturalism. By announcing a religion which proclaimed that each man could gain salvation for himself without the mediation of priests or reference to gods, he would increase the respect for human nature and raise the tone of morality. 'It is a foolish idea to suppose that another can cause us happiness or misery.'[21] After Buddha did his work, the belief in the permanence and universality of natural law became almost an instinct of the Indian mind.

We shall see later that the world of experience according to Buddha does not require for its explanation any God. The law of karma will do. There is the implication of the existence of the Highest, but it is not a matter of logical demonstration. Buddha endorses the Upaniṣad hypothesis and anticipates Paul's judgment: 'O the depths of the riches both of the wisdom and knowledge of God! How unsearchable are His judgments, and His ways past finding out.'[22]

The Upaniṣads were a sealed book to the people at large. Their teaching was lost in a jumbled chaos of puerile superstition.[23] There were people who advocated tapas to bend the gods to their will. A dialogue of Buddha with an ascetic mentions twenty-two methods of self-mortification in respect of food and thirteen about clothing. The beauty of renunciation was eclipsed by the barbarism of superstition. Those who attempted to raise their souls ran the danger of degrading themselves into beasts. The masses of men were addicted to the ceremonies and observances prescribed by those who live on food provided by the faithful and whom Buddha describes as 'tricksters, droners out of holy words for pay, diviners,

21. Bodhicaryāvatāra.

22. Romans xi. 33.

23. Lalitavistara describes the state of India at the time Buddha preached in these words: 'While at Uruvelā Śākya called to mind all the different forms of penances which people in his time were in the habit of submitting to and which they thought raised the mind above all carnality. "Here," he thought, "am I born in the Jambūdvīpa among people who have no prospect of intellectual redemption, crowded by *Tīrthikas*, or revealers of the truth, with diverse wishes, and at a time when their faculties are wriggling in the grasp of the crocodile of their carnal wants. Stupid men who seek to purify their persons by diverse modes of austerity and penance, and inculcate the same. Some of them cannot make out their mantras; some lick their hands; some are uncleanly; some have no mantras; some wander after different sources; some adore cows, deer, horses, hogs, monkeys or elephants. Seated at one place in silence with their legs bent under them, some attempt greatness. Some attempt to accomplish their penance by inhaling smoke or fire, by gazing at the sun, by performing the five fires, resting on one foot or with an arm perpetually uplifted or moving about the knees ... some pride themselves on their saluting Brahmā, Indra, Rudra, Viṣṇu, Devī, Kumāra"....'

exorcists, ever hungering to add gain to gain.'[24] The priest who pretended to be the channel of divine power dominated the religion of the country. Buddha has nothing but warm admiration for the prophet of the soul, the true Brāhmin, who was required to say, 'Silver and gold have I none.' But when the prophet became a priest, and amassed silver and gold, he lost the power and the prestige born of spiritual gifts, and could no more say to the lame man, 'Rise up and walk.' He ceased to cure the sick by initiating them into the life of spirit, but assuming high airs, he pretended to be in the confidence of the gods and addressed the needy: 'Son, make a sacrifice to god and a payment to me, and thy sins will be forgiven thee.' The system of salvation by silver could not answer to the deeper needs of the human heart. To the mass of men religion consisted in regular ceremonial, prayer and penance, purifications and prohibitions applicable to almost all relations of human life. Buddha felt the hollowness of the host of beliefs which people were wont to regard as articles of faith. He hated that men should play the fool for nothing. He raised his voice in indignant protest against superstition and unreason and bade his disciples cease playing with trifles and realise the spiritual laws of the world. He denied the divinity of the gods and undermined the authority of the Vedas.

Buddha felt most intensely the inevitable defects of an age of criticism and enlightenment, when ancient faith was undermined and the fancies of theology were disappearing like the shapes of a dream. Men's souls were full of unrest, and desolating discord, and those unable to believe were looking out for a doctrine. The quest of the age was reflected in the spirit of early Buddhism. Buddha laid his finger on the heart's desire for the true, the good and the beautiful.

In the collapse of creeds and the disintegration of systems, it was the task of Buddha to provide a firm foundation for morality. As in the Greek world the larger and more comprehensive metaphysical systems of Plato and Aristotle were followed by the ethical speculations of the Stoics and the Epicureans, so it happened in the ancient India. When the foundations of philosophy became shaken, the principles of conduct attracted the attention of thinkers. If ethics is made to rest on the shifting sands of metaphysics or theology, it has an uncertain tenure. Buddha wished to build it on the rock of facts. Ancient Buddhism resembles positivism in its attempt to shift the centre from the worship of God to the service of

24. Rhyṣ Davids, *Buddhist India*, p. 215; see also *Dialogues of the Buddha*, 15.

man. Buddha was not so keen about founding a new scheme of the universe as about teaching a new sense of duty. It was his privilege to start a religion independent of dogma and priesthood, sacrifice and sacrament, which would insist on an inward change of heart and a system of self-culture. He made it clear that salvation does not depend on the acceptance of doubtful dogmas or doing deeds of darkness to appease an angry God. It depends on the perfection of character and devotion to the good. The moral law is not the chance invention of an exceptional mind, or the dogma of a doubtful revelation, but the necessary expression of the truth of things. Ignorance of truth is, according to Buddha, the cause of all misery. To deny the moral value of austere asceticism, to repudiate the popular religion, to despise the Vedic ceremonialism, in short, to make a religion of philosophy, is a great speculative venture, the daring of which we cannot rightly estimate. We find in the early teaching of Buddhism three marked characteristics, an ethical earnestness, an absence of any theological tendency and an aversion to metaphysical speculation.

Buddha had to reckon with the decline of the sense for the supernatural and the ideas of faith. In a period of self-questioning and self-testing, when men learned to look with a sharper eye on all that has hitherto been unthinkingly accepted, it is impossible to exempt faith from criticism. When serious thinkers dismissed the soul as a phantom, and immortality as a hallucination, it was no use trying to demonstrate their reality. Buddha adopted the critical spirit, but wished to set limits to it. His attitude was a perfect contrast to the spirit of scepticism, indifference and flippancy which characterised the materialist thinkers; yet he gathers up and concentrates the illumination of the age and gives us a penetrating criticism of traditional beliefs. After all, systems of thought and practice are only working hypotheses by which successive ages try to satisfy the aspirations and harmonise the results of advancing knowledge and growing insight. The environment is changed, knowledge has increased. The spirit of scepticism is afoot. Traditional religion has become unbelievable. Thinking men were devising some larger theories with which to walk through life and bring the ineradicable aspirations of human nature into harmony with the obvious data of experience. Buddha stood forth as the spokesman of the age. He was deeply influenced by the reaction setting in against the popular beliefs. There is no mistaking the fact that he merely accelerated what the stream of events was already rolling onward. He focussed the spirit of the age and gave a voice to the vague and unsystematised feelings of thinking men. He was at once the prophet and the exponent of the time spirit. Hegel compares the man of genius in relation to his age to one who places the last and the locking stone in an arch. Many hands help to build the structure, but it is in his hand alone that it becomes a complete work, sure and self-sustained. Such a master's hand was that of Buddha, one of the greatest of India's thinkers. Buddha's relation to his predecessors is analogous to that of Socrates to the Sophists. While in one sense his system is an expression of the current of criticism, it was also destined to stem the tide by strengthening the spiritual though not the religious view of reality. Immortality may be unbelievable and God may be inconceivable, yet the demands of duty are absolute.

We cannot consider Buddha a rationalist. Rationalism is defined as 'the mental habit of using reason for the destruction of religious beliefs.'[25] Buddha did not set out with the intention of reaching negative results. Being a disinterested seeker after truth, he did not start with any prejudice. Yet he is a rationalist, since he wished to study reality or experience without any reference to supernatural revelation. In this matter Buddha is at one with modern scientists, who are of opinion that the idea of supernatural interference should not be introduced into the logical interpretation of natural phenomena. Buddha had so firm a grip of the connectedness of things that he would not tolerate miraculous interferences of the cosmic order or magical disturbances of mental life.

Feeling that there was no use in making an appeal to faith in an age which had lost all faith in faith, he relied on reason and experience and wished to lead men by mere force of logic to his views. He wanted to establish a 'religion within the bounds of pure reason,' and thus put an end to both superstition and scepticism. He rarely assumes the prophetic rôle. He is a dialectician, arguing with his opponents to lead them to liberation. He presents to his followers the experience through which he himself has passed, and exhorts them to verify for themselves his views and conclusions. 'The doctrine is not based on hearsay, it means 'come and see.''[26] 'Buddha does not liberate men, but he teaches them how to liberate themselves as he has liberated himself. Men adhere to his preaching of the truth, not because it comes from him, but because, aroused by his word, a personal knowledge of what he preaches arises in the light of their minds.'[27] His

25. Benn, *History of English Rationalism in the Nineteenth Century*, vol. i., p. 4.
26. Saṁyutta Nikāya, iii.
27. Oldenberg, *Buddha*.

method is that of psychological analysis. He endeavoured to rid himself of all illegitimate speculation, build from the raw material of experience, and assist the spiritual growth of suffering humanity by an honest and unbiased expression of the results of his thought and experience. According to him, 'If a man sees things as they really are, he will cease to pursue shadows and cleave to the great reality of goodness.' Laying aside metaphysical speculations, he traces out the reign of law and order in the world of experience. Understanding, according to him, is to be limited to the field of experience, the laws of which it can explore.

VI

BUDDHA AND THE UPANIṢADS

For a revelation of the struggles of spirit and the experiences of the soul, Buddha had ready to hand that supreme work of the Indian genius, the Upaniṣads. Early Buddhism is not an absolutely original doctrine. It is no freak in the evolution of Indian thought. Buddha did not break away completely from the spiritual ideas of his age and country. To be in open revolt against the conventional and legalistic religion of the time is one thing; to abandon the living spirit lying behind it is another. Buddha himself admits that the dharma which he has discovered by an effort of self-culture is the ancient way, the Aryan path, the eternal dharma. Buddha is not so much creating a new dharma as rediscovering an old norm. It is the venerable tradition that is being adapted to meet the special needs of the age. To develop his theory Buddha had only to rid the Upaniṣads of their inconsistent compromises with Vedic polytheism and religion, set aside the transcendental aspect as being indemonstrable to thought and unnecessary to morals, and emphasise the ethical universalism of the Upaniṣads. Early Buddhism, we venture to hazard a conjecture, is only a restatement of the thought of the Upaniṣads from a new standpoint. Rhys Davids says: 'Gautama was born and brought up and lived and died a Hindu.... There was not much in the metaphysics and principles of Gautama which cannot be found in one or other of the orthodox systems, and a great deal of his morality could be matched from earlier or later Hindu books. Such originality as Gautama possessed lay in the way in which he adopted, enlarged, ennobled and systematised that which had already been well said by others; in the way in which he carried out to their logical conclusion principles of equity and justice already acknowledged by some of the most prominent Hindu thinkers. The difference between him and other teachers lay chiefly in his deep earnestness and in his broad public spirit of philanthropy.'[28] 'It is certain that Buddhism has acquired as an inheritance from Brāhmanism not merely a series of its most important dogmas, but what is not less significant to the historian, the bent of its religious thought and feeling, which is more easily comprehended than expressed in words.'[29] The contempt for ritualism was common to him and the Upaniṣads. Buddhism shared with the rest of Aryan India the belief in the law of karma and the possibility of attaining nirvāṇa. That sorrow or suffering is the essential fact of life on earth is admitted by almost all schools of Indian thought, the Upaniṣads included. Buddha himself was not aware of any incongruity between his theory and that of the Upaniṣads. He felt that he had the support and sympathy of the Upaniṣads and their followers. He classed the Brāhmins along with the Buddhist mendicants, and used the word as one of honours in reference to the Buddhist arhats and saints. Buddhism, in its origin at least, is an offshoot of Hinduism. 'Buddhism grew and flourished within the fold of orthodox belief.'[30] Throughout this account of early Buddhism we shall endeavour to show how the spirit of the Upaniṣads is the life-spring of Buddhism.

VII

SUFFERING

From his spiritual experience, Buddha became convinced of the four noble truths, that there is suffering,[31] that it has a cause,[32] that it can be suppressed,[33] and that there is a way to accomplish this.[34]

The first noble truth is the tyranny of pain. Life is suffering. 'Now, this is the noble truth concerning suffering. Birth is painful, decay is painful, disease is painful, death is painful, union with the unpleasant is painful; painful is the separation from the pleasant, and any craving that is unsatisfied, that too is painful. In brief, the five aggregates[35] which spring from attachment are painful.'[36] in the age of Buddha men of keen intellect

28. *Buddhism*, pp. 83–84.
29. Oldenberg, *Buddha*, p. 53.
30. Rhys Davids, *Buddhism*, p. 85.
31. Duḥkha.
32. Samudaya.
33. Nirodha.
34. Mārga.
35. Body, feeling, perception, will and reason.
36. *Foundation of the Kingdom of Righteousness*, p. 5.

and deep feeling were asking, What does all this weary round of existence mean? and Buddha addressed his appeal to the men who were longing for a way of escape, a resort to nirvāṇa, where the wicked cease from troubling and the weary are at rest. Insistence on suffering is not peculiar to Buddhism, though Buddha emphasised it overmuch. In the whole history of thought no one has painted the misery of human existence in blacker colours and with more feeling than Buddha. The melancholy foreshadowed in the Upaniṣads occupies the central place here. Possibly the ascetic ideals of an unreasoned exaltation of poverty, glorification of self-sacrifice, and an obsession of renunciation cast a hypnotic spell over Buddha's mind. To make people long for escape from this world, its blackness is a little overdrawn. We may try all we can to spread comfort and happiness and suppress all social injustice, yet man will not have satisfaction. Buddha concludes, existence is pain, the struggle to maintain individuality is painful, and the fluctuations of fortune are frightful.[37] In the Dhammapada, it is said: 'Not in the sky nor in the depths of the ocean, nor having entered the caverns of the mountain, nay such a place is not to be found in the world where a man might dwell without being overpowered by death.' The most moral hero and the greatest work of art must one day be cast down and consumed in death. All things pass away. Our dreams and hopes, our fears and desires—all of them will be forgotten as though they had never been. The great aeoms will sweep on, the unending generations will hurry past. None can resist the universal supremacy of death. Death is the law of all life. The evanescence of all human things is a source of melancholy to which many are subject. Our mind cannot grasp the substance of what it aims at, nor our lives realise

37. 'The pilgrimage (saṁsāra) of beings,' Buddha says, 'has its beginning in eternity. No opening can be discovered, from which proceeding, creatures, mazed in ignorance, fettered by a thirst for being, stray and wander. What think ye, disciples, whether is more, the water which is in the four great oceans, or the tears which have flown from you and have been shed by you, while ye strayed and wandered on this long pilgrimage and sorrowed and wept, because that was your portion which ye abhorred and that which ye loved was not your portion? A mother's death, a brother's death, the loss of relations, the loss of property, all this have ye experienced through long ages, and while ye experienced this through long ages, more tears have flowed from you and have been shed by you, while ye strayed and wandered on this pilgrimage, and sorrowed and wept, because that was your portion which ye abhorred, and that which ye loved was not your portion, than all the water which is in the four great oceans.' Saṁyutta Nikāya; Oldenberg, *Buddha*, pp. 216–217.

the visions it sees. All fulfilment of desire is attended with pain. The misery of human nature, with its eternal longing, which creates wants much in advance of man's power of satisfying them, cannot but make us feel that life is a curse. Tormented by thought, cheated by chance, defeated by the forces of nature, oppressed by the massive weight of duty, the horror of death, the dread consciousness of coming lives where the tragedy of existence will be repeated, the individual cannot help crying, 'Let me escape, let me die.' The remedy for all the woes of earth lies in getting out of it.

To the thinking, the unutterable sadness of transcience and the pitiful ineffectualness of virtue are the striking facts. Kant in his article on the 'Failure of Every Philosophical Attempt in Theodicy' (1791), refuting the optimism of Leibniz, asks: 'Would any man of sound understanding who has lived long enough and has meditated on the worth of human existence care to go again through life's poor play, I do not say on the same conditions, but on any conditions whatever?' The gloominess and grief of the great philosophers are perhaps the products of their thought. Those who feel but do not think have a better lot.

We cannot help feeling that Buddha overemphasises the dark side of things. The Buddhist view of life seems to be lacking in courage and confidence. Its emphasis on sorrow, if not false, is not true. The predominance of pain over pleasure is an assumption. Nietzche had Buddha in mind when he said, 'they meet an invalid, or an old man, or a corpse, and immediately they say, life is refuted.' After all, the value of life seems to rise with its evanescence. If the beauty of youth and the dignity of age are transient, so are the travail of birth and the agony of death. There is a tendency in Buddhism to blacken what is dark and darken what is grey. The outlook is restricted on principle to all that is sharp, bitter and painful in life.

But Buddhism would justify Buddha's attitude by saying that every religion exaggerates the suffering of life, for the aim of religion is the redemption from sin and suffering. With a happy world there would have been no need for religion. How can we escape from this world of death? is the question which the Upaniṣads ask, and Buddha is now asking it with a renewed force. Naciketas, the Brāhmin, asked Yama, Death, in the Kaṭha Upaniṣad: 'Keep thou thy houses, keep dance, and song for thyself. Shall we be happy with these things, seeing thee?'[38] The Buddhist asks: 'How is there laughter, how is there joy, as the world is always burning? Why do ye

38. i. 1. 26.

not seek a light, ye who are surrounded by darkness? This body is wasted, full of sickness and frail; this heap of corruption breaks to pieces. Life indeed ends in death.'[39]

If pessimism means that life on earth is not worth living unless it be in purity and detachment, then Buddhism is pessimism. If it means that it is best to be done with life on earth for there is bliss beyond, then Buddhism is pessimism. But this is not true pessimism. A system is pessimistic if it stifles all hope and declares 'to live on earth is weariness and there is no bliss beyond.' Some forms of Buddhism do declare this and are justly called pessimistic. So far as the early teaching of Buddha is concerned, it is not that. It is true that it considers life to be an unending succession of torments, but it believes in the liberating power of ethical discipline and the perfectibility of human nature. Again, though the suffering of creation weighs upon Buddha's mind, it does not seem to be purposeless. Desire is there to impel us to the supreme effort to abandon all desire. Each man has his own burden to bear, and every heart knows its own bitterness, and yet through it all goodness grows and progress becomes perfection. The world with all its suffering seems adapted to the growth of goodness. Buddha does not preach the mere worthlessness of life or resignation to an inevitable doom. His is not a doctrine of despair. He asks us to revolt against evil and attain a life of a finer quality, an ārhata state.

VIII

CAUSES OF SUFFERING

In answering the second question of the causes of suffering Buddhism has recourse to psychological analysis and metaphysical speculations. 'Now this is the noble truth of the origin of suffering. Verily it is the craving thirst that causes the renewal of becomings, that is accompanied by sensual delights, and seeks satisfaction, now here, now there—that is to say, the craving for the gratification of the senses, or the craving for prosperity.[40]

The Upaniṣads have already indicated the cause of suffering. To them the eternal is bliss and the transient painful. *Yo vai bhūmā tad amṛtam anyad ārtam.* The eternal unchanging is the truth, freedom and happiness, but the world of birth, old age and death is subject to suffering. The real is

39. Dhammapada, xi. 146. 148.

40. *Foundation of the Kingdom of Righteousness*, p. 6.

not to be found in the not-self, which is subject to origination and decease. It is there where these have no dominion. There is sorrow because all things are transient. They vanish as soon as they occur. The law of causality conditions all being which is in a state of perpetual becoming, arising and passing away. 'There are three things, O King, which you cannot find in the world. That which, whether conscious or unconscious, is not subject to decay and death, that you will not find. That quality of anything (organic or inorganic) which is not impermanent, that you will not find. And in the highest sense there is no such thing as being possessed of being.'[41] 'And that which is transient, O monks, is it painful or pleasant?' 'Painful, Master.'[42] Sorrow is one with transiency. Desires cause suffering, since we desire what is impermanent, changeable and perishable. It is the impermanent of the object of desire that causes disappointment and regret. All pleasures are transient. The fundamental proposition of the system that life is sorrow is dogmatically accepted from the Upaniṣads.

Buddha establishes that there is nothing permanent, and if only the permanent deserved to be called the self or Ātman, then nothing on earth is self. Everything is *anattā* or not-self. 'All are impermanent, body, sensation, perception, Saṅkhāras and consciousness, all these are sorrow. They are all not-self.' Nothing of them is substantial. They are appearances empty of substance or reality. What we consider the self is a succession of empty shows too insignificant to be worth fighting about. If men quarrel about them, it is because of their ignorance. 'On what existing do decrepitude and death come into existence, and on what do they depend? On birth taking place, decrepitude and death come into existence, and they depend on birth ... on ignorance subsiding, ideas subside, and on its cessation is their cessation, on the cessation of ideas is the cessation of apprehension.'[43] Ignorance is the main cause out of which false desire springs. When knowledge is attained suffering is at an end. Ignorance and false desire are the theoretical and the practical sides of one fact. The empty abstract form of false will is ignorance, the concrete realisation of ignorance is false will. In actual life the two are one. To the Buddhist, as to the Indian thinkers in general, knowledge and will are so closely related that no distinction is drawn between them. The same word *cetanā* is used to signify both thinking and willing. As we shall

41. Milinda, iv. 7. 12; see also Bhikkhunīsaṁyutta; Dhammapada, v. 47–48; and Oldenberg: *Buddha*, pp. 218–219.

42. See Majjhima Nikāya, iii. 19; Buddhaghoṣa; Atthasālinī, E.T., p. 74.

43. Lalitavistara.

see, exercises of thought are looked upon as preparatory to the purifying of heart and will. Ignorance of truth is the antecedent condition of all life. For one clear, piercing, scrutinising glance is enough to make us feel that nothing on earth, wife or child, fame or honour, love or wealth is worth pursuing. 'For all that is, when clung to falls short.'[44]

A wonderful philosophy of dynamism was formulated by Buddha 2,500 years ago, a philosophy which is being recreated for us by the discoveries of modern science and the adventures of modern thought. The electro-magnetic theory of matter has brought about a revolution in the general concept of the nature of physical reality. It is no more static stuff but radiant energy. An analogous change has pervaded the world of psychology, and the title of a recent book by M. Bergson, *Mind Energy,* indicates the change in the theory of psychical reality. Impressed by the transitoriness of objects, the ceaseless mutation and transformation of things, Buddha formulated a philosophy of change. He reduces substances, souls, monads, things to forces, movements, sequences and processes, and adopts a dynamic conception of reality. Life is nothing but a series of manifestations of becomings and extinctions.[45] It is a stream of becoming.[46] The world of sense and science is from moment to moment. It is a recurring rotation of birth and death. Whatever be the duration of any state of being, as brief as a flash of lightning or as long as a millennium, yet all is becoming. All things change. All schools of Buddhism agree that there is nothing human or divine that is permanent. Buddha gives us a discourse on fire[47] to indicate the ceaseless flux of becoming called the world.[48]

> Worlds on worlds are rolling ever,
> From creation to decay,
> Like the bubbles on a river,
> Sparkling, bursting, borne away.[49]

44. Majjhima Nikāya, 32.
45. Pātubhāvo-uppādo.
46. 'All things are in a state of flux.' 'Reality is a condition of unrest.' (Heraclitus, *Fragments*, 46 and 84.)
47. Cf. Heraclitus, 'This world is an eternally living fire.' Buddha and Heraclitus both use fire, the most mutable of the elements, to represent the metaphysical principle of becoming.
48. Mahāvagga, i. 121.
49. Shelley, *Hellas*.

Though the flame maintains itself unchanged in appearance, every moment it is another and not the same flame. The steam is sustained in its flow by ever new waters. The becoming of all that is, is the central fact of Buddhism. Absolute reality is not the property of anything on earth. 'It is impossible that what is born should not die.'[50] 'Whatever is subject to origination is subject also to destruction.'[51] Necessary and inexorable is the dying of all that is born. The difference is only in the degree of duration. A few may last for years, and others for a brief while. Change is the stuff of reality. There is neither permanence nor identity with regard to the world. It is only the transmitting of force. The idea might have arisen from reflection on consciousness and the apparent transitoriness of all objects of nature. Uninterrupted change is the feature of our conscious life. The living universe is a reflection of our mind. Each single phenomenon is but link in the chain, a transitory phase of evolution, and the several chains constitute the one whole, *dharmadhātu*, or the spiritual universe. Buddha adopts the golden mean even here. 'This world, O Kaccāna, generally proceeds on a duality, on the "it is" and the "it is not." But, O Kaccāna, whoever perceives in truth and wisdom, how things originate in the world, in his eyes, there is no "it is not".... Whoever, Kaccāna, perceives in truth and wisdom how things pass away in this world in his eyes there is no "it is" in this world.... "Everything is"—this is one extreme, O Kaccāna. 'Everything is not' is another extreme. The truth is the middle.'[52] It is a becoming without beginning or end. There is no static moment when the becoming attains to beinghood. No sooner than we conceive it by the attributes of name and form than it has changed to something else.[53]

How do we come to think of things, rather than of processes in this absolute flux? By setting our eyes to the successive events. It is an artificial attitude that makes sections in the stream of change, and calls them things. Identity of objects is an unreality. Out of the conditions and relations we build a seemingly stable universe. In dealing with the world we have to employ relations of different kinds, such as substance and quality, whole and part, cause and effect, which are mutually involved. The eight principal relative conceptions which we ignorantly regard as absolute are origination

50. Abhidharmakośavyākhyā.
51. Mahāvagga, 1–23.
52. Saṁyutta Nikāya. Oldenberg: *Buddha*, p. 249.
53. See Saṁyutta Nikāya, xxii. 90. 16.

and cessation, persistence and discontinuance, unity and plurality, coming and going. Even the modes of existence and non-existence are mutually dependent, so that one is possible only in relation to the other. All these relations are contingent and not necessary. They are not true, as Kant would say, of things in themselves.[54] They operate only in our world, i.e. the world of appearance or phenomena. So long as we look upon these limited and relative conceptions as absolutely true, we are subject to ignorance, the cause of life's misery. When we know the truth of things, we shall realise how absurd it is for us to worship isolated products of the incessant series of transformations as though they were eternal and real. Life is no thing or state of a thing, but a continuous movement or change. It is the Bergsonian attitude in germ.

Identity of objects is only another name for continuity of becoming. A child—a boy—a youth—a man—an old man are one. The seed and the tree are one. The banyan tree a thousand years old is one and the same plant with the seed out of which it has grown. It is the succession that gives the appearance of an unbroken identity. Though the substance of our bodies as well as the constitution of our souls changes from moment to moment, still we say it is the same old thing or the same old man. A thing is only a series of states of which the first is said to be the cause of the second, for they seem to be of the same nature. The seeming identity from moment to moment consists in a continuity of moments which we may call the continuity of an ever changing identity. The world is a number of accidents ever changing and being renewed at every breath and each moment disappearing, only to be replaced by a similar set. In consequence of this rapid succession, the spectator is deceived into the belief that the universe is a permanent existence, even as a glowing stick whirled round produces the appearance of a complete circle. A useful convention makes us give names and forms to the individual. The identity of name and form is no evidence of the identity of the inner reality. Again, we are naturally led to imagine a permanent core, but it is an abstraction of thinking. We say it rains, while there is no 'it' at all. There is nothing but movement, no doer but deed, nothing else but a becoming.

To account for the continuity of the world in the absence of a permanent substratum, Buddha announces the law of causation and makes it the

54. Time, according to Budhhaghoṣa, is 'a notion abstracted by mere usage from this or that event.' Atthasālinī, E.T., p. 78.

basis of continuity. The law of universal causation, with its corollary of the eternal continuity of becoming, is the chief contribution of Buddhism to Indian thought. Existence is transformation. It is a series of successive states. All things undergo the changes indicated in *utpāda* (origination), *sthiti* (staying), *jarā* (growth), and *nirodha* (destruction). 'Know that whatever exists arises from causes and conditions, and is in every respect impermanent.' Whatever has a cause must perish. 'Anything whatever born, brought into being and organized, contains within itself the inherent necessity of dissolution.' 'All component things must grow old.' Every substance is organic, and its existence is only a continuity of changes, each of which is determined by its pre-existing conditions. A thing is only a force, a cause, a condition. It is called a dharma. 'I will teach you the dharma,' says Buddha, 'that being present, this becomes; from the arising of that, this arises. That being absent, this does not become; from the cessation of that, this ceases.'[55] For Buddha, as for the Upaniṣads, the whole world is conditioned by causes. While the Upaniṣads say that things have no self-existence as such, but are products of a causal series which has no beginning or end, Buddha says things are the products of conditions. The Upaniṣads are as clear as early Buddhism, that in this world of unresting change and eternal becoming there is no firm resting place for man.

That which constitutes being in the material realm of things is only the *paṭiccasamuppāda*, or the origin of one thing in dependence on another. Causality is always self-changing or becoming. The essence of a thing, its dharma, is its immanent law of relation. There is no *being* which changes. There is only a self-changing or self-forming. We cannot say, as in the Nyāya philosophy, that one thing is the cause of something else. For a thing is what it is, and it cannot become something else. As the world process is affiliated to conscious growth, so is the force of causality related to inner motivation. Organic growth is the type of all becoming. The past is drawn up into the moving flow. The difficulty of external causation is due to the fact that in the outside world our knowledge is confined to relations of phenomena. But in our inner consciousness we know that our will determines acts. The same force operates throughout. Schopenhauer calls it the 'will.' Buddha calls it 'karma.' It is the one reality, the thing in itself of which the whole world is the working out. In the external world causation becomes uniform antecedence. That is the cause, given which another occurs. After all the trouble of modern philosophy, causation is not defined

55. Majjhima Nikāya, ii. 32.

in more adequate terms. Students of natural science like Karl Pearson ask us to replace the idea of causation by the category of correlation. Cause and effect represent earlier and later stages of a continuous process. We describe the course of events by the aid of the formula of causality, but do not explain why things happen as they do. Ultimate causes may be the province of metaphysics, but observation is limited to secondary causes. The aim of Buddhism is not philosophical explanation, but scientific description. So Buddha answers the question of the cause of any given state of a thing by describing to us the conditions of its coming about, even in the spirit of modern science.

The causal evolution is not to be viewed as a mechanical succession of movements, in which case the world process becomes a series of extinctions and fresh creations, but is one state working itself up to another state or informing it with a ceaseless pulsation. It is the determination of the present by the past. Buddhism believes in transitive causation, where one state transmits its *paccayasatti*, or causal energy, to some newly conceived germ. Causal relations are of the type of the seed growing into the tree, where the one is necessary for the other. All life is force. Though we can never see the working of the force, it is there; in consciousness we feel its presence. The world-process is of the nature of a self-acting development. It *appears* to be a series of incessantly succeeding phenomena, while it is a continuous development comparable to an indivisible melody. There is a cohesion of the past with the present which is broken up into a succession of before and after in our external treatment of nature. Then life becomes just one thing after another, and causality becomes mere succession, as Nāgasena asserts.

The doctrine of impermanence held in common by the Upaniṣads and early Buddhism is developed by later Buddhism into the view of momentariness. But to say that things are anitya or impermanent is different from saying that they are momentary or kṣaṇika. Buddha holds that only consciousness is momentary and not things, for he says: 'It is evident that the body lasts one year.... A hundred years and even more. But that which is called mind, intellect, consciousness, keeps up an incessant round by day and by night, of perishing as one thing and springing up as another.'[56] It was Buddha's interest to show that body, mind, etc., are not the true

56. Saṁyutta, ii. 96. Buddha does not say so definitely as Bergson does that the difference between the two, consciousness and matter, is only a difference of tension, or rhythm, or rate of moving.

self. They are not the permanent. Impermanence when predicated of things in general does not mean momentariness. It is only when Buddha speaks of mind that he uses the analogy of a flame. The flame of a lamp is a succession of flames each of which lasts only an instant, and thought (*citta*) process is of the same type. He clearly distinguishes the momentary character of mental processes from the impermanent nature of non-mental reality. When this momentary character is extended to all existence we get the *kṣaṇikavāda*. Later Buddhists believe that all existence is momentary. Permanent existence, they argue, is a self-contradiction. Existence or sattva means practical efficiency, or arthakriyākāritva. Existence is the capacity to produce some change in the order of things. The seed exists since it produces shoots. Permanent things, however, cannot possess this power of producing changes. If things were unchanged in past, present and future, there would be no reason why they should produce different effects at different points of time. If it is said that the potential power is permanent, and it becomes actual when certain other conditions are fulfilled, it is replied that whatever has power to do a thing does it, and whatever does not do it has no power. If the conditions bring about the change, then they alone exist and not the permanent thing. If existence means causal efficiency, then things that exist are momentary. 'Strictly speaking, the duration of the life of a living being is exceedingly brief, lasting only while a thought lasts. Just as a chariot wheel in rolling rolls only at one point of the tyre, and in resting rests only at one point; in exactly the same way the life of a living being lasts only for the period of one thought. As soon as that thought has ceased the living being is said to have ceased.'[57] On this view of momentariness with which Buddhism became identified very early in its career, the nature of movement is hard to grasp. When a body seems to move, what happens is that it is continuously renewed. It is reborn each moment, as a flame which is always being renewed and never remains even for a moment identical with itself.

Nature is one continuous vibration, an infinite growth bound by an iron chain of causality. It is a continuous whole, one and indivisible. Anything that happens sends a throb through the whole circle of existence, which is only another name for ceaseless change. Even in the mere mechanism of a soulless universe Buddhism sees an eternal cosmic law or ordered procedure. It is 'a mighty maze, but not without a plan.'[58] The

57. Visuddhimagga, chap. viii.
58. Pope.

wheel of the cosmic order goes on 'without maker, without known beginning, continuously to exist by nature of concatenation of cause and effect.'[59]

The order of the universe is called in Pāli, Niyama, or the process of going on. Some time before the period of Buddhaghoṣa (fifth century AD), and after the collection of the piṭakas, five orders were distinguished and named Kammaniyama, or order of act and result; Utuniyama, or physical inorganic order; Bījaniyama, or order of plants, the organic order; Cittaniyama, or order of conscious life; Dhammaniyama, or order of the norm, or the effect of nature to produce a perfect type. It is Kammaniyama that declares that good and bad actions result in desirable and undesirable results. It represents the universal fact that certain acts, bodily, mental, etc., eventually result in pain to the doer and his fellows while other acts bring happiness to both. It is the sequence of deed and effect that Kamma emphasises.

This huge world of life and motion, which is always becoming, always changing, growing, striving, has yet a law at the centre of it. This is the main distinction between early Buddhism and Bergsonism. To Bergson life means the absence of law, to Buddha all life is an illustration of a general law. The Buddhistic conception of life and law lights with its splendour the discoveries of science and gives meaning to the deepest instincts of man. The certainty of law is able to lift the awful weight which the suffering of life has laid upon the human spirit and fills the future with hope, for the individual can reach beyond the struggle and suffering inseparable from life if only he strives for it.

The fundamental difference between Buddhism and the Upaniṣads seems to be about the metaphysical reality of an immutable substance, which is the true self of man as well. We have to decide whether it is the idea of Buddha to look upon the universal order as coming out of nothing and going back to nothing. It is true that Buddha finds no centre of reality or principle of permanence in the flux of life and the whirl of the world, but it does not follow that there is nothing real in the world at all except the agitation of forces. The vital question is that of the original cause which set the wheel in motion. Who gave the impetus? If the mind is a flux and the object world another, is there or is there not a whole in which the two have their being? If our attention is confined to the phenomenal world, we cannot say on what the world rests, elephant on tortoise or tortoise on

59. Buddhaghoṣa, Visuddhimagga, xvii.

elephant, whether the causality of the world is the creation of God, or the evolution of a substance, or a natural unfolding out of its own interior. Buddha simply accepts the facts of experience. Things change. There is no being in the world, but only becoming. In such a state the supreme reality is the law of change, and that is causality. Buddha does not speak of any final cause or chance. The universe is governed by necessity. There is no chaotic anarchy or capricious interference. Oldenberg expresses the difference between the Brāhmanical and the Buddhistic conceptions in these words: 'The speculation of Brāhmins apprehended being in all becoming, that of the Buddhists becoming in all apparent being. In the former case substance without causality, in the latter causality without substance.'[60] This description exaggerates the dominant aspects of the two systems, which are agreed on the fundamentals, though there is a difference in the distribution of emphasis. For the Upaniṣads as much as for Buddha, 'the universe is a living whole, which, apart from violence and partial death, refuses to divide itself into well-defined objects and clear-cut distinctions.'[61] It is an undivided movement. The Upaniṣads do not posit a mere being exclusive of becoming. They do not regard the world of becoming as an illusion. Even Oldenberg admits that the thinkers of the Upaniṣads perceived an aspect of being in all becoming. They do not look upon the world of becoming as an unrelated procession of states. It may be appearance, but yet it is the appearance of reality. The Upaniṣads exclude the idea of absolute change by calling attention to the fact that there is a permanent underlying the flux. Changes are alternations in the special determinations, or accidents of a permanent substance. While the whole is unchangeable, the changes are the relative determinations of aspects of the whole, and these successive phases are bound by law. Buddha does not say that all changes involves a permanent that changes, nor does he say that change alone is permanent, as some of his followers interpret him. He is indifferent to the 'being' of things and finds the reality relevant to our practical interests in growth. But even if we hold with Nāgasena that we have only sequence, we cannot help asking, if everything is conditioned, is there an unconditioned? Without it causality contradicts itself. If each phenomenon is referred to another as its sufficient reason and that again to another, we cannot in the nature of the case find a sufficient reason for anything. We must somehow

60. *Buddha*, p. 251.
61. Bradley.

get beyond the category of cause to some being which is its own cause and remains one with itself in spite of all its changes. When we say that the transient is known as transient, we oppose it to the eternal, and the question of the reality of the eternal is raised. Either we should look upon the ultimate reality as a growing principle, or we must admit some permanent element which manifests and maintains itself in the whole process of change. In any case a principle of being or identity is admitted.

According to Aristotle, identity is necessary for all change. All change involves a permanent that changes. We cannot think of change without a permanent. It is the truth contained in Kant's *Second Analogy of Experience.* 'Without the permanent, no relations in time are possible.' The succession of 'B' upon 'A' means that 'A' is over before 'B' begins. The relation between them called succession cannot exist for either 'A' or 'B,' but only for something present to each of them. If there were nothing but successive events in the world, nothing but 'A' vanishing before 'B' begins, 'B' before 'C' begins, and so on, there could be no succession. The possibility of any successon implies a relative permanence. There must be something not in the succession but permanent that can carry on each vanishing moment of the succession and add it to the next. Even if we grant that all change implies a relative permanent, still the possibility of everything being relatively permanent implies an absolute permanence. We cannot resolve the whole into a network of relations, a mere mass of connections with nothing to be connected. It is like the flight without the bird. Thinghood is not exhausted by mutual relations. Buddha, limiting his attention to the world of experience, regards being as a continuous process. It is the view popularised by Bergson in modern philosophy, that the reality of the phenomena lies in the transition or becoming, but not in the things viewed. Avidyā gives us the illusory view of static substances. Knowledge gives us insight into the impermanence of things, but yet the changes are all self-changes, which obey an immanent law of causality.

If we accept the momentariness view, we have to admit causation and continuity with their correlates of permanence and identity, or resolve the world into a devil's dance of wild forces, and give up all attempts at comprehending it. Śaṁkara points out the inconsistency between causation with its implication of permanence and the momentariness doctrine thus: 'According to the Buddhists everything has a momentary existence. So when the second moment arrives, the thing which was existing in the first moment ceases to exist, and an entirely new thing springs up.

Accordingly, you cannot maintain that the preceding thing is the cause of the succeeding thing, or that the latter is the effect of the former. The preceding thing, according to the theory of momentariness, has ceased to be when the succeeding moment arrives; that is to say, the former becomes non-existent when the thing of the succeeding moment comes into being, and therefore cannot be regarded as producing the latter, since non-existence cannot be the cause of existence.'[62] The validity of this objection is admitted by some later Buddhists,[63] who argue that there is a permanent element underlying all changes. Mr Sogen says: 'The substratum of everything is eternal and permanent. What changes every moment is merely the phase of a thing, so that it is erroneous to affirm that according to Buddhism the thing of the first moment ceases to exist when the second moment arrives.'[64]

Confining his attention to the relative world of becoming, Buddha did not posit, like the thinkers of the Upaniṣads, a universal, all-sustaining life beating in every human heart, and the centre of the world. We cannot, however, deny the reality of the absolute simply because it is inaccessible to knowledge. If all that is, is conditioned, when the conditions are exhausted we get a blank. Oldenberg observes: 'The conditional can only be thought of as conditioned through another conditional. If we follow the dialectic consequence solely, it is impossible on the basis of this theory of life to conceive how, where a series of conditions has run out, annihilating itself, anything else is to be recognised as remaining but a vacuum.'[65] Buddha, agreeing with the Upaniṣads, holds that the phenomena of the world as known to our intellect possess only a conditioned existence. Our intellect compels us to posit an unconditioned being as the condition of the empirical series. This necessary being is not itself a member of the series. To be free from the law of contingency and dependence, it must be a non-empirical condition. Yet it cannot be detached completely from the empirical series, for in this case the latter would become unreal. Everything seems to be, yet not to be; it is at once being and becoming. Every event compels us to pass beyond it into some preceding form of existence, out of which the event has come as its evolved equivalent. This theory that everything existing is and is not, is real and unreal, suggests the idealistic view of becoming,

62. V.S., chap. ii. 11 ff.
63. E.g., the sarvāstivādins.
64. *Systems of Buddhistic Thought*, p. 134.
65. Oldenberg, *Buddha*, p. 277.

which is only an evolution of being. This is the main tendency of Buddha's teaching. Every existence is a mediation of two opposites, and so far as this world is concerned it is not possible for us to separate being and non-being. If we try to isolate either of them and determine it strictly by itself, it crumbles again, leaving mere nothingness behind. The empirical real is the intermediate thing, the progress, the movement from not-being to being, the becoming. Buddha is convinced of the futility of the logic which attempts to deal with objects of sense or thought as though they were fixed and static entities instead of phases in an eternal process or realisation. His silence on the absolute indicates that the eternal substance is not in his view available for the explanation of phenomena. Experience is all that is open to our knowledge, and the unconditioned lies beyond experience. There is no need to waste our time in fruitless efforts to grasp what always eludes us. A strict interpretation of the relativity of human knowledge compels us to admit the impossibility of demonstrating the existence or otherwise of a permanent element. Though Buddhism and the Upaniṣads refuse to see ultimate reality of substance or being in the ever changing sequence, the difference at most is that while the Upaniṣads assert a reality beyond change or becoming, Buddhism adopts a suspense of judgment on this question. In no sense is this healthy non-committal attitude to be construed into a denial of an ultimate being. It is impossible to think that Buddha recognised nothing permanent in this rush of the world, no resting-place in the universal turmoil where man's troubled heart can find peace. However much Buddha tried to refuse to reply to the question of the ultimate reality which lay beyond the categories of the phenomenal world, he did not seem to have had any doubt about it. 'There is an unborn, an unoriginated, an unmade, an uncompounded; were there not, O mendicants, there would be no escape from the world of the born, the originated, the made and the compounded.'[66] Buddha believed in an ontological reality that endures beneath the shifting appearances of the visible world.

IX

THE WORLD OF CHANGE

Is the becoming of the world real and objective? The main tendency of Buddha is to represent the universe as a continuous flow, which is *nissatta*,

66. Udāna, viii. 3.

or nonentity, *nijjīva*, or soullessness. All that is, is dhamma or grouping of conditions. It is unreal, but not non-existent. Yet there are passages in the early teaching of Buddha which countenance a purely subjective interpretation of the world. The world of object is conditioned by the individual as subject. It is within each of us. 'Verily, I declare into you, that with this very body, mortal as it is, and only a fathom high, but conscious and endowed with mind, is the world, and the waxing thereof and the waning thereof and the way that leads to the passing away thereof.'[67] Buddha tells the monk who is worried about the question of what remains after liberation: 'The question is to be put thus; 'Where no more is there earth, or water, or fire, or wind? Where are dissolved both long and short, and large and small, and good and bad? where are subject and object wholly remainderless melted away?' The answer is: 'By the undoing of consciousness wholly remainderless all is melted away.'[68] On the subject the world rests; with it it arises and with it it passes away. The world of experience is through and through such stuff as our dreams are made of. Hard facts of the world are a series of sensations. We do not know whether there are things to which our ideas refer. The rotation of the world is consequent on the force of karma and ignorance. There are also passages which support the interpretation that the particulars of the world are individuation of the one reality, which has neither particularity nor individuality. These are forms, which reality assumes, when it becomes an object of knowledge. While the former view dissolves the world into a dream positing nothing behind the flux, the latter reduces the world of knowledge to an appearance of a trans-empirical reality.[69] The latter is more Kantian while the former is more Berkeleyan. We may say that the latter interpretation corresponds to the hypothesis of Schopenhauer that the metaphysical principle is the will to live, and things and persons are varied objectifications of the one will to live. It is also sometimes suggested that our imperfection called ignorance breaks up the one continuous cosmic process into the individual persons and separate things. Statements are not wanting to the effect that composite substances disappear when true

67. Rhys Davids, *Dialogues of the Buddha*, i. p. 279. It is also suggested that the world does not exist for the enlightened one.

68. Dahlke, *Buddhist Essays*, p. 310.

69. *Kathāvatthu* (translated by Aung and Mrs Rhys Davids under the title of *Points of Controversy*) mentions among the unconditioned reals, space, nirvāṇa and the four truths.

knowledge arises, leaving behind the truth of the primary elements. The Leibnizean view that simple things are permanent while complex things are bound to be dissolved is familiar to early Buddhistic speculation. It looks upon the soul also, however, as a combination, and therefore subject to dissolution. The simple indestructible elements are conceived materially as earth, water, light, air, to which the Vaibhāṣikas add a fifth, ether. That an absolute śūnya or void abstract space is the reality may be traced to some passages, such as Buddha's answer to Ānanda inquiring about the cause of earthquakes: 'This great earth, Ānanda, is established on water, the water on wind, and the wind rests upon space.'[70] 'Venerable Nāgasena, there are found beings in the world who have come into existence through karma, and others who are the result of a cause, and others produced by the seasons. Tell me, is there anything that does not fall under any of these three heads?' 'Yes, there are two such things, space and nirvāṇa.'[71] Buddha has not left any clear account of the world of becoming. Ever so many suggestions are made, and they are all developed in a one-sided manner by the later schools of Buddhism. Nāgasena takes up a very subjective attitude. To him a thing is nothing but the complex of its characters. There is nothing real in the body apart from fleeting sensations. Things are only mental symbols for complexes of sensations. One of the four schools contends that matter is the phantasmal play of the phenomena of mind. Another, that mind is all. A third holds to the philosophy of the void or śūnyavāda, and urges that the world is neither real nor unreal, nor both nor neither. Buddha did not feel called upon to solve the problem of external reality; to him it was enough to note that man stands helpless in the middle of the stream of becoming, which he can neither check nor control; that he is bound to toss about in the dark unfathomable depths of saṁsāra so long as he is possessed by the thirst for life; and that in this restless world there is no possibility of peace. 'It is not the time to discuss about fire, for those who are actually in burning fire, but it is the time to escape from it.'[72]

X

THE INDIVIDUAL SELF

The dualism of body and mind is a part of becoming, a distinction of aspects in a whole; for all things are related to each other as aspects of one

70. Dīgha Nikāya, 207.
71. Milinda, iv.
72. Majjhima Nikāya, vol. i., p. 29.

continuous evolution. While life is eternal it is not always bound up with consciousness. Any point in the universe becomes a point of reference in relation to which all other things in the universe may be conceived to be in motion, and when such a point of reference is also conscious, we call it an individual subject. Perception of the truth of things requires subjective centres.

The individual subject is the empirical life of man, which grows and changes. The Upaniṣads declare emphatically that the true self of man is not to be identified with the body or the mental life which grows. Yet the union of mental and material qualities makes the individual. Every person as every thing is a synthesis, a compound. The Buddhists call it a saṁskāra, an organization. In all individuals, without exception, the relation of the component parts to one another is ever changing. It never the same for two consecutive moments. Man is a living continuous complex, which does not remain the same for the two moments, and yet continues in an endless number of existences without being completely different from itself.[73] While both mind and body are in ceaseless change, impermanence is more marked and the flow more rapid in mind that in body, so that if we wish to speak of anything as permanent it must be rather of body than of mind.[74]

Individuality is an unstable state of being which is ever growing. Rhys Davids says: 'There can be no individuality without putting together, there can be no putting together, no confection, without a becoming; there can be no becoming without a becoming different; and there can be no becoming different without a dissolution, a passing away, which sooner or later will be inevitably complete.'[75] It is a perpetual process with nothing permanent. Nothing here is permanent, neither name nor form.[76] To the five ascetics of Isipatana in Benares, headed by Koṇḍañña, the second sermon was delivered on the non-existence of the soul: 'The body is not the eternal soul, for it tends towards destruction. Nor do feeling, perception, disposition and intelligence together constitute the eternal soul, for were it so, it would not be the case that consciousness likewise tends towards

73. See Mahāniddesa, p. 117; Visuddhimagga, viii; W.B.T., p. 150.

74. Saṁyutta Nikāya, ii. 94 and 95. According to the great text of the Hīnayāna Abhidharmamahāvibhāṣāśāstra, a day of twenty-four hours contains six thousand four hundred millions ninety-nine thousand nine hundred and eighty kṣaṇas or moments, and the five skandhas are repeatedly produced and destroyed in every kṣaṇa. (See Yamakami Sogen, *Systems of Buddhistic Thought*, p. 11.)

75. *The Religious Systems of the World*, p. 142.

76. Mahāvagga, i. vi. 38 ff.

destruction.' 'Our form, feeling, perception, disposition and intelligence are all transitory, and therefore evil, and not permanent and good. That which is transitory, evil and liable to change, is not the eternal soul. So it must be said of all physical forms whatsoever, past, present, or to be, subjective or objective, far or near, high or low: 'this is not mine, this I am not, this is not my eternal soul.'[77] Dhammadinna in Veddallasutta says: 'The ignorant unconverted man regards the self as bodily form, or as something having a bodily form, or bodily form as being in the self, or the self as being in the bodily form; or else he regards the self as feeling, or as something having feeling, or feeling as being in the self, or the self as being in the feeling.' The argument is repeated with the other skandhas. There is no self (or Ātman) or person (pudgala) or living being (sattva) or principle of life (jīva) which is permanent. We have no consciousness of any such changeless entity or eternal principle in man.[78] We have only linkages of causes and effects. Man seems to be a complex composed of five skandhas. The theory of the skandhas is developed out of the nāmarūpa of the Upaniṣads. Here our point is that besides constituent elements, rūpa (the material) and nāma (the mental), we seem to have nothing more.

In the Suraṅgama Sutta, Ānanda's pitiful attempts to locate the soul inside the body or outside it, behind the sense organs, etc., are discussed.[79] We search in vain for a permanent soul in the substance of the brain, or the relics of sense, or the constituents of individuality. The postulation of an unconnected force called the soul seemed to the Buddhists to go against the law of karma, for people look upon the soul as a sort of jack-in-the-box, somehow the chief agent of all activities. According to Mrs Rhys Davids: 'The anti-attā argument of Buddhism is mainly and consistently directed against the notion of a soul, which was not only a persistent unchanging, blissful transmigrating superphenomenal being, but was also a being wherein the supreme Ātman or world soul was immanent, one with it, in essence and as a bodily or mental factor issuing its fiat.'[80] The Ātman of the Upaniṣads is, however, not the transmigrating self. Another misconception of the Upaniṣad definition of the soul repudiated by Buddha is that which

77. Mahāvagga, i. 21.

78. See Saṁyutta Nikāya, iv. 54.

79. Western psychologists indulge in such attempts to locate the soul in the body, nervous system, brain, and a particular point in it.

80. *Buddhist Psychology*, p. 31.

regards the Ātman as an abstract unity excluding all differences. If it is so, it is certainly a nonentity, as Indra said long ago.

A different reason which led Buddha to be silent about the soul was the conviction that the master instinct to affirm the ordinary self is the hidden root of all spiritual evil. He repudiates the popular delusion of the individual ego and disputes the reality of the surface self. He is emphatic about the false views of self. The objects with which we identify ourselves are not the true self. 'Since neither self nor aught belonging to self, brethren, can really and truly be accepted, as not the heretical position which holds: 'this is the world and this is the self, and I shall continue to be in the future, permanent, immutable, eternal, of a nature that knows no change, yea, I shall abide to eternity,' is not this simply and entirely a doctrine of fools?'[81] It is the false view that clamours for the perpetual continuance of the small self that Buddha refutes. We never remain the same for two moments together, and for what self is it then that we desire everlasting continuance?[82] Buddha repudiates the animism which projects a self into every object. He denies the existence of the unknown substratum which some posit as the support of qualities, since its nature is hidden from us. This useless occult, unknown and unknowable substance, Buddha rightly denies. Sometimes the liberated soul is conceived after the analogy of the human being. In his early wanderings Buddha approached the renowned sage Āḷāra Kālama and became his disciple, learning the successive degrees of ecstatic meditation. Āḷāra taught the view that the individual soul when it abolishes itself is set free. 'Having abolished himself by himself, he sees that naught exists, and is called a nihilist; then, like a bird from its cage, the soul escaping from the body is declared to be set free; this is that supreme Brahman constant, eternal, and without distinctive signs, which the wise who know reality declare to be liberation.' Buddha objected to this doctrine on the ground that the liberated soul was still a soul; whatever the condition it attained be, it was subject to rebirth, and the 'absolute attainment of our end is only to be found in the abandonment of everything.'

Buddha clearly tells us what the self is not, though he does not give any clear account of what it is. It is, however, wrong to think that there is no self at all according to Buddha. 'Then the wandering monk Vacchagotta spake to the Exalted One, saying: "How does the matter stand, venerable Gotama, is there the ego?" When he said this, the Exalted One was silent.

81. Majjhima Nikāya, i. 138. Cf. B.G., iii. 27.

82. See Inge, *Proceedings of the Aristotelian Society*, vol. xix. p. 284.

"How then, venerable Gotama, is there not the ego?" And still the Exalted One maintained silence. Then the wandering monk Vacchagotta rose from his seat and went away. But the venerable Ānanda said to the Exalted One: "Wherefore, sire, has the Exalted One not given an answer to the questions put by the wandering monk Vacchagotta?" If I, Ānanda, when the wandering monk Vacchagotta asked me: "Is there the ego," had answered: "The ego is," then that, Ānanda, would have confirmed the doctrine of the Samaṇas and Brāhmaṇas who believe in permanence. If I, Ānanda, when the wandering monk Vacchagotta asked me: Is there not the "go?" had answered: The ego is not," then that, Ānanda, would have confirmed the doctrine of the Samaṇas and the Brāhmaṇas, who believe in annihilation.' About this dialogue Oldenberg remarks: 'If Buddha avoids the negation of the existence of the ego, he does so in order not to shock a weak-minded hearer. Through the shirking of the question as to the existence or non-existence of the ego is heard the answer to which the premises of the Buddhist teaching tended, the ego is not.'[83] We cannot agree with this view that Buddha deliberately disguised the truth. Were Oldenberg correct, then nirvāṇa would mean annihilation, which Buddha repudiates. Nirvāṇa is not a lapse into a void, but only a negation of the flux and a positive return of the self to itself. The logical conclusion from this would be that something is, though it is not the empirical self. This is also in agreement with Buddha's statement that the self is neither the same as nor entirely different from the skandhas. It is not a mere composite of mind and body, nor is it the eternal substance, exempt from the vicissitude of change.[84] The discussion of the burden and its bearer makes out that the skandhas which are the burden and the pudgala which is the bearer are distinct entities. If they were identical, there is no need to distinguish between them. 'O, ye mendicants, I am going to point out to you the burden as well as the carrier of the burden: the five states are the burden and the pudgala is the carrier of the burden; he who holds that there is no soul is a man with false notions.'[85] To be born is to take up the burden; to lay it down is to attain bliss or nirvāṇa.

83. *Buddha*, p. 273.

84. In Puggalapaññatti we have a discussion of three principal theories regarding the nature of Ātman: Śāśvatavāda, which holds that the soul truly exists in this life and the future; the Ucchedavāda, that the soul truly exists only in this life; and the third theory that the soul does not exist in this life or the next.

85. W.B.T., p. 161; Sarvābhisamayasūtra quoted in Uddyotakara's Nyāyavārttika, iii. 1. 1.

Buddha emphasises the fact that we transcend experience when we make assertions about the permanent soul behind phenomena. While agreeing with the Upaniṣads that the world of origination, decease, and suffering is not the true refuge of the soul, Buddha is silent about the Ātman enunciated in the Upaniṣads. He neither affirms nor denies its existence. For so long as we swear by dry logic we cannot prove the reality of the soul as Ātman. The unknowable Ātman said to underlie our self is an inscrutable mystery. Some say it is, and it is open to others to say that it is not. Buddha exhorts us to be philosophical enough to recognise the limits of philosophy. A true psychology is possible only if we repudiate the metaphysical bias in favour of or against the soul. The psychologists of the middle of the nineteenth century tried to discuss psychological problems in the spirit of Buddha, even as physicists and biologists deal with their subject matter without defining matter or life. Buddha contents himself with a description of psychical phenomena, and does not venture to put forth any theory of the soul. Rational psychologists attempt to describe the nature of the soul, its finiteness or otherwise.[86] To posit a soul seemed

86. The difference between the two positions is brought out in the following passage from one of our greatest living psychologists, Professor Stout: 'It is a fact recognised explicitly or implicitly by everyone that the manifold and constantly changing experiences that enter into the life history of an individual mind are in some sense owned by a self or ego which remains one and the same throughout their vicissitudes. But when we begin to inquire into the precise nature of the unity and identity ascribed to the self and the precise sense in which its experiences belong to it, we are confronted with a fundamental divergence of views. On the one hand it is maintained that, just as the unity of a triangle, or of a melody, or of an organism consists merely in the special mode in which its parts are connected and correlated so as to form a specific kind of complex, so the unity of what we call an individual mind consists merely in the peculiar way in which what we call its experiences are united with each other. On this view, when we say that a desire is someone's desire we merely mean that it enters as one constituent among others into a connected totality of experiences, having a certain sort of unity and continuity which can belong to experiences only and not to material things. In opposition to this doctrine, it is strenuously maintained by others that the identical subject is not merely the unified complex of experience but the distinct principle from which they derive their unity, a something which persists through them and links them together. According to these writers it is an inversion of the truth to say that the manifold experiences through their union with each other form a single self. On the contrary, it is only through their relation to the single self as a common centre that they are united with each other. Of these two conflicting theories I feel bound to accept the first

to Buddha to step beyond the descriptive standpoint. What we know is the phenomenal self. Buddha knows that there is something else. He is never willing to admit that the soul is only a combination of elements, but he refuses to speculate on what else it may be.

The Upaniṣads arrive at the ground of all things by stripping the self of veil after veil of contingency. At the end of the process they find the universal self which is none of these finite entities, though the ground of them all. Buddha holds the same view, though he does not state it definitely. He denies the immortality of the fleeting elements which constitute the complex empirical individual. He denies the unphilosophical or the theological view sometimes put forward in the Upaniṣads that the Ātman is of the size of a thumb, which is said to escape from the body at death through an aperture in the suture of the skull. He also allows that the subject self is indemonstrable. Our introspection cannot seize it, yet we must assume it, for it is the subject that sees all else. Without it we cannot account for even the empirical self. Train of ideas, bundle, heap, collection are all metaphors, and involve a unifying agency. Without this immanent principle the life of man becomes inexplicable. So Buddha consistently refuses to deny the reality of the soul. Ancient Buddhist thinkers noticed this apparently uncertain attitude of Buddha towards the question of the self, and some have held that Buddha taught from motives of expediency both the existence and the non-existence of the self.

Nāgārjuna, in his commentary on the Prajñāpāramitā Sūtra, says: 'The Tathāgata sometimes taught that the Ātman exists, and at other times he taught that the Ātman does not exist. When he preached that the Ātman exists and is to be the receiver of misery or happiness in the successive lives as the reward of its own karma, his object was to save men from falling into the heresy of nihilism (ucchedavāda). When he taught that there is no Ātman in the sense of a creator or a perceiver or an absolutely free agent, apart from the conventional name given to the aggregate of the five skandhas, his object was to save men from falling into the opposite heresy of externalism (śāśvatavāda). Now, which of these two views represents the truth? It is doubtless the doctrine of the denial of Ātman. This doctrine, which is so difficult to understand, was not intended by Buddha for the ears of those

---

and reject the second. The unity of the self seems to me indistinguishable from the unity of the total complex of its experiences.' (*Some Fundamental Points in the Theory of Knowledge*, p. 6.)

whose intellect is dull and in whom the root of goodness has not thriven. And why? Because such men, by hearing the doctrine of an-Ātman, would have been sure to fall into the heresy of nihilism. The two doctrines were preached by Buddha for two very different objects. He taught the existence of Ātman when he wanted to impart to his hearers the conventional doctrine; he taught the doctrine of an-Ātman when he wanted to impart to them the transcendental doctrine.'[87]

XI

NĀGASENA'S THEORY OF SELF

When we pass from the direct teaching of Buddha to its interpretation by Nāgasena and Buddhaghoṣa a negative complexion is cast over the silence or the agnosticism of the original teaching of Buddha. Buddhist thought is torn away from its ancestral stem and planted in a purely rational soil. The logical results of the philosophy of becoming are drawn out with rigour. Phenomenalistic doctrines which remind us of Hume are developed with great skill and brilliance. Buddha makes psychology the fundamental discipline from and through which metaphysical problems are to be approached. Our attention according to him should shift from the absolute mind of metaphysical speculation to the human mind of psychological observation. Human consciousness apparently is the playground of rising and vanishing ideas. With his eye for the continual change and movement of ideas and consciousness and insistence on the exact method of psychological observation, Nāgasena dismisses the immortal soul as an illegitimate abstraction, and reduces the self of man to a unified complex exhibiting an unbroken historical continuity. In him, therefore, the

87. Similarly, Dharmapālācārya says in his commentary on the Vijñānamātraśāstra: 'The existence of the Ātman and of the dharmas, i.e. of the ego and of the phenomenal world, is affirmed in the sacred canon only provisionally and hypothetically, and never in the sense of their possessing a real and permanent nature.' Āryadeva, too, the most prominent of Nāgārjuna's disciples, says in his commentary on the Mādhyamikaśāstra: 'The Buddhas, in their omniscience, watch the natures of all living beings and preach to them the Good Law in different ways, sometimes affirming the existence of the Ātman and at other times denying it. Without an adequate development of one's intellectual powers, no one can attain nirvāṇa, nor can one know why evil should be eschewed. It is for the people who have not reached this stage that the Buddhas preach the existence of Ātman.' (Se Yamakami Sogen, *Systems of Buddhistic Thought*, pp. 19–20).

negative position of the non-existence of the soul is explicitly affirmed. He even goes to the length of saying that his designation Nāgasena indicates nothing permanent.[88] Things are names, concepts perhaps. Chariot is a name as much as Nāgasena. There is nothing beneath the properties more real. The immediate data of consciousness do not bear out the existence of any unity which we can imagine.

'And Milinda began by asking, "How is your Reverence known, and what, sir, is your name?"

'"I am known as Nāgasena, O king, and it is by that name that my brethren in the faith address me, yet this is only a generally understood term, a designation in common use. For there is no permanent individuality (no soul) involved in the matter."

'Then Milinda called upon the Yonakas and the brethren to witness: "This Nāgasena says there is no permanent individuality (no soul) implied in his name. Is it now even possible to approve him in that?' And turning to Nāgasena, he said: 'If there be no permanent individuality (no soul) involved in the matter, who is it, pray, that gives to you members of the Order your robes and food and lodging and necessaries for the sick? Who is it that enjoys such things when given? Who is it that lives a life of righteousness'? Who is it who devotes himself to meditation? Who is it who attains to the goal of the Excellent Way, to the nirvāṇa of Arhatship? And who is it who destroys living creatures? Who is it who takes what is not his own? Who is it who lives an evil life of worldly lusts, who speaks lies, who drinks strong drink, who (in a word) commits any one of the five sins which work out their bitter fruit even in this life? If that be so, there is neither merit nor demerit; there is neither doer nor causer of good or evil deeds; there is neither fruit nor result of good or evil karma. If, most reverend Nāgasena, we are to think that were a man to kill you there would be no murder, then it follows that there are no real masters or teachers in your Order, and that your ordinations are void.... You tell me that your brethren in the Order are in the habit of addressing you as Nāgasena. Now what is that Nāgasena? Do you mean to say that the hair is Nāgasena?"

'"I don't say that, great king."

'"Or the hairs on the body, perhaps?"

'"Certainly not."

'"Or is it the nails, the teeth, the skin, the fresh, the nerves, or the brain, or any or all of these, that is Nāgasena?"

'And to each of these he answered no.

88. Milinda, ii. 1. 1.

'"Is it the outward form then (rūpa) that is Nāgasena, or the sensations (vedanā), or the ideas (samjñā), or the syntheses, the constituent elements of character (saṁskāra), or the consciousness (vijñāna) that is Nāgasena?"

'And to each of these he answered no.

'"Then is it all these skandhas combined that are Nāgasena?"

'"No, great king."

'"But is there anything outside the five skandhas that is Nāgasena?"

'And still he answered no.

'"Then thus, ask as I may, I can discover no Nāgasena. Nāgasena is a mere empty sound. Who then is the Nāgasena that we see before us?"

'And the venerable Nāgasena asked Milinda the king: 'Did your Majesty come here on foot, or in a chariot?

'"I did not come on foot; I came on a chariot."

'"Then if you came, sire, in a chariot, explain to me what that is. Is it the pole that is the chariot."

'"I did not say that."

'"Is it the axle that is the chariot?"

'"Certainly not."

'"Is it the wheels, or the framework, or the ropes, or the yoke, or the spokes of the wheels, or the goad, that are the chariot?"

'And to all these he still answered no.

'"Then is it all these parts of it that are the chariot?"

'"No, sir."

'"But is there anything outside them that is the chariot?

'And still he answered no.

'"Then thus, ask as I may, I can discover no chariot. Chariot is a mere empty sound. What then is the chariot you say you came in?" And he called upon the Yonakas and the brethren to witness, saying: "Milinda the king here has said that he came in a chariot. But when asked in that case to explain what the chariot was, he is unable to establish what he averred. Is it, forsooth, possible to approve him in that?"

'And Milinda said: "I have spoken no untruth, reverend sir. It is on account of its having all these things—the pole and the axle, the wheels and the framework, the ropes and the yoke, the spokes and the goad—that it comes under the generally understood term, the designation in common use, of "chariot."

'"Very good. Your Majesty has rightly grasped the meaning of 'chariot.' And just so it is on account of all those things you questioned me about, the thirty-two kinds of organic matter in a human body, and the five constituent elements of being—that I come under the generally understood term, the designation in common use, of 'Nāgasena.' For it was said, sire, by our Sister Vagira in the presence of the Blessed

One: 'Just as it is by the condition precedent of the co-existence of its various parts that the word "chariot" is used, just so is it that when the skandhas are there we talk of a "being."'"'[89]

From the silence of Buddha on the question of the 'soul,' Nāgasena drew his negative inference that there was no soul. The word self is dropped altogether, and only states of self are spoken of. The self is a stream of ideas. The several states of self possess a common character, and we abstract this common element and call it the self or Ātman. If it is argued that there is such a thing as consciousness of self or the intuition of self, the Buddhists reply that it is a psychological impossibility. As when we deal with things like chariot, etc., we imagine something underlying the properties, even so do we unjustly imagine a soul underlying mental states. The idea of a soul when analysed comes to this, that certain qualities exist together. As body is a name for a system of qualities, even so soul is a name for the sum of the states which constitute our mental existence.[90] Without the qualities there is no soul, as there is no river without the two banks, the water and the sand, and no chariot without the wheels, the poles, the axle and the body.[91]

Nāgasena recognises the distinction between thoughts and things. In every individual he admits there are nāma and rūpa, mind and body. Only mind is not a permanent self any more than body is a permanent substance. Ideas, states, modifications come and go, attract us for a while, occupy our attention, and then disappear. We imagine that there is a permanent self which binds all our states and preserves them all, but this assumption is not justified by actual experience. In the manner of Hume he argues that we do not find anywhere in our experience anything answering to the conception of self. We do not perceive anything simple and continuous. Any idea which has no corresponding impression is an unreality. Things are what they are perceived to be. 'For my part, when I enter most intimately into what I call *myself*, I always stumble on some particular perception or other, of heat or cold, light or shade, love or hatred,

89. Milinda, ii. 1. 1.

90. 'The very existence of ideas constitutes the soul,' according to Berkeley, though this does not represent his later view. (*Works*, vol. iv., p. 434).

91. The Bodhisattva said to a pilgrim: 'Will you have a drink of Ganges water fragrant with the scent of the forest?' The pilgrim gives the answer back in the words: 'What is the Ganges? Is the sand the Ganges? Is the water the Ganges? Is the nether bank the Ganges? Is the further bank the Ganges?' The Bodhisattva retorted: 'If you except the water, the sand, the hither bank and the further bank, where can you find any Ganges?' (*Jātaka Tales*, no. 244).

pain or pleasure. I never can catch myself at any time without a perception and never can observe anything but the perception. When my perceptions are removed for any time as by sound sleep, so long am I insensible of myself, and may truly be said not to exist. And were all my perceptions removed by death, and could I neither think nor feel, nor see, nor love, not hate, after the dissolution of my body, I should be entirely annihilated, nor do I conceive what is further requisite to make me a perfect nonentity. If any one, upon serious and unprejudiced reflection, thinks he has a different notion of *himself*, I must confess I can reason no longer with him. All I can allow him is, that he may be in the right as well as I, and that we are essentially different in this particular. He may, perhaps, perceive something simple and continued which he calls himself, though I am certain there is no such principle in me. But setting aside some metaphysicians of this kind, I venture to affirm of the rest of mankind that they are nothing but a bundle or collection of different perceptions, which succeed each other with an inconceivable rapidity, and are in a perpetual flux and movement. Our eyes cannot turn in their sockets without varying our perceptions. Our thought is still more variable than our sight, and all our other senses and faculties contribute to this change; nor is there any single power of the soul which remains unalterably the same, perhaps for one moment.'[92] Again, a little further on, Hume writes: 'What we call mind is nothing but a heap or bundle of different perceptions united together by certain relations, and supposed, though falsely, to be endowed with a certain simplicity and identity.' Nāgasena, like Hume, feels himself to be under an intellectual obligation to regard all terms as jargon to which no imaginable meaning could be attached, and so is obliged to dispense with the subtle soul which to him expresses an impossible meaning. What is not felt is not real. We know only that there is suffering, but not that there is a subject that suffers.[93] Nāgasena rightly says that he does not know the self substance, that in which the qualities inhere according to Descartes, the unknown support of Locke. We have no idea of it, and we cannot presume to give any intelligible account of its relation to the qualities which it is supposed to support. Modern psychology has made the expression psychology without a soul, first used by Lange, current coin, and admits

92. Hume's *Works*, vol. i., pp. 3 ff.

93. M. Taine remarks: 'There is nothing in ego except the train of its events.' Soul, according to voltaire, is a 'vague, indefinite term for an unknown principle of effects, known and felt by us, which has generally been taken for the origin or cause of life, or for life itself.'

that soul is only a label attached to the bundle of sensations, emotions and sentiments. William James considers the term soul to be a mere figure of speech to which no reality corresponds. 'The word explains nothing and guarantees nothing, its successive thoughts are the only intelligible things about it.' Some realists who approach the problems of philosophy in the scientific spirit of early Buddhism do not accept the theory of the soul.[94] The notion of an inner principle different from and mysteriously related to outer responses is considered a superstition. Non-empirical explanatory essences are all eliminated. Self, then, is a generic idea standing for a collection of mental states. It is sum total of conscious contents.[95] Nāgasena is perfectly logical. If we do not, with Plato, hold that behind every individual being like chariot there is a universal lurking, we need not think that the complex man has a self behind him.

If sense is for us the measure of the universe, then experience becomes the feeling of each moment. Self is nothing more than an isolated momentary perception. The life of self, or what we popularly call mind, lasts only so long as the indivisible, momentary consciousness lasts. According to William James, the pulse of the present moment is the real subject. 'Consciousness may be represented as a stream.... Things which are known together are known in single pulses of that stream.' The real subject 'is not an enduring being; each subject lasts but for a moment. Its place is immediately taken by another which exercises its function, that is, to act as the medium of unity. The subject for the time being knows and adopts its predecessor, and by so doing appropriates what its predecessor adopted.'[96] The self logically becomes a transitory state of consciousness. Each conscious phenomenon called the mind is not a modification of any eternal mind stuff or the appearance of an Ātman, but only a highly complex compound constantly changing and giving rise to new combinations. On this view we cannot account for the relative permanence and unity of experience. Bertrand Russell states that there is an empirically given relation

94. Perry, *Philosophical Tendencies*, pp. 271 ff.

95. It is said in Visuddhimagga: 'Just as the word chariot is but a mode of expression for axle, wheels and other constituent members, placed in a certain relation to each other, but when we come to examine the members one by one, we discover that in an absolute sense there is no chariot; just as the words house, fist, lute, army, city, tree, are only modes of expression for collections of certain things disposed in a certain manner, in exactly the same way the words living being and ego are only modes of expression for a complex of bodily and non-bodily constituents.'

96. *Principles of Psychology*.

between two experiences which constitutes their being what is commonly called experiences of the same person, and we might therefore regard the person simply as the particular series of experiences between which this relation holds, dispensing with him altogether as a metaphysical entity. There is continuity, but no identity. The consciousness of two successive moments have no substantial identity. What is felt in the previous moment is already dead and gone, and even as we think our experiences flit away. Each state is an isolated individual, appearing for a moment and immediately vanishing, giving place to another, which has a similar fate. The impression of continuity is produced by the close crowding in of impressions, even as the continuity of a circumference is made up of a number of small points. Russell is of opinion that each of us is not one man but an infinite series of men, of whom each exists just for one moment. In successive states of consciousness we are different beings, and even continuity of existence between them is hard to comprehend. When the one is present, the other is irrevocably dead and gone. How can even the past condition the present?[97] The emphasis on the continuity as well as the transitoriness of mental states seems to be inconsistent. The persistence of the past in the present involved in the law of karma is not accounted for.

The mysterious soul refuses to be eliminated. Acts of perception and memory become impossible without it. We cannot rightly define a perception and cannot know even that consciousness is a succession. If mind is only successive perceptions, there is nothing that perceives. One perception cannot perceive another. The greatest contribution of Kant to

97. In the very useful introductory essay Mr Aung has prefixed to his translation of Anuruddha's Abhidhammattha-Saṅgaha, he sums up Aniruddha's explanation of the phenomenon of memory in these words: 'Each mental state is related to the next in at least four different modes of relation (paccaya): proximity (anantara), contingiuty (samanantara), absence (n'atthi) and abeyance (avigata). This fourfold correlation is understood to mean that each expired state renders service (upakāra) to the next. In other words, each, on passing away, gives up the whole of its energy (paccayasatti) to its successor. Each successor, therefore, has all the potentialities of its predecessors and more. This being so, the mental element or the principle of recognition or perception (saññā) in each of the mental states that take part in a memory process, with all its heritage of the past, is a recognising under favourable circumstances, in the image reproduced or the idea revived of the original object by the very marks which were observed by its predecessors in a certain intuition or reflection. Thus the subject has come to regard the image as the copy, and the idea as the counterpart of the original object intuited or reflected upon' (p. 14).

modern thought is the principle that the different kinds of empirical consciousness must be connected in one self-consciousness. This is the basis of all knowledge, whether of ourselves as individuals or of the world as systematically connected according to law. Knowledge implies the determination of the successive feelings by a subject not in the succession. Without the synthesis of self, experience would remain a mere rhapsody of distinct perceptions and would never become knowledge. An experience in which we have only feelings one after another is not an experience of objects at all. This central truth of all idealism was enunciated in unambiguous terms some centuries before Kant by the great Indian philosopher Śaṁkara. Śaṁkara criticises the doctrine of momentariness or kṣaṇikavāda in his commentary on the Vedānta Sūtras.[98] He argues that our consciousness cannot be momentary since it belongs to a permanent individual. If an individual does not exist, then recognition and memory become unintelligible. If it is said that these phenomena do not require a permanent individual, for what happens at one moment may be recalled at another distinct moment, even as we recollect today what we did yesterday, Śaṁkara says, then our judgments would always remain. 'I remember that *somebody* did something yesterday,' and not as they actually run, 'I remember that *I* did a particular thing yesterday.' It may be said that the consciousness of identity is illusory, for between a momentary cognition of yesterday and another such cognition of today there is a similarity which we wrongly interpret as an identity of the perceiving consciousness. But such an argument will not hold, since we cannot make a judgment of similarity if there are not two things, and if the momentariness doctrine is true, we cannot admit the existence of two things. It follows that we must admit the permanence of the perceiving consciousness, since there is no other way in which the past cognition and the present may be held together and compared, so that a judgment of similarity may result. If the past is to be recognised in the present, the permanence of the percipient is necessary. Even if such recognition be admitted to be based on similarity, the recognition of the similarity itself requires the identity of the subject. Again, we cannot admit that the judgment of similarity explains everything. When I say I recognise the man I met yesterday, I do not mean that my cognition is similar to the cognition of the previous day's, but that the objects of the two are identical. Mere similarity is inadequate to explain

98. ii. 2. 18–32.

the experience of recognition. Besides, there is no possibility of doubting our own selves. Even if I doubt whether what I see today is the same as what I saw yesterday, I never doubt whether I that see something today am the same self that saw something yesterday. Thus Śaṁkara argues against the momentariness view as applied to the perceiving subject, and contends that without a subject no synthesis, no knowledge, no recognition is possible.[99]

Nāgasena did not raise the question of knowledge and so evaded these problems. Otherwise he would have realised that the two terms subject and object, between which the knowledge relation holds, cannot stand for the same thing.

XII

PSYCHOLOGY

Whatever may be the view of the metaphysical reality of the soul, the Buddhists as a class attempt to deal with the individual life without any reference to a permanent self, for even if it has any meaning it seems to be too recondite to be of any service to us. We have now to notice the Buddhist analysis of the self. 'When one says "I," what he does is that he refers either to all the skandhas combined or any one of them, and deludes himself that that was "I."'[100] The being which undergoes existence is a composite one formed of skandhas or aggregates, which are five in number for human beings and fewer for others. The mind has the unity of a system.[101] It is a composite of mental forces.

The elements of individuality are distinguished into two broad divisions, nāma and rūpa. Even in the Upaniṣads these constitute the phenomenal self. Through them the pure being of Brahman is spread out in the objective sphere. Nāma answers to the mental and rūpa to the physical factors.[102] Body and mind are viewed as mutually dependent;

99. Commentary on, ii. 2. 25.

100. Saṁyutta Nikāya, iii. 130.

101. Dr McDougall writes: 'We may fairly define a mind as an organised system of mental or purposive forces.'—(*Psychology*.)

102. 'It is called rūpam because it manifests, rūpyati' (Saṁyutta Nikāya, iii. 86). What reveals itself to the senses is called rūpam. It is used to refer to matter and material qualities, objects perceived, and what Mrs Rhys Davids calls 'realms of attenuated matter.' See her Editorial Note in Buddhaghoṣa's Atthasālinī, E.T. See also W.B.T., pp. 184 ff, where it is made to include the four elements, the body, the senses, and even the sensations.

'whatever is gross is form or rūpa; whatever is subtle is nāma. The two are connected one with the other, and therefore they spring into being together. As a hen does not get a yoke or an egg shell separately but both arise in one, the two being intimately dependent one on the other; just so, if there were no nāma, there would be no form. What is meant by nāma in that expression being intimately dependent on what is meant by form, they spring up together. And this is, through time immemorial, their nature.'[103] The Buddhists, along with Indian psychologists in general, believe in the material or organic nature of mind or manas.

As to the distinction between the outer and the inner, the objective and the subjective, the following passage is pertinent: 'Which are the states which are ajjhatta (personal, subjective, internal)? Those states which for this or that being, related to the self, to the individual, to one's own, are referred to the person ... and which are the states that are bahiddha (non-personal, objective and external)? Those states which for this or that other being, for other individuals, related to the self, to the individual, to one's own, are referable to the person.' All are dharmas or mental presentations, ideas in Locke's sense, whatever is the immediate object of perception, thought or understanding. The individuality of man, consisting of both rūpa and nāma, body and mind, is said to be a congeries of mental states. In Book I of Dhammasaṇgaṅi those mental states or dharmas which reveal the nature of mind or nāma, the states of internal sense, are discussed. In Book II the states revealing the rūpa or the outer world, the products of external sense, are given. Dharma is a comprehensive term including the objects of external and internal senses. The phenomena of the world are divided into two classes: (1) Rūpiṇo, having form, the four elements and their derivatives; (2) arūpiṇo, not having form, modes or phases of consciousness, i.e. the skandhas of feeling, perception, synthesis and intellect. Rūpa means at first sight the extended universe as distinct from the mental one, the world seen as distinct from the unseen mind, the arūpiṇo. Slowly it comes to signify the worlds in which it is possible for us to have rebirth, for these are also capable of being seen. It is well for us to note that the early Buddhist did not care to carry his researches deeper, since his main interest was ethical. He argued to the nature of the external world from the physical basis of his own being.

Nāma, the mental, includes citta, heart or emotion, vijñāna, or consciousness, and manas, or mind. We have also as a division of nāmarūpa

103. Milinda, 2. 8.

the five skandhas, which are: (1) Rūpa, material attributes; (2) Vedanā, feeling; (3) Saṁjñā, perception; (4) Saṁskāras, or mental dispositions and will; (5) Vijñāna, or reason. These terms are not used with any strict connotation. They constitute the complex grouping of self. Cetana or will has a number of co-efficients. 'Saṁskāra' includes a miscellaneous host of tendencies, intellectual, affectional and volitional, and has for its specific function synthesis. Vijñāna is intelligence which comprehends abstract contents.[104] It is not conditioned by sense contact, while feelings, perceptions and dispositions are.

The scheme, which shows a pretty high development of the power of introspective analysis, agrees with modern psychology in fundamentals. It recognises broadly the distinction between body and mind, the physical and the psychical aspects of the individual. In the psycho-physical organism, the part that is relatively stable is the body, or rūpakāya, and the unstable one is the mind. On the mental side we have perception, conception, feeling or affection and conation or will. The first three can be easily traced to Saṁjñā and Vedanā, and Vijñāna. Vedanā is affectional reaction.[105] It is mental experience, awareness and enjoyment, and has the three qualities of pleasant, painful and neutral, resulting from contact with objects of sense, and itself producing taṅha, craving or desire. Saṁjñā is the recognition of the general relations as well as the perception of all kinds, sensuous and mental.[106] We have here distinct cognition. The series of cognitions called cittasaṁtāna goes on uninterruptedly through the successive existences. The object of consciousness may be either an object of sense or of thought.

According to Buddhaghoṣa, consciousness first comes into touch with its object, and then perception, feeling and volition arise. It is, however, not possible to break up the unitary conscious state into several successive stages answering to feeling, perception, etc. 'In one whole consciousness,

104. It has eighty-nine subdivisions, and comprises the distinct consciousness of what is transmitted through the organs of seeing, hearing, smelling, tasting, touching, and the sixth sense, manas, as well as the discrimination of good, bad and indifferent. These aggregates with their subdivisions, 193 in number, exhaust all the elements, material, intellectual and moral, of the individual. See Rhys Davids: *Buddhism*, pp. 90–93; Aniruddha, *Compendium of Philosophy*, Pāli Text Series, pp. 16, 88.

105. Milinda, ii. 3. 10. See also Buddhaghoṣa's Atthasālinī, E.T., p. 54.

106. Milinda, ii. 3. 11.

it cannot be said that this comes first and that next.'[107] It is interesting to know that Buddhaghoṣa looked upon Vedanā or feeling as the most complete awareness and enjoyment of the object.[108]

We may here notice the theory of sense perception of the early Buddhists. The visual sensation of the blue image arises when the colour blue which is given and the organ of the eye meet. Sometimes a distinction is drawn between hetu, cause, and pratyaya, or condition; while the visual sensation is *conditioned* by the eye and the object, the blue colour, it is said to be *caused* by the preceding cognition. The objects of sense are of five classes: sight, sound, smell, taste and touch. Buddhaghoṣa distinguishes these into asaṁpattarūpa, or those where the organism does not come into contact with the objective sources of the objects, as sight and sound, and saṁpattarūpa, smell, taste, etc., which are only modifications of touch. Democritus regarded all sensation as touch or its development. The fivefold objects are called pañcārammaṇa. When the organ and the object come into contact sensation arises. As matter of fact, the flux of consciousness is only 'the sequence of states of mind caused by the casual impact of sense and object. The phassa, or the contact, takes place 'as when two rams are butting together.' The eye is one and the object another, and the compact is the union of the two.'[109] The Dhammasaṅgaṇi holds that external phenomena are caused by the impinging on and modification of the internal or personal rūpa by way of sense. There are other views which

107. Atthasālinī, pp. 143–144.

108. Feeling 'has (1) experiencing as characteristic, (2) enjoying as function, (3) taste of the mental properties as manifestation, and (4) tranquillity as proximate cause. (1) There is no such thing as feeling in the four planes of existence without the characteristic of experiencing. (2) If it be said that the function of enjoying the object is obtained only in pleasurable feeling, we reject that opinion and say: let it be pleasurable feeling or painful feeling or neutral feeling, all have the function of enjoying (anubhavana) the object. As regards enjoying the taste of an object, the remaining associated states enjoy it only partially; of contact there is (the function of) the mere touching, of perception the mere noting or perceiving, of volition the mere co-ordinating, if consciousness the mere cognising. But feeling alone, through governance, proficiency, mastery, enjoys the taste of an object ... therefore it is said that enjoyment or experience is its function. (3) The mere presence or feeling as such is referred to by calling its manifestation 'tasting a mental property' (cetasika). (4) And inasmuch as a tranquillised body enjoys bliss or happiness, feeling has tranquillity as its proximate cause' (Atthasālinī, E.T., pp. 145–146).

109. Milinda, ii. 3. 9; see also Majjhima, i. 3.

make the eye and the objects condition each other. Without the eye there is no visible world, and without a world no seeing eye.[110]

The objects of thought are also of five classes: (1) Citta, mind; (2) Catasika, mental properties; (3) Pasāda rūpa, sensitive qualities of the body, and sukuma rūpa, subtle qualities of the body; (4) Paññatti, name, idea, notion, concept; (5) Nirvāṇa. These are Dhammārammaṇa, where Dhamma means the mental presentation. No definite account is given of the way in which sense experience is transformed into knowledge of meaning and ideas. It is said that the mind, which is regarded as a material organ, forms out of the sensations the intellectual ideas and notions. We do not know

110. Mrs Rhys Davids gives the following summary of the account of sense perception contained in the Dhammasaṅgaṇi:

A. The Senses.

First, a general statement relating each sense in turn, (*a*) to nature the four elements; (*b*) to the individual organism and affirming its invisibility and its power of impact.

Secondly, an analysis of the sensory process in each case, into—

(*a*) A personal agency or apparatus capable of reacting to an impact not itself.

(*b*) An impinging 'form' or form producing an impact of one specific kind.

(*c*) Impact between (*a*)and (*b*).

(*d*) Resultant modification of the mental continuum, viz., in the first place, contact (of a specific sort); then hedonistic result, or intellectual result, or presumably both. The modification is twice stated in each case, emphasis being laid on the mutual impact, first as causing the modification, then as constituting the object of attention in the modified consciousness of the persons affected.

B. The Sense-Objects.

First, a general statement, relating each kind of sense-object in turn to nature, describing some of the typical varieties, and affirming its invisibility, except in the case of visual objects and its power of producing impact.

Secondly, an analysis of the sensory process in each case as under A, but, as it were, from the side of the sense-object, thus:—

(*a*) A mode of form or sense-object, capable of producing impact on special apparatus of the individual organism.

(*b*) The impact of that apparatus.

(*c*) The reaction or complementary impact of the sense-object.

(*d*) Resultant modification of the mental continuum, viz., in the first place contact (of a specific sort), then hedonistic result, or intellectual result, or presumably both. The modification is twice stated, in each case emphasis being laid on the mutual impact, first as causing the modification, then as constituting the object of attention in the modified consciousness thus affected. (*Buddhist Psychology*, pp. li–liv.)

how it happens. Citta, which is both thing and thought, is said to work up the sensations into the concrete stream of consciousness. The seventh book of Abhdhamma piṭaka is called Patthāna, or relations. The Buddhist recognises how all consciousness is a relation of subject and object. In all these processes we are assuming the activity of vijñāna, the peculiar function of which is recognition,[111] which is a purely intellectual reaction.

Conation or will of modern psychology cannot easily be traced in the Buddhist analysis. Yet it is quite as fundamental and ultimate as cognition or affection. In the Buddhist theory, will is the most dominant aspect of consciousness, the basal element of human life. There is no ground to think that will in Buddhist psychology is a resultant of the integration of the five skandhas. We may say that vijñāna, vedanā and saṁskāra roughly correspond to knowledge, feeling and will. Childers in his dictionary brings the concepts answering to modern conation under saṁskāras. They include chando, desire, and viriyam, effort. This latter, according to Mrs Rhys Davids, assists all other faculties. In Aristotle we find that conative effort is the vital element in appetite, passion, choice or will. Mrs Rhys Davids is of opinion that though there are no indications of a clearly developed psychology with its nice distinctions between appetite, desire and choice, still we have the main lines between the psychological fact of willing and the ethical judgment of it clearly drawn. In the Piṭakas she thinks there is a 'pretty consistent discrimination in the employment of terms connoting volition between psychological import only and ethical or moral implication. In two parallel passages in the Dhammasaṅgaṇi, for instance, the term which best conveys the meaning of bare simple conation or consciousness of energy, namely viriyam, as well as all its synonyms and complementary terms–trying and striving, effort and endeavour, zeal and ardour, vigour and resistance, persistent striving , sustained desiring and exertion, grasping of a weight—is used to describe, in part, both the state or quality of mind which is morally good and that which is morally bad. To all such terms, then, when used of psychological activity, Buddhism attaches no blame any more than we should. When, on the other hand, the sacred writings wish to convey ethical values in terms of volitional import, either distinct and special words are used, or else the term of volition is explicitly qualified as referring to an object of perverted desires, or to a morbid state of will; want to wish (ākaṅkhā) becomes craving or thirst (taṇhā), for desire (chando) we get lust (chandorāgo), lusts of the flesh (kāma-rāgo), sensual delight (nandirāgo), or else some qualifying

111. Milinda, ii. 3. 12.

phrase, desire for form (rūpachando), and so forth.'[112] Everything is made a modification of will. Modern psychology emphasises the conative or purposive nature of all mental life. Sometimes the conation has a theoretical interest, sometimes practical. To adopt Professor Alexander's language: 'Theoretical acts of mind are such as subserve the continuance of the object before the mind without alteration of it. Practical acts are such as alter the objects.' Cognition and conation 'are not distinguishable elements in every psychosis, but every species of conation assumes two different forms, theoretical or practical, according to the different interests which the conation possesses.'[113] Generally theory ends in practice. Cognitions are eminently practical. Buddhist psychology is right when in the doctrine of pratītyasamutpāda it says that perceptions excite desires. The object on which conation is directed may be sensed, perceived, imaged, remembered or thought. Cognition and will become the theoretical and practical varieties of conation. Physiological psychology adopts the sensory-motor circuit as the unit. Of it the afferent part answers to cognition, the efferent to the conative. The whole process is looked upon as one, and these two are distinguished in it as elements. Where all mental life is conational, will represents the active pursuit of the end, transforming it from an ideal into a reality. Even here the practical aspect is the dominant one. The theoretical cognition arises when the practical expression is arrested or inhibited. The mere joy of contemplation is also a conative development where the practical interest is the delight itself. Feeling, again, is not independent of conation. It accompanies all acts. Professor Stout has given up the old tripartite classification of mental states and reverts to the ancient bipartite analysis of mind, bringing the affective and conational elements together under the name of interest as against the element of cognition. If we discard the separateness of cognition and make it the theoretical aspect of conation we get to the Buddhist emphasis on conation as the central fact of mental life.

Though there is no transcendental Ātman, its place, according to M. Poussin,[114] is taken by vijñāna. That which passes from life to life is vijñāna.[115] We are said to have vijñāna santāna, or continuum. This is not a permanent, unchanging, transmigrating entity, but a series of individual

112. J.R.A.S., 1898, p. 49.
113. *British Journal of Psychology*, 1911, p. 244.
114. *Journal Asiatique*, 1902. This view is probably later than the piṭakas.
115. W.B.T., p. 207.

and momentary consciousnesses, a regular procession of states. The vijñāna series is distinct from vedanā, or feelings, and is autonomous and independent of physical processes.

Buddhist psychology may best be described as associationist. For each group of dharmas the antecedent facts which determine their appearance in consciousness are sought out according to certain laws, and explanations remarkable for that age are suggested. To the question why do we have particular ideas when particular impressions occur, Nāgasena replies: 'Because of their being an incline, and because of their being a door, and because of their being a habit, and because of their being an association.' The incline is explained in terms which remind us of modern physiological psychology and its law of neural habit. 'When it rains, where will the water go to?' 'It will follow the slope of the ground.' 'And if it were to rain again, where would the water go to?' 'It would go the same way as the first water had gone.'[116] Dr McDougall writes: 'We have good reason to believe that the passage of impulse through a chain of neurons leaves that chain more or less permanently altered in such a way that its resistance to the passage of the impulse is in some degree diminished.' The path by which the discharge takes place becomes according to the law of neural habit one of lowered resistance.[117] The Buddhist explanation is, of course, a psychological insight, and not the result of a study of anatomy and physiology of the brain, sciences then, perhaps, hardly in existence. The conditions of recall are also mentioned.

Speaking of the duration of mental states, it is said every state of consciousness has three phases: genesis (uppāda), development (thiti), and dissolution (bhaṅga). Each of these occupies an infinitesimal division of time, an instant, a kṣaṇa. The space of three instants in which a state of consciousness becomes, exists and vanishes is called a cittakṣaṇa. Some Buddhists are of opinion that there is not even an instant for which the conscious state is steady. It simply grows and decays with no static interval, however infinitesimal it might be. Vissuddhimagga says: 'The being of a past moment of thought has lived, but does not live nor will it live. The being of a future moment will live, but has not lived nor does it live. The being of the present moment of thought does live, but has not lived nor will it live.'[118]

116. ii. 3. 7.
117. *Physiological Psychology*, pp. 125–6.
118. W.B.T., p. 150.

Every conscious state is said to be a disturbance of the stream of being which is the flow of subconscious existence. Buddhist psychology recognised unconscious life. It is called vidhimutta, or free from process, as distinct from vidhicitta, or waking consciousness. The two are divided by the threshold of consciousness, the manodvāra, or the door of mind. It is there where the stream of simple being or bhavāṇga[119] is cut off or arrested. Bhavāṇga is subconscious existence, or more accurately existence free from waking consciousness.[120]

A consistent theory of phenomenalism cannot account for the elaboration of similar impressions into general notions or the cognisance of unity in diversity. Buddhist psychology gives us an analysis of mental states, but does not raise the question of the necessity of a subject in the process of attention, will, etc. It speaks of feelings and relations, but does not ask whether they can exist apart from a combining consciousness. The subject of activity according to the Buddhists is the sum total of the organic and mental dispositions and acts. 'By name and form are deeds done,' and this of course is an ever changing composite. We are even told that we should not ask who experiences contact but only conditioned by what is their contact.[121] Our sense of individuality is an illusion. Yet we speak as if the 'I' attains rebirth or reaches nirvāṇa. Buddhaghoṣa explain it in this way: 'Just as in the case of those elements of being which go under the name of tree, as soon as at any point the fruit springs up, it is then said "the tree bears fruit" or the "tree has fructified," so also in the case of those groups which go under the name of "god" or "man," when a fruition of happiness or misery springs up at any point, then it is said that 'god' or 'man' is happy or miserable.'[122] Though the present self may not be the past, it is yet the outcome of the past, the resultant of the series.[123]

119. Bhava, being; aṅga, part. Bhavāṅga means both organic existence and subconscious existence. All is alive; only in some cases we have consciousness and in others not.

120. Nineteen kinds of bhavāṅga are distinguished. Of them ten are possible in kāma loka, five in rūpa loka and four in arūpa loka. According to Mrs Rhys Davids: 'Consciousness is only an intermittent series of psychic throbs associated with a living orgnanism, beating out their coming to know through one brief span of life' (*Buddhist Psychology*, p. 16). Bhavāṅga is subconscious existence when subjectively viewed, though objectively it is sometimes taken to mean nirvāṇa.

121. See Saṁyutta Nikāya, ii. 13.

122. W.B.T., p. 241.

123. 'When, O Great King, a man lights a candle, will not the candle burn through the night?' 'Yes, sure, it will burn through the night.' 'How then, O Great King, is the

The conception of the soul retains enough meaning to make rebirth significant. The difficulty is that, if there be no permanent soul, then punishment has no meaning. At the time of the punishment the individual is no longer the same being who committed the crime. But there is enough identity to justify punishment. There is no metaphysical entity to justify punishment; yet the individual is not a haphazard succession of unconnected phenomena but a living complex, a chain of causes and effects, physical, psychical and moral. The king asks Nāgasena: 'He who is born, Nāgasena, does he remain the same or become another?' 'Neither the same nor another.' 'Give me an illustration.' 'Now, what do you think, O king, you were once a baby, a tender thing, and small in size, lying flat on your back, was that the same as you who are now grown up?' 'No. That child was one and I am another.' 'If you are not that child, it will follow that you have had neither mother nor father, no, nor teacher.'[124] The re-born man is not the dead man, yet not different from him. He arises from him. Every day we are new, and yet not quite new. There is persistent continuity as well as unceasing change. Buddhaghoṣa says: 'If taking any continuous series an absolute sameness obtained, then, for example, sour cream could not arise from milk. And if there were absolute difference, the milk could not generate sour cream in the ordinary course of things.' There is neither absolute identity nor absolute difference. The whole is a series. The new creation is so immediate on the old that for all practical purposes it may be taken as the continuance of the same. There is a continuity of karma. Rebirth is new birth. Even in the Upaniṣads the unique ever-growing impermanent self it is that wanders in the world of saṁsāra and is the object of retributive justice. Rebirth requires the persistence of this ego. Through the conceptions of impermanence and causality a dynamic conception of self is evolved. Each experience as it rises and passes leads up to or becomes or ends in another experience, moment or phase of life, which sums up the whole past. In terms suggestive of M. Bergson's theory of memory, the Buddhists contend that there is no separate memory, for the whole past is contained in the present as a causative influence or force pursuing it throughout. 'That which we have felt, sought, willed from infancy is here

---

flame, during the first watch of the night, the same that it is in the second watch?' 'No, sir.... But the light burns the whole night adhering to the same matter.' 'So also, O Great King, the chain of the elements of things is joined together. One element is always coming into being, another is always ceasing and passing away. Without beginning, without end, the change continues.' (Milinda.)

124. Milinda.

now, bending over the present moment which goes merging into it, pressing against the gate of consciousness which would leave it without.'[125] The past bites into the present and leaves its mark on it.

XIII

PRATITYASAMUTPĀDA, OR THE DOCTRINE OF DEPENDENT ORIGINATION

The coming into being of life which is suffering, as well as its cessation, is accounted for by the doctrine of Pratītyasamutpāda. 'Then the Blessed One, during the first watch of the night, fixed his mind upon the chain of causation, in direct and in reverse order: "From ignorance spring the saṁskāras (conformations), from the saṁskāras springs consciousness, from consciousness spring name and form, from name and form spring the six provinces (of the six senses, eye, ear, nose, tongue, body or touch and mind), from the six provinces springs contact, from contact springs sensation, from sensation springs thirst (or desire), from thirst springs attachment, from attachment springs becoming, from becoming springs birth, from birth spring old age and death, grief, lamentation, suffering, dejection and despair. Such is the origin of this whole mass of suffering. Again, by the destruction of ignorance, which consists in the complete absence of lust, the saṁskāras are destroyed; by the destruction of the saṁskāras, consciousness is destroyed; by the destruction of consciousness, name and form are destroyed; by the destruction of name and form, the six provinces are destroyed; by the destruction of the six provinces, contact is destroyed; by the destruction of contact, sensation is destroyed; by the destruction of sensation, thirst is destroyed; by the destruction of thirst, attachment is destroyed; by the destruction of attachment, becoming is destroyed; by the destruction of becoming, birth is destroyed; by the destruction of birth, old age and death, grief, lamentation, suffering, dejection and despair are destroyed. Such is the cessation of this whole mass of suffering."'[126] Warren believes that the 'full formula in its present shape is a piece of patchwork put together of two or more that were current in Buddha's time.' It is based on the truths that man is bound to the wheel of life, and it is possible for him to free himself from these bonds by arresting the transitive character of causation. A view similar to this theory

125. *Creative Evolution*, p. 5.
126. Mahāvagga, i. 1. 1–3; S.B.E., xiii; see also Milinda, ii. 3. 1.

of the wheel of causation is suggested in the Upaniṣads.[127] The wheel of causation is sometimes distinguished into elements derived from the past life, those from the present and those of the future.[128]

The will to live is the ground of our existence. Its negation is our salvation. The greatest sin of man is to have been born, as Schopenhauer is fond of quoting from Calderon. It is this simple fact that is elaborated in the causal chain. It embodies the second great truth that suffering originates from desire, and sums up the conditions of existence. The Nidānas are the twelve successive causes where each one conditions the next. With the exception of the first, avidyā, or ignorance, and the last, jarāmaraṇa, old age and death, the nidānas are called the ten karmas or acts. In early Buddhism, these are not so much substances as phases of being. There is no fixity about the number or order of the nidānas. In the doctrines of the pratītyasamutpāda and the nidānas we find formulated a series of terms expressing the interrelated or mutually dependent order obtaining throughout the world of sentient existence.

The first factor in this series is avidyā, or ignorance. The false sense of 'I' is the central support of individual being. It is the bearer of karma as well as its breeder. Individuality is the product of avidyā and karma, even as the flame is the fiery spark as well as the fuel that feeds it. Avidyā hides

127. The eight fetters of the vital air, speech, tongue, eye, ear, mind, hands and skin and their auxiliaries, mentioned in the Upaniṣads (Bṛh., iii. 2), may be the basis of the doctrine. The word Brahmacakra, or the wheel of Brahma, occurs in the Śvetāśvatara Upaniṣad (vi. 1). It is called in early Buddhism bhavacakra, or the wheel of existence.

128. The following table brings out the distinction. See Majjhima Nikāya 140; Mahāpadāna suttanta, ii.

1. Those due to the past life	Avidyā, or ignorance. Saṁskāras, or predispositions or tendencies.
2. Those due to the present life	Vijñāna, or consciousness of self. Nāmarūpa, or mind and body. Ṣaḍāyatana, or the sense organs. Sparśa, or contact. Vedanā, or emotion. Taṇhā, or craving. Upādāna, or clinging or attachment
3. Those of the future life	Bhava, or coming to be. Jāti, or rebirth. Jarāmaraṇa, old age and death.

the nature of life, which is sorrow.[129] The stress on ignorance is nothing peculiar to Buddhism. 'Things are what they are,' as Bishop Butler says, 'and the consequences of them will be what they will be; why then should we desire to be deceived?' Yet we do deceive ourselves every day. Buddha asks us to face facts, know what they are and mean. It is ignorance consisting in assuming as real what is not, that produces the craving for life. It impels us to live and enjoy the world. The lust for life is considered by Buddha to be ignoble, stupid, moral bondage, one of the four mental intoxicants. If man is to be relieved from the misery of mundane existence, the false desire should be rooted out and the rage to life suppressed. Ignorance in early Buddhism is the cause of egoism, or the I-sense. It makes the individual feel himself to be separate from the rest of existence, unrelated to the order of the world. We cling to our little self, struggle hard to perpetuate it, and continue it through all eternity.[130] Individual existence is an evil, desire is the outer expression of it. Men are unhapphy simply because they are alive. The source of all sorrow is the affirmation of life. The force of ignorance is so great that in spite of the worst suffering men display a tenacious clinging to life.

The second link in the chain is saṁskāras. The word saṁskāra comes from a root which means to prepare or arrange. It stands for the product as well as for the process of making. It suggests how all things that are made have existence only in the making, how all being is becoming. Saṁskāra is translated 'synthesis' or 'conformation.' It also means action, pure and impure, action possessing merit to be rewarded or guilt to be punished, here or hereafter. In the wide sense of the term it means the will force or the spirit energy which determines the new existence. In the Majjhima Nikāya we read: 'It happens, my disciples, that a monk, endowed with faith, endowed with righteousness, endowed with knowledge of the doctrine, with resignation, with wisdom, communes thus with himself: 'Now then could I, when my body is dissolved in death, obtain rebirth in a powerful princely family.' He thinks this thought, dwells on this thought, cherishes this thought. These saṁskāras and internal conditions which

129. 'No world or thing here below ever fell into misery without having first fallen into folly.' (Carlyle, *Latter-Day Pamphlets.*)

130. 'Men overlook the fact that they are really no more separate than a bubble in the foam of an ocean wave is separate from the sea, or than a cell in a living organism is separate from the organism of which it forms a part.' (Rhys Davids, *The Religious Systems of the World*, p. 144.)

he has thus cherished within him and fostered lead to his rebirth in such an existence. This, disciples, is the avenue, this the path which leads to rebirth in such an existence.' The train of thought is repeated with reference to the several classes of men and gods until its application is made to the highest condition of nirvāṇa. The saṁskāra may also be for the abolition of all saṁskāras or the gaining of wisdom and deliverance.

In the causal nexus the third item is consciousness, from which name and form arise. 'If consciousness, Ānanda, did not enter into the womb, wound name and form arise in the womb?' 'No, sir.' 'And if consciousness, Ānanda, after it has entered into the womb were again to leave its place, would name and form be born into this life?' 'No, sir'. 'And if consciousness, Ānanda, were again lost to the boy or to the girl while they were yet small, would name and form attain growth, increase and progress?' 'No, sir.'[131] At death, while the other elements, body, feelings, perceptions vanish, vijñāna or consciousness persists, as the connecting link between the old and the new. Only when we attain nirvāṇa or deliverance does it completely disappear. It is the element of consciousness which becomes the germ of the new being when the old being dies. This germ seeks in the womb the material stuff from which a new state of being is formed. If consciousness does not find the necessary material structure, it cannot develop. 'If, Ānanda, consciousness were not to find name and material form as its resting-place, would then birth, old age and death, the origin and development of sorrow, reveal themselves in succession?' 'No, sir, they would not.'[132]

The world of objects stands opposed to the conscious subject. If there is no subject, there is no object. As we have seen, the activity of the six senses depends on the world which arises from the impressions produced when the senses come into touch with objects. The rise of impressions constitutes birth, their cessation, death. The two, consciousness and name and form, are inter-dependent. From them the six fields, eye, ear, nose, tongue, body and manas or mind, arise. Thence are developed the organs necessary for communication with the external world and the objects of the world, forms, sounds, colours, tastes, tangibility and thoughts. Thoughts are said to exist objectively confronting manas or mind, even as visible bodies exist before the eyes. Sometimes it is said that the eye is the product of seeing, the ear of hearing.

131. Mahānidāna Sutta.
132. Mahāpadāna Sutta and Saṁyutta Nikāya, i.

From feeling arises taṇhā or thirst or longing, which leads us from birth to birth. It is the potent cause of life and suffering. We are because we thirst for being. We suffer because we thirst for pleasure; 'Whomsoever thirst holds in subjection that thirst, that contemptible thing which pours its venom through the world, his suffering grows as the grass grows. Whosoever holds it in subjection.... suffering falls off from him as the water drops from the lotus flowers.'[133] 'As, if the root be uninjured, even as a hewn tree grows up anew mightily, so, if the excitement of thirst be not wholly dead, suffering ever and anon breaks out again.'[134] Taṇhā or thirst in its threefold form is the cause of all suffering.[135]

From thirst comes clinging or upādāna. The flame of thirst clings to the fuel of upādāna. Wherever it may go the flame has the fuel clinging to it. Deliverance is the extinction of thirst, and bondage is clinging to things. Only by the cessation of clinging can the soul be delivered from sinful existence.

From clinging to existence comes becoming or bhava, which Candrakīrti interprets as the karma which brings about rebirth.[136] From becoming comes birth, from birth come old age and death, pain and lamentation, sorrow, anxiety and despair.

The whole scheme seems dogmatic. It aims at showing that vijñāna, or consciousness of 'I,' does not reside in an eternal soul, but is a continuous phenomenon arising by way of cause and effect. It elaborates the answer contained in the second and third truths of the origin and the extinction of suffering. The vanity of all existence should be understood before the pain of existence can be abolished. The individuality to which we cling is only a form, an empty appearance occasioned by ignorance, the first and the root cause. The persistence of ignorance is indicated by the persistence of individuality. It is not a question of the individual manufacturing sorrow; he is himself a form of sorrow. The sense of 'I' which generates the illusion is itself an illusion. Individuality is the symptom as well as the disease. According to the Upaniṣads the life history of the individual is continued so long as there is ignorance in the understanding and leanness in the soul. In the *Theologia Germanica* it is stated: 'Nothing burneth in hell but self-will,' and this self-will is avidyā actualising itself. It is the cause as well as the product, the deceiver as well as the deceived. Ignorance and

133. Dhammapada, v. 335.
134. Dhammapada, v. 338.
135. See Mahāvagga, i. 1. 2.
136. Punarbhavajanakaṁ karma. Mādhyamika Vṛtti.

individuality are mutually dependent. Individuality means limitation, and limitation means ignorance. Ignorance can cease only with the cessation of the possibility of ignorance, namely, individuality. The whole world is a prey to ignorance, and so it suffers. From the monarh to the mendicant, from the creeping thing of earth to the shining deva of heaven, everything suffers. 'There are five things which no samana and no Brāhmaṇa and no god, neither Māra, nor Brahmā, nor any being in the universe can bring about: that what is subject to sickness should not be sick, that what is subject to death should not die, that what is subject to decay should not decay, that what is liable to pass away should not pass away.'[137] Individuality born of avidyā is the crux of all life, the original sin of all existence.

The whole scheme rests on avidyā, but we are not told how exactly this avidyā arises. The beginning of the circuit is not apparent. We cannot find its cause. It seems to be a blind end or an incomprehensible reality which we must accept unthinkingly. To Buddha everything that lives, moves and displays individual existence does so through the power of avidyā. Its presence is attested by the fact of existence. When we see a swinging pendulum we infer that it must have received a push. We infer avidyā to be the antecedent condition of all existence. There is nothing prior to it, for the process of the world is beginningless. Buddha seems to assert the eternity of ignorance. In the chain of causation it is put first, for through it comes willing and through willing existence. When we ask what is it of which we are ignorant, early Buddhism says we are ignorant of the true nature of 'I and of the four noble truths. The cause of existence is a pre-existence like the present, where knowledge of the four sacred truths was not acquired. In the Upaniṣads the cause of all suffering is traced to the avidyā, pertaining to the fundamental identity of the ego with the soul of the world, which leads to egoity. In both, egoity is the result of avidyā, in both it is the non-possession of the saving knowledge that hides from us the truth.

Buddha recognises that ignorance is nothing absolute. It comes into play that it may abolish itself. The metaphysical problem of the rise of ignorance seems to be evaded. We cannot account for it. We cannot say it is real, for it can be sublated. Nor is it unreal, for in that case it could not produce anything. But Buddhism does not consider avidyā to be a cause by courtesy. It is really the source of all existence. Perhaps the Upaniṣad theory is truer. The manifold world has the power of concealing reality at the same time that it manifests it. This power is the the central force, the

137. Aṅguttara Nikāya, ii. Oldenberg, *Buddha*, p. 217.

non-being, which pushes reality into outward manifestation. This explanation is not possible until we explicitly posit a central reality. So long as such a central being is not admitted, the nature of avidyā and its origin will remain unsolved. But everything in Buddhism is favourable to the Upaniṣad hypothesis. Avidyā is not absolutely useless. It provides room for the possibility of deliverance from itself. If nirvāṇa is more than extinction, the truth more than a mere passing shadow, then individuality is not absolute non-being, but a mixture of being and non-being, and avidyā is not falsehood so much as lack of knowledge. When it is abolished truth remains. Later Buddhist writers like Aśvaghoṣa speak of an abrupt upheaval of avidyā out of the Tathatā, the sudden rise of the individual will out of the universal. Vasubandhu explains the individuals as the imperfect reflections of the one universal mind. Avidyā, then, is the śakti or the force of the absolute which brings about the procession of individual existences from out of the universal. It is the principle of negativity at the very heart of reality. Behind it our finite intellect cannot penetrate. Buddhistic metaphysics becomes satisfactory and intelligible only if it is completed by some form of absolute idealism.

XIV

ETHICS

Long to the watcher is the night
To the weary wand'rer along the road,
To him who will not see truth's light,
Long is the torment of his chain of births.

So reads a Buddhist proverb.[138] Life on earth is a pilgrimage in a strange land which the true knower is not anxious to prolong. Buddha points a way out of the inward contradiction characteristic of human life. Redemption from suffering is the motive of Buddha's teaching. To escape from the pervasive evil of existence is the goal of moral life. Salvation consists in the unmaking of ourselves. While nirvāṇa is the highest goal, all forms of conduct which lead to it positively or bring about an undoing of rebirth are good, and their opposites bad. The ordinary standards of mundane values require modification.

138. Oldenberg, *Ancient India*, p. 94.

The ethics of Buddhism is based on its psychology.[139] All sound philosophy and true ethics require correct psychological analysis. The psychology of Buddhism is elaborated in the interests of ethics. The Buddhist discipline, the culture of the will, etc., require some theory of the way in which sensations are produced and attention developed. Buddhism analyses the moral personality of man and finds the principle of moral causation operating in its growth. Even the repudiation of the Ātman theory has an ethical motive. Will, according to Buddhism, is man's distinctive endowment by virtue of which he is an ethical being. The doctrine of karma or moral causation exhibits all existence as born of desire. With Kant, Buddha would say that the only thing in the world which possesses an absolute value is the good will, the will freely determined by the moral law. All human beings are capable of willing the good as good. Individuality ceases when, with the wearying of the will, action ceases. Action ceases when delight of the senses in objects ceases. This delight ceases by the recognition of the transiency of life. We must try to break up the composite self so as to prevent fresh formations. Escape from the chain of rebirth into the bliss of life eternal is the ideal of Buddhism, as of many other Indian and non-Indian systems. The Orphic Brotherhood yearned to be delivered from the grievous wheel of re-incarnations and Plato believed in a beatific condition where we can eternally contemplate the archetypes of truth, goodness and beauty.

Karma is an act both intellectual and volitional. It is doubly qualified, being a mental intention issuing in an effect. Psychologically every act has three sides: (1) the volitional preparation, (2) the act itself, and (3) what is called the 'back' of the act, the feeling of regret or remorse which follows the act. The first is the intention or the resolve. Though it is not the act itself, it is not meaningless. Again, every choice and every act possesses a real worth and value, transient in time but permanent in character. Some acts have their retribution immediately, some after a time, perhaps in the next existence. Acts are distinguished into two kinds: (1) those which are pure, free from āsravas, and (2) those which are impure or tainted by them. The pure ones, free from passion, desire and ignorance, do not entail any retribution, do not lead to but destroy fresh individual existence. They prepare the way for nirvāna. Meditation on the four noble

139. Martineau was wrong when he said that 'psychological ethics are altogether peculiar to Christendom.' (*Types of Ethical Theory*, vol. i, p. 14).

truths by which one tries to enter the paths of arhatship is a pure act, above good or evil consequence. All other acts are impure from this standpoint, and among the impure ones which have as their general feature accompaniment by some reward or retribution in this life or later, a distinction is made into good and bad acts. Different standards are adopted. Good acts are those which lead to the conquest of passions, desires, and illusions of the ego. Bad acts are those which lead to unpleasant retributions. Again, good acts are those done with the motive of happiness in the world hereafter (lokottara), bad acts are those done with the idea of gaining happiness here below. The former destroy desire and lead to a cancelling of the rewards of other acts. Their eventual fruit seems to be nirvāṇa or deliverance. Again, good acts are those which aim at the welfare of others, bad acts those which aim at self-advantage. These different criteria agree with one another. The acts which lead to a conquest of passion or a really good life hereafter are those which aim at the world welfare. They possess the three features of absence of lust (alobha), absence of hatred (adveṣa), and absence of delusion (amoha). The bad acts which aim at self-interest and happiness on earth and lead to the bondage of birth are born of a false vision (mithyādṛṣti), lust and hatred.[140] Moral evil is due to ignorance or mistaking the value and nature of things.

The system enunciated by Buddha is free from the extremes of self-indulgence and self-mortification. Buddha found after six years of ascetic life that the true way 'cannot be attained by one who has lost his strength.' 'There are two extremes which he who has gone forth ought not to follow–habitual devotion, on the one hand, to the passions, to the pleasure of sensual things; and habitual devotion, on the other hand, to self-mortification, which is painful, ignoble, unprofitable. There is a middle path discovered by the Tathāgata—a path which opens the eyes and bestows understanding, which leads to peace, to insight to the higher wisdom, to nirvāna. Verily it is the Aryan eightfold path. That is to say: right beliefs, right aspirations, right speech, right conduct, right mode of livelihood, right effort, right mindedness and right rapture.'[141] This eightfold path represents the morality of Buddhism.

Right belief has the first place. What we do reflects what we think. Wrong acts issue from wrong beliefs. Mostly we do not realise that the elements of self will go down to dust in death and so cling to individuality. To remove

140. See W.B.T., pp. 216–18.

141. First sermon on setting in motion the Wheel of the Law.

wrong views, right knowledge is necessary. In Buddhist psychology will and intelligence go together.

Right aspiration is a product of right vision. 'It is the longing for renunciation; the hope to live in love with all; the aspiration of true humanity.'[142] Giving up the idea of separateness, the aspirant works for the whole. The resolve must be a real one, according to the Mahāyāna, making the aspirant say: 'I must bear the burden of all creatures.'[143]

Aspirations must be turned to activities. They must find expression in right speech, right action, and right living. 'To abstain from falsehood, to abstain from back-biting, to abstain from harsh language, and to abstain from frivolous talk is called right speech.'

Right action is unselfish action. Buddha does not believe in ceremonialism, prayer and ritual, spell and sacrifice. 'Better homage to a man grounded in the dharma than to Agni for a hundred years.' When once a Brāhmin put it to him that bathing in the Bahuka river washes a sinner of his sin, Buddha retorted: 'The Bahuka, the Adhika cannot purify the fool of his sin, bathe he himself ever so often ... No river can cleanse the doer of evil, the man of malice, the perpetrator of crime. To the pure it is ever the holy month of Phaggu. To the pure it is always a perpetual fast. To the man of good deeds it is a vow everlasting. Have thy bath here, even here, O Brāhmin, be kind to all beings. If thou speakest not false, if thou killest not life, if thou takest not what is given thee, secure in self-denial—what wouldst thou gain by going to Gaya? Any water is Gaya to thee.'[144] 'Not superstitious rites,' says Aśoka, 'but kindness to servants and underlings, respect to those deserving of respect, self-control coupled with kindness in dealing with living creatures, these and virtuous deeds of like nature are verily the rites that are everywhere to be performed.' 'Pious regulations are of small account, whereas meditation is excellent.'[145] Buddha did not declare open war against the ceremonialism of the times, but tried to infuse moral significance into its forms and thus undermine it. 'Anger, drunkenness, deception, envy, these constitute uncleanliness; not the eating of flesh.'[146] Again, 'neither abstinence; nor going naked, nor shaving the head, nor a rough garment, neither offerings to priests, nor sacrifices to the gods will

142. Suttavibhaṅga.

143. Vajradvaja Sutta.

144. Laksmīnarsu, *Essence of Buddhism*, p. 230.

145. Aśoka Pillar Edict, vii.

146. Cf. 'It is not that which entereth into a man that defileth him, but that which cometh out.'

cleanse a man who is not free from delusions.' Buddha was against the worship of the ugly and the repulsive embodied in certain morbid types of asceticism. His sweet reasonableness comes in his condemnation of unnatural forms of asceticism.

Buddhism insists on purity of motive and humility in life. Of the pāramitās, or perfections which help us to attain nirvāṇa, śīla has an important place. The distinction between śīla, or morality, and dāna, or charity, is one between passive and active virtue, nivṛtti and pravṛtti. Śīla is the observance of rules like that of non-violence, dāna implies active self-sacrifice and helping those in need of help. It is living for the good and benefit of all beings. The ideal disposition of charity is brought out in the story of Yuan Chwang, who, when he was about to be sacrificed for the goddess Durgā by pirates, thought: 'Let me return and be born here below that I may instruct and convert these men, and cause them to practise themselves in doing good and giving up their evil deeds, and thus by diffusing far and wide the benefits of the dharma to give rest to all the world.'

Right action leads to right living, free from lying and deceit, fraud and chicanery. Thus far the stress has been on conduct, but inner purification is also attended to. The aim of all endeavour is to remove the causes of sorrow. Subjective purification is needed for it. The last three of right effort, right thought and right tranquillity refer to it.

Right effort consists in practising control of passions so as to prevent the rise of bad qualities. An inhibition of the bad and a reinforcement of the good by mental avoidance and concentration is what this means. If we want to expel an undesirable idea which haunts our mind, Buddha recommends the following five methods: (1) Attend to some good idea. (2) Face the danger of the consequences of letting the bad idea develop into action. (3) Turn attention away from the bad idea. (4) Analyse its antecedents and so nullify the consequent impulse. (5) Coerce the mind with the aid of bodily tension. By aśubhabhāvanā, or reflection on the evil, we acquire a disgust for all that is corrupt. 'Reverend Sir, have you seen a woman pass this way?' and the elder said, 'I cannot say whether it is a woman or a man that passed this way. This I know that a set of bones is travelling on this road.'[147] Without right effort there can be no enlightenment. Through it alone can we destroy anger, envy, pride and attachment to objects.

147. M. Poussin describes the force of true insight as distinct from intellectual knowledge in these words: 'Whosoever understands the truth of suffering, under

Right effort cannot be isolated from right thinking. To avoid mental unsteadiness, the mind that plays and roves[148] is to be controlled. Emotions are to Buddhism as to stoicism, 'failures, disturbances of moral health, and if indulged become chronic diseases of the soul.' They destory all healhty endeavour. Even spiritual pride endangers moral progress. 'Whosoever is pure and knows that he is pure and finds pleasure in knowing that he is pure becomes impure and dies with an impure thought. Whosoever is impure and knows that he is impure and makes effort to become pure dies of a pure thought.' 'On the mind depends dharma, on the practice of dharma depends enlightenment.[149]

While the five skandhas are said to constitute an exhaustive account of the nature of the human being, so long as he is looked upon as a unit of the empirical world, we get a slight modification of this view when we turn to the Buddhist emphasis on intuitive knowledge, called prajñā. The theory of knowledge based on the skandhas is sensationalism. The concept of prajñā compels a change in it. Prajñā stands for the highest activity of the human mind, and has supreme value from the religious point of view. Attempts are no doubt made in the Pāli canon and Visuddhimagga to bring prajñā under one of the skandhas. In the Sutta piṭaka it is allied to vijñāna. In the Abhidharma it is brought under the saṁskāras. The Kathāvatthu refers to and refutes a heretical view which would class one form of prajñā, divyacakṣu, or the heavenly eye, under the rūpaskandha. In Buddhaghoṣa's day saṁjñā, vijñāna and prajñā represented simple and complex modes of human insight. It is the most reasonable interpretation. The skandhas represent the empirical point of view and lay stress on the knowledge the individual has when he regards himself as a separate entity. When the individual nature is transformed into unity with the whole, prajñā displaces the empirical knowledge. The

its fourfold aspect, will acknowledge the falsehood of vulagar notions, and will see pleasure and existence as transitory and painful, but he will not destroy his innate desire of pleasure, his thirst after existence. What is to be gained is a profound and efficacious feeling of the miseries of life, of the impurity of the body, of universal nothingness, to such a degree that the ascetic should see a woman as she really is, as a skeleton furnished with nerves and flesh, as an illusion made up of carnal desire. Mind will thus be freed from love, hatred and from every passion.' (*Transactions of the Third International Congress of Religions*, vol. ii, p. 41).

148. Tatratatrābhinandinī.

149. Cittādhīno dharmo dharmādhīno bodhiḥ.

unregenerate cultivate vijñāna, while the regenerate develop prajñā. There is a steady growth from sense-cognition to true insight. The two are not independent, but the latter is an expansion of the earlier. Prajñā terminates in bodhi or enlightenment.

Mental culture is not so much a suppression of the senses as a cultivation of them to see the truth. In the Indriyabhāvanā Sutta Buddha asks a pupil of Pārāśarya how his master teaches the culture of sense. The answer is given that the senses are trained to the extent when they fail to fulfil their functions. The eye sees no object and the ear hears no sound. Buddha rejoins that this would mean that the blind and the deaf have their senses best cultivated. A true sense-culture means a training of the senses so as to discriminate all forms of sense-consciousness and estimate their real worth. Spiritual insight is an expansion and development of intellectual vijñāna and sense-perception. Buddha seems to admit the reality of an absolute which we intuit in the state of prajñā. 'Serene, pure, radiant lookest thou, Sāriputta, whence comest thou?' 'I have been alone, Ānanda, in rapture of thought ... till I rose above perception of the world without into an infinite sphere of cognition, and this again melted into nothing.... Insight came, and I discerned with the celestial vision the way of the world, the tendencies of men, and their coming to be, past, present and yet to come. And all this arose in me and passed without one thought of ego-making or of mine-making.' On this insight into a transcendent reality only a philosophy like that of the Upaniṣads can be built. Buddha shrank from it, for systematic philosophy had to wait for a later day. He gives us only a series of standpoints and shrewd psychological observations.

While the previous stage refers to prajñā or insight, we have next dhyāna, or meditation, with its result of tranquillity or samādhi. Dhyāna is highest contemplation, and takes the place of prayer in Buddhism. This aspect of early Buddhism is developed in the Hīnayāna school. Dhyāna has four stages: the first, of gladness and joy arising from a life of solitude accompanied by insight, reflection, contemplation and inquiry, and freed from all sensuality; the second, of elation, and internal calm and a deep peace of mind, without any conscious reflection; the third, of the total absence of all passions and prejudices, where ātmamoha, or lust of self, is completely stilled; and the fourth, of self-possession, and complete tranquillity, without care and joy, for all that gives joy or care is put aside.[150]

150. Childers states the idea thus: 'The priest concentrates his mind upon a single thought. Gradually his soul becomes filled with a supernatural ecstasy and serenity,

Dhyāna is the steady endeavour to bring the mind into harmony with all that is. It is a deliberate effort to eliminate egotism and be lost in the truth. A part of the daily life of the members of the Buddhist saṅgha consists in the practice of contemplations. The modes of training the heart and the mind are borrowed from the prevailing beliefs. We are asked to cherish the moods of loving-kindness (maitrī), compassion (karuṇā), cheerfulness (muditā), and impartiality (upekṣā). These are the four sublime moods or Brahma vihāras. They are the systematic attempts to make the sentiments of love, sympathy, etc., extend over ever-widening groups till the whole world of humanity, nay, of sentient beings is included. The forty subjects of meditation and the four ecstatic moods tend to diminish passion and lead us from the dominion of the senses. A life of meditation of the highest restores us to the real truth. We cannot help asking what is the object on which dhyāna or spiritual contemplation is to be exercised.

There is no reference to grace in Buddhism. It is only a question of self-development. Man can develop by effort and training a strength and a virtue that can render him independent of all things. None can prevail against him if he conquers himself. 'Not even a god can change into defeat the victory of a man who has vanquished himself.'[151] because Buddha demands love of humanity and discipline of mind indepednent of a religious sanction, there are people who exclaim that Gautama Buddha was the positivist August Comte born 2,000 years too soon!

Both the Buddhist dhyāna and the yoga doctrine emphasise the physical and hygienic conditions necessary for mental training. Control of the body is a preparation for enlightenment. Tapas is replaced by psychological exercises leading to spiritual insight. Exercises of spiritual abstraction whereby the individual withdraws his powers from the external world and realises the stillness of the ego are common to all yogic theories. In the four states of dhyāna we have a progressive and methodical abstraction from the plurality of the phenomenal world. Dhyāna is not a desultory

---

while his mind still reasons upon and investigates the subject chosen for contemplation; this is the first jhāna. Still fixing his thought upon the same subject, he then frees his mind from reasoning and investigation, while ecstasy and serenity remain, and this is the second jhāna. Next, his thoughts still fixed as before, he divests himself of ecstasy and attains the third jhāna, which is a state of tranquil serenity. Lastly, he passes to the fourth jhāna, in which the mind, exalted and purified, is indifferent to all emotions alike of pleasure and of pain.' (*Dictionary*, p. 169.)

151. Dhammapada, 105.

reverie, but a set exercise to heighten the powers of mind by closing the avenues of sense. M. Poussin says: 'The mind once concentrated and strengthened by exercise with the clay disk, or any other exercise of the same kind, is successively to abandon its contents and its categories. The ecstatic starts from a state of contemplation, coupled with reasoning and reflection; he abandons desire, sin, distractions, discursiveness, joy, hedonic feeling; he goes beyond any notion of matter, of contact, of difference; through meditation on void space, knowledge without object, contemplation of nothingness, he passes into the stage where there is neither consciousness nor unconsciousness, and finally he realises the actual disappearance of feeling and notion. It is a lull in the psychological life which coincides with perfect hypnosis.'[152] We cannot say with any definiteness or certainty whether greater freedom of mind and clarity of imagination can be obtained by a shutting out of sense impressions or a hypnotic exhaustion of the outer senses. Modern science in this department is still in its infancy. Buddhism along with the rest of Indian thought believed it to be so, and the belief persists even today. It is generally accepted in India that when mental states are checked and sense impressions suspended, the empirical self is reduced to the lowest point and the universal self shines forth. The ideals of yogic practice are different in different metaphysical systems. In the Upaniṣads it is union with or realisation of Brahman. In Patañjali's Yoga it is insight into truth. In Buddhism it is attainment of the Bodhisattva condition or realisation of the emptiness of the wrold.

Buddha did not consider every trance to be necessarily good. It must aim at the right end, namely, the eradication of desire. Buddha realised that there were those who took to yogic exercises to acquire supernatural powers. Buddha refined the practice by telling them that even such powers could be acquired only through the practice of righteousness and wisdom.[153] Buddha forbade his disciples to work miracles for display. Acquisition of supernatural powers does not confer any spiritual advantage. The yogic beliefs of Buddhism are to be seen clearly in the Lamaism of Tibet.

The eightfold path is sometimes divided into four stages, where each is marked by the breaking of the fetters, which are ten in number, which bind man to earth. The first of these fetters is the delusion of a personal self

152. *The Way to Nirvāṇa*, p. 164.
153. See Ākhankheya Sutta, S.B.E., vol. xi.

(satkāyadṛṣṭi), the mother of all egoism. The realisation that there is no permanent self, that what is, is only an aggregation of skandhas, may tempt us into the path of self-indulgence and scepticism. This has to be guarded against. The second obstacle is called scepticism (vicikitsā). It is a cloak for idleness or vice. We must also give up the belief in the efficacy of the purificatory rites and ceremonies. Rituals do not help us to free ourselves from lust, hatred and ignorance. He who is released from the delusion of the ego, from doubt of Buddha and his doctrines, and from belief in ceremonial rites, is said to have entered the first stage in the noble path. He is called the Śrotāpanna, or he who has got into the stream. About this state Dhammapada says: 'Better than sovereignty over the earth, better than going to heaven, better than lordship over all worlds, is the reward of the first step in holiness.'[154] The two next obstacles to be overcome are sensuality (kāma) and malevolence (pratigha). When these are conquered he attains the second stage of the noble path. He is Sakṛdāgāmin, or he who will once be re-born in the world of men. The deficiencies are minimised though not abolished. Those who have reduced the cardinal errors of lust, resentment and glamour return to the world once before they attain final release. When these two impediments are completely destroyed he becomes Anāgāmin. Though he is not free from all error, there is no more chance of falling backward. The impediments yet to be overcome are craving (rāga) for material and immaterial pleasures in this world or another, pride (māna), self-righteousness (auddhatya), and ignorance of the true nature of things. When these fetters are burst he reaches the goal, becomes an arhat[155] (literally worthy), and attains the blessedness of nirvāṇa. The causes of his suffering are exhausted and the impurities are washed away. He is no more subject to rebirth. The arhat condition is a state of blissful sanctification. Nirvāṇa is the goal of Buddhism, and arhatship terminates in it. Upādhiśeṣanirvāṇa is the arhatvaphala, or the fruition of sanctification. The arhat is still a man. It is when he dies that the ceases to exist. Then is the oil in the lamp of life spilt and the seed of existence withered. He vanishes from creation and attains Parinirvāṇa, or the annihilation of the elements of being.[156]

154. Dhammapada 178.

155. Arhat is a common word used in pre-Buddhistic times for anyone who attains the ideal of his religion.

156. See *The Religious Systems of the World*, pp. 148, 149.

The Buddhist morality is more individual than social. In our lives we have to imitate the example of Buddha. Stress is not laid on convention and authority. When Buddha was asked by Ānanda about instructions touching the order, he answered: 'Be ye lamps unto yourselves; be ye a refuge to yourselves; betake yourselves to no external refuge; hold fast to the truth as a lamp; hold fast as a refuge to the truth; look not for refuge to any-one besides yourselves.'

Conduct is broadly distinguished into well-being and ill-being. The former springs out of unselfishness and results in acts of love and compassion, the latter is rooted in egoism and results in acts of malice, etc. Actions become good by the avoidance of the ten transgressions; the three bodily sins, of murder, theft and adultery; the four sins of speech, lying, slander, abuse, and idle talk; and the three sins of mind, covetousness, hatred and error. We have also other classifications of sinful conduct. Sensuality, desire for rebirth, ignorance, metaphysical speculation, are four kinds of sinful conduct. Sometimes the whole is summed up in simple formulas, apparently negative, but really positive, which say, kill no living thing, do not steal, do not commit adultery, do not speak untruths, do not drink intoxicating liquors. These rules emphasise the need for self-control in five different directions. Positively they mean control anger, the desire for material possessions, the lusts of the flesh, cowardice and malevolence (the chief cause of untruthfulness), and the craving for unwholesome excitement. The result of this self-control will be to bring happiness to himself and others and develop positive virtue. Control of anger leads to growth of gentleness, control of covetousness leads to the spread of charity, control of lust to purity in love. Sometimes the ideal virtues are stated to be ten in number. Charity, purity of conduct, patience, strenuousness, meditation, intelligence, employment of right means, resoluteness, strength and knowledge. Sometimes the ethical discipline of śikṣa is put down in the three rules of morality, culture and insight. In Milinda we find that good conduct, perseverance, mindfulness, meditation and wisdom constitute the virtuous life.[157] The codes of duties of the Upaniṣads and early Buddhism are not different in essentials.[158]

We may turn to the motive or inspiration of moral life. Avoidance of pain and quest of pleasure are the springs of all conduct. Nirvāṇa is the

157. ii. 1. 7–15.

158. Suicide is wrong, for putting an end to life is no cure for the illusion of the ego.

highest sukha or bliss. Modern hedonists contend that happiness is found in the increase of life in its length and breadth. The Buddhists claim that it lies in the dissolution of the conditions of selfishness and ignorance which lead to renewed existence. Eternal salvation is what Buddha sets before man at the end of the narrow path of knowledge, virtue and austerity, and not any small end of wealth, conquest or power. It is confusion of mind which leads the self to identity itself with small interests. This confusion is common in the world. 'I do not see any living being in the three worlds who does not prefer this own self to anything.'[159] Selfishness is caused by imperfect understanding and consequent confusion of the bounds of individuality.Unselfishenss is the result of the right perception of the truth. The true good is attainable only by a suppression of the subjectivity of self and the development of the universal consciousness. It is a sublimated selfishness that tells us that we should give up our selfish craving. Compassion for the suffering of others is the impelling motive of altruism. We are all comrades in suffering, subject to a common doom. All creatures in heaven and earth, even those lower than ourselves in the scale of being, are subject to the law of moral perfection. The whole existence, divine, human and animal, in all its spheres is linked together by the chain of moral causation. It is this community of nature which underlies the system of Buddha, though it is not explicitly recognised anywhere. The raw material of human nature is not completely egoistic. Unselfish conduct is not unnatural. We need not think that egoistic action is the only intelligible action. To say that each individual is outside of the other is a half truth. There is also a vital and organic union of all beings. The development of this uniting consciousness or the attainment of fullness of knowledge, peace and joy is nirvāṇa. Freedom is the expansion into the universal consciousness, the widening out of our feeling and sympathy for all that is. 'The disciple lets his mind pervade one quarter of the world with thoughts of love, and so the second ... and thus the whole wide world....'[160] While, strictly speaking, Buddhist morality has no supernatural sanction, still for the ordinary man the hope of heaven to be reached after death is kept quite intact.

The conditions of virtue are independent of outer things. It makes little difference what you are, prince or peasant, for all are imperfect. A true

159. Saṁyutta, i.
160. Mahāsudassana Suttanta.

and honest life alone counts. Buddhism insists not so much on the performance of duty as on the transformation of the whole being. Those arrayed like Solomon in all his glory, magnificent in physique and proud in intellect, are not the really great. Without humility, charity and love, life is death at the core.

The charge of intellectualism is repeated against the ethics of Buddhism. Knowledge is no doubt emphasised, for ignorance is said to be the root cause of sorrow and suffering. It is the possession of truth that brings about a reform in mind. Selfish desire cannot arise in a mind enlightened by true wisdom. So the liberated soul is called Buddha, the knower.[161] Virtue is knowledge of the good. Yet Buddha recognises that this knowledge cannot dissolve the body built of karma, though it prevents the building of fresh karma. We have also to realise that by knowledge Buddha did not mean mere intellectual learning. It is not acquaintance with theological dogmas or esoteric mysteries, but knowledge of which morality is the necessary condition. It is a life of truth which we can acquire only by clearing the soul of the darkening influence of passion and impulse. Knowledge is not something to be packed away in some corner of our brain, but what enters into our being, colours our emotion, haunts our soul, and is as close to us as life itself. It is the over-mastering power which through the intellect moulds the whole personality, trains the emotions and disciplines the will. That doctrinal belief is not what is meant by knowledge is brought out in Tevijja Sutta.[162] To the question, What shall I do to be saved? Buddha gives the answer in the spirit of the Upaniṣads. Salvation consists in the overcoming of selfishness, theoretically the illusion of the ego, and practically the craving of self. The acquisition of truth, Buddha again and again repeats, depends on these conditions: (1) Śraddhā, or faith;[163] (2) Darśana, or sight. Mere faith will not do. Truths acquired at second-hand on the

161. 'Here Brāhmanical speculation anticipates Buddhism in diction as well as in thought ... when he who has come to know the Ātman is mentioned in the Śatapathabrāhmaṇa as "delivered," the word then used for knowing is that word (pratibuddha), which also signifies awaking, the word which the Buddhists are accustomed to use when they describe how Buddha has in a solemn hour under the aśvattha tree gained the knowledge of the delivering truth or is awake to the delivering truth; the same word from which also the name "Buddha," that is, the "knowing," the "awake," is derived.' (Oldenberg, *Buddha*, p. 52.)

162. iii. 1. 2.

163. Majjhima, i. 71.

authority of other people remain external to our minds, and do not become part of our lives. 'Now, O monks, are you going to say we respect the master and, out of respect for him, we believe this and that? You must not say so. Is not what you will say to be true, that exactly which you have by yourselves seen, known and apprehended?'[164] (3) Bhāvanā, or cultivation. It is meditation or pondering over truth unceasingly till we practically become one with it and live it. The higher life cannot be entered upon by the undisciplined, and yet the crown of human life is the direct perception of the truth which makes all false notions impossible. Aristotle closes his ethics with contemplation as the ultimate good, after giving us a long survey of relative goods. Buddha looks upon prajñā as the highest possession, but takes care to add that prajñā without love and benevolence is impossible, and even if possible, quite barren. Mystic contemplation without practical goodness is not perfection.[165]

Another complaint made against Buddhist ethics is that it is ascetic. If asceticism means suppression of desire, then Buddhist ethics is ascetic. Desire builds the house of existence. It is its nature to flee endlessly and restlessly from all that it has. It knows no peace. In a lower form it is unregenerate impulse, craving, or taṇhā, while the rationalised taṇhā is desire. The extinction of taṇhā is possible only by the extirpation of desire. This can be achieved by strenuous volition, or chanda. Buddha does not advocate mere passivity. For the wrong desires cannot be suppressed by quiescence, but only by a strong will and purpose.

Buddha insists not on an abolition of will or a turning away from the world, but on a hot contest with desire, an active wrestling with evil. 'If the critic would dwell more on the positive tendencies in Buddhist ethics, he might discern under the outward calm of mien of the Buddhist sage, in literature and art, a passion of emotion and will not paralysed or expurgated, but rendered subservient to and diffused around deep faith and high hope. For there is no doctrine, not even excepting Platonism, that sees in life, in the life that now is, greater possibilities of perfection. Nor is there any system, not excepting that of the Christian, which sees in the evolution of human love a more exalted transcendence of the lower forms of that emotion.'[166] Buddha does not want a suppression of emotion

164. Majjhima, i.
165. Dhammapada, 183.
166. Mrs Rhys Davids, J.R.A.S., 1898, p. 55.

and desire, but asks for the cultivation of true love for all creation. This glowing emotion must fill the whole universe and result in an outflow of abounding goodwill. 'Our mind shall not waver, no vile speech will we utter; we will abide tender and compassionate, loving in heart, void of secret malice; and we will be ever suffusing such a one with the rays of our loving thought, and from him forthgoing we will be ever suffusing the whole world with thought of love far-reaching, grown great and beyond measure, void of ill-will and bitterness.'[167] The legendary stories contained in the Jātakas illustrate the deep love and compassion exhibited by Buddha in his previous lives.[168] Buddha's doctrine is the middle way between luxury and asceticism, and so he shrank from all excess and avoided extremes. He does not ask us to suppress desire but only divert it. The same conclusion may be reinforced by the Buddhist analysis of feeling. A state of consciousness is never good in itself, but good or bad by its effects. If the effect is well-being, we have sukha (pleasure); if ill-being, we have duḥkha (pain); if neither, we have a neutrally toned feeling. All creatures aim at well-being; only they are mostly satisfied with relative well-being. A few there are who aspire after absolute well-being or happiness. Buddha asks us to suppress the will to live on the lower plane and cultivate the will to live well and gain the ultimate peace. If quietude and calm are admired, it is because they are aids to concentration. Will is to be controlled and not repressed. Without a disciplined exercise of the will nothing great can be accomplished. When a young prince asks him how long it would take to graduate in his doctrine, Buddha points out that, as in the art of riding, even there everything depends on whether the pupil brings the five conditions of confidence, health, merit, energy and intelligence.[169]

We are asked to put down not all desires, but only the wrong desires by a strenuous effort of will.[170] 'I preach asceticism in as much as I preach

167. Majjhima Nikāya, 21.

168. In Tāranātha's *History of Indian Buddhism* we have the story of the monk Āryasaṅgha, who saw a certain dog snapping and barking at people, with the lower part of its body eaten and gnawed by worms. Moved by compassion, Āryasaṁgha thought within himself, 'If I do not rid this dog of these worms, the poor creature will die; if, however, I take the worms from off her and throw them away, the worms will die.' Wherefore he resolved to cut some flesh from his own body upon which to put the worms, and did so!

169. Majjhima, 65.

170. Mahāparinibbāna Sutta, vii.

the burning away of all conditions of the heart that are evil. One who so does is the true ascetic.' Besides, the ascetic discipline of Buddha has in view the mind's inward landscape, and not the body's outer fortunes. As a matter of fact, Buddha allows the care of the body, though not attachment to it. 'Have you ever at any time been hit in battle by an arrow?' 'Yes, I have.' 'And was the wound anointed with ointment, smeared with oil and bandaged with a strip of fine cloth?' 'Yes, it was.' 'Did you love your wound?' 'No.' 'In exactly the same way the ascetics do not love their bodies; but without being attached to them, they take their bodies in order to advance in the religious life.'[171]

Buddha allowed decent dress, regular food, shelter and medical treatment, even to the Bhikṣus. He knew that bodily torture was injurious to strength of mind, so necessary for the understanding of philosophical truths. Buddha refined asceticism and discriminated between the true and the false. He condemned the morbid exaggerations of certain ugly types of asceticism. A knife if it be caught by the blade cuts the hand. False asceticism leads to the downward path. To him asceticism does not mean severing the ties of life, but the rooting out of egoism. The ascetic is not he who punishes the body, but he who purifies the soul. Asceticism is only detachment from the things that distract our desires, 'the cares of the world and the deceitfulness of riches and the lusts of outer things.' In the Upaniṣads we find that Naciketas dismisses with supreme contempt the transient pleasures of the world in his eagerness to know the Brahman who lives beyond death, dwelling in the depths. Insistence on renunciation is necessary for all healthy life. When the nun Gautamī asked Buddha to teach her the quintessence of the dharma, he said: 'Of whatsoever teaching thou art sure that it leads to passion, and not to peace; to pride, and not to humility; to the desiring of much, and not the desiring of little; to the love of society, and not to the love of solitude; to idleness, and not to earnest striving; to a mind hard to pacify, and not a mind easy to pacify—that, O Gautamī, that is not dharma.'[172] Meditation in solitude was advised as means for cultivating spiritual calm and detachment.

It is not possible for Buddhism to discard its past. From the early Vedic times there had been in India ascetic tempers who had cut themselves adrift from the responsibilities of life and wandered free. We have seen in

171. Milinda, p. 73.
172. Dahlke, *Buddhist Essays*, p. 215.

the Upaniṣads how, in their love for the supreme, some 'relinquish the desire for children, the struggle for wealth, the pursuit of worldly weal, and go forth as mendicants.' The Brāhmanical codes recognised the right of these to sever themselves from the duties of life and the observance of rites. The ideal man of India before whom the prince and the peasant bow is the ascetic who walks about alms-bowl in hand, through streets and alleys, from house to house, without uttering a word or making a request. Of the mendicants, Jacobi says: 'There can be no doubt from the laws laid down respecting them that they had a recognised position about the eighth century BC.' The Buddhist Bhikṣus are the mendicants living on alms, taking the vow of poverty, and devoting themselves to the spreading of the gospel of Buddha. Of course, Buddha did not expect all men to become ascetics. He divides men into two classes, those who are still attached to the world and its life, upāsakas, or laymen, and those who by self-mortification are delivered from it, śramaṇas, or ascetics.[173] Despite his great respect for worldly virtues, Buddha believed that the fulfilment of worldly duties is not directly helpful to salvation. 'Full of hindrances is household life, a path defiled by passion; free as the air is the life of him who has renounced all worldly things. How difficult is it for the man who dwells at home to live the higher life in all its fullness, in all its purity, in all its bright perfection! Let me then cut off my hair and beard, let me clothe myself in the orange-coloured robes, and let me go forth from a household life into the homeless state.'[174] There is no consistency, however, on this point, for according to Majjhima Nikāya a man may attain nirvāṇa without being a monk. Though Buddha condemned morbid ascetic practices, it is a surprise to find that the discipline demanded of the Buddhist brethren is more severe in some points than any referred to in the Brāhmanical texts. Though theoretically Buddha admits the possibility of gaining salvation without austere asceticism, still in practice it seems to be necessary for almost all according to him.

Saṅgha is the Buddhistic brotherhood, which the disciples join in order to realise the perfect life. It is a religious order to which members are admitted on the performance of certain vows and the profession of faith. It is open to all without exception. In the beginning Buddha took an unfavourable view of women. When Ānanda asked him how a man should

173. Cf. the different orders of St Francis.
174. Tevijja Sutta, i. 47.

act in the presence of a woman, Buddha answered: 'Avoid looking at her ... if it is necessary to look, do not speak to her; if it be necessary to speak, then keep wide awake.'[175] When the widowed queen of Suddhodana decided to adopt the life of the hermitage and came to Buddha for conversion, accompanied by the wives of 500 princes, Buddha refused three times, since their admission would perplex the minds of many who had entered the order. When again they came with bleeding feet and dusty dress, Ānanda asked: 'Are Buddhas born into the world only for the benefit of men? Assuredly it is for the benefit of women also.' Thereafter they were admitted. Since earthly suffering affected all, the way out of it must be open to all who choose to accept it. Only those afflicted with sickness and disease and confirmed criminals, also those whose admission would interfere with existing rights, such as soldiers, debtors and slaves, sons whose parents do not consent, and children were kept out. The Saṅgha is an organised brotherhood formed of monks and mendicants. The ascetics of the Brāhmanical religion did not possess any such organised corporation. The spirit of proselytism consciously attempted by the Buddhists is responsible for this organised action. The Buddhist monk has no power to save or condemn. He is not a worker of miracles or a mediator between God and man, but only a leader. The Saṅgha contains both lay members and monks. While the lay member assents to the doctrine, the monk is the missionary. The rules of the Buddhist Saṅgha were borrowed from the Brāhmanical codes, though they were adapted to missionary purposes. The relation between Buddha and his disciple or between the monks and the followers is one of teacher and pupil.

There is a good deal of misconception about Buddha's attitude to caste. He does not oppose the institution, but adopts the Upaniṣad standpoint. The Brāhmin or the leader of society is not so much a Brāhmin by birth as by character. In the time of Buddha the caste system was in a confused condition, where the distinctions were based on birth rather than on qualities. 'The Brāhmin who has removed all sinfulness, who is free from haughtiness, from impurity, self-restrained, an accomplished master of knowledge, who has fulfilled the duties of holiness, such a Brāhmin justly calls himself a Brāhmin. He that gives way to anger and feels hatred, a wicked man, a hypocrite, he that embraces wrong views and is deceitful, such a one is an outcast, and he that has no compassion for living things.'

175. Mahāparinibbāna Sutta, v. 23.

'Not by birth is one a Brāhmin, not by birth is one an outcast; by deeds is one a Brāhmin, by deeds is one an outcast.'[176] All men had the power to become perfect. Buddha himself is an exmaple of that perfection of knowledge to which any man might attain by meditation and self-control. It is idle to think that certain men were doomed to helotry and infamy and others to virtue and wisdom. So members of all castes were admitted into the monastic order. Anybody could embrace Buddhism and attain to the highest rank by becoming a member of the Saṅgha. In this way Buddha undermined the spirit of caste, which later developed inhuman practices. But this is not foreign to the Brāhmanical theory, which also looked upon the highest status of the Sannyāsin as above caste. We cannot say that Buddha abolished caste, for the religion of Buddha is an aristocratic one. It is full of subtleties that only the learned could understand, and Buddha has always in view the Samaṇas and the Brāhmaṇas. His first converts were the Brāhmin priests and the rich youth of Benares. We cannot say that Buddha effected any social revolution. Even birth in a Brāhmin family Buddha allows to be a reward for merit.[177] He was a spiritual reformer in that he won for the poor and the lowly a place in the kingdom of God. 'The still very prevalent notion that Buddhism and Jainism were reformatory movements, and that more especially they represented the revolt against the tyranny of caste, is quite erroneous. They were only a protest against the caste exclusiveness of the Brāhmanical ascetics; but caste as such, and as existing outside their doors, was fully acknowledged by them. Even inside their orders admission, though professedly open to all, was at first practically limited to the higher castes. It is also significant for the attitude of these orders to the Brāhmanic institutions of the country that, though in spiritual matters their so-called lay adherents were bound to their guidance, yet with regard to ceremonies such as those of birth, marriage and death, they had to look for service to the old Brāhmanic priests.[178] Buddha was not a social reformer. He felt most intensely that suffering was bound up with selfishness, and he preached a moral and mental discipline designed to root out the conceit of self. Buddha's whole spirit was other-worldly, and he had not the burning enthusiasm for the earthly kingdom so necessary for a social reformer or a national leader. 'Buddha's

176. See Vasala Sutta, Vāsettha Sutta, and Dhammapada, chap. xxvi.
177. See Hardy, *Manual of Buddhism*, p. 446.
178. Hoernle, *Calcutta Review*, 1898, p. 320.

spirit was a stranger to that enthusiasm, without which no one can pose as the champion of the oppressed against the oppressor. Let the state and society remain what they are; the religious man who as a monk has renounced the world has no part in its cares and occupations. Caste has no value for him, for everything earthly has ceased to affect this interest; but it never occurs to him to exercise his influence for its abolition or for the mitigation of the severity of its rules for those who have lagged behind in worldly surroundings.'[179] in the world of thought both Upaniṣads and Buddhism protested against the rigours of caste. Both allowed the highest spiritual dignity to the poor and the humble, but neither rooted out the Vedic institutions and practices, though on this point Buddhism is a little more successful than Brāhmanism. But the passion for social reform was practically unknown to even the best minds of those times. Democracy is a modern motive of social reform.

We have already said that Buddha did not interfere with the domestic ritual which continued to be performed according to the Vedic rules.[180] So far as the authority of the Veda on doctrinal matters is concerned, Buddha does not accept it. As a general rule he denounces all exoteric or secret doctrines: 'O disciples, there are three to whom secrecy belongs and not openness—to women ... to priestly wisdom ... to false doctrine.'[181] 'I have preached the truth without making any distinction between exoteric and esoteric doctrines, for in respect of the truths, Ānanda, the Tathāgata has no such thing as the closed fist of a teacher who keeps something back.'[182] Buddha himself was a reviler of the Vedas. He protested against that part of the Vedas which countenanced animal sacrifices. At any rate, such is the opinion of Jayadeva, the author of Gītagovinda, and Rāmacandra Bhāratī, the author of Bhaktiśataka, otherwise called Buddhaśataka.

XV

KARMA AND REBIRTH

The law of karma is not imposed from without, but is worked into our very nature. The formation of mental habits, the increasing proneness to

179. Oldenberg, *Buddha*, pp. 153–154.
180. See Bhandarkar, *A Peep into the Early History of India.*
181. Aṅguttara Nikāya.
182. Mahāparinibbāna Sutta.

evil, the hardening influcene of repetition which undermines the effective freedom of the self, whether we know it or not, are comprehended under the law of karma. We cannot escape from the effects of our acts. The past in a real sense produces the present and the future. The law of karma is the principle working out justice in human relations. 'It is through a difference in their karma that men are not all alike. But some are long lived, some short lived, some healthy, and some sickly, etc.'[183] Without this explanation men would feel themselves to be the victims of an immense injustice. It also helps to make the sufferer resigned, because he feels that through suffering he is wiping out an old debt. It makes the enjoyer courteous, for he must do good again to deserve it. When a persecuted disciple came to Buddha with broken head and streaming wounds, Buddha told him: 'Suffer it to be so, O Arhat ... you are now feeling results of your karma that might have cost you centuries of suffering in purgatory.' It insists on individual responsibility and the reality of a future life. It recognises that the retribution of sin depends on the status of the sinner. If a man weak in mind and morals does an evil deed, it may lead him to the inferno. If a good man does it he may escape with a small pain in this life. 'It is as if a man were to put a lump of salt into a small cup of water, the water would be made salt and undrinkable. But if the same lump of salt were put into the river Ganges, the water of the Ganges would not be perceptibly tainted.'[184]

The theory of karma is much older than Buddhism, though it gets a logical justification in the philosophy of becoming. Men are temporary links in a long chain of causes and effects where no link is independent of the rest. The history of an individual does not begin at his birth, but has been for ages in the making.

When karma becomes the supreme principle superior to gods and men, it is difficult to assign any place to the initiative and endeavour of man. If everything that happens is determined by it, it is hard to see why the individual should take thought of what he does. He cannot but act in harmony with the law. Salvation is another name for acquiescence in the course of things. Such a conception again and again crops up in the history of thought. The Greek held that there was an inexorable destiny higher than man or god which could not be altered by effort or prayer. The same dread fate appears in the faith of the Calvinists and the Kismet of the

183. Milinda. See Majjhima, iii. 203, and Buddhaghoṣa: Atthasālini, p. 88.
184. Aṅguttara Nikāya, i. 249.

Muslisms. Nobody can learn even from Buddha if he has not already been destined for it or done enough merit to deserve it. We admit that Buddha did not give a straight answer to the question of freedom, but put it aside as a problem of speculation. Yet his system allows the possibility of free action and ultimate conquest over the whole law of karma.[185] His insistence on energy and endeavour and struggle against hate and error is not consistent with a denial of freedom. His scheme has a place for repentance, or saṁvega. The following suggestions may enable us to reconcile the Buddhist emphasis on karma with freedom. The chief argument in support of determination even in modern thought is that from causation. Karma, according to Buddhism, is not a mechanical principle, but is organic in character. The self grows and expands. There is no self, but only an evolving consciousness which may be spread out in a series of states. Though the present is determined by the past, the future remains open and depends on the direction of our will. The determination of the present by the past is not, however, a merely mechanical one. The law of karma tells us that there is continuity between the past and the present, that the present accords with the past. This does not mean that the present is the only possible outcome of the past. 'O priests, if anyone says that a man must reap according to his deeds, in that case there is no religious life, nor is any opportunity offered for the entire extinction of misery. But if anyone says, O priests, that a reward a man reaps accords with his deeds, in that case, O priests, there is a religious life, and opportunity is afforded for the entire extinction of misery.'[186] A mechanical misinterpretation of the law of karma conflicts wih the claims of ethics and religion.

The whole difficulty of the problem is due to the psychological orientation of Buddha's outlook. The analysis of the self into a sum of qualities, tendencies and dispositions, is perfectly legitimate for psychological science with its restricted object. For psychology which traces the rise and growth of mental presentations and establishes causal connections among them determinism holds. But it can never adequately explain the constitution of the unitary self. If we do not emphasise the subjective factor, the principle for which alone mental facts are facts of mind, we misinterpret the nature of the self. When we isoalte it from its contents, it becomes a logical abstraction, which is not what determines our activities. Our whole

185. See Milinda, iv. 8. 39–41.
186. Aṅguttara Nikāya, iii. 99.

self at any moment is the subject of our activity, and it has in it the capacity to transcend its past. The self apart from the contents is characterless and barren; the contents alone without the self support perfect determinism, for the concrete self freedom is a fact. To say that nothing happens without a cause is not inconsistent with holding that the present state of the self may act as a cause. Buddhism only protests against the unscientific view of indeterminism which regards freewill as an incalculable force which somehow interferes with the orderly working of mind. There is more in the world than mechanical law, though there is a perfect natural history of the thoughts and desires of the individual. Karma asserts this orderliness of natural process as well as spiritual growth. It is not intended to remove responsibility or invalidate effort, for nothing great can be achieved without effort.

When we attain the highest condition, it is said that karma has no effect. All the past deeds with their results vanish for ever. The condition of freedom is beyond good and evil. It is often said that morality ceases to be of transcendental worth when moral acts are looked upon as an obstruction to final bliss, in so far as they inevitably bring about a reward and maintain the round of existence. We must get rid of both merit and demerit to escape from this life. All moral conduct is a preparation for the final state. When the ideal is realised the struggle ceases. There is no effect to be produced in any future existence. It is the Upaniṣad doctrine that whatever the individual who has attained liberation does, he does without attachment. It is not deeds in themselves that bring about results, but deeds springing from selfish desires. The highest condition is therefore above moral rules and the operation of the law of karma, yet morality has an organic bearing on the end.

The rotating wheel is the symbol of the series of lives determined by the principles of karma. The dissolution of the old is the formation of the new. Death is nothing but birth cradled in flames. Throughout life there are changes. Birth and death are vital changes to which we attach names. When the mass of actions meant to receive retribution here is exhausted, death occurs. The wheel of life presents us with fresh opportunities where, if we choose, we may improve our fate. In this wheel are not only men, but all living things constantly ascending and descending.

Buddha, following the Brāhmanical theory, presents hell for the wicked and rebirth for the imperfect. A heaven is also recognised. 'On the dissolution of the body after death, the well-doer is reborn in some happy state in heaven.'[187] Sometimes both heaven and hell are looked upon as temporary states before rebirth happens. Early Buddhism popularised the conception of rebirth by the tales of the Jātakas relating the previous births of Buddha and the many deeds of self-sacrifice by which he prepared himself for the final victory over evil in the great conflict under the Bo tree. It is said that we can see the infinite past of every life if we develop certain supernatural powers.

There is no such thing in Buddhism as the migration of the soul or the passage of an individual from life to life. When a man dies his physical organism, which is the basis of his psychical dissolves, and so the psychical life comes to an end. It is not the dead man who comes to rebirth but another. There is no soul to migrate. It is the character that continues.[188] Buddhism does not explain the mechanism by which the continuity of karma is maintained between two lives separated by the phenomenon of death. It simply assumes it. We are told that the successive lives are linked by a chain of natural causation. The resulting character builds up a new individuality which gravitates automatically to the state of life for which it is fitted. It is said that owing to the strength of karma the consciousness of the dying man begets or begins a series of states of consciousness coupled with a subtle organism, the last of which takes up its abode in some matrix.[189] The decisive element is generally looked upon as the last thought which becomes the essence of the moral and intellectual life of the dying man. It is the force which remains as a desire for new life when death occurs. There must not only be this karma or force resulting from actions, but also upādāna, or clinging to existence. Since life is a combination, if the separated elements do not come together, there would be no life. There must be a force at work which tends to recombine the scattered elements. Under the pressure of this force of attraction called upādāna, a new combination results. Karma could do nothing without it. Karma is an informing principle waiting for its material.

'For when in any existence one arrives at the gate of death, either in the natural course of things or through violence; and when by a concourse of intolerable, death-dealing pains, all the members, both great and small, are loosened and wrenched apart in every joint and ligament; and the body,

187. Mahāparinibbāna, i. 24.
188. See Abhidharmakośa, iii. 24.
189. See Poussin, *The Way to Nirvāṇa*, pp. 83–84.

like a green palm-leaf exposed to the sun dries up by degrees; and the eyesight and the other senses fail, and the power of feeling, and the power of thinking and vitality are making the last stand in the heart—then consciousness residing in that last refuge, the heart continues to exist by virtue of karma, otherwise called the predispositions. This karma, however, still retains something of what if depends on, and consists of such former deeds as were weighty, much practised, and are now close at hand; or else this karma creates a reflection of itself or of the new mode of life now being entered upon, and it is with this as its object that consciousness continues to exist.

'Now, while consciousness still subsists, inasmuch as desire and ignorance have not been abandoned and the evil of the object is hidden by that ignorance, desire inclines the consciousness to the object; and the karma that sprang up along with the consciousness impels it toward the object. This consciousness being in its series thus inclined toward the object by desire and impelled toward it by karma, like a man who swings himself over a ditch by means of a rope hanging from a tree on the higher bank, quits its first resting-place and continues to subsist in dependence on objects of sense and other things, and either does or does not light on another resting-place created by karma. Here the former consciousness, from its passing out of existence, is called passing away, and the latter, from its being reborn into a new existence, is called rebirth. But it is to be understood that this latter consciousness did not come to the present existence from the previous one, and also that it is only to causes contained in the old existence, namely, to karma or predisposition, to inclination ... that its present appearance is due.'[190]

A distinction is made between animals, ghosts and men on the one hand, gods and creatures in hell or demons on the other.[191] The latter are apparitional and their birth-consciousness can make for itself a new body out of unorganised matter. With animals, ghosts and men birth-consciousness presupposes physical circumstances, and if they are not realised at the moment of death, the dying consciousness cannot be continued at once

190. Buddhaghoṣa Visuddhimagga, chap. xvii; see W.B.T., pp. 238–239. For an example of an attempt made by mediaeval Buddhist psychology to account for rebirth or conception, or patisandhi, we may refer to the reader to Mr Aung's translation of Anuruddha's Abhidhammatthasaṅgaha, specially the Introductory essay.

191. See Aung and Rhys Davids, *Compendium of Philosophy*, pp. 137–139.

into the birth-consciousness of a new being. For such being an intermediary existence in a short-lived Gandharva form is allowed. This Gandharva, like a discarnate spirit, creates at the earliest opportunity with the help of conceptional elements the proper embryo.

The causal explanation of continuity accounts for rebirth also. The man who is reborn is the heir of the action of the dead man. Yet he is a new being. While there is no permanent identity there is at the same time no annihilation or cutting off. The new being is what its acts have made it. This theory of the survival of karma is suggested in the Upaniṣads, in the conversation between Ārtabhāga and Yājñavalkya in the Bṛhadāraṇyaka Upaniṣad.

While the main tendency of Buddhism is to make karma the surviving element, there are also indications that vijñāna is sometimes assigned that function. 'All that we are is the result of what we have thought.' Vijñāna is said to constitute in a real sense the substance of our soul.'[192] It only shows the close kinship between vijñāna and karma, thought and will. In the highest condition of nirvāṇa we are free from karma as well as vijñāṇa, and all sorrow ceases with the disruption of personality. Karma keeps going the life process, and when it is exhausted individual existence terminates.

XVI

NIRVĀṆA

'Now this is the noble truth as to the passing of pain. Verily it is the passing away so that no passion remains, the giving up, the getting rid of, the emancipation from, the harbouring no longer of this craving thirst.' Buddha did not face the question of the nature of nirvāṇa directly. He felt that his mission was not so much to unveil the secrets of blessedness as to win men to its realisation. To him the all-absorbing topic was the suffering of life. The word nirvāṇa literally means 'blowing out' or 'cooling'. Blowing out suggests extinction. Cooling suggests not complete annihilation, but only the dying out of hot passion. 'The mind released is like the extinction of a flame.'[193] These two implications of nirvāṇa are to be met with as the

192. It is interesting to know that even according to Hume personal identity arises solely from the 'smooth and uninterrupted progress of thought along a train of connected ideas.'

193. Dīgha Nikāya, ii. 15. See also Majjhima 72, where Buddha compares nirvāṇa to the expiring flame which has no more any hay or wood to burn.

negative and the positive sides of the one ultimate state of being which cannot be adequately described in terms of thought. At any rate, nirvāṇa, according to Buddhism, is not the blessed fellowship with God, for that is only a perpetuation of the desire for life. That Buddha means only the extinction of false desire and not all existence comes out from a large number of passages. Nirvāṇa is only the destruction of the fires of lust, hatred and ignorance. Only in this sense of nirvāṇa can we understand Buddha's attainment of bodhi at the age of thirty-five and his spending the remaining forty-five years of his life in active preaching and doing good. Sometimes a distinction is drawn between two kinds of nirvāṇa: (1) Upādhiśeṣa, where only the human passions are extinct, and (2) Anupādhiśeṣa, where all being is extinct. According to Childers, the former indicates the condition of a perfect saint where the five skandhas are still present, though the desire which attracts us to being is extinct. In the latter we have the cessation of all being consequent on the death of the saint. It seems to be a distinction between the free whose external life continues and those whose external life ceases. Whenever it is said that people attain nirvāṇa in this world, the Upādhiśeṣa nirvāṇa is meant. It is the arhatship which becomes parinirvāṇa when the arhat disappears from the world of the transitory. The distinction of Upādhiśeṣa and Anupādhiśeṣa thus corresponds to that between nirvāṇa and parinirvāṇa, dying out and complete dying out.[194] There is no strict usage on this question.[195] Even parinirvāṇa cannot mean absolute non-being. It only means absolute perfection of being. 'Final deliverance is declared by the sage Buddha to be nothing other than a flow of faultless states of consciousness.'[196] It is mental repose free from stress and conflict. The suppression of the evil tendencies is accompanied by a simultaneous spiritual progress. Nirvāṇa, which is the consummation of the spiritual struggle, is a positive blessedness. It is the goal of perfection and not the abyss of annihilation. Through the destruction of all that is individual in us, we enter into communion with the whole universe and become an integral part of the great purpose. Perfection is then the sense of oneness with all that is, has ever been and can ever be. The horizon of being is

Śvetāśvatara Upaniṣad (iv. 19) speaks of the Paramātman as the fire the fuel of which has been consumed. See also Nṛsiṁhottaratāpanīya Up. 2.

194. Milinda, ii. 2. 4.

195. See Oldenberg, *Excursus on Nirvāṇa*, iii.

196. S.S.S.S., ii. 4. 21.

extended to the limits of reality. It is a kind of existence devoid of egoity, a timeless existence, full of 'confidence, peace, calm, bliss, happiness, delicacy, purity, freshness.'[197] There are passages in Milinda which indicate that Buddha after parinirvāṇa ceased to exist. 'The Blessed One passed away by that kind of passing away in which no root remains for the formation of another individual. The Blessed One has come to an end and it cannot be pointed out of him that he is here or there. But in the body of his doctrine he can be pointed out.'[198] We cannot worship Buddha because he is no more, and so we worship his relics and doctrines.[199] Nāgasena lends colour to the conception of nirvāṇa as extinction, or cessation of all activities (cittavṛttinirodha), cessation of all becoming (bhavanirodha), yet we feel that to some early Buddhists nirvāṇa meant completeness of being, eternal beatitude exalted high above the joys and sorrows of the world. 'The Tathāgata, O Vaccha, when thus liberated from the category of materiality, is deep, immeasurable, difficult to fathom, like the great ocean.' The nun Khemā assures Pasenadi of Kosala that death releases the Tathāgata from the empiricial existence of the five skandhas. Sāriputta rebukes Yamaka for holding the heretical view that a monk in whom sin is ended would be cut off. Max Müller and Childers, after a systematic examination of all passages relating to nirvāṇa conclude that 'there is not one passage which would require that its meaning should be annihilation.' It is clear that it is the false individuality that disappears while the true being remains. Even as the rainbow is a mixture of fact and imagination, so is individuality a combination of being and non-being. The falling raindrops are the rūpa, the line of light is the nāma, and the product of their crossing is bhava, or the rainbow, which is an appearance, an illusion. But it has something real as its basis that is eternal. 'The world rests upon me only in so far as it, as the known, stands opposed to me, as the knower. Only the form can be known, not that upon which it is based. Wherefore the world can only be done away with through knowledge—i.e. only in so far as it is form. Only so far as it is form does it arise and pass away, is it a becoming, and becoming can have an ending. That, however, upon which form is based, the elementary—that is being; and never and nowhere can being pass into non-being; never and nowhere can what is eternal

197. Milinda, ii. 2. 9; iii. 4. 6; ii. 1. 6.

198. Milinda, iii. 5. 10. It suggests the thought embodied in George Eliot's *Choir Invisible*, or Maeterlinck's *Blue Bird*, the survival in the memory of posterity.

199. iv., 1; see also Samyutta, i.

come to an end.'[200] Nirvāṇa is an eternal condition of being, for it is not a saṁskāra, or what is made or put together, which is impermanent. It continues while its expressions change. This is what lies behind the skandhas, which are subject to birth and decay. The illusion of becoming is founded on the reality of nirvāṇa. Buddha does not attempt to define it, since it is the root principle of all, and so is indefinable. It is said that in nirvāṇa, which is compared to deep sleep, the soul loses its individuality and lapses into the objective whole. According to the view emphasised in later Mahāyāna works, what is the bhavāṅga, or the stream of being. The wind of ignorance blows over it and stirs its equal flow, causing vibrations in the ocean of existence. The sleeping soul is wakened and its calm unfettered course is arrested. It wakes up, thinks, builds an individuality and isolates itself from the stream of being. In deep sleep these barriers are broken. Nirvāṇa is getting back into the stream of being and resuming the uninterrupted flow. Even as no thought waves perturb the stream of being when a man sleeps, so also in nirvāṇa do we have peaceful rest. Nirvāṇa is neither annihilation nor existence as we conceive it, but is becoming one with the eternal reality, which Buddha does not explicitly admit. Only since it is beyond the horizon of human thought we are obliged to employ negative terms to describe it. It is a condition transcending subject-object relations. In it there is no trace of self-consciousness. It is a state of activity which is not subject to causality, for it is unconditioned freedom[201] It is a state real and enduring, though not existent in the world of time and space. The psalms of the elders and the nuns are full of eloquent descriptions of the deep joy and the immortal delight of nirvāṇa surpassing all description. The individual consciousness enters into a state where all relative existence is dissolved. It is the silent beyond. In one sense it is self-extinction, in another absolute freedom. It is the fading of the star in the brilliant rise of the sun or the melting of the white cloud in the summer air. To think that nirvāṇa is annihilation is according to Buddha 'a wicked heresy.'[202]

Though the nirvāṇic condition is represented as implying the highest kind of activity, still it is viewed predominantly in a negative way as passive. In an age when this world, full of life, bustle and excitement, gave no hope to men who were growing tired to existence, the perfect condition comes

200. Dahlke, *Buddhist Essays*, p. 258.
201. Cf. Śūnyatānimittapraṇihitam.
202. Saṁyutta, iii. 109.

to be represented as more restful than romantic, a state of peace and happiness, stillness and calm, rest and refreshment. The ceaseless flux of rebirth is felt with such power that nirvāṇa, or the condition in which the flux is said to be stayed, is hailed as a blessed release.

Buddha, with the Upaniṣad thinkers, refused to allow any speculations about the condition of men who attain nirvāṇa, since it is not an object of knowledge. Yet in the way of the Upaniṣads he gives descriptions of it both positive and negative. In the Tevijja Sutta he even allows it to be called union with Brahmā. Since such a description does not consist with the view which makes Buddha a negative thinker, denying any abiding principle in man and the world, Rhys Davids says: 'In holding out a hope of union with Brahmā as a result of the practice of universal love, the Buddha is most probably intended to mean a 'union with Brahmā' in the Buddhist sense, that is to say, a temporary companionship as a separate being with the Buddhist Brahmā, to be enjoyed by a new individual not consciously identical with its predecessor. It is just possible that the *argumentum ad hominem* should be extended to this part of the sutta, and that the statement in iii. I should be taken to mean: 'This (universal love) is the only way to that kind of union with your own Brahmā which you desire.' But such a yielding to heretical opinion at the close of his own exposition of the truth would scarcely be imputed to a Buddha.'[203] Rhys Davids forgets that it is no heresy according to Buddha. If we look upon nirvāṇa as a positive condition we must admit the reality of a permanent. Logic is a hard task-master. Buddha is obliged to admit a permanent principle. 'There is, O disciples, a something that is not born, not produced, not created, not compounded. Were there not, O disciples, this something not born ... there would be no possible exit for what is born.'[204] It is also clear that the reduction of self to a number of skandhas is not ultimate. If the self is merely an impermanent compound of body and mind, qualities and functions, then when it disappears there is nothing which is delivered. We destroy our desires, burn our karma and are lost for ever. Freedom becomes extinction. But nirvāṇa is timeless existence, and so Buddha must admit the reality of a timeless self. There is a being at the back of all life which is unconditioned, above all empirical categories, something which does not give rise to any effect and is not the effect of anything else. 'Of

203. Introduction to Tevijja Sutta, S.B.E., vol. xi., p. 161.
204. Udāna, viii. 3, and Itivuttaka, 43.

nirvāṇa we cannot say that it has arisen, or that it has not arisen, or that it can arise; that it is past or future or present.'[205] Nirvāṇa is the simultaneity which is the support of all succession. Concrete time loses itself in the eternal. The shifting nature of the world conceals the stable reality. Only such a view is necessary to complete Buddha's account of nirvāṇa. Buddha did not trouble himself about the definition of these transcendental concepts which he felt to be real, for they did not help life and progress. In accord with his teaching about Māluṇkyāputta's questions that he would discuss only those problems that have a bearing on progress in peace, holiness and enlightenment, and not others, he disallowed the question of the ultimate goal. A deliberate dismissal or an evasive answer to such a vital problem cannot suppress the tendency to raise it. It is an instinct of the human mind that engenders the problem. And when Buddha failed to give an orthodox solution, different schools derived different conclusions from his attitude. Some reduce nirvāṇa to śūnyatā, vacuity and nihility. Bishop Bigandet says: 'By an inexplicable and deplorable eccentricity, the system promises men as a reward for their moral efforts the bottomless gulf of annihilation.' According to Mrs Rhys Davids, 'the nirvāṇa of Buddhism is simply extinction.' Oldenberg inclines to a negative view.[206] Dahlke frequently suggests it. In one place he writes: 'Only in Buddhism does the conception freedom from pain remain purely a negative thing and not a positive in disguise–heavenly bliss.[207] According to these writers nirvāṇa is the night of nothingness, the darkness where all light is extinguished. Such a one-sided reading of Buddha's theory is not new. Buddha, after having declared that the condition of the liberated one is inconceivable, continues: 'Teaching this, explaining this, I am falsely, without reason, wrongly, not truthfully accused by some.... 'An unbeliever is the samaṇa Gotama, the real entity's destruction, annihilation, dying away is what he preaches.' What I am not, what is not my doctrine, that I am accused of.'[208] Strange to say, there are others who look upon the Buddhist nirvāṇa as so positively pleasurable that they charge Buddha with hedonism. Evidently, two different views were developed very early on the basis of Buddha's utterances. Buddha's real attitude is probably, that nirvāṇa is a state of perfection inconceivable by us, and if we are obliged to offer descriptions of it, it is

205. Milinda.
206. See *Buddha*, p. 273.
207. Buddhist *Essays*, p. 48.
208. Majjhima, 22.

best to bring out its inconceivability by negative descriptions, its richness of content by positive predicates, realising all the time that such descriptions are at best approximations only.

XVII

ATTITUDE TO GOD

In the prevailing religion of the period of Buddha, the dominant feature was the spirit of barter established between gods and men. While the Brahman of the Upaniṣads was high and noble, yet ever so many gods, the heavenly orbs as well as the material elements, plants as well as animals, mountains as well as rivers, were popularly accepted. The unbridled license of a wild imagination deified all possible objects of the world, and as if these were not enough, added to them monsters, shapes and symbols of fancy. The Upaniṣads, no doubt, shattered the authority of these gods in the world of thought, but did not disturb their sway in the world of practice. So men were not wanting who paraded the gods as the creators of the world and governors of the universe able to affect for good or ill the destiny of man. Buddha realised that the only way to remove the haunting fear of the gods, the threatened torments of the future and the corruption of the human spirit, inclined to buy the goodwill of the gods by flattery and praise, was to destroy the gods once and for all. The idea of a first cause does not help us in moral progress. It leads to inaction and irresponsibility. If God exists, He must be the sole cause of all that happens, good as well as evil, and man can have no freedom of his own. If He abhors wickedness and disowns the authorship of evil, then He is not a universal agent. We expect to be forgiven by God.[209] If the grace of God is all powerful, if it can make in an instant a saint of a criminal, we are tempted to be indifferent to the virtuous life and cultivation of character. Character building is so much labour lost. Heaven and hell merely happen to be the reward of virtue and vice. If evil-doing means hell, men feel that hell is a long way off, while simple pleasure is next door to us. Buddha had to oppose the prevailing view and declare that virtue and happiness, vice and suffering are organically related.[210] The uncertain nature of philosophical speculation which indulged in all sorts of fancies, and the practical conviction which made men throw the burden on gods rather than rely on their own efforts,

209. 'God will forgive me, for that is His business' (Heine).
210. See Aṅguttara Nikāya, 6. 1.

led Buddha to confine his teaching to this world. A strictly scientific attitude sees no god in the thunderbolt or angels in heaven. Religious illusion was dissolved by the natural interpretation of things. The hypothesis of a personal God seemed inconsistent with it. The law of karma requires us to reject all notions of favouritism, caprice and arbitrariness. The majesty of God and the prestige of Providence pale before this principle of karma. Not a hair can drop from the head, not a stone can fall to the ground without the decree of karma. A God who can neither adapt nor alter, neither produce nor modify, is no God at all. Moreover, it is not easy to reconcile the heart-rending facts of life with the belief in a loving God. The suffering of the world is intelligible only on the hypothesis of karma. It explains all about the world of living beings, inhabitants of hell, animals, ghosts, men and gods. There is nothing superior to karma. Though Buddha admits the existence of deities like Indra, Varuṇa, etc., for purposes of explanation they are unnecessary. Even they are involved in the round of births and cannot interfere with the solemn law of moral causation.[211] There is no divine author of our being. A man is born from his own deeds. Even what parents he has depends on his karma. 'My action is my possession ... my inheritance ... the matrix which bears me ... the race to which I belong.... My refuge.' The view of the orthodox that there is a supreme personal creator, Īśvara, and the view of the materialists (svabhavavāda) that the development of the world is due to the innate independent power of things, are both repudiated by the Buddhists. The diversity of the world comes from acts.[212] Actions bear a fruit of mastery. They create and organise the material things necessary to their reward. If a man is destined to be born a sun god, then not only is he born, but he gets an abode, a celestial palace, a moving chariot, etc., as the fruit of mastery.[213] Even so at the beginning of the cosmic period of the whole material universe is created by the mastering energy of the acts to be enjoyed by the future inhabitants. The receptacle of the world (bhājanaloka) is the fruit of the mastery of the acts of all living beings (sattvaloka).

The traditional arguments in support of the existence of God were disputed by the early Buddhists. The proof that as a watch implies a watchmaker, even so the world implies a God is offensive to them. We

211. See *Dialogues of Buddha*, i. pp. 280 ff, 302.
212. Karmajaṁ lokavaicitryam, Abhidharmakośa, iv. 1.
213. Adhipatiphala.

need not have a conscious cause. Even as the seed develops into the germ, and the germ into the branch, we can have production without a thinking cause or a ruling providence. Thoughts and things are the fruit of acts even in the same way as pleasant and unpleasant sensations are. Milinda compares the cycle of existence determined by karma to a wheel which recoils on itself or with the reciprocal generation of the hen from the egg, and the egg from the hen. Eye, ear, body and spirit come into contact with the world, occasioning sensation, desire, action, etc., and the fruit of these is again an eye, an ear, a body, a spirit that will make a new being. This is the everlasting law of righteousness. We cannot alter its course. Buddha, more a teacher than a saviour, helps us to see the truth. He does not imagine a world-maker far back in the ages, beginning the series of saṁsāra. The flow of the world has no other cause beside itself. To him the cosmological argument had no force. Enough if we know how things happen. We need not go behind the order of the world. Though an explanation by antecedent conditions is no final truth, still to man nothing more is open. A first cause which is itself unaccused seems to be self-contradictory. The necessity of conceiving every cause as effect which has its cause in a preceding one makes the conception of an uncaused cause absolutely unthinkable. Similarly, the teleological argument is untenable in view of the obvious imperfection of the world. The world seems to be an ingenious contrivance for inflicting suffering. Nothing could be more elaborate and masterly in its perfection than this scheme of pain. A perfect Creator cannot be the author of this imperfect world. Neither a benevolent God nor caprice, but a law which works with a fatal logic, is the truth of things. Buddha would agree with Spinoza in the view that the world is neither good nor bad, neither heartless nor irrational, neither perfect nor beautiful. It is man's anthropomorphism that makes him look upon the cosmic process as a sort of human activity. Nature obeys no laws imposed from without. We have only necessities in nature.[214]

214. In a conversation with Anāthapiṇḍika Buddha is said to have argued the question thus: 'If the world had been made by Īśvara, there should be no change nor destruction, there should be no such thing as sorrow or calamity, as right or wrong, seeing that all things, pure and impure, must come from him. If sorrow and joy, love and hate, which spring up in all conscious beings, be the work of Īśvara, he himself must be capable of sorrow and joy, love and hatred, and if he has these, how can he be said to be perfect? If Īśvara be the maker, and if all beings have to submit silently to their maker's power, what would be the use of practising

XVIII

THE IMPLICATIONS OF KARMA

The oppressing sense of the mechanical saṁsāra produces a passionate longing for an escape from it. This pessimistic outlook is inevitable so long as the premises are granted. On account of its metaphysical agnosticism

---

virtue? The doing of right or wrong would be the same, as all deeds are his making and must be the same with their maker. But if sorrow and suffering are attributed to another cause, then there would be something of which Īśvara is not the cause. Why, then, should not all that exists be uncaused too? Again, if Īśvara be the maker, he acts either with or without a purpose. If he acts with a purpose, he cannot be said to be all perfect, for a purpose necessarily implies satisfaction of a want. If he acts without a purpose, he must be like the lunatic or suckling babe. Besides, if Īśvara be the maker, why should not people reverently submit to him, why should they offer supplications to him when sorely pressed by necessity? And why should people adore more gods than one? Thus the idea of Īśvara is proved false by rational argument, and all such contradictory assertions should be exposed.' (Aśvaghoṣa's Buddhacarita.) 'If, as theists say, God is too great for man to be able to comprehend Him, then it follows that His qualities also surpass our range of thought, and that we can neither know Him nor attribute to Him the quality of a creator' (Bodhicaryāvatāra). If the world has not been created by Īśvara, may not all existence be a manifestation of the absolute, the unconditioned, the unknowable behind all appearances? 'Said the Blessed One to Anāthapiṇḍika: "If by the absolute is meant something out of relation to all known things, its existence cannot be established by any reasoning (hetuvidyāśāstra). How can we know that anything unrelated to other things exists at all? The whole universe, as we know it, is a system of relations: we know nothing that is, or can be, unrelated. How can that which depends on nothing and is related to nothing produce things which are related to one another and depend for their existence upon one another? Again, the absolute is one or many. If it be only one, how can it be the cause of the different things which originate, as we know, from different causes? If there be as many different absolutes as there are things, how can the latter be related to one another? If the absolute pervades all things and fills all space, then it cannot also make them, for there is nothing to make. Further, if the absolute is devoid of all qualities (nirguṇa), all things arising from it ought likewise to be devoid of qualities. But in reality all things in the world are circumscribed throughout by qualities. Hence the absolute cannot be their cause. If the absolute be considered to be different from the qualities, how does it continually create the things possessing such qualities and manifest itself in them? Again, if the absolute be unchangeable all things should be unchangeable too, for the effect cannot differ in nature from

Buddhism could not emphasise the Upaniṣad idea of a divine plan of saṁsāra arranged to help the spiritual evolution of man. The whole conception without a spiritual background seems to be devoid of any point except it be to convince us of the purposelessness of all existence. But the necessity of karma and the reality of spirit are different ways of expressing the one truth. While karma does not consist with special miracles, it need not be interpreted as excluding a constant spiritual activity. It disallows only the capricious God, who is not found everywhere and always, but here and there and at rare intervals. Abstract intellect which moves among ideas and concepts reduces the concrete reality of the world to the most general terms. There are in the Upaniṣads also such abstract representations of Brahman divorcing it from its concrete existence in life and consciousness. The Infinite is beyond the reach of vision and thought. Such a transcendental conception which we may call indifferently an infinite zero or an inexpressible reality, the nameless nihil, indefinable,[215] self-less[216] and base-

---

the cause. But all things in the world undergo change and decay. How then can the absolute be unchangeable? Moreover, if the absolute which pervades all is the cause of everything, why should we seek liberation? For we ourselves possess this absolute and must patiently endure every suffering and sorrow incessantly created by the absolute' (Aśvaghoṣa's Buddhacarita). S.S.S.S. gives an account of the arguments of later Buddhism against the theistic systems of Nyāya-Vaiśeṣika. (1) We cannot maintain the creatorship of God logically. (2) If He is the Lord of the world, He leads men to the practice of unrighteousness also. (3) If He is the authority for religious scriptures, how can His contradictory language be authoritative? (4) If He is only the agent for the virtuous, then He is not infinite, not being all. (5) Has He in creation any end in view, any self-interest in the matter? If He has, He is imperfect; if He has not, why did He trouble about creation at all? Does He undertake to do that which is profitless? If His activity be mere diversion, He seems to play like a little child. (6) The existence of a God makes man helpless, for being unavoidably impelled by Him he goes to heaven or hell. (7) What is the good of suggesting that people are totured for the pleasure of the Lord? (8) If He is free to bestow boons, He may do so even upon the wicked and the vicious, and it is open to Him to send the virtuous to hell. (9) If He bestows gifts according to the karmas of the individuals, then all men are lords like Him. Being devoid of freedom in the matter of granting gifts, why is He to be called the Lord of all? (iv. 23–38). It is to be noted that the three works here referred to belong to later Buddhism.

215. Anirdeśyam.

216. Anātmyam.

less,[217] is of no use in life. Buddha calls it the fiction of the metaphysician.[218] This warning was needed at a time when people were losing their moral energy in the ecstatic apprehension of the absolute. At best, since the reality of such an infinite is incapable of verification, we must leave it an open question. Buddha asks us to suspend judgment where knowledge is impossible. If relativity is a necessary condition of thought, then it applies to the thought of God also. Let us therefore give up the attempt to define the absolute and look at pratyak, or the actual, and not at the parāk, or the transcendent. We have definite knowledge of the phenomenal flow. By his own insistence on the causal connections of phenomena, he seems to support the view that there is no ultimate spirit behind this ancient shoreless sea of forms incomprehensibly interchanging, no unknown God who with His protean magic or māyā shapes and reshapes for ever all cosmic being. Still, the explicit teaching of the Upaniṣads, which is nowhere denied by Buddha,[219] is necessary to give completeness to the doctrine of Buddha. According to both the Upaniṣads and Buddhism, it is the fate of man's life to be restless, capricious and tragic. But this pain is not the whole of it. The Upaniṣads argue that the paradox of the world, its caprice, its tragedy, are the witnesses to the life of the spirit. They are there to provoke the spiritual power of man and give him victory. Contradiction is at the heart of things, because the world is spiritual. Buddha admits that we should conquer the passions of sin to attain the joy of spirit. It is misleading to think that the lowly passions are all and caprice is at the centre of the universe. Buddha allows that endurance is the essence of spirituality, courage the vital energy of truth. If we exaggerate one essential element of a divine arrangement, then we tend to look upon the world as godless. A whole view tells us that it is possible for us to catch the rhythm and pulse beat of the spirit that is working even through the so-called caprice of nature. Without such an idea there will be no gleam of purpose in the world. The theory that the world is moving to a higher morality and a deeper wisdom will lose its sense. Surely Buddha does not view the world as purposeless

217. Anilayanam.

218. Brahmajāla Sutta, i. 26.

219. There is no passage where the Buddhist texts refer to the Brahman of the Upaniṣads, even for polemical purposes. 'The Brahman as the universal one is not alluded to by the Buddhists either as an element of an alien or of their own creed, though they very frequently mention the God Brahmā.' (Oldenberg: *Buddha*.)

un-reason. It is not a becoming without end or aim, mere sound and fury signifying nothing. Such a view would be the death of all idealism. Buddha discerned in the succession of events the working out of a deep design. The world of passing events reflects the reality of an idea, call it karma or the law of righteousness. There is no law against this law. Except against the background of this absolute eternal value, the show of the world is a mere phantasmagoria. The discipline of karma is purifying and remedial. Its operation is the energising of a vital law. It is the business of man to so order his life as to bring it into harmony with this law. The world was, is and will be ruled by righteousness. While a personal creator is disputed by Buddha, this eternal principle is not. Buddha will not say that the principle of karma is an entirely mindless energy. It is not an unintelligent principle that frames the ions and the electrons, that gathers the atoms into molecules and the worlds. There is nothing to tell us that Buddha denied the reality of an eternal self-sustaining spirit, the active mind of the universe. While we cannot know more about God than that He is an absolute law, we perceive enough from this world of relativity to compel us to recognise an invisible spirit. This law is only the expression of a divine mind, if we can indulge in a theological phrase.

The law contradicts theism, only if theism implies arbitrary interference and suppression of law and order. Such action of God is unnatural. Only children and savages could believe in an interfering God. To refute meaningless interference is not to deny the reality of a supreme spirit. For the conception of order, natural and moral, does not supersede the final agency of spirit. Simply because we cannot comprehend the spiritual source and sustaining centre, we need not deny its existence. The absoluteness of the moral law which Buddha assumes requires a central spirit about which he is silent. Our belief that events will continue to happen in accordance with the forecasts of reason, and things in the future will not be uninterpretable chaos, is grounded in a spiritual view of the universe. Even on the most unsympathetic view we have to say that Buddha abolished religion of the popular type which rests largely on craven fear or worship of power, and strengthened religion in the sense of trust in righteousness. He held the universe to be a spiritual one, not a mere mechanism but a dharmakāya, pulsating with life. Dharma is the warp and the woof of all that lives and moves. Every natural cause is the revelation of the spirit at work. Scepticism about the spiritual basis of the world is inconsistent with disinterested conduct. And Buddha need not be charged with such a paradoxical position.

XIX

PRACTICAL RELIGION

The religious instinct of man requires a god, and so in the practical religion of Buddha he himself was deified, in spite of his own caution. For when Sāriputta said to him. 'Such faith have I, Lord, that methinks there never was and never will be either monk or Brahmā who is greater and wiser than Thou,' he replied: 'Grand and bold are the words of thy mouth; behold thou hast burst forth into ecstatic song. Come, hast thou, then, known all the Buddhas that were?' 'No, Lord.' 'Hast thou known all the Buddhas that will be?' 'No, Lord.' 'But at least thou knowest me, my conduct, my mind, my wisdom, my life, my salvation.' 'No, Lord.' 'Thou seest that thou knowest not the venerable Buddhas of the past and the future; why then are thy words so grand and bold?'[220] Yet the nature of man is irrepressible. Buddha, the eye of the world (lokacakṣus), the model we have to imitate, he who reveals to us the path to perfection, who considers himself to be nothing more than a knower who has discovered the path and made it possible for others to walk in his footsteps, becomes the sole refuge and the only god of the masses.[221]

Buddha adopts popular theology which consoles us by building up other worlds when he admits the reality of Brahmā and other gods.[222] Only he makes all his gods mortal. He denies the first cause of the universe, a creator or controller of karma, but acquiesces in popular beliefs and speaks of intercourse between men and gods. He admits spiritual exercises which help us in securing life in the lower worlds of form and no form. To secure greater prestige for Buddhism, it is even suggested that the gods Brahmā and Sakka (Indra) are converts to Buddhism. They are as much in need of saving knowledge as men. All this is in accordance with the Brāhmanical

220. Mahāparinibbāna Sutta.

221. Cf.: 'So also, O Brāhmin, of those beings who live in ignorance and are shut up and confined as it were in an egg, I have first broken the eggshell of ignorance, and alone in the universe obtained the most exalted universal Buddhahood. Thus am I, O Brāhmin, the oldest and the noblest of beings.' (Oldenberg, *Buddha*, p. 325). Buddha is only amārgadarśaka.

222. See Mahāgovinda Sutta and Tevijja Sutta.

tradition, where the gods are said to reach the divine status by pious deeds, sacrifices and penances. When their reserve of puṇya or merit is exhausted, by their experience of divine pleasures, they pass out into other forms. There are stories in which the gods struggle for life and power, prestige and pre-eminence. When new aspirants for divine rank heap up penances and merit which entitle them to divinity, the old gods put obstacles in the way.[223] Buddhism adapts the old gods to its new doctrine by making them all subordinate to the Buddhist monk aiming at nirvāṇa. 'Brahmā is overpowered by avidyā, Viṣṇu is embraced by great illusion which it is difficult to discriminate. Śaṁkara holds Pārvatī in his own person, owing to excessive attachment, but in this world the great muni, the Lord, is without avidyā, without illusion, and without attachment.'[224]

XX

THEORY OF KNOWLEDGE

Taking up next the Buddhist theory of knowledge, we find that, unlike the materialist, the Buddhist admits the validity of inference in addition to perception,[225] though there is a difference between the Buddhist theory of inference and the Naiyāyika's. The Buddhist maintains that connexions could be established between causes and effects, while the Naiyāyika admits other forms of invariable concomitance as well. According to the former, we can argue from effects to causes; according to the latter, not only from effects to causes, but also from signs to things signified. This distinction is due to the Buddhist doctrine of becoming. Though inductive generalisations based on inseparability may not be always valid, they are valid with regard to causal successions. That all horned animals have divided hoofs is an empirical generalisation observed to be valid within the limits of experience, though it may not be absolutely valid. So far as inference to fire from smoke is concerned, it cannot be denied, for denying it, it is impossible to live.

How can we establish causal relations between two phenomena? The early Buddhist says that if A precedes B, and the disappearance of A means the disappearance of B, other things remaining the same, then A is the cause

223. The purāṇic stories of the type of Menakā and Viśvāmitra illustrate this fact.

224. Bhaktiśataka by Rāmacandra, 3.

225. See S.S.S.S., iii. 4. 4. 18–22. Early Buddhism, however, seems to have accepted analogy and authority also. Maitreya discarded analogy and Dignāga discarded authority. See J.A.S. of Bengal, 1905, p. 179.

of B. This is the method of difference. Later Buddhists develop this doctrine by emphasising the immediate antecedents of the cause. They also insist that we must be careful that no other circumstances are altered. So they state the full doctrine of causal inference in five steps, whence it is called pañcakāraṇi: (1) In the first stage we perceive neither the cause nor the effect. (2) The cause appears. (3) The effect appears. (4) The cause disappears. (5) And the effect disappears. Of course, relations of co-existence such as those of genus and species can also be established, though in a different manner. If we notice a number of instances of the association of a certain character with certain others, and if we have never perceived the one without the other, we suspect some fundamental identity between the two. And if the suspicion is confirmed and identity established, then the generalisation follows. If we know an object to be a triangle, we may call it a figure, for the generic features must be present in the specific. It cannot be a triangle were it not also a figure. So among successions the causal ones, and among co-existences the genus-species ones, warrant generalisations, according to the Buddhists.

We are not sure that Buddha adhered to these canons of truth. The pessimistic view of life, the belief in saṁsāra, heaven and hell are all taken bodily from the thought systems which prevailed in his day. It only shows that the most radical account of reality cannot dispense with the past history of mind. If we leave aside this part of Buddha's doctrine accepted by him without analysis and criticism from previous thought, we feel regarding the rest of his philosophy that he was more or less consistent. He declines to apply his thought to first causes as well as to final causes. He is concerned with actual existence and not ultimate reality. To a Brāhmin lost in philosophical truths about the eternity and the non-eternity of the world, Buddha says that he has nothing to do with theories. His system is not a darśana, or a philosophy, but a yāna, or a vehicle, a practical method leading to liberation.[226] Buddha analyses experience, discerns its true nature. Since they adopt the method of analysis, the Buddhists are sometimes called analytic thinkers or vibhajyavādins. Buddha confines his attention to the world and leaves the gods at rest, expecting in return that they will leave him at rest. He adopts an attitude of pragmatic agnosticism about transcendental realities. This alone is consistent with the facts of experience, the deductions of reason and the laws of morality. Nothing is denied, but

226. Majjhima Nikāya.

the background is left open for any future reconstruction. We must carefully note that this does not mean that Buddha is a sceptic who seeks rest in negation. All that he says is, let us make ourselves perfect first without quarrelling about the goal of perfection. So indifferent was he to metaphysical doctrines that among the early followers of Buddha we find some who hold to the Brāhmanical views. The Brahmajāla sutta tells us of disciples who speak openly against Buddha's views. Buddha's sermons are addressed to his Brāhmin and Buddhist followers together. So long as we are of the earth earthly, Buddha asks us to give up the attempts to define the indefinable and indulge in those 'love-affairs of the understanding,' the discussions of metaphysical problems. He would not say anything to compel belief or work miracles to persuade the unbelieving. Inward impulse will lead to the truth, and so his disciples were exhorted to practise love and charity. Not philosophy, but peace alone purifies the soul. When we have the deeper illumination born of moral life, we shall have the true enlightenment, and why should we try to forestall it with our weak understanding?

The striking fact is that Buddha passes over in silence all questions of metaphysical import on the ground that they are ethically unimportant. What exactly is the significance of Buddha's silence? Did he know the truth and yet refuse to divulge it? Was he a negative dogmatist, denying soul and God? Or did he consider such discussions unprofitable? Was it his idea that the speculative tendency was a weakness which ought not to be encouraged? Many of the students of early Buddhism consider that Buddha abolished God and cast off the soul, and that it is more definitely atheistic than we have here represented it to be. That such a negative interpretation is supported by Nāgasena, Buddhaghoṣa as well as the Hindu thinkers who criticise the system is well known. Nor do we deny that Buddhism became identified very early in its career with a negative metaphysic. We submit, however, that this negative view is not actually expounded by Buddha himself, but is an interpretation of his silence on ultimate problems, thought out by his early followers. This silence may be indicative of either ignorance of the ultimate truth or a deep desire to point a way of salvation open to all, whether they are possessed of a metaphysical bent or not. The silence of Buddha may be interpreted therefore as the expression of an attitude of atheism, or of agnosticism, or of a moral earnestness and deep love for humanity. In our account of Buddhism, we have frequently urged that Buddha's specific declarations against the denial of self, against the confounding of nirvāṇa with annihilation and in favour of the reality of an unconditioned to which we can escape from the conditional, cannot be easily reconciled with a negative philosophy. The fact that Buddha felt that he was in the possession of truth and could lead men on to it militates against the second view of agnosticism. If he did not know the truth, he would not have considered himself to be a Buddha or the enlightened. The third hypothesis remains that Buddha knew all about the ultimate problems, but did not announce them to the multitudes who came to hear him for fear that he might disturb their minds.[227] This view seems to us to be the most satisfactory. On one occasion Buddha took some dry leaves into the hollow of his hand and asked his disciple Ānanda to tell him whether there were any other leaves besides those in his hand, to which Ānanda replied: 'The leaves of autumn are falling on all sides, and there are more of them than can be numbered.' Then the Buddha said: 'In like manner I have given you a handful of truths, but besides these there are many thousands of other truths more than can be numbered.[228] There are other truths, according to Buddha, than those of the phenomenal world which he has revealed. If a man is moral, he will see for himself those other truths. It is Buddha's self-imposed mission to insist on the moral preparation necessary for the enlightenment of the kind he has himself attained. This attitude of Buddha has philosophical justification. He recognised the limits of human knowledge and drew a boundary line separating the logically knowable from the unknowable. He felt that our senses apprehend becoming, and things which become are not real. Yet, with the Upaniṣads, he recognises the mystery of the infinite. When the finite intelligence takes upon itself the infinite task of encasing eternity in time, and immensity in space, it is paralysed by paradoxes. We cannot imagine the unimaginable. Every attempt to think being, to comprehend reality, turns it into a phenomenon. Reality must escape the grasp of the human mind, for man himself is a product of avidyā. Knowledge with its distinction between I and Thou is not final. There is an impenetrable veil separating man and the truth. Yet this truth or wisdom, which we cannot perceive or know, is not unreal. "Where does wisdom dwell, Nāgasena?" "Nowhere, O king." "Then, sir, there is no such thing as wisdom." "Where does the wind dwell, O king?" "Not anywhere, sir." "So there is no such thing as wind?" Buddha contends

227. See B.G., iii. 26.
228. Quoted in Ānandācārya's Brahmadarśanam, p. 10.

that the reality of the absolute is logically indemonstrable, but never does he assert that it has no existence. His opinion may be put in the words of Goethe's Faust:

> Who dares to name Him,
> Who to say to Him, I believe?
> Who is there ever with a heart to dare
> To utter 'I believe Him not'?

Buddha does not like the idea of basing the reality of Brahman on Vedic authority, for when once we admit the evidence of revelation, there is no end to it. So in the Tevijja Sutta, Buddha compares those who believe in Brahman on the authority of the Vedas and seek union with him, to those who build a staircase at the junction of four roads to mount up to a high mansion as to which they can neither see nor know either where it is, or how it is, or what it is built of, or whether it exists at all. It is also true that Buddha does not encourage attempts to fathom the depths of the unknown.[229] It is a waste of valuable time to be discussing things for which our intellects are inadequate. From the past history of metaphysical disputes, moreover, Buddha learns that the solid earth and moral law begin to rock under our feet when we attempt to fly in the attenuated atmosphere of speculation. So he asks us to turn back to mother earth and not be taken in by the idle flapping of our wings in the vacuum of the absolute. Deep interest in metaphysical problems betrays to him on the part of the questioners a speculative spirit. So it is put down as one of the five heresies.[230] It is the ethical obsession of Buddha that is responsible for his indefiniteness on metaphysical problems. Unwilling to add to the confusion of the times, Buddha asks us to confine ourselves to the limits of the comprehensible.

There seems to be some similarity between Kant and Buddha in their attitude to metaphysical problems. Both lived in an age when the field of philosophy was divided into the opposite camps of metaphysical dogmatism and scepticism. Both felt the need for looking deeper into the foundations of the dogmatic procedure of reason and were anxious to safeguard the validity of ethical principles. Both ask us to give attempts to comprehend logically

229. Francis Bacon, in the spirit of Buddha, observes that final causes, like the vestal virgins dedicated to God, are barren.

230. Cullavagga, ix. 1. 4.

super-sensible realities. To both metaphysics is incapable of solving the problems which reason suggests about the hidden nature of things. The moment we try to grasp them intellectually we shall be lost in antinomies and contradictions. Both look upon the moral law as the supreme guide of life, a law above gods and men, from everlasting to everlasting. Doubt (or vicikitsā) of the moral law is a grievous sin fatal to salvation.

As to the tendency to steer clear of ultimate problems, we cannot help saying that it was unfortunate. Man cannot but philosophise. When Buddha says that what is given is conditioned, the question naturally arises, is there an unconditioned? Is that unconditioned only the whole of the conditions or an absolute first? The problems whether the world has a beginning, whether the soul is immortal, whether man is a free agent, whether there is a supreme cause of the world, have a vital relation to the highest aspirations of humanity and refuse to be set aside. Though it is not open to us to solve them, it is not possible for us to desist from raising them. The dignity of man is not compromised if he is not able to know the truth of things, but yet the same dignity demands that he should not be indifferent to it. Buddha tells us that we should beware of the temptation of casting a glance into the depths, since it is not given to us to fathom the abyss. But his dogmatic denunciation of the futility of extra-empirical inquiries did not gain its end.[231] The history of Buddhism points to the inevitability of metaphysics. It is a living proof of the truth that we fight against metaphysics only to fall into it.

231. 'So long as it is thought possible to reach that distant goal of knowledge, so long it is vain for a wise simplicity to protest that we can do very well without it. The pleasure of advancing knowledge makes it readily take the appearance of a duty, and a deliberate self-restraint of reason seems to show, not the simplicity of wisdom, but a stupidity which hinders the elevation of our nature. For questions as to the nature of spirit, as to freedom and predestination, as to the future state, etc., at once set in motion all the powers of the intelligence, and draw men by their importance into a fever of speculation which subtilises and decides, dogmatises and controverts, with every new semblance of insight. It is only when such discussions give place to a philosophy which tests its own procedure and takes account not only of objects, but also of their relation to the mind of man, that the limits can be drawn closer and the boundary stones laid, which will henceforth prevent speculation from passing beyond its proper sphere. It needs some philosophy to discover the difficulties that surround many conceptions, which are treated by the ordinary consciousness as easy and simple. A little more philosophy drives away the illusion of knowledge which still remains and persuades us that such objects lie entirely beyond the horizon of man's intelligence.' (Caird, *Philosophy of Kant*, vol. i., p. 142.)

There is not always a virtue in vagueness, for the indefiniteness of Buddha's metaphysics enabled his disciples to fasten different systems on to what he said. His cautious and careful attitude developed into negative systems, and his teaching fell a prey to the very dogmatism which he was anxious to avoid. In Nāgasena, as we have seen, the supreme reality becomes a baseless assumption. He repudiates the distinction between the knowable or the phenomenal and the noumenal that is not knowable. Knowledge of things is no longer considered to be relative. It is true and absolute. There is nothing beyond experience. The real and the experienced are identical. The relative is the absolute. A true metaphysic must be a theory of experience, and not a guesswork as to what is at the back of it hiding itself under a veil. We have to accept the fact that the world has neither limits in space nor commencement in time. We must not employ the hypothesis of a cause distinct from the world to account for it. Other followers of Buddha tried to round off Buddha's deliverances on the nature of this world by their own schemes of metaphysics.

XXI

BUDDHISM AND THE UPANIṢADS

The inquirer who desires to reconstruct remote forms of thought has not here the sure key which consecutive progress or logical evolution can give him. Buddha, in his deep hatred of darkness and love of light, wished to abandon all mystery. This procedure favoured clear and definite thought, but had its own defects. The teaching of Buddha became deficient in depth and lacking in organic character. His ideas stood out in hard outlines broken off from each other. The organic inter-connections were not clear. The atmosphere which alone could weld together the different elements into a spiritual whole was implicitly present. Human reason, which is arhitectonic in its nature, must regard its ideas and principles as parts of a possible system, and this instinct of the mind requires us to show how the teaching of Buddha has a unity of principle underlying it. The only metaphysics that can justify Buddha's ethical discipline is the metaphysics underlying the Upaniṣads. Buddhism is only a later phase of the general movement of thought of which the Upaniṣads were the earlier. 'Many of the doctrines of the Upaniṣads are no doubt pure Buddhism, or rather Buddhism is on many points are consistent carrying out of the principle laid down in the Upaniṣads.'[232] Buddha did not look upon himself as an

232. Max Müller, S.B.E., xv.; Introduction, p. xxxvii.

innovator, but only a restorer of the ancient way, i.e. the way of the Upaniṣads. Both Buddhism and the Upaniṣads repudiate the authority of the Vedas so far as their philosophy is concerned. In practice both entered into an alliance with beliefs alien to their spirit, so that many who accepted theoretically their teaching were practically worshipping other gods. In this matter Buddhism was less compromising than the Upaniṣads. Both of them protest against the mechanical theory of sacrifices and ritualistic extravagances. Both emphasise that there is no release from rebirth either by the performance of sacrifice or practice of penance. It is the perception of the truth, the knowledge of reality, which is the basis of all existence, that will liberate us. The tendency to deny the substantial reality of the individual is common to both. The feeling that this life is suffering, and the life hereafter is that for which we sigh, is accepted by both. They exhort us to get rid of life's fitful fever. The vital teaching of the Upaniṣads, the oneness of all life, is accepted by Buddha. To both life is one great pilgrimage in which we either drop downwards or climb upwards. The tendency towards universalism of Buddhist ethics is nothing new. That the absolute reality is incomprehensible by intellect is admitted by both. The descriptions of the absolute as neither void nor not void nor both nor neither remind us of many passages of the Upaniṣads. If there is nothing real, and if it is ordained that we should be eternally ignorant, we will not have the insatiable curiosity that devours us. In the explanations of soul, world and other problems we come across the Upaniṣad phrases of nāmarūpa, karmavipāka, avidyā, upādāna, arhat, śramaṇa, Buddha, nirvāṇa, prakṛti, Ātman, nivṛti, etc. Buddhism helped to democratise the philosophy of the Upaniṣads, which was till then confined to a select few. This process demanded that the deep philosophical truths which cannot be made clear to the masses of men should for practical purposes be ignored. It was Buddha's mission to accept the idealism of the Upaniṣads at its best, and make it available for the daily needs of mankind.[233] Historical Buddhism means the spread of the Upaniṣad doctrines among the peoples. It thus helped to create a heritage which is living to the present day. Such democratic upheavals are common features of Hindu history. When the treasures of the great sages were the private property of a few, Rāmānuja, the great Vaiṣṇava teacher, proclaimed the mystic texts to even the pariahs. Buddhism, we might say, is a return of Brāhmanism to its own fundamental principles. Buddha is not so much a revolutionist who rode to success on

233. See Holmes, *The Creed of Buddha*.

the crest of the wave of reaction against the Upaniṣad theory as a reformer whose aim was to remould the prevalent theory of the Upaniṣads by bringing into prominence its neglected truths. The central defect of Buddha's teaching is that in his ethical earnestness he took up and magnified one-half of the truth and made it look as if it were the whole. His distaste for metaphysics prevented him from seeing that the partial truth had a necessary complement and rested on principles which carried it beyond its self-imposed limits.

XXII

BUDDHISM AND THE SĀṀKHYA SYSTEM

There are some thinkers who are of opinion that Buddhism and Jainism are both based on the Sāṁkhya theory. Burnouf thinks that Buddhism is only a carrying out of the principles of the Sāṁkhya. According to Weber it is not impossible that the Kapila of the Sāṁkhya system and Gautama Buddha were one and the same person, and in support of this guess he mentions the fact of Buddha's birth in Kapilavastu. It is a common assumption of these systems that life is suffering. They both accept the lower and the ephemeral gods of Brāhmanism, while they are silent about the existence of the supreme eternal deity. Wilson writes that certain propositions about the eternity of matter, the principles of things and final extinction are common to Sāṁkhya and Buddhism. According to Jacobi and Garbe the Sāṁkhya propositions of duality and the enumeration of tattvas are older than Buddhism. It is true that the Sāṁkhya theory of creation and the Buddhist doctrine have some similarities.[234] The 'four noble truths' of Buddhism correspond to the four truths of Sāṁkhya as put in the Sāṁkhyapravacanabhāṣya: '(1) That from which we deliver ourselves is pain. (2) Deliverance is the cessation of pain. (3) The cause of pain is want of discrimination between prakṛti and puruṣa, which produces the continued union. (4) The means of deliverance is discerning knowledge.' Kapila rejects sacrifices, prayers and ceremonies as much as Buddha.

The Buddhists admit that Kapila, the sage to whom the Sāṁkhya books ascribed the origin of their philosophy, lived several generations before Buddha, and that Sāṁkhya ideas prevailed at the time of Buddha. In the

234. Avidyā is parallel to pradhāna, saṁskāra to buddhi, vijñāna to ahaṁkāra, nāmarūpa to tanmātras, ṣaḍāyatana to indriyas (see Kern: *Manual of Buddhism*, p. 47, footnote 6). The pratyayasaṅgha of the Sāṁkhyas and the pratītyasamutpāda of the Buddhists closely resemble each other.

first suttanta of Dīghanikāya, where sixty-two different theories of existence are mentioned, a view similar to the Sāṁkhya is also found. 'On what grounds and for what reasons do the recluses and the Brāhmins, who are believers in the eternity of existence, declare that both the soul and the world are eternal,' and that 'the souls are many also?' Buddha must have known the beginnings of the system, though not the system itself. That the world was evil and salvation was isolation from prakṛti may have been very suggestive to Buddha. The Sāṁkhya conception of psychic process may even have been at the bottom of the Buddhist theory of skandhas. But there is no question that the Sāṁkhya *system* is a much later growth summing up the work of centuries. The Sāṁkhya Sūtras (i. 27–47) refute the Buddhist tenet of the momentary duration of external objects, which succeed each other in a perpetual flux, and the doctrine that things exist only in perception, and have no objective reality, and there is nothing but śūnya. The sūtras, moreover, presuppose a knowledge of the schools of Buddhism and are later than the schools themselves.

XXIII

SUCCESS OF BUDDHISM

In a country where Brāhmanism had been for more than a thousand years the prevalent religion, Buddhism succeeded in undermining it, and in about two hundred years came to be recognised as the state religion of India. Not even such propagandist religions as Islam and Christianity had anywhere, in the history of the world, such marvellous success. Nor can it be said that Buddha pandered to the passions and prejudices of people. He did not offer any cheap relief from the sins of the soul or put up salvation to auction. There is no appeal to human selfishness, since Buddhism demands a rigorous renunciation of all the pleasures men care for. The causes of the success of Buddhism as a religion are the three jewels, or triratna, of (1) Buddha; (2) the dharma, or the law; and (3) the saṅgha, or the brotherhood. The singular personality and career of Buddha, the friend of humanity, the contemner of the exalted, the ascetic hero, had a tremendous effect on the minds of men. Speaking of the person of the founder, Barth writes: 'We must set clearly before us the admirable figure ... that finished model of calm and sweet majesty, of infinite tenderness for all that breathes and compassion for all that suffers, of perfect moral freedom and exemption from every prejudice.'[235] 'He never spake but good and wise words. He was the light of the world.'[236] It would have been a surprise if his magnanimity and moral elevation did not appeal to the imagination of the people. The idea of human brotherhood undermined the growing rigours of caste. The institution of the saṅgha and its spirit of discipline attracted many. The Buddhist monks, like their founder, forsook all to preach the Truth. The elevated morality taught by Buddha, that only the pure in heart shall attain salvation, sums up the Law and the Prophets. Buddha justified the practice of the good even to those who did not believe in a personal God. No other independent ethics gives us a more thrilling message of universal benevolence. At a time when bloody sacrifices were not yet out of fashion, the teaching of mercy to all creation had a tremendous effect. His opposition to ceremonialism contributed largely to recommend his doctrine to the masses. The sublime grandeur of Buddha's teaching may be gathered from the following utterances of his: 'Never in this world does hatred cease by hatred—hatred ceases by love.' 'Victory breeds hated, for the conquered is unhappy.' 'One may conquer a thousand men in battle,

235. *The Religions of India*, p. 118.

236. Even in the Middle Ages Marco Polo heard of Buddha and wrote of him: 'Had he been a Christian, he would have been a great saint of our Lord Jesus Christ, so holy and pure was the life he led.' 'There is unquestionably much in common between the character and teaching of the founders of the two religions. Both are represented as infinitely critical and infinitely wise. Both desired beyond all things the salvation of mankind. Both proclaimed a royal law of love, the love of our neighbour and ourselves, the Buddha, indeed, including among the objects of our charity those poor relations of ours which we call the brute creation. Thou shalt hurt no living being.' Both required of their disciples the forsaking of all and the following of the master. Both taught the utter vanity of earthly good, insisted on self-denial and exhibited compassion as the highest law of life. Both inculcated the supreme necessity of purity of thought and intention. Both prescribed the non-resistance of evil, the overcoming of evil with good. Both had a special tenderness for the young, the poor, the suffering, the outcast. In the accounts which have come down to us of the lives of both, there are the most remarkable parallelisms; and what is more important and significant, the personality of both must be accounted even now the strongest religious forces in the world, drawing the hearts of men by a spiritual magnetism through so many ages.' (W.S. Lilly, *Many Mansions*, p. 62). 'Among heathen precursors of the Truth I feel more and more that Sākyamuni is the nearest in character and effect to Him Who is the Way the Truth and the Life.' (*Memoirs of Bishop Milman*, p. 203.)

but he who conquers himself is the greatest victor.' 'Let a man overcome anger by kindness, evil by good.' 'Not by birth, but by his conduct alone, does a man become a low caste or a Brāhmin.' 'Hide your good deeds and confess before the world the sins you have committed.' 'Who would willingly use hard speech to those who have done a sinful deed, strewing salt, as it were, upon the wound of their fault?' No voice like Buddha's ever thundered into our ears the majesty of the good. It is the flaming ideal of righteousness that helped Buddhism to succeed as a religion. The missionary spirit contributed considerably to the spread of the gospel. Buddha bade his disciples: 'Go into all lands and preach this gospel. Tell them that the poor and the lowly, the rich and the high, are all one, and that all castes unite in this religion as do the rivers in the sea.' Buddhism succeeded so well because it was a religion of love, giving voice to all the inarticulate forces which were working against the established order and the ceremonial religion, addressing itself to the poor, the lowly and the disinherited.

REFERENCES

Buddhist Suttas, S.B.E., vol. xi.
The Dhammapada and Sutta Nipāta, S.B.E., vol. x.
The Questions of King Milinda, S.B.E., vols. xxxv and xxxvi.
Warren, Buddhism in Translations.
Rhys Davids, Buddhism.
Rhys Davids, Buddhist India.
Rhys Davids, The Dialogues of Buddha.
Mrs Rhys Davids, Buddhism.
Mrs Rhys Davids, Buddhist Psychology.
Mrs Rhys Davids and Aung, Anuruddha's Compendium of Philosophy.
Mrs Rhys Davids and MaungTin, The Expositor.
Poussin, The Way to Nirvāṇa.
Kern, Manual of Indian Buddhism.
Hopkins, The Religions of India, chap. xiii.
Holmes, The Creed of Buddha.
Coomaraswamy, Buddha and the Gospel of Buddhism.

CHAPTER VIII

Epic Philosophy

■ The readjustment of Brāhmanism—The epics—The Mahābhārata—Date—Its importance—The Rāmāyaṇa—the religious ferment—The common philosophical ideas—Durgā worship—Pāśupata system—Vāsudeva-Kṛṣṇa cult—Vaiṣṇavism—Pāñcarātra religion—The suspected influence of Christianity—The cosmology of the Mahābhārata—The Sāṁkhya ideas in the Mahābhārata—Guṇas—Psychology—Ethics—Bhakti—Karma—Future life—Later Upaniṣads—The Śvetāśvatara Upaniṣad—The Code of Manu—Date—Cosmology and ethics. ■

I

THE READJUSTMENT OF BRĀHMANISM

While systems of revolt were agitating the eastern part of the country, in the west, the home of the Brāhmins, great changes were taking place, though unconsciously. When new communities professing strange beliefs were being freshly taken into the Aryan fold, the old Vedic culture had to undergo a transformation agreeable to the new hordes who were actually swamping the country, or fail to aryanise them. It had either to expand and remodel its own religion, to accommodate new beliefs, or die and disappear. The pride of the Aryan would not allow him to throw open the right of sacrifices to the new-comers; but they could not be left uncared for. Since the assimilation of the new beliefs was the one condition of continued existence, Aryan culture undertook, not without trouble and repugnance, the gigantic task of taking in the new beliefs and adapting itself to the moral needs of the new-comers. The aryanisation was essentially a spiritual process. The Brāhmin tried to allegorise the myth and symbol, the fable and legend, in which the new tribes delighted. He accepted the worship of the tribal gods, and attempted to reconcile them all with Vedic culture. Some of the later Upaniṣads describe the attempts to build a Vedic religion on non-Aryan symbolism. The Pāśupata, the Bhāgavata and the Tāntrik developments, belong to this period of social upheaval through which the aryanisation of vast multitudes in pre-Buddhistic India proceeded. They were so moulded and developed under

Aryan influence that it is to-day difficult to maintain that they had not their origin in the early Upaniṣads and the Vedas. The epics of the Rāmāyaṇa and the Mahābhārata speak to us of this growth of the Vedic religion during the period of the Aryan expansion in India.

II

THE MAHĀBHĀRATA

The Mahābhārata describes the great war waged in ancient times between the two branches of the one royal family, that of the Bhāratas. It is mentioned in the Śatapatha Brāhmaṇa[1] that 'the greatness of the Bhāratas neither the men before nor the men after them have ever attained to.' The epic relates the heroic deeds of valour which were performed in the great war fought about the thirteenth or the twelfth century BC according to R.C. Dutt and Pratt.[2] Colebrooke puts it in the fourteenth century BC, and Wilson, Elphinstone and Wilford are of the same view. Macdonell writes: 'There can be little doubt that the original kernel of the epic has, as a historical background, an ancient conflict between the two neighbouring tribes of the Kurus and the Pāñcālas, who finally coalesced into a single people. In the Yajur-Veda these two tribes already appear united, and in the Kāṭhaka king Dhṛtarāṣṭra Vaicitravīrya, one of the chief figures of the Mahābhārata, is mentioned as a well-known person. Hence the historical germ of the great epic is to be traced to a very early period, which cannot well be later than the tenth century BC.'[3] The original event seems to be a non-Aryan one, if we may judge from the bloodthirst of Bhīma, the polyandry of Draupadī and such other incidents. But it was soon converted into an Aryan story. It has become a national epic, with tales from different parts of the country worked into a single whole. It appeals to all whether in Bengal or South India, in the Punjab or the Deccan. It was the aim of the Mahābhārata to satisfy the popular mind, and it could do so only by accepting the popular stories. It conserves in a collected form all the ancient beliefs and traditions of the race. It is so comprehensive in its scope that there is a popular saying that what is not in the Mahābhārata is not to be found in the land of the Bhāratas. By bringing together the social and the religious ideas of the different peoples assembled on the soil of India, it

1. xiii. 5. 4.
2. Dutt, *Ancient Hindu Civilisation.*
3. *Sanskrit Literature*, pp. 284–285.

tried to impress on the minds of men the fundamental unity of the Bhāratavarṣa. Sister Nivedita writes: 'The foreign reader, taking it up as sympathetic reader only and not as scholar, is at once struck by two features: in the first place, its unity in comelexity; and in the second, its constant effort to impress on its hearers the idea of a single centralised India, with an heroic tradition of her own as formative and uniting impulse.'

III

DATE AND AUTHORSHIP

It is now agreed that the present Mahābhārata is an enlarged edition of an earlier tradition called the Bhārata. According to the opening chapter of the Mahābhārata, the Bhārata Saṁhitā as originally composed by Vyāsa, contained 24,000 verses, though Vyāsa enlarged it into a work of 6,000,000 verses, of which only a lakh now exist. But even this Bhārata must have been based on lays, ballads and versified traditions of the events of the war. Ballads and songs recording the doughty deeds of great heroes, singing the praises of great warriors, the beauty of queens, the pomp of court, could have been composed only when the echoes of the war were in men's ears. From the earliest times in the west of India, in the land of the Kuru-Pāñcālas, and in the east, in the land of the Kosalas, the local bards were singing the heroic deeds of their tribal heroes. These songs could never have been fixed, since they were orally transmitted, and should have undergone modification in each age. Brāhmanism had to reckon with these traditions, thoughts and aspirations which were not its own. The Bhārata is the first attempt at effecting a reconciliation between the culture of the Aryans and the mass of fact and fiction, history and mythology which it encountered. Being nearer the war, it must have been a simple heroic poem, with not much of didactic purpose or philosophical synthesis. It might have been composed about 1100 BC or so.[4] Soon new material accumulated, and the taks of assimilation became well-nigh impossible. Yet it was attempted, and the Mahābhārata is the result. It bears on its face the unsatisfactory alliance between the folksongs and the superstition of the new communities and the religious spirit of the Aryans. Vyāsa[5] made the best of a bad bargain and wove into a colossal poem the floating mass

4. Mr Vaidya fixes the date of the earlier work at about 3100 BC

5. It is very doubtful whether any one individual can be credited with the authorship of the work.

of epic tradition, hero worship, stirring scenes of strife and warfare, dressing up the new gods of uncertain origin and doubtful morality in the 'cast-off clothes' of the Vedic deities. It is clear that while the balled stage is the first, the Bhārata is the next. It must have been composed even when the religion was ritualistic and polytheistic. Those portions of the Mahābhārata which inculcate the worship of the Vedic gods, Indra and Agni, are the relics of this stage. Women in those days possessed great freedom and caste was not rigorous. There was no element of sectarianism, no philosophy of the Ātman or theory of the avatāras. Kṛṣṇa appears as a historical character. The next stage of thought represents the period when the Greeks (Yavanas), the Parthians (Pahlavas) and the Scythians (Śakas) entered the country. We have now the trimūrti conception that Brahmā, Viṣṇu and Śiva are different forms of the One Supreme, fulfilling the different functions of creation, preservation and destruction. The deeds of might originally attributed to Indra are now transferred to Viṣṇu and in some cases to Śiva. What was originally a heroic poem becomes a Brāhmanical work, and is transformed into a theistic treatise in which Viṣṇu or Śiva is elevated to the rank of the Supreme. The Bhagavadgītā, perhaps, belongs to this stage, though as a rule the philosophical portions of the Mahābhārata should be assigned to the last stage. In Books XII and XIII we have discussions on philosophy, religion, politics and law. When Brāhmanism ceased to be the religion of a few, by assimilating the indigenous beliefs and religious practices of its surroundings, a philosophic restatement of the ancient wisdom became necessary. Many efforts to combine the absolutism of the Upaniṣads with the theistic beliefs of the people in a synthetic whole were made, though not with any genuine principle of reconciliation. The author of the Bhagavadgītā, with true speculative insight and synthetic power, initiates a new philosophical and religious synthesis, which forms the background of the theistic systems of a later day. Containing within itself productions of different dates and authorship, the Mahābhārata has become a miscellaneous encyclopaedia of history and mythology, politics, law, theology and philosophy.[6]

6. We do not know exactly when the Mahābhārata was composed. We may be pretty certain that about the time of the rise of Buddhism the Mahābhārata was known. Macdonell is of opinion that 'the original form of the epic came into being about the fifth century BC' This view is confirmed by the absence of any reference to Gautama Buddha in the epic. Pāṇini is familiar with the characters of the story (Gaviyudhibhyāṁ sthiraḥ, 8. 3. 95; Vāsudevārjunābhyāṁ vuṇ, 4. 3. 98). The

The Mahābhārata is sometimes called the fifth Veda. It is looked upon as a work of authority on conduct and society.[7] It is intended to teach even the weak and the lowly the rules of ethical conduct.[8] The Buddhist scriptures were thrown open to all, while the sacred books of the Brāhmins were confined to the three higher classes. Hence the necessity for a fifth Veda open to all.

IV

THE RĀMĀYANṆA

The Rāmāyaṇa of Valmīki is essentially an epic work, and is not of the miscellaneous character of the Mahābhārata. Its hero Rāma, the model of virtue, the pattern of perfection, is made the incarnation of Viṣṇu, who took form on earth for the repression of wrong and the inculcation of virtue. What was originally an epic poem is transformed into a Vaiṣṇava treatise. It is not so universal in its scope as the Mahābhārata. It has the finish and the system indicative of no complex authorship. We may,

---

Āśvalāyana Sūtras mention the work called Mahābhārata in addition to the Bhārata (Gṛhya Sūtras, 3. 4. 4). We have an inscription of the Gupta kings, from which the existence of the Mahābhārata in that period is evident. The poet Bhāsa takes many of his plots from the Mahābhārata. Aśvaghoṣa refers to the Bhārata in his Buddhacarita and Saundarananda. Baudhāyana in his Dharma Sūtras quotes a verse found in the Yayāti upākhyāna and another verse found in the Bhagavadgītā (2. 2. 26; 2. 22. 9), and he is said to belong to 400 BC. From all these evidences it may be inferred that the Mahābhārata was well established about the time of Buddha. We cannot, however, decide with any accuracy the particular periods of history represented by its component parts. Even after the fifth century BC we cannot say that it was not added to or altered in parts by later writers who wished to harmonise its teachings with their own advanced notions of religion and morality. There are some who think that parts of the poem are as late as the Purāṇas, and that it was growing till the sixth century AD. 'It has been conclusively shown that the poem was recognised in AD 300, and by AD 500 was essentially the same as it now exists' (Bühler and Kirste, *Contribution to the Study of the Mahābhārata*). In spite of it all, it is not wrong to say that the bulk of the work has remained the same from 500 BC up till the present day.

7. Āśvalayana Gṛhya Sūtras, 3. 4. 4.

8. Sāyaṇa in his commentary on the Black Yajur-Veda says that the Mahābhārata and the Purāṇas are designed to teach the law of duty to women and the Śūdras, who were not allowed to read the Vedas (see *Bibliotheca Indica*, vol. i., p. 2).

however, distinguish two stages in it, the earlier epic phase and the later religious adaptation. If we take Books II–VI of the Rāmāyaṇa and leave out of consideration Books I and VII, which are admitted to be later additions, we shall see that the main substance of the poem is secular. Rāma is only a good and great man, a high-souled hero, who utilised the services of the aboriginal tribes in civilising the south, and not an avatār of Viṣṇu. The religion it reflects is frankly polytheistic and external. We have the Vedic gods with Indra as their chief. The new divinities of Kāma, Kubera, Kārtikeya, Gaṅgā, Lakṣmī and Umā, the wives of Viṣṇu and Śiva, deified animals like Śeṣa the snake, Hanumat the monkey, Jāmbavat the bear, Garuḍa the eagle, Jaṭāyu the vulture, and Nandi the bull, receive prominent mention. Sacrifice is the mode of worship. Though Viṣṇu and Śiva maintain their pre-eminence, worship of snakes, trees and rivers is also to be met with. Ideas of karma and rebirth are in the air. There are, however, no sects. In the second stage we have references to the Greeks, the Parthians and the Scythians. There is an attempt to make Rāma an avatār of Viṣṇu.

For purposes of philosophy and religion, the Rāmāyaṇa is not so important as the Mahābhārata, though it reflects more truly the customs and beliefs of the times. It is sometimes looked upon as a protest against Buddhistic monasticism, since it glorifies the domestic virtues and makes out that there is no need to give up home life for the sake of freedom.

Since the Rāmāyaṇa refers to Buddha as a nāstika,[9] or a denying spirit, its composition is said to be of a later date than that of the Mahābhārata, though its story may be of an earlier period.

The interesting portions for a student of Indian philosophy in the Mahābhārata are the Sanatsujātīya, the Bhagavadgītā, the Mokṣadharma and the Anugītā. When Arjuna asked Kṛṣṇa at the end of the war to repeat what he had told him at the commencement, Kṛṣṇa said that he could not command the state of the yoga in which he uttered the Gītā, and so gave a substitute for it in what is called the Anugītā. Apart from the attempt of the Bhagavadgītā to reconcile different views, we have in the Mahābhārata only a collection of different beliefs, a syncretism, but not a system. The Anugītā points to the existence of a large number of philosophical schools. 'We observe the various forms of piety to be as it were contradictory. Some say piety remains after the body is destroyed; some say that it is not

9. Ayodhyā Kāṇḍa.

so. Some say everything is doubtful, and others that there is no doubt at all. Some say the permanent principle is impermanent, others that it exists, still others that it exists and does not exist. Some say it is single, others that it is twofold, and others that it is both. Some Brāhmins who know Brahman and perceive the truth believe that it is one; others that it is distinct; and others again, that it is manifold. Some say that both time and space exist, others that it is not so.'[10] Conflicting ideas are collected together in one whole. We come across the polytheism of the Vedas, the monism of the Upaniṣads, the dualism of the Sāṁkhya, the deism of the Yoga, the monotheism of the Bhāgavatas, the Pāśupatas and the Śāktas. Postponing to the next section a detailed consideration of the different religious views, we may here refer to the mass of philosophical ideas which were held as the common property of the thinkers of the Mahābhārata.

V

COMMON IDEAS OF THE AGE

Since there are different philosophical tendencies in the Mahābhārata, we cannot say definitely what canons of authority it accepts. Generally the Vedic scriptures are considered to be valid. Pratyakṣa, or perception, anumāna, or inference, and āgama, or authority, are recognised. Sometimes the four canons of the Nyāya system are mentioned.[11] It certainly opposes those who repudiate the authority of the Veda. The nāstika creed of the dissenters[12] is refuted by Pañcaśikha, a follower of the Sāṁkhya.[13] The lokāyatas are also mentioned.[14] The dialectical pundits (hetumantaḥ), who deny the reality of souls and despise immortality, 'wander over the whole earth.'[15] A reference to the Jains may be found in the passage where a priest is said to have 'tramped around Benares, astounding the people, clothed in air ... like a mad man.'[16] Opposition to Buddhism is also found. 'What makes you so glorious?' asks one woman

10. Chap. xxiv.
11. xii. 56. 41.
12. ii. 31. 70.
13. Śāntiparva, 218.
14. i. 70. 46.
15. xii. 19. 23.
16. xiv. 6. 18.

of another, and the reply is: 'I did not wear the yellow robe or bark garments, nor go shorn or with matted hair.'[17] Heresy and repudiation of the Vedas were thought of as landing us in hell and a cycle of low births. 'The reason why I was born a jackal,' says a character in the Mahābhārata,[18] 'is that I was a counterfeit pundit, a rationalist and critic of the Vedas, being devoted to logic and the useless science of reasoning, a proclaimer of logical arguments, a talker in assemblies, a reviler and opposer of priests in arguments about Brahman, an unbeliever, a doubter of all, who thought myself a pundit.' The Purāṇas and the Itihāsas are also accepted.[19] Here and there there is doubt of the value of the Vedic authority. 'Deceitful is the Veda.'[20] The Upaniṣad view, that for those who had abandoned routine the Vedas are useless, is perhaps reflected here.

The religion accepted by the Mahābhārata is the Vedic one, though it carries its past into a greater future. Preserving its identity, it attempts to do justice to the new gods. Indra has grown very weak. Viṣṇu, the solar deity, has his attributes embodied in Agni and Sūrya. Yama retains his greatness, though he becomes a judge, a dharmarāja. 'Yama is not death as some think. He is one that gives bliss to the good and woe to the bad.'[21] Vāyu and Varuṇa remain shorn of their prestige. Prajāpati is left untouched, and for some time, prior to the rise of Śiva and Viṣṇu, was the highest deity. The early Pāli literature of Buddhism reflects this stage. The second stage is marked by the conception of the trimūrti. Brahmā, Viṣṇu and Śiva were regarded as different aspects of the supreme, though co-ordinate in rank. Megasthenes was familiar with this idea. Viṣṇu and Śiva became supreme over other gods, though they had not then acquired any clear-cut distinctness. They very easily melted into each other.[22] A hymn is addressed to Śiva having the form of Viṣṇu and Viṣṇu having the form of Śiva.[23] The third stage arises when Kṛṣṇa the epic hero is identified with Viṣṇu. The cult of Kṛṣṇa supersedes both animistic superstitions and Vedic ritualism. The dance of Kṛṣṇa on the head of Kālīya means the

17. xiii. 123. 8; see also xii. 18. 32.
18. xii. 180. 47–48.
19. xii. 343. 20.
20. xii. 329. 6.
21. v. 42. 6.
22. iii. 189. 5.
23. iii. 39. 76.

suppression of the worship of nāgas or serpents by that of Kṛṣṇa. The defeat of Indra by Kṛṣṇa symbolises the suppression of Vedic orthodoxy by the Viṣṇu cult.

The henotheistic tendency is still prevalent. 'I am Nārāyaṇa, I am creator and destroyer, I am Viṣṇu, I am Brahmā, I am Indra the master god, I am king Kubera, Yama, Śiva, Soma, Kāśyapa and also Prajāpati.'[24] Upaniṣad monism asserts its rights and reduces the different gods into manifestations of the one supreme Brahman. Divine immanence is freely taught. The Brahman of the Upaniṣads becomes invested with a distinct personality, and is called Īśvara, who appears under different names, Śiva, Viṣṇu, Kṛṣṇa.[25] Bhakti, or intense love of God, which is not motived by any desire, is the essential feature of the Mahābhārata religion. The un-individualised Brahman cannot serve as an object of worship; the theistic religion of the Mahābhārata therefore transforms the Brahman into an Īśvara. It is aware, however, that the impersonal absolute is the more real of the two.[26] It is superior to the manifested Vāsudeva. 'That is real which is indestructible and eternal and unmodifiable.'[27] The emphasis, however, is on the personal Vāsudeva, and from the religious point of view there is support for it in the Upaniṣads.[28]

The Mahābhārata is able to accept different popular beliefs on account of its vaguely felt conviction that they are all different ways of approaching the one truth. 'In all the five systems of knowledge, the same Nārāyaṇa is preached and worshipped according to different methods and ideas; ignorant persons do not know him in this way.' We see in the epics the gradual modification of the old Vedic religion into modern Hinduism. The Śākta, the Pāśupata or the Śaiva and the Pāñcarātra systems, which belong to the āgama class, and are therefore non-Vedic, enter into the Hindu religion. We have also image worship in temples, pilgrimages to sacred places gradually introduced. Since a knowledge of the different systems of religions we meet with in the Mahābhārata is essential for understanding the attempts made in the scholastic period to interprete the Brahma Sūtras, let us deal briefly with them.

24. iii. 189. 5.
25. Patañjali speaks of Śiva Bhāgavatas; see Mahābhāṣya, ii. 76.
26. Śāntiparva, 339. 21–28.
27. Ibid., 162. 10.
28. See Kaṭha, i. 2. 20; Śvet. iii. 20; vi. 21; Muṇḍaka, iii. 2. 3.

VI

DURGĀ WORSHIP

Durgā worship is mentioned in the Mahābhārata at the beginning of the Bhīṣma parva. Kṛṣṇa advises Arjuna to make an obeisance to Durgā before the commencement of the battle and pray for success.[29] In the first stage she is only a virgin goddess worshipped by the wild tribes of the Vindhyas. She soon becomes the wife of Śiva, and is addressed as Umā. In the Mārkaṇḍeyapurāṇa and two hymns of the Hari-vaṁśa,[30] she becomes the centre of a great cult. Early in the seventh century Bāṇa wrote his Candī Śataka.

Śakti worship, there is no doubt, prevailed originally among the non-Aryans, and was gradually adopted by the Aryans. Since she was a fierce goddess looked upon as controlling the destructive forces of the world, she is made the wife of Rudra. Attempts are made to affiliate her with the goddesses of the Ṛg-Veda, Rudrāṇī, Bhavānī, etc. Devīsūkta,[31] which is interpreted as in honour of the primal energy of life, is made the basis of Śāktaism. The sixth verse of its reads: 'I bend the bow for Rudra, to cut off the evil doing hater of the Brahman. I fight for man. I pervade heaven and earth.' She is the energy drawing forth from Paramātman the whole universe from ākāśa downwards. 'I wander like the wind bringing forth all things.'[32] In the Kena Upaniṣad we have Devī bringing the devas, who grew arrogant by their victory over the asuras, to their senses and finally appearing before Indra in the form of a beautiful woman, Umā Haimavatī, to offer him supreme knowledge. She later becomes the māyāṣakti of Brahman. A philosophical explanation is offered that the supreme spirit cannot perform the three functions of creating, preserving and destroying without the help of its energy. When Īśvara creates, he is dominated by the energy

29. Chap. xxiii. Many names are given to her, such as Kumārī (maiden), Kālī (black or time as destroyer), Kapālī (the wearer of skulls), Mahākālī (the great destroyer), Caṇḍī (the fierce), Kānṭāravāsini (the dweller in the forest). There is a hymn in the Virāṭaparva (chap. vi) sung by Yudhiṣṭhira in praise of Durgā. She is referred to as the slayer of Mahiṣa, a goddess dwelling in the Vindhya mountains delighting in wine, flesh and animal sacrifices. She is also looked upon as Kṛṣṇa's sister, dark blue in colour like him.

30. Chaps. lix and clxvi; see also Avalon, *Hymns to the Goddess.*

31. R.V., x. 125.

32. x. 13. 8.

known as Vāk, or speech, when he preserves, by that of Śrī or Lakṣmī; when he destroys, by that of Durgā. Śakti is the Īśvarī, the source, support and end of all existence and life. In spite of attempts to aryanise the Śakti cult, the limitations of its origin are visible in the practices of some Śāktas even to-day.

VII

THE PĀŚUPATA SYSTEM

In the Mahābhārata we find a theology named Pāśupata centring round the god Śiva.[33] The Rudra of the Ṛg-veda (i. 114. 8), the personification of the destructive powers of nature, becomes in the Śatarudrīya, the lord of cattle, paśūnām patiḥ. In the Brāhmaṇas, Śiva becomes the distinctive term for Rudra. The Pāśupata system continues the tradition of Rudra-Śiva.

We have an account of the Pāsupata system in Sarvadarśanasaṁgraha[34] and Advaitānanda's Brahmavidyābharaṇa. Śaṁkara[35] criticises the theology in his commentary on the Vedānta Sūtras. The five chief categories are the following: (1) Kāraṇa, or cause. The cause is the Lord, the pati, the eternal ruler, who creates, maintains and destroys the whole existence. (2) Kārya, or effect. It is what is dependent on the cause. It includes knowledge or vidyā, organs or kalā, and individual souls, or paśu. All knowledge and existence, the five elements and the five qualities, the five senses and the five organs of action, and the there internal organs of intelligence, egoism and mind are dependent on the Lord. (3) Yoga, or discipline. It is the mental process by which the individual soul gains God. (4) Vidhi, or rules. It relates to the practices that make for righteousness. (5) Duḥkhānta, or the end of misery. It is final deliverance or destruction of misery, and obtaining an elevation of spirit, with full powers of knowledge and action. The individual soul even in the ultimate condition has its own individuality, and can assume a variety of shapes and do anything instantly.

33. It is mentioned as one of the five schools of religious doctrine in the Nārāyaṇīya section (Śāntiparva, 349. 5. 64). In the Vanaparva, Arjuna obtains the weapon from Paśupati, the lord of cattle, who is looked upon as dwelling in the Himalayas with his wife Umā, Pārvatī or Durgā, attended by a number of beings called gaṇas, or hosts. He is associated with the Rudra of the Ṛg-Veda who had his hosts of Maruts called gaṇas, and as their leader is styled Gaṇapati.

34. Chap. vi.

35. S.B., ii. 2. 37–39.

Praśastapāda, the early commentator on the Vaiśeṣika Sūtras, and Uddyotakara the author of the gloss on the Nyāya Bhāṣya, were followers of this creed.

VIII

VĀSUDEVA-KṚṢṆA

We now pass to the most important religious doctrine of the Mahābhārata, the Vāsudeva-Kṛṣṇa cult, which is the basis of the Bhagavadgītā as well as of modern Vaiṣṇavism. Garbe traces four different stages in the growth of the Bhāgavata religion. In the first stage it had an existence independent of Brāhmanism. The central features of this stage, which in the opinion of Garbe continued till 300 BC, are the founding of a popular monotheism by Kṛṣṇa-Vāsudeva, its alliance with Sāṁkhya-Yoga, the deification of the founder of the religion and a deepened religious sentiment on the basis of bhakti. The anti-Vedic character of this religion, which is criticised by the commentators of the Vedānta Sūtras, belongs to this stage. The brāhminising of the religion, the identification of Kṛṣṇa with Viṣṇu, and the pre-eminence of Viṣṇu, as not merely a great god but as the greatest of them all, belong to the second period, which is about 300 BC. The word Vaiṣṇava as the name of the sect of Viṣṇu worshippers occurs in the Mahābhārata.[36] In the Vedic worship of Viṣṇu there is no reference to grace. The third stage is the transformation of the Bhāgavata religion into Vaiṣṇavism and the incorporation of the elements of the philosophical schools of the Vedānta, the Sāṁkhya and the Yoga. This process took place according to Garbe from the Christian era up till AD 1200. Then comes the last stage of philosophic systematisation attempted by the great theologian Rāmānuja. We are here concerned with the first two stages.

The Bhāgavata religion with Vāsudeva as the central figure, taught to Nārada by the Lord in the Śvetadvīpa, is said to be the same as the doctrine of the Harigītā[37] and that of the Bhagavadgītā.[38]

36. xviii. 6. 97.

37. Śāntiparva, 346.

38. 348. 53. It is a monotheistic or ekāntika religion. The names Nārāyaṇīya. Sātvata, Ekāntika, Bhāgavata and Pañcarātra are used as equivalents. The chief sources for this school are the Nārāyaṇīya section of the Mahābhārata, the Śāṇḍilya Sūtras, the Bhāgavata Purāṇa, the Pañcarātra Āgamas, and the works of the Āḷvārs and Rāmānuja. Nāradapāñcarātra mentions as the chief works on the subject

In the Nārāyaṇīya section of the Mahābhārata is found the story of Nārada's visit to Badarikāśrama to see Nara and Nārāyaṇa. Finding there Nārāyaṇa performing some religious rites, Nārada with a perplexed mind asked whether there was anything the supreme Lord had himself to worship. Nārāyaṇa answered that he worshiped the eternal spirit, his original substance. Eager to see it, Nāraga goes to Śvetadvīpa, where the great Being tells him that he is not to be seen by one who is not absolutely devoted to him. The religion of Vāsudeva is explained to Nārada. Vāsudeva is the supreme soul, the internal ruler of all. Living beings are represented by Saṁkarṣaṇa, who is a form of Vāsudeva. From Saṁkarṣaṇa springs Pradyumna or mind, and from Pradyumna Aniruddha or self-consciousness arises. These four are forms of the Supreme. The Mahabhārata suggests that different views were entertained about the number and nature of these Vyūhas or forms.[39] The Bhagavadgītā does not mention them, and the Vedānta Sūtras criticise the theory on the ground of its inconsistency with the accepted view of creation. There is also a mention of the avatāras, Varāha, Nārasiṁha, Vāmana, Paraśurāma, Śrī Rāma, and 'he who will come into existence for the destruction of Kaṁsa at Mathurā.' Buddha is not mentioned as an avatāra. The story of Uparicaravasu related by Bhīṣma to Yudhiṣṭhira knows nothing of the theory of vyuhas or forms.[40] From it

Brahmavaivarta Purāṇa, the Bhāgavata, the Viṣṇu Purāṇa, the Bhagavadgītā and the Mahābharāta (ii. 7. 28–32; iii. 14. 73; iv. 3. 154). Rāmānuja's works are not useful for our present purpose, since they belong to the twelfth century AD and make a deliberate attempt to reconcile the Upaniṣad monism with the Bhāgavata religion. Even the Bhāgavata Purāṇa is not of much value since, according to tradition, its author took it up when he felt that he did not do justice to the devotional element in the Mahābhārata (i. 4 and 5). It was at the instance of Nārada that he made devotion the central feature of the Bhāgavata Purāṇa. The Nārada Sūtras and the Śāṇḍilya Sūtras are later than the Mahābhārata and the Bhāgavata, since the former mentions Śuka and Vyāsa (N.S., 83), and the latter quotes freely from the Bhagavadgītā (9. 15). Thus our chief source is the Nārāyaṇīya section of the Mahābhārata.

39. Śāntiparva, 348. 57.

40. Uparicaravasu adopted the religion of the Pāñcarātra system originally promulgated by Citraśikhaṇḍins. This system was expounded by the Ṛṣis in the presence of the great Lord, who said: 'You have composed a hundred thousand excellent verses, which contain rules for all the affairs of men and are in harmony with the Vedas ... and lay down precepts about the religion of action as well as that of contemplation. This śāstra will be handed down from person to person until it

two things are clear: that the Bhāgavata religion is a monotheism, and its way of salvation is devotion or bhakti. Slaughter of animals is avoided. It is because Buddha made the same protest against animal sacrifices that he is made an avatār of Viṣṇu. The religion inculcates a combined pursuit of bhakti and karma.[41] It does not demand ascetic renunciation.[42]

Vāsudeva is the first and prominent name of the Bhagavat.[43] 'The eternal God, mysterious, beneficent and loving, should be known as Vāsudeva.'[44] The name occurs in the Bhāgavata mantra.[45] It is sometimes said that the name Bhagavat indicates that the religion is a development of an old Vedic cult. We read in the Vedas of a deity called Bhaga, considered to be the bestower of blessings. Bhaga gradually came to mean goodness, and according to the rules of Sanskrit grammar, the god possessing goodness comes to be known as Bhagavat. The worship of such a god constitutes the Bhāgavata religion. The Viṣṇu Purāṇa says that glory (aiśvarya), righteousness (dharma), fame (yaśas), property (sampat), knowledge (jñāna), and renunciation (vairāgya), are called Bhaga, and he who possesses them the Bhagavat.[46] Gradually Vāsudeva became identified with Nārāyaṇa and Viṣṇu.

---

reaches Bṛhaspati. From him the king Vasu will obtain it, and become my devotee.' King Vasu performs a sacrifice of horses in which Bṛhaspati acts as priest and Ekata, Dvita and Trita act as overseers, or sadasya. No animal is killed on the occasion. The God appears only to the king and accepts his offering. Bṛhaspati is provoked, and the overseers tell him that the great Lord appears only to them who are favoured by His grace. They relate the story of the Śvetadvīpa, where 'there are men possessing the lustre of the moon, devotees of the god, who possess no senses, do not eat anything, are absorbed in Him who is bright like the sun. It is there that we heard the great teaching that the supreme God is not to be seen by one who is not devoted to Him.' See Bhandarkar: Vaiṣṇavism.

41. Śāntiparva, 334–351.

42. Compare: Pravṛttilakṣaṇaś caiva dharmo nārāyaṇātmakaḥ. Śānti, 347. 80–81.

43. See B.G., vii. 10.

44. Bhīṣmaparva, chap. lxvi.

45. Om namo bhagavate vāsudevāya.

46. vi. 5. 74. The Bhāgavata religion is also called the Sātvata religion, since Vāsudeva is given that name (Ādiparva, 218, 12). The Bhāgavata mentions the Sātvatas as worshippers of the Bhagavat (ix. 9. 49). They along with Andhakas and Vṛṣṇis were Yādava tribes (Bhāgavata, 1. 14. 25; 3. 1. 29). Megasthenes also alludes to them. The aryanisation resulted in the identification of Vāsudeva with

From the beginning Viṣṇu was marked out for a great destiny. In the Vedas he is the god of three strides. He dwells inscrutable in the bright realm of light, 'where even the birds dare not fly.'[47] 'To reach the highest place of Viṣṇu' is the ambition of man in the Upaniṣads.[48] Even in the Vedas Viṣṇu was entrusted with the work of the deliverance of man from distress.[49] In the Śatapatha Brāhmaṇa[50] it is said that 'men are Viṣṇus.' He is the great helper of the gods against the asuras according to Aitareya Brāhmaṇa. He assumes the form of a dwarf to recover the earth for the gods from the asuras.[51] We find the name Nārāyaṇa for the first time in Śatapatha Brāhmaṇa,[52] though there it is not connected with Viṣṇu.[53]

How does Kṛṣṇa become associated with Vāsudeva-Nārāyaṇa? In the Mahābhārata sometimes he is distinguished from them.[54] But soon he

---

Nārāyaṇa and later Viṣṇu. We cannot be sure that at the time of the Bhagavadgītā Viṣṇu stands for the supreme reality. In it he is only an Āditya. In the Nārāyaṇīya section of the Mahābhārata Vāsudeva and Nārāyaṇa are identified. The old Vedic conception of two birds dwelling in a tree, friends and associates of each other, might have given rise to the stories of the eternal friendship of Nara and Nārāyaṇa, the individual soul and God. The onlooker is Nārāyaṇa, and the eater of the fruit is Nara. Nārāyaṇa, the eternal soul of the universe, is the resting-place of men (M.B., xii. 341). Manu says that the waters were called Naras, and since the Supreme had them for His resting-place he is called Nārāyaṇa (i. 10; see also R.V., x. 82. 5 and 6). He is the origin of the whole world, the Supreme God represented as lying on the body of a huge serpent in the ocean of milk. Metaphor apart, He is the self-conscious Lord of the universe confronted by the principle of not-self. It is from Him that Nārada is supposed to get his monotheistic religion.

47. R.V., i. 155. 5.

48. Katha, 1. 3. 9.

49. R.V., 6. 49. 13.

50. v. 2. 5. 2–3.

51. Śat. Brāh., i. 2. 5. 5; Tait. Brāh., i. 6. 1. 5.

52. xii. 3. 4. 1.

53. In Taittirīya Āraṇyaka, Nārāyaṇa appears as 'the deity, eternal, supreme and lord,' and receives the name of Hari (Tait. Ar., x. 11. 1). In the Mahābhārata Nārāyaṇa is called an ancient ṛṣi (see also R.V., 10. 90, and M.B., v. 49. 5–20; vii. 200. 57). During the period of the Brāhmaṇas Nārāyaṇa assumes a cosmic character, and in the Mahābhārata he is identified with Viṣṇu. Thus in the Bhīṣma parva of the Mahābhārata, Vāsudeva, Nārāyaṇa an Viṣṇu are used as equivalent terms (chaps. lxv. and lxvi).

54. xii. 334. 18.

becomes identified with the Supreme. Megasthenes, the Greek ambassador to the court of Candragupta (300 BC), mentions the fact that Kṛṣṇa was worshipped then at Mathura. If we try to trace the ancestry of Kṛṣṇa, we find it to be the name of a Vedic ṛṣi who composed a hymn.[55] He is said to be a descendant of Aṅgiras.[56] In the Chāndogya Upaniṣad we find Kṛṣṇa, the son of Devakī, as a pupil of ṛṣi Ghora,[57] an Āṅgirasa. It is clear that from the time of the Vedic hymns down to the Upaniṣad period there was a tradition about Kṛṣṇa as a Vedic thinker. But in another passage of the Ṛg-Veda Kṛṣṇa is spoken of as a non-Aryan chief waiting on the banks of Aṁśumatī with an army of 10,000 to fight Indra.[58] Sir R.G. Bhandarkar believes that a nomadic tribe of cowherds called ābhīras were worshippers of a boy-god.[59] They were a non-Aryan tribe with unrefined manners. The stories of libertinism relating to the life of Kṛṣṇa may have been derived from these wandering tribes.[60] According to Mr Vaidya, Kṛṣṇa belongs to the Yādava race of Kṣatriyas, who came in the second invasion of the Aryans, a community still pastoral in its habits, which found its habitation on the banks of the Jumna.[61] Other indologists, like Weber and Dutt, contend that the Pāṇḍavas were a non-Aryan people, with the peculiar custom of brothers marrying a common wife. In them prevailed the Kṛṣṇa cult, and the writer of the Mahābhārata tries to show that by their devotion to Kṛṣṇa they were led to victory. The wars and incidents of the Pāṇḍavas, a people from outside the pale of Brāhmanism, was worked up with a religious motive into the epic, and they were themselves admitted into

55. R.V., viii. 74.

56. See Kauṣītaki Brāh. xxx. 9; Pāṇini. iv. 1. 96.

57. iii. 17.

58. viii 96. 13–15. The later legends relating to Kṛṣṇa's turning the Gopas away from the worship of Indra, and the consequent indignation of Indra, which resulted in the pouring of incessant rain, and Kṛṣṇa's feat of lifting up the Govardhana hill over the heads of the Gopas to protect them from the rain, may all be based on this incident narrated in the Ṛg-Veda. In the Atharvasaṁhitā Kṛṣṇa is described as having slain the giant Keśi. Buddhistic works also mention his name (see Lalitavistara.) We have evidence to believe that the worship of Kṛṣṇa was prevalent when Jainism arose, for we find that the whole story of Kṛṣṇa is reproduced with slight alterations in the life of the 22nd Tīrthaṅkara Ariṣtanemi, who was a famous Yādava. See S.B.E., vol. xxii., pp. 276–279.

59. Mausalaparva, chap. vii.

60. Vaiṣṇavism, etc., pp. 36–38.

61. *Epic India*, chap. xviii.

the Aryan fold under the name of the Bhāratas. Garbe believes Kṛṣṇa to have lived about two hundred years before Buddha, to have been the son of Vāsudeva, to have founded a monotheistic and ethical religion, and to have been eventually deified and identified with the god Vāsudeva, whose worship he founded. In the Mahābhārata we have a combination of all traditions about Kṛṣṇa that survived till then, a non-Aryan hero, a spiritual teacher, and a tribal god.

We see in the Mahābhārata the process by which Kṛṣṇa is made into a supreme deity. In some places he is represented as worshipping Mahādeva.[62] There are contexts where his divinity is denied.[63] In Sabhāparva Śiśupāla contests Kṛṣṇa's claim to rank as god; Bhīṣma defends it: 'Whoever says that Kṛṣṇa is a mere man is of dull intellect (mandadhīḥ).' From this it is obvious that there was strong opposition to the deification of Kṛṣṇa. He is sometimes looked upon as the warrior Lord of Dvāraka. Occasionally he becomes a religious preacher of monotheism, which has for its object of worship Bhagavat, the adorable. Sometimes he is identified with Bhagavat himself. The Mahābhārata contains several layers of thought superimposed one upon another in the course of ages representing Kṛṣṇa in all the grades, from a historical character to an avatār of Viṣṇu.

It is clear that the editors of the Mahābhārata felt that some popular hero must be made the rallying centre to counteract the mighty influence of the heretical sects. The figure of Kṛṣṇa was ready to hand. There were, however, certain acts which were not characteristic of a divine being associated with his life, such as the Rāsa-līlā, or the circular dance with the Gopis, Jalakrīḍā, or water sport, and vastrāpaharaṇa, or carrying away of clothes. These demanded some explanation. King Parīkṣit asked Śuka to clear his doubt: 'The Lord of the universe was incarnate to establish religion and destroy irreligion. Did he, being the revealer, master and preserver of religious laws, violate them by committing the unholy act of adultery?' The answer is: 'The violation of religious laws by the gods and the daring acts of the glorious do not bring any stains, as fire is not stained by feeding on impure substances. But those that are not gods should never commit such deeds, even in thought. If a man foolishly drinks poison in imitation of Śiva, he is sure to die. The words of the gods are true, but their acts are sometimes true and sometimes not.'[64] But the ingenuity of the

62. See Droṇaparva.
63. Muir, O.S.T., iv. pp. 205 ff.
64. Bhāgavata, Book x. 33. 26–29.

Brāhmin will not leave it there. He will allegorise and attempt to sanctify the whole life of Kṛṣṇa and mystify the atmosphere. The Gopīs symbolise people who found God by devotion without learning. The desertion of home and husband by milkmaids is a symbol of the soul's self-surrender to the heavenly Bridegroom. Bṛndāvana is the heart of man. Rādhā and the Gopīs are entangled in the māyā of the world. The flute of Kṛṣṇa is the voice of God. To follow him means to sacrifice name and fame, cast away dignity and self-respect, and give up home, family and all. Those who care for social safety and peace cannot respond to the call of the infinite. To love God is to take up the cross. The surrender of the soul to the heavenly Bridegroom who is common to all and special to each—a metaphor not peculiar to India—involves the desertion of earthly come and husband. The greatest sacrifice of all must be made before God can be possessed. We hear in Vaiṣṇava poetry the constant refrain, 'I am become a harlot for thy sake.' Many a folktale is interpreted in this mystic manner, and incidents of doubtful morality are metamorphosed into relations of God and the individual soul. Yet with the best will in the world to recast history, to allegorise facts and invent explanations, we cannot accept the life of Kṛṣṇa as described in the Purāṇas. These incidents together with the story of Kṛṣṇa's childhood and Balarāma's weakness of drink clearly indicate the non-Aryan origin of Kṛṣṇa. If to-day Kṛṣṇa is the most popular Indian god, it is because the author of the Bhagavadgītā makes him the spokesman of the highest religion and philosophy. When Kṛṣṇa became a god, his other names, Keśava, Janārdana, etc., were transferred to Vāsudeva, and the stories of his being the son of Devakī were assigned to the original god, and even to-day we have contradictory descriptions of him as a high spiritual soul, with keen philosophical insight, and a popular hero not quite knightly in his behaviour.

The Bhāgavata system, with its worship of Vāsudeva-Kṛṣṇa, is also called the Pāñcarātra religion. We do not know the origin of this name. In the Padmatantra it is said: 'The five other great śāstras are like darkness in the presence of this, therefore it is currently known by the term Pāñcarātra.'[65] The name, perhaps, may be due to the fact that the system combines five different doctrines. We cannot be sure that we have an account of this religion in its purity even in the Nārāyaṇīya section of the

65. i. 1. 69. For a different view of the origin of the name see Schrader, *Introduction to Pāñcarātra*.

Mahābhārata, for the Vedic adaptation seems to have begun even then. The Āḷvārs of South India, the earliest of whom may be said to belong to the fifth century AD, adopt this doctrine. The term 'āḷvār' means one who is immersed in god-love. There are twelve āḷvārs recruited from all castes, and their works, which are in Tamil, are called Prabandhas, or songs in praise of some form of Viṣṇu, full of piety and devotion. These constitute the Vaiṣṇava Veda. Rāmānuja, the commentator of the Vedānta Sūtras, belongs to a later period, being the sixth in apostolic succession from Nādamuni, who was initiated into the faith by Nammāḷvār. The Bhāgavatas are the direct forerunners of Vaiṣṇavism in India. The followers of the Pāñcarātra were apparently not allowed originally to adopt the Vedic forms of worship. They themselves seem to base their views on what are called the Pāñcarātra Āgamas.[66]

The Āgamas generally classify the topics of discussion under the four heads of—(1) knowledge (jñāna), (2) meditation (yoga), (3) construction and establishment of images (kriyā), and (4) rites (caryā or saṁskāras). The central god is Vāsudeva-Kṛṣṇa, with his four vyūhas. The immanence of god Krsna is insisted on: 'Everything is Kṛṣṇa from Brahmā to a reed.'[67] Viṣṇu, the supreme by means of his śakti or energy, which has a double aspect of kriyā and bhūti, answering to force and matter, effects the creation of the world. The relation between Viṣṇu and his energy is said to be one of inseparable connexion or inherence, like that of substance and attribute. Rāmānuja accepts from the Pāñcarātra theory the distinct existence of Brahman, the individual souls and the world. The way of sacrifice yields to the worship of images in temples. The religion becomes more emotional. Bhakti, or devotion, is insisted on. A chief feature of modern Vaiṣṇavism derived from this system is the doctrine of prapatti, or absolute self-surrender. God helps those who without any other hope fall at His feet. The question arises, How can a just God excuse the sinning souls? The system elevates Lakṣmī, the consort of God, to the place of the mediator. The strict justice of God is tempered by the mercy of Lakṣmī, who knows not

66. Many of them are referred to in Vedāntadeśika's Pāñcarātrarakṣā. This, along with the Āgama-prāmāṇya of Yāmunācārya of the tenth century and the Pāñcarātra section fo the Vedānta Sūtras (ii. 2. 39–42), are our data for the system. The Vaiṣṇavite who looks upon the Āgamas as revealed by Nārāyana himself never troubles about fixing a date for them.

67. Ābrahma stambaparyantam sarvam Kṛṣṇaś carācaram (Nārada Pāñcarātra).

what it is to punish.[68] This mediator is of the very nature of God, and does the work when called upon by the devotee. The favour of Lakṣmī is a necessary prelude to that of God Himself. Even past karmas may be forgiven. Prapatti seems to be the way by which the individual soul attains to the supreme spirit, and it is quite as efficacious as any other method, Sāṁkhya or Yoga.[69] Among the worshippers of Viṣṇu there is no caste. Jābāla Brāhmaṇa says: 'The people of the Kirāta tribe, of the Hūṇas ... are purified of their sins by their mere contact with those who have their heart knit in Viṣṇu.' The followers of this school did not very much care for the varṇāśrama (the caste regulations) as did the Smārtas, or those who adhered to the Vedic śāstras.

It is a debated question whether the Pāñcarātra, Bhāgavata or Sātvata religion was in its origin Aryan or non-Aryan. Some contend that it was non-Aryan, because its worship was non-Vedic. It did not adopt the Vedic rites or saṁskāras and its doctrine of the birth of jīvas and minds from Saṁkarṣaṇa was opposed to Vedic theories. Yāmunācārya in his Āgamaprāmāṇya notices the several objections against the authoritativeness of the Āgamas and refutes them all. The considerations urged against are that their contents are of a different spirit from those of the Vedas, that they do not mention rites and ceremonies like the Agnihotra or the Jyotiṣṭoma, that they even rebuke the Vedas, and that they are not accepted by the twice-born or the Dvijas. On the other hand, they are practised by the Sātvatas, apparently a non-Aryan tribe.[70] There is too much of black magic and superstition.[71] The system is not counted in the traditional list of doctrines. Even Bādarāyaṇa, if we accept Śaṁkara's view, does not support it. It has its own peculiar system of ceremonies, branding, etc. To such objections, Yāmunācārya replies that the system is related to the Vedas, it is accepted as authoritative by Bādarāyaṇa in the Mahābhārata and the Bhāgavata, and also by such reputed seers like Bhṛgu and Bhāradvāja, that the Bhāgavatas are the best of Brāhmins, and that the name Sātvata does not refer to a caste, but stands for those who possess the quality of sattva in a predominant degree. Rāmānuja follows Yāmunācārya. The very need for defence seems to show that it took some

68. Nityam ajñātanigrahā.
69. Śāntiparva, 348. 74.
70. Manu, 10. 23. 5.
71. Kshudravidyā pracurata.

time for the system to be accepted as Vedic. Some of the essential elements of modern Vaiṣṇavism, such as image worship, branding the body, the wearing of the ūrdhvapuṇḍra (the vertical mark), are due to the Pāñcarātra religion.

Under whatever name it be called, there is no doubt that the religion is a very old one, perhaps as old as Buddhism itself, if not older, but since the Nārāyaṇīya section in which the religion is described speaks of Nārada's adventures in the Śvetadvīpa, or the white island, where the residents were ekāntins or monotheists, it is sometimes argued that the monotheism is borrowed from Christian sources. Dr Seal says: 'This Nārāyaṇīya record, in my opinion, contains decisive evidence of an actual journey or voyage undertaken by some Indian Vaiṣṇavas to the coasts of Egypt or Asia Minor, and makes an attempt in the Indian eclectic fashion to include Christ among the avatārs or incarnations of the supreme spirit Nārāyaṇa, as Buddha came to be included in a later age.'[72] Weber is of the same opinion.[73] Lassen agrees with it. He thinks it probable that certain Brāhmins might have learnt to know of Christianity in a land lying to the north-west of their mother country, and might have brought to India some Christian tenets. He believes, however, that this land is Parthia, where 'the tradition that the apostle Thomas had preached the gospel is old.' But monotheism is not unknown in Vedic literature. The Chāndogya Upaniṣad mentions the Ekāyana religion as one of the śāstras learnt by Nārada.[74] The Bhāgavata religion does not possess any elements fundamentally foreign to Indian religious thought. 'For one who is intimate with the intellectual life of ancient India the doctrine of bhakti is entirely conceivable as a genuine product of India,'[75] according to Garbe. 'No shadow of evidence has up to now been brought forward to support the theory that the conception of bhakti is derived from Christianity. The religious significance contained in the word bhakti has nothing exclusively about it that is specially Christian. Not only have devotion to God and faith in Him developed themselves gradually in other monotheistic religions, but even beyond the circle of monotheistic ideas the two conceptions are to

72. *Vaiṣṇavism and Christianity*, p. 30.

73. I.A., 1874. 'An investigation into the origin of the festival of Kṛṣṇa Janmāṣṭamī.'

74. vii. 1. 4.

75. Garbe, *Philosophy of Ancient India*, p. 84.

be found. And particularly in India we possess all the essentials on the strength of which we have to regard bhakti as 'indigenous' fact, as Barth says, since monotheistic ideas are to be found prevalent from the time of the Ṛg-Veda onward through almost all the periods of the religious history of India, and the powerful longings after the divine, peculiar to the Indian soul from yore, must have developed such sentiments as divine love and divine faith in a popularly conceived monotheism.' The Śvetadvīpa, or the white island, is, according to the cosmology of the age, a part of India which is north of Mount Meru. Christianity, after all, reached India only in the second or the third century AD. We have evidence to show that the monotheistic religion prevailed much earlier. Vāsudeva's name occurs in Pāṇini's grammar.[76] According to Sir R.G. Bhandarkar, Pāṇini flourished 'in the beginning of the seventh century before the Christian era, if not earlier still.'[77] Buddhist and Jaina scriptures refer to the bhakti school.[78] M. Senart writes that the word *bhaktimān* used in Theragāthā is borrowed by Buddhism from an earlier Indian religion. 'If there had not previously existed a religion made up of the doctrines of Yoga, of Viṣṇuite legends, of devotion to Viṣṇu-Kṛṣṇa worshipped under the title of Bhagavān, Buddhism, would not have come to birth at all.'[79] Barth says:[80] 'The ancient Bhāgavata, Sātvata or Pāñcarātra sect, devoted to the worship of Nārāyāṇa and its deified teacher, Kṛṣṇa Devakīputra, dated from a period long anterior to the rise of the Jains in the eighth century BC.' In his comment on Pāṇini, Patañjali says that Vāsudeva is the name of the worshipful, that is God.[81] We have also archaeological evidence to prove the priority of the Bhāgavata religion to the rise of Christianity. The Besnager inscription of the second century BC[82] mentions the erection of a flagstaff with Garuḍa's image in it in honour of Vāsudeva by Heliodora, the Bhāgavata. The Ghosuṇḍi inscription speaks of the worship of Bhagavat Saṁkarṣaṇa and Vāsudeva. A third inscription of the first century BC existing at Nanaghat contains an adoration of Saṁkarṣaṇa and Vāsudeva. From all this it is evident that the monotheistic religion of India is

76. iv. 3. 98.
77. *Bombay Gazetteer*, vol. i., part ii., p. 141.
78. Theragāthā, 370.
79. *Indian Interpreter*, 1910, pp. 177–178.
80. I.A., 1894, p. 248.
81. J.R.A.S., 1910, p. 168.
82. *Epigraphica Indica*, vol. x.

absolutely independent of any foreign influences, and is the natural outcome of the life and thought of the period.

IX

EPIC COSMOLOGY

In cosmology the Mahābhārata accepts the Sāṁkhya theory, though not consistently. It makes both puruṣa and prakṛti aspects of the one Brahman. The world is regarded as a development from Brahman. The self is said to send out from itself the guṇas, the constituents of nature, as a spider emits a web.[83] The same idea of the productive activity of Brahman is found in other forms. We have also the view that from Brahman was created the god Brahmā, who sprang forth from a golden egg, which forms the body of all creatures. The conception of the cosmic egg survives. The Sāṁkhya duality becomes more explicit sometimes. Nature is other than the puruṣa, though the latter is conceived as cosmic. Both puruṣa and prakṛti are derived from one principle. Prakṛti creates under the control of puruṣa,[84] or puruṣa impels to activity the creative elements.[85] Elsewhere it is also mentioned that all activity rests in prakṛti, that puruṣa never acts, and if it considers itself as active it is deluded.[86] The idea is also found that though creation and destruction are the work of prakṛti, still prakṛti is only an emanation from puruṣa, into which it resolves itself from time to time.[87] We do not think that, except by implication, the māyā theory is contained in the epic. The evolution of the world is described after the Sāṁkhya system in many places in the Mahābhārata.[88]

There is no doubt that the Sāṁkhya ideas were slowly maturing in this period, though they were not formulated into a system. The chief features of the Sāṁkhya system as found in the Mahābhārata may be noted, since most of the subsequent thought accepts the psychology and the cosmology of the Sāṁkhyas, though not their metaphysics and religion. The Sāṁkhya enumeration of the elements is accepted by the Mahābhārata.[89] We have

83. xii. 285. 40.
84. xii. 314. 12.
85. xii. 315. 8.
86. xii. 222. 15–16; see also B.G., vi. 37.
87. xii. 303. 31 ff.
88. See Aśvamedhaparva, 35. 20–23, and 47. 12–15.
89. See Śāntiparva, 303–308; Anugītā, xi. 50. 8; xii. 306. 39–40.

a near approach to the classical theory in the Anugītā,[90] where the order of development is given. From the unevolved is produced the great Mahat, from it individuation or ahaṁkāra, from it the five elements, and from them, on the one hand, the qualities of sound, smell, etc., and on the other the five vital airs, while from individuation arise the eleven organs of sense, the five of perception, the five of action and mind. The *system* of the Sāṁkhya is yet distant, since the puruṣa is counted in some passages as the seventeenth, surrounded by the sixteen qualities, and not the twenty-fifth. Describing the twenty-five elements in many places, the Mahābhārata adds a twenty-sixth, called Īśvara.[91] All this shows that it was a period when reflection was very busy on the Sāṁkhya problems.

The Mahābhārata assumes the doctrine of the guṇas. The constituents of prakṛti are the three qualities of sattva (goodness), rajas (passion), and tamas (darkness). They are present throughout all things, though in different degrees. Beings are classified into gods, men and beasts according as the one or the other quality predominates.[92] These three are the fetters of the soul. 'They are seen mixed up. They are attached to one another and likewise follow one another.... There is no doubt of this, that as long as there is goodness (sattva), so long darkness (tamas) exists. As long as goodness and darkness exist, so long is passion (rajas) said to exist. They perform their journey together in union and move about collectively.'[93] Nīlakaṇṭha, commenting on this, observes: 'However much sattva may be increased, it is still held in check by the tamas, and thus there is the continual relation of that which checks and that which is checked between the three qualities. They exist together though varying in strength.' Tamas is the quality of inertia, or in man, the spirit of stupor. It aims at the satisfaction of the senses. Its end is pleasure. Its character is ignorance. If it is controlled, the man is said to be temperate. Rajas is the emotional energy exciting desires. It makes man restless and long for success and power; when subdued, it has its gentle side of affection, pity, love. It is intermediate between tamas, which leads to ignorance and falsehood, and sattva, which develops insight into reality. Sattva is the intelligent side of man. It promotes stability of character and fosters goodness. It alone is

90. 14. 40–42.
91. Śāntiparva, 308; see also 306. 29; 310. 10.
92. Anugītā, 14. 36–38.
93. Anugītā, chap. xxiv.

competent to guide men aright. Its virtue is practical wisdom, its end right performance of duty. No man is devoid of these qualities. The three qualities have their stronghold relatively in mind, life and body. Tamas, or the principle of inertia, is strongest in our material nature or physical being, rajas in our vital nature, which works against the physical, sattva in our mental nature. Strictly speaking, they are present in mixed form in every fibre of our psychical make-up. Taking up the volitional side of conscious life, the tamas element predominates in our lower appetites, with their ceaseless recurrence of wants and satisfactions. The rajas element prevails in our desires for power and profit, for success and adventure. The element of sattva aims at a happy balance or adjustment of self to environment and an inner harmony.[94] These three by their interaction determine the man's character and disposition. All human souls therefore are grouped into inert, restless and good. Among the twice-born classes, the Vaiśyas, or the traders, represent the lowest; the Kṣatriyas, with their competitive ways of thinking and efforts to overreach others, form the intermediate stage; while the Brāhmins constitute the highest class. When referred to God, the three guṇas lead to the conceptions of Viṣṇu, Brahmā and Śiva. The guṇas are the essential powers of the divine, which are not merely existent in a perfect equilibrium of quietude, but also in divine action. The tamas in God is a calm subduing all actions, the rajas is His will capable of effective and blissful action, and the sattva is the self-existent light of the divine being. These three qualities which are everywhere intertwined account for all activities of nature. The world is a play of these modes. The variety of phenomena arises through the interaction of the equilibrium, motion and inertia. 'The guṇas are born in guṇas and are dissolved in them.'[95]

The teachers of the Sāṁkhya, Kapila, Āsuri and Pañcaśikha,[96] are mentioned, though there are differences between the Sāṁkhya system and that of Pañcaśikha.[97]

We do not agree with Deussen in his view that epic philosophy constitutes the transition between the idealism of the Vedānta and the

94. Cf. Plato's three elements of appetite, spirit, reason, and his three classes of society.

95. Śāntiparva, 305. 23.

96. Anugītā, xii. 319. 59; xii. 218. 14.

97. See Keith, *Sāṁkhya System*, pp. 39–40.

realism of the Sāṁkhya. Both are assumed in it. Though the Sāṁkhya had not in the epic developed many of its characteristic features, still the essentials were all there. The Yoga philosophy is assumed, though the technical terms of Patañjali's system are yet absent.[98]

In psychology, the Mahābhārata accepts the five senses of hearing, touch, sight, taste and smell, answering to the five elements of earth, water, fire, air and ākāśa. The contact of sense with object is not enough to produce perception. The feeling has to be conveyed by the manas, to buddhi and then to the soul. 'Seeing cannot take place by the eye alone without the aid of mind.'[99] Buddhi is the deciding factor, since manas is only a transmitting agent.[100] As to the nature of the soul, some believed with the Sāṁkhya that it was an immovable passive spectator of prakṛti, the source of action and change, sensation and thought. The atomic character of soul is also mentioned with approval. In addition to the individual souls, it believed in a supreme soul, or Puruṣottama. The Upaniṣad theory is of course present. The Ātman is called Kṣetrajña when bound in body, and Paramātman when freed from it and the guṇas.[101] The conception of the liṅga śarīra, or the subtle body, is also to be met with.[102]

X

ETHICS

Ethics as the pursuit of happiness is given an important place in the Mahābhārata. 'All beings desire pleasure and seek to avoid pain.'[103] 'What we desire is pleasure (sukham), and what we hate is pain (duḥkham).'[104] In this world the two are mixed up.[105] But both pleasure and pain are anitya, or ephemeral. The goal of human endeavour is to gain a state where we can accept pleasure or pain with calm and composure.[106] Dharma, or righteousness, is the stable condition which gives man perfect satisfaction. It helps him to gain salvation as well as peace and happiness on earth.

98. See xii. 237. 6–7.
99. Śāntiparva, 311. 17.
100. Ibid., 251. 11.
101. See Śāntiparva, 187. 24.
102. See Vanaparva, 296. 16.
103. Śāntiparva, 139. 61.
104. Ibid., 295. 27.
105. Ibid., 190. 14; 25. 23; Vanaparva, 260. 49.
106. Śāntiparva, 25. 16.

Though dharma leads to mokṣa, the two are distinguished as the means and the end. In the enumeration of the four ends of man (puruṣārthas) dharma, artha (wealth), kāma (desire), and mokṣa, the to are distinguished. The rules for gaining salvation constitute the mokṣa dharma. In the narrower sense, dharma means the ethical code as distinct from the religious, though it has also the freedom of the soul in view.

Apart from certain general principles, like truth-speaking, non-violence, dharma is relative and dependent on the conditions of society. It has always a social implication. It is the bond which keeps society together.[107] If we do not preserve dharma, there would be social anarchy, and wealth and art will not flourish. Dharma develops the solidarity of society.[108] It aims at the welfare of all creation.[109] 'Whatever is not conductive to social welfare, or what ye are likely to be ashamed of doing, never do.'[110] According to the Mahābhārata, the sum total of duties is contained in the maxim, 'Thou shalt not do to others what is disagreeable to thyself.'[111] The caste duties are ordained on account of their instrumental value. 'To support the state by force and not shaving one's head is the duty of a Kṣatriya.'[112] Of course, the really moral virtues are regarded as superior to the caste functions. 'Truth, self-control, asceticism, generosity, non-violence, constancy in virtue—these are the means of success, not caste nor family.'[113] 'Virtue is better than immortality and life. Kingdom, sons, glory, wealth—all this does not equal one-sixteenth part of the value of truth.'[114] Though women had no right to the Vedic sacrifices, they were allowed to go on pilgrimages, read epics and worship God in spirit and understanding.[115]

Dharma is not conceived in any hedonistic spirit. It is not the mere satisfaction of desires. Accumulation of pleasures cannot give us true happiness. 'The desire for happiness does not cease by the mere enjoyment of pleasures.'[116] Whatever we get, we try to get beyond. 'The silkworm dies

107. 'Dhāraṇād dharmam ity āhur dharmo dhārayate prajāḥ.' Karṇaparva, 69. 59.

108. Lokasaṁgraha or samājadhāraṇa.

109. Sarvabhūtahitam.

110. Śāntiparva, 124. 66; 261. 9; 109. 10.

111. Pandit, 1871, p. 238.

112. 'Daṇḍa eva hi rājendra kṣatradharmo na muṇḍanam.' Śāntiparva, 23. 46.

113. iii. 181. 42.

114. iii. 34. 22.

115. iii. 37. 33; see also iii. 84. 83.

116. Na jātu kāmaḥ kāmānām upabhogena śāmyati. Ādiparva, 75. 49. See also Manu, ii. 94.

of its wealth.'[117] Nothing finite can satisfy the hunger for the infinite. It may be necessary for us to suffer for the sake of dharma. True joy entails suffering.[118] Discontent is the spur of progress.[119] We should control our minds and tame our passions. When we become purified in heart and possessed of truth we are not likely to go wrong for fear of offending men or avoiding pain. The development of this attitude requires discipline of mind and will. In some places extreme asceticism is advocated. Since pleasure and pain are interdependent, the only way of freeing ourselves from them is by the destruction of tṛṣṇā, or thirst.[120] Through training we acquire a state incomparably greater than the satisfaction of desire or the gaining of Indra's heaven.[121] There does not seem to be any consistent attitude towards yoga and asceticism in the Mahābhārata. We hear of ṛṣis standing on one leg, or devoured by vermin, on the other hand those who are easily irritable like Durvāsas. The idea of tapas is prominent, though we hear sometimes of protests against it. 'The red garment, the vow of silence, the threefold staff, the water-pot—these only lead astray. They do not make for salvation.'[122] Retirement from the world is not allowed until the individual fulfils the duties of the other stages. A story is related in the Mahābhārata which points out how very important it is to live in the world before leaving it. An anchorite who had left the world before marrying came in his wanderings to a terrible place, the pit of hell. There he found his father and grandfather and all his ancestors suspended one below another on the open mouth of the abyss. The rope which prevented them from falling into it was slowly being gnawed by a mouse, representing the force of Time. So many well-known voices reminded him of accents he heard when a child appealing in the words 'save us,' 'save us.' The only hope of salvation for the long line of ancestors was the birth of a son. The anchorite understood the lesson, returned home and married.

If we are to fulfil our duties as members of society, how are we to know what our duties are? The pure and perfect are laws unto themselves. The imperfect have to accept laws made by others and recognised by society. Ācāra, or custom, is the main rule.[123] The rules will assume the

117. xii. 330. 29.
118. Vanaparva, 233. 4.
119. Sabhāparva, 55. 11. Asaṁtoṣa śriyo mūlam.
120. Śāntiparva, 25. 22; 174. 16.
121. Ibid., 174. 48; 177. 49.
122. xii. 321. 47.
123. Anuśāsanaparva, 104. 157; Manu, i. 108.

form of commands and feel like restraints, since they check the superficial tendencies of our nature.[124] If conflicts of duties arise we have to follow the example of the great. The need of a lovable personality to inspire and influence is recognised. 'Logic is not conclusive, the scriptures differ, the saying of no ṛṣi is valid, the truth of dharma seems to be hidden in secret; the way of the great is to be followed.'[125] The truly great are the atmajñānis, or those who possess spiritual knowledge.

Some general rules are prescribed, such as, avoid extremes.[126] Even too much of patience is forbidden.[127] Though the principles of truth and ahiṁsā are recognised as imperative, still the Mahābhārata contemplates exceptions to them.[128] The law of truth speaking has no intrinsic value, since truthfulness, which means love of humanity, is the only unconditioned end.[129] Yet knowing the danger of allowing exceptions to rules the Mahābhārata insists on prāyaścitta, or purification, for those, who transgress the law of truth-speaking.[130]

Sin is recognised and the significance of confession with repentance is understood. The true penitent should say, 'I will not do so again.' Bhakti, or loving faith in God, is regarded as a means of attaining moral purity. In some passages it is said that we can again the highest only by wisdom and not karma, however good and meritorious. We pass from birth to birth, 'so long as the piety which dwells in the practice of concentration of mind for final emancipation has not been learnt.'[131]

The Mahābhārata believes in the force of karma, or the fatality of the act. It accepts the Upaniṣad theory that all creatures are bound by karma and are released by wisdom.[132] Sometimes the karma of the forefathers affects even their descendants.[133] Attempts are made to reconcile the law of karma with the freedom of man. While the general tendency of the karma theory is to the effect that there is no room for independence by the side of its

124. See Mīmāṁsā Sūtras, i. 1. 2; M.B., Śāntiparva, 29. 4. 29.

125. Vanaparva, 312. 115.

126. Ati sarvatra varjayet.

127. Vanaparva, 28. 6 and 8.

128. Śāntiparva, 109. 15–16.

129. Yad bhūtahitam atyantam etat satyam matam mama. Śāntiparva, 329. 13; 287. 16.

130. viii. 104–109.

131. Anugītā, iii. 23.

132. 'Karmaṇā badhyate jantun vidyayā tu pramucyate.' Śāntiparva, 240. 7.

133. Ibid., 129. See also Manu, iv., 170, and Ādiparva, 80. 3.

iron necessity, still there are redeeming features. Human effort can modify karma. Karma is compared to a fire which we can by our effort fan into a flame or extinguish altogether. Different kinds of karma are recognised: prārabdha, saṁcita and āgāmi. The karmas that have begun to bear fruit in connection with this body from among the stock of impressions of actions in the previous human birth are called prārabdha-karmas. The other impressions due to the past birth are called saṁcita, or seed-like impressions. Those impressions newly received by actions in this life are called āgāmi karmas. The two latter can be overcome by real jñāna and expiatory rites, while the prārabdhakarmas cannot. By the grace of God we can destroy the force fo saṁcita and āgāmi. It is also admitted that success in any enterprise depends not merely on karma, but on the effort of the individual. The operation of the law of karma does not, however, limit the power of God. The law of karma is an expression of the nature of God. Viṣṇu is said to be the embodiment of the law, its ground and energy.[134]

On the question of future life we have no clear account in the Mahābhārata. The way of the gods is distinguished from that of the fathers, and a third place of hell is admitted. Immortality is not 'living glorious like a king.'[135] It is eternal happiness in a heaven where there are no sufferings of hunger or thirst, death or old age. It is the final condition of bliss to be attained by a true yogin. To the warrior, 'happiness in Indra's heaven' is promised. The stars were looked upon as the souls of the departed sages. Arjuna finds them to be great heroes slain in battle. The highest goal, however, is declared to be union with God. The Sāṁkhya theory that the spirit is freed from empirical existence when it realises its distinction from nature is also referred to. 'When an embodied self properly perceives the self concentrated, then there is no ruler over him, since he is the lord of the triple world. He obtains various bodies as he pleases ... he attains Brahman.'[136]

XI

THE ŚVETĀŚVATARA UPANIṢAD

Some of the later Upaniṣads belong to this period, and purport to restate the teaching of the early Upaniṣads. They mark an advance in thought and reflect the growth of the mind of the country in the intervening period.

134. M.B., xiii. 149.
135. vii. 71. 17.
136. Anugītā, 4.

They attach themselves to some tendency of religion or school of philosophy. There are Upaniṣads which specifically teach the Yoga practices or the Sāṁkhya principles or the Vedānta system. The Jābāla upholds an extreme asceticism and asks us to root out all desires. The Maitrī Upaniṣad also adopts a pessimistic attitude.[137] It makes a synthesis of the Sāṁkhya and the Yoga views. An attempt is made to trace the twenty-four tattvas of the Sāṁkhya system to the supreme Brahman. The Maitrī, the Dhyānabindu, and the Yogatattva Upaniṣads extol the Yoga method. The Amṛtabindu Upaniṣad teaches that the jīvas are parts of Brahman in the sense that limited spaces are parts of one universal space. It gives an advaitic interpretation. 'That verily is partless Brahman which is beyond all thought, unstained. Knowing "that Brahman am I," one becomes immutable.' The one appears as many on account of upādhis, or limitations. 'As one and also as many is He seen, like the moon in water.'[138] The Kaivalya Upaniṣad makes sannyāsa, or world renunciation, the only path to mokṣa.[139] It insists on jñāna,[140] and argues the non-dependence of the self on objects. 'Whatever in the three states (of waking, dreaming and sleeping) is the object of enjoyment, the enjoyer and the enjoyment itself, from these distinct am I, the witness, the pure intelligence, the ever good.'[141] Some other Upaniṣads insist on contemplation, worship of a personal god and symbolic meditation. There are Upaniṣads which make out that Viṣṇu or Śiva is the supreme Lord of the universe, and insist on the path of devotion. The Mahānārāyaṇa, the Rāmatāpannīya, the Śvetāśvatara, the Kaivalya and the Atharvaśiras Upaniṣads are examples. Most of these are chiefly occupied in reconciling the conflicting tenets of the Sāṁkhya, the Yoga and the Vedānta philosophies, and belong to a period posterior to the formulation of the systems. It may be useful to describe the contents of the Śvetāśvatara Upaniṣad since we have in it an attempt parallel to that of the Bhagavadgītā, with this difference that Śiva is here the supreme Lord.

It is a post-Buddhistic Upaniṣad, since it is familiar with the technical terms of the Sāṁkhya and the Yoga philosophies. It mentions the name of Kapila, though Śaṁkara believes that the name refers to Hiraṇyagarbha, who is brown or gold coloured. The reference to the she-goat of three

137. i. 2–4.
138. 8 and 12.
139. i. 1.
140. 9 and 10.
141. 18.

colours[142] is sometimes taken as an indication of the three guṇas of the Sāṁkhya philosophy. But Śaṁkara interprets it as a reference to the three original elements of the Upaniṣads, fire, water and earth. Chapter ii of the Uapaniṣad is full of references to the Yoga system. The word 'liṅga' is used perhaps in the Nyāya sense.[143] This Upaniṣad seems to assume a knowledge of Buddhistic speculations such as those of time (kāla), nature (svabhāva), or succession of works (karma), or chance, or elements, or puruṣa. In speaking of the highest reality the Upaniṣad uses such names as Hara, Rudra, Śiva.[144] The popular god of Brāhmanism is given the attributes of Brahman.

Deussen calls the Śvetāśvatara Upaniṣad 'a monument of theism,' for it teaches a personal god, creator, judge and preserver of the universe. Hara the Lord rules over the individual selves and the world of matter. The Upaniṣad repudiates the theory of naturalism, which makes svabhāva the cause of the universe.[145] The latter theory believes that the universe is produced and sustained by the natural and necessary action of substances according to their own properties. On such a view there would be no need for a supreme being.

The reality of God cannot be proved by logic. It can only be realised by faith and meditation.[146] 'When absorbed in this concentration the yogi sees by the true nature of his own self, which manifests like a light the true nature of Brahman, which is unborn, eternal, free from all effects of nature, he gets released from all bonds.'[147] 'He has no visible form; no one sees Him with the eye. Those who know Him by the heart and understanding, as seated in the heart, become immortal.'[148] He is the master of nature and soul the cause of bondage and release, the eternal of all things, the self-born.[149] Divine immanence is also admitted. He is the dweller in the heart of man concealed in all beings. 'Thou art woman, thou art man, thou art the youth and even the maid, thou art the old man trembling on his staff, thy face is the universe.'[150]

142. iv. 5.
143. vi. 9.
144. i. 10; iii. 4 and 7; iv. 10 and 12.
145. vi. 1.
146. vi. 13.
147. ii. 15.
148. iv. 20.
149. vi. 16; vi. 7; vi. 13.
150. iii. 11. 14. 16; iv. 3. See also Mahānārāyaṇa, ii. 7; Kaivalya, 9 and 10.

The Upaniṣad is aware of the reality of the impersonal Brahman, of which the three tendencies or developments are God, world and self. 'Where there is no darkness, there is neither day nor night, neither existence nor non-existence, there is the all-blessed even alone.'[151] He is called 'nirguṇa,' though theistic interpreters say that this word means that the Supreme is devoid of evil qualities.[152] There is no doubt that the Śvetāśvatara admits the reality of a supreme Brahman above the changing world,[153] beyond space,[154] imperturbable, free from change becoming and causality.[155] It is the pure basic consciousness by the light of which everything shines,[156] and is described as 'without parts, without action, without faults, without ignorance or misery.'[157] From this Supreme three unborn elements proceed, the all-knowing God, the imperfect self, and the world of prakṛti, which has in it the materials of enjoyment and suffering.[158] These three are not ultimately different. They are three aspects of the one Brahman.[159] The absolute of the Upaniṣads becomes the highest element, an individual among individuals. The personal Lord is the composite Brahman, the eternal support of jīva and matter.[160] All theism has this ambiguity about it. The religious needs of human consciousness demand that the ultimate principle is to be conceived as good,[161] the friend and refuge of all,[162] the giver of desired objects.[163] Since it is hard to contemplate an impersonal Brahman, a personal lord is provided.[164] 'Brahman is conscious intelligence, one without parts, without a body. For helping the devotee in his practice of devotion, symbols and forms have been attributed to Him.'[165] The Śvetāśvatara identifies the two, the personal and the impersonal, though

151. iv. 18.
152. vi. 11.
153. iii. 14.
154. iii. 20.
155. v. 13; vi. 5.
156. vi. 14.
157. vi. 19.
158. i. 9.
159. i. 12. Trividham brahmam etat. See also i. 7.
160. Saṁyuktam etat.
161. iii. 5.
162. iii. 17.
163. iv. 11.
164. Kaivalya, 24.
165. Rāmatāpanīya, i. 7. See Kaivalya, 18.

it makes the personal the creation of the impersonal Brahman, if such an act as creation be allowed. In relation to the world and the individuals in it, the absolute assumes personality. So long as the individual clings to his own individuality, the absolute is an other and so a personal god. But when the individual surrenders his individuality, the two become one.

We come across the theory of māyā, and God is said to be the controller of māyā. The Sāṁkhya account is accepted with modifications. Prakṛti ceases to be an independent power, but becomes of the very nature of God.[166] The world is created by God's own power (devātmaśakti).[167] 'As a spider spins its web with threads from its own body, so has the one God brought forth the world substance from out His own being and covered Himself therewith.'[168] The God makes manifold the one.[169] There is, however, no suggestion that the world is a delusive appearance. It is admitted that it hides from our vision the supreme reality.[170] The world is māyā, since we do not know how the impersonal develops into Īśvara, the world and the souls. Māyā in the sense of divine power is also admitted. Prakṛti is called māyā, since the self-conscious Īśvara develops the whole world through the force of not-self. Māyā in the sense of avidyā is recognised, since the display of the world hides the one spirit in it all. These different significations are not irreconcilable, though confusion will result if we do not carefully distinguish them.

The theory of kalpas is put forth as a compromise between the accounts of creation given in the Upaniṣads and the endlessness of saṁsāra. According to the latter, actions of each life-history issue in the next life. Each life thus presupposes an earlier and there cannot be any first life, and so there cannot be any creation of the world at a particular point. We yet hear of the creation of the world as an event recurring periodically from all eternity. The universe once created persists through an entire kalpa, or world period, after which it returns into the supreme God, only to issue again from Him. The cause of this re-issue is that the works of the soul still survive and demand a fresh creation or a renewed existence for their expiation. The idea of a periodical dissolution and recreation of the universe is common

166. iv. 9–10.
167. i. 3.
168. vi. 10.
169. vi. 12. Ekaḥ rūpam bahudhā yaḥ karoti.
170. v. 1.

to the Bhagavadgītā, the Śvetāśvatara and epic thought.[171] 'He dwells in all creatures and burning with fury at the end of time, He as lord dashes to pieces all created things.'[172] 'He is the God who many times spreads forth one net after another in space and again draws it in.'[173] The later Upaniṣads make much of this idea. 'It is He who, when the universe is dissolved, remains alone on the watch, and it is He who then (again) from the depths of space wakens to life the pure spirits.'[174] For the single creation of the Upaniṣads, we get an eternally recurring process, a recreation occurring after each dissolution, determined by the actions of the souls.

Being a theistic religion, the Śvetāśvatara draws a distinction between the worshipper and the worshipped,[175] soul and God, though it is a distinction of degree. By meditating on God, by devoting oneself to Him, the ignorance of man is dispelled.[176] Bhakti is inculcated and the grace of God is said to be the cause of the freedom of man.[177] But God is not capricious and in granting His favours is guided by certain principles. The doctrine of prapatti, or self-surrender, is suggested.[178] There is an appearance of conflict between meditation and worship. 'This absolute Brahman should be thought as eternal and as always in one's own soul, for beside Him there is nothing to be known; knowing the individual soul as the enjoyer, the objects of enjoyment, and dispenser, all these three even as Brahman, he obtains liberation.[179]

The soul after death has to take one of the three paths: that of the gods acquired by knowledge, that of the fathers acquired by good karma, and the lower one which evildoers traverse.[180] We are released from all bonds when we know the Creator.[181] Till then, we shall have to assume various bodily forms in accordance with the nature of our desires. 'In this wheel of Brahma (brahma-cakra), which is the support as well as the end of all beings,

171. B.G., ix. 7; see also viii. 17–19.
172. iii. 2. Śvetāśvatara Up.
173. v. 3; see also vi. 3–4.
174. Maitrī Up., vi. 17.
175. iv. 6–7; 1. 8.
176. 1. 10; iv. 4–6.
177. iii. 20; see also 1. 16. 2. 2. 3. 12. 6. 6 and 21.
178. vi. 18.
179. i. 12.
180. v. 7.
181. v. 13.

which is infinite, roams about the pilgrim soul when it fancies itself and the supreme Ruler different; it obtains immortality when it is uplifted by Him.'[182]

XII

THE CODE OF MANU

Before we take up the Bhagavadgītā we may refer briefly to the Code of Manu, to which a high position is assigned among the smṛtis. Attempts are made to relate the author of this law book with the Manu mentioned in the Vedas.[183] In the Ṛg-Veda he is often called the father Manu.[184] He is the founder of the social and moral order, who first settled the dharma. He is the progenitor of mankind. Though he may not be an individual law-giver, the dharmaśāstra ascribed to him is held in great respect. 'A smṛti opposed to Manu is not approved.'[185]

Sir William Jones assigns to the Code of Manu a very early date, 1250 BC. Schlegel holds that its date cannot be later than 1000 BC. Monier Williams puts it at about 500 BC.[186] Weber considers the text to be more recent than the latest parts of the Mahābhārata. The author is familiar with Vedic literature, and refers to previous legislators and traditions. Weber, Max Müller and Burnell think that the versified edition of the Mānavadharmaśāstra is a later rendering of an older treatise in prose. It is said to be 'a work belonging to the Mānavas, one of the six subdivisions of the Maitrāyaṇīya school of the Black Yajur-Veda, of which a few adherents still exist in the Bombay Presidency.' In support of the opinion Burnell quotes Whitney.[187] From the nature of its style and language, the Code of Manu is assigned to the epic period. Like the Mahābhārata and the Purāṇas, this book is of a popular character intended for those who cannot get to the fountain head. It shows the close relation between law and religion. Its main purpose is not philosophy Medhātithi recognises the philosophical portions to be more or less prefatory in their character. The philosophical views found in chapters i and ii are substantially the same as those of the Purāṇas.

182. i. 6.
183. R.V., viii 27.
184. R.V., i. 80. 16; i. 124. 2; ii. 33. 13.
185. See Taittirīya Saṁhitā, ii. 2. 10. 2; iii. 1. 9. 4.
186. *Indian Wisdom*, p. 215.
187. Burnell, *The Ordinances of Manu*, Introduction, p. xviii.

As Colebrooke asserts in his essays, we have in Manu the Pourāṇik Sāṁkhya mixed up with the Vedānta.[188] The account of creation given in Manu has nothing distinctive about it.[189] It is based on the hymn of creation of the Ṛg-Veda. The ultimate reality is Brahman, which soon manifests a dualism between the self-existent Hiraṇyagarbha and darkness. 'He desiring to produce begins of many kinds from his own body, first with a thought created the waters and placed his seed in them. That seed became a golden egg equal to the sun in brilliancy; in that egg he himself was born as Brahmā, the progenitor of the whole world ... that divine one who resided in the egg divided it into two halves, from which he formed heaven and earth, and between them the middle sphere, the eight points of the horizon and the eternal abode of the waters.... Thence he drew forth the mind, the self-sense, and then the great principle soul and all products affected by the three qualities, and in their order he five organs which perceive the objects of sensation.' Regarding the ultimate metaphysical position of the book, much discussion centres round the statement: 'This existed in the shape of darkness unperceived, destitute of distinctive marks, unattainable by reasoning, unknowable, wholly immersed as it were in deep sleep.'[190] Darkness (tamaḥ) is generally interpreted as mūlaprakṛti, the root evolvent of the Sāṁkhya philosophy. 'Tamobhutam' means absorbed in this prakṛti. Rāghavānanda, the Vedāntin commentator, makes 'tamaḥ' mean avidyā, or ignorance. The world is said to be evolved from the darkness through the causal efficiency of Hiraṇyagarbha in the order accepted by the Sāṁkhya system. The world is also called the śarīra, or the body of the Hiraṇyagarbha, and the souls his creation. The explanation of the account of creation varies with the opinions of the critics themselves. The doctrine of guṇas,[191] the conception of trimūrti,[192] and the idea of sūkṣmaśarīra,[193] or the subtle body, are all to be met with.

The Code of Manu is essentially a dharmaśāstra, an ethical code. It glorifies custom and convention at a time when they were being undermined. The loosening of traditional doctrine lightened the hold of

188. *Miscellaneous Essays*, vol. i., p. 249.
189. i. 5 ff.
190. Āsīd idaṁ tamobhūtam aprajñātam alakṣaṇam
Apratarkyam avijñeyam prasuptam iva sarvataḥ. i. 5.
191. xii. 24.
192. i. 10.
193. xii. 16–17.

dogma and authority. Respectability is the reply of common sense to reckless romanticism. Manu bases his ordinances on ancient usages which prevailed in the Hindu settlements on the banks of the Ganges. He admits Vedic sacrifices[194] and regards caste as an ordinance of God.[195] He favours asceticism, and yet he tells us that we have to surrender only the desires opposed to dharma.[196] Along with much that is defective there are some flashes of genius and insight. 'To be mothers were women created, and to be fathers men.'[197] 'He only is a perfect man who consists (of three persons united), his wife, himself and his offspring.' The husband is declared to be one with the wife.[198] Social duties are to be fulfilled first and foremost. 'A twice-born man who seeks final liberation, without having studied the Vedas, without having begotten, and without having offered sacrifices, sinks downwards.'[199] 'The tapas of a Brāhmin is concentrated study, of the Kṣatriya protection of the weak, of the Vaiśya trade and agriculture, of the Śūdra service of others.'[200]

Moral conduct is that which has a predominance of the quality of sattva and that which does not make for future existence.[201] He is the ideal hero who has conquered all. Pain is subjection to other people and pleasure is subjection to self.[202] 'He who sacrifices to the self alone, equally recognising the self in all creative beings and all creative beings in the self, becomes self-governing, self-luminous.'[203] Morality, however, is relative to the effects of our acts on future life. Conduct which has a tendency to bring about a good birth is good conduct, while that which brings about a bad birth is bad conduct. But both of these are inferior to that supreme conduct which enables us to reach perfection or cessation from rebirth.

We cannot say that Manu is an exclusive advocate of the established order whose system provides no scope for progress. There are according

194. iii. 76.
195. i. 31.
196. iv. 176.
197. ix. 96.
198. ix. 45.
199. vi. 37.
200. See Bhagavan Das, *Hindu Social Organisation* and The International Journal of Ethics, October, 1922, on *The Hindu Dharma*.
201. xii. 89.
202. iv. 1. 160. Sarvam paravaśam duḥkham sarvam ātmavasaṁ sukham.
203. xii. 91; see also 118.

to him four ways of determining right and wrong: Veda, smṛti, ācāra and conscience. The three former make for social order, but social progress is guaranteed by the last. We can do what is agreeable to our conscience (ātmanaḥ priyam).[204] We are allowed to do whatever is convincing to our reason.[205] Manu admits the value of the inner witness, the voice of God within us, the antarātmā.[206]

REFERENCES

TELANG, Bhagavadgītā, Anugītā, etc., S.B.E., vol. viii.
HOPKINS, The Great Epic of India, chap. iii.
C.V. VAIDYA, Epic India, chap. xvii.
R.G. BHANDARKAR, Vaiṣṇavism, Śaivism, etc.
HEM CHANDRA RAY CHAUDHURI, Early History of the Vaiṣṇava Sect.
BÜHLER, The Laws of Manu, S.B.E., vol. xxv.

204. ii. 12.
205. Manaḥ pūtam samācaret, vi. 46.
206. iv. 161.

CHAPTER IX

The Theism of the Bhagavadgītā

■ The importance of the Gītā in Indian thought—Its universal significance—Date—Relation to the Mahābhārata—The Vedas—The Upaniṣads—Buddhism—The Bhāgavata religion—The Sāṁkhya and the Yoga—Indian commentaries on the Gītā—The Gītā ethics is based on metaphysics—The problem of reality—The real in the objective and the subjective worlds—Brahman and the world—Puruṣottama—Intuition and thought—Higher and lower prakṛti—The avatārs—The nature of the universe—Māyā—Creation—The individual soul—Plurality of souls—Rebirth—The ethics of the Gītā—Reason, will and emotion—Jñāna mārga—Science and philosophy—Patañjali's Yoga—The Jñāni—Bhakti mārga—The personality of God—The religious consciousness—Karma mārga—The problem of morality—The moral standard—Disinterested action—Guṇas—The Vedic theory of sacrifices—Caste—Is work compatible with mokṣa?—The problem of human freedom—The integral life of spirit—Ultimate freedom and its character. ■

I

THE BHAGAVADGĪTĀ

The Bhagavadgītā which forms part of the Bhīṣma parva of the Mahābhārata is the most popular religious poem of Sanskrit literature. It is said to be 'the most beautiful, perhaps the only true philosophical song existing in any known tongue.'[1] It is a book conveying lessons of philosophy, religion and ethics. It is not looked upon as a śruti, or a revealed scripture, but is regarded as a smṛti, or a tradition. Yet if the hold which a work has on the mind of man is any clue to its importance, then the Gītā is the most influential work in Indian thought. Its message of deliverance is simple. While only the rich could but off the gods by their sacrifices, and only the cultured could pursue the way of knowledge, the Gītā teaches a method which is within the reach of all, that of bhakti, or devotion to God. The poet makes the teacher the very God descended into humanity. He is supposed to address Arjuna, the representative man, at a great crisis

1. William von Humboldt.

in his life. Arjuna comes to the battlefield, convinced of the righteousness of his cause and prepared to fight the enemy. At the psychological moment he shrinks from his duty. His conscience is troubled, his heart is torn with anguish and his state of mind, 'like to a little kingdom, suffers then the nature of an insurrection.' If to slay is to sin, it is a worse sin to slay those to whom we owe love and worship. Arjuna typifies the struggling individual who feels the burden and the mystery of the world. He has not yet built within himself a strong centre of spirit from which he can know not only the unreality of his own desires and passions, but also the true status of the world opposing him. The despondency of Arjuna is not the passing mood of a disappointed man, but is the feeling of a void, a sort of deadness felt in the heart, exciting a sense of the unreality of things. Arjuna is ready to repudiate his life if necessary. He does not, however, know what is right for him to do. He is faced by a terrible temptation and passes through an intense inward agony. His cry is a simple yet tremendous one, significant of the tragedy of man, which all who can see beyond the actual drama of the hour can recognise. The mood of despair in which Arjuna is found in the first chapter of the Gītā is what the mystics call the dark night of the soul, an essential step in the upward path. The further stages of illumination and realisation are found in the course of the dialogue. From the second chapter onwards we have a philosophical analysis. The essential thing in man is not the body or the senses, but the changeless spirit. The mind of Arjuna is switched on to a new path. The life of the soul is symbolised by the battlefield of Kurukṣetra, and the Kauravas are the enemies who impede the progress of the soul. Arjuna attempts to recapture the kingdom of man by resisting the temptations and controlling the passions. The path of progress is through suffering and self-abnegation. Arjuna tries to evade the rigorous ordeal by subtle arguments and specious excuses. Kṛṣṇa stands for the voice of God, delivering his message in thrilling notes, warning Arjuna against dejection of spirit. The opening chapter shows great insight into the heart of man, its conflict of motives, the force of selfishness and the subtle whisperings of the Evil One. As the dialogue proceeds the dramatic element disappears. The echoes of the battlefield die away, and we have only an interview between God and man. The chariot of war becomes the lonely cell of meditation, and a corner of the battlefield where the voices of the world are stilled, a fit place for thoughts on the supreme.

The teacher is the favourite god of India, who is at once human and divine. He is the god of beauty and love, whom his devotees enthrone on the wings of birds, on the petals of flowers, on whatever they most delight in of all that lives on earth. The poet vividly imagines how an incarnate God would speak of Himself. There is support for the poet's device to make Kṛṣṇa say that he was Brahman. In the Vedānta Sūtras,[2] the Vedic passage where Indra declares himself to be Brahman is explained on the hypothesis that Indra is only referring to the philosophical truth that the Ātman in man is one with the Supreme Brahman. When Indra says 'Worship me,' he means 'worship the God I worship.' On a similar principle Vāmadeva's declaration that he is Manu and Sūrya is explained. Besides, the Gītā teaches that an individual freed from passion and fear and purified by the fire of wisdom attains to the state of God. Kṛṣṇa of the Gītā stands for the infinite in the finite, the God in man concealed within the folds of flesh and the powers of sense.

The message of the Gītā is universal in its scope. It is the philosophical basis of popular Hinduism. The author is a man of deep culture, catholic rather than critical. He does not lead a missionary movement; he addresses no sect, establishes no school, but opens the way to all the winds that blow. He sympathises with all forms of worship, and is therefore well fitted for the task of interpreting the spirit of Hinduism which is unwilling to break up culture into compartments and treat other forms of thought and practices in a spirit of negation.[3] The Gītā appeals to us not only by its force of thought and majesty of vision, but also by its fervour of devotion and sweetness of spiritual emotion. Though the Gītā did much to develop spiritual worship and undermine inhuman practices, still on account of its non-critical attitude it did not destroy altogether false modes of worship.

The tone of the Gītā is dogmatic, and its author does not suspect that is is possible for him to err. He gives the truth as he sees it, and he seems to see it in its entirety and many-sidedness, and to believe in its saving power. 'In the Gītā there is a sage that speaks in the fullness and enthusiasm of his knowledge and of his feelings, and not a philosopher brought up in any school who divides his material in conformity to a settled method and arrives at the last steps of his doctrines through the clue of a set of systematic ideas.'[4] The Gītā stands midway between a philosophical system and a poetic inspiration. We do not have here the illimitable suggestiveness

2. i. 1. 30.
3. B.G., iii. 29.
4. *Indian Antiquary*, 1918, p. 3. Garbe's Introduction to the Bhagavadgītā.

of the Upaniṣads, since it is a deliberately intellectual solution of the problem of life. It is designed to meet a situation complicated by troubles of conscience and confusion of mind.

The main spirit of the Gītā is that of the Upaniṣads; only there is a greater emphasis on the religious side. The thin abstractions of the Upaniṣads could not satisfy the many-sided needs of the soul. The other attempts to solve the secret of life were more theistic in their texture. The author of the Gītā found that men could not be made to love logic. So he took his stand on the Upaniṣads, drew out their religious implications, galvanised them into a living system by incorporating with them popular mythology and national imagination.

II

DATE

The question of the date of the Bhagavadgītā cannot be easily settled. Since it forms a part of the Mahābhārata, it is sometimes doubted whether it is an interpolation added to the text at a later period. According to Talboys Wheeler, that 'Kṛṣṇa and Arjuna on the morning of the first day of the war, when both armies are drawn out in battle array and hostilities are about to begin,' should 'enter into a long and philosophical dialogue respecting the various forms of devotion which lead to the emancipation of the soul,' is unnatural. Telang, agreeing partially with this judgment, argues that the Bhagavadgīta is an independent work appropriated by the author of the Mahābhārata for his own purposes.[5] Though a philosophical discussion may be 'incongruous and irrelevant' at the beginning of the battle, still there is no doubt that only grave crises such as the battlefield stimulate in thinking minds thoughts about the ultimate values. Only then do spiritually disposed minds acquire the tension necessary to break the barricades of sense and touch the inner reality. It is possible that Arjuna might have had pointed advice from his friend Kṛṣṇa which the poet worked up into the poem of seven hundred verses. The author of the Mahābhārata is anxious to elaborate the principles of dharma whenever he has an opportunity, and he does so in the present context.

There are internal references to the Bhagavadgītā in the Mahābhārata which clearly indicate that from the time of the composition of the

5. S.B.E., vol. viii., Introduction, pp. 5–6.

Mahābhārata the Gītā has been looked upon as a genuine part of it.[6] The stylistic resemblances between the Gītā and the Mahābhārata show that they belong to one whole.[7] In the main views about other systems of philosophy and religion, there is also agreement. Karma is preferred to akarma.[8] The attitude to the Vedic sacrifices,[9] the statements of the order of creation,[10] the account of the Sāṁkhya theory of guṇas,[11] and Patañjali's Yoga,[12] and the description of Viśvarūpa,[13] are more or less the same. Nor can we say that the principles of reconciliation are peculiar to the Gītā.

Even when we assign the Bhagavadgītā to the Mahābhārata as a genuine part of it, we cannot be sure of its date, since there are products of different periods included in it. Telang in a learned introduction to his Bhagavadgītā deals with the general character of its teaching, its archaic style, its versification and its internal references, and argues that the work belongs to a period earlier than the third century BC. Sir R.G. Bhandarkar thinks that the Gītā is at least as old as the fourth century BC. Garbe assigns the original Gītā to 200 BC, and the present form of it to AD 200. Śaṁkara (ninth century AD) comments on it, and Kālidāsa knows it. In his Raghuvaṁśa[14] there is found a passage akin to a Gītā verse. Bāṇa refers to the Gītā, and these two authors belong to the fifth and seventh century AD. The Purāṇas (second century AD) contain many Gītās composed after the manner of the Bhagavadgītā. Bhāsa in his Karṇabhāra has a passage which reads like an echo[15] of a verse from the Gītā. Bhāsa is sometimes assigned to the second or the fourth century AD, and sometimes to the second century BC. Even on the former view, the Gītā must have been earlier. Bodhayāna's Gṛhya Sūtras are familiar with Vāsudeva worship, and contain a statement attributed to the Lord (Bhagavān), which seems to be a quotation from the Bhagavadgītā.[16] This is also true of his Pitṛmedha Sūtras. If Āpastamba

6. Ādi Parva, 2. 69; 1. 179; 2. 247.
7. Tilak, Gītā-rahasya, Appendix; S.B.E., vol. viiii., Introduction.
8. B.G., chap. ii; Vanaparva, chap. xxxii.
9. Śāntiparva, 267; see also Manu, chap. iii.
10. B.G., chaps. vii and viii; Sāntiparva, 231.
11. B.G., xiv and xv; Aśvamedhaparva, 36–39; Śāntiparva, 285 and 300–311.
12. B.G., chap. vi; Śāntiparva, 239 and 300.
13. Udyogaparva, 170; Aśvamedhaparva, 55; Śāntiparva, 339; and Vanaparva, 99.
14. 10. 31. Cf. B.G., 3. 22.
15. Hato pi labhate svargaṁ jitvā tu labhate yaśaḥ. Cf. B.G., ii. 37.
16. 2. 22. 9. Cf. B.G., ix. 26.

belongs to the third century BC,[17] then Bodhayāna is earlier by a century or two. We shall not, I believe, be far wrong if we assign the Gītā to the fifth century BC[18]

III

RELATION TO OTHER SYSTEMS

Almost all the views which prevailed in the age influenced the author of the Gītā, who brings to a focus the rays of religious light cast at random in the world about him. It is necessary for us to note the exact relations between the Gītā on the one hand and the Vedas, the Upaniṣads, Buddhism, the Bhāgavata religion and the systems of Sāṁkhya and Yoga on the other.

The Gītā does not throw overboard the authority of the Vedas. It considers the Vedic injunctions to be quite valid for men of a particular cultural status. One cannot attain perfection, according to the Gītā, without obeying the ordinances of the Vedas. Sacrificial acts are required to be performed without any expectation of reward.[19] After a particular stage, the performance of Vedic rites tends to become an obstacle to the attainment of supreme perfection. The exalted character of the Vedic gods is not accepted. Though the Vedic observances secure for us power and wealth, they do not take us straight to freedom. Deliverance can be found by the discovery of self. When the secret of salvation is in our possession there is no need for the performance of Vedic karmas.[20]

The philosophic background of the Gītā is taken from the Upaniṣads. Some verses are common to the Upaniṣads and the Gītā.[21] The discussions of Kṣetra and the Kṣetrajña, Kṣara and Akṣara are based on the Upaniṣads. The account of the supreme reality is also derived from the same source. Bhakti is a direct development of the upāsana of the Upaniṣads. The love for the supreme involves the giving up of all else. 'What shall we do with

17. S.B.E., vol. ii., Introduction, p. xliii. Cf. vol. xiv., p. xliii.

18. If the references in the Dharma Sūtras are regarded as interpolated texts, then the Gītā may be assigned to the third or the second century BC.

19. xvii. 12.

20. ii. 42–45; ix. 20–21.

21. B.G., ii. 29, and Kaṭha Up., ii. 7; B.G., ii. 20; viii. 11, and Kaṭha Up., ii. 19; ii. 15; B.G, iii. 42, and Kaṭha Up., iii. 10; B.G., vi. 11 and Śvet, Up., ii. 10; B.G., vi. 13, and Śvet. Up., ii. 8.

progeny, when we have got this being, this world to live in?'[22] Ideas of devotion to the supreme, the conquest of self and the attainment of a condition of peace and serenity are in the atmosphere of the period. Disinterested work is defended even in the Upaniṣads.[23] That non-attachment results from an elevated state of mind is brought out in the Upaniṣads.[24] The practical and the religious tendencies of the Upaniṣads are so developed as not to supersede the teachings of earlier thinkers. The cold flawless perfection was no doubt a magnificent explanation of the world, but it was not quite suited to be a transforming power of life. The vogue of the Bhāgavata religion inclined the author of the Gītā to give a glow and a penetrating power to the absolute of the Upaniṣads. He made it into a personal Īśvara, called by the different names of Śiva, Viṣṇu, etc. All the same, the author is aware that he is only revivifying a dead past and not propounding a new theory. 'This imperishable yoga I declared to Vivasvat, and he taught it to Manu, Manu to Ikṣvāku,' and this secret is now revealed to Arjuna by Kṛṣṇa.[25] This passage indicates that the message of the Gītā is the ancient wisdom taught by Viśvāmitra, the seer of Gāyatrī, and the ṛṣi of the third cycle of the Ṛg-Veda and Rāma, Kṛṣṇa, Gautama Buddha, and other teachers of the Solar line. The full name of the Gītā, as it is evident from the colophon at the end of each chapter, is the Upaniṣad of the name of the Bhagavadgītā. The traditional account of the relation between the Gītā and the Upaniṣads is contained in the passage now almost too familiar for quotation, that 'the Upaniṣads are the cows, Kṛṣṇa is the milker, Arjuna the calf, and the nectar-like Gītā is the excellent milk.'

The Bhāgavata religion was the immediate stimulus to the synthesis of the Bhagavadgītā. It is actually suggested that the teaching of the Gītā is identical with the doctrine of the Bhāgavatas. It is sometimes called the Harigītā.[26]

There is no mention of Buddhism, though some of the views of the Gītā are like those of Buddhism. Both protest against the absolute authority fo the Vedas and attempt to relax the rigours of caste by basing it on a less untenable foundation. Both are the manifestations of the same spiritual upheaval which shook the ritualistic religion, though the Gītā was the more

22. Bṛh. Up., iv. 4. 22.
23. Īśā. Up.
24. Chān. Up., iv. 14. 3; Brih., iv. 4. 23.
25. iv. 1–3.
26. Śāntiparva, 349. 10.

conservative, and therefore less thorough going protest. Buddha announced the golden means, though his own teaching was not quite true to it. To prefer celibacy to marriage, fasting to feasting, is not to practise the golden mean. The Gītā denounces the religious madness of the hermits and the spiritual suicide of saints who prefer darkness to daylight and sorrow to joy. It is possible to attain salvation without resorting to the cult of narrowness and death. The word nirvāṇa occurs in the Gītā,[27] but this does not show any borrowing from Buddhism, since it is not peculiar to it. In the descriptions of the ideal man the Gītā and Buddhism agree.[28] As a philosophy and religion, the Gītā is more complete than Buddhism, which emphasises overmuch the negative side. The Gītā adopts the ethical principles of Buddhism, while it by implication condemns the negative metaphysics of Buddhism as the root of all unbelief and error. It is more in continuity with the past, and therefore had a better fortune than Buddhism in India.

According to Garbe, 'the teachings of the Sāṁkhya-Yoga constitute almost entirely the foundation of the philosophical observations of the Bhagavadgītā. In comparison with them the Vedānta takes a second place. Sāṁkhya and Yoga are often mentioned by name, while the Vedānta appears only once (Vedāntakṛt, xv. 15), and then in the sense of Upaniṣad or treatise. Accordingly, when we think merely of the rôle which the philosophical systems play in the Gītā as it has been handed down to us, and when we consider the irreconcilable contradictions between the Sāṁkhya-Yoga and the Vedānta, which can only be done away with by carefully distinguishing between the old and the new, the Vedāntic constituents of the Bhagavadgītā prove not to belong to the original poem. Whether we investigate the Gītā from the religious or the philosophical side, the same result is reached.' The terms Sāṁkhya-Yoga when they occur in the Gītā do not represent the classical schools of Sāṁkhya and Yoga, but only the reflective and the meditative methods of gaining salvation.[29] Besides, during the period of the Gītā there was no clear-cut distinction between the Sāṁkhya-Yoga on one side and the Vedānta on the other, which alone can justify Garbe's interpretation. Fitz-Edward Hall is more

27. vi. 15.

28. ii. 55–72; iv. 16–23; v. 18–28; xii. 13–16. Cf. Dhammapada, 360–423; Suttanipāta, Munisutta, i. 7 and 14.

29. B.G., ii. 39; iii. 3; v. 4–5; xiii. 24. In xviii. 13 there is a reference to the philosophy of Sāṁkhya. Madhva quotes a verse from Vyāsa Smṛti, where Sāṁkhya means knowledge of spirit, ātmatattvavijñānam. See his commentary on B.G., ii. 40.

correct when he says: 'In the Upaniṣads, the Bhagavadgītā, and other ancient Hindu books, we encounter, in combination, the doctrines, which after having been subjected to modifications that rendered them as wholes irreconcilable, were distinguished at an uncertain period into what have for many ages been styled the Sāṁkhya and the Vedānta.'[30] The psychology and the order of the creation of the Sāṁkhya are accepted by the Gītā, though the metaphysical implications of the Sāṁkhya are rejected by it.[31] Kapila's name is mentioned, though not that of Patañjali. We cannot, however, be sure that this Kapila is the founder of the Sāṁkhya system. Even if it be so, it does not follow that the system in all its details was elaborated by that time. The terms buddhi or understanding, ahaṁkāra or self-sense, and manas or mind, occur, though not always in their Sāṁkhya significations. The same is true of prakṛti.[32] While the Sāṁkhya deliberately avoids the question of the existence of God, the Gītā is most anxious to establish it.

Though the distinction between puruṣa and prakṛti is recognised, the dualism is overcome. Puruṣa is not an independent element, but only a prakṛti or form of God. The psychical intelligence is the higher nature. When we deal with the Sāṁkhya system we shall see how it looks upon all the modes of prakṛti or nature as phenomena implying a permanent subject to whom they appear and for whom they exist. Though prakṛti or nature is unconscious, its activities are purposive, meant as they are for the freedom of the soul. The teleological character of its activities is not in accord with its alleged unconsciousness. In the Gītā the difficulty is overcome. There is a spiritual fact behind the play of prakṛti or nature. Puruṣa or soul is not the independent reality which it is in the Sāṁkhya system. Its nature is not mere awareness, but bliss also. The Gītā does not recognise any ultimate distinctness of individual souls.[33] It also believes in the existence of an Uttamapuruṣa, or supreme soul. Yet the character of the individual soul and its relation to nature as given in the Bhagavadgītā show the influence of the Sāṁkhya theory.[34] Puruṣa is the spectator, and not the actor. Prakṛti does everything. He who thinks 'I act' is mistaken. To realise the separateness of puruṣa from prakṛti, soul from nature, is the end of

30. Preface to Sāṁkhyasāra, p. 7.
31. ii. 11–16, 18–30; ii. 27–29; v. 14; vii. 4; xiii. 5.
32. iii. 33; iv. 6; vii. 4; ix. 8; xi. 51; xiii. 20; xviii. 59.
33. vii. 4; xiii. 20–22; see also V.S., 2. 1. 1., and S.B. on it.
34. Sāṁkhya Kārikā, 62; B.G., xiii. 34.

life. The theory of the guṇas or qualities is accepted. 'There is no entity on earth or heaven among the devas that is free from the three qualities born of prakṛti.'[35] The guṇas constitute the triple cord of bondage. So long as we are subject to them we have to wander in the circuit of existence. Freedom is deliverance from the guṇas. The physiological account of the internal organs and the senses is found here as in the Sāṁkhya.[36]

The Gītā refers to yoga practices also. When Arjuna asks Kṛṣṇa as to how mind, which is admittedly fickle and boisterous, can be brought under control, Kṛṣṇa answers by saying that abhyāsa, or practice, and vairāgya, or indifference to worldly objects, should be acquired.[37]

IV

THE TEACHING OF THE GĪTĀ

At the time of the Gītā many different views about ultimate reality and man's destiny prevailed. There were the Upaniṣad traditions based on the intuition of the soul, the Sāṁkhya doctrine that liberation can be obtained by freeing oneself from contact with nature, the Karma Mīmāṁsā view that by fulfilling our duties we attain perfection, the way of devotional feeling which holds that by attaining exaltation of the heart, the gladness of freedom can be obtained, and the Yoga system, which declares that man is free when the quiet life of the soul takes the place of the vari-coloured light of the world. The supreme spirit is viewed either as an impersonal absolute or a personal lord. The Gītā attempts to synthesise the heterogeneous elements and fuse them all into a single whole. That is why we find in it apparently conflicting views about the end of freedom and the means of discipline. Finding that the Gītā is not a consistent piece of doctrine, different writers try to account for it in different ways. Garbe and Hopkins suppose that several writers in different centuries have been at work upon it. According to Garbe the original Gītā was written in the second century BC as a theistic tract, based on the Sāṁkhya-Yoga, though in the second century AD it was adapted by the upholders of the Upaniṣad monism. 'These two doctrines—the theistic and the pantheistic—are mixed up with each other, and follow each other, sometimes quite unconnected and

35. xviii. 40; xiv. 5.

36. iii. 40–42; xiii. 5.

37. See B.G., vi. 33–34. Śaṁkara sees a reference to the Nyāya system in x. 32. See S.B.G. on it.

sometimes loosely connected. And it is not the case that the one is represented as a lower exoteric and the other as the higher esoteric doctrine. It is nowhere taught that theism is a preliminary step to the knowledge of the reality or that it is its symbol, and that the pantheism of the Vedānta is the ultimate reality itself; but the two beliefs are treated of almost throughout as though there was indeed no difference between them, either verbal or real.'[38] Hopkins makes the Gītā a Kṛṣṇaite version of a Viṣṇuite poem, which was itself a late Upaniṣad. Keith believes that it was originally an Upaniṣad of the type of the Śvetāśvatara, but was later adapted to the cult of Kṛṣṇa. Holtzmann looks upon it as a Viṣṇuite remodelling of a pantheistic poem. Barnett thinks that different streams of tradition became confused in the mind of the author. Deussen makes it a late product of the degeneration of the monistic thought of the Upaniṣads, belonging to a period of transition from theism to realistic atheism.

There is no need to accept any of these conjectures. The Gītā is an application of the Upaniṣad ideal to the new situations which arose at the time of the Mahābhārata. In adapting the idealism of the Upaniṣads to a theistically minded people, it attempts to derive a religion from the Upaniṣad philosophy. It shows that the reflective spiritual idealism of the Upaniṣads has room for the living warm religion of personal devotion. The absolute of the Upaniṣads is revealed as the fulfilment of the reflective and the emotional demands of human nature. This change of emphasis from the speculative to the practical, from the philosophical to the religious, is also to be found in the later Upaniṣads, where we have the saviour responding to the cry of faith. The Gītā attempts a spiritual synthesis which could support life and conduct on the basis of the Upaniṣad truth, which it carries into the life-blood of the Indian people.

The question whether the Gītā succeeds in gathering up the different tendencies of thought into a true whole remains to be answered in the course of our study. The Indian tradition has always felt that incongruous elements are fused together in it, while the Western scholar has persisted that the brilliant fragments refuse to coalesce even in the skilled hands of the author. There is no use of dogmatising in the very premises of the discussion.[39]

38. I.A., December 1918.

39. There are several commentaries on the Gītā by Indian writers, of which the chief are those by Vṛttikāra, Śaṁkara, Rāmānuja, Madhva, Vallabha, Nimbārka and Jñāneśvar. Ānandagiri says that the Vṛttikāra Bodhāyana, the author of a voluminous commentary on the Vedānta Sūtras, also wrote a vṛtti or gloss on the

The context in which the Gītā is said to be delivered points out how its central purpose is to solve the problem of life and stimulate right conduct. It is obviously an ethical treatise, a yoga śāstra. The Gītā was formulated in a period of ethical religion and so shared in the feeling of the age. Whatever peculiar adaptations the term yoga may have in the Gītā, it throughout keeps up its practical reference.[40] Yoga is getting to God, relating oneself to

---

Gītā (see Ānandagiri on S.B.G., ii. 10). According to him the Gītā teaches the method of the combined pursuit of Jñāna and Karma. Neither of them by itself leads to freedom. Śaṁkara believes that Jñāna or wisdom is the highest means to perfection, and contends that the identity of the individual soul with the supreme Brahman is to be realised by intuitional wisdom. The manyness of the world is traced to the imperfection of man. All action is the cause of bondage, since it is dependent on the false sense of duality. When true wisdom abolishes our ideas of duality, the soul is saved, and no action has any meaning thereafter. The other paths of Karma or work, Bhakti or devotion, Yoga or self-control, lead only to wisdom or Jñāna. See S.B.G., iii. 1. Rāmānuja distinguishes jīva or cit, world or acit, and God or Īśvara, and makes the two former constitute the body of God. In metaphysics he adopts thus a modified monism, and in practice insists on the path of devotion. He suggests by implication that the rules of caste should be maintained throughout. Both Śaṁkara and Rāmānuja subordinate Karma, though with different motives. Madhva repudiates the theory of māyā and accepts an ultimate distinction between the absolute Brahman and the individual souls. For him, also, devotion to God is the supreme way to bliss. Though Vallabha declares that Brahman and the purified soul are one, he yet makes jīva a part of Brahman. The world of māyā is not false, since māyā is only a power separated from Īśvara by his will. Grace of God is the only way by which the individual could be freed. According to Nimbārka the world and the souls are dependent on God in whom they exist, though in a subtle condition. His theory is called dualistic non-dualism. Jñāneśvar makes Patañjali's yoga the aim of the teaching of the Gītā. When there are so many views of the Gītā adopted by able minds, the task of the student is not an easy one. Its bold and brilliant syntheses and reconciliations do not always give us exact information as to how contradictory ideas are to be logically combined. There is no denying that the Gītā fosters a life of spirit. There is a romantic twilight which captures the imagination and uplifts our nature, so long as we are religiously minded and rely on dogmatic thought. But the critical intellect has to work on it with care before it can deduce a consistent system from it.

40. Yoga is practice as distinct from Sāṁkhya or knowledge. See Śvetāśvatara Upaniṣad, 'Sāṁkhyayogādigamyam,' knowable by knowledge and practice. Yoga also means karma, see Gītā, iii. 7; v. 1. 2; ix. 28; xiii. 24. The yoga of the Lord is spoken of as His wondrous power. See ix. 5; x. 7; xi. 8. Yoga also means getting things which we do not have. See ix. 22.

the power that rules the universe, touching the absolute. It is *yoking* not merely this or that power of the soul, but all the forces of heart, mind and will to God. It is the effort of man to unite himself to the deeper principle. We have to change the whole poise of the soul into something absolute and uncompromising and develop the strength to resist power and pleasure. Yoga thus comes to mean the discipline by which we can train ourselves to bear the shocks of the world with the central being of our soul untouched. It is the method or the instrument, upāya, by which the end can be gained. Patañjali's yoga is a system of psychic discipline by which we can clear the intellect, free the mind of its illusions and get a direct perception of reality. We can discipline the emotions and realise the supreme by a soul-surrender to God. We can train our will so as to make our whole life one continuous divine service. We can also perceive the divine in the nature of our being, watch it with ardent love and aspiration, till the spark grows into an infinite light. All these are different yogas or methods leading to the one supreme yoga or union with God. But no ethical message can be sustained if it is not backed up by a metaphysical statement. So the yoga śāstra of the Gītā is rooted in brahmavidyā, or knowledge of the spirit. The Gītā is a system of speculation as well as a rule of life, an intellectual search for truth as well as an attempt to make the truth dynamic in the soul of man. This is evident from the colophon at the end of each chapter, which has come down to us from a date which is unknown, that it is the yoga śāstra, or religious discipline of the philosophy of Brahman, 'brahmavidyānāṁ yogaśāstre.'

V

ULTIMATE REALITY

The problem of ultimate reality is here approached, as in the Upaniṣads, by the two ways of an analysis of the objective and of the subjective. The metaphysical bent of the author is clearly revealed in the second chapter, where he gives us the principle on which his scheme is based: 'Of the unreal there is no being, and of the real there is no non-being.'[41] The objective analysis proceeds on the basis of a distinction between substance and shadow, the immortal and the perishable, the akṣara and the kṣara. 'There are these two beings in the world, the destructible kṣara and the indestructible akṣara. The unchanging one is the akṣara.'[42] We cannot say

41. ii. 16.
42. xv. 16.

that the 'unchanging one' here referred to is the supreme reality, for in the very next verse the Gītā declares that 'the supreme being is another called the highest self, Paramātman, who as the inexhaustible Lord pervading the three worlds supports them.'[43] The author first distinguishes the permanent background of the world from its transitory manifestations, the prakṛti from its changes. Within this world of experience, 'imau loke,' we have the perishable and the permanent aspects. Though prakṛti is permanent when compared with the changes of the world, still it is not absolutely real, since it depends on the supreme Lord.[44] This supreme spirit is the true immortal, the abode of the eternal.[45] Rāmānuja, to suit his own special theory, makes kṣara stand for the principle of prakṛti, and akṣara for the individual soul, and regards Puruṣottama, or the supreme self, as superior to both these. It is possible for us to interpret the conception of Puruṣottama as that of the concrete personality which is superior to the false abstractions of the infinite and the finite. The only difficulty is that Brahman, declared to be the basis of the finite, cannot be looked upon as a mere abstraction. The Gītā distinguishes between the finite or the impermanent, and the infinite or the permanent. Whatever is limited or transitory is not real. All becoming is an untenable contradiction. That which becomes is not being. If it were being, it would not become. Since the things of the world are struggling to become something else, they are not real. Transitoriness marks all things on earth. In the background of our consciousness, there is the conviction that there is something that does not pass away. For nothing can come out of nothing. That ultimate being of reality is not the ever-changing prakṛti. It is the supreme Brahman. It is the eternal or rock-seated being, *kūṭasthasattā*, while the world is only timeless, endless existence, *anādipravāhasattā*. 'He sees truly who sees the supreme Lord abiding alike in all entities and not destroyed though they are destroyed.'[46] This eternal spirit dwells in all beings, and is therefore not a qualitatively distinct other to the finite. The Gītā believes in the reality of an infinite being underlying and animating all finite existences.

43. xv. 17.

44. It is said that 'there is another being unmanifested and eternal and distinct from this unmanifested principle, which is not destroyed when all existences are destroyed' (viii. 20).

45. viii. 21.

46. xiii. 27, see also viii. 20.

The individual self is ever unsatisfied with itself and is struggling always to become something else. In its consciousness of limitation, there is a sense of the infinite. The finite self which is limited, which ever tries to rise beyond its sad plight, is not ultimately real. The true self has the character of imperishableness. The Gītā tries to find out the element of permanence in the self, that which is always the subject and never the object. Kṣetra is the place or the object, and Kṣetrajña is the knower of the object or the subject.[47] What is known is not a property of the knower. In the self of man, there is the element of the knower that remains constant behind all changes. It is the eternal, immutable, timeless self-existence. Breaking up the individual self into its component parts of body, mind, soul, the Gītā tries to discover the element which *is* always. The body is not the permanent subject, for it has an end, being only a fleeting frame.[48] The sense life is brief and mutable.[49] The empirical mind is ever changing. All these are only objects for a subject, the instruments through which the soul works. They have no existence in their own right. The inner principle, the source of all knowledge, is in the words of the Gītā 'greater than the senses, the mind and the understanding.'[50] It is the element which combines and is present throughout even in deep sleep. This function of combination cannot be attributed to the senses or the understanding or a combination of these.[51] The principle of the subject is the indispensable basis on which the object world, including the empirical self, is based. If we drop the subject, the object vanishes. But the subject does not vanish even though the object disappears. The Gītā gives eloquent descriptions of this undying element. It is the lord of the body. 'He is not born nor does He die, nor having been, does He cease to be any more. Unborn, eternal, everlasting, ancient, He is not slain when the body is destroyed.'[52] 'Weapons do not reach it, flame does not burn it nor water wet it. Wind does not dry it. It is impenetrable, uncombustible ... perpetual, all pervading, stable, immovable, ancient.'[53]

About the nature of the supreme self, the Gītā account is rather puzzling. 'This inexhaustible supreme self, being without beginning and

47. xiii. 1 and 5–6.
48. ii. 13. 11. 18.
49. ii. 14.
50. iii. 42.
51. xiii. 6.
52. ii. 20.
53. ii. 22–25.

without qualities, does not act and is not tainted, though stationed in the body.'[54] It is viewed as a mere spectator. The self is akartṛ, non-doer. The whole drama of evolution belongs to the object world. Intelligence, mind, senses are looked upon as the developments of the unconscious prakṛti, which is able to bring about this ascent on account of the presence of spirit. The subject self is within us calm and equal, uncaught in the external world, though its support, source and immanent witness.

We have in the actual individuals of the world combinations of subject and object.[55] The empirical individuals are the divine principle of subject limited by contexts of object. In the world the subject and the object are always found together.[56] Only the object has not an ultimate transcendental existence. The subject superior to the object is the basis of the object. 'When a man sees all the variety of existence as rooted in one and all as emanating from that, he becomes one with the supreme.'[57] When the confusion with the object terminates, the subject in all is found to be the same. When Kṛṣṇa urges Arjuna not to grieve for the dead, he says that death is not extinction. The individual form may change, but the essence is not destroyed. Until perfection is obtained, individuality persists. However repeatedly the mortal frame is destroyed, the inner individuality preserves its identity and takes on a new form. Buoyed up by this faith, man has to work for self-knowledge. Our imperishableness is guaranteed either by way of endlessness or perfection. It is the unfolding of our implicit infinitude. It is by this affirmation of the soul, by this vindication of the intuition of the Upaniṣads, that the Ātman, or the pure subject, remains unaffected, even though our body be 'dust returning unto dust,' that Kṛṣṇa stills the unrest of Arjuna's mind.

> Never the spirit was born; the spirit shall cease to be never,
> Never was time it was not; end and beginning are dreams;
> Birthless and deathless and changeless remaineth the spirit for ever,
> Death hath not touched it at all, dead though the house of it seems.[58]

In the spirit of the Upaniṣads the Gītā identifies the two principles of the Ātman and the Brahman. Behind the fleeting senses and the body

54. xiii. 31.
55. xiii. 27.
56. xiii. 20–21.
57. xiii. 31.
58. Sir Edwin Arnold's translation.

there is the Ātman; behind the fleeting objects of the world there is Brahman. The two are one, being of identical nature. The reality of this is a matter of each man's experience to be realised for himself. Any endeavour to define the unchanging in terms of the changing fails. There is, however, no attempt in the Gītā to prove that the absolute discerned by intuition is the logical foundation of the world, though this is implied. If the world is to be an experience and not a chaotic confusion, then we require the reality of an unconditioned absolute. We should, however, be very careful not to oppose the infinite and the finite as two mutually exclusive spheres. This will lead us to a false view of the infinite. What strikes us at first is the distinction between the passing finite and the real infinite. But if this were all, then the infinite becomes finitised, converted into something limited, since the opposed and the excluded finite becomes the limit of the infinite. It is wrong to conceive the infinite as something pushed out of the being of the finite. It is the finite itself in its truth. It is the infinitised finite, the real in the finite, and not something lying side by side with it. If we overlook the infinite in the finite, we get an endless progress peculiar to the world of finitude or saṁsāra. This very endlessness is the sign of the infinite within the sphere of the finite. The finite reveals itself as nothing more than the infinite made finite. The distinction between the infinite and the finite is only a characteristic of loose thinking. In truth there is only the infinite, and the finite is nothing more than the finitisation of the infinite. It follows that terms like transcendence and immanence are inapplicable, since these assume a distinct 'other' to the absolute. Any category of thought is inadequate for the purposes of the absolute. It is described as neither being nor non-being, neither formed nor unformed.[59] The Gītā reiterates the Upaniṣad principle that the real is the immutable self-existence behind the cosmic world, with its space, time and causality.

The Gītā assets the truth of an advaita or non-dualism in philosophy. The supreme Brahman is the immutable self-existence 'of which the Vedāntins speak, to which the doers of the austerities attain.' It is the highest status and supreme goal of the soul's movement in time, though it is itself no movement, but a status original, eternal and supreme. In the unalterable eternity of Brahman, all that moves and evolves is founded. By it they exist; they cannot be without it, though it causes nothing, does nothing and determines nothing. The two, Brahman and the world, seem to be opposed

59. xiii. 12.

in features. Even though we repudiate the reality of saṁsāra and look upon it as a mere shadow, still there is the substance of which it is the shadow. The world of saṁsāra shows its unreality by its constant struggle to overreach itself, but the absolute Brahman is its own end, and looks to no end beyond itself. Since the world of saṁsāra is based on the absolute, the latter is sometimes said to be both the changeless and the changing. The endless details and the oppositions of the saṁsāra are there just to turn the mind in the direction where all oppositions are overcome and successions are embraced in a successionless consciousness. While all possible relatives and opposites are only based on it, it is not opposed to them, being their very substratum. We do not know how exactly the world of saṁsāra is based on the absolute Brahman, though we are sure that without the absolute there would be no saṁsāra. Thee is the silent sleeper as well as the seething sea. We do not know how exactly the two are related. We conceal our ignorance by the use of the word māyā. The two are one, yet they seem different, and the seeming is due to māyā. The transcendental reality, though untouched by the changes, still determines them. From the philosophical point of view we are obliged to stop here. 'Who could perceive directly and who could declare whence born or why this variegated creation?'[60]

The same problem when applied to the individual self becomes one of the relation of the free subject to the object. The bond between the immortal witness self and the flowing changes of consciousness, we do not know. Śaṁkara in this difficulty adopts the hypothesis of adhyāsa or super-position. The two, subject and object, cannot be related by way of saṁyoga or contact, since the subject is partless. The relation cannot be samavāya, or inseparable inherence, since the two are not related as cause and effect. Śaṁkara concludes, 'that it must be of the nature of mutual adhyāsa, i.e. it consists in confounding them as well as their attributes with each other, owing to the absence of a discrimination between the nature of object and that of subject, like the union of mother-of-pearl and silver or of rope and snake when they are mistaken the one for the other owing to the absence of discrimination. The union of the two is itself apparent, mithyājñāna, and it vanishes when a man attains to right knowledge.'[61] This theory is not found in the Gītā, however much it may be implied by it.

The metaphysical idealism of the Upaniṣads is transformed in the Gītā into a theistic religion, providing room for love, faith, prayer and devotion.

60. Taittirīya Brāhmaṇa, ii. 8–9.
61. S.B.G., xiii. 26.

So long as we do not have the vision of the absolute, but are working from the side of the empirical world, we can account for it only on the theory of the supreme godhead of Puruṣottama. The impersonality of the absolute is not its whole significance for man. The Gītā, anxious to adapt the Upaniṣad idealism to the daily life of mankind, supports a divine activity and participation in nature It tries to give us a God who satisfies the whole being of man, a real which exceeds the mere infinite and the mere finite. The supreme soul is the origin and cause of the world, the indivisible energy pervading all life. Moral attributes are combined with the metaphysical.[62] The Gītā refuses to commit the fallacy of taking distinctions for divisions. It reconciles all abstract oppositions. Thought cannot act without *creating distinctions and reconciling them*. The moment we think the absolute, we have to translate the truth of intuition into terms of thought. Pure 'being' is gone over into 'nothing,' and we have left in our hands a unity of being and nothing. This unity is as real as thought itself. Of course the Gītā does not tell us of the way in which the absolute as impersonal non-active spirit becomes the active personal Lord creating and sustaining the universe. The problem is considered to be intellectually insoluble. The mystery clears up only when we rise to the level of intuition. The transformation of the absolute into God is māyā or a mystery. It is also māyā in the sense that the transformed world is not so real as the absolute itself.

If through logic we try to understand the relation of the absolute to the world we assign to it a power or śakti. The inactive qualityless absolute, unrelated to any object, is converted by logic into the active personal Lord possessing power related to prakṛti or nature. We have 'Nārāyaṇa brooding over the waters' the eternal 'I' confronting the pseudo-eternal 'not I.' This latter is also called prakṛti or nature, since it generates the world. It is the source of delusion, since it hides the true nature of reality from mortal vision. The world is organically connected with the Puruṣottama. All things partake of the duality of being and non-being from Puruṣottama downwards. The element of negation is introduced into the absolute, and the unity is forced to unfold its inwardness in the process of becoming. The 'ancient urge to action' is located in the heart of Puruṣottama. The original unity is pregnant with the whole course of the world, which contains the past, the present and the future in a supreme now. Kṛṣṇa shows to Arjuna the

62. B.G., viii. 9 and 13.

whole viśvarūpa (worldform) in one vast shape.[63] In the radiance of eternity Arjuna sees nameless things, the form of Kṛṣṇa bursting the very bounds of existence, filling the whole sky and the universe, worlds coursing through him like cataracts. Contradiction constitutes the main spring of progress. Even God has the element of negativity or māyā, though He controls it. The supreme God puts forth His active nature or svāmprakṛtim and creates the jīvas, who work out their destinies along lines determined by their own nature. While all this is done by the supreme through his native power exercised in the perishable world, he has another aspect untouched by it all. He is the impersonal absolute as well as the immanent will. He is the causeless cause, the unmoved mover.

> He is within all beings—and without—
> Motionless, yet still moving; not discerned
> For subtlety of instant presence; close
> To all, to each; yet measurelessly far;
> Not manifold, and yet subsisting still
> In all which lives.
> The light of lights, he is in the heart of the dark
> Shining eternally.[64]

The supreme is said to be possessed of two natures higher, parā, and lower, aparā, answering to the conscious and the unconscious aspects of the universe. The lower parkṛti produces effects and modifications in the world of nature or of causes; the higher prakṛti gives rise to the puruṣas or the intelligent souls, in the world of ends or values. The two belong to one spiritual whole. Madhva cites a verse to this effect: 'There are two prakṛtis for God, jaḍa, or unconscious, and ajaḍa, or conscious; the former is unmanifested prakṛti; the latter is Śrī or Lakṣmī, which upholds the former. She is the consort of Nārāyaṇa. With these two Hari creates the world.'[65] The Gītā accepts the Sāṁkhya theory of the evolution of the manifold from the homogeneous indeterminate matter, determined by the presence of spirit or puruṣa. Only the presence of puruṣa necessary to stimulate prakṛti to activity must be a real presence. It is therefore more correct to say

63. B.G., chap. xi; vi. 29; vii. 8–9; viii. 22; x.
64. xiii. 15–18. Sir Edwin Arnold's translation.
65. Commentary on vii. 5.

that all activity is due to the combined effort of puruṣa and prakṛti, though the element of intelligence is more prominent in the subjective and that of matter in the objective world. Both of them form the nature of the one Supreme. They are the constitutive stuff of the world.[66] That is why the Lord is said to be the support of the world as well as the all-illumining light of consciousness. The author of the Gītā does not describe the way in which the one nature of God manifests itself at one stage as unconscious matter, at another as conscious intelligence, and how these two products of one primal source appear to be antagonistic to each other during the course of the world progress.[67]

While dwelling in man and nature the Supreme is greater than both. The boundless universe in an endless space and time rests in Him and not He in it. The expression of God may change, but in Him is an element which is self-identical, the permanently fixed background for the phenomenal alternations. The diversified existence does not affect His identity.[68] 'As the mighty air everywhere moving is rooted in space so all things are in Me.'[69] Yet space is space even without the 'moving airs.' The Lord is not tainted by the qualities of creation. The world as the expression of His nature does not detract from the self-sufficiency of God. Yet we cannot know the nature of God apart from the constitution of the world. If the identical principle is emptied of all content, of all that constitutes progress in knowledge and life, the God-in-Itself may become unknowable. It is also true that if we lose ourselves in the world, the reality may be hidden from our vision. It is necessary for us to know what God is independent of all relations to objects, and how He maintains Himself throughout all changes He brings about. Simply because relatedness to objects cannot

66. Rāmānuja says: 'From the connection between the unintelligent prakṛti and the intelligent embryo cast into it (14. 3) there results the origin of all beings, which beginning from the gods and ending with immovable things are all mixed up with the non-intelligent thing.' (R.B.G., 13. 2). Rāmānuja, however, holds that these beings possess an ultimate existence distinct from that of Īśvara, though the Gītā is definite that the undivided Brahman is not really divided, but only seems to be so (vibhaktam iva, 13. 16).

67. We are not, therefore, in a position to institute any comparison between the Gītā conception of the Puruṣottama, or the whole, and Bergson's theory of an eternal durée, or of the Gītā doctrine of puruṣa and prakṛti with Bergson's conception of life and matter.

68. M.B., Śāntiparva, 339–344.

69. ix. 6; ix. 10.

be excluded, we need not think that the subject has no self-identity. If the expression is confused with the spirit, the Gītā theory will become one of cosmotheism. The author of the Gītā, however, explicitly repudiates such suggestions. The whole world is said to be sustained by one part of God, 'ekāṁśena.'[70] In the tenth chapter Kṛṣṇa declares that He is manifesting only a portion of His endless glory. The immutability of the absolute and the activity of the Īśvara are both taken over in the conception of Puruṣottama.

The personal Puruṣottama is from the religious point of view higher than the immutable self-existence untouched by the subjective and the objective appearances of the universe. He is looked upon as an impartial governor ever ready to help those in distress. Simply because He sometimes inflicts punishments we cannot call Him unjust or unkind. Śrīdhara quotes a verse which reads: 'Even as a mother is not unkind to her child whether she fondles or beats him, so also Īśvara, the determiner of good and evil, is not unkind.'[71] The impersonal absolute is envisaged as Puruṣottama for the purposes of religion. The idea of Puruṣottama is not a wilful self-deception accepted by the weak heart of man. While the dry light of reason gives us a featureless reality, spiritual intuition reveals to us a God who is both personal and impersonal. The principle of reconciliation is contained in the Upaniṣads. The Īśā Upaniṣad looks upon the real as both the mobile and the immobile. To dwell on either exclusively results in a darkness of knowledge or of ignorance. The Gītā tries to make a synthesis of the imperishable self and the changing experience. The supreme spiritual being with energy in Puruṣottama; the same in a state of eternal rest is Brahman. Śaṁkarānanda quotes a verse which says: 'There are two forms of Vāsudeva, the manifested and the unmanifested; the Parabrahman is the unmanifested, and the while world of moving and unmoving things is the manifested.'[72] The Supreme has two aspects of the manifested and the unmanifested; the former is emphasised when prakṛti is assigned to its nature and Jīva is said to be a part of it.[73] The stress is on the same side when Kṛṣṇa says: 'Whatever is glorious, good, beautiful and mighty, understand that it all proceeds from a fragment of my splendour.'[74] When Kṛṣṇa calls upon us to become his devotees, when he shows the viśvarūpa,

70. x. 42.
71. Commentary on the Gītā, iv. 8.
72. Commentary on the Gītā, iv. 11.
73. xv. 7.
74. x. 41.

or the world-form, whenever he uses the first person, we have references to the manifested aspect of the Supreme.[75] This side of divine nature is involved in the work of creation, where it loses itself in the succession of time and the waves of becoming. Beyond it all is another status, the silent and the immutable, than which there is nothing higher. The two together form the Puruṣottama. If we try to make out that the personal Lord is the highest metaphysical reality we get into trouble. 'I will declare that in the object of knowledge, knowing which one reaches immortality, the highest Brahman, having no beginning or end, which cannot be said to be existent or non-existent.'[76] The author of the Gītā frequently reminds us that the manifested aspect is a creation of his own mystic power, or yoga māyā.[77] 'The undiscerning ones, not knowing my transcendental and inexhaustible essence, than which there is nothing higher, think me, who am unperceived, to have become perceptible.'[78] On ultimate analysis the assumption of the form of Puruṣottama by the absolute becomes less than real. It is therefore wrong to argue that according to the Gītā the impersonal self is lower in reality than the personal Īśvara, though it is true that the Gītā considers the conception of a personal God to be more useful for religious purposes.

Before we pass on to the cosmology of the Gītā, we may note the relation between the conception of Puruṣottama and Kṛṣṇa, thus raising the question of the avatārs or incarnations.

Whether Kṛṣṇa is identical with Puruṣottama or only a limited manifestation of Him is a question on which there is difference of opinion. The theory of avatārs is mentioned in the Gītā. 'Even though I am unborn and inexhaustible in my essence, even though I am Lord of all beings, still assuming control over my own prakṛti, I am born by means of my māyā.'[79] The avatārs are generally limited manifestations of the Supreme, though the Bhāgavata makes an exception in favour of Kṛṣṇa, and makes him a full manifestation, 'Kṛṣṇas tu bhagavān svayam.' The form given to him is indicative of his all-comprehensiveness. The peacock feathers of his head are the variegated colours which flood man's eyes. The colour of his complexion is that of the sky, the garland of wild flowers typifies the grandeur of the solar and the stellar systems. The flute he plays upon is that by which

75. ix. 34; xiv. 27; xviii 65.
76. R.B.G., xiii. 12.
77. vii. 25.
78. vii. 24.
79. iv. 6.

he gives forth his message. The yellow garment with which he decks his person is the halo of light which pervades space, the mark on his chest is the emblem of the devotion of the devotee which he proudly wears out of love to man. He stands in the devotee's heart, and so great is his grace to man that his feet, which symbolise it, are put one over the other so that they may have their full effect. Śaṁkara and Ānandagiri look upon Kṛṣṇa as only a partial manifestation of the supreme godhead.[80] Kṛṣṇa, in the opinion of the author of the Gītā, is the Puruṣottama. 'The foolish mistake me, clad in human form, ignorant of my supreme nature, the great Lord of all beings.'[81]

The theory of avatārs brings to mankind a new spiritual message. The avatārs are the militant gods struggling against sin and evil, death and destruction. 'Whensoever righteousness languishes and unrighteousness is on the ascendant, I create myself. I am born age after age, for the protection of the good, for the destruction of the evildoers and the establishment of the law.'[82] It is an eloquent expression of the law of the spiritual world. If God is looked upon as the saviour of man, He must manifest Himself whenever the forces of evil threaten to destroy human values. According to Hindu mythology, whenever the forces of vice and wickedness, a Rāvaṇa or a Kaṁsa are in the ascendant, the representatives of the moral order, Indra, Brahmā, etc., along with Earth, which is said to suffer most, go to the court of Heaven and cry aloud for a world redeemer. The work of redemption, however, is a constant activity, though on occasions it becomes accentuated. The normal self-manifestation of God becomes emphatic when the world-order grows disproportionately evil. An avatār is a descent of God into man, and not an ascent of man into God. Though every conscious being is such a descent, it is only a veiled manifestation. There is a distinction between the self-conscious being of the divine and the same shrouded in ignorance. The human being is as good as an avatār, provided he crosses the māyā of the world and transcends his imperfection. The creator Puruṣottama is not separated from his creatures. The two do not exist apart. He is always fulfilling himself in the world. Man comes to full consciousness by actualising his potentiality. It becomes indifferent,

80. Aṁśena saṁbabhūva, or born of a part. Śaṁkara. Ānandagiri, commenting on it, says that it is an illusory form created by his own will. Svecchānirmitena māyāmayena svarūpeṇa.

81. ix. 11.

82. iv. See also Tevijja Sutta; Mahānirvāṇa Tantra, iv.

then, whether we say God limits Himself in the form of man or man rises to God working through his nature. Yet an avatār generally means a God who limits Himself for some purpose on earth, and possesses even in His limited form the fullness of knowledge.

The philosophical intellect tries to relate the avatārs, or the ideals of perfection, to the great onward march of the world. The superior souls who focussed representative ages in their own selves became the embodiments of God in a special sense. These examples of men who established supremacy over their nature and made their outward substance reveal the God within are more effective for struggling individuals. From them can man take courage and try to grow into their stature. They are the moulds into which the seeking soul tries to cast itself, that it might grow towards God. What has been achieved by one man, a Christ or a Buddha, may be repeated in the lives of other men. The struggle towards the sanctifying of the earth or the revealing of the God-ideal has passed through several stages in the evolution on earth. The ten avatārs of Viṣṇu mark out the central steps. The growth in the sub-human or the animal level is emphasised in those of the fish, the tortoise and the boar. Next we have the transition between the animal and the human worlds in the man-lion. The development is not completely fulfilled when we come to the dwarf. The first stage of man is that of the brutish, violent, uncivilised Rāma with his axe, who devastates the rest of humanity; later we get the divine spiritual Rāma, who consecrates family life and affections, and Kṛṣṇa, who exhorts us to enter into the warfare of the world; and after him Buddha, who, full of compassion for all life, works for the redemption of mankind. Last of all we have the avatār yet to come, the militant God (Kalki) who fights evil and injustice with the sword in hand. Great crises in human progress are signalised by the appearance of avatārs.

VI

THE WORLD OF CHANGE

To know the exact place of the māyā theory in the Gītā, it is necessary to distinguish the different senses in which the word is employed, and the exact bearings of the Gītā on them all. (1) If the supreme reality is unaffected by the events of the world, then the rise of these events becomes an inexplicable mystery. The author of the Gītā does not use the term māyā in this sense, however much it may be implied in his views. The conception of a beginningless, and at the same time unreal, avidyā causing the illusion of the world does not enter the mind of the author. (2) The personal Īśvara is said to combine within himself sat and asat, the immutability of Brahman as well as the mutation of becoming.[83] Māyā is the power which enables him to produce mutable nature. It is śakti, or the energy of Īśvara, or ātmavibhūti, the power of self-becoming. Īśvara and māyā in this sense are mutually dependent and are both beginningless.[84] This power of the supreme is called māyā in the Gītā.[85] (3) Since the Lord is able to produce the universe by means of the two elements of His being, prakṛti and puruṣa, matter and consciousness, they are said to be māyā (higher and lower) of God.[86] (4) Gradually māyā comes to mean the lower prakṛti, since puruṣa is said to be the seed which the Lord casts into the womb of prakṛti for the generation of the universe. (5) As the manifested world hides the real from the vision of the mortals, it is said to be delusive in its character.[87] The world is not an illusion, though by regarding it as a mere mechanical determination of nature unrelated to God, we fail to perceive its divine essence. It becomes the source of delusion. The divine māyā becomes avidyāmāyā. It is so, however, only for us mortals, shut off from the truth; to God who knows it all and controls it, it is vidyāmāyā. Māyā to man is a source of trouble and misery, since it breeds bewildering partial consciousness which loses hold of the full reality. God seems to be enveloped in the immense cloak of māyā.[88] (6) Since the world is only an effect of God, who is the cause, and since everywhere the cause is more real than the effect, the world as effect is said to be less real than God the cause. This relative unreality of the world is confirmed by the self-contradictory nature of the process of becoming. There is a struggle of opposites in the world of experience, and the real is above all opposites.[89]

83. ix. 19.
84. See Śāṇḍilya Sūtras, ii. 13 and 15.
85. xviii. 61; iv. 6.
86. iv. 16.
87. vii. 14; vii. 25.
88. Māyā which does not produce avidyā is said to be sāttvikī māyā. When it is polluted it breeds ignorance, or avidyā. Brahman reflected in the former is Īśvara, while that reflected in the latter is jīva, or the individual self. This is later Vedānta, see Pañcadaśī, i. 15–17. The Gītā is not aware of this view.
89. ii. 45; vii. 28.

There is, however, no indication that the changes of the world are only imaginary.[90] Even Śaṁkara's non-dualism admits of real changes in the world; only the first change of Brahman into the world is regarded by him as an appearance, of vivarta. The word is a real emanation from the supreme Puruṣottama; only from the ultimate point of view it is not real, since it is ever at war with itself. The Gītā repudiates the view that 'the world is untrue, without any fixed basis, devoid of any ruler, brought about by union caused by lust and nothing else.'[91] It follows that in the world we have a real development presided over by Īśvara. We cannot say that the Gītā looked upon the world as real only so long as we lived in it. There is no suggestion that the world is a troublous dream on the bosom of the infinite. While living in the world of becoming, it is possible, according to the Gītā, to possess the immortality of timeless self-existence. We have the supreme example of Puruṣottama, who makes use of the world undeluded by it. When we transcend māyā, time, space and cause do not fall away from us. The world does not disappear, but it only changes its meaning.

Puruṣottama is not a remote phenomenon in some supreme state beyond us all, but is in the body and heart of every man and thing. He maintains all existences in relation to one another. The world of souls and matter is the effect of his nature. God does not create the world out of a nothingness or a void, but from His own being. In the praḷaya condition the whole world, including jīvas, exists in the divine in a subtle state. In the manifested state they are cut off from one another and forget their identity of source. All this is his sovereign yoga. The world is compared to a tree 'with root above and branches below.'[92] Prakṛti is a general feature of the world. The interminable antagonisms, the mutual devourings of the various forms of existence, the evolving, the differentiating, the organising and the vivifying of matter are all due to prakṛti. 'Earth, water, fire, air, space, mind, buddhi or understanding, self-sense or ahaṁkāra are the eight-fold divisions of my prakṛti.' This is God's lower nature. That which vitalises these and sustains the world is His higher.[93] Rāmānuja writes: 'The prakṛti, or the material nature of the universe, is an object of enjoyment; that which is other than this, which is insentient and object

90. iii. 28; iv. 6; vii. 14; xiv. 23.
91. xvi. 8.
92. xv. 1.
93. vii. 4–5; see also R.B.G. on vii. 4–5.

of enjoyment, is the life principle jīva, which is of a different order. It is the enjoyer of the lower one, and is in the form of intelligent souls.' The Gītā supports Rāmānuja's view of reality, if we ignore its absolutist background and emphasise the idea of Puruṣottama with its dual nature of consciousness and matter. The metaphor of beads and string, according to Rāmānuja, points out how 'the totality of intelligences and non-intelligent things, both in their state of cause and in the state of effect, which form my body, are like a number of gems on a string that hangs from me, who have my being in the Ātman.'[94]

The individual soul is said to be a portion of the lord, mamaivāṁśah.[95] Śaṁkara is not faithful to the intention of the author of the Gītā when he says that 'aṁśa,' or part, indicates an imaginary or apparent part only. It is a real form of Puruṣottama. Śaṁkara's position is correct if the reference is to the indivisible Brahman, who is partless, but then even Puruṣottama is imaginary, since there is in him an element of not-self. The actual individual is a kartṛ or doer; so he is not the pure immortal spirit, but the personal self, which is a limited manifestation of God. This portion is kept distinct on account of the form which it draws to itself, the senses and the mind. As the prakṛti has a definite magnitude, duration and vibration, even so does puruṣa acquire a definite extent and reach of consciousness. The universal is embodied in a limited context of a mental-vital-physical sheath. 'Puruṣa joined with prakṛti enjoys the qualities born of nature and the cause of its birth, good or evil, is its connexion with the qualities.'[96]

VII

THE INDIVIDUAL SELF

The individuals are subject to māyā, or delusion, being lost in outer appearances.[97] Birth in the world of saṁsāra is the result of imperfection. Rotation in the circle of existence is inevitable so long as we are blind to the truth. We get rid of individuality when we transcend māyā and realise our true status. Any form the individual assumes is doomed to be

94. R.B.G., vii. 7.
95. xv. 7.
96. xiii. 21.
97. vii. 13; 26. 27.

superseded. The individual always tries to become something else. The infinite character cannot become fully explicit in any finite existence. It ever keeps on transcending its own finite self until the becoming reaches its end in being and the finite is taken over into the infinite. The finite world is an endless progress, an infinite perfectibility, an ever approximating approach to an ever-growing object of desire. It follows that all distinctions based on becoming and connexions with prakṛti are only transient. The eternality and plurality of puruṣas is assumed in the Gītā when its thought rests at the level of Puruṣottama. The jīvas, than, are only distinct fragments of Puruṣottama individualised. From the standpoint of absolute truth, their individuality is dependent upon the object element. Even in this world those acts indicative of separate individuality are not due to the immortal actionless spirit, but are derived from the forces of prakṛti. 'The qualities born of prakṛti constrain everybody to some action.'[98] If the puruṣas are eternal, it cannot be any delusion to think that they are the doers and are different from each other. The Gītā says: 'He whose mind is deluded by egoism thinks himself the doer of actions which are wrought by the qualities of prakṛti.' 'Qualities move among qualities.'[99] It is a confusion with the object that is responsible for the false view of individuality. The basis of distinction is then not-self, while the self is the same in all, 'dog or dog-eater.'[100] It is easy for Śaṁkara to press all these passages into the service of his non-dualism. He says: 'Nor are there what are called ultimate differentiae, or antyaviśeṣas, as the basis of individual distinctions in the self, since no evidence can be adduced to prove their existence in relation to the several bodies. Hence Brahman is homogeneous and one.'[101] We need not assume indefinable marks of individual identity to account for the distinctions of the world. Individuals are different because of their embodiments. As the Mahābhārata says: 'A man bound up with guṇas is a jīvatma, or individual soul; when freed from them, he is paramātma, or supreme soul.'[102] Passages which proclaim the identity of the individual with the supreme are interpreted by Rāmānuja in a different way. For example, the declaration that 'Brahman in each possesses hands and feet everywhere and

98. iii. 5.
99. iii. 27–28.
100. v. 18; xiii. 2. 22.
101. S.B.G., v. 19.
102. Śāṇtiparva, 187. 24.

envelops all' is taken by Rāmānuja to mean that 'the purified nature of the Ātman, by virtue of its being devoid of the limitations of the body and such other objects, pervades all things.'[103] Again, when the Gītā says that the Puruṣa in each is 'the witness, the permitter, the supporter, the enjoyer, the great lord and the supreme self,' Rāmānuja is perplexed. 'Such a puruṣa, by virtue of his connexion with guṇas, produced by the prakṛti, becomes the great ruler only with reference to this body, and the highest Ātman only with reference to this body.'[104]

From an occasional singular or plural usage we cannot draw any inference about the ultimate nature of the soul. When the stress is on the empirical side the plural number is used. 'Never did I not exist, nor thou, nor these rulers of men; and no one of us will ever hereafter cease to exist.'[105] It is easy to infer from this a doctrine of the eternal plurality of souls. Rāmānuja observes: 'the Lord Himself declares that the distinction of the self from the Lord as well as from other selves is the highest reality.' Śaṁkara, on the other hand, urges 'as the self, the Ātman, we are eternal in all the three periods of time (past, present and future).' He believes that the plural is used with reference to the bodies, which are different, as is clear from the next verse relating to rebirth and not with reference to self. Metaphysically there is only one spirit.[106]

The Gītā believes in rebirth until the ultimate state is reached. Birth following upon imperfection is bound to death, and vice versa. Birth and death occur as infancy, youth and age occur to a man's frame.

Nay, but as when one layeth
His wornout robes away
And taking new ones, sayeth
'These will I wear to-day.'
So putteth by the spirit
Lightly its garb of flesh,
And passeth to inherit
A residence afresh.[107]

103. R.B.G., xii. 13.
104. R.B.G., xiii. 23; see also xiii. 33.
105. R.B.G. and S.B.G., ii. 12.
106. viii. 4; xiii. 31.
107. ii. 22. Sir Edwin Arnold's translation. See also ii. 13; ii. 27.

Death only changes the scene. The instrument through which the player can express himself must be intact. The gradual failure of powers in old age, or their temporary failure in illness, though physical, reacts on the core of mind's being. When the body dies he is supplied with a new instrument. Our life does not die with us: when one body wears out it will take another. The kind of birth depends on the character we have developed. We are born in celestial regions, or as men on earth, or in the animal world, according as we develop character in which sattva, rajas or tamas predominates. Every step we gain is conserved for us. When Arjuna asks Kṛṣṇa about the fate of those who are not able to attain perfection, whether they go to ruin, Kṛṣṇa says that a man who does good never goes to ruin, but he obtains another birth 'when he recovers the mental characteristics of his former life, and with them he again struggles onward for perfection.'[108] There is a conservation of all values. None can lose the way of the supreme if his heart is set on it. Rebirth continues till the goal is reached.[109] The sūkṣma śarīra, or the subtle body, consisting of the senses and the mind, survives death and is the bearer of character.[110] Rebirth is a discipline by which we can perfect ourselves. There is also a reference to the path of the gods through which the saṁsārins pass.[111] The third path of the sinful is also mentioned.[112]

VIII

ETHICS

The distinctness of particular persons, their finiteness and individuality, are only accidental, and do not represent the underlying truth. The individual will not gain the secret of peace, stable and secure, until he breaks down his apparent self-completeness and independence. True freedom means self-transcendence or union with the highest through logic, love or life. The end we seek is becoming Brahman or touching the eternal, *brahmasaṁsparśam*. This is the only absolute value.[113]

It is in the power of all to destroy evil, to eliminate the corruption of the flesh, to redeem the lower nature and rescue the senses from bondage

108. vi. 44–5.
109. vii. 19.
110. xv. 8.
111. viii. 23–26.
112. ix. 12; xvi. 19–21.
113. vi. 20, 23, 27 and 28.

to passion. Each struggling individual will have to make a sustained endeavour to look into the truth with his won eyes, judge with his own reason, and love with his own heart. A half-truth won for ourselves is worth more than a whole truth learned from others.

Man is a complex of reason, will and emotion, and so seeks the true delight of his being through all these. He can reach the end by a knowledge of the supreme reality, or by love and adoration of the supreme person, or by the subjection of his will to the divine purpose. There is the impulse in him forcing him to get beyond his little self in these different directions. The end is the same whichever standpoint we adopt. It is the harmonious efficiency of the several sides of our life by which truth is attained, beauty created and conduct perfected. The Gītā is emphatic that no side of conscious life can be excluded. The several aspects reach their fulfilment in the integral divine life. God himself is sat, cit and ānanda, reality, truth and bliss. The absolute reveals itself to those seeking for knowledge as the Eternal Light, clear and radiant as the sun at noon-day in which is no darkness; to those struggling for virtue as the Eternal Righteousness, steadfast and impartial; and to those emotionally inclined as Eternal Love and Beauty of Holiness. Even as God combines in Himself wisdom, goodness and holiness, so should men aim at the integral life of spirit. The obstructions of the road are not operative when we reach the end. It is true that in the finite life of the individual there seems to be some kind of antagonism between contemplation and action. This is only a sign of our imperfection. When Kṛṣṇa is asked about the particular method to be adopted, he clearly says that we need not worry about this question, since the different pathways are not ultimately distinct, but lead to the same goal, and are found together in the end though they cross and recross one another on the road. Man does not function in fractions. Progress is correlated and not dissociated development. Knowledge, feeling and will are different aspects of the one movement of the soul.

The Gītā tries to harmonise the different ideals of life current at the time and correct their extravagances. Intellectual inquiry, strenuous self-sacrifice, fervent devotion, ceremonial observance and yogic exercises were looked upon as affording access to the divine.[114] The Gītā synthesises them

114. Cf. Plotinus: 'There are different roads by which this end (of spiritual apprehension) may be reached: the love of beauty which exalts the poet; that devotion to the One and that ascent of science which make the ambition of the philosopher; that love and those prayers by which some devout and ardent soul tends in its moral

all and shows the exact place and value of each of them. It believes in the effectiveness of a combined attack. The harmonising ideal which all these different methods have in view is the increasing solidarity of the individual with the universe presided over by Puruṣottama.

Madhusūdana Sarasvatī considers that the Gītā adopts the three methods indicated in the Upaniṣads, karma or work, upāsana or worship, and jñāna or wisdom, and devotes six chapters to each in succession. Whatever be the truth of it, it emphasises the three great divisions of conscious life. The Gītā recognises that different men are led to the spiritual vision by different approaches, some by the perplexities of the moral life, some by the doubts of the intellect, and some by the emotional demands for perfection.

IX

JÑĀNA MĀRGA

The logical mind, unable to acquiesce in the partial, tries to grasp the totality of things, and finds no rest until it is anchored in the truth. It is buoyed up by the undying faith in its destiny to acquire supreme truth.[115] The Gītā recognises two kinds of knowledge, that which seeks to understand the phenomena of existence externally through intellect, and that which by the force of intuition grasps the ultimate principle behind the apparent series. When subject to the logical intellect, the spirit of man tends to lose itself in nature and identify itself with its activities To grasp the truth of existence in its source and reality within, it has to free itself from the snare of false identification. The intellectual apprehension of the details of existence is called vijñāna, as distinct from jñāna, or the integral knowledge of the common foundation of all existence. These two are only different sides of one pursuit. All knowledge is knowledge of God. Science and philosophy both try to realise the truth of the oneness of things in the eternal spirit. Scientific knowledge is said to be dominated by rajas, while spiritual knowledge is permeated by the quality of sattva. If we mistake

---

purity towards perfection. These are the great highways conducting to that height above the actual and the particular, where we stand in the immediate presence of the Infinite, who shines out as from the deeps of the soul.' (Letter to Flaccus.)

115. 'Blessedness consists in love towards God, and this arises from knowledge.' (Spinoza). 'With certain persons the intellectual effort to understand the universe is a principal way of experiencing the Deity.' (Bradley.).

the partial truths of science for the whole truth of spirit, we have the inferior knowledge, where the lowest quality of tamas predominates.[116] The truth of the soul is a hypothesis so long as we are at the level of science. The endless becoming covers up the being. Science dispels the darkness oppressing the mind, shows up the incompleteness of its own world, and prepares the mind for something beyond it. It stimulates humility, since by its means we cannot know all. We are hemmed in between the forgetfulness of what was and the uncertainty of what shall be. To indulge in the imaginative desire to become acquainted with the first causes of things and the destiny of mankind, science admits, is a vain pursuit. If we want to get at the ultimate truth science has to be supplemented by another discipline. The Gītā holds that paripraśna, or investigation, is to be combined with service, or sevā.[117] For the development of the intuitive power we require a turning of the mind in another direction, a conversion of the soul. Arjuna could not see the truth with his naked eyes, and so asked for the divine sight or spiritual vision.[118] The viśvarūpa is a poetic exaggeration of the intuitional experience where the individual possessed by God sees all things in Him. The Gītā believes that for attaining this spiritual vision the individual should learn to live within and fix his mind on the highest reality. What hides the truth from our vision is not merely the fault of intellect, but also the passion of selfishness. Ajñāna is not intellectual error, but spiritual blindness. To remove it we must cleanse the soul of the defilement of the body and the senses, and kindle the spiritual vision which looks at things from a new angle. The fire of passion and the tumult of desire must be suppressed.[119] The mind, inconstant and unstable, must be steadied into an unruffled lake, that it might mirror the wisdom from above. Buddhi, or the power of understanding and discrimination, needs to be trained.[120] The way in which this power operates depends on our past habits. We should so train it as to bring it into agreement with the spiritual view of the universe.

It is as a means of mental training that the Gītā accepts the yoga system. The yoga discipline gives the directions by which we can lift ourselves from

116. xviii. 20–22.

117. iv. 34.

118. xi. Cf. the Prophet's words, 'Lord, open his eyes that he may see.' See also the vision of Ezekiel and Exodus xxxiii. 18, Revelation, chap. iv., and Saddharma Puṇḍarīka, chap. i.

119. iv. 39.

120. ii. 44.

our mutable personality into a super-normal attitude, where we possess the key which is the secret of the whole play of relations. The essential steps of the yogic discipline are: (1) purification of mind, body and senses, that the divine may take possession of them; (2) concentration or withdrawal of the consciousness from the dispersed movement of thoughts running after the senses and fixing it on the Supreme; and (3) identification with the real when we reach it. The Gītā is not so very systematic as Patañjali's Sūtras, though the different sādhanas or instruments are referred to.[121]

The Gītā offers us certain general principles acceptable to thinkers of all shades of opinion. We are asked to have faith or śraddhā,[122] subdue the riotous impulses and hold fast in thought to God. An atmosphere of stillness and calm is necessary for the spiritual vision. In the silence following the firm control of the mind we can hear the voice of the soul. The true yoga is that which brings about spiritual impartiality, or samatvam.[123] 'Where the mind flickereth not like a lamp in a sheltered spot; where seeing the self by the self, one is satisfied in himself; where one experiences the absolute bliss known only to understanding, but ever beyond the senses, and standing where one swerves not from the truth; where no other gain is considered greater, and, where placed, one is not moved by the greatest pain—that state free from misery is yoga.'[124] It is not necessary for all to practise yoga in order that they may attain the spiritual insight. Madhusūdana Sarasvatī quotes a verse from Vaśiṣṭha: 'To suppress mind with its egoism, etc., yoga and jnāna are the two means. Yoga is the suppression of mental activity (vṛtti-nirodha), and jñāna is true comprehension (saṁyagavekṣaṇam). For some yoga is not possible, for others jñāna is not possible.'[125] The spiritual intuition may also be helped by work and worship.[126]

While admitting the relevancy of the yoga discipline for spiritual training in some cases, the Gītā is not unconscious of its dangers.[127] By mere fasting and such other methods we may only weaken the powers of the senses, while our relish for sense-objects may be intact. What is wanted

121. Chap. vi.
122. iv. 39.
123. ii. 48.
124. vi. 19–26.
125. Commentary on the Gītā, vi. 29.
126. iv. 42.
127. ii. 59–61.

is control of senses and indifference to the attractions of material objects. This is possible only with the rise of knowledge.

Spiritual intuition which is more perceptual in character[128] is not uncritical conviction. It is supported by scientific judgment. It is a union of knowledge with austerity and passion, the most complete experience that we can possibly have, where we have no more confusion of mind, but enjoy true peace and rest of spirit.[129]

When once the fullness of cognitive experience is reached, the other sides of consciousness, emotion and will, make themselves felt. The vision of god in the spiritual illumination is attained in an atmosphere of joy. The whole life-aspiration becomes one continuous adoration of the infinite. The knower is also a devotee and the best of them.[130] 'He who knows me worships me.'[131] To know the truth is to lift up our hearts to the Supreme, touch Him and adore Him.[132] There is also a practical influence. The more profoundly we are conscious of our true nature, the deeper is our insight into the real needs of others. The good becomes 'not merely the key-stone of knowledge, but the polestar of conduct' in the famous phrase of Nettleship. We have the example of Buddha, the greatest jñāni or seer, whose love for humanity led to his ministry of mankind for forty years.

It is sometimes argued that knowledge or intelligence is indifferent to morality. Intelligence, it is said, is not an essential part of character. Intellectually we make only mistakes or errors of judgment; morally we do wrong. The intellect is neither good nor bad, since it can be used to promote or destroy good life. All this may be true of our analytic understanding. Jñāna, or the wisdom of the Gītā, carries us beyond one-sided views and narrow standpoints to the comprehensive truth, where we feel that the differences between men are not ultimate, and that no conduct which is based on false distinctions can be good. We see that the lives of men have a common root, and that a self-existent eternal spirit is living and operating in all individual lives. When this truth is perceived, sense and self lose their power.[133]

128. ix. 2, Pratyakṣāvagamam.
129. iv. 35; v. 18–21.
130. vii. 17.
131. xv. 19.
132. x. 8–9.
133. ii. 59.

X

BHAKTI MĀRGA

The Bhakti mārga, or the path of devotion, indicates the law of the right activity of the emotional side of man. Bhakti is emotional attachment distinct from knowledge or action.[134] Through it we offer our emotional possibilities to the divine. Emotion expresses a living relation between individuals, and becomes instinct with the force of religious feeling when it binds God and man. If we do not love and worship, we become shut within the prison of our own egoism. This way, when rightly regulated, leads us to the perception of the Supreme. It is open to all, the weak and the lowly, the illiterate and the ignorant,[135] and is also the easiest. The sacrifice of love is not so difficult as the tuning of the will to the divine purpose or ascetic discipline, or the strenuous effort of thinking. It is quite as efficacious as any other method, and is sometimes said to be greater than others, since it is its own fruition, while others are means to some other end.

The origin of the Bhakti mārga is hidden in the mists of long ago. The upāsana theory of the Upaniṣads and the devotional way of the Bhāgavatas have influenced the author of the Gītā. He struggles to develop an order of ideas belonging to the religious level of the Upaniṣads to which they were not able to give free and unambiguous utterance. The absolute becomes in the Gītā 'the understanding of them that understand, the splendour of the splendid,'[136] the first of gods and men, the chief of the ṛṣis, as well as death which ravishes all.[137] Admitting that meditation of the unmanifested absolute leads to the goal, Kṛṣṇa urges that it is a hard process.[138] It offers no foothold for the finite man from which he could approach it. The love which we feel for an object involves an element of separateness. However closely love may unite, the lover and the beloved remain distinct. We have to rest content with a dualism even as thought does; but it is not correct to describe the monism which transcends the dualism as a descent to a lower grade. Devotion to the Supreme is possible only with a personal God, a concrete individual full of bliss and beauty.

134. Śāṇḍilya Sūtras, i. 4–5 and 7.
135. ix. 32; see also xi. 53–54.
136. vii. 10.
137. x. 20–25. 3.4.
138. xii. 5.

We cannot love a shadow of our minds. Personality implies a capacity for fellowship, or communion, or a feeling together. There is the personal need for a personal helper. So God, into whose being the heart of love enters, is not the God who revels in bloodshed, not one who sleeps in serene abstraction while hearts heavy-laden cry out for help. He is love.[139] He who gives up his whole to God and falls at His feet finds the gates of spirit lie open. The voice of God declares, 'This is My word of promise, that he who loveth Me shall not perish.'[140]

It is not a rigid law of recompense that binds God to the world. The consequences of deeds may be averted by means of devotion to God. This is no supersession of the law of karma, since the law requires that even devotion should have its reward. Kṛṣṇa says: 'Even if a man of evil conduct turns to me with a sole and entire love, he must be regarded as a saint,' because he has turned to God with a settled will, and has therefore become a soul of righteousness. The Lord by Himself does not receive the sin or the merit of any.[141] Yet He has so arranged the scheme of things, that nothing happens without producing its effect. In a sense it is true that 'the Lord enjoys all sacrifices and penances.' It is in this way that we have to reconcile apparently contradictory views expressed in passages like 'none is hateful to Me and none dear,' and 'the devotees are dear to Me.'[142] Man is the object of God's constant care.

The nature of love towards God or bhakti is indescribable even 'as the taste of the dumb person.'[143] The essential features of this emotional attachment may, however, be stated. There is the adoration of something looked upon as absolutely perfect. Since the object is perfection, nothing less than the highest conceivable will do. Nārada in his sūtras brings in the analogy of human love,[144] where also the finite individual transcends himself and reaches out towards an ideal. Only the ideal very frequently reveals its actual nature. The object of devotion is the highest being, or Puruṣottama. He is the illuminator of souls as well as the vivifier of the world. God is not to be identified with the different elements which seem

139. Śaraṇāgatavatsalaḥ.
140. ix. 31.
141. ix.; v. 15.
142. ix. 29; xii. 14–20; see also xvi. 16.
143. Nārada Sūtras, 51–52.
144. Ibid., 23.

to be the ultimate realities at a lower level, nor is He the lord of sacrifices as the Mīmāṁsakas imagine. He is not to be confused with the several personal agencies which the mind of man attributes to the natural forces. He is not the puruṣa of the Sāṁkhyas. He is all these and more.[145] The author of the Gītā emphasises how God lives in each individual. If the Supreme were quite foreign to the individual consciousness, He could not be an object of worship; if He were absolutely identical with the individual, even then worship is not possible. He is partly the same as and partly different from the individual. He is the divine Lord associated with prakṛti or Lakṣmī, in whose hands lies the measure of desirable things. The prospect of union with Him is a vision of delight. 'Fix thy mind in Me, into Me let thy understanding enter; thou shalt surely live with Me alone hereafter.'[146] All other love is only an imperfect manifestation of this supreme love. We love other things for the sake of the eternal in them. The devotee has a sense of utter humiliation. In the presence of the ideal he feels that he is nothing, and such an utter prostration of the self is the indispensable pre-requisite of true religious devotion. God loves meekness.[147] The individual feels himself to be worthless apart from God. His devotion expresses itself as either love for God (prīti), or misery due to the absence of God (viraha). The self cannot but reject itself as worthless dross when it discovers the supreme value of the object to which it attaches itself. The devotee throws himself entirely on the mercy of God. Absolute dependence is the only way. 'Merge thy mind in Me, be My devotee, prostrate thyself before Me, thou shalt come even unto Me. I pledge thee My troth, thou art dear to Me. Abandoning all dharmas, come unto Me alone for shelter; sorrow not, I will liberate thee from all sins.'[148] God insists on undivided devotion, and assures us that He will take up our knowledge and our error and cast away all forms of insufficiency and transform all into His infinite light and the purity of the universal good. Again, there is the continual desire to serve the ideal. The devotee 'looks only on the object of his devotion, talks only about Him and thinks only of Him.'[149] Whatever he does he does for the glory of God. His work is absolutely unselfish, since it is indifferent to its fruits. It is an utter self-giving to the transcendent.[150] When the devotee

145. viii. 4.
146. xii. 8.
147. Nārada Sūtras, 27, dainyapriyatvam.
148. B.G., xviii. 64–66.
149. Nārada Sūtras, 55.
150. B.G., ix. 28.

surrenders himself completely into the hands of the ideal, we do not have a blind intensity of feeling. It is an open-armed surrender in which feeling is displaced by life. God becomes the ruling passion of the mind. The devotee reaches his end, becomes immortal and satisfied in himself. He does not desire anything, sorrows not; he is filled with joy and peace—rapt in the spirit.[151] Bhakti, or true devotion, according to the Gītā, is to believe in God, to love Him, to be devoted to Him and to enter into Him. It is its own reward.

For the true bhakti, we require first of all Śraddhā or faith. The highest reality has to be assumed or taken on faith till it reveals itself in the devotee's consciousness.[152] Since faith is a vital element, the gods in whom the people have faith are tolerated. In view of the unlimited variety of the habits and minds of men, liberty of thought and worship is allowed to the individual. Some love is better than none, for if we do not love, we become shut up within ourselves. The infinite presents itself to the human soul in a variety of aspects. The lower gods are forms or aspects of the one Supreme. The Gītā ranks the avatārs of the divine as lower than Puruṣottama; Brahmā, Viṣṇu and Śiva, if they are not names for the Supreme acting as creator, preserver and destroyer, are also subordinated to Puruṣottama.[153] The worship of Vedic gods is admitted.[154] Out of a feeling of pity, the Gītā allows freedom to the multitudes worshipping kṣudra devatas or petty divinities. So long as worship is done with devotion it purifies the heart and prepares the mind for the higher consciousness.[155]

The philosophical justification of this tolerant attitude is suggested though not worked out. A man is what his thoughts are. Whatever he has faith in, that he will attain to. The world is a purposive moral order, where the individual obtains what he desires. 'Those who make vows to the gods go to the gods; those who make vows to manes go to them.'[156] 'Whichever form any worshipper wishes to worship with faith, to that form I render his faith steady. Possessed of that faith, he seeks to propitiate that deity, and obtains from it those beneficial things which are really given by Me.'[157] As Rāmānuja observes: 'From Brahmā to a reed, all things that live in the

151. Nārada Sūtras, 4–7. Mattaḥ, stabdhaḥ, ātmārāmaḥ.
152. iv. 40.
153. xi. 37.
154. ix. 23.
155. vii. 21–23.
156. ix. 25; see also xvii. 3.
157. vii. 20–21.

world are subject to birth and death caused by karma, therefore they cannot be helpful as objects of meditation.' Only the true Lord Puruṣottama can serve as the object of devotion. The lower forms are stepping-stones to it. In chapter x we are called upon to fix our mind on particular objects and persons displaying power and grandeur to an extraordinary degree. This is called pratīka upāsana. In chapter xi the whole universe assumes the form of God. In chapter xii we dwell on the presiding God. Only the highest can give us freedom. Other devotees reach finite ends, while the devotees of the Supreme reach infinite bliss.[158]

The forms which bhakti takes are contemplation of God's power, wisdom and goodness, constant remembrance of Him with a devout heart, conversing about His qualities with other persons, singing His praises with fellow-men and doing all acts as His service.[159] No fixed rules can be laid down. By these different movements the human soul draws near to the divine. Several symbols and disciplines are devised to train the mind to turn godward. Absolute devotion to God is not possible unless we give up our desires for sense-objects. So yoga is sometimes adopted.[160] The impulse may take any form of adoration, from external worship to a periodical reminder to free us from the preoccupations of life. The Gītā asks us sometimes to think of God, excluding all other objects. This is a negative method.[161] It also requires us to look upon the whole world as a supreme manifestation of God.[162] We have to realise God in nature and self, and so regulate our conduct as to make it expressive of the divine in man. Supreme devotion and complete self-surrender, or bhakti and prapatti, are the different sides of the one fact. The Gītā recognises that the one infinite God can be approached and worshipped through any of His aspects. This tolerant spirit has made Hinduism a synthesis of different kinds of worship and experience, an atmosphere unifying many cults and creeds, a system of thought or a spiritual culture based on the fact that the one truth has many sides.

In the highest fulfilment of devotion, we possess a sense of certitude about the object. The experience is self-certifying in character. It is its

158. Anto brahmādibhaktānām madbhaktānām anantatā.... Madhva's commentary on the Gītā, vii. 21.

159. Nārada Sūtras, 16–18.

160. Ibid., 47–49.

161. B.G., xviii. 73.

162. Chaps. vi and xi.

own proof, svayam pramāṇam. Logical discussions are not of much avail. The true devotees do not worry about vain discussions concerning God.[163] This is the highest kind of bhakti, from which there is no transition to anything else. It is devotion that is constant, *nirantara*, unmotived *nirhetuka*.[164] Few there are who are willing to serve God for naught. The Gītā has not the weakness of emotional religions which deny knowledge and will for the sake of love. While all devotees are dear to the Lord, the possessor of wisdom is the dearest of all.[165] The other three classses of devotees, the suffering, the seeker of knowledge and the selfish, may have petty aims and cease to love God when their desires are fulfilled, but the seer worships Him ever in purity of spirit.[166] Bhakti, or intense love for God, becomes then a fire, scorching, burning and consuming all linitis of individuality. The vision of truth is revealed. Without this restraint of the spiritual truth, the Gītā religion might lapse into emotionalism, and devotion itself might become a mere carnival of feeling.

What begins as quiet prayer, a longing for the sight of the beloved, ends in an irresistible rapture of love and delight. The worshipper becomes incorporate with God's being. He feels the force of the truth of the oneness of God in the universe. 'Vāsudevaḥ sarvam iti.' He escapes from the loneliness of life and the insignificance of a world where he was a mere particular to one where he becomes the instrument of the central Spirit.[167] The largest human personality is only a partial expression of it. The genuine nature of each individual is the eternal spirit revealing itself in time and space. Knowledge and devotion become interdependent.[168] True devotion issues in unselfish conduct. The devotee is consumed by an all-embracing beneficent love that seeks not its own or any return for its overflowing. It is like the divine love that brought the universe into being, maintains it and lifts it up to itself. Not the devotee but the power of spirit acts in him in a divine freedom. Absolute self-surrender and the dedication of all work to God mark the conduct of the true devotee. He has thus in him the content of the highest philosophy as well as the energy of the perfect man. Though here and there we come across passionate souls who do not worry about

163. Nārada Sūtras, 58 and 75.
164. B.G., vii. 17–18; viii. 14–22; Bhāgavata, iii. 29–12.
165. vii. 17.
166. xviii. 5.
167. B.G., xviii. 46; vii. 19; viii. 7.
168. Nārada Sūtras, 28–29.

the affairs of the world, still the ideal devotee of the Gītā is one in whom love is lighted up by knowledge and bursts forth into a fierce desire to suffer for mankind. Tilak quotes a śloka from Viṣṇu Purāṇa, which says: 'Those who give up their duties and sit down uttering the name Kṛṣṇa, Kṛṣṇa, are really the enemies of God and sinners. Even the Lord took birth in the world for the sake of righteousness.'[169]

It is obvious that for those who insist on devotion as the final nature of spiritual life, the end is not an immersion in the eternal impersonal, but a union with the Puruṣottama. The Gītā, however, recognises nirguṇa bhakti, or devotion to the qualityless, as superior to all else. Then the absolute becomes the most ultimate category.[170] When devotion is perfected, then the individual and his God become suffused into one spiritual ecstasy, and reveal themselves as aspects of one life. Absolute monism is therefore the completion of the dualism with which the devotional consciousness starts.

XI

KARMA MĀRGA

Through divine service or karma we can also reach the highest. Karma is act or deed, even that by which the impersonal becomes personal.[171] Karma is said to be beginningless, and the exact manner by which the work of the world process is hard to understand.[172] At the end of creation the whole world is said to lie in the form of a subtle karma seed ready to sprout again at the next start.[173] Since the world process is dependent upon the Lord, we can call Him the lord of karma.[174] We are committed to some action or other. It is necessary to see to it that our conduct promotes the interests of righteousness, which at the same time results in spiritual rest and satisfaction. Karma mārga is the path of conduct by which the individual thirsting for service can reach the goal.

At the time of the Gītā many different views of right conduct prevailed, viz. the Vedic theory of the observance of rites and ceremonies, the Upaniṣad doctrine of a search after truth, the Buddhistic idea of the giving up of all

169. See B.G., ix. 30; cf. 1 John ii. 9–11, iv. 18–20.
170. See Bhāgavata, iii. 29; vii. 14.
171. vii. 24–25.
172. iv. 17.
173. viii. 18–19.
174. vii. 22.

actions and the theistic view of the worship of God. The Gītā tries to round them all into a consistent system.

The Gītā recognises that it is through work that we are brought into relation with the rest of the world. The problem of morality has significance only in the human world. The self of man alone of the objects of the world possesses a sense of responsibility. The individual aspires after spiritual happiness, but he cannot derive it from the material elements of the world. The pleasure which he strives after is of different kinds. What is derived from a deluded mind and false desires has more of tamas in it; what is derived from the senses has more of rajas, and the pleasure of self-knowledge has more of sattva in it.[175] The highest satisfaction can come only when the individual ceases to look upon himself as an independent agent and feels that God in His infinite grace guides the world. The spirit in man is satisfied if it sees the spirit in the world.[176] Good work is that which helps us to the liberation of the individual and the perfection of spirit.

Right conduct is whatever expresses our real unity with God, man, and nature; wrong conduct is whatever does not bring out this essential structure of reality. The unity of the universe is the basic principle. Good is whatever advances towards completeness, and evil is whatever is inconsistent with it. This is the essential difference between Buddhism and the Gītā. Buddhism no doubt made morality central to the good life, but it did not sufficiently emphasise the relation of moral life to spiritual perfection or the purpose of the universe. In the Gītā we are assured that even though we may fail in our efforts, the central divine purpose can never be destroyed. It points out that the soul of the world is just, in spite of all appearances to the contrary. The individual fulfils his destiny when he becomes the instrument of the increasing purpose of God.

The finite centres should look upon themselves as members of an organism and work for the sake of the whole. The false claim to absoluteness and the wrong view that his independence is limited by that of others should be abandoned. The true ideal is loakasaṁgraha, or the solidarity of the world. The spirit of the whole works in the world. The good man should co-operate with it and aim at the welfare of the world.[177] The Gītā repudiates the notion of individual claims. The best people have

175. ii. 71; vi. 22. 15. 28; xii. 12; xvii. 62; xviii. 36–38.
176. Plato, *Republic*, ix.
177. v. 25; xii. 4.

the largest burdens to bear. The venture of finite beings implies evil that has to be overcome. We cannot shrink from the task of fighting sin and injustice. The hesitating Arjuna was persuaded by Kṛṣṇa to fight, not for love of glory or lust of kingdom, but for the sake of the law of righteousness; but when we fight injustice we should do so, not in passion or ignorance which brings grief and disquiet, but in knowledge and with love for all.[178]

Sense control becomes a characteristic of the good man. Passion imprisons our spiritual nature. It deadens discretion and fetters reason. To give full rein to the untamed impulses is to enslave the soul dwelling in the body.[179] The Gītā requires us to develop a spirit of detachment and indifference to the results of action, the spirit of yoga, or impartiality.[180] True renunciation consists in this. Giving up acts out of ignorance is tyāga mixed with tamas; giving up acts out of fear of consequences such as bodily suffering is tyāga with rajas in it; doing work in a spirit of detachment without fear of consequences is the best form, since it has more of sattva in it.[181]

It is necessary to understand the exact bearing of the Gītā on the question of work. It does not support an ascetic ethics. The Buddhistic theory of inaction is interpreted in a more positive way. True inaction is action without any hope of reward. Analysing the nature of the act of karma, the Gītā distinguishes the mental antecedents from the outer deed, and calls upon us to control the former by suppressing all selfishness.[182] Naiṣkarmya, or abstention from action, is not the true law of morality, but niṣkāmatā, or disinterestedness.[183] Passion, anger and covetousness, the three ways to hell, are to be overcome.[184] All desires are not bad. The desire after righteousness is divine.[185] The Gītā, instead of demanding a rooting out of our passions, asks for a purifying of them. The physical-vital nature is to be cleansed, the mental-intellectual nature is to be purified, and then the spiritual nature finds its satisfaction.[186] The Gītā is certain that inertia

178. xi. 55.
179. vi. 46; viii. 27.
180. vi. 46; viii. 27.
181. xvii. 7–9, 11–12.
182. xviii. 18.
183. v. 11; xviii. 49.
184. ii. 62–63; xvi. 21.
185. vii. 11.
186. Puṣti, tuṣti and śānti are the respective ideals of the vital, the intellectual and the spiritual sides of human nature.

is not liberty. 'Nor indeed can embodied beings completely relinquish action.'[187]

The eye cannot choose but see,
We cannot bid the ear be still,
Our bodies feel where'er they be
Against or with our will.[188]

Rest is not on earth; it is all life for ever. Work keeps up the circuit of the world, and each individual should try his best to keep it going.[189] The whole setting of the Gītā points out that it is an exhortation to action. Work is inevitable till we attain freedom. We have to work for the sake of freedom, and when we attain it, we have to work as instruments of the divine. Then, of course, there is no more work necessary for preparing the mind or purifying the heart. The freed souls have no rules to obey, they do what they please, but the vital point is they do something.[190]

The Gītā asks us to act in a way when action does not bind. The Lord Himself acts for the sake of humanity. Though from the absolute standpoint He is self-contained and desireless, He has always something to accomplish in the world. Even so is Arjuna asked to fight and do his work. The free souls have also the obligation to help others to discover the divine in themselves. Service of humanity is worship of God.[191] To work desirelessly and impersonally for the sake of the world and God does not bind us. 'Nor do these works bind Me, enthroned on high, unattached to actions.'[192] The Gītā draws a distinction between sannyāsa and tyāga: 'Sannyāsa is renouncing all interested works; tyāga is giving up the fruit of all work.'[193] The latter is more comprehensive. The Gītā does not ask us to abhor the common business of life, but demands the suppression of all selfish desires. It is a combination of pravṛtti, or work, and nivṛtti, or withdrawal, that the Gītā upholds. Mere withdrawal is not true renunciation. The hands may be at rest, but the desires may be busy. What binds is not work, but the spirit

187. xviii. 11.
188. Wordsworth.
189. iii. 10. 16.
190. Bṛh. Up., vi. 4. 22; S.B., iii. 32.
191. xviii. 46.
192. ix. 9; iv. 13–14.
193. xviii. 2.

in which it is done. 'The giving up of karmas by the ignorant is really a positive act; the work of the wise is really inaction.'[194] The inner life of spirit is compatible with active life in the world. The Gītā reconciles the two in the spirit of the Upaniṣads. Action in the way indicated by the Gītā is skilled action. 'Yogaḥ karmasu kauśalam,' yoga is skill in works.[195]

Whatever we do has to be done not in subjection to an external law, but in obedience to the inner determination of the soul's freedom. This is the highest kind of action. Aristotle says: 'He is best who acts on his own convictions, while he is second best who acts in obedience to the counsel of others.'[196] To the unregenerate the scriptures are the authority. The injunctions of the Vedas are only external, and do not bind us when we reach the highest condition, where we act naturally in accordance with the law of spirit.

All work has to be done in purity of motive. We have to exclude from our minds subtle shades of selfishness, preferences for special forms of work, desire for sympathy and applause. Good karma, if it is to purify the mind and lead us to wisdom, should be performed in this spirit. The selfish regoist who looks upon himself as a god on earth and hunts after sense-pleasures is a demon adopting materialism in metaphysics and sensualism in ethics.[197]

The theory of the guṇas or qualities plays an important part in the Gītā ethics.[198] The bondage to guṇas causes the feeling of limitedness. The bonds belonging to mind are erroneously attributed to the self. Though action saturated with sattva is said to be the best kind of action,[199] it is also urged that even sattva binds, since a nobler desire brings about a purer ego. For full freedom all egoism should cease. The ego, however pure it may be, is an obstructing veil and binds itself to knowledge and bliss. Getting beyond all qualities and occupying an impersonal cosmic outlook form the ideal state.[200]

The Gītā transforms the Vedic theory of sacrifices and reconciles it with true spiritual knowledge.[201] The outer gift is a symbol of the inner

194. Aṣṭāavakragītā, xviii. 61.
195. ii. 50, 48; iii. 3; iv. 42; vi. 33, 46.
196. Ethics, i. 4–7.
197. xvi. 8, 42.
198. xiv. 5.
199. xviii. 23.
200. xiv. 19.
201. iv. 24–27.

spirit. The sacrifices are attempts to develop self-restraint and self-surrender. The true sacrifice is the sacrifice of the sense delights. The god to whom we offer is the great Supreme, or the Yajña Puruṣa, the lord of sacrifices.[202] We have to feel that all objects are divinely appointed means for the realisation of the highest ends and engage ourselves in work, resigning it all to God. Whether we eat or drink or whatsoever we do we should do all to the glory of God. A yogin always acts in God, and his conduct becomes a model for imitation by others.[203]

The Gītā lays down several general principles for the regulation of human conduct. The golden mean is advised in some passages.[204] The Gītā recognises the caste divisions as well as the theory of the stages of life. Men on a lower level of feeling and thought cannot all of a sudden be lifted up into a higher state. The humanising process takes a long time, sometimes several generations. The Gītā broadly distinguishes four fundamental types of individuals answering to the four stages of the upward ascent. Basing caste on qualities,[205] the Gītā requires each individual to do the duties imposed by his caste.[206] Svadharma is the work in agreement with the law of one's being. We worship God by doing our ordained duties.[207] God intends every man for some work in connection with society. The constitution of the social order is said to be divine. Plato supports an analogous doctrine. 'The ruler of the universe has ordered all things with a view to the excellence and preservation of the whole, and each part, as far as may be, has an action and passion appropriate to it ... for every physician and every skilled artist does all things for the sake of the whole, directing this effort toward the common good, executing the part for the sake of the whole, and not the whole for the sake of the part.'[208] Though originally framed on the basis of qualities, caste very soon became a matter of birth. It is hard to know who has which qualities. The only available test is birth. The confusion of birth and qualities has led to an undermining of the spiritual foundation of caste. There is no necessity why men of a particular birth should always possess the character expected of them. Since the facts of life do not answer to the logical ideal, the whole institution of caste is

202. iv. 33.
203. iii. 21.
204. vi. 16–17.
205. iv. 13.
206. ii. 31.
207. xviii. 46–47.
208. *Laws*, x. 903B. Jowett's version.

breaking down. While it is easy to condemn the system from our present-day knowledge, we have to recognise in fairness to it that it attempted to build a society on a basis of mutual goodwill and co-operation and remedy the dangers of a competitive view of society. It recognised the supremacy not of wealth, but of wisdom, and its judgment of values is correct.

The last of the four stages is that of sannyāsa, where the individual is called upon to withdraw from life.[209] This stage, it is sometimes said, is to be entered on when the body is shrinking and the subject feels unfit for work.[210] True sannyāsa is the giving up of selfish desires, and this is possible even while we live as householders.[211] It is not right to say that, in the view of the Gītā, we cannot attain mokṣa or freedom unless we resort to the last stage of sannyāsa.

Action performed in the spirit indicated by the Gītā finds its completion in wisdom.[212] Egoism is eliminated and a sense of the divine is kindled. If we do the will we shall know of the doctrine. In that stage there is also a heartfelt devotion to the divine. Thus karma mārga leads us to a condition where emotion, knowledge and will are all present.

From our account it is clear that the path of service leads to mokṣa; only it is not karma in the sense of the Pūrva Mīmāṁsā. Vedic sacrifices do not lead us to freedom. They have only an instrumental use. They prepare the mind for higher wisdom. But karma performed as a sacrifice to God, and in a spirit of disinterestedness and impersonality, is quite as efficacious as any other method, and there is no need to subordinate it to the method of wisdom as Śaṁkara does, or that of devotion as Rāmānuja believes. In the interests of their own views, they make out that it was only to flatter Arjuna and coax him into action that Kṛṣṇa declares the path of karma to be superior.[213] We cannot suppose that Arjuna was called upon to act with a lie in his soul. Nor is he an ajñānin who has to work for the sake of purifying his mind and heart. It is not possible for us to look upon Janaka, Kṛṣṇa and others as persons who indulge in works because they are men of imperfect wisdom. Nor is there need to think that after attaining wisdom there is no possibility for work. Janaka says that the true preaching was declared to him, which was to do karma, after killing selfish desires by

209. Manu, vi. 33–37; M.B., Śāntiparva, 241. 15; 244. 3.
210. Manu, vi. 2; M.B., Udyogaparva, 36. 39.
211. B.G., v. 3.
212. Chap. iv.
213. S.B.G., v. 2; vi. 1–2; xviii. 11; R.B.G., v. 1; iii 1.

wisdom. Even Śaṁkara allows that after the attainment of wisdom some karmas are necessary to sustain the body.[214] If some acts are allowed, it is only a question of degree how much the freed soul does. If the individual is afraid of becoming once again subject to karma, it means that his sense-control is not perfect.[215] Even if we believe that as Brahman is different from the world, so is Ātman from the body, there is nothing to prevent the body from performing acts.[216] The Gītā, however, admits that men are of different temperaments, and some are inclined to withdrawal and others to service, and they will have to act according to the law of their own being.[217]

Before we pass from this section it is necessary to note the views of the Gītā on the question of human freedom. The will of man seems to be determined by past nature, Beredity, training and environment. The whole world seems to converge in the nature of the individual. Except indirectly, the determination by nature cannot be called an ordinance of God. 'All existences follow their nature, and what shall coercing it avail?'[218] Human effort seems to be vain, since God in the centre of things seems to whirl all individuals 'as if mounted on a machine.'[219] If the will determined by nature were all, there is no human freedom. The Buddhists declare that there is no self, but only karma acts. The Gītā recognises a soul superior to the mechanically determined will. Whatever may be the truth of the ultimate state of the soul, when freed from bondage to nature, at the moral level it has a separate independent existence. The Gītā believes in human freedom. Kṛṣṇa, after describing the whole philosophy of life, asks Arjuna to 'do as he chooses.'[220] There is no omnipotence of nature over the human soul. We are not obliged to follow the dictates of nature. We are actually warned against our likes and dislikes, which are 'the besetters of the soul in its path.' A distinction is made between what is inevitable in the make-up of nature which we cannot suppress and those wanderings and confusions which we can get rid of. Those beings whose souls have not struggled to the surface are driven by the current of nature. Human individuals in whom intelligence predominates check the process of nature.

214. iii. 8.
215. xviii. 7; iii. 6.
216. iv. 21; v. 12.
217. M.B. Śāntiparva, 339–340.
218. xviii. 59–60; see also iii. 33, 36.
219. xviii. 61.
220. Yathecchasi tathā kuru, xviii. 63.

They refer all activities to the intelligent will. They do not lead unexamined animal lives, unless they are dominated by passion. 'What propels a man to sin, often seemingly against his will, and as if constrained by some secret force?' The answer is given that 'it is lust, which instigates him ... it is the enemy of man on earth.'[221] It is possible for the individual to control his passion and regulate his conduct by reason. Śaṁkara writes: 'As regards all sense-objects, such as sounds, there necessarily arises in each sense love for an agreeable object, and aversion to a disagreeable object. Now I shall tell you where lies the scope for personal exertion and for the teaching of the śāstras. He who would follow the teaching should at the very commencement rise above the sway of affection and aversion.'[222] Karma is only a condition and not a destiny. This follows even from the Gītā analysis of the act where fate is only one of five factors. For the accomplishment of any act, five elements are necessary. They are adhiṣṭhāna, or basis, some centre from which to work; kartṛ, or a doer; karaṇa, or the instrumentation of nature; ceṣṭā, or effort; and daiva, or fate. This last is the power or powers other than human, the cosmic principle which stands behind modifying the work and disposing of its fruits in the shape of act and its reward.

XII

MOKṢA

Whatever be the method we pursue, wisdom, love or service, the end reached is the same, union of the soul with the highest. When the mind is purified and egoism is destroyed, the individual becomes one with the supreme. If we start with the service of man, we end by becoming one with the supreme, not merely in work and consciousness, but in life and being. Love culminates in the ecstasy of devotion, where soul and God become one. Whatever route we approach by, we end in seeing, experiencing and living the divine life. This is the highest form of religion or life of spirit, called jñāna in the wider sense of the term.

Jñāna as the method of attaining spiritual reality is distinct from jñāna as the spiritual intuition, which is the ideal. Śaṁkara correctly observes that mokṣa, or direct perception of God, is not an act of service or devotion,

221. iii. 37; vi 5–6.
222. S.B.G., iii. 34.

or for that matter cognition, however much it may be led up to by it. It is an experience or a direct insight into truth. It is to attain God that the different paths are tried. The Gītā is not wholly consistent in its evaluation of the different routes to reality. 'Try to know Me. If you cannot contemplate Me, practise yoga. If you are not equal to this, try to serve Me by dedicating all your work to Me. If even this is found hard, do your duty regardless of consequences, giving up all desire for fruits.'[223] Again: 'Better indeed is wisdom than constant practice; meditation is better than wisdom; renouncing the fruit of action is better than meditation; on renunciation follows peace.'[224] Each of the methods is preferred sometime or other.[225] In the mind of the author any method will do, and what the method is is left to the individual's choice. 'Some by meditation, others by reflection, others by action, others by worship ... pass beyond death.'[226]

The supreme experience is freedom, and the word jñāna is employed to refer to both the goal of the adventure as well as the path leading to it. On account of this confusion some have been led to think that jñāna as a path is superior to the other methods of approach, and that cognition alone persists, while the other elements of emotion and will fall out in the supreme state of freedom. There does not seem to be any justification for such an opinion.

Freedom or mokśa is unity with the supreme self. It is called by different names: mukti, or release; brāhmī sthiti being in Brahman, naiṣkarmya, or non-action; nistraiguṇya, or the absence of the three qualities; kaivalya, or solitary salvation; brahmabhāva, or the being of Brahman. In the absolute experience there is a feeling of the oneness of all. 'The Ātman is in all beings, and all beings are in the Ātman.'[227] The state of perfection exceeds the fruits of righteousness, resulting from the observance of Vedic rites, performances of sacrifices and all other methods.[228]

We have already said that different interpretations are given as to the place of work in the ultimate condition. The Gītā is not clear on the point whether there is any basis of individuality in the ultimate state. The final

223. xii. 9–11.
224. xii. 12.
225. vi. 46; vii. 16; xii. 12.
226. xiii. 24–25, xviii. 54–56.
227. vi. 29.
228. viii. 28.

condition is called siddhi, or perfection; parāsiddhi, or supreme perfection; parāṁgatim, or the supreme goal; 'padam anāmayam,' or the blissful seat; śānti, or quietude; 'śāśvatam padam avyayam,' the eternal indestructible abode.[229] These expressions are colourless, and do not tell us whether there is a continuance of individuality in the state of freedom. There are texts which assert that the released are not troubled about the concerns of the world. They have no individuality, and therefore no basis for action. Duality disappears and work becomes impossible. The freed man has no qualities. He becomes one with the eternal self.[230] If prakṛti acts, and if the eternal is independent of the modes of prakṛti's workings, then in the state of mokṣa there is no ego, no will, no desire. It is a condition beyond all modes and qualities, impassive, free and at peace. It is not mere survival of death, but the attaining of the supreme state of being, where the spirit knows itself to be superior to birth and death, infinite, eternal, and unconditioned by manifestations. Śaṁkara takes his stand on these passages and interprets the freedom of the Gītā in the sense of the kaivalya of he Sāṁkhyas. If we have a body clinging to us, nature will go on acting till the body is shaken off as a discarded shell. The impersonal spirit is detached from the workings of the body. Even Śaṁkara recognises that there will be life and action so long as there is the body. We cannot escape from the instrumentalism of nature. The Jīvanmukta, or the freed soul, possessing the body, reacts to the events of the outer world, though he does not get entangled in them. There is no suggestion of the transformation of the whole nature into the immortal dharma, the law of the infinite power of the divine. Spirit and body are an unreconciled duality, and the spirit can attain its perfection only when the sense of the reality of the body is shaken off. On this view we cannot think of the action of the highest Brahman, since the basis of all activity, the unstable formation in the bosom of the infinite, the temporary phenomenon is dissolved. A perfect relinquishment of our point of view seems to be the end of all progress. Śaṁkara is emphatic that our view of the infinite is not its true measure. The fullness of its life cannot be comprehended by us from our human standpoint. Adopting this view, he urges that those verses of the Gītā which imply the plurality of spirits do not refer to the ultimate state, but only to relative conditions.

229. xii. 10; xvi. 23; xiv. 1; vi. 45; viii. 13; ix. 32; xvi. 22–23; ii. 51; iv. 39; v. 12; xviii. 62; xviii. 56.

230. Ātmaiva, vii. 18. He obtains my nature, madbhāvaṁ yāti, viii. 5; see also viii. 7.

We have other verses which suggest that action is possible even for the freed souls. The men of insight and wisdom imitate the supreme Lord and act in the world.[231] The highest condition is not a laya or a disappearance in the supreme, but one of individuality. The freed spirit, though centred in impersonality, possesses its own individuality as a part of the divine soul. Even as Puruṣottama, who has the whole universe suffused through His being, acts, the liberated individuals should act. The highest state is one of dwelling in Puruṣottama.[232] Those who have attained it are freed from rebirth and attain to the status of God.[233] Release is not obliteration of individuality for all eternity, but a state of blissful freedom of the soul with a distinct existence in the presence of God. 'My devotees come to me.'[234] The author of the Gītā seems to believe in a continuance of conscious individuality even in freedom. As a matter of fact, some passages suggest that the freed do not become God, but only attain sameness of essence with God.[235] Freedom is not pure identity, but only qualitative sameness, an elevation of the soul to God-like existence, where petty desires have no power to move. To be immortal is to live in the eternal light. We do not cease to be selves, but deepen our selfhood, efface all stains of sin, cut asunder the knot of doubt, master ourselves, and are ever engaged in doing good to all creatures. We do not free ourselves from all qualities, but possess the sattva quality and suppress the rajas.[236] Rāmānuja insists on this view, and makes out that the freed soul is in constant union (nityayukta) with God, and his whole life and being reveal it. Knowledge streams from the light in which he lives, and in his love for God he is practically lost. We seem to possess here a supreme existence attained not by a total exclusion of nature, but by a higher spiritual fulfilment of it. On this view we act and live in God; only the centre of activity shifts from the human self to the divine. The divine energy is felt to be pulsating through the whole world, taking different forms in different things. Each soul has its centre and circumference in God. The view of Rāmānuja holds to the truth of spiritual personality as a factor even in the highest experience.

There are then two conflicting views in the Gītā about the ultimate

231. iv. 14–15.
232. Nivasiṣyasi mayyeva.
233. xviii. 21; iv. 10. Madbhāvam āgatāḥ.
234. vii. 23; see also ix. 25; iv. 9.
235. xiv. 2. Mama sādharmyam āgatāḥ.
236. Śāntarajasam, vi. 27.

state, one which makes the freed soul lose itself in the impersonality of Brahman and attain a peace beyond the strife of the world, and the other where we possess and enjoy God, being lifted above all suffering and pain and the eagerness of petty desires, which are the badges of subjection. The Gītā being a religious work insists on the ultimateness of a personal God, and calls for a full flowering of the divine in man to its utmost capacity of wisdom and power, love and universality. From this we cannot, however, conclude that the Gītā view is opposed to that of the Upaniṣads. The controversy is only a particular application of the general problem whether the absolute Brahman or the personal Puruṣottama is the highest reality. In the discussion of Gītā metaphysics we have said that the Gītā does not repudiate the ultimate reality of the absolute Brahman, but it suggests that from our point of view this absolute reveals itself as the personal Lord. There is no other way for thought, human and limited as it is, to envisage the highest reality. Adopting the same standpoint, we may say that the two views of the ultimate state of freedom are the intuitional and the intellectual ways of representing the one condition. From our human standpoint the absolute seems to be a passive, relationless identity, making all action impossible while it is not really so. If we want to give positive descriptions of it, then Rāmānuja's account is the only available one. To make out that the two, the absolute and the personal God, are one, the Gītā says that in the highest reality impersonality and personality are combined in a manner that is incomprehensible to us. Even so the freed spirits may have no individuality, and yet have one by self-limitation. It is in this way that the Gītā harmonises the ever immobile quietism of the timeless self with the eternal play of the energy of nature.

Whatever the truth be regarding the state of the freed after death, so long as he continues to live in the world, he is committed to some action or other. Śaṁkara sees in his activity the modes of nature's working, and Rāmānuja the actions of the supreme. These are two different ways of expressing the impersonality of action. His work is done in a freedom of the soul and with an inner joy and peace which does not depend on externals for its source or continuance. The freed souls throw off the listlessness of scepticism. All darkness is dispelled from their countenances. They show in their animated looks and firm voice that they have the vitality of a spiritual persuasion which they do not and cannot distrust. They are not subject to the dominion of flesh or attraction of desire. They are not cast down in adversity or elated in prosperity. They are strangers to anxiety, fear and anger. They possess an easy mind and the unspoiled virgin outlook of a child.[237]

The freed soul is beyond all good and evil. Virtue is transcended in perfection. The mukta rises above any mere ethical rule of living to the light, largeness and power of spiritual life. Even if he should have committed any evil acts which would in ordinary circumstances necessitate another birth on earth, no such thing is necessary. He is freed from ordinary rules and regulations. Absolute individualism is the view of the Gītā so far as the end is concerned. It would be a dangerous doctrine if these freed men should imitate Nietzsche's super-man, who has no patience with the weak and the unfit, the defective and the delinquent. Though they are freed from social obligations, the free spirits of the Gītā freely approve of them. The liberated do not suffer any vexation in themselves or cause vexation to others.[238] It is their second nature to work for the welfare of the world. These noble souls regard with equal mind all things of the earth. They stand for a dynamic creative spiritual life, and see to it that the social regulations tend to the fuller spiritual unfolding or expression of human life. They do their appointed work, niyatam karma, ordained by the divine will which works in them.

While the Gītā insists much on social duties, it recognises a supra-social state. It believes in the infinite destiny of the individual apart from human society. The sannyāsin is above all rules, caste and society. This symbolises the infinite dignity of man, who can strip himself of all externals, even wife and children, and be self-sufficient in the solitude of the desert if he has his God with him. It is not an ascetic ideal that the sannyāsin adopts. He may be aloof from society, yet he has compassion for all. Mahādeva, the ideal ascetic, seated in the Himalayan snows, readily drinks poison for the saving of humanity.

REFERENCES

Telang, Bhagavadgītā. S.B.E., vol. viii.
Tilak, Gītārahasya.
Aurobindo Ghosh, Essays on the Gītā.

237. Cf. Bālabhāvas tathā bhāvo niścinto yoga ucyate. Jñānasaṁkalinī Tantra.
238. xii. 15.

CHAPTER X

Buddhism as a Religion

The history of Buddhism after the death of Buddha—Aśoka—The Mahāyāna and the Hīnayāna—Northern and southern Buddhism—Literature—Hīnayāna doctrines—Metaphysics, ethics and religion—The rise of the Mahāyāna—Its monistic metaphysics—The religion of the Mahāyāna—Its resemblance to the Bhagavadgītā—The ethics of the Mahāyāna—The ten stages—Hīnayāna and Mahāyāna ethics compared—Nirvāṇa—Decline of Buddhism—The effects of Buddhism on Indian thought.

I

SECTS OF BUDDHISM

Even in the lifetime of Buddha there were tendencies to schism among his followers,[1] though they did not develop or account of the magnetic personality of the founder. After his death they became emphasised. The Hīnayānists believe that the Theravāda is identical with the three piṭakas as now existing in Ceylon and compiled at the first council at Rājagṛha. This first council tried, against much opposition, to relax the rigours of asceticism and make some softening changes in the rules. A second council took place at Vaiśāli about a hundred years after the first one. It considered the theory and practices of the Vinaya, or the rules of the order, and debated whether any indulgences should be allowed or not. After a severe struggle, the more orthodox party, Sthaviras,[2] or the elders, succeeded in condemning the indulgences. The progressive party, or the Mahāsaṅghikas, which was defeated, had large numbers to support them. They held a council called the Mahāsaṅgīti, or the great council. We have the story of this great council, from the orthodox point of view, described in Dīpavaṁśa.[3] It is said to have overturned religion and 'broken up the old scriptures,' 'distorted the sayings and doctrines of the Nikāyas,' and 'destroyed the spirit of Buddha's teaching.' The main point of difference between the orthodox and the progressive sections seems to have been on the question of the attainment

1. Witness the attempts of Devadatta.
2. Pāli Theras.
3. 5.

of Buddhahood. The Sthaviras held that it was a quality to be acquired by a strict observance of the rules of the Vinaya. The progressives maintained that Buddhahood was a quality inborn in every human being, and by adequate development it was capable of raising its possessor to the rank of a tathāgata. The Sthaviravāda, or the orthodox view, is said to be the lineal ancestor of Ceylonese Buddhism. Buddhism even in the second century of its existence had broken up into eighteen sects, all of them claiming to be the original faith. We do not know further details of the course of Buddhism till Aśoka's time.[4] When Aśoka, the Mauryan emperor, adopted Buddhism two centuries and a half after Buddha's death, there was a vigorous expansion of Buddhism. What was only a local sect of Hinduism for nearly three centuries after the death of Buddha became largely through the endeavours of Aśoka a world religion.[5] All over this vast empire, which extended from the valley of Kabul to the mouths of the Ganges and from the Himalayas to the south of the Vindhya mountains, he gave orders that his edicts should be engraven on stone pillars, so that they might abide for ever. He sent missionaries to all parts of India, from Kashmir to Ceylon, even to countries not under his sway. The thirteenth edict states that he sent missionaries to Antiochous II of Syria, Ptolemy II of Egypt, Antigonos Gonatos of Macedonia, Magas of Cyrene and Alexander II of Epirus. In the third century BC Buddhism entered Kashmir and Ceylon, and penetrated slowly into Nepal and Tibet, China, Japan and Mongolia. Aśoka's son Mahendra, it is said, was made the head of the Buddhist church of Ceylon. In view of the tendency for new practices to creep into the Buddhist religion, Aśoka emphasised the moral side of Buddhism.[6] The increased respect paid to the order already attracted many men of doubtful views into it, and as the Mahāvaṁśa says, 'heretics assumed the yellow robe in order to share in its advantages; whenever they had opinions of their own they gave them forth as doctrines of the Buddha, they acted according to their own

4. 'We know, whether from native or foreign sources, very little of what happened during the century and half that followed after the Buddha's death.' Rhys Davids, *Buddhist India*, p. 259.

5. See V. Smith, *Aśoka*, p. 22.

6. Aśoka mentions in one of his inscriptions that he caused a stūpa (memorial building) of Kanakamuni to be put up for a second time. It is obvious that people had already taken to building stūpas, making pilgrimages, etc. The fact that Kanakamuni was looked upon as a past Buddha shows that even then there was the belief in the series of Buddhas.

will, and not according to what was right.'[7] A third council met at Pāṭaliputra[8] under the presidentship of Tissa, son of Moggalī, with the object of purifying the doctrine.

The new rulers of India, the Yavanas, the Śakas, the Kṣātrapas, the Satavāhanas, the Pahlavas and the Kuṣaṇas, many of whom were of foreign nationality, readily adopted the Buddhist religion. Though Brāhminism had its representatives in the South and the West, yet the great majority were Buddhistic. Under he Guptas, who came to power in the first century AD (319 AD?), Brāhmanism revived. We read of Samudragupta's Aśvamedha sacrifice in the inscriptions of Candragupta at Madhura and Skandagupta in Behar. We have also many other monuments of Brāhmanic revival. The sectarian worship of Śiva and Viṣṇu becomes popular. Subandhu in his Vāsavadattā tells us that Buddhist doctrines were attacked by the followers of Jaimini.[9] Prākrit, the chief language of the Buddhists, yielded to Sanskrit, as is evident from the Buddhist Sanskrit inscriptions of the era. Buddhism imitated Brāhmanism in making a god of Buddha. Images of Buddha were set up, devotion to a personal being developed, and Nāgārjuana, a contemporary of Kaniṣka, gave a distinct form to this type of Buddhism, called the Mahāyāna, though it was shaping itself even before his time. Mahāyānism seems to be the culmination of the movement which led to the secession of the Mahāsaṁghikas from the Theravādins. The decline of early Buddhism, the rise of Mahāyānism and the revival of Brāhmanism all synchronised. The Mahāyāna follows the canon drawn up by the council in Kaniṣka's time, held at Jalandhara in the Punjab. The original doctrine was much enlarged, new material was added, and a good deal of popular magic and superstition was incorporated with it. Of course, it is the younger branch with Sanskrit, while the Hīnayana is the older, with Pāli as its language. The latter claims to represent the teaching of Gautama in its original form, and to preserve the rationalistic, monastic, and puritanic elements of his teaching. The Mahāyāna develops the doctrine in a mystical, theological and devotional way. The Hīnayāna has maintained its supremacy in Ceylon and Burma, the Mahāyāna in Nepal and China. A sharp opposition between the inwardness of the Hīnayāna, which withdraws from the visible world, and the adaptation to the world conditions

7. 38–39.
8. 252 BC
9. Kecij Jaiminimatānusāriṇa iva tathāgatamatadhvaṁsinaḥ.

characteristic of the Mahāyāna, runs throughout the subsequent history of the Buddhist religion. The latter is the great way meant for all, while the Hīnayāna is the little way fit only for a select few. In the South, where the Hīnayāna was the ruling faith, Kaniṣka's council is not acknowledged. Hīnayāna Buddhism was called Southern Buddhism, since it prevailed in southern countries like Ceylon, while Mahāyāna is called the Northern, since it flourished in the North, Tibet, Mongolia, China, Korea and Japan. But this division seems to be an artificial one. Rhys Davids observes: 'There is not now, and never has been, any unity either of opinion or of language in what is called Northern or in what is called Southern Buddhism.'[10] When we realise that almost all Buddhist canonical literature, wherever it might have extended, arose in the North of India, and recognise that the two are not separate compartments, but possess traces of mutual influence, we see that it is not necessary to call one northern and the other southern. It is clear, however, that the distinction between the Hīnayāna and the Mahāyāna was current even before the fourth century AD. Fahian and Yuan Chwang mention the Hīnayāna, and it also occurs in the *Lalitavistara*.

The Hīnayāna bases itself on the Pāli canon, while many of the Sanskrit works of Buddhism belong to the Mahāyāna. The Mahāyāna Buddhism possesses no canon, since it does not represent any homogeneous sect.[11]

10. *Buddhist India*, p. 173.

11. The most important works of the school are the following nine: (1) Aṣṭasāhasrikāprajñāpāramitā, (2) Gaṇḍavyūha, (3) Daśabhūmīśvara, (4) Samādhirāja, (5) Laṅkāvatāra, (6) Saddharmapuṇḍarīka, (7) Tathāgataguhyaka, (8) Lalitavistara, (9) Suvarṇaprabhāsa. The Prajñāpāramitā (AD 200) deals with the six perfections of a Bodhisattva, especially with the highest prajñā or wisdom, the knowledge of the doctrine of Śūnya. An abridged edition of it, attributed to Nāgārjuna, is the Mahāyāna Sūtras, from which Nāgārjuna derives his own Mādhyamika Sūtras. The Gaṇḍavyūha celebrates the Bodhisattva Mañjuśrī, and teaches the doctrines of śūnyatā, dharmakāya and the redemption of the world by bodhisattvas. The Daśabhūmiśvara (AD 400) details the ten stages by which Buddhahood is reached. Samādhirāja, or the king of meditations, is a dialogue describing the various stages of contemplation through which a bodhisattva can attain the highest enlightenment. The Laṅkāvatāra Sūtra (AD 400) describes the Yogācāra views. The Saddharma-Puṇḍarīka, or the lotus of the law (AD 250), makes Buddha a god above gods, an immeasurably exalted being who has lived for countless ages and will live for ever. According to it every man can become a Buddha who has heard his preaching and performed meritorious acts. Even those who adore

II

HĪNAYĀNA BUDDHISM

The Hīnayāna Buddhism is a logical development of the principles of the canonical works. The unsystematic views expressed in them and discernible in Milinda are later developed into the system embodied in the Abhidharmas of the Vaibhāṣikas (the Sarvāstivādins) and the works of Buddhaghoṣa and Abhidharmasaṁgraha. According to the Hīnayāna Buddhism all things are momentary.[12] The so-called permanent entities, space and nirvāṇa, do not exist. They are names of negations. All being consists of momentary entities called dharmas. There is no thinker, but only thoughts; no feeler, but only feelings. It is a pure phenomenalism maintaining the non-existence of substances or individuals.[13] It believes

---

relics and erect stūpas attain the highest enlightenment. Lalitavistara, as its title signifies, gives a detailed account of the sport of Buddha. It looks upon the life-work of Buddha as a diversion of the supreme being. Edwin Arnold's *Light of Asia* is based on it. The contents of Suvarṇaprabhāsa are partly philosophical and partly legendary. It deals also with tantra ritual. The two Sukhāvatīvyūhas, as well as the Amitāyurdhyāna Sūtra, Vajracchedikā, or the Diamond Cutter, are popular in Japan. The Sukhāvativyūha (AD 100) contains a detailed account of the land of bliss and praises Amitābha. Kāraṇḍavyūha, akin to the later Hindu Purāṇas, is devoted to the exaltation of Avalokiteśvara, the Lord who looks down with compassion on all things, the typical bodhisattva, who in the exercise of infinite pity refuses Buddhahood till all beings are saved. The yearning for universal salvation is powerfully expressed in it. Mahāvastu, the book of great events, is called a Hīnayāna work, and belongs to the heretical sect of the Lokottaravādins, who regard Buddha as a supernatural being. It contains many Mahāyānist doctrines, such as an enumeration of the ten states of a bodhisattva, hymns to Buddha, emphasis on the worship of Buddha as a means to salvation. Aśvaghoṣa's Buddhacarita (first century AD), is one of the chief classics of Mahāyāna Buddhism. This author's works include Saundarananda kavya, which deals with the conversion of Nanda, half-brother of Buddha. Vajrasūci, or the Diamond Needle, is also attributed to him. Āryaśūra is a poet of Āśvaghoṣa's school (fourth century AD). He composed a famous Jātakamāla, or garland of jātakas. Śāntideva's Śikṣāsamuccaya (seventh century) is a manual of Mahāyāna teaching. Bodhicaryāvatāra is a religious poem of great merit. For a detailed account of these Mahāyāna works see Nariman: *Literary History of Sanskrit Buddhism*, and Rājendral Lal Mitra: *Nepalese Buddhist Literature*. The dates here given are only probable.

12. Yat sat tat kṣaṇikam.
13. Pudgalanairātmya.

in the absolute existence of dharmas, small and brief realities which, grouped as cause and effect, crate the pseudo-individuals.

The goal of existence is the attainment of nirvāṇa or cessation of consciousness. All consciousness is a feeling for something, and therefore bondage.[14] There is no speculation in the Hīnayāna about what remains after nirvāṇa.

The arhat ideal is the distinguishing-mark of the Hīnayāna, which believes in the possibility of emancipation through one's own powers. The method is contemplation and meditation[15] on the four truths. The Hīnayāna Buddhism is indefinite about the Buddhahood of those who reach arhata, nor does it suggest that every creature may attain Buddhahood. We cannot help feeling that the ideal of the arhat, the perfect egoist, who is useless to others, is untrue to the real personality of Buddha, the man of pity and compassion, though the dependence on the saviour Buddha of the Mahāyāna faith is also untrue to the teaching of the original Buddha, however useful it may be. The Hīnayāna ideal may be justly summed up in the statement of Ibsen: 'There are actually moments when the whole history of the world appears to me like one great shipwreck, and the only important thing seems to be to save oneself.'

The arhata is the highest condition, the state of sainthood, when the fire of passion is extinguished, where there is no more karma to bind us to rebirth. Buddha is said to have attained this state at the beginning of his ministry. The attainment of nirvāṇa on earth by self-control does not require the aid of any supernatural power. The greatest of all beings, Buddha himself, is to be revered simply because of the example and the teaching he has left us and for nothing more. The Hīnayānists try to achieve the goal in the solitude of their cells, segregated from the common life of men. In the Khaggavisāṇa Sutta family life and social intercourse are strictly prohibited. 'To him who leads a social life affections arise and the pain which follows affection.'[16] The followers of the Hīnayāna are called upon to shut their eyes as they pass along the highways of the world, lest their sight should rest on any outward beauty. A wise man 'should avoid married life as if it were a burning pit of live-coals.'

14. W.B.T., p. 162.
15. Darśana and bhāvanā.
16. ii.

In friendship of the world anxiety is born,
In household life distraction's dust springs up.
The state set free from home and friendship's ties
That, and that only, is the recluse's aim.[17]

He who wants to attain nirvāṇa according to Visuddhimagga should resort to the cremation ground, which is a school of many exquisite virtues, and imparts to us the lesson that the world and the self are unreal. We cannot reach our goal by means of a life of love and activity. The lack of warmth and passionlessness of the arhat ideal are not inspiring. It may well be that in those days of loosely knit social life, these beliefs had a great value. But the world cannot become a monastery. We cannot have a compulsory conscription of men, women and children into cloisters. Disgust of life does not represent all that is substantial in the life of man. True asceticism is not indifference to the suffering of the world, but the building up of a silent centre even in the furious activity of life. We must be spiritual enough to possess our souls in the noise of the blatant world, and not merely in the peace and silence of an anchorite's apartment. Early Buddhism, unlike the Hīnayāna, required us to look for our opportunities in the retreats of misery and the haunts of pain, the clamour of the crowd and the tumult of traffic.

The Hīnayāna developed an anthropomorphic conception, based on the popular polytheism, and believed in one supreme Creator and many subordinate deities. These gods were neither omnipotent nor omniscient. They were introduced simply because meditation is an essential stage of discipline. The historical Buddha was glorified, even deified, and thus the need for an object of reverence was met. The gods are said to have paid their homage at his birth and death. Buddha is the God over gods, devātideva, supreme in knowledge and power, and yet there is no defined relation of the worshipper and the worshipped. Strictly speaking, Buddha is only a preacher, a guide to truth. He is neither divine nor supernatural. He is different from other saints who have also attained bodhi, for he not only discovered the truths of salvation, but also declared them to the world. In the orthodox Hīnayāna, Buddha was but a man like other men, only with greater genius and power of intuition. Worship of Buddha is merely an act of commemoration. Some conservative followers of this religion held

17. Muni Sutta of Sutta Nipāta, i. 12; quoted in Milinda, iv. 5. 1.

that we could imitate Buddha, though we are not qualified for his perfection.[18] They cherished the hope of being born in the good resort of the heavenly worlds and finishing their journey on the way of bodhi at some future time. The Hīnayāna seems to have practically ignored Gautama's advice regarding speculation about the unseen. Admitting first Buddha, then the munis entering on the path leading to Buddhahood, and then the Hindu deities, the Hīnayāna became practically a polytheism. Philosophical phenomenalism and religious polytheism with monarchical tendencies are what we have here. The Hīnayāna is a colourless religion denying God in doctrine, though allowing worship of Buddha in practice. There is no devotion or bhakti, which implies a living God.

The Hīnayāna Buddhism is not merely a way to nirvāṇa, but also teaches us the way to rebirth into the world of Brahmā by the grace and help of holy saints. Heaven and hell are accepted. The view is an expression of weariness or disgust with the endless strife of becoming, of the relief found in mere ceasing from effort. It is not a healthy-minded doctrine. A sort of world hatred is its inspiring motive. It prefers negative and philosophically strict definitions, while the Mahāyāna aims at positive and religious expressions. The former represents more faithfully the historical traditions of Buddha, while the latter aspires to please the masses by promising to fulfil the needs of the heart. By its abstract and negative tendencies the Hīnayāna became the incarnation of dead thought and the imprisonment of spirit. It gives us neither a warm faith for which to live nor a real ideal for which to work.

III

THE MAHĀYĀNA

If the doctrines belonging to the period between the rise of Buddhism and the time of Aśoka perhaps represent early Buddhism, the views that prevailed in the time of Aśoka may be said to be the Hīnayāna doctrine. The tendencies that developed during the period from Aśoka to Kaniṣka and became explicit thereafter form the Mahāyāna Buddhism. A cold, passionless metaphysics devoid of religious teaching could not long inspire enthusiasm and joy. The Hīnayāna ignored the groping of the spirit of

18. One section of the Hīnayānists called the Lokottaravādins makes Buddha a superhuman being, lokottara, who comes down to the world to save mankind for a short time.

man after something higher and wronged the spiritual side of man. The philosophical atheism of the Hīnayāna is the skeleton in the box, the diseased worm in the beautiful flower. The wronged sides of human nature asserted their rights and rebelled against the cold understanding with an imperious violence which was as tyrannical and exclusive as that of the understanding had been. The famishing soul and the thirsting fancy sought to derive nourishment from the suggestive symbolism of the prevailing religion. The life of Buddha could arouse emotion. Naturally Buddha was made a god. He was the realisation of the moral idea, the law personified. The metaphysically minded Hīnayānist, out of loyalty to the teaching of Buddha, might have hesitated, torn off the thin disguise for despair, and looked upon Buddha as no more than human. But a faith which failed to quicken the flame of devotion had either to undergo modification or perish.

In ethics the monastic tendency with all its consequences of detachment from the world's affairs, the morbid suppression of all human interests and pleasures, the impossible extinction of natural life proved unsatisfying to human nature. Man is bound to the world he tries to escape from. If freedom from servitude to the not-self means the extinction of self, then death is our goal. Buddha meant by freedom triumph over not-self, but not its destruction. The Mahāyānists contend that Buddha is no preacher of penance. He does not shut his eyes to the world when he attains nirvāṇa, but offers light to it that it may reach its goal. 'I would be a guard to them that have no protection, a guide unto the traveller, a ship, a well spring, a bridge, for the seekers of that shore; I would be a lamp to such as need a lamp, a bed for the weary that need a bed, the very slave of such as need service.'[19] In the Hīnayāna, nirvāṇa became negatively interpreted as extinction of all being. It is not possible for ordinary man to fall in love with annihilation.

The negative philosophy of the Hīnayāna could not become a popular religion. When Buddhism became universal in spirit and embraced large masses, the Hīnayāna could not serve. A religion more catholic than the Hīnayāna, a less ascetic ideal was required. When Buddhism spread throughout India and even beyond it, it ceased to set itself up in opposition to the prevailing religions, but insinuated itself slowly into other forms. In the formative stages of the Mahāyāna Buddhism there were successive

19. Bodhicaryāvatāra.

movements of the nomadic tribes from outside into the country. Hordes of half-civilised tribes captured parts of the Punjab and Kashmir.[20] Many of the aliens adopted the religion and language, culture and civilisation of the Buddhist peoples whom they conquered. Kaniṣka, the most powerful of the princes, himself became a Buddhist. The centre of power moved from the East to the West. Pāli gave place to Sanskrit. The uncivilised soaked in superstitious practices did not embrace Buddhism without transforming it. They reduced the higher religion to the level of their understanding. Though there were doctrinal differences between the Mahāyāna Buddhism and the Brāhmanical views, still the complexion it assumed for its followers was nothing new or unheard of in the times. The Mahāyāna found that it could capture the peoples' minds only if it gave up the icy coldness of some forms of early Buddhism and framed a religion which could appeal to the human heart. It imitated the successful experiments of Hinduism embodied in the theism of the Yoga, of the later Upaniṣads and of the Bhagavadgītā.

The Mahāyāna Buddhism gives us positive ideas of God, soul and human destiny. 'The Mahāyāna, or Great Vessel, is so called by its adherents in contradistinction to the Hīnayāna, or little vessel, of primitive Buddhism; the former offers to all beings in all worlds salvation by faith and love as well as by knowledge, while the latter only avails to convey over the rough sea of becoming, to the farther shore of nibbāna those few strong souls who require no external spiritual aid nor the consolation of worship. The Hīnayāna, like the "unshown way" of those who seek the "Nirguṇa Brahman," is exceeding hard; whereas the burden of the Mahāyāna is light, and does not require that a man should immediately renounce the world and all the affections of humanity. The manifestation of the body of the Law, says the Mahāyāna, is adapted to the various needs of the children of the Buddha; whereas the Hīnayāna is only of avail to those who have left their spiritual childhood far behind them. The Hīnayāna emphasises the necessity of saving knowledge, and aims at the salvation of the individual, and refuses to develop the mystery of nibbāna in a positive sense; the Mahāyāna lays as much or greater stress on love, and aims at the salvation of every sentient being, and finds in nirvāṇa the One Reality, which is

20. It is still a question whether Buddhism entered China in its older form of the Hīnayāna or the younger form of the Mahāyāna, but however this may be, the Mahāyāna soon grew predominant, and has been in the ascendant till today.

"void" only in the sense that it is free from the limitations of every phase of the limited or contingent experience of which we have empirical knowledge.'[21] The Hīnayāna protests against the Mahāyāna as an accommodation of the pure teaching to the necessities of human nature. Anyway, while it stands as an example to the world of releasing the highest through knowledge, the Mahāyāna requires us to take part in the world, evolving new social and religious ideals. The absence of the supernatural and the consequent lack of any scope for imagination, the morbid way of solving the central problems of life, the reduction of nirvāṇa to extinction and ethical life to a monastic asceticism, made the Hīnayāna a religion for the thinking and the strong in spirit, while a new development had to arise for the emotional and the worshipful.

IV

THE MAHĀYĀNA METAPHYSICS

We shall notice here the general philosophical principles of the Mahāyāna, postponing to a later section a detailed discussion of its two important schools, the Śūnyavāda, which holds that all is void, and the Vijñānavāda, which declares that nothing exists except in consciousness. While the Hīnayāna looks upon the soul as a complex of transitory elements or skandhas, the Mahāyāna holds that even these elements are not real. This does not mean that there is nothing real. A metaphysical substratum is admitted. This reality in its ontological aspect is called Bhūtatathatā, or the essence of existence. In its religious aspect it is called Dharmakāya. It is the highest principle which harmonises all contradictions. It is also called Nirvāṇa, since it brings absolute peace to the torn heart. It is Bodhi, or wisdom. It directs the course of the world and gives shape to all. Mahāyāna metaphysics is monistic in character. All objects in the world are of one reality. The nature of this reality is beyond language and description. 'Things in their fundamental nature cannot be named or explained. They cannot be adequately expressed in any form of language. They are beyond the range of perception, and have no distinctive features. They possess absolute sameness, and are subject neither to transformation nor to destruction. They are nothing else but one soul, for which tathatā is another

21. A. Coomaraswamy, *Buddha and the Gospel of Buddhism*, pp. 226–227.

designation.'[22] 'There is then neither that which speaks nor that which is spoken of; neither that which thinks nor that which is thought; when you conform to tathatā and when your subjectivity is completely obliterated, it is then that you will be said to have insight.'[23] The absolute is free from relativity, individuality and conditionedness, though it is the self-existent and the source of all. It is 'the effulgence of great wisdom; the universal illumination of the dharmadhātu (universe), the true and adequate knowledge, the mind pure and clean in its nature; the eternal, the blessed, the self-regulating and the pure, the immutable and the free.'[24]

The world of experience is phenomenal and not real. It is compared to a dream, though it is not without meaning. The Mahāyāna Buddhists liken the universe to a māyā, mirage, flash of lightning or froth.[25] All things of the world have the three aspects of (1) quintessence, (2) attributes, and (3) activities. If we take a jar, its quintessence is the earth, its attribute is the form of the jar, and its activity is to keep water. The attribute and activity are subject to law of birth and death, while the quintessence is indestructible. The waves of the ocean may be high or low, but the water itself neither increases nor decreases. The whole universe has its unchanged aspect as well as its changeable one. Bhūtatathatā is the former, the absolute which persists throughout all space and time as the basis of all. This universal eternal substratum answers to the Brahman of the Upaniṣads.[26] In the realm of absolute truth or paramārtha we have nothing else. But in the region of relative truth or saṁvrti we have the one made many by name and form. The absolute has the two states of the unconditioned and the conditioned, the realm of being proper and that of life and death. The Mahāyāna holds a middle position regarding the nature of the world. It is neither real nor unreal. It affirms that it actually exists, but denies its absolute reality. Waves exist, but not absolutely. The world is a phenomenon, impermanent, subject to flux and change. Since the reality pervades all, everything individual is

22. Suzuki's version of *The Awakening of Faith*, p. 56.

23. Ibid., p. 58.

24. Ibid., p. 96.

25. *Lalitavistara*.

26. The Mahāyānists seemed to have been aware of the similarity of their position to the Upaniṣad view. So the Laṅkāvatāra Sūtra says, that 'the explanation of the Tathāgatagarbha as the ultimate truth and reality is given in order to attract to our view even those who have superstitious faith in the Ātman theory.'

the whole potentially, or, in religious language, every individual is a potential Buddha. The Avataṁsaka Sūtra says: 'There is not even one living being that has not the wisdom of the tathāgata. It is only because of the vain thoughts and affections, that all beings are not conscious of this.' The individual souls are aspects of the absolute. As water is the essence of the waves, so the tathatā is the reality of persons. That which passes from existence to existence is the ego, which is not the imperishable soul. The passing ego is an embodiment of the permanent reality, and everything on earth has a quintessence of the uncreate and eternal reality. 'In the one soul we may distinguish two aspects, the soul as pure being and the soul in saṁsāra ... the two are so closely inter-related that one cannot be separate from the other.'[27]

The rise of the world is accounted for as usual by a metaphysics of metaphors. Ignorance or avidyā is said to be the cause of the world. 'All things on account of our confused subjectivity appear under the forms of individuation. If we could overcome this subjectivity, the signs of individuation would disappear, and there would be no trace of a world of objects.'[28] 'When the mind of all creatures which in its own nature is pure and clean, is stirred up by the wind of ignorance, the waves of mentality make their appearance. These three, mind, ignorance and mentality, have no absolute existence.'[29] Neither subjectivity nor the external world which is negated is real. 'As soon as subjectivity is rendered empty and unreal, we perceive the pure soul manifesting itself as eternal, permanent, immutable, completely comprising all things that are pure.'[30] The explanation of the world is that there is in reality no world at all but avidyā produces it. Whence did this negative principle of ignorance come? No answer is given. It is there,

27. Suzuki, *Awakening of Faith*, p. 55.

28. Ibid., p. 36.

29. P. 68.

30. In the enlightened condition we know that all things are the one absolute reality. Aśvaghoṣa writes: 'All so-called illusory phenomena are in truth from the beginning what they are; and their essence is nothing but the one soul. Though ignorant minds that cling to illusory objects cannot understand that all things are in their nature the highest reality (paramārtha), all Buddha tathāgatas being free from clinging are able to have an insight into the true nature of things—therefore the mind that is saturated with subjectivity is annihilated, all things are understood and omniscience is attained.' (Suzuki, *Awakening of Faith*, p. 126. See also p. 60.)

and it breaks the silence of the absolute, and starts the wheel of saṁsara, transforming the one into the many. We project the element of avidyā into pure being hypothetically, illusorily, apparently. The world of experience is a manifestation of pure being conditioned by avidyā. However illusory in its ultimate nature, avidyā must exist in the being of tathatā. Aśvaghoṣa suggests that the avidyā is a spark arising from the unfathomable depths of pure being. He identifies it with consciousness. This awakening of consciousness marks the first step in the rise of the world from the self-identity of tathatā or pure being. Then the distinctions of subject and object arise. The original being was the absolute, where the subject and the object merged into one. Though it is different from absolute nothingness, we cannot give a logical description of it. The moment we come back from that stage which we are said to realise in bodhi or perfect enlightenment, we seem to possess the world of contrasts and relations. Avidyā starts the cosmic process. Intellectually we can only stay that this element of negativity is in the very heart of the absolute. Why? Because it is there. The jewel is in the lotus;[31] the self-creative force is in the absolute. The real and the phenomenal are not ultimately different. They are two moments of the same thing, one reality with two aspects. The universe would be utterly unmeaning, absolutely unreal, if it were not in some way the expression of the real. The realm of birth and death is the manifestation of the immortal. It is the appearance in time and space, the actualisation of the absolute. The ultimate reality is sarvasattva, the soul of all things, real and imaginary. 'This pure being becomes birth and death (saṁsāra), in which are revealed the quintessence, the attributes and the activity of the Mahāyāna or the great reality. (1) The first is the greatness of quintessence. The quintessence of the Mahāyana as pure being exists in all things, remains unchanged in the pure as well as in the defiled, is always one and the same (samatā), neither increases nor decreases, and is void of distinction. (2) The second is the greatness of attributes. Here we have the Tathāgata's womb, which contains immeasurable and innumerable merits (puṇya) as its characteristics. (3) The third is the greatness of activity, for it produces all kinds of good works in the world phenomenal and super-phenomenal.'[32]

31. Cf. Om maṇi padme hum.
32. Suzuki, *The Awakening of Faith*, pp. 53–54.

V

THE MAHĀYĀNA RELIGION

The rebellion of man against his nature cannot last long. The needs of the human heart stand in the way of the unimpeded march of the critical spirit. There were passages enough even in the canonical writings to satisfy the heart of man. In Majjhima Nikāya (22) it is said that even those who have not entered into the paths 'are sure of heaven,' 'if they have love and faith towards Me.' It is an echo of the Gītā doctrine of bhakti. The Mahāyāna uses these texts and believes in a saviour God. There is no unity in the Mahāyāna religion. It suffered religious superstitions gladly. Wherever it prevailed, India, China, Korea, Siam, Burma and Japan, the indigenous religions were tolerated, while it took care to teach them a new respect for life, kindness to animals and resignation. So long as men conformed to certain ethical rules and respected the order of monks, the Buddhist teachers did not feel called upon to condemn the superstitious usages. It does not matter what gods you worship, so long as you are good. The protean character of Mahāyāna Buddhism is due to this tendency. In each of the countries where it was adopted it had a separate history and doctrinal development.

It does not concern us here to narrate the history of the later fortunes of the Buddhist faith in countries beyond the limits of India. If the Buddhist religion started with a grim, austere, self-repressive code, and ended with temple courts crumbling, mouldering and worn, it is due to its tolerant spirit. It is impossible for crude and rude tribes to become converts to Buddhism without making their own contribution to it. The freedom of opinion in religious matters is in consonance with the metaphysical views of the Mahāyāna. All religions are revelations of the same Dharmakāya and bring out some aspects of truth. Dharma is the all-pervading spiritual force, the ultimate and the supreme principle of life. The first attempt at personifying dharma is in the conception of Ādi Buddha, the first cause, the eternal God, superior to all things, the supreme, the first of all the Buddhas, without equal or comparison.[33] Even this Ādi

33. The Sūtrālaṁkāra criticises the doctrine of Ādi Buddha on the ground that no one can become a Buddha without proper equipment (saṁbhāra) of merit and knowledge, but this means a long past.

Buddha is a metaphysical conception remote from life and experience, and not an active force in touch with the world which he is said to have brought into being. The work of saving the world is done by the Buddhas, or the beings endowed with the highest intelligence and love. There have been an infinite number of these Buddhas in the past, and there will be an infinite number in future. Since the goal of every individual is to become a Buddha, there are many Buddhas. These who are secure in their own prospect of emancipation delay accepting it for the good of others. They are all transitory manifestations of the One Eternal Being. The historic Buddha is one such manifestation of the moral ideal. He is not the One Reality, but a god among many others. Amitābha sits on one side of him, and Avalokiteśvra, who saves the faithful by his grace, on the other.[34] The supreme Being is viewed in different aspects to suit the needs of different men. 'I reveal the law in its multifariousness with regard to the inclinations and dispositions of creatures, I use different means to rouse each according to his own character.'[35] Many of the Vedic gods become aspects of the One Supreme. Nāgārjuna by his precept and practice taught that the Hindu gods of Brahmā, Viṣṇu, Śiva and Kālī had the attributes assigned to them in the Brāhmanical scriptures, and were proper objects of propitiation. The traditional gods of the Hindus were fitted into a new system, where separate places and functions were assigned to them.[36] Mahāyānism is so called because it included a vast number of bodhisattvas, archangels and saints, which are only the ancient gods of Vedic Aryans thinly disguised by Buddhistic symbolism. There is no doubt that in giving a large place to bhakti or devotion the Mahāyāna scheme of salvation opened the breaches to Tantrikism and other mystic forms.[37]

34. Aśvaghoṣa, *Awakening of Faith*, Suzuki's translation, p. 68.

35. Cf. Bhagavadgītā, ix. 44 ff., and Saddharmapuṇḍarīka, ii.

36. Indra becomes Śatamanyu and Vajrapāṇi, with his own kingdom of heavens (svarga), called Trayastṛṁśaloka. Brahmā had his chief characters transferred to Mañjuśrī, the lamp of wisdom. Sarasvatī continued to be one of his wives, the other being Lakṣmī. Avalokiteśvara or Padmapāṇi has the attributes of Viṣṇu or Padmanābha. Virūpākṣa is one of the names of Śiva, though in Buddhistic legend he is one of the four kings. Gaṇeśa is taken over both as Vināyaka and demon Vinataka. The Sapta tathāgatas are the seven ṛṣis. Ajita formed with Śākyamuni and Avalokiteśvara a triad.

37. Cf. Col. Waddell's description of Mahāyāna Buddhism as 'a mysticism of sophistic nihilism.'

The monistic metaphysics of the Mahāyāna has given rise to an apparently polytheistic religion, but we should note that the several gods are subordinate to a single head. This unity of the Mahāyāna religion may be brought out by relating it to the doctrine of the three kāyas, which is allegorical in its significance. The Dharmakāya is the timeless, unconditioned spiritual reality of dharma. It is not a personal being revealing itself in a single historical figure, but is the all-pervading ground, which without suffering any modification assumes a variety of forms. The Dharmakāya answers to the impersonal absolute, the Brahman of the Upaniṣads. It is not so much the body of the law as the fathomless being or the norm of all existence.[38] When the absolute principle assumes name and form, we have the transformation of the Dharmakāya into the Saṁbhogakāya. The substance which persists becomes the subject which enjoys. The Brahman is now the Īśvara. He is the God in heaven, determined by the name and form, omniscient, omnipresent, omnipotent, the Ādi Buddha, supreme over all the Buddhas. When we pass to the Nirmāṇakaya, we get the several manifestations of this one activity into avatārs, or incarnations.

Every Buddha partakes of the nature of the three kāyas. The very nature of the Buddha is the bodhi, or enlightenment. But till he attains absolute nirvāṇa he possesses and enjoys the fruit of his deeds as a bodhisattva, and has a beatific body, or saṁbhogakāya. The historical Buddhas are these real Buddhas, sovereigns of celestial worlds appearing on earth to redeem mankind. 'I am one of a long series of Buddhas. Many were born before and many will be born in future. When the wickedness and violence rule over the earth, Buddha takes his birth to establish the kingdom of righteousness on earth.'[39] 'The exalted one appears in the world for salvation to many people, for joy to many people, out of compassion for the world, as a blessing, a salvation, the joy of gods and men.'[40]

So far as the Mahāyāna is concerned, there is practically nothing to distinguish it from the religion of the Bhagavadgītā. The metaphysical conception of Dharmakāya, or the ultimate foundation of existence, corresponds to the Brahman of the Gītā. As Kṛṣṇa calls himself the Supreme One, even so Buddha is made into a Supreme God. He is not an

38. This is evident from its synonyms, Svabhāvakāya, or nature-body; Tattva, suchness; Śūnya, the abyss; the Nirvāṇa; the eternal liberty; Samādhikāya, or the rapture body.

39. Cf. this with the Gītā, iv. 7–8.

40. Aṅguttara Nikāya.

ordinary deity, but the devātideva, the paramount God of gods.[41] He is the creator of all bodhisattvas.[42] That Buddha reached bodhi, enlightenment at Gaya, is a fancy of the unregenerate. 'I am the father of the world, sprung from myself,' says Buddha of himself, 'it is only because I know how the fatuous are of perverted sense and blind that I, who have never ceased to exist, give myself out as departed.'[43] Buddha has been from eternity. His enormous love for humanity is brought out by the parable of the burning house.[44] All beings are his children.[45] 'The Tathāgata, having left the conflagration of the three worlds, is dwelling in peace in the tranquillity of his forest abode, saying to himself all three worlds are my possession, all living beings are my children, the world is full of intense tribulation, but I myself will work out their salvation.' 'To all who believe me I do good, while friends are they to me who seek refuge in me.'[46]

The doctrine of the three kāyas is applied to the individual human being. In all beings there is the Dharmakāya, or the permanent reality; immediately over it we have the body of enjoyment, or the Saṁbhogakāya, the spirit individualised, and then the Nirmāṇakāya, where the mind is defiled.

VI

ETHICS

The ethical ideal of the Mahāyāna is the bodhisattva, as distinct from the arhat of the Hīnayāna. Bodhisattva literally means 'one whose essence is perfect knowledge.' But historically it means 'one who is on the way to the attainment of perfect knowledge, a future Buddha.' The term was first used of Gautama Buddha during the period of his search for liberation. It therefore came to mean 'a Buddha designate,' or a man destined to become a Buddha in this or in some future life. When once nirvāṇa is attained, all earthly relations come to an end. A bodhisattva out of the abundance of his love for suffering humanity stops short of nirvāṇa. Weak man in times of stress and sorrow requires a personal guide, and these lofty beings, who can tread the path of the nirvāṇa, engage themselves in the task of leading

41. Saddharmapuṇḍarīka, vii. 31.
42. Ibid., xiv.
43. Saddharmapuṇḍarīka, xv. 21. See B.G., iv. 9.
44. *Lotus*, chap. iii; Mahāvagga, i. 21.
45. *Lotus*, p. 89.
46. Lalitavistara, viii. Cf. B.G., vii. 16.

men into the true way of knowledge. The Hīnayāna ideal of complete absorption, or arhattva, the lonely journey on the trackless path of eternity, this isolated bliss is, according to Mahāyāna, the temptation of the Māra.[47]

The career of an aspirant to Buddhahood represented in the early Buddhism by the eight-fold path is here elaborated into ten bhūmis or stages. The first stage is the joyful (pramuditā) one characterised by the rise of the thought of bodhi.[48] It is here that the bodhisattva makes those pregnant resolutions (praṇidhāna) which determine the future course. The resolution of Avalokiteśvara not to accept salvation until the last particle of dust shall have attained to Buddhahood before him is such a vow. The insight is developed gradually so as to render the heart pure and the mind free from the illusion of self. The recognition of the impermanence of things enlarges the aspirant's compassionate nature, and we get next the stage of vimalā, or purity. In it we have the practice of morality and the exercise of wisdom (adhicitta). In the next stage the bodhisattva engages himself in the various bhāvanās which enable him to annihilate anger, hatred and error, had promote faith, compassion, charity and disinterestedness. This is the third stage (prabhākarī), where the seeker shines with patience and forbearance. The bodhisattva, to surrender all traces of egoism, trains himself in good work and applies himself specially to the cultivation of virtues connected with bodhi (bodhipakṣa dharma). It is the fourth radiant stage (arciṣmatī). Then ones the seeker begin a course of study and meditation to understand the four noble truths in their true light. It is the fifth invincible (sudurjayā) stage where dhyāna and samādhi predominate. As a result of moral practice and meditation, the seeker turns to the basic principles of dependent origination and non-substantiality. This stage is called abhimukhī, or 'turned towards.' Here prajñā reigns. Yet he is not completely free from passion, and still has the desires of becoming a Buddha and the intention of saving mankind. He devotes himself to the attainment of that knowledge which would enable him to effect his aim of universal salvation. He is now in the seventh stage, called dūraṁgamā. When he is

47. Aṣṭasāhasrikāprajñāpāramitā, xi. To use William James's picturesque expression, if at the last day all creation was shouting hallelujah, and there remained one cockroach with an unrequited love, that would spoil the peace of a bodhisattva, though not the absorption of the arhat.

48. Cittotpāda.

free from the eager desire for the particular, his thoughts are not bound to any special objects, and he becomes immovable (acala). This is the eighth stage where the supreme virtue of (anutpattikadharmacakṣuḥ) seeing all things such as they are, i.e. rooted in tathatā, dominates. The activity of the bodhisattva is tainted by no duality or selfishness. He is not content with tranquil repose, but is actually engaged in the teaching of dharma to others. It is the ninth stage, that of the good ones (sādhumatī) when all his acts are unselfish, done without desire. It is said to Gautama Buddha that there is not a single spot in this vast earth where He has not in some past life denied his life for the sake of others. The bodhisattva of the Mahāyāna answers to the awakened of the Upaniṣads, the Saviour of Christianity, the superman of Nietzsche, for he helps the world, which is powerless to accomplish its end by itself. The bodhisattva becomes a tathāgata in the tenth stage, a cloud of dharma (dharma-megha). Salvation means conformity of life to dharma. It is the manifestation of universal love of men and animals. Mahāyāna Buddhism has two stages higher than the arhatship, namely, the bodhisattva and the Buddha. The doctrine of the bodhisattva is so characteristic of the Mahāyāna that it is sometimes called the Bodhisattvayāna, or obtaining deliverance by practising the virtues of a bodhisattva.

The principles of moral life are dāna (charity), vīrya (fortitude), śīla (morality), kṣānti (patience), and dhyāna (meditation), and crowning all, prajñā, the home of peace and blessing. The severity of monasticism is relaxed. Whether you should become a monk or not depends on your character and temperament. It is possible to reach the goal though married. Asceticism and poverty, so common in Hīnayāna ethics, are almost exceptional. To follow Buddha's commands is the way to salvation. Stress is also laid on faith in God or bhakti. In his commentary on the Prajñāpāramitā, Nāgārjuna says: 'Faith is the entrance to the ocean of the laws of the Buddha an knowledge is the ship on which one can sail in it.' The Mahāyāna does not believe in the possibility of emancipation through one's own powers. The help of a saviour is necessary. Prayer and worship have a meaning so long as we are on the path, though not when we reach the end. The doctrines of karma, or the continuous working of our deeds good or bad, is tempered by mercy, which finds expression in the easier way of salvation by faith. Three classes of Śrāvakas or hearers, Pratyeka Buddhas, and Bodhisattvas are recognised. Piety is the means adopted by the first, knowledge by the second, devotion to the spiritual weal of others by the third.[49]

While the Hīnayāna made nirvāṇa attainable by a few only through the life of a monk, the Mahāyāna taught that every man could aim at becoming a bodhisattva, and even low caste men could attain salvation by the practice of virtue and devotion to Buddha. The ethical humanism and universalism characteristic of the Mahāyāna are quite in the spirit of early Buddhism. It was Buddha's mission to extend the blessings of salvation to all mankind. 'Go ye now, O Bhikṣus, for the benefit of the many, for the welfare of mankind, out of compassion for the world. Preach the doctrine which is glorious in the beginning, glorious in the middle and glorious in the end, in spirit as well as in letter.' To the Hīnayāna morality is essentially a negative process, purging the soul of worldly desire and evil. The bodhisattva ideal is more positive. The doctrine specially associated with it is that of parivarta, or turning over of ethical merit to the advantage of others. It reminds one of the doctrine of vicarious atonement, which proceeds on the view of the oneness of life. No man lives to himself alone. The good or evil of one affects the whole.

Whether the metaphysical truth that nothing on earth is real, and the ethical law that we should work and suffer for our neighbour, can be reconciled or not, is a problem for the Mādhyamika system. Apparently, the bodhisattva of the Mahāyāna still harbours the illusion or the moha, that he must save the world.

In the Mahāyāna the emphasis is not on nirvāṇa, but on the obtaining of bodhi or enlightened sainthood. Nirvāṇa is freedom of the soul. Gradually it came to mean the happy state of concentration centred on eternity. Kramamukti, or steady attainment of freedom, is instituted, as in the Brāhmanical systems to give solace to the heart of man which longs for immortal bliss. The existence of Buddhas after the end of their earthly career is admitted. The idea of nirvāṇa is displaced by a paradise with hell opposed to it. On the road to sanctity or the bodhisattvahood, the individual enjoys numerous existences on celestial planes. Mahāyāna indulged rather over much in these celestial existences and postponed the question of ultimate nirvāṇa. When, however, the question is taken up, it is answered in the traditional Buddhist manner. It means freedom from

49. See Aṅguttara Nikāya, ii. 245.

rebirth,[50] the cutting off of the chain of existence,[51] the rooting out of desire, spite and ignorance,[52] or an unconditioned being.[53] Since our existences are conditioned, nirvāṇa is unconditioned being. It is not non-existence pure and simple, but real freedom, where ignorance is overcome. What happens to a bodhisattva when he becomes a Buddha? Is he reabsorbed into the absolute being, or does he retain his individuality? The Mahāyāna is not clear on this point, though it inclines mostly to the latter alternative. To become a Buddha is to become one in essence with the infinite. Aśvaghoṣa describes the perfect condition thus: 'It is like the emptiness of space and the brightness of the mirror, in that it is true, real and great. It completes and perfects all things. It is free from the condition of destructibility. In it is reflected every phase of life and activity in the world. Nothing goes out of it, nothing enters into it, nothing is annihilated, nothing is destroyed. It is one eternal soul, no forms of defilement can defile it; it is the essence of intelligence.' According to Asaṅga, nirvāṇa is the union with the Great Soul of the universe, or Mahātman. The Mahāyānists are anxious to make out that nirvāna is not annihilation.

VII

THE FALL OF BUDDHISM IN INDIA

The vital reason for the disappearance of Buddhism from India is the fact that it became ultimately indistinguishable from the other flourishing forms of Hinduism, Vaishṇavism, Śaivism and Tantrik belief. India had a more popular religion, a cult which could satisfy her imagination by its picturesqueness. The old Buddhism, which denied the very being of God, offered no hope of human immortality and looked upon all life as misery, love of life as the greatest evil, and end of man as the extinction of all desire, lost its power. Mahāyānism was unable to acquire the prestige of primitive Buddhism, and so proved weak and vacillating in its conflicts with

50. Punarjanmanivṛtti. Aśvaghoṣa, Buddhacarita, xv. 30.

51. Nāgārjuna.

52. Ratnakūṭa Sūtra.

53. Vajracchedikā. The Bodhicaryāvatāra makes it the giving up of the world and egoims. The Ratnamegha accepts this definition. The Prajñāpāramitā considers nirvāṇa to be profound, fathomless being. Candrakīrti identifies nirvāṇa with śūnyatā, or knowledge, which puts an end to all illusions.

Brāhmanical religion. Moreover, it grew weaker as it spread wider. It had developed elaborate superstitions which dissatisfied the people at large. Throughout its conquests it did not aim at the suppression of other religions, but tied to suffuse them with its own ethical spirit. It accommodated itself to all men and to all times, with the result that paradises were added and animistic ideas introduced. This tendency of compromise was its strength as well as its weakness. The spirit which breathes in the XIIth Edict of Aśoka, that 'there should be no praising of one's sect and decrying of other sects, but on the contrary a rendering of honour to other sects for whatever cause honour may be due to them,' was the characteristic feature of Mahāyānism. It adopted the tactics later sanctified by St Paul, who became a Jew to the Jews and all things to all men that he might gain a few at least. In each country Mahāyānism had its own form.[54] When it gave place to devotion, bhakti and salvation, it opened the flood-gates to all forms of superstition. Hideous extravagances had to be defended with futile dialectic. Mystic forms of animism were smuggled into the great sphere of truth. Its hospitality to the stories of magic, clairvoyance and ghost-seeing weakened it. The disciples surrounded with cheap marvels and wonders the lonely figure with a serene soul, simple and austere in the yellow robes, walking with bared feet and bowed head towards the city of Benares. To inspire the outer world with respect for the figure of the master, honest propagandists developed rather dishonest history. It is impossible to believe Buddha to be the son on a mortal father. To make a god of him, stories were invented 'Under the overpowering influence of these sickly imaginations the moral teachings of Gautama have been almost hid from view. The theories grew and flourished, each new step, each new hypothesis demanded another; until the whole sky was filled with forgeries of the brain, and the nobler and simpler lessons of the founder of the religion were smothered beneath the glittering mass of metaphysical subtleties.'[55] The Buddhistic monks lost their old apostolic fervour. The monasticism of Buddhism became as bad as any priesthood. 'Not mendicant monks, devoted to a pure life, but opulent churches with fat priests; not simple discourses calculated

54. These developments of Mahāyāna are described in Hackmann's *Buddhism as a Religion*. The historian of Buddhism will have to take into account the Avataṁsaka, the Dhyāna and the Mantra schools, as well as the Chinese Tientai and the Japanese Nichiren.

55. Rhys Davids, *Buddhism*.

to awaken the moral and religious consciousness, but subtle arguments on discipline and metaphysics, were now what Buddhism represented.'[56] The life of Buddhism was choked by the mass of superstition, selfishness and sensuality which surrounded it. The result was that when Yuan Chwang visited India he found the realities of primitive Buddhism swamped by the rubbish of myth and legend. The faith which was glorious in the days of Aśoka, and not without inspiration even so late as the time of Kaniṣka, was lost in a wilderness of marvels and miracles such as those of endless Buddhas and immaculate conceptions.

In addition to the degeneration of Buddhism there was the stronghold of the past. The life of the people was dominated by the Brāhmanical faith. Even Buddhism could thrive only by accepting Brāhmanical gods. Early Buddhism included Indra, Brahmā and other divinities. The new converts carried into it much of their reverence for the old gods. The Hīnayāna accepted Brahmā, Viṣṇu and Nārāyaṇa in their own names. The Mahāyāna, we have seen, never seriously opposed itself to the Hindu doctrines and practices. It elaborated the mythology and spoke of a hierarchy of divine grades and capacities, at the head of which was Ādi Buddha. While the Brāhmins looked upon Buddha as an incarnation of Viṣṇu, the Buddhists returned the compliment by identifying Viṣṇu with Bodhisattva Padmapāṇi, called Avalokiteśvara. Religion became a private affair, and the Brāhmin ascetics were looked upon as the brethren of the Buddhist samanas. Brāhmanism and the Mahāyāna faith affirmed identical philosophical and religious views. The pertinacity characteristic of the Indian mind showed itself in a monistic idealism in philosophy and freedom of worship in religion (iṣṭadevatārādhana). The Mahāyāna metaphysics and religion correspond to the Advaita metaphysics and theism. In serving the needs of a large majority of men, it became holy a feeble copy of the Bhagavadgītā. A gradual process of intellectual absorption and modifications developed to such an extent as to countenance the theory that Mahāyānism was only a sectarian phase of the great Vaiṣṇava movement.[57] The Hīnayāna, with its more ascetic character, came to be

56. Hopkins.

57. The transition of Buddhism into Vaiṣṇavism may be seen in Pure of Orissa, where a temple originally dedicated to Gautama Buddha is now the dwelling of Kṛṣṇa, in the form of Jagannātha (Lokanātha). The only relic of Buddhism we find there is that men of all castes eat the food cooked in the house of God.

regarded as a sect of Śaivism. Buddhism found that it had nothing distinctive to teach. When the Brāhmanical faith inculcated universal love and devotion to God and proclaimed Buddha to be an avatār of Viṣṇu, the death knell of Buddhism in India was sounded. Buddhism repeated the merits as well as the faults of Hinduism. The hand of the immeasurable past, with its congenial fancies and inherited beliefs, again took hold of the country, and Buddhism passed away by becoming blended with Hinduism.

Buddhism died a natural death in India.[58] It is an invention of the interested to say that fanatic priests fought Buddhism out of existence. It is true that Kumārila and Śaṁkara criticised Buddhistic doctrines, but the resistance offered by Brāhmanism to Buddhism is the natural resistance of an old organisation to a new development which came to have nothing really new. The violent extermination of Buddhism in India is legendary. Buddhism and Brāhmanism approached each other so much that for a time they were confused and ultimately became one. Slow absorption and silent indifference, and not priestly fanaticism and methodical destruction, are the causes of the fall of Buddhism.

The history of Buddhism is decisive on a crucial problem of life. It establishes the enormous difficulty of having a pure morality, independent of spiritual sanctions. It failed to bring to India a real spiritual deliverance in spite of the fact that it laid powerful emphasis on a severely simple life of pure goodness. Early Buddhism provided a rallying centre for revolting individuals. The Hīnayāna by its exaggerations betrayed the central weakness of Buddhist systems. The Mahāyāna, in trying to correct the deficiency of the Hīnayāna, went to the other extreme and contradicted the spirit of Buddha by allowing all sorts of superstitions to meddle with spiritual life. Uncompromising devotion to the moral law is the secret of the strength of Buddhism, and its neglect of the mystical side of man's nature the cause of its failure.

VIII

INFLUENCE OF BUDDHISM ON INDIAN THOUGHT

Buddhism has left a permanent mark on the culture of India. Its influence is visible on all sides. The Hindu faith has absorbed the best of its ethics. A new respect for life, kindness to animals, a sense of responsibility and

58. See Monier Williams, *Buddhism*, chap. vii.

an endeavour after higher life are brought home to the Indian mind with a renewed force. The Brāhmanical systems, as a result of Buddhist influence, cast into the shade those parts of their religion which were irreconcilable with humanity and reason.[59] The Mahābhārata has echoes of the fine side of Buddhism. 'By conquest hatred is increased, and by hatred hatred is not destroyed.'[60] After Buddhism it became wellnigh impossible for Indian thought to adopt a hopeful view of the world. The standards which till then satisfied the mind of man could no more be sustained. Human existence is an evil and mukti is freedom from being. Later systems of thought accept it. Nyāya counted birth (janma) and activity (pravṛtti) among evils.[61] Both good and evil are undesirable since they involve rebirth. We return to the world to enjoy the reward or undergo the punishment. To be born is simply to die. To be happy is not to be born. The revolt of spirit against matter has dominated the history of Indian thought since the time of Buddha. All thinkers subsequent to him have lived in the shadow of the great renunciation. The end of life is symbolised by the robe of the sannyāsin. The evil of desire is exaggerated.[62] The world is bound by desire.[63] Indian thought was forced to reckon with the reflections of Buddhism on the instability of life and the doctrine of relativity. Some of Buddha's misunderstandings and some of his deeper insights have affected the course of subsequent thought. The best things of the world die before they are re-born, and even so has Buddhism perished in India, to be born again in a refined Brāhmanism. Buddha to-day lives in the lives of those Indians who have not given up their past traditions. His presence is felt in all around. Throughout worshipped as a god, he has a place in the mythology which is still alive, and so long as the old faith remains without crumbling down

59. In a work called Ācāramayūkha, ascribed to one Śaṁkara, the following five objectionable things are prohibited: (1) oblations to fire, (2) the killing of cows for sacrifices, (3) self-torturing austerities, (4) the use of flesh in the sacrificial feasts to the manes of the ancestors, and (5) marrying the widow of the deceased brother. Agnihotraṁ gavālambhāṁ sannyāsam phalapaitṛkam devareṇa sutotpattiḥ kalau pañca vivarjayet. See also Nirṇayasindhu, iii. Another reading has 'aśvālambhaṁ' for 'agnihotraṁ.'

60. Udyogaparva, 71. 56 and 63.

61. N.S., i. 2; iv. 55.

62. Janma duḥkhaṁ jarā duḥkhaṁ, jāyā duḥkham punaḥ punaḥ;
Āśāśāḥ paramaṁ duḥkham, nirāśāḥ paramaṁ sukham.

63. Āśayā badhyate loke.

before the corrosive influence of the new spirit, Buddha will have a place among the gods of India. His life and teaching will compel the reverence of mankind, give ease to many troubled minds, gladden many simple hearts, and answer to many innocent prayers.

REFERENCES

Saddharma Puṇḍarīka, S.B.E., xxi.

Buddhist Mahāyāna Texts, S.B.E., 1.

Suzuki, Mahāyāna Buddhism.

Suzuki, The Awakening of Faith.

Coomaraswamy, Buddha and the Gospel of Buddhism.

CHAPTER XI

The Schools of Buddhism

■ Introduction—The four schools of realism and idealism—The Vaibhāṣikas—Nature of reality—Knowledge—Psychology—The Sautrāntikas—Knowledge of the external world—God and nirvāṇa—The Yogācāras—Their theory of knowledge—Nature of Ālayavijñāna—Subjectivism—Criticism of it by Śaṁkara and Kumārila—Individual self—Forms of knowledge—The Yogācāra theory of the world—Avidyā and Ālaya—Nirvāṇa—Ambiguity of Ālayavijñāna—The Mādhyamikas—Literature—The Mādhyamika criticism of the Yogācāra—Phenomenalism—Theory of relations—Two kinds of knowledge—Absolutism—Śūnyavāda—Nirvāṇa—Ethics—Conclusion. ■

I

THE FOUR SCHOOLS OF BUDDHISM

Buddha used critical analysis as the way to truth. He insisted on observation and reasoning. His religion was not dogmatic. A saying is attributed to Buddha to the effect: 'One must not accept my law from reverence, but first try it as gold is tried by fire.'[1] By leaving the metaphysical background free for the flight of the speculators, Buddha increased the uncertainty about the ultimate foundations of things. Early Buddhism contained germs capable of development along different lines. The same thoughts do not always grow in others as they do in their founders. So when speculative thinkers stripped Buddhism of much that was living and personal, it became reduced to a number of abstract positions from which different thinkers according to their inclinations developed different systems. Experience according to Buddha was the only substantial datum open to us, the real existence, the ultimate fact that all thought must reckon with. The empiricism of Buddha led to a thorough criticism and disintegration of conventional beliefs. The empiricism of the Buddhist schools is an intelligent application of the

1. Unfortunately, this philosophic spirit declined when large numbers accepted Buddhism as a religion. Faith in Buddha's words increased. 'All that the Lord Buddha has said is well said,' said Aśoka. In the Divyāvadāna it is declared: 'The sky will fall with the moon and stars, earth with its mountains and forests will ascend, oceans will be dried up, but the Buddhas speak not wrongly.'

critical method to experience itself. Through the pressure of logic rather than of set design, Buddhism resulted in different schools of thought. At a very early date after Buddha's death, differences of belief and practice began to appear. Even at the time of the Council at Vaiśāli, there were doctrinal disputes which led to the great meeting, Mahāsaṅgha of the seceders, who themselves split up into eight different schools. The Theras who convened the Vaiśālī Council also developed in the second century BC a number of schools, though their main branch supported the Sarvāstivāda or the realistic theory that everything exists. The Pāli canon bears witness to the opposed movements of thought, and Kathāvatthu deals with many of these sects and schools.[2] Hindu thinkers do not refer to these schools of Buddhist thought which arose before the first century BC. According to them there are four chief Buddhist schools, of which two belong to the Hīnayāna and two to the Mahāyāna. The Hīnayāna schools are the Vaibhāṣikas and the Sautrāntikas, who are realists or Sarvāstivādins, believing that there is a self-existent universe actual in space and time, where mind holds a place on equal terms with other finite things. The Mahāyāna schools are the Yogācāras, who are idealists, and the Mādhyamikas. The Yogācāras contend that thought is self-creative and all producing. It is the ultimate principle, and even the ultimate type and form of reality. The Mādhyamika philosophy is a negative critical system, formulating the metaphysical background of the Mahāyāna Sūtras. The Mādhyamikas are sometimes called Sarvavaināśikas or nihilists.[3]

The tendencies of the speculative systems of Buddhism, though they were long in existence, were formulated and codified only after the time of Kaniṣka. The systems of Hindu thought criticise these schools, thus indicating that the latter belong to a period earlier than the Hindu systems themselves. We shall not be far wrong if we assign them to the second century AD, though some of the more distinguished exponents of this or that school

2. See J.R.A.S., 1891, and Journal of the Pāli Text Society, 1904–1905.

3. I-tsing, of the sixth century, says: 'Those who worship the bodhisattvas and read the Mahāyāna Sūtras are called the Mahāyānists (the great), while those who do not perform deeds are called the Hīnayānists (the small). There are but two kinds of the so-called Mahāyāna. First, the Mādhyamika, second, the Yoga; the former profess that what is commonly called existence is in reality non-existence, and every object is but an empty show, like an illusion, whereas the latter affirm that there exist no outer things in reality, but only inward thoughts, and all things exist only in the mind.' (Takakusu's *I-tsing*, p. 15.)

may belong to a later era. In the third century after Buddha's death the Vaibhāṣikas came into prominence, and the Sautrāntikas in the fourth century after his death. The Mādhyamikas according to Āryadeva, came into existence five hundred years after Buddha's death. Asaṅga, the founder of the Yogācāra school, is at least as late as the third century AD. Buddhist philosophic thought reached its most vigorous life in the fifth, sixth and seventh centuries.

II

THE VAIBHĀṢIKAS

The speculative schools attached to the Hīnayāna belong to the Sarvāstivāda or pluralistic realism.[4] The Vaibhāṣikas are so called because they consider the language of the other schools to be absurd, viruddhabhāṣā,[5] or because they attached themselves to the Vibhāṣā or the commentary on the Abhidharma. They reject the authority of the Sūtras altogether and acknowledge only the Abhidharma. They appeal to experience, which bears unimpeachable witness to the nature of things. By experience they mean knowledge produced by direct contact with the object. The world is open to perception. It is wrong to think that there is no perception of the external world. For without perception there can be no inference. We cannot derive a vyāpti or universal proposition if we do not have perceptions for our data. To speak of an inference absolutely independent of any objects perceived is opposed to all common sense.[6] So objects are of two kinds, the perceived and the inferred, the sensible and the cogitable. Though

4. The Sarvāstivādins, otherwise called Hetuvādins or causationalists, consider seven works to be of importance, of which the chief is Kātyāyanīputra's *Jñānaprasthāna* composed about three hundred years after Buddha's death. The commentary on this called the *Mahāvibhāṣā* was compiled by five hundred arhats under the leadership of Vasumitra, probably after the great council under Kaniṣka. A summary of it is found in Vasubandhu's *Abhidharmakośa*. Yaśomitra is the author of the *Abhidharmakośavyākhyā*. Fragmentary parts of *Udānavagga*, *Dhammapada* and *Ekottarāgama* are influenced by the Sarvāstivāda. Aśvaghoṣa's *Buddhacarita*, in spite of its emphasis on devotion to Buddha and Āryaśūra's *Jātakamālā*, seem to belong to this school. Bhadanta (third century AD), Dharmatrāta, Ghoṣaka and Buddhadeva are other prominent exponents of this view, though they do not agree with one another on all points.

5. See S.D.S.

6. Sakalalokānubhavavirodhaś ca.

here and there external objects may be known to exist by inference, still as a rule perception points to their existence. A distinction is made between the inner world of ideas and the outer world of objects. There is a difference in the way things hang together in thought and the way in which they hang together in nature. The Vaibhāṣikas are natural dualists who maintain the independent existence of nature and mind. Epistemologically their theory is a naïve realism. The mind is conscious of objects Our knowledge or awareness of things not mental is no creation, but only discovery. Things *are* given to us. The substance of things has a permanent existence throughout the three divisions of past, present and future.

The permanent substances are not the transitory phenomena, but the elements which underlie them. Some Sarvāstivādins maintain the eternal existence of the noumenal counterparts of the five skandhas or elements of things. They avoid the difficulty of causation, since according to them cause and effect refer to two phases of one thing. Water is the common substance of ice and steam. The phases are momentary, but the substratum is permanent. Āryadeva puts this view of cause in the following words: 'The cause never perishes, but only changes its name when it becomes an effect having changed its state. For example, clay becomes the jar having changed its state, and in this case the name clay is lost and the name jar arises.'[7]

7. Compare the view elaborated in Abhidharmakośabhāṣya: 'Are we to think that wood perishes by contact with flames?—*Yes,* for we no longer see the wood when it is burnt, and no reasoning is worth the evidence of our senses. *No*—it is a matter of reasoning; for even if we no longer see the wood, that may be the outcome of the fact that it perishes of itself and ceases to be renewed. The non-existence of the wood which you say is caused by fire is a pure nothingness, a nonentity, and nonentity cannot be an effect and cannot be caused. Besides, if destruction or non-existence which succeeds existence had sometimes a cause it would always, like births, have a cause. And you willingly admit that flame, sound and thought are momentary by nature' (iv. 2). 'If things perish without cause from their very nature, as objects thrown into the air fall, then they must perish in the moment of their birth, and they cannot exist beyond the moment in which they actually receive being; for if destruction, being without cause does not take place at the very birth of the thing, it will not take place later, for the thing remains what it is' (ibid.). If you say the thing ripens grows older, etc., what grows older, what changes, is a series. The notion of change is contradictory. 'That the same thing should become other than it is is absurd. That the thing should remain the same and its characters become different is absurd' (ibid. iv. 2). If things are momentary, then they perish of themselves without any cause. A flame dies because it is momentary and not because it is blown out. We cannot destroy what exists, nor can we destroy what does not exist.

The objects we see cease to exist when they are not perceived. They have but a brief duration like a lightning flash. The atoms are immediately separated and their aggregation is but instantaneous. Things exist for four moments, those of production, existence, decay and death. Still, it is not perception that makes them into objects. The objects have an existence independent of our perception even though they cease to exist the moment we cease to perceive. The Vaibhāṣikas, however, as well as the Sautrāntikas admit the permanent reality of the underlying elements or their extra-mental existence. No definite account is given of the relation between the underlying reality and the phenomenal manifestations. The view of the elements or the noumenal counterparts of things is not clear. We are often told that even these elements are momentary. They are sometimes reduced to mere hypostatised concepts.[8] The self called pudgala has no existence apart from the elements of personal life. The unity of the individual is a fiction for the continuous flow of mental states. The theory rests on naturalistic assumptions, and when strictly developed takes us to materialism or sensationalism. Realising that we are dealing with transitory phenomena, the Sautrāntikas argue that the underlying substances are inferred by us and not directly perceived.

The Vaibhāṣikas and the Sautrāntikas admit the reality of an outer world. Objects are distinguished by them into the bāhya, or the external, and the abhyantara, or the internal. Under the former they have bhūta, or the elements, and bhautika, or objects belonging to the elements. Under the latter they have citta, or intelligence, and caitta, or those belonging to intelligence.[9]

8. See the Journal of the Pāli Text Society, 1913–1914, p. 133.

9. We may take not of the subjective and the objective classifications noticed in Vasubandhu's Abhidharmakośa. The subjective classification is simple. We have the five skandhas or constituents of being, the twelve āyatanas or locations, and the eighteen dhātus or bases. The objective classification deals with two kinds of objects, the asaṁskṛta dharmas (non-composite) and the saṁskṛta dharmas (composite). Of the non-composite dharmas, which are not produced by things, which are self-existent and exempt from change, i.e. origin, growth and destruction, there are three: (1) Pratisaṁkhyānirodha, (2) apratisaṁkhyānirodha, (3) ākāśa or space. Of the composite dharmas there are four kinds: (1) The eleven rūpadharmas (rūpa equals matter), (2) the one citta (mind), (3) the forty-six caitta dharmas, and (4) the fourteen cittaviprayukta, or non-mental composites. The seventy-two composite dharmas and the three non-composite dharmas exhaust all the things. The word dharma means a number of things in Buddhism, such as law, rule, faith, religion,

There are only four elements, and not five: earth, which is hard; water, which is cool; fire, which is warm; and air, which is mobile. The fifth element, ākāśa, is not recognised. The external objects are the results of the gathering together of the ultimate atoms according to their capacity. The atomic theory is accepted by the Vaibhāṣikas and the Sautrāntikas. All objects are ultimately reducible to atoms. The Vaibhāṣikas maintain that the atom has six sides, and yet is one, for the space within the atom cannot be divided. They also hold that the atoms can be perceived in a mass, though we cannot see them singly, even as we see a mass of hair, but not a single hair.[10] An atom is the smallest particle of rūpa, according to Vasubandhu.[11] It cannot be placed anywhere or trampled on or seized or attracted. It is neither long nor short, neither square nor round, neither curved nor straight, neither high nor low. It is indivisible, unanalysable, invisible, inaudible, untastable and intangible.[12] The atoms cannot penetrate one another. The Vaibhāṣikas and the Sautrāntikas do not admit double or triple atoms, though they allow indefinite atomic aggregations. Compound substances are composites of primary elements. Bodies which are the objects of sense are aggregates of atoms. Material things which offer resistance to sense-organs are collections of the fourfold substrata of rūpa, colour, smell, taste and touch. The unit possessing this fourfold quality is the paramāṇu, or the ultimate atom which defies analysis. The paramāṇus become perceptible when they combine. The perceptible atomic unit is the aṇu, which is a combination of paramāṇus. The atoms are the same in all the elements possessing the qualities of earth, air, fire and water. Though material things have the qualities of the four different elements, yet it happens that in some cases some elements display their active energy, while others are in a potential condition. In hard metal the earth element, in the liquid stream the water element, in the burning flame the fire element predominates. The Sarvāstivādins distinguish two worlds, the bhājanaloka, the universe as the abode of things, and the sattvaloka, the world of living beings. The first serves the second. The Cittaviprayukta dharmas are composite energies

---

worldly phenomena, things, state: here it is used for any existing object. See Sogen: *Systems of Buddhistic Thought.*

10. The Nyāya Sūtras hold that the atom is transcendental, not perceptible to the senses. N.S., ii. 1. 36; iv. 2. 14.

11. Paramāṇu is the minutest form of rūpa. It cannot be pierced through or picked up or thrown away.

12. Abhidharmamahāvibhāṣā.

distinct from matter and mind, such as prāpti and aprāpti. They are not actual, but only potential and become actually existent when they attach themselves to a mental or a material basis.

The non-composite elements are three: ākāśa, which is free from all distinction and limitless. It is an eternal, all-pervading positive substance.[13] It *is*, though it is devoid of form (rūpa), and is not a material thing (vastu). Apratisaṁkhyānirodha is the non-perception of dharma, caused by the absence of pratyaya or conditions, and not produced by knowledge.[14] It is intense concentration on one subject, so that all other influences sink into silence. Pratisaṁkhyānirodha is the positive fruition of transcendental knowledge, the highest idea of the Sarvāstivādin. The nirvāṇa of this school is neither quite the same as existence conditioned by the skandhas nor different from it. Since the Vaibhāṣikas recognise the permanent existence of the atoms of the skandhas, nirvāṇa cannot be a condition altogether independent of the skandhas. Śaṁkara criticises the three non-composite or asaṁskṛta dharmas as avastu (non-substantial), abhāvamātram (only negatively discernible), and nirupākhya (devoid of form).[15] It is true that they are indefinable, but that does not mean they are unreal.

The true instruments of knowledge open to us are perception and conception. Perception (or grahaṇa) gives us truth, since it is free from any imagination or kalpanā. But it only gives us indefinite presentations. Conception or cognition (adhyavasāya) does not give us knowledge, though it is definite, for it is ideal or imaginary. Perception is not illusory, but indefinite. Conception is illusory, though definite. An absolutely undetermined object of perception does not exist. It is indeed difficult to distinguish the given and the ideal aspects of the objects of knowledge. There seems to be an inconsistency here in the Vaibhāṣika theory, for if perception is so indefinite, how can we say that it gives us knowledge of the reality of things? It may be that through perception we bump against reality, and feel that there is something real. But to ascertain the nature of the object with which we come into collision, inference is necessary.

The perceiver or upalabdhṛ is vijñāna and the substratum of consciousness (citta or mind) is permanent. Memory is a cittadharma, or a quality of citta. The sense-objects are rūpa (colour or form), taste, smell, touch and sound. Answering to these five sense-objects, we have five sense-

13. This is also the view of the Nyāya.
14. Vasubandhu.
15. V.S. Commentary, ii. 2. 22–24.

organs. After grasping the external objects, the indriyas arouse the citta or mind and excite vijñāna or consciousness. These indriyas which grasp the object are material in their nature. Each has two parts, the principal and the auxiliary. In the case of sight, the optic nerve is the principal and the eyeball is the auxiliary. There are said to be six kinds of discrimination according to the five sense-organs and the sixth mind, which is the internal sense. By means of the sixth sense of mind, we know not only the particular colours, but colour as such or sound as such. Citta, according to Vasubandhu, is one with mind, vijñāna or discrimination.[16] There is no soul distinct from vijñāna or citta.

According to this school Buddha is an ordinary human being, who, after attaining the qualified nirvāṇa by his Buddhahood and final nirvāṇa by his death, lost his being. The only divine element in Buddha is his intuitive knowledge of the truth, which he attained without the aid of others.

III

THE SAUTRĀNTIKAS

The second school of the Hīnayāna is that of the Sautrāntikas.[17] The Sautrāntikas admit the extra-mental existence of the phenomenal world. Only we do not have a direct perception of it. We have mental presentations through which we infer the existence of external objects. They must exist because there cannot be perception without an object of perception.[18]

Mādhava describes the arguments by which the Sautrāntikas infer the existence of an external world in his Sarvadarśana-saṁgraha: 'Cognition

16. The mind is called citta because it observes (cetati), manas because it considers (manyate), and vijñāna because it discriminates (vijānate). Abhidharmakośa, 2.

17. Of the origin of the term Sautrāntika, Mādhava says: 'The name Sautrāntika arose from the fact that the venerated Buddha said to some of his disciples, who asked what was the ultimate purport (anta) of the aphorism (sūtra), be Sautrāntikas' (S.D.S., p. 332). It may well be that the Sautrāntikas are so called because of their adherence to the Sutta Piṭaka, or the section consisting of the discourses of Buddha to the rejection of the two other Piṭakas. The Sautrāntikas take their stand on the sūtras. There are two divisions among them, those who reject every other appeal than that to the word of the master, and those who admit other proofs. Kumāralabdha, a contemporary of Nāgārjuna, is said to be the founder of the system. Dharmottara, the logician, and Yaśomitra, the author of the commentary on Vasubandhu's Abhidharmakośa, are followers of the school.

18. Locke's *Essay*, iv. 4. 3.

must ultimately have some object since it is manifested in duality.... If the object proved were only a form of cognition, it should manifest itself as such, and not as an external object.' Modern logic might look upon this as a confusion between objectivity and externality. If it is said that the internal principle manifests itself as if it were something external, the Sāutrāntikas reply: 'This is untenable, for if there be no external objects, there being no genesis of such, the comparison, 'as if they were external,' is illegitimate. No man in his senses would say Vasumitra looks like the son of a childless mother.'[19] We infer the objective existence from certain properties, even as 'nourishment is inferred from a thriving look, as nationality from language and as emotion from expression.'[20] Again: 'Consciousness by itself is everywhere alike, and if it were all, the world must be one. We have, however, now blue, now red. These must be due to differences in the objects themselves.' The varieties of forms of consciousness indicate the existence of external objects. Besides, 'those things which while a thing exists manifest themselves only at times must depend on something else than that thing.' Consciousness manifests itself only at times as blue and so forth. Again: 'That is knowledge of the subject (ālayavijñāna) which concerns the ego. And that is knowledge of the object (pravṛttivijñāna) which manifests blue, etc.' Lastly, this external world does not rise into being at our will. To account for the involuntary nature of sense-perceptions, we must admit the reality of a world able to produce sound, touch, colour, taste, smell, pleasure, pain, etc. The world is therefore external to consciousness. Our belief in it is based on inference. We may ask whether its existence is so absolutely self-evident and demonstrable that it can resist the shock of doubt. As Descartes puts the objection, 'may it not be that some malignant spirit is playing upon our minds and awaking in them the ideas of things that have no reality.' We then seem to be brought to the Yogācāra view that the immediate objects of consciousness of which we have any certainty are our ideas. No lying spirit can deceive us about them. When once the unity of thought and being is broken up, when we separate the consciousness of self from the immediate consciousness of the world, both of them lose their life. The Mādhyamika theory consistently disposes of both self and not-self, and leads us to an absolute unity lifted beyond the distinction of self and not-self.

19. P. 27.
20. P. 28.

While holding that there can be no perceptual knowledge of objects without external objects, the Sautrāntikas contend that these outer objects are only momentary. All things are momentary.[21] If the objects which determine the forms of consciousness are only momentary, how do we get the illusion of permanent objects? 'The forms of the object penetrate one after the other into the understanding; the illusion of simultaneity is caused by the swiftness of the proceeding. Just so as an arrow passes through the eight leaves of a flower, as it were, at the same time, and a firebrand appears as a circle.' The Sautrāntikas are hypothetical dualists, or cosmothetic idealists, to use Hamilton's expression. They deny any immediate knowledge of an independent world, but admit the reality of it to account for our perceptions and images. Through conscious presentations objects are apprehended. There is no doubt that so far as psychological fact is concerned, the Vaibhāṣikas are on better ground. When we perceive, the Sautrāntika says we have an idea or presentation. The unsophisticated individual whose mind is not debauched by psychological learning confirms the Vaibhāṣika account when he says that he perceives a tree and not an idea from which he infers the tree. To import the results of psychological analysis into the naïve mind of the experiencing individual is to commit the psychologist's fallacy. The individual sees the tree which is not himself. To say that he apprehends an idea which he later refers to an external thing is a distortion of plain facts. Modern psychology confirms the Vaibhāṣika theory that perception is an act of consciousness, which stands in relation to a non-mental existent physical object.

Dharmottara in his Nyāyabinduṭīkā, a commentary on Dharmakīrti's Nyāyabindu, regards saṁyak-jñāna or right knowledge as the sole means for the accomplishment of all desires a man may have. While the truth of a judgment consists in its agreement with the objects, the test of truth is successful activity. All knowledge is purposive. It starts with the presentation of an idea and terminates with the fulfilment of the desire that is prompted by it. As both perception and inference help us in the realisation of our desires, they are valid forms of knowledge. Only in perception, the presentation is direct, while in inference it is mediated by the liṅga or the reason. Dreams and illusions are examples of wrong knowledge.

Admitting the reality of the external world, the Sautrāntika goes on to explain the process of knowledge. Knowledge arises on the basis of four

21. S.S.S.S., iii. 3. 16.

conditions, which are: (1) data, or ālambana; (2) suggestion, or samanantara; (3) medium, or sahakāri; and (4) dominant organ, or adhipatirūpa. 'From blue data, the form of blue arises in the understanding, which manifestation is styled a cognition (jñāna). From suggestion there is a revival of old knowledge. The restriction to the apprehension of this or that object arises from the medium, light, as one condition and the dominant organ as the other.'[22] Dharmakīrti, in his Nyāyabindu, defines perception as a presentation determined exclusively by the object and free from all mental impositions (kalpanā). Obviously it is nirvikalpa or indeterminate knowledge, since savikalpa or determinate knowledge involves the conceptual activity of the mind. Dharmakīrti is of opinion that names and relations are imposed by the mind, while the senses reveal the objects accurately unless they are themselves perverted by organic or extraneous causes. This pure perception, free from all traces of conceptual activity, is said to give us the object in its own nature (svalakṣaṇam). It is, however, difficult to decide in our actual perceptions, which are by no means pure, what are the respective contributions of the object and the mind.

The atomic theory is accepted by the Sautrāntikas with very little difference from the Vaibhāṣikas. For the Sautrāntika, ākāśa is the same as the ultimate atom, since both are notions and nothing more.[23]

In opposition to the Vaibhāṣikas and the Mādhyamikas, the Sautrāntikas maintain that thought can think itself, and that we can have self-consciousness.[24] Though the end of a finger cannot touch itself, a lamp illuminates itself and another.[25] This theory is quite compatible with realism.

Yaśomitra, the Sautrāntika and the commentator of the Abhidharmakośa of Vasubandhu, dealing with the reality of God, argues: 'The creatures are created neither by Īśvara, nor by Puruśa (spirit), nor by Pradhāna (matter). If God was the sole cause, whether the God was Mahādeva, Vāsudeva or another, whether spirit or matter, owing to the simple fact of the existence of such a primordial cause, the world would have been created in its totality at once and at the same time. For it cannot be admitted that three should be a cause without an effect; but we see the creatures coming into existence not simultaneously, but successively, some from wombs, some from buds. Hence we have got to conclude that there is a series of causes, and that God

22. S.D.S., p. 30.
23. S.S.S.S., iii. 3. 5.
24. Svasaṁvitti.
25. Bodhicaryāvatāra, ix. 15.

is not the sole cause. But it is objected that the diversity of causes is due to the volition of the Deity; 'Let now such and such a creature be born, let another creature be born in such and such a way.' It is in this way that is to be explained the phenomenon of the appearance of creatures, and that it is proved that God is the cause of them all. To this we reply that to admit several acts of volition in God is to admit several causes, and that to make this admission is to destroy the first hypothesis, according to which there is one primordial cause. Moreover, this plurality of causes could not have been produced except at one and the same time, since God, the source of the distinct acts of volition which have produced this variety of causes, is Himself alone and indivisible. The sons of Śākya hold that the evolution of the world has no beginning.'[26]

IV

THE YOGĀCĀRAS

Āryāsaṅga or Asaṅga and his younger brother Vasubandhu, the teacher of Dignāga, founded the Vijñānavāda or the idealist view of the Yogācāra.[27]

The school is called Yogācāra, since it declares that the absolute truth or bodhi manifested in the Buddhas is attainable only by those who practise

26. Quoted in Nariman, *Literary History of Sanskrit Buddhism*, pp. 284–285.

27. Originally an adherent of the Sarvāstivāda school, Asaṅga became the chief exponent of the Yogācāra doctrine. He explains his doctrine in his Yogācārabhūmiśāstra, Mahāyānasūtrālaṁkāra, a work consisting of memorial verses in various metres, and a commentary on the latter by himself. Vasubandhu is said to have lived about the last quarter of the fourth century. Takakusu and Jacobi assign him to the latter part of the fifth century. Other opinion puts him *circa* AD 300. Vasubandhu's pupil, Guṇaprabha, was the guru or teacher of Śrī Harṣa, the king of Kanouj and the friend of Yuan Chwang. This fact favours Jacobi's opinion that Vasubandhu lived about the second half of the fifth century. Vasubandhu is distinguished for his profound learning and perverseness of thought. He is the author of Abhidharmakośa, a Hīnayāna work. In later life he was converted by his brother Asaṅga to the Mahāyāna doctrine, and wrote several commentaries on the Mahāyāna texts. Aśvaghoṣa is also a follower of the Yogācāra school. His chief work is Mahāyānaśraddhotpāda, or The Awakening of faith in the Mahāyāna (translated by Suzuki in the Open Court Series). Aśvaghosa's authorship of this work is not beyond doubt. He is a Brāhmin of Eastern India, who lived in the first century AD. He is said to have been the spiritual adviser of the famous Kuṣan king, Kaniṣka. (The date of Kaniṣka is unsettled, some, Boyer, Oldenberg, and Haraprasād Śāstri, putting it in the first century AD and others first century BC. Sir

Yoga. The title Yogācāra brings out the practical side of the philosophy, while Vijñānavāda brings out its speculative features. The principle of critical analysis is applied not only to the individual ego and the material objects, but also to the dharmas, or the elements of things, and an idealism which reduces all reality to thought relations is developed.

The representative theory of perception adopted by the Sautrāntika takes us naturally to the subjectivism of the Yogācāra. Our data in knowledge are a disordered medley, which the Sautrāntikas say come to us from without, supplied by things which exist. We do not know what these things are. If objects of our knowledge are only ideas in our mind, which have a representative character, since they are referred to objects beyond themselves and are considered to be images and effects of things existing outside the thinking subject, it is difficult to comprehend their nature. They are said to be symbolic of something beyond themselves. If we start with ideas unreferred, their later reference to objects need not be true. The existence of an outer world is a fiction. Even if it exists it can never be known. We can never get behind the screen and know what causes the ideas. 'Our senses testify not, but that we have certain ideas. And if we draw conclusions from the testimony which the premises will not support, we deceive ourselves.'[28] When the Sautrāntika maintains that we have ideas and through them we infer things, it is clear that if there were external bodies we cannot know

---

R.G. Bhandarkar is of opinion that Kaniṣka lived in the third century AD. J.R.A.S., Bombay Branch, vol. xx.) Aśvaghośa is also the author of Buddhacarita. The Laṅkāvatārasūtra describes a visit paid to Rāvaṇa in Ceylon by Buddha, who answered a number of questions according to the doctrine of the Yogācāra school. It is an important text of this school, though Mādhyamika tenets are not wanting in it. The Abhisamayālaṁkārāloka and the Bodhisattvabhūmi are other works of the same school. Among the distinguished thinkers of this persuasion may be mentioned Nanda, Dignāga, Dharmapāla and Śīlabhadra. The last was Professor at Nalanda, from whom Yuan Chwang acquired the knowledge of Buddhist philosophy. Dignāga, the author of Nyāyabindusubhāṣitaṣaṁgraha, Pramāṇasamuccaya, was a South Indian philosopher and pupil of Asaṅga or Vasubandhu Dignāga is regarded by some as a contemporary of Guṇaprabha, and assigned to AD 520 to 600. It is not improbable that Kālidāsa refers to him in his Meghadūta, and if so, he must have flourished about the time of Kālidasa. The words are: Adreḥ śṛṅgaṁ harati—dignāgānām pathi pariharan sthūlahastāvalepan. Suguira says that Dignāga was a native of Andhra. See his *Hindu Logic as preserved in China and Japan*, p. 33.

28. Reid, *Works*, p. 286.

them, and if they were not, even then we will have as much reason to think they were.[29] If a cause is necessary for ideas, that cause need not necessarily be the outer world. Even with regard to ideas which are not voluntarily produced, all that we can say is that there must be some cause. The Sautrāntika does not face the consequences of his representative theory of knowledge, since he starts with the assumption of two substances.

The task of the Yogācāra was like that of Berkeley, to expose the baseless and self-contradictory character of the unknown absolute matter of the Sautrāntika, and persuade us to drop all ideas of such an external existence. We have no warrant for supposing the cause of all ideas to be material substance. Matter is an idea and nothing more. Things are clusters of sensations. The objects of knowledge are either ideas actually imprinted on the sense, or those perceived by attending to passions and operations of the mind. External objects independent of consciousness are not intelligible. The Yogācāras ask: 'Does the external object apprehended by us arise from any existence or not? It does not arise from an existence, for that which is generated has no permanence; nor does it not arise from an existence, for what has not come into being has no existence.'[30] Again, 'Is the external object a simple atom or a complex body? It cannot be the latter, for we do not know whether it is part or whole that is apprehended. It cannot be an atom, since it is supersensible.' We cannot cognise atoms, and about the aggregates of atoms we cannot say whether the aggregates are different or not from the atoms. If they are different from the atoms, they can no longer be regarded as composed of atoms. If they are not different from atoms, i.e. if they are one with them, they cannot be the causes of the mental representations of gross bodies. Besides, if the objects are momentary, then they last only an instant, and knowledge which is an effect can arise only after the cause ceases to be, and so it can never arise at all. At the moment of cognition the object would have ceased to be. It comes to this, that for perceiving an object we need not have an object. Even if objects exist they become objects of knowledge through ideas which take the form of objects. Since the latter are all we need, there is no necessity to assume external objects. Since we are conscious of ideas and things together, the two are not different. All the properties we know, length, size, taste, etc.,

29. Berkeley, *Principles of Human Knowledge*, section 7.
30. S.D.S., p. 24.

are subjective. There are no objects independent of us, and when we speak of such we use words only. Outer objects are non-existent. The apparent phenomena around us are produced by mental operations within. They appear and disappear like swiftly vanishing clouds. The so-called outward things, stars and planets, are really mental experiences arising in an established order which may somehow be counted upon.[31] We read into external nature what exists only in our own minds. If we ask for the explanation for the actual varieties of ideas, the Yogācāra refers us to the impressions left by previous ideas. Our dream experiences are full of ideas which arise from previous mental impressions without any external objects. Even so is waking experience to be explained.[32] All dharmas or things and their qualities are constituents of consciousness. Our consciousness by its two functions of khyāti or perception and vastuprativikalpa or interpretation develops the world of experience. The Yogācāra traces the activity of consciousness to the beginningless instinctive tendencies working in it.[33]

The Yogācāras are supporters of Vijñānavāda. They deny the real existence of all except vijñāna or consciousness. 'Sarvam buddhimayaṁ jagat;' the whole world is ideal. Whatever we may say about the natural world said to be beyond, internal experience cannot be denied. Our knowledge may not be a record of the truths of nature, but nobody can deny its existence. Knowledge is. Its presence is potent. This theory has

31. Cf. Einstein's theory of relativity, which makes out that even length is not an absolute property of the rod, but depends on the relative velocity and position of the rod and the observer.

32. According to the logic of Dignāga, existence means the capacity for producing an effect, arthakriyākāritva. External things are not real. A permanent thing is inactive. Does it possess, at the moment when it was accomplishing its present act, the power to accomplish its past and future? If so, it will accomplish them all at once. For it is not usual that anything capable of an act should postpone. If not, it will never accomplish them, as a stone which cannot produce a bird now will never produce one. If it is said that the permanent thing produces such and such an effect by reason of the co-operation of other factors, then if the factors are external, the latter are active; if they give a new power to the permanent things, then the first being who lacked this capacity perished, and a new being possessing this capacity is born. It is difficult to attribute to permanent things identical with themselves a successive activity, so they are all transitory.

33. See Laṅkāvatāra Sūtra.

the support of early Buddhism, which holds that all that happens is the result of thought and is made up of it. 'All that we are is the result of what we have thought; it is founded on our thoughts; it is made up of our thoughts.' The psycho-physical organism which continues after the death of a man is said to be created in the matrix by the rebirth of consciousness. Since the Yogācāras do not admit the dependence of consciousness on external objects and hold that it is self-subsistent, their view is called the Nirālambanavāda. The distinction of material and mental dharmas disappears, since all dharmas are mental.

When the Mādhyamika argues that even vijñāna is unreal, since we cannot have consciousness without an object of which we are conscious, the Yogācāra replies: 'If all is nothing, then nothing itself becomes the criterion of truth, and the Mādhyamika has no right to discuss with others of a different way of thinking. He who accepts nothing as real can neither prove his position nor disprove his opponent's case.'[34] When the Mādhyamika considers all things to be śūnya or void, even this absence of characteristics must designate a something. The Bodhisattvabhūmi puts it thus: 'For śūnya (vacuity) to be a justifiable position, we must have firstly the existence of that which is empty, and then the non-existence of that by the absence of which it is empty; but if neither exists, how can there be a vacuity?' We wrongly superimpose the notion of a serpent on a rope. The rope exists, the serpent does not. Therefore the rope is void of serpent. Similarly, the qualities and characteristics as form, etc., commonly attributed to things may not exist. Though the denotable properties may not exist, the substratum exists. The distinctions of jñāna and jñeya, knowledge and knowable, are based on something. The simile of a dream is used to illustrate this position. The visions of a dream are independent of anything to be seen. The elephants we see in a dream do not exist. They are products of mind wrongly made objective. The form ākṛti of elephant is taken by the thought under the influence of the impression (vāsanā) left by the visual knowledge. Even the knowledge that we touch an elephant is a knowledge assumed by thought. Since there is really no knowable, there is really no knowledge. There is no matter rūpa, nothing outside the thought, yet for all these imaginary entities also there must be some substratum, and that according to the Yogācāras is vijñāna.

34. S.S.S.S., iii. 3–4.

The Yogācāras are frankly idealistic. What is, is merely one homogenous vijñāna, which is not an abstract, but a concrete reality. The thinking being becomes conscious of its existence and identity of the subject only by knowing objects. The whole system of facts is placed within the individual consciousness. The ālaya, with its internal duality of subject and object, becomes itself a little world. It is confined to its own circle of modifications. The world of reality is deprived of its independence and reduced to a mere dance of ideas or thought relations. The ālaya, which is a continually changing stream of consciousness, is contrasted with Ātman, which is immutable, though the Yogācāras are not clear about the exact significance of the ālaya. The ālaya is sometimes the actual self, developing and ever-growing.[35] It receives impressions and develops the germs deposited in it by karma, or experience, and is continually active. It is not merely the superficial self, but the great storehouse of consciousness which the yogins find out by meditation. Through meditation and other practices of self-examination, we realise that our waking or superficial consciousness is a fragment of a wider whole. Every individual has in him this vast whole of consciousness the great tank, of the contents of which the conscious self is not fully aware.[36] Our personal consciousness knows but a small fraction of the sum total of our conscious states, the ālayavijñāna. There are indications that the ālayavijñāna was sometimes used in the sense of the absolute self. It is said to be without any origination, existence and extinction, utpādasthitibhaṅgavarjam.[37] It is the permanent background of the endless variety of feelings and ideas, common to all minds. It alone exists; individual, intellectual products are mere phenomena, phases of the ālaya. It is the sole foundation of the false belief in the existence of the world. All things in the universe are in it. Particular phenomena are manifestations of the ālaya according to the number and nature of the conditions. We in our ignorance break up this consciousness into several elements. 'What is of the nature of consciousness is indeed indivisible, but by those whose vision is confused it seems to be, as it were, differentiated into the perceived object, the perceiving subject and

35. Cf. Gentile's neo-idealism with its insistence on thought and the historical character of reality.

36. The Yogācāras accepted the doctrine of the subconscious which William James has called the most important step taken by psychology in recent years.

37. Laṅkāvatāra Sūtra.

the perception itself.'[38] Again, 'there exists in reality only one thing, and that is of the nature of the intelligent principle of consciousness, and its oneness is not destroyed by the varied character of its manifestations.[39] Māna, the means of knowledge, meya, the object of knowledge, and phala, the resulting knowledge, are distinctions within the whole of vijñāna. Objects arise from the successive modifications of mind. The Laṅkāvatāra Sūtra says: 'Cittam exists; not the objects perceptible by sight. Through objects visually cognised, cittam manifests itself in body in one's objects of enjoyment, residence, etc. It is called the ālaya of men.' Vijñāna constitutes the whole universe. Things of nature are only the other of it. Vijñāna is the whole, itself and the other. We see the gradual transition from the psychological to the logical self. All things are related to vijñāna. There is nothing outside thought. There cannot be any absolute opposition between thinking subject and the world of objects which he thinks. Thought is the beginning and the end of all knowledge. Remove thought, all will vanish into nothing. The individual who thinks is not merely an individual, he is part of all he knows, and all he knows is part of him. The reality outside knowledge, the thing in itself of Kant, is a creation of the mind. The idea of something else behind thought causing it, is simply another thought and no more. Thought is the only reality we have to reckon with. It is that which knows and the object which it knows. If this is the view of the Yogācāra, then the external world becomes a negation or the non-ego, which a thinking being sets up within, and in conflict with which it attains to consciousness. The priority and productivity of thought is the central thesis here. Thought is the structure as well as the stuff of reality. It presupposes no datum or reality external to itself, call it what you will, space or nature. It knows only so far as it thinks itself to be the object of its knowledge. Thought contains everything in itself. If the object constituted by the subject detaches itself from the subject, and shuts itself up in impenetrability, then it is eviscerated of its reality. In this sense thought is no other than God. The Yogācāra, when he teaches the immanent existence of all things in vijñāna, when he makes out that the ālaya is common to all individuals, that while the phenomenal self differs, the transcendental self is the same in all, is adopting this view. Ālayavijñāna is the absolute totality, originality and creativity, unconditioned itself by time and space, which are modes of existence of

38. S.S.S.S., iii. 2–4.
39. S.S.S.S., iii. 2–6.

the concrete and empirical individuality. Things of nature are deposits from the great sea of thought. They can all be taken back into its transparent unity and simplicity, which is the mother sea of consciousness, out of which things arise and into which they again return. It is the living base from which come the members which again withdraw themselves. It is the highest or perfect knowledge in which no thing is known, no difference is felt. It is always the same, and therefore perfect. Ālaya becomes the universal subject, and not the empirical self.

While then, metaphysically, all is due to the one reality which is thought, the Yogācāras sometimes reduce the matter opposed to the empirical individual to a mere sensation or collection of sensations. The world is not merely the contents of this or that consciousness. Solidity, distance, hardness and resistance are not mere ideas of the finite mind. By maintaining that they are, the Yogācāra's view becomes crudely subjectivist. It cannot account for the world organism which precedes the birth of human consciousness. Nor can it account for the seeming reality of a common world which renders our ordinary life possible. While we are willing to admit that it was not the intention of the Yogācāra school to make the world of space and time dependent or contingent on individual consciousness, yet we cannot help saying that, in their eagerness to refute naïve realism, they confused psychological and metaphysical points and countenanced a crude mentalism. The confusion is increased by the employment of the same term, vijñāna, to indicate both the changing and the unchanging aspects of mental life. We have the skandha vijñāna, which is a phenomenal effect of karma, and the ālayavijñāna, which is the ever active, continuous, spiritual energy dwelling in all. The reality of the world depends on the latter. An absolute consciousness must exist for the objects to exist and be known. This does not mean that the world is mere consciousness. Yet such an inference is often made by the Yogācāras.

The Yogācāras threw overboard the easy-going assumption of the realists who looked on mind as a self-contained thing confronted in experience by other self-contained things. Going behind the two substances of matter and mind, they tried to discover a comprehensive reality including the two. With true insight they recognised that what is really constructive of the object world is intelligence or vijñāna, which is more than merely individual. Within this vijñāna arises the distinction between subject and object. The ālayavijñāna is the foundational fact of reality revealing itself in individual minds and things. The distinction between subject and object is a distinction made by knowledge itself within its own field, and not a relation between two independent entities, as the Vaibhāṣikas and the Sautrāntikas assumed. The ālayavijñāna is the whole containing within itself, the knower and the known. Unfortunately, we notice the tendency to identify the ālayavijñāna with skandhavijñāna, which is only a property of the finite mind. If foundational knowledge is confused with the activities of particular subjects in space and time, we are upon the slope which leads to the precipice of scepticism. Almost all the non-Buddhist critics of the Yogācāra theory overlook the element of truth contained in it (albeit overlaid with a mass of error) and repudiate it as mere mentalism.

Śaṁkara criticises the theory that the world has no existence except in the human mind on several grounds. It fails to account for the variety of perception. How can we account for the sudden noise when we are enjoying a sunset? To say that things and ideas are presented together does not mean that they are one. Inseparable connection is different from identity. If all cognitions are empty of content, then the consciousness that there are no things is also empty. The comparison of waking to dream is due to a confusion. Dream experience is subjective and private, while the waking is not so. Objects of waking, knowledge endure, while dream objects last only during dreams. Śaṁkara argues that there is a real difference between dreaming and waking. We may dream of travelling great distances, and if the two, dreaming and waking were identical, then we should get up at the place to which we have travelled, not as we actually do at the same place where we were when we began to dream. If it is said that the two are not continuous, and it is open to us to infer the falsity of dreams from waking, as much as waking from dreams, Śaṁkara replies, that since waking experience is the one experience which affects us practically, we infer that dreams are false. If the Buddhist seems to infer the falsity of the waking world, he must have access to some experience to contradict the waking one. If he admits any such higher experience he would allow that there is something permanent after all, and so the momentariness theory vanishes and Vedāntism is established. We cannot perceive non-existent things. Śaṁkara takes his stand on psychological facts. 'We are always conscious of something,' and not merely conscious. Nobody when perceiving a post or a wall is conscious of his perception only. We are conscious of the object of perception, a post or a wall. A dream chair is not part of the dreaming mind any more than the chair on which we sit in waking life is part of the mind of the sitter. To be dependent on mind is not to be a part of mind. The statement that the perceptual consciousness takes on the form of the thing cognised so that we are never conscious of a thing, but only of a form belonging to our consciousness, is according to Śaṁkara absurd. If from the start there were no objects, he asks, how could perception take on the form of objects? It is because objects exist that consciousness is able to take on their form. Otherwise consciousness would be free to take on any form it pleased. If it is said that our consciousness of things as external is illusory, that we see objects as if they were external, whereas in reality they are not, Śaṁkara asks, if really there were nothing external, how can we have even an illusion of externality? If there were no such thing as a snake at all, if we did not know of it, we could not imagine it in the rope. Therefore external objects must exist.[40]

Kumārila argues that there is a distinction between waking and dreaming. 'For us, dream cognition is certainly falsified by the perception of the waking cognition contradicting it. While for you, what would constitute the difference between the reality of waking cognition and dream consciousness, both of which you hold to be equally false?'[41] To the objection that the waking cognitions are invalidated by the insight of the yogis, Kumārila says: 'Such yogic cognition is not found to belong to any person in this life; and as for those who have reached the yogic state, we know not what happens to them.'[42] If the Nirālambanavādin cites the Nyāya theory in his support to the effect that judgment and inference are explained by it on the basis of ideas of subject and predicate of the constituent propositions, and that these do not necessitate the external reality of objects, Kumārila replies that the Nyāya accepts the reality of external objects and proceeds on that basis.[43] To trace the differences of ideas to impressions leads us to anyonyāśraya, or mutual dependence and infinite regress. We can have no differentiation of the pure form of the idea. Vāsanā or impression brings about a distinction in the apprehender, but not in the object apprehended,[44] and vāsanā itself is inexplicable. 'Ideas being momentary and their dispersion total (leaving no trace behind), there being no association of the impressed and the impresser (since the two do not in any case appear together), there can be no vāsanā.' The two moments

40. See also Udayana, Ātmatattvaviveka.
41. v. 3. 88–89. Ślokavārttika.
42. 93–94.
43. 167–175.
44. 180–1.

not being together cannot be related by way of impression. Even if they were together, they could not be related, since both are momentary and cannot operate on each other.[45] If properties of previous cognitions persist in subsequent ones, we cannot say that they are destroyed totally. It is the need for a permanent consciousness, which is capable of impressions and preserving the vāsanās, that makes the Yogācāras look upon ālaya as a permanent entity, yet they are obliged by their Buddhist presuppositions to look upon it as ever changing. Hence the unsatisfactoriness of the Yogācāra doctrine. Śaṁkara's criticism hits off the point well. Unless there exists one continuous principle which cognises everything, we cannot account for knowledge. If ālayavijñāna is looked upon as the permanent self, the distinctive feature of Buddhism that there is nothing permanent is gone. The philosophical impulse led the Yogācāras to the Upaniṣad theory, while the Buddhist presuppositions made them halting in their acceptance of it.

The Yogācāras, however, felt that reducing the world to a mere relation of ideas would be to deprive reality of all its meaning. The phenomenal existence of the world with its distinction of subject and object is accepted by them. Mādhava writes: 'Nor must it be supposed that on this hypothesis, the juice, the energy and the digestion derivable from an imaginary and an actual sweetmeat will be the same.'[46] This reminds us of Kant's famous distinction between the imaginary and the real hundred dollars. Psychologically the Yogācāras admit the distinction of subject and object. But critical analysis reveals to them that these are all differences within a whole which the Yogācāra identifies with vijñāna or thought. The empirical self finds an object over against itself, without which its own conscious life is not possible. That which the empirical self finds given is not for the absolute, a mere contingent datum. The word is as real as the particular self and independent of it, though dependent upon the universal consciousness. We need hardly point out how very similar the latter view of the ālayavijñāna is to the philosophy of Fichte, which looks upon all experience as that of a self-conscious subject. To him the self is both act and product in one. The ego affirms or posits itself, and it does so by oppositing or distinguishing from itself a non-ego. By this process of limitation or negation the ego brings into being the element of otherness. The absolute ego differentiates into a multiplicity of finite egos at once other than itself and modes of itself.

45. 182–5.
46. S.D.S., p. 26.

The world in space and time appears to be real, because of our imperfect apprehension. Our intellect, though fundamentally free from the modes of subject and object, still, thanks to the succession of unreal ideas or to the beginningless predispositions,[47] develops diverse distinctions between the percipient and the percept. Our buddhi is twofold, cognitional and non-cognitional. The former leads to a correct apprehension of truth, the latter which is dependent on a fundamental insensitiveness is evolved out of the skandhas, āyatanas and the dhātus (or the material components of the body), and is the source of avidyā, and is not an authoritative criterion of truth.[48] Every individual has the vijñāna in which the germs of all things exist in their ideality. The objective world does not exist in reality, but by means of the subjective illusion created by avidyā the individual projects the germs in the ālayavijñāna to the outside world, and imagines that they are as they seem to him to be. We have again subjectivism here, since the objective world is reduced to mind stuff. 'In the all-conserving consciousness or ālaya, avidyā obtains, and from non-enlightenment starts that which sees, that which represents, that which apprehends and the objective world, and that which constantly particularises.'[49] The empirical ego comes from a commingling of the ālaya with avidyā, and this empirical ego has for its correlate the empirical world, and both are phenomenal and are transcended in the ālaya. The metaphysical is the truth of the psychological.

All thoughts excepting those of a Buddha have a three-fold nature or character: (1) the imagined nature (parikalpita), (2) dependent or caused nature (paratantra), and (3) absolute or metaphysical nature (parinișpanna). Our dream experiences come in the first class. Thought externalises itself in the form of dream figures. Such wrongly objectified objects of cognition are the bodily organs, things known by them and the material universe. In the idea of the ego, ahaṁdṛṣṭi, thought presents itself to itself, as object and subject of cognition. From the opposition of duality arise the so-called categories of being, non-being, essence, etc. The dual nature results from the fact that we consider the so-called objects which are only forms of thought to be external and existing in themselves, even as a dreamer believes in the reality of dream elephants when he notices them. This duality has no metaphysical reality, but is a product of imagination, parikalpa or vikalpa, which imposes on thought the categories of subject and object.

47. Anādivāsanāvaśāt (S.D.S., ii. 26).
48. S.S.S.S., iii. 4. 6–7.
49. Aśvaghoṣa, *Awakening of Faith*, p. 75.

But whence do thoughts derive their origin? What is the law according to which they appear in an ordered succession? They are not produced by the external objects of the realists. Nor are they due to an immutable Ātman, as the Vedāntins argue, nor are they autonomous. Thoughts are dependent one upon another. M. Poussin writes: 'All the Buddhist philosophers, maintainers of the doctrine of karma, had to admit that thoughts, although momentary, do not perish altogether, but originate new thoughts, sometimes after a long interval of time. As long as they believed in the existence of matter and considered man as a physico-psychical complex, it was not difficult for them to explain the interdependence of thoughts.' The six classes of cognitions had a material support and exterior excitements, and it was possible to explain all the psychological facts, including memory, with these six cognitions. But the idealists had to work out a system of psychology without the hypothesis of any material element. They say 'that the cognitions acknowledged by the realist schools, visual ... mental cognitions create seeds (bīja), which will ripen in due time without any interference except for the power of the bodhisattvas into new visual ... mental cognitions. Now these seeds are not a part of the visual ... mental cognitions which arise in succession between the sowing and the ripening of the seeds; for example, the cognition of blue which will emerge tomorrow in a certain series of cognitions named "I" depends on yesterday's cognitions of belief. But its seed is not to be found in any of the cognitions of which I am conscious today. Therefore we must add to the sixfold cognition of the primitive psychology another group of cognitions which the modern philosopher would style unconscious or subliminal images; these are the seeds of actual cognition; they are created by actual cognition; beside and below the actual cognition they flow as a series of momentary subliminal images which proceed, owing to an uninterrupted self-reproduction; this series bears the old supply of seeds, is enlarged by the sowing of new seeds, and will stop when the series have borne fruit and no new seeds sown.'[50] If no new seed is sown and the old stock is exhausted, we pass beyond the second stage of knowledge and reach the third, called parniṣpanna. The duality of subject and object is realised to be accidental to thought, being produced by the misconception of imagination. To know thought in its metaphysical aspect, duality has to be overcome. True, when once it is freed from duality it becomes ununderstandable, beyond expression. No

50. E.R.E., vol. ix., p. 850.

character (viśeṣa) can be predicated of it; it can be said only to exist (bhavati eva). It is therefore defined as vastumātra, simply thing, or cittamātra, mere thought.

It is open to us to look upon parikalpitasatya as positive error, as when we mistake a rope for a snake; paratantrasatya as relative knowledge, as when we recognise a rope as a rope; and pariniṣpannasatya as metaphysical insight, as when we recognise that rope is a mere concept and has no being as a thing in itself. Nāgārjuna reduces the first two to one, saṁvṛti satya, and calls the third paramārtha. Parikalpita is the illusory knowledge of Kant, which is purely subjective, being unconditioned be the categories. It cannot stand critical judgment and has no practical efficiency. Paratantra is the empirical knowledge of Kant, relative and conditioned. Through this categorised knowledge the absolute reality, free from all conditions, cannot be known. It is possible for us to rise to the metaphysical insight since the one universal dwells in all. It exists whole and undivided in every single thing, entirely free from all forms of the phenomena. Plurality is possible because of subjection to time and space, which are the principles of individuation. The ālaya is free from diversity, though its phenomena are innumerable in space and time. The highest state which transcends all opposites, in which the positive and the negative are one and the same (bhāvābhāvasamānatā), is called by the Yogācāras tathatā, or pure being.[51]

Agreeing with the realists, the Yogācāras divide all things in the universe into the two groups of saṁskṛta, or composite, and asaṁskṛta, or non-composite. The composite dharmas are also similarly divided as in the realist schools, though in them the first place is given to rūpa, or matter, while the Yogācāras give it to citta, or mind. Citta or mind is the ultimate source of all things. This citta has two aspects, lakṣaṇa or phenomenal, bhāva or noumenal. The former deals with its changeableness, the latter with its immutability. It has two functions, attending to objects and receiving impressions. Altogether its dharmas are eight, the five dependent on the sense-organs, the sixth of the internal sense, the seventh of vijñāna which speaks of them, and the eighth of the ālayavijñāna.[52]

51. See Mahāyānasūtrālaṁkāra.

52. Śaṁkara says: 'With reference to this doctrine we make the following remarks: "Those two aggregates, constituting two different classes, and having two different causes which the Buddhists assume, viz., the aggregate of the elements and elementary things whose cause the atoms are, and the aggregate of the five skandhas, cannot, on Buddhist principles, be established, i.e. it cannot be explained how the aggregates

The asaṁskṛta dharmas are six: Ākāśa is the limitless, free from all change, which is identified with mere being; Pratisaṁkhyānirodha is the cessation of all kinds of kleśas or sorrows, attained through the power of perfect knowledge; Apratisaṁkhyānirodha is cessation acquired without the aid of perfect knowledge. Acala is the state of disregard for all power and pleasure, and Saṁjñāvedanānirodha is that where vedanā (feeling) and saṁjñā (perception) do not act. These five are not independent, but are different names conventionally employed to denote the noumenal aspect of the universe. We may call them the different stages by which the highest reality can be attained. Dharmapāla says: 'All these five conventional terms are given to several stages of manifestation and parts of pure being.' This takes us to the true metaphysical absolute of the Yogācāra school, viz., tathatā. 'This is the transcendental truth of everything, and is termed tathatā, because its essential nature is real and eternal. Its nature is beyond the reach of language. Is is indefinable.'[53] Lest we mistake it for nothingness, it is called bhāva, or existence. Asaṅga says: 'It can neither be called existence nor non-existence. It is neither such nor otherwise. It is neither born nor destroyed. It neither increases nor decreases. It is neither purity nor filth. Such is the real lakṣaṇa or nature of the transcendental truth.'

---

are brought about. For the parts constituting the (material) aggregates are devoid of intelligence, and the kindling of intelligence depends on an aggregate of atoms having been brought about previously. And the Buddhists do not admit any other permanent intelligent being, such as either an enjoying soul or a ruling lord, which could effect the aggregation of the atoms. Nor can the atoms and skandhas be assumed to enter on activity on their own account, for that would imply their never ceasing to be active. Nor can the cause of aggregation be looked for in the so-called abode (i.e. the ālayavijñāna pravāha, the train of self-cognition), for the latter must be described either as different from the single cognitions or as not different from them. In the former case it is either permanent, and then it is nothing else but the permanent soul of the Vedāntins; or non-permanent, then being admitted to be momentary merely, it cannot exercise any influence and cannot therefore be the cause of motion of the atoms. And in the latter case we are no further advanced than before. For all these reasons the formation of aggregates cannot be accounted for. But without aggregates there would be an end of the stream of mundane existence, which presupposes these aggregates."' (*Commentary on Vedānta-Sūtras*, edited by G. Thibaut, pp. 403–4). Avidyā is no explanation of the formation of aggregates, for 'How can it be the cause of that without which as its abode it is not capable of existence? Besides the notion of causality is itself unintelligible.'

53. Vasubandhu.

Pure being or tathatā is also called ālayavijñāna, in its dynamic aspect, when it is combined with the principle of individuation or negativity. The moment we make pure being into vijñāna or cit, we introduce the element of individualism. The ālaya has difference eternally in its own heart. We have the self-realising consciousness, an absolute of the Hegelian type.[54] The moment we descend from the absolute being to the ālayavijñāna we get in addition to consciousness a principle of space, in addition to being a non-being. Space is nothing but a mode of particularisation, and has no real existence of its own. The whole phenomenal world is due to the particularisation of the confused mind. If the confusion clears up, the modes of relative existence vanish. Space is real and eternal in a limited sense.[55] The contingent appearances traceable to avidyā do not affect the pure spirit. We seem to have what later Vedānta calls vivartavāda, or phenomenalism. 'The appearance of duality in the unity of cognition is an illusion.'[56] Again: 'The internal principle manifests itself as if it were external.'[57] The one truth is seen in the form of a world through the force of avidyā. We cannot say in what sense all things are in the absolute. If all are in it, there is no meaning in development. If they are not, if the absolute produces them, then it cannot remain unaffected by what it produces. The avidyā which is the cause of all experience, which obtains the moment we have the ālayavijñāna, cannot be accounted for. 'Though all modes of consciousness and mentation are products of avidyā, avidyā is in its ultimate nature identical and not identical with enlightenment. In one sense it is destructible, in another it is not.'[58] Enlightenment and non-enlightenment are one, as all kinds of pottery, though different are made of the same clay.'[59] Tathatā is the first principle. Ālaya with avidyā comes

54. 'That there is one spiritual self-conscious being of which all that is real is the activity or expression; that we are related to the spiritual being, not merely as parts of the world which is its expression, but as partakers in some inchoate measure of the self-consciousness through which it at once constitutes and distinguishes itself from the world; that this participation is the source of morality and religion, this we take to be the vital truth which Hegel had to teach.' (T.H. Green, *Works*, vol. iii., p. 146.)
55. Suzuki, p. 107.
56. S.D.S., p. 27.
57. Ibid.
58. Suzuki, p. 67.
59. Ibid., pp. 73–74.

next. Next we have the empirical subjects and objects, which grow feeding upon each other.

Every individual has in him the higher principle bound up with a selfish individuality. Individuality clings to us so long as we are subject to avidyā. The differences among men are due to the force of ignorance. 'Though all beings uniformly have the same quality, yet in intensity, the ignorance or principle of individuation, that works from all eternity, varies in such manifold grades so as to outnumber the sands of the Ganges.'[60] Saṁsāra is the going on or pravṛtti of the particularising tendency due to the defilement of our thought. Vāsanās, or tendencies, and karma, or work, keep up uninterruptedly the continuance of the circuit. Ālaya, or citta, is the source of the objects we perceive, and has in it potencies determined by our past conduct which are bound to develop. All dharma, pain, pleasure, good and bad conduct, are the outer manifestations of the potential seeds stored in the ālaya. Some of these seeds are full of defilement,[61] and so make for saṁsāra. Others are free from defilement,[62] and so tend to liberation. It is the presence of the transcendental element that helps us to think of higher ideas.

But the mere presence of the absolute will not lead to liberation. A distinction is made between *raison d'être* (hetu) and cause (pratyaya). The combustible nature of the wood is the *raison d'être* of the fire; but we must set fire to it, or it will not burn. Even so, though the presence of the absolute may be the *raison d'être* of salvation, still the practice of wisdom and virtue is necessary. Asaṅga writes: 'By not clinging to wealth or pleasures, by not cherishing any thoughts to violate the precepts, by not feeling dejected in the face of evils, by not awakening any distraction or indolence of attention while practising goodness, by maintaining serenity of mind in the midst of disturbance and confusion of the world, and finally by always practising single-mindedness (ekacitta) and by the right comprehension of the nature of things, the bodhisattvas recognise the truth of vijñānamātra, the truth of the origin of all in consciousness.' The Yogācāras practise yoga. Yoga helps us to acquire intuitive insight. Discursive understanding gives us dependent or empirical knowledge. The metaphysical truth requires yogic discipline. When the mind is clear of all prejudice or illusion, it reflects the truth.[63]

60. Ibid., p. 89.
61. Sāsravabīja.
62. Anāsravabīja.
63. See the last book of Spinoza's *Ethics*, where he makes out that the infinite in man whose essence is light and harmony will be liberated from the world of darkness

Nirvāṇa is purification of mind, its restoration to its primitive simplicity or radiant transparency. 'When by constancy of reflection we rid ourselves of all prejudgments, there arises knowledge freed from the illusions which take the form of objects, and this is called Mahodaya, the grand exaltation or emancipation.'[64] The Vijñānamātra Śāstra distinguishes four kinds of nirvāṇa. (1) Nirvāṇa is a synonym for dharmakāya, the undefiled essence present in all things. This nirvāṇa is possessed by every sentient individual, pure and spotless, in its native being. (2) Upādhiśeṣa nirvāṇa, or that which has some residue left. It is a state of relative being which, though freed from all affection, all hindrance, is still under the fetters of materiality which cause suffering and misery. (3) Anupādhiśeṣa nirvāṇa, or that which has no residue. It is a complete liberation from all fetters. (4) The nirvāṇa which means absolute enlightenment, and has for its object the benefiting of others, is the highest kind of nirvāṇa.

While the Yogācāra theory did a great service to the science of logic, by pointing out the necessity of thought for all reality, it betrayed its weakness by its frequent denial of all non-mental reality and experience. The use of the term ālayavijñāna is too indefinite. It is sometimes considered a synonym for tathatā, when it is identified with vastumātra, the mere abstraction of being, the pure existentiality, the Hegelian Seyn, the ultimate which remains when we abstract from every fact and form of existence. Again, it is considered to be a phenomenon of the mind including other phenomena in its scope. It is also the cosmic mind with the principle of negativity in it. Sometimes it is equated with the stream of consciousness within the individual. The indefiniteness of the theory on such a central issue has exposed it to a good deal of legitimate criticism.

V

THE MĀDHYAMIKAS[65]

The Mādhyamika philosophy is an ancient system which can be traced to the original teaching of Buddha. Buddha called his ethical teaching the

---

and discord, when the passions are subdued. So long as the mind is the prey of passions, it mistakes the unreal for the real. When the fluctuations of mind which arise from these passions are destroyed, the intuition of the true 'existence of things' becomes possible.

64. S.D.S., p. 26.

65. Of the Mādhyamika philosophy, the main text is the Mādhyamika Sūtras

Middle (madhyama) Way, and repudiated the two extremes of an exaggerated asceticism and an easy secular life. In metaphysics he condemned all extreme positions, such as that everything exists, or that nothing exists. The Mādhyamika philosophy tries to adopt the mean between extreme affirmation and extreme negation. We have in Nāgārjuna one of the greatest thinkers of India, a far more vigorous sifting of the contents of experience than we found in either the subjectivists or the realists. He is sustained by an unselfish intellectual enthusiasm and philosophical ardour, which aim at thoroughness and completeness for their own sake. His philosophy is nearer now to scepticism, now to mysticism. His scepticism is due to his realising the essential relactivity of thought. Yet he has faith in an absolute standard of reality. His scepticism is Buddhistic, while his absolutism derives from the Upaniṣads. In the true philosophic spirit Nāgārjuna reveals the paradoxes which our everyday consciousness veils by means of a more or less thoughtless phraseology and indifference to

---

of Nāgārjuna, a South Indian Brāhmin, who, according to Kumārajīva who translated his biography into Chinese in AD 401, lived about the middle of the second century AD, though the tradition of his system may be assigned to the first century of the Christian era. There is also a view that Nāgārjuna lived in the first century before Christ. Sarat Chandra Das is of opinion (see *Indian Pundits in the Land of Snow*, p. 15) that Nāgārjuna converted Dhorabhadra, who lived in 56 BC, to Buddhism, if the account of Indian history preserved in the Archives of the Dalailama are to be believed. The Chinese traveller Yuan Chwang holds that Nāgārjuna lived in Southern Kosala, 400 years after the death of Buddha, and obtained supreme enlightenment as a bodhisattva. Dr Vidyābhūṣaṇ places Nāgārjuna about AD 300. In no case could he have been later than AD 401, when Kumārajīva translated the life of Nāgārjuna into Chinese. Moreover, Nāgārjuna assumes a knowledge of the definitions of the sixteen categories as given in the Nyāya Sūtras, and wrote a treatise on the pramāṇas. In it Nāgārjuna reduced the syllogism of five members into one of three. In another work on logic, called Upāyakauśalyahṛdaya Śāstra, we find a clear exposition of the art of debate. In the Vigrahavyāvartanī Kārikā, Nāgārjuna criticises the Nyāya theory of pramāṇas, and perhaps Vātsyāyana knew Nāgārjuna's views. The Sanskrit Commentary on the Mādhyamika Sūtras which we possess is by Candrakīrti, who probably lived in the first half of the seventh century AD. Śāntideva, of the seventh century AD, is named sometimes among the Mādhyamikas and at other times among the Yogācāras. In his works, Bodhicaryāvatāra, Śikṣāsamuccaya, he recognises two kinds of truth, saṁvṛti and paramārtha, and accepts the doctrine of śūnya. 'Make thy merit sure by deeds full of the spirit of tenderness and the śūnya' (Śikṣāsamuccāya, v. 21). The other systems of thought criticise the Mādhyamika theory.

reflection. The Yogācāra suggests the relational view of reality from which Nāgārjuna develops his scepticism. But the positive part of his philosophy is not different from the Advaitic interpretation of the Upaniṣad view. It is a serious mistake to suppose that we have in Nāgārjuna only a revival of the Upaniṣad doctrine. He seems to draw his inspiration from the Upaniṣads, though his philosophy is developed within the shadow of and with special reference to the Buddhistic views. The result is a type of thought which has never existed before, though it is supposed to be derived from the Prajñāpāramitā. It is perhaps better to point out that the general view places the Śūnyavāda earlier than the Vijñānavāda, though one can never be sure of it. The two perhaps developed side by side. Anyway, our order of treatment helps us to see the logical relations of the two systems.

VI

THEORY OF KNOWLEDGE

If we cannot pass from perceptions to the objects they are supposed to refer or represent, how can we pass beyond perceptions to a self-consciousness which is said to perceive? We cannot credit thought with a reality which we deny to the external world, since both are groups of passing phenomena. We do not know what consciousness is apart from seeing, feeling, willing, etc. Substance is not different from attributes. Were it so, it is beyond apprehension. There is, therefore, no need to look upon the external world as a phenomenon of the internal, or make the subject all-pervasive. The Yogācāras accounted for the empirical world by positing a continuous subject. The argument is pushed a step beyond this and the very shadow of the soul is given up. If the Yogācāras are right, then there are no objects to be known. Even Vijñāna cannot exist if there are no objects to be known.[66] No object means no subject. Thus the Mādhyamika abolishes the constant ālaya and sets the stream of ideas adrift. If there are no objective relations discoverable, there is no world at all. External objects as well as internal states are both void, śūnya. The Mādhyamika says that we are dreaming even when we are awake. Through the pressure of logic, the Mādhyamika infers the final inexplicability of subject and object. The explanations of science and common sense which assume their validity are interesting and valuable, but they are not the final truth. Before we attempt to define the

66. S.S.S.S., iii. 1. 18.

exact significance of the Mādhyamika theory of the phenomenality of the world, let us consider the arguments by which the Mādhyamika establishes his view.

The Mādhyamika, as the name implies, adopts a position midway between extreme affirmation and extreme negation. If the world were real, no changes can occur in it at all. Improvement and enlightenment are possible only if the world is plastic and in a state of constant becoming. As Candrakīrti, commenting on Nāgārjuna, observes: 'If everything has its own self-essence, which makes it impossible to pass from one state to another, how could a person desire to ascend, if he ever so desire, higher and higher on the scale of existence?' We cannot do anything in a world perfect and real. So it must be unreal. Nāgārjuna asks: 'If you negate the doctrine of śūnya, you negate causation. If there were such a thing as self-essence, the multitudinousness of things must be regarded as uncreated and imperishable, which is tantamount to eternal nothingness. If there were no emptiness, there would be no attainment of what has not yet been attained, nor would there be the annihilation of pain nor the extinction of all the passions.'[67] The nature of the world as an evolving process compels us to deny absolute reality to it. It seems clear from this that while Nāgārjuna denies absolute being to the world, he does not reduce it to mere nothing.

The Mādhyamika theory of the phenomenal nature of the world follows from the doctrine of pratītyasamutpāda, or dependent origination. A thing is a mass of dharmas following one another in unbroken succession. The individual human being is a collection of dharmas, since every thought, sensation, or volition is a dharma. A carriage is the name of a collection of material dharmas; a man is a collection of material and mental dharmas which constitute his pseudo-individuality. Apart from dharmas, carriage and man have only an ideal existence, an existence of designation (prajñapti) Dharmas alone exist, but they are doomed to destruction. Dharmas are moments in a continuous series. Every thought may have as its determining cause or pratyaya a great number of dharmas, more or less external to itself, object of vision, visual organ, etc., but its cause or hetu property so-called is the thought immediately preceding it, even as every moment of the duration of the flame depends on the oil, the wick, etc., though it is truly a continuation of the preceding moment of the flame. Nothing is by itself. Everything depends on something else. The Mādhyamikas do not dismiss

67. Chap. xxiv.

all dharmas as well as their collections as unreal, though they look upon them as phenomenal and momentary.[68] Yet it must be admitted that in the excitement of the argument they sometimes suggest that they are utterly non-existent.

If incapacity to explain is sufficient reason to deny the reality of a thing, then neither external objects nor inner souls are real. The Yogācāras argue that external objects are unreal, since we cannot say whether they arise from existence or not, whether they are simple atoms or complex bodies. Nāgārjuna accepts the principle underlying this theory, that the unintelligible is the unreal, but he adds that on this showing even consciousness or vijñāna is unreal, seeing that we cannot say anything consistent about it. It is in this connection that Nāgārjuna develops his theory of relations. The Yogācāras urge that all things have their being through relations of consciousness. We do not know of any other medium than a thinking consciousness through which alone things can subsist. Nāgārjuna admits that relations constitute the world. The world is a mere complex of these relations. The hosts of heaven, the furniture of earth, all the bodies which compose this mighty frame of the world have no substantial existence. They are hypostatised relations. But the relations themselves are unintelligible. Nāgārjuna shows that the whole world of experience is an appearance, a mere network of unintelligible relations. Matter and soul, space and time, cause and substance, motion and rest, are all alike the baseless fabric of the vision which leave not a rack behind. Reality must at least be consistent. But the categories through which we construct our reality or experience are unintelligible and self-contradictory. Intelligibility is the minimum expected of reality, but the relations of experience do not possess even that. Things which are not consistent may be actual, but they are not real. We are reminded of the attempt of Bradley, since the general principle is the same in the two cases. Of course, we have not here the luminous systematic application which constitutes the greatness of Bradley's metaphysics. Nāgārjuna's attempt is neither so full nor so methodical as Bradley's. He lacks the latter's passion for system and symmetry, but he is aware of the general principle, and his work has a unity in spite of much that is deficient as well as redundant.

68. 'When we come rationally to examine things, we cannot ascertain the nature of anything; hence all things must be declared to be inexplicable and devoid of any assignable nature or character.' (Laṅkāvatāra Sūtra, ii. 173.)

The category of gati or motion cannot be explained. We cannot understand its nature. A thing cannot be in two places at one time. 'We are not passing a path which has already been passed. Nor are we passing that which is yet to be passed. The existence of a path which has neither been passed nor is yet to be passed is beyond comprehension.'[69] The path may be divided into two sections, that which is already passed and that which has yet to be passed. There is no third possible. The first is over, the second is not yet, so passing is an impossibility. The consequences of this denial of motion are developed in the succeeding verses.[70] Since there is no passing, there can be no passer.[71] There cannot be an agent without passing, and yet how can an agent pass? 'Inasmuch as you are not beginning to pass a path which has already been passed, nor are you beginning to pass what has not yet been passed, nor what is being passed, what then are you beginning to pass?'[72] We cannot assert the identity of the passer and the passing, since there cannot be a passer without the act of passing. If we say that the passer is different from the passing, we maintain that there can be an act of passing without the passer as well as a passer without the fact of passing. They are neither identical with nor different from each other, and the only conclusion is that the passer, the path and the act of passing are unreal.[73] Nor can we say that the act of staying or rest (sthiti) is real. Motion, change and rest are all unintelligible. It may appear that in all this Nāgārjuna is creating artificial difficulties, since change and motion are facts. There is no doubt that they are actual, but the question is, how can we intelligibly conceive them? So long as we are philosopohising, we cannot stop short of complete explanation. Motion and rest cannot be completely explained, and so they are not final truths, but only relative terms, useful conventions.

In chapter vii Nāgārjuna takes up the question of composite substances or saṁskṛtas which come into existence, continue and cease to exist.[74] If the three, origination, continuance and extinction, separately do not characterise a saṁskṛta, how can they be jointly and simultaneously in one and the same object? If the object be without extinction and continuance at the time of its origination, then it is not called a saṁskṛta.

69. Mādhyamika Sūtras, ii. 1.
70. ii. 2–5.
71. ii. 6. 7. 8.
72. ii. 12.
73. ii. 14. 18.
74. Utpāda sthiti-bhaṅga-samāhāra-svabhāvam.

It is the same with the two other qualities. Yet all the three cannot be at the same moment. Light and darkness cannot exist simultaneously, so saṁskṛtas are not real. In chapter xxi he takes up the question of the origination and extinction, (saṁbhava vibhava) and proves their unreality. From the critical point of view, neither production nor destruction is possible. In chapter xix the conception of time, as including past, present and future, is declared to be an unintelligible category. The past is a doubtful report, and the future an indeterminate forecast. What is experienced in the present seems to be all that is. But we can have no present apart from the past and the future. Time, then, seems to be a form of thought, fabricated out of emptiness.[75]

A thing is known to us through its qualities. When we apprehend all the qualities, we are said to know the thing, and when we do not know them, we do not know the substance. In chapter v Nāgārjuna deals with this question, with special reference to the elements of earth, water, fire, air, ākāśa or ether, and consciousness or vijñāna, and argues that there is no substance prior to attributes, for that would mean an attributeless substance.[76] Where then can the attributes exist? They seem to be neither in substance without attributes, nor in themselves, and they can be nowhere else. Substance, again, cannot exist beyond the attributes, and there is nothing which is not a substance or an attribute. An attribute flings us back to a substance, and the substance leads us to attribute, and we do not know whether the two are one or different. Chapter xv treats of svabhāva, or inherent property, and shows that neither existence nor non-existence can be proved to be the essential property of substance. Qualities, like colour, hardness, softness, smell, taste, etc., are subjective. They exist because there are senses. There would be no colour without the eye, no sound without the ear. The qualities then depend on conditions other than and different from themselves. They are not independently real, since they depend on our sense-organs. They cannot exist in themselves. Since qualities exist in relation to sense-organs, they are all dependent on the senses, and so Nāgārjuna does not distinguish qualities into primary and secondary. Since all qualities are appearances only, the things in which they reside cannot be real. If the thing is related to the qualities, then the 'appearance' character of the qualities should affect the thing as well. We are never aware of things

75. Te ākāśasthitena cetasā kālaṁ kurvanti.
76. Chap. i.

which possess these qualities. Our knowledge is confined to qualities. The thing so-called is beyond experience, and therefore belief in it is a dogmatic assumption. We cannot say that these qualities and not some others belong to the thing. If substance is merely the glue which binds or keeps the qualities together without allowing them to clash with each other, then it becomes only a relation. Substance is then an abstract relation of qualities, and cannot exist apart from consciousness, which is the vehicle through which it is created. Substance and quality are correlative, and neither can be applied to reality as a whole. What absolutely exists is neither substance nor quality, which are mutually dependent. Provisionally in our experience we may accept substance to be that in which qualities inhere, since we cannot imagine qualities, such as weight, form, etc., apart from an underlying substratum. As a matter of fact, Nāgārjuna believes that things seem to be real in virtue of the relationships of causality, dependence, contiguity and conditionality.

The contradictions of the causal relations are brought out in chapter iv of the Mādhyamika Sūtras. 'An object as separate from its cause is not perceptible, and the cause of the object as separate from the object itself cannot be perceived. If the cause of the object is separate from the object itself, then you assert that the object is causeless. But to assert the existence of the cause of an object is not reasonable, for an object without cause does not exist.' Nāgārjuna argues that an effect separate from cause or cause separate from effect is non-existing. A thing is born neither from itself nor from another, nor from both, nor without cause. Production seems to be logically impossible.[77] Nothing real can be spoken of as coming to existence, nor can it be said that the pot this moment non-existent next moment becomes existent. That will be to assert a contradiction. When we know that things have no absolute existence, we see that they cannot produce others with such existence. If we speak of causes, we do so at the expense of logic, indulging in makeshifts of subject and object, substance and attribute, space and time. Absolutely speaking there is no cause or effect,

77. S.S.S.S., chap. iv. 7. 9, puts the argument thus: 'What is non-existent cannot be produced by any cause, such as a square circle; if origination is admitted to be desirable in the case of what is existent, then it produces only that which has been already produced. One and the same thing cannot be both existent and non-existent. Nor can we say that one and the same thing is distinct from both existence and non-existence.'

no production or cessation.[78] Sometimes cause is taken as the whole sāmagri or totality, which is also shown to be arbitrary and difficult to comprehend.[79] From this discussion it follows that the conception of change is unintelligible. A changes into B. Nāgārjuna argues, if A could become B, it must always have been B, else it cannot become B. But it could not have been B, for then there is no point in saying that it has become B. The process of change is unintelligible. Causaton cannot account for change, since it itself is an impossible conception.

A quality stands to substance in the relation of dependence. The two exist in virtue of a certain relationship. The cognition and the cognisable stand in such a relation. Absolutely both are unreal, but relatively they seem to exist, and so long as one thing depends on another, neither is existent in itself.

A phenomenon occupying a certain time or place stands to another in another time or palce in the relation of contiguity, but that spatial relations are relative and that there is no absolute priority or posteriority are quite obvious.

The part stands to the whole in the relation of conditionality, as the threads to the cloth. There is no cloth apart from the threads, and there are no threads apart from the cloth. Neither has absolute existence. No whole without parts, no parts without a whole. The two seem to exist in virtue of the relationship of conditionality. But it is only seeming or saṁvṛti. No objects of the universe absolutely exist. They appear to exist through relations.

The question of self is taken up in chapter vi. The general principle that there is no substance apart from qualities leads to the conclusion that there is no self apart from states of consciousness. There is no soul prior to acting, feeling and thinking. In chapter ix Nāgārjuna says: 'Some say that the entity (soul), whose act it is to see, hear and feel, existed prior to the acts. But how can we know that it existed prior to the acts? ... If soul could exist prior to and therefore without the act of seeing, cannot seeing take place independent of soul? The soul and the acts of seeing presuppose each other. Again, if it did not exist prior to all hearing, seeing, etc., how can it exist prior to each? If it is the same that sees, hears and feels, it must have existed prior to each. The soul does not exist in the elements from which the acts of seeing, hearing and feeling proceed.' The soul cannot be known until

78. Chap. xxi.
79. Chap. xx.

the acts of seeing, etc., take place. So it did not exist prior to these acts. Nor does it become existent posterior to them. For if the acts of seeing, etc., could take place independently of the soul, what is the use of bringing in the latter? The soul and the acts of seeing are simultaneous to each other. Unless they are independent of each other, they cannot exist simultaneously.[80] Nāgārjuna applies to the self the arguments which the Yogācāras used to undermine external reality. If the properties which we read into the outer universe do not involve a permanent reality called matter, why should the existence of ideas involve a self which is not an idea? The uninterrupted series of momentary mental states is all we mean be self. We know nothing about the nature of consciousness as such. It is a steam, an evolving field of presentations unrolling before us. Belief in a permanent self is as daring and dogmatic according to Nāgārjuna as the parallel belief in a material world. That objects of consciousness are arranged in psychological sequences so as to constitute separate minds is a mere speculation. Things are just what they seem to be. We cannot even talk of a stream of ideas. If we admit the reality of a soul, apart from conscious states, it is only for practical purposes. The mutual dependence of self and its states, the agent and his acts, is also brought out in chapter viii. 'The doer is so called in relation to the deed, and the deed is so called in relation to the doer. Absolutely speaking, there is neither doer nor doing.'[81]

Knowledge is impossible of explanation. Sensations generate ideas, even as ideas generate sensations. The plants produce the seed and the seed again the plant. Perception is not self-existent. 'You are not seeing that which had already been seen. Nor are you seeing that which has not yet been seen; the object of seeing which has neither already been seen nor has yet to be seen is non-existent.'[82] 'The sense of seeing does not see it, nor does that which is not a sense of seeing do it. What third, then, is it that sees?'[83] The seer, the seeable, and the act of seeing, answering to the passer,

80. The Nyaya system refers to this view of Nāgārjuna, and says in reply: 'If thus you deny perception, etc., then nobody can establish the existence of the objects of sense. If there are no objects of sense, no objections can be raised with regard to them. So your objections are altogether groundless. If you deny all evidences, then your objections lose value; if you admit the validity of your objections, then you agree to the variety of perceptions, etc.'

81. xvi. x.

82. iii. 3.

83. iii. 4.

the passable and the act of passing are all unthinkable. Perception and perceived objects exist in relation to each other. If there is no vision, there is no colour; and if there were no colours, there would be no visual perceptions. 'As the son is dependent upon father and mother, even so is the visual sensation dependent on eyes and colours.' And we can never be sure that what we perceive is not altogether our own. The same thing appears differently to different persons and to the same person at different times. In chapter xiv saṁsarga, or contact, is analysed and rejected. The changes and states come and go, and even succession cannot be maintained unless that which feels is a unity which persists through succession. But this unitary self is itself a difficult conception.

Again, what about general properties (jāti)? Are they to be found independent of the individuals characterised by them (jātimat), or are they always found in the individuals only? All our knowledge depends upon difference. What is a cow? Not a horse, not a sheep. It means a cow is not a not-cow. Instead of saying a cow is existent, we say it is non-existent as a horse or a tree. All our knowledge is relative and sustained by differentiation. The horse is non-existent, the world is non-existent. We do not know what these are. The dilemma is put thus: We cannot know the nature of a thing apart from its distinction from others. We cannot know its distinction from others apart from a knowledge of its own nature.[84] One thing takes us to another, and there is no end to this process. We cannot get the final explanations of things.[85] All things are relative. Nothing is self-existent, since everything is based on an endless series of causes and effects. All properties of things are relational, and not absolute. We work with schemes of relations which also do not coalesce. Things we see now are not seen in deep sleep. What is found in dreams is not found when we are awake. If anything were really existent, it should be found in all the three states. Thought cannot know itself and cannot know another. Truth must be equated with silence. Knowledge is an impossibility.[86] Such is the conclusion of Nāgārjuna's fierce logic.

There is no God apart from the universe and no universe apart from God, and both are equally appearances. If Nāgārjuna thus ridicules the

84. Yasmān na hi svabhāvānām pratyayādiṣu vidyate,
Avidyamāne svabhāve, parabhāvo navidyate.
85. Rūpādivyatirekeṇa yathā kumbho na vidyate,
Vāyvādivyatirekeṇa tathā rūpaṁ na vidyate. (Chap. i.)
86. Chap. xxvii.

idea of God, let us remember that it is the deist's God that he repudiates. He is sincere in his devotion to the true God, the Dharmakāya of the Mahāyāna Buddhism.

With a daring logic he shows how the world, composed of birth, life and death, is unreal.[87] Suffering,[88] saṁskāras[89] or mental tendencies, bondage, liberation,[90] and all actions[91] are unreal. They are due to relations, the nature of which we can never comprehend. Nāgārjuna has the courage to face the conclusions of his logic, however unpalatable they may be to the religious interests of mankind. He rounds off his system by saying that in reality there is no Buddha or tathāgata,[92] and from the absolute standpoint there is not even any distinction between truth and error at all. When there is nothing real, there is no possibility of misunderstanding anything.[93] The four noble truths of suffering[94] and the conceptions of nirvāṇa[95] are all unreal. In the very first stanza of his Mādhyamika Śāstra he says: 'There is no death, no birth, no distinction, no persistence, no oneness, no manyness, no coming in, no going forth.' There is nothing real. The negative truth of this is already given. No positive demonstration is necessary. We require a cause for that which is, and not for that which is not. The world has only phenomenal existence, and things are neither transient nor eternal, neither produced nor destroyed, neither the same nor different, neither coming forth nor passing away, except in appearance. The world is nothing more than an ideal system of qualities and relations. We believe in relations which cannot be intelligibly explained. It is the higher superstition of science, that the categories useful in the world of experience are ultimately real, that Nāgārjuna explodes.

The world of experience is an illusion bred by relations. The categories of cause and effect, part and whole, which are not self-existent, but mutually dependent, make up the world. They give us the provisional seeming reality which is the object of saṁvṛti, or conventional knowledge. They are suited

87. Chap. xi.
88. Chap. xii.
89. Chap. xiii.
90. Chap. xvi.
91. Chap. xviii.
92. Chap. xxii.
93. Chap. xxiii.
94. Chap. xxiv.
95. Chap. xxv.

to the determinations of the reciprocal relations of phenomena. When they attempt to express the true essence of existence, they contradict themselves. They are working ideas without ultimate philosophical significance. We may mention here that while Bradley contends that thought establishes relations between terms that are not themselves reducible to relations, Nāgārjuna accepts a position similar to that of Green, that the reality of experience is a relational one, except for the absolute, which stands behind. To Bradley, in the world of common sense and science, there is always something that cannot be reduced to relations. To Nāgārjuna there is nothing of that nature here. Yet Nāgārjuna is not a mere destructive sceptic, but a constructive thinker. There is an ultimate truth which science cannot reach. He pulls to pieces all experience, so that he may reveal the absolute behind it. The phenomenal world involves real oppositions, and the noumenal is pure affirmation. We cannot help thinking of something behind the world we see, hear and feel. The colour, the form and the sound which we perceive are not homeless attributes of nothing. In chapter iv Nāgārjuna tells us that śūnyatā is a conclusion forced on him, and not assumed by him at the start. To take it for granted would be to commit the fallacy of sādhyasama, *petitio principii*. Phenomenalism is forced on him. The question of logic as theory of knowledge is how experience is possible. Nāgārjuna exhibits the conditions which render experience possible, shows their un-intelligibility, and infers the non-ultimate character of experience. The whole show of Nāgārjuna's logic is a screen for his heart, which believed in an absolute reality. The outer scepticism was in the interests of the inner truth. Nature is an appearance, yet there is the eternal foundation, the infinite, from which everything springs and into which everything retires. Only when talking about it we must drop all categories relative to our empirical life. We cannot say what it is, whether it is free or conscious. The questions themselves imply the transference to the infinite reality of the conditions of our finite existence. To refuse to define the infinite spirit is not to deny it. The reality of the absolute involves the phenomenality of the world. 'The skandhas are empty, all things have the character of emptiness, they have no beginning, no end, they are faultless and not faultless, they are not imperfect and not perfect, therefore, O Sāriputta, here in this emptiness there is no form, no perception, no name, no concept, no knowledge.'[96]

96. Larger Prajñāpāramitāhṛdayā Sūtra, p. 148. S.B.E., xlix.

Admitting that the world of knowledge is relational, the Yogācāras posited the reality of vijñāna which relates. Nāgārjuna takes up the concept of vijñāna as self, and shows its inadequacy. If the vijñāna is a definite self, then it is not the ultimate principle. If it is the infinite spirit, it is wrong to attribute to it the empirical category of selfhood. The absolute is just the absolute, and we cannot say anything of it. All thinking is relative, and the absolute when thought becomes a kind of relative; we cannot think of it as self-conscious personality without setting up some dummy to relate it to.

VII

DEGREES OF TRUTH AND REALITY

Nāgārjuna's theory of phenomenalism seems to require us to abandon the whole scheme of values as an illusion. When everything becomes unreal, good and evil are also unreal, and we need not strive to attain the state of nirvāṇa and free ourselves from miseries which do not exist. We cannot live taking life to be an illusion. It seems to be wellnigh impossible to base moral life on a detected illusion. Though the miseries are unreal, when judged by the absolute standard, they are real so far as our present existence is concerned. To one who has realised the paramārtha there is no problem at all. For he has reached nirvāṇa, but those who are entangled in the world have to work. Morality is not jeopardised, since the course of illusion is irresistible to all on earth. The illusion is so vital to human life that the distinction of good and evil remains unaffected whatever might happen to it in the higher condition. Nāgārjuna recognises two kinds of truth, absolute and empirical. 'The teaching of Buddha relates to two kinds of truth, the relative, conditional truth, and the transcendent absolute truth.'[97] By means of this distinction the otherwise insoluble contradiction between absolute nihilism and ethical life is avoided. While the higher leads to nirvāṇa, only through the lower can the higher be reached. Saṁvṛti is the product of man's reason. It is the cause of the universe and its phenomena. It literally means a covering or screen which keeps off the truth. There is no need to prove its existence since it is its own evidence. A dreaming man cannot deny his dreaming by any argument, since every argument used by him is as false as the thing which it goes to prove or

97. Chap. xxiv.

disprove. When we wake up we can prove the falsity of the object seen in a dream. Even so the falsity of saṁvṛti or practical truth can be proved by the attainment of paramārtha or absolute truth. No amount of saṁvṛti argumentation can discredit saṁvṛti itself. In it everything happens as if things were composed of real and substantial dharmas. The distinctions of subject and object, truth and error, bondage and liberation are valid at this level. Ultimately saṁvṛti is no truth at all, since it is all a dream or a delusion. All things in the world, its beautiful illusions like Buddha and sacred hopes of nirvāṇa, are shattered to pieces. The commonplace objection, that if all is illusory, even the idea of illusion must be illusory, does not shock Nāgārjuna. The dialectical difficulties lead him to the acceptance of an absolute answering to paramārtha or eternal truth. To the objection, that if everything is void, if nothing arises or passes away, there cannot be any distinction between good and evil, truth and error, Nāgārjuna replies that the supreme truth which will quench all craving and bring inward peace lies concealed by saṁvṛti or the conventions of our common life. Strictly speaking, there is no existence, no cessation of being, no birth or deliverance. The real is śūnya in the sense that there is nothing concrete or individual. It does not mean that it is absolute nothingness or a blank featureless being.[98] It is empty, as distinct from saṁvṛti, which is said to be real. Nāgārjuna quotes Buddha to the effect: 'There is no woman, no man, no life, no sentient being, no self. All these dharmas are unreal, non-existent, like dreams, fictions, like the reflection of the moon in the water.'

Reason is condemned as defective only to make room for faith. It is a faith sustained by knowledge, and not bred by ignorance. It is not a mere empty play of fancy, but is based on reason. If the absolute and the relative truths were unrelated, we would be involved in absolute scepticism. Knowledge cannot be vindicated, even as the knowledge of phenomenon or appearance if it were absolutely severed from the knowledge of noumenal reality. Nāgārjuna points out that without resorting to practical truth the transcendental truth cannot be attained.[99] The truth of intellect is not to be brushed aside, even though it is not final. It is not the supreme

98. Cf. But whereso'er the highways tend,
Be sure there's nothing at the end.
R.L. Stevenson.

99. Vyavahāram anāśritya paramārtho no deśyate, chap. xxiv.

power which some philosophers take it to be. The highest truth which is not revealed by intellect is to the finite mind only a postulate. We can believe it though we cannot see it. No man can say that he has known it as he has known objects of experience. Yet he feels that some such hypothesis is necessary to round our experience. The facts in our hands demand completion in the manner indicated. Yet the plan is not spread out before us. The truth is hovering over our hearts and will descend into them if we are ready. We must transcend our limitations. Absence of perfect insight is quite consistent with belief in its necessity. Though the idea cannot be brought within the range of logical argument, yet the faith is a grounded one. Only such is true faith, the evidence of things not seen.

Adopting a very abstract standpoint, Kumārila criticises Nāgārjuna to the effect that: 'It must be admitted that that which does not exist never exists, and that which exists is absolutely real, and therefore there can be no assumption of two kinds of truth.'[100] Śaṁkara believes that the Mādhyamika theory supports the mere nothingness of the world. Udayana, under the same impression, asks: 'Is the conception of śūnya or void, a fact or not? If it is not a fact perceived by and through one, how can you say that the world is śūnya? If it is a fact, is it self-evident or perceived by and through some one else? Then, the existence of some one else and what he perceived must both be admitted.'

Nāgārjuna recognises different kinds of existence. The objects of hallucination do not exist in the same sense in which the objects of perception exist, though both of them as facts of mind belong to the same order. All things and persons are collections of dharmas, and the difference between the two is determined by the nature of the dharmas which group themselves. In the case of things similar dharmas enter. In the case of persons it is not so. While our vital organs, etc., renew themselves without any essential modification, the mental dharmas are subject to great changes. The objects of hallucination have no extra-mental existence, while those of experience live in the context of experience, and to that extent are independent of the subject. Nāgārjuna recognises that the world exists in the sense of having a position in time and space, though it does not involve permanence or persistence. The object of experience has a certain fixity due to its spatial position and temporal context. We can become aware of it under certain conditions, and repeat that experience also. It is

100. Na satyadvayakalpanā. Ślokavārttika, 115, 3. 10.

trans-subjective, being an object common to all normal experience under appropriate conditions. The purely mental state is neither extended nor determined by spatial relations, and is of a transient nature, and directly apprehended by one subject only. Material existence has thus a greater certainty than the purely mental. Images are transient, changing with the flow of consciousness, while objects of sense-perception are relatively certain and capable of reinstatement in consciousness in accordance with definite conditions. Existence in the world means position in time, space and the causal system, though not absolute self-existence. This does not mean that they are non-existent. The Lalitavistara says: 'There is no object which is existent, neither is there any which is non-existent.' The world is not absolutely real, nor is it absolute nothingness, for the latter is an impossible conception. By śūnya, therefore, the Mādhyamika does not mean absolute non-being, but only relative being. It is Śaṁkara's empirical existence. To say that the things are not substantial in the sense of self-existent is one thing. To say that they are not only non-substantial, but that they do not exist at all, is quite another. We seem to get tendencies of both these views in the Mādhyamika writings, while the former seems to be their true position. The pratītyasamutpāda doctrine, that it is the nature of dharmas to be produced by concurrent causes, and what is so produced is not produced in itself, and therefore does not exist in itself, shows only that the actually existent things are not ultimately real. Śūnya in this sense means production by causes or dependence. The Buddhist realists, the Sautrāntikas and the Vaibhāṣikas, on the other hand, lay no stress on the view that what is produced by causes does not exist in itself, and is without any substantiality, and is therefore śūnya or void. 'All is declared śūnya, empty, because there is nothing that is not the product of universal causation.'[101] The śūnyavāda of the Mādhyamikas is negatively the non-existence of substances and positively the ever-changing flux of saṁsāra. It is sometimes said that the Mādhyamikas assert that the dharmas do not exist at all either in reality or in appearance. They are to be compared only with such impossible things like the daughter of a barren woman. We may describe the beauty of such a woman, and yet the object described along with the description is non-existent. This view does not represent the intentions of Nāgārjuna, however much some of his statements may lend themselves to such an interpretation. One such statement is the

101. Chap. xxiv.

following: 'Do we not experience the dharmas?' Nāgārjuna says: 'Yes, even as the monk with diseased eyes sees hair in an alms bowl. As a matter of fact, he does not see it, for the knowledge of it does not exist any more than its object. This is proved by the fact that a man with healthy eyes has no thought about the hair.' When the individual gains absolute truth, he knows things in their true nature, and will not then affirm their existence. They no more appear to him, and so absolute knowledge means no knowledge of things. The whole world is like a magical show. The saint free from avidyā is not subject to it: what seemingly exists is an illusion. Since to the Mādhyamikas all thoughts and things are void, they are sometimes called Sarvavaināśikas. This view, that the world with its suns and stars is nothing more than a baseless appearance, is quite in consonance with the popular classification of the four Buddhist schools into the Vaibhāṣikas, or presentationists, who admit the perceptibility of external objects; the Sautrāntikas, or representationists; the Yogācāras, or subjectivists; and the Mādhyamikas, or nihilists. But we do not think that this view is true to the teaching of Nāgārjuna, who is not the common conjurer who wishes to prove that the chair we sit on is not a chair. Existence in the only possible sense of continuous production of phenomena he admits, though he denies to it absolute reality.

VIII

ŚŪNYAVĀDA AND ITS IMPLICATIONS

The term śūnya is variously understood. To some it means nothingness, to others a permanent principle, transcendent and indefinable, immanent in all things. The former is true of the world of experience; the latter of the metaphysical reality. Even the illusory structure cannot be sustained in the atmosphere of a void. All negation depends on a hidden affirmation. Absolute negation is impossible. Total scepticism is a figment, since such scepticism implies the validity of the sceptic's judgment. Nāgārjuna admits the existence of a higher reality, though with the Upaniṣads he considers it to be not an object of experience. 'The eye does not see and the mind does not think; this is the highest truth, wherein men do not enter. The land wherein the full vision of all objects is obtained at once has by the Buddha been called the paramārtha, or absolute truth, which cannot be preached in words.'[102] 'It cannot be called void or not void, or both or neither, but

102. Chap. iii.

in order to indicate it, it is called the void.'[103] There is fundamental reality, without which things would not be what they are. Śūnyatā is a positive principle. Kumārajīva, commenting on Nāgārjuna, observes: 'It is on account of śūnyatā that everything becomes possible, without it nothing in the world is possible.' It is the basis of all. 'O Subhūti, all dharmas have for their refuge śūnyatā; they do not alter that refuge.'[104] Śūnyatā is the synonym of that which has no cause, that which is beyond thought or conception, that which is not produced, that which is not born, that which is without measure.'[105] As applied to the world of experience, śūnyatā means the ever-changing state of the phenomenal world. In the dread waste of endlessness man loses all hope, but the moment he recognises its unreality he transcends it and reaches after the abiding principle. He knows that the whole is a passing dream, where he might sit unconcerned at the issues, certain of victory.

About the ultimate reality we cannot say anything. To attain truth we must cast aside the conditions which are incompatible with truth. The absolute is neither existent nor non-existent, nor both existent and non-existent, nor different from both non-existence and existence.[106] To the Mādhyamikas reason and language apply only to the finite world. To transfer the finite categories to the infinite would be like attempting to measure the heat of the sun by the ordinary thermometer. From our point of view the absolute is nothing.[107] We call it śūnyam, since no category used in relation to the conditions of the world is adequate to it. To call it being is wrong, because only concrete things are. To call it non-being is equally wrong.[108] It is best to avoid all descriptions of it. Thought is dualistic in its functions, and what is, is non-dual or advaita. Buddha is reported to have said: 'What description can be given and what knowledge devised of an object which cannot be represented by the letters of the alphabet? Even this much of description that it does not admit of representation by the letters of the alphabet is made by means of attributing letters to the

103. Śūnyam iti na vaktavyam aśūnyam iti vā bhavet
Ubhayaṁ nobhayaṁ ceti prajñāptyarthaṁ tu kathyate.
104. Prajñāpāramitā.
105. Aṣtasāhasrikā Prajñāpāramitā, chap. xviii.
106. Astināsti ubhaya anubhaya iti catuṣkotivinirmuktaṁ śūnyatvam. Mādhava. S.D.S.
107. Śūnyaṁ tattvam.
108. Tatra astitā vā nāstitā vā na vidyate nopalabhyate.

transcendent, absolute, signified by the term śūnyatā.' 'The real state of dharma is like nirvāṇa, indescribable, incomprehensible, without birth or death, beyond the reach of thought and language.'[109] It is in this sense of transcending all relations that Duns Scotus says: 'God is not improperly called nothing.' 'For thought, what is not relative, is nothing.'[110]

While the absolute is free from all modes of limitations and cannot be thought by our finite consciousness, still, on account of avidyā inherent in human mind, it manifests itself in the phenomenal world. Avidyā is the principle of relativity. Of course, the world reflects the permanent substance, otherwise we cannot attain paramārtha through saṁvṛti, which Nāgārjuna admits. The essence of things is śūnya in both senses of the term. 'The objects that we perceive now were śūnya in the past and will be śūnya in the future. All things in their nature have śūnya for their essence.' It is avidyā that makes us attribute existence to things which do not exist. The knowledge of the truth is called Mahavidyā and its opposite is avidyā.

The śūnya of Nāgārjuna will remind the reader of Hamilton's unconditioned or Spencer's inscrutable power. On account of its non-relational character, it is compared sometimes to the One of Plotinus, the substance of Spinoza, and the neutrum of Schelling. To the mind weary with the agitation of the world it has a great appeal.[111] The highest is immobile in its absoluteness, and seems to be the negation of all becoming. The moment the element of negation is asserted, its absoluteness is compromised. On such a view, if the absolute is all real, then it cannot have any principle of negation. Such a boundless being may seem a dead, dull

109. Chap. xviii.

110. Bradley. According to the Mahopaniṣad, Brahman is 'śūnya or void, tuccha or trivial, abhāva or non-existent, avyakta or unmanifest, adṛśya or invisible, acintya or inconceivable, and nirguṇa or qualityless.' Yogasvarodaya describes Brahman whose nature is reality, wisdom and joy as śūnya. *Śūnyaṁ tu saccidānandaṁ niḥśabdabrahmaśabditam*. Cf. also Kabir: 'They call Him emptiness who is the Truth of truths, in Whom all truths are stored.' (Tagore's translation.)

111. Cf. Faber's hymn:

O Lord, my heart is sick,
Sick of this everlasting change,
And life runs tediously quick
Through its unresting race and varied range,
Change finds no likeness of itself in Thee,
And makes no echo in Thy mute eternity.

nothing. Negation seems to be as necessary as affirmation. Without it we have not the element of distinction, and consequently life or manifestation is impossible. If pure being were alive and real, we should be obliged to think in it a principle of distinction, of negativity. Nāgārjuna would look upon such an argument as 'human, much too human.' Our incapacity to define the nature of the absolute or understand the mystery of the relation between the finite and the infinite need not persuade us to the belief that it is nothing. The proof of the absolute reality and its fullness of being is the nirvāṇic bliss attained by mystics. If the Yogācāra be later than the Mādhyamika theory, we can easily understand the logic of the development. An intellectual account of Nāgārjuna's absolute will lead us to the theory of ālayavijñāna. From our finite level, Nāgārjuna's absolute seems to be immobile in its absoluteness. To the Yogācāra it is universal consciousness, which is ever growing. Things and persons are not outside it, but in it. They are in its perpetual process, included in the consciousness of the absolute. To the Mādhyamikas the things seem external to pure being, bound in by their own finiteness, closed by their existence, and we do not know how they are related to the infinite being. Ālayavijñāna is not a state, but a process. It is spirituality, vijñana objectifying itself or expressing itself in the object world. The highest way in which thought can envisage the absolute is by looking upon it as consciousness, cit, vijñāna. In it we have both affirmation and negation, identity and difference. The Yogācāra theory is akin to that type of Hegelianism which puts self-consciousness at the centre of things. The Mādhyamika theory is an advaitism of the type of Śaṁkara or of Bradley, for the concept of self to it is not ultimate. The idea of self is after all a relation, and it is not logical to make the absolute subject to any relation whatsoever.

IX

CONCLUSION

Though the world is phenomenal, we take it to be real, through the pressure of past habit. To arrive at nirvāṇa we have to follow the ancient path, and put an end to all misery by giving up false notions of the reality of things. Pain and misery as well as happiness and joy are due to our avidyā. Mind is the source of all trouble and unhappiness. Ethical relations have their value in the finite world.

It has been shown that saṁsāra is a mere show. If we understand its truth, then it is nirvāṇa. The truth is the absolute. Tathāgata is absence of particular being, and the world is also absence of definite being.[112] All that is said of śūnya is true of nirvāṇa. It is beyond the realm of relative expression. We cannot say whether it is śūnya or aśūnya, or both or neither.[113] Conventionally we say Buddha exists. Strictly we cannot say even that. Nāgārjuna says: 'That is called nirvāṇa which is not wanting, is not acquired, is not intermittent, is not non-intermittent, is not subject to description and is not created.' When nirvāṇa is obtained, ignorance terminates, and the bonds of existence are loosened. The unconditioned, uncreate, formless, alone remains. It is even said that nirvāṇa is not something to be attained. Only ignorance has to be got rid of.

Those who strive after final attainment or mukti must practise hard the six transcendental virtues of charity, morality, patience, enterprise, meditation and supreme wisdom, and attain perfection in them. If we ask, how can a bodhisattva who knows the unreality of all try to lift others from their sin?, the answer may be given in the words of Vajracchedikā: 'He who has entered on the path of the bodhisattvas should thus frame his thought: All beings must be delivered by me in the perfect world of nirvāṇa, yet after I have delivered these beings, no being has been delivered. And why? Because, O Subhūti, if a bodhisattva had any idea of beings, he could not be called a bodhisattva.'[114] 'A gift should not be given by a bodhisattva as accepting objects as real.'[115] Strictly speaking, even the presumption of the reality of a bodhisattva is untrue.

The Vaibhāṣikas started with a dualistic metaphysics, and looked upon knowledge as a direct awareness of objects. The Sautrāntikas made ideas the media through which reality is apprehended, and thus raised a screen between mind and things. The Yogācāras quite consistently abolished the things behind the images, and reduced all experience to a series of ideas in their mind. The Mādyamikas, in a more daring and logical manner, dissolved mind also into a mere idea, and left us with loose units of ideas and perceptions about which we can say nothing definite. English empiricism repeats this logical movement. The starting-point of the mechanist logic of Locke and his successors was to conceive of subject and object as interacting, finite entities, and the content of knowledge as the product of

112. Chap. xxii. 16. See also xxv. 12.
113. Chap. xxii. 11.
114. S.B.E., xlix. p. 132.
115. Ibid., p. 1.

this interaction. Through such knowledge, which contains neither of the factors of which it is said to be the product, we cannot know either the subject or the object. We see the logical consequence of such a theory in the scepticism of Hume, where self and world are reduced to sequences of mental states. The English side of the movement is thus summed up by Reid: 'Ideas were first introduced into philosophy in the humble character of images or representatives of things, and in this character they seemed not only to be inoffensive, but to serve admirably well for explaining the operations of the human understanding. But since men began to reason clearly and distinctly about them, they have, by degrees, supplanted their constituents and undermined the existence of everything but themselves.... These ideas are as free and independent as the birds of the air.... Yet, after all, these self-existent and independent ideas look pitifully naked and destitute when left thus alone in the universe, set adrift without a rag to cover their nakedness.'[116] Knowledge is not possible, experience is unintelligible, and philosophy could go no further without a radical reconsideration of its fundamental position.

From the metaphysical point of view, the two-substance theory of the Vaibhāṣikas becomes loaded on the side of mind when we come to the Sautrāntikas. The Yogācāras dropped the outer world and put mind in the centre of things, and the Mādhyamikas affirmed that neither individual selves nor material objects could be held to be ultimately real: the real is the absolute. While the Yogācāras confidently apply the concept of self-consciousness to the absolute, the Mādhyamikas consider self as well as not-self to be equally unreal. Personality is not ultimate.

We need not say that the Advaita Vedānta philosophy has been very much influenced by the Mādhyamika doctrine. The Alātaśānti of Gauḍapāda's Kārikās is full of Mādhyamika tenets. The Advaitic distinction of vyavahāra, or experience, and paramārtha, or reality, correspond to the saṁvṛti and the paramārtha of the Mādhyamikas. The Nirguṇa Brahman of Śaṁkara and Nāgārjuna's śūnya have much in common. The force of avidyā introducing the phenomenal universe is admitted by both. The keen logic which breaks up the world into a play of abstractions, categories and relations appears in both. If we take an Advaita Vedāntin like Śrī Harṣa, we find that he does little more than develop the Mādhyamika theory, expose the self-contradictions of the categories we work with, such as cause and

116. *Works*, p. 109.

effect, substance and attribute, and deny the reality of things on account of the impossibility of adequately explaining them. According to the Khaṇḍana of Śrī Harṣa, things are anirvacanīya, or indescribable; according to the Mādhyamika vṛtti they are niḥsvabhāva, or devoid of essence. To be indefinable and to be characterless are, after all, the same. With the Buddhist's attitude to the unseen, Nāgārjuna does not dwell much on the positive absolute, though he admits its reality. By his negative logic, which reduces experience to a phenomenon, he prepares the ground for the Advaita philosophy. It is a strange irony that the great exponents of the two doctrines look upon themselves as supporting antagonistic positions.

REFERENCES

Sarvadarśanasaṁgraha, chap. ii.
Sarvasiddhāntasārasaṁgraha.
Śaṁkara's Commentary on the Vedānta Sūtras.
Nāgārjuna's Mādhyamika Sūtras.
YAMAKAMI SOGEN, Systems of Buddhistic Thought.

APPENDIX

Further Consideration of Some Problems[1]

■ The Method of Approach—The Comparative Standpoint—The Upaniṣads—Early Buddhism—The Negative, the Agnostic and the positive Views—Early Buddhism and the Upaniṣads—The Schools of Buddhism—Nāgārjuna's Theory of Reality—Śūnyavāda and the Advaita Vedānta. ■

My book on *Indian Philosophy* has been kindly received, and I take this opportunity to thank my critics for their appreciation and sympathy. I propose to deal here with a few controversial issues that the first volume has raised, such as the method of philosophical interpretation, the value of comparative studies, the teaching of the Upaniṣads, the alleged atheism of Buddha, and the metaphysics of Nāgārjuna.

I

The historian of philosophy must approach his task, not as a mere philologist or even as a scholar but as a philosopher who uses his scholarship as an instrument to wrest from words the thoughts that underlie them. A mere linguist regards the views of ancient Indian thinkers as so many fossils lying scattered throughout the upheaved and faulty strata of the history of philosophy, and from his point of view any interpretation which makes them alive and significant is dismissed as far-fetched and untrue. A philosopher, on the other hand, realises the value of the ancient Indian theories which attempt to grapple with the perennial problems of life and treats them not as fossils but as species which are remarkably persistent. The reactions of the human mind to the problems of philosophy which are recorded in the Upaniṣads or the Dialogues of Buddha are to be met with in a reincarnated form in some of the most flourishing systems of the present day. Though the sayings of the ancient Indians may be scattered, ambiguous and unco-ordinated, there is no reason to assume that their logic was as full of lacunæ as are their literary remains. It is the task of creative logic, as distinct from mere linguistic analysis, to piece together

1. This essay appeared in *Mind*, vol. xxxv., N.S. No. 138.

the scattered data, interpret for us the life they harbour and thus free the soul from the body. Max Müller wrote: 'What I feel is, that it is not enough simply to repeat the watchwords of any ancient philosophy, which are easily accessible in the Sūtras, but that we must at least make an attempt to bring those ancient problems near to us, to make them our own, and try to follow the ancient thinkers along the few footsteps which they left behind.'[2] Collection of facts and the accumulation of evidence are an important part, but only a part, of the task of the historian who attempts to record the manifold adventures of the human spirit.[3] He must pay great attention to the logic of ideas, draw inferences, suggest explanations and formulate theories which would introduce some order into the shapeless mass of unrelated facts. If the history of philosophy is to be more than a bare catalogue of facts about dead authors and their writings, if it is to educate the mind and enthral the imagination, the historian should be a critic and an interpreter and not a mere mechanical 'ragpicker.'

II

The cultivated in both east and west desire now a mutual understanding, and nothing is so useful for it as comparative studies. There are dangers to which the method is open, since it is very difficult to be discriminating for the European scholar or the Indian interpreter. The works in the 'Religious Quest of India' series written by European missionaries living in India, though they mark an advance on the publications of the missionaries of a previous generation, are not unprejudiced accounts of Indian thought, since they are written with the explicit aim of presenting Christianity as

2. *Six Systems of Indian Philosophy*, p. 293.

3. Cp. Hegel: 'For, in thought and particularly in speculative thought, comprehension means something quite different from understanding the grammatical sense of the words alone, and also from understanding them in the region of ordinary conception only. Hence we may possess a knowledge of the assertions, propositions, or of the opinions of philosophers; we may have occupied ourselves largely with the grounds of and deductions from these opinions and the main point in all that we have done may be wanting—the comprehension of the propositions.' Hegel compares such non-philosophical historians of philosophy, 'to animals which have listened to all the tones in some music, but to whose senses the unison, the harmony of their tones has not penetrated.'—*History of Philosophy*, E.T., vol. i, p. xxv.

the final goal of Indian thought and quest. Many of the Western students of Indian culture are convinced that Indians have been stunted in soul from the beginning and that it is quite beyond them to find out for themselves anything worth while in philosophy or religion, not to speak of science, art and literature. They are certain that the Western nations had held for all time the monopoly of effective culture and philosophising. They attempt to establish the higher antiquity and superiority of the European civilisation and trace everything great and good in Indian thought to the Christian era. They declare that many of the achievements for which the ignorant give credit to the Indian are really borrowings from Greece. They are inclined to date the hymns of the Ṛg-Veda and the civilisation reflected in them much later than Babylonian and Egyptian cultures.

While the Western scholar is inclined to dismiss as unfair all attempts to compare the 'crude and primitive' speculations of ancient India with the mature systems of the West, there are not wanting critics in India who feel a sort of old pride injured when they find Indian thought compared with the Western. They think that, in matters of religion and philosophy, at any rate, India is far superior to the West, and that Western thought is *jejune* and primitive when compared with the Indian.

With these judgments one sympathises or not according to one's taste. But mutual understanding is not possible without mutual respect and sympathy born of it. If we are true to history, we shall see that each nation has had its own share of the inner light and spiritual discovery. No cultural or religious imperialist, who has the settled conviction that he alone has all the light and others are groping in darkness, can be a safe guide in comparative studies. The reliable interpreter should adopt the empirical method of investigation with a reasonable exercise of intelligence and imagination. While he should discuss Indian views in terms of modern thought and relate them to the problems of the day, he must be cautious and careful in the use of his terms, which may be really different though apparently equivalent. He must avoid substituting modern arguments for ancient lines of thought. In an enterprise of this kind, one is always liable to be accused of reading the one into the other, but there is this difficulty in all historical work. The only safeguard against this risk is through the adoption of the comparative method. We should then be able to bring out what is characteristic of each tradition and appreciate its value.

III

Many of my critics were puzzled by my discussion of the Upaniṣads, since I did not fly a banner and fix a label to my view. My criticism of the theory of 'illusion,' generally associated with Śaṁkara's metaphysics and supported by Deussen, led some of my critics to imagine that I was opposed to Śaṁkara's view. My indifference to personal theism made it equally clear to some others that I was not friendly to Rāmānuja's interpretation. But if one is not a follower of Śaṁkara or of Rāmānuja or any other classical interpreter, it is assumed that one can only be a reveller in strange unphilosophical confusion. I submit that my interpretation of the Upaniṣads is not an unreasonable one, though it may seem to differ from this or that tradition in this or that point.

Scholastic explanations overwhelm the teaching of any original genius. We tend to see Socrates with the eyes of Plato, or Plato with the eyes of Aristotle or Plotinus. The Upaniṣads are generally interpreted in the light of one or the other of the great commentators. My endeavour was to show how the Upaniṣads lent themselves to divergent developments and whether it was not possible to give a coherent account of their teaching which would do justice to the main principles of the two chief interpreters, Śaṁkara and Rāmānuja. If we can find a single point of view from which the different interpretations can be reconciled and understood—it may be that no such point of view exists—but if one can be found, it is likely that we can understand the teaching of the Upaniṣads better. In philosophical interpretation, the most coherent view is the most true.

The Upaniṣads speak with a double voice in describing the nature of ultimate reality. They sometimes make it the absolute which cannot be characterised by the phenomenal categories; at other times they identify it with the supreme person whom we are to adore and worship. As the result of this, we have two views about the nature of the world. In some passages, the world is regarded as an accident of Brahman (the absolute) and in others as organic to God. A careful reader perceives these two tendencies running through the Upaniṣads, one which regards the absolute as pure being and makes the world an accidental appearance (vivarta) of it, and the other which looks upon the absolute as a concrete person of whom the word is the necessary expression.[4] The former view is nearer Śaṁkara's and the latter nearer Rāmānuja's. I confess that 'it is difficult to decide

4. See pp. 168, 172–173, 184–186, 202.

whether it is the Advaita (or non-dualism) of Śaṁkara or the modified position of Rāmānuja that is the final teaching of the parent gospel.'[5]

The only intelligible reconciliation between two such apparently discordant notes seems to be through the device of a duality of standpoints. When we rise above the intellectual level and intuit the nature of reality, we see that there is nothing but the absolute, and the world is only the absolute, and the problem of the relation between the two does not arise, since the absolute and the world are not two distinct entities which require to be related. When we envisage the absolute from the human end, through the logical categories, we tend to view it as a whole which binds together the different elements in it. The absolute is looked upon as a personal God by whose power of self-expression or māyā the world is sustained. The absolute as pure being (Śaṁkara) and the absolute as a person (Rāmānuja) are the intuitional and the intellectual representations of the one supreme fact.[6] As these two lines of thought cross and re-cross in the Upaniṣads, Śaṁkara and Rāmānuja were able to support their views from them. As we shall see, Śaṁkara adopts this device of a duality of standpoints in attempting to harmonise the different texts of the Upaniṣads.

IV

In my account of early Buddhism, I attempted to make out that it is 'only a restatement of the thought of the Upaniṣads' with a new emphasis.[7] In spite of the absence of any specific reference to the Upaniṣads, it is admitted that the teaching of Buddha is considerably influenced by the thought of the Upaniṣads.[8] Indifference to Vedic authority[9] and ceremonial piety,[10] belief in the law of karma, rebirth[11] and the possibility of attaining mokṣa or nirvāṇa[12] and the doctrine of the non-permanence of the world and

5. Pp. 258–259.
6. See pp. 168, 172, 180–181, 184–185, 258–259.
7. P. 361; see also pp. 375 ff.
8. As orthodox a Hindu thinker as Kumārila declares that even the Buddhist views of subjectivism, momentariness and non-self theory derive their inspiration from the Upaniṣads. 'Vijñānamātraksaṇabhanganairātmyādivādānām api upaniṣatprabhavatvam.' *Tantravārttika*, i. 3. 2.
9. Muṇḍaka Up., i. 1. 5.
10. Ibid., 2, 7–10; Bṛh. Up., i. 4. 15.
11. Chān. Up., v. 10. 7; Kaṭha, v. 7; Śvet, v. 11–12.
12. Chān. Up., iv. 15. 5–6; Bṛh., vi. 2. 15; Śvet, i. 7. 8. 11.

the individual self[13] are common to the Upaniṣads and Buddha. While Buddha adopts the position of the Upaniṣads in holding that absolute reality is not the property of anything on earth, that the world of saṁsāra is a becoming without beginning or end, he does not definitely affirm the reality of the absolute, the self and the state of liberation. He does not tell us about the state of the enlightened after death, whether it is existent, non-existent, both or neither, about the nature of the self and the world, whether they are eternal, non-eternal, both or neither, whether they are self-made, made by another, both or neither. As a matter of fact these questions were reserved issues on which Buddha did not allow any speculation. While there is no doubt that Buddha refused to dogmatise on these problems, it is still an interesting question, if it can be answered at all, what exactly the implications of this refusal are.

The three questions, whether there is an absolute reality exempt from the changes of the world, whether there is a permanent self distinct from the changing aggregates, and whether nirvāṇa is a state of positive being, are different sides of the one fundamental problem of metaphysics. If there is an ultimate reality which is not subject to the laws of the world of change, then nirvāṇa is the attainment of this sphere of reality and the enlightened one is the permanent self. If there is not an absolute reality, then there is no permanent self and nirvāṇa is nothingness. The former view is nearer the religious idealism of the Upaniṣads and the latter is nearer the negative rationalism of scientific metaphysics.

Whatever Buddha's personal views may have been, he declined to engage in discussions about metaphysical questions on the ground that they were not helpful to the seeker of salvation. His avoidance of all metaphysical themes is irritating in its vagueness to the modern historian of philosophy, who is anxious to give a label to every thinker and system of thought. But Buddha eludes his grasp. Was his silence an apology for uncertainty? Was he a mentally timid man afraid of speaking out, or was he merely sitting on the fence? Was his mind vague and hazy, or was he attempting to avoid the danger of being deceived? Was he facing both ways, indifferent to the

13. The changing character of the world is denoted by the word 'jagat.' Īśā Up., 1; Bṛh. Up., iii. 1. 3; cf. 'sarvam mṛtyor annam,' Bṛh., iii. 2. 10; also i. 3. 28. In Kaṭha, i. 12, svarga or heaven is described as a place where hunger and thirst, sorrow, old age and death are absent. The futility of the greatest earthly pleasures is brought out in Kaṭha, i. 26–28.

positive and the negative implications of his teaching? There are only three alternatives open to us. Buddha admitted the reality of the absolute, or did not admit its reality, or did not know the truth about it. Let us try to determine whether his thought was negative, positive or agnostic in character.

At once we are confronted by the difficulty that we do not possess any written record of Buddha's teachings. The Pāli Canon came into its present shape long after the death of Buddha. It contains matter, some very old and some rather late. It is therefore difficult to say with certainty how much of the Canonical Buddhism is due to Buddha himself and how much is later development. In ancient India, many of the discourses and utterances of the teachers were preserved in memory by their disciples and transmitted to the generations that followed. Such has been the case with the great Vedic literature. The same is true of Buddha, who founded in his lifetime a regular order and gathered round himself a body of disciples who became the representatives of his teaching. Though we cannot be sure that we have the *ipsissima verba* of Buddha, there is no doubt that we possess, to a considerable extent, the substance and the profound depth of his teaching. If we doubt the authenticity of Buddha's great deliverances on the four noble truths, the eightfold path, and the exhortations attributed to him in the *Mahāparinibbāna Sutta* and *Sutta Nipāta*, we may as well doubt the authenticity of the teachings attributed to Vājñavalkya, Śāṇḍilya and Uddālaka.[14] Attempts are made to date the agnostic or the negative or the positive passages as earlier and assign them to Buddha and treat others as the contributions of his followers, in the interests of this or that interpretation of early Buddhism. But to start with the idea that all passages which conflict with one's reading of Buddha's silence are later, is to argue in a circle; for the ground on which they are regarded as later is just that they contain indications of a different outlook. Taking our stand on the texts which are generally acknowledged to be Buddha's, let us try to find out what metaphysical standpoint they suggest.

14. According to Rhys Davids, the four greater Nikāyas and the greater part of such books of the lesser Nikāya as *Itivuttaka* and *Sutta Nipāta* are as old as 400 BC and that of the Vinaya, *Mahāvagga, Cullavagga* i.–x. is as old as 300 BC. From the representations of the Buddhist stories and legends on the reliefs and monuments of Sanchi, etc., it is clear that about the middle of the third century BC we had a body of Buddhist texts designated Piṭtakas and divided into five Nikāyas.

V

The negative interpretation of his silence is the most popular one. Hindu thinkers, early Buddhists and many modern students of Indian thought adopt this view.[15] Buddhist studies aroused much interest in the West during the second half of the nineteenth century, when men's minds were swayed by scientific metpahysicians like Herbert Spencer and Auguste Comte. Naturally Buddhist scholars felt that the silence of Buddha was a cloak for negative rationalism. Buddha shrank from confessing his faith for fear that he might startle his followers out of their wits. If we accept this view, not only does Buddha's philosophy become incoherent, but his character also is compromised. There are so many passages, admittedly Buddha's, which cannot be accounted for on this view. Besides, the success of Buddha's teaching at a time when the great gods Viṣṇu and Śiva were rising into prominence will be difficult to explain. We have evidence to show that the early converts to Buddhism were religiously minded. The *Mahāsudassana* and *Cakkavattisīhanāda Suttantas* reveals to us that the minds of the early Buddhists were filled with the legend of the Sun-God. A negative creed was not likely to impress the Jaṭilas or fire-worshippers who were among the early converts to Buddhism.[16] A philosophy which denies the reality of an ultimate spirit, repudiates the reality of the self and promises men annihilation as the reward of a virtuous life, is not likely to kindle in the human heart any enthusiasm for its founder or fervour for his teaching. To assume that such a barren rationalism appealed to the Indian heart of the sixth century BC is to ignore all laws of psychology. So careful a scholar as Professor Berriedale Keith declines to believe that Buddha was a negativist. He holds that the passages of the Pāli Canon which interpret the practical agnosticism of Buddha as a definite negativism are not to be taken as a serious account of Buddha's teaching.[17]

VI

The second alternative of agnosticism, which does not apparently commit us to any definite view, has had the valuable and impressive support of

15. Cp. Professor Macdonell: Buddha 'left no doubt about the goal to which his teaching led, the cessation of all the saṁskāras, annihilation of all the skandhas, eternal death.'—*Hindustan Review*, 1923, p. 93.

16. *Mahāvagga*, i. 15 ff.

17. *Buddhist Philosophy*, pp. 47 ff.

Professor Keith. He says: 'It is quite legitimate to hold that the Buddha was a genuine agnostic, that he had studied the various systems of ideas prevalent in his day, without deriving any greater satisfaction from them than any of us today do from the study of modern systems, and that he had no reasoned or other conviction on the matter. From the general poverty of philosophical constructive power exhibited by such parts of the system as appear essentially Buddha's, one is inclined to prefer this explanation.' 'Agnosticism in these matters is not based on any reasoned conviction of the limits of knowledge; it rests on the twofold ground that the Buddha has not himself a clear conclusion on the truth on these issues, but is convinced that disputation on them will not lead to the frame of mind which is essential for the attainment of nirvāṇa.'[18]

The 'agnostic' interpretation which makes out that Buddha refused to give answers to metaphysical questions simply because he had none to give, is hardly fair to Buddha's genius. If Buddha had himself no theory of life, it would have been impossible for him to give a larger meaning and a greater depth to lie. It cannot be that Buddha voyaged through life without a chart, for then his system would be unintelligible and his passion for humanity inexplicable. If Buddha had no clear convictions on the nature of the ultimate goal of all striving, if he had no light on the mystery of nirvāṇa, how could he say that by perfecting one's nature one would attain the bliss inexpressible? The designation of 'Buddha,' 'the enlightened,' which he assumed leads us to infer that he had some definite views, right or wrong, on the ultimate questions. The depth of conviction which comes out in many exhortations to his disciples to follow the Norm to reach the truth, is hardly intelligible on the hypothesis of agnosticism. 'Let a man of intelligence come to me,' says he, 'honest, candid, straightforward; I will instruct him, teach him the Norm, and if he practice according as he is taught, then to know for himself, and to realise that supreme religion and goal for the sake of which clansmen go forth from the household life into the homeless state will take him—only seven days.'[19] Buddha must be either an impostor or a deluded man to talk in this strain, if he had no clear views on the ultimate questions.

Besides, this interpretation does not reckon with the passages where Buddha says that he does not give out all the truths known to him. In the

18. Ibid., pp. 63 and 45.
19. *Udumbarikā Sīhanāda Suttanta*. Dīgha N., iii. 56.

Pāsādika Suttanta,[20] he tells us that he does not reveal the truths in his possession, which are not likely to help one in one's moral growth. Saṁyutta Nikāya relates an incident, where Buddha, taking a bunch of leaves in his hand, explained to the assembled monks that, as the leaves in the forest outnumbered the leaves in his hand, so the truths which he knew but had not taught, outnumbered the truths which he had taught. While Buddha taught less than he knew and believed, his disciples seem to have believed rather less than what he had taught them.

Professor Keith is not inclined to regard the agnosticism of Buddha as a reasoned one. Though it is not logically argued out, the view that it is difficult to solve ultimate problems by empirical understanding is familiar to the thinkers who preceded Buddha. If Buddha refused to say whether the world had a beginning or not, it may well be that either alternative seemed to him to be unsatisfactory. If Buddha 'had studied the various systems of ideas prevalent in his time,' the somewhat reasoned agnosticism of the Upaniṣads would leap up to his eyes.

It is admitted that the agnosticism of Buddha, if it is absolute and not merely pragmatic as in the case of the Upaniṣads, is not creditable to his philosophic power, and those who adopt this view of Buddha's silence are inclined to rate him as a philosopher of indifferent quality. But this is purely a matter of personal opinion. Buddha's critical attitude to the different metaphysical theories—the sixty-two described in the *Brahmajāla Sutta* and the ten raised only to be set aside as not tending to salvation in the *Poṭṭhapāda Sutta*[21]—as well as to the religious practices of his time, shows that Buddha is a thinker and critic of no mean order. To imagine that he was not a close thinker would be to deny metaphysical capacity to one who disputed many metaphysical schemes. It would be a strange insensibility for which there is little proof. Besides, no thinking man, not, at any rate, one of Buddha's intellectual and moral stature, could live without some sort of belief about transcendent values.

Those scholars who support the hypothesis of agnosticism do so since that view alone fits in with their faith that Buddha's teaching is emphatically a species of primitive thought. They reject other interpretations on the ground that they are too logical to be primitive. We need not say that the view which pictures Buddha as a narrowminded rationalist, an indifferent

20. Ibid., iii. 134.
21. Dīgha N., 1. 187 ff.

psychologist and a bad philosopher, is hardly calculated to convince or even trouble those who do not share the assumptions of the critics. Such a vague dreamer is obviously one who could never have had any large religious influence even in the India of the sixth century BC.

VII

If we believe that Buddha was not a vague dreamer or a hypocrite, but a sincere and earnest soul of an anti-dogmatic turn of mind, then a chance phrase or a significant touch may contain, to the careful observer, the clue to his general position which is the permanent background of his life and thought. The spirit of this metaphysics will be all-pervading though it may be seldom expressed.

The emphasis laid by Buddha on the impermanence and non-substantiality of the world is plainly in harmony with the depreciation of all empirical existence which we find in the Upaniṣads.[22] The crucial question is, whether Buddha's condemnation of the world of experience is the result of his acceptance of an absolute reality, as in the case of the Upaniṣads. When one says that one does not believe in reality or God, one only means that one does not believe in the popular ideas of them. When Buddha scrapped inadequate conceptions, it can only be in comparison with a more adequate one. As a matter of fact, nowhere did Buddha repudiate the Upaniṣad conception of Brahman, the absolute. In the *Kathāvattu*, where different controversial points are discussed, there is no reference to the question of the reality of an immutable being. All this indicates, if anything, Buddha's acceptance of the Upaniṣad position. Besides, the famous sermon at Benares suggests strongly the reality of an absolute realm. The descriptions of the absolute as neither existent nor non-existent, nor both nor neither, remind us of similar passages in non-Buddhist texts where they are used to deny not the absolute but empirical descriptions of it.[23]

Why, then, did Buddha not admit in express terms the reality of the absolute? Buddha refused to describe the absolute, for that would be to take a step out of the world of relativity, the legitimacy of which he was the first to contest in others. The absolute is not a matter of empirical observation.

22. 'The wise seek not the stable (dhruvam) among things which are unstable (adhruveṣu) here,' Kaṭha Up., iv. 2.

23. R.V., x. 129. 1–2; Bṛh. Up., ii. 5. 19; iii. 8. 8; Iśā Up., 4 and 5: Kaṭha Up. iii. 15; Muṇḍaka, i. 1. 6; ii. 2. 1; Śvet, vi. 11; Maitrī, iv. 17.

The world of experience does not reveal the absolute anywhere within its limits. The Upaniṣads admit as much and warn us against applying the categories of the phenomenal world to the ultimate reality. The seer of the Upaniṣads, when called upon to describe the nature of the absolute, kept silent, and when the question was repeated, he persisted in his silence and ultimately declared that 'the Ātman is silence' (Śānto'yam ātmā).[24] 'Where the eye goes not, speech goes not, nor the mind; we know not we understand not how one would teach it.'[25] It is 'other than the known and above the unknown.'[26] Often the Upaniṣads give negative descriptions of the absolute.[27] But the conception of the absolute as something unknown and incomprehensible, without beginning or end, without shape, substance or dwelling-place, is too exalted for ordinary people. So the Upaniṣads indulge in positive descriptions to satisfy the interests of religion and make known that the unutterable absolute is none the less positive in character. While the Upaniṣads did not dare to be loyal to the tremendous admission of the incomprehensibility of the absolute, Buddha, more consistently, refuses to apply any category of the empirical world to the absolute reality. While he makes out that the absolute is not the world of change, that the self is not the empirical determinations of bodily form, perceptions, feelings, dispositions, and intellect, that nirvāṇa is not empirical being, he does not say that these are,[28] since they are incapable of logical verification. Their reality is intuited by the freed, and others have to accept it on authority. But when once authority is admitted, there is no reason why the authority of the Vedas should not be accepted in favour of the Vedic gods. There is no reason why Buddha's view should rank higher than ever so many dreams of the human heart and shadows of the human mind which people are called upon to accept on the authority of others. The Upaniṣads assert and Buddha agrees, that it is not possible for us to attain theoretical certainty on the ultimate questions, and those who profess to have attained it are charlatans anxious to impose on the vulgar. While Buddha destroyed the dogmatism of his predecessors he did not wish to substitute any dogmatism of his own in its place; for such a procedure would encourage disputations

24. S.B., iii. 2. 17.

25. Kena Up., i. 3; see also Kaṭha Up., vi. 12–13; Muṇḍaka, iii. 1. 8.

26. Kena, i. 4.

27. Bṛh. Up., ii. 3. 6; iii. 8. 8; iii. 9. 26; iv. 2–4; Kaṭha, iii. 15; Muṇḍaka, i. 6.

28. Cp. Augustine: 'We can know what God is not, but not what He is,' *Trinity*, vii. 2.

which hinder spiritual growth. Buddha declares that he does not reveal the truths he knows, not only because they are not helpful to the seeker of liberation but also because men hold different opinions regarding them.[29] In his time, fruitless discussions had become almost a mental disease. The Hindu thinkers seemed to Buddha to be neglecting the deeper needs of life in their anxiety to grapple with the bottomless issues of thought. So Buddha exhorted his followers to withdraw from the strife of systems and direct their attention to religion as the life and the way leading to the attainment of truth. Truth will work itself out in us, when we free ourselves from prejudices, let reality reflect itself in us and modify our very being. Truth is to be found in life itself. It is not a matter of learned controversy but a spiritual necessity. In view of the obvious limits to the logical investigation of reality, Buddha did not think it his duty to satisfy the metaphysical craving, though he had definite views on the metaphysical questions.

Within the limits allowed by logic, Buddha describes the ultimate principle of the universe as the law or the dharma. The precise significance of the concept of dharma will become clear if we look into its previous history in Vedic literature. We have in the Ṛg-Veda the conception of ṛta as moral and physical order. It is not the creation of God but is itself divine and independent of the gods who are said to be its custodians. The moral order of the world controlling the problems of life in its different spheres of law, custom and morality is called Dharma. In the *Bṛhadāraṇyaka Upaniṣad* it is said that, after creating the classes of Kṣatriyas, Vaiśyas and Śūdras, the supreme 'created a better form, the law of righteousness (dharma). There is nothing higher than the law of righteousness (dharmāt param nāsti).... Verily, that which is the law of righteousness is truth (satyam).... Verily both these (satyam and dharma) are the same thing.'[30] The Vedic ṛta stands for both satya and dharma.[31] In the *Taittirīya Upaniṣad*, the

29. *Udāna*, p. 11; Saṁyutta N., v. 437; Dīgha N., i. 179. To impress the incomprehensible character of the absolute by the adoption of the attitude of silence is a well-known device. When Vimalakīrti was asked to describe the nature of the absolute, he remained silent, and Bodhisattva Ma juśri exclaimed, 'Well done! Well done! Non-duality is truly above words.' *Vimalakīrti Sūtra*. Cp. Suzuki: *Mahāyāna Buddhism*, pp. 106–107.

30. i. 4. 14. See also Bṛh. Up., iv. 15. 1. Iśā Up., 15; 'The face of the real is covered over with a golden vessel; O Pūṣan, do thou uncover that, for one *whose law is the real* (satyadharmāya) to see.' See also R.V., iv. 5. 5; vii. 104. 8; ix. 113. 4; x. 190. 1.

31. Ṛta has for its negative an-ṛta which is a-satya as well as a-dharma.

perfected soul who has felt the unity of his soul with that of the world sings, 'I am the firstborn of ṛta (or the Real), earlier than the gods and the centre of the immortal.'[32] Similarly, in the *Kaṭha Upaniṣad*, where a passage from the Ṛg-Veda[33] is substantially repeated, ṛta is identified with the supreme spirit.[34] The supreme Brahman is both ṛta and satya.[35] The identity of dharma and ṛta with satya is a doctrine as old as the Ṛg-Veda and the Upaniṣads. The one absolute reveals itself to the philosophically minded as Eternal Truth or Reality, and the way to it is through wisdom (jñāna) and faith (śraddhā). This is the view which the Upaniṣads emphasise. To those religiously inclined, the absolute seems to be Eternal Love and the way to it is through love (prīti) and devotion (bhakti). This view is stressed by some of the later Upaniṣads, the *Bhagavadgītā* and the Purāṇas. Those who are ethically disposed look upon the absolute as Eternal Righteousness and hold that we can attain it through service and self-sacrifice. The one absolute which is at once Light, Love and Life reveals itself in different ways to the seekers of different temperaments.

Buddha's whole attitude is a predominantly ethical one, and naturally the ethical aspect of the absolute, its character as righteousness, appeals to him most. The place assigned by the Upaniṣads to Brahman is given to dharma by Buddha.[36] Dharma controls all things. In the *Agañña Suttanta*, the evolution of the world and the gradation of beings in it are said to be

32. Aham asmi prathamajā ṛtā'sya, pūrvam devebhyo nābhā'yi.

33. iv. 40. 5; see also Vājasaneyi Saṁhitā, x. 24; xii. 14; Tait. Saṁ., iii. 2. 10. 1; Śat. Brāh., vi. 7. 3. 11; Tait. Āran., vi. 1. 5. 6. Rangarāmānuja, commenting on Kaṭha, v. 2. Identifies ṛtam with aparicchinnasatyarūpabrahmātmakam.

34. V., 2; see Śaṁkara on Tait,. iii. 10 and Kaṭha, v. 2.

35. Ṛtam satyam param brahma. Tait. Āran., vi. 13. 27. 12.

36. Cp. Rabindranath Tagore: 'This dharma and the Brahman of the Upaniṣads are essentially the same ... Dharma in Buddhism is an eternal reality of Peace, Goodness and Love for which man can offer up the homage of his highest loyalty, his life itself. This dharma can inspire man with almost superhuman power of renunciation, and through the abnegation of self lead him to the supreme object of his existence, a state that cannot be compared to anything we know in this world, and yet of which we can at least have a dim idea, when we know that it is only to be reached, not through the path of annihilation, but through immeasurable love. Thus to dwell in the constant consciousness of unbounded love is named by Lord Buddha, Brahmavihāra, or moving in Brahman,' *Viśvabhāratī Quarterly*, 1924, pp. 385–386.

conditioned by the principle of dharma.[37] Brahmacakra or the wheel of Brahman becomes dhammacakka or the wheel of the law, The path of the Brahman is called the way of the dharma.[38] The eightfold path is called indiscriminately the Brahmayāna or the dharmayāna. The Tathāgata is said to have Brahman or dharma as his body. He is said to become one with Brahman or one with dharma.[39] There are many passages in the Pāli Canon where we are called upon to pay homage and reverence to the dharma.[40] In *Milinda*, dharma is personified as the god of righteousness.[41] Dharma is the highest reality and the things of the world are dharmas, as they are the manifestations of the one ultimate principle.

On the ground that bodily form, perceptions, feelings, dispositions and intellect are non-permanent, Buddha, denies to them the character of self.[42] The changing character of the empirical self is illustrated by the metaphors of fire and the movement of water. The Sermon at Benares does not deny the existence of a self distinct from the changing empirical aggregates. Buddha declines to deny the reality of a permanent self in his conversation with Vacchagotta. The *Laṁkāvatāra*, a work written centuries after Buddha, suggests that Buddha accepted the 'self' theory only to beguile his hearers. It is unnecessary to assume that Buddha lowered his standards for the sake of expediency, when other explanations are available. When Buddha argues that nirvāṇa can be normally attained before the bodily

37. Dīgha N., iii. 80 ff.

38. Saṁyutta N., i. 141; v. 5; *Theragātha*, 689.

39. Buddha when he attained nirvāṇa is said to have become 'dharma-dhātusvabhāvātmaka.'

40. Saṁyutta N., ii. 138; Anguttara N., ii. 20.

41. Cp. Śat. Brāh., xiii. 4. 3. 14. Cp. Poussin: 'If the Buddhists admit neither judge nor creator, at least they recognise a sovereign and infallible justice—a justice of wonderful insight and adaptability, however mechanically it acts.... In my opinion it is a calumny to accuse the Buddhists of atheism; they have at any rate taken full cognisance of one of the aspects of the divine' (quoted in *Buddha's Way of Virtue*, p. 13). Mr Saunders says: 'His (Buddha's) serene faith in righteousness and in reality of the unseen, intangible values may be called religious; and we may well believe that knowing his people and their genius for religion, he believed that he might safely leave them to work out a religious interpretation of this law of causality.' Mr Saunders thinks that Buddha's insistence on the law of karma and dharma is a 'notable contribution to an ethical theism' (*Epochs of Buddhist History*, p. 3).

42. See *Mahāvagga*, i. 6. 38; Majjhima N., 35; *Mahānidāna Sutta*: Dīgha N., ii. 66.

death of the sage, and equates it with happiness of the highest order accompanied by the consciousness of the destruction of all rebirth, he tacitly admits the reality of the self. When he declares that the character of the enlightened one is beyond nature, and protests against the accusation that he teaches the destruction of the real,[43] he admits that the destruction of the five constituents does not touch the real self. The *Dhammapada* makes the self the lord of self and the witness of its good and evil.[44] In the Sāṁkhya and the Advaita Vedānta, we have an exclusion from the self of all that belongs to the not-self, in the spirit of the Upaniṣads and Buddhism.

But Buddha could not confirm the reality of the self on empirical evidence. So he declines to answer questions about the non-phenomenal self, whether it was one with or different from the aggregates.[45] He did not so much deny the permanent self as speculations about it. Referring to six different speculations about the nature of the self, Buddha says: 'This, O monks, is a walking in mere opinion, a resorting to mere views, a barren waste of views, an empty display of views.'[46] Pudgalavāda or belief in a permanent self was held by one branch of Buddha's early disciples. *Kathāvattu* attributes it to the Sammitiyas and Vajjiputtakas. We have in the Saṁyutta Nikāya the sūtra of the burden-bearer.[47] The Buddhist commentators, Buddhaghoṣa, Vasubandhu, Candrakīrti and Yaśomitra, who are inclined to a negative interpretation of Buddha's teaching, explain it away, though it is difficult to believe that the changing aggregates are both the burden and the bearer thereof.

It is generally admitted at the present day that it is wrong to identify nirvāṇa with an 'eternity of nothingness.' The word 'nirvāṇa' means literally extinction, and what is extinguished is 'craving, sorrow, rebirth.'[48] The earliest conception of nirvāṇa is that it is an inexplicable state which can be attained even here and now[49] by the complete destruction of thirst (taṇhā) and the defilements of mind.[50] It is a real condition where saṁsāra

43. *Alagaddūpama Sutta*: Majjhima N., i. 140.
44. 160.
45. Majjhima N., i. 256.
46. Sīlācāra: *Dialogues of Buddha*, vol. i., p. 6.
47. iii. 25.
48. *Mahāvagga*, vi. 31. 7; S.B.E., vol. xiii.
49. See *Brahmajāla Sutta*: D.N., i.
50. Nandī saṁyojano loko vitakkasa vicāranā
Taṇhāya vippahānena nibbānam ity ucyati.
Sutta Nipāta, 1109; see also 1087.

terminates and an ineffable peace is attained.[51] *Apaṇṇka Sutta* describes nirvāna in words suggestive of the mokṣa of the Upaniṣads. 'Not tormenting himself, not tormenting others, already in this lifetime, no longer hungry, extinguished, come to coolness, feeling himself well, he dwells with self that has become Brahman.'[52] The beautiful poetry of the Thera- and the Therī-gāthas is inspired by ideas of the freedom and joy of nirvāṇa.

We cannot adequately describe the nature of nirvāṇa since it is not an object of logical knowledge. Though it is felt by those who share it as strongly positive, conceptually it is a negative state. Nirvāṇa is the negation of the empirical being bound by the law of karma or saṁsāra. 'There is, O monks, that which is neither earth nor water, neither fire nor air, neither infinity of space nor infinity of consciousness, nor nothingness nor perception, neither this world nor that world, neither sun nor moon.' 'Where there is neither death nor birth, there neither is this world nor that, nor in between—it is the end of sorrow.'[53] But it is not non-being. 'There is something unborn, unoriginated, unmade, uncompounded; were there not such a thing, there would be no escape from that which is born, originated, made and compounded.'[54] There is thus authority for the interpretation of nirvāṇa as something uncreate and endless[55] or as an uncompounded element different from the passing world.[56] *Udāna* alludes to the fate of the enlightened who have attained nirvāṇa. Even as the path of the fire when extinguished cannot be traced, even so the path of those who are completely freed cannot be traced. The Upaniṣads[57] compare the supreme self with the fire the fuel of which has been consumed. Only the extinction of the fuel does not destroy the fire which ceases to be visible.[58] As the

51. Majjhima N., 139. Cp. Professor Keith: 'That nirvāṇa is real ... doubtless accords with the general tone of the Canon itself' (*Buddhist Philosophy*, p. 83).

52. Anattantapo aparantapo diṭṭhe ve dhamme nicchāto nibbuto sītibhūto sukhapaṭisaṁvedī brahmabhūtena attanā viharati.—M.N., i. 412.

53. *Udāna*, viii. 1; see also ii. 10, and *Itivuttaka*.

54. *Udāna*, viii. 3. 10. Cp. Chān. Up., viii. 13. 1, where the Brahma-world into which the perfected pass is said to be uncreated, akrtam. The state of release is described as uncreated, akṛtaḥ—Muṇḍaka Up., i. 2. 12.

55. *Milinda*, p. 261.

56. See *Psychological Ethics*, pp. 367 ff.

57. Śvet Up.

58. Cp. Keith: 'There is no doubt that the Indian idea of the extinction of fire was not that which occurs to us of utter annihilation, but rather that the flame returns to the primitive, pure, invisible state of fire in which it existed prior to its manifestation in the form of visible fire' (*Buddhist Philosophy*, pp. 65–66).

Upaniṣads distinguish ultimate release (mokṣa) from the attainment of heaven (svarga), so Buddha distinguishes nirvāṇa from existence in paradise and warns his followers that desire for blissful existence in the formless world (arūpaloka) is one of the fetters which prevent the attainment of nirvāṇa.

Buddha evidently admitted the positive nature of nirvāṇa. Sāriputra dismisses Yamaka's view of nirvāṇa as the night of nothingness, as a heresy.[59] In the interesting conversation between King Pasenadi of Kosala and the nun Khemā, it is admitted that nirvāṇa is an ineffable state which does not lend itself to empirical description. The deep nature of the Tathāgata cannot be fathomed, even as the sands of the Ganges or the waterdrops in the ocean cannot be reckoned.[60] Buddha refuses to answer all questions about the nature of nirvāṇa, since the questions impede moral progress[61] and nirvāṇa is inconceivable (ananuvejjo). 'Whereof one cannot speak, thereof one must be silent.'[62]

VIII

The scientifically minded students of Buddhism tend to interpret the teaching of Buddha as a negative rationalism. Those who are impressed by the futility of modern attempts at metaphysical system-building are inclined to construe Buddha's doctrine as one of agnosticism; and if they come across inconvenient passages, they declare that they are the work of Buddha's followers. Professor Keith recognises that a positive philosophy affirming the reality of the absolute, the self and nirvāṇa, can be traced to the Canon, but he is reluctant to attribute it to the Buddha himself and so gives the credit for it to 'a section at any rate of his early followers.'[63] The different readings of Buddha's silence on metaphysical questions are motived

59. Saṁyutta N., iii. 109.
60. Ibid., iv. 374; Majjhima N., i. 487.
61. Saṁyutta N., ii. 223; Majjhima, 63.
62. Cp. Aurobindo Ghosh: 'The ideal of nirvāṇa was only a negative and exclusive statement of the highest Vedāntic spiritual experience' (*Ārya*, vi., p. 101). According to Friedrich Heiler, 'nirvāṇa is, although it might sound a paradox, in spite of all conceptional negativity nothing but "eternal salvation" after which the heart of the religious yearns on the whole earth' (quoted in the *New Pali-English Dictionary*). The later schools of Buddhism, which interpret nirvaṇa as conscious union with the universal Buddha or the awakening of the Buddha-self in the human heart, are nearer Buddha's teaching than those which view it as the cessation of all existence whatsoever.
63. *Buddhist Philosophy*, pp. 63–64.

by different acts of faith.[64] An impartial historian must strive not only for accuracy in his statements but also justice in his appreciations. While it is his duty to recognise the inconsistencies in a system, he must endeavour, if his interpretation is to be fruitful, to account for them by discriminating the essential from the accidental. It is not fair to insist on negativism or agnosticism where another explanation is not merely possible but is probably more in accordance with the ideas of the teaching of the early Canon. The 'agnostic' interpreter makes Buddha's silence a cloak for ignorance and the 'negative' interpreter looks upon it as an act of cowardice. On the former view, Buddha did not know the truth, but tried to save his face by evading all questions and asserting that they were unnecessary. On the latter he had definite views, but since he had not the courage to oppose established opinions, he kept his views to himself. Those who regard Buddha as one of the world's greatest men, of whom what Plato said of Socrates in the *Phædo* is not untrue, that he was 'the best, and also the wisest and most righteous of his time,' may be excused if they do not agree with the assumptions of the 'negative' and the 'agnostic' interpreters. If we do not want to compromise the philosophical power or the moral greatness of Buddha, we must accept the positive interpretation. It alone accounts for Buddha's metaphysical commissions and omissions and his ethical teaching which is a logical deduction from his metaphysics. It relates Buddha to his spiritual surroundings and makes his thought continuous with that of the Upaniṣads. The history of a nation's thought is an organic growth and not a mere succession of change on change.

IX

If Buddha accepts the metaphysical standpoint of the Upaniṣads, how is it that Buddhism is regarded as a heresy by the Hindu thinkers? What is the explanation for the cleavage between the Hindu and the Buddhist systems of religion and culture?

64. Referring to the place of faith in the interpretation of philosophies of an earlier age, where we are wholly confined to written records, 'usually fragmentary, often second-hand or of doubtful authority,' Professor Burnet says: 'A man who tries to spend his life in sympathy with the ancient philosophers will sometimes find a direct conviction forcing itself upon him, the grounds of which can only be represented very imperfectly by a number of references in a footnote. Unless the enumeration of passages is complete—and it can never be complete—and unless each passage tells exactly in the same way, which depends on its being read in the light of innumerable other passages not consciously present to memory, the so-called proofs will not produce the same effect on any two minds' (*Greek Philosophy*, pp. 1–2).

The Hindu quarrels not so much with the metaphysical conceptions of Buddha as with his practical programme. Freedom of thought and rigidity in practice have marked the Hindu from the beginning of his history. The Hindu will accept as orthodox the Sāṁkhya and the Pūrva Mīmāṁsā systems of thought, regardless of their indifference to theism, but will reject Buddhism in spite of its strong ethical and spiritual note, for the simple reason that the former do not interfere with the social life and organisation, while the latter insists on bringing its doctrine near to the life of the people.

In deducing the consequences of the Upaniṣad philosophy with incomparable beauty and logic, Buddha showed the inconsistencies in the beliefs and practices of those who paid lip allegiance to the Upaniṣads. While the bold speculators of the Upaniṣads adventured on the naked peaks of the absolute, the masses of men were allowed to worship their little gods and perform the sacrificial ceremonies which they were supposed to demand. The elaborate sacrificial religion failed to command the confidence of the thoughtful in Buddha's time. As a matter of fact, the Vānaprasthas and the Yatis were exempted from them, and the doubt naturally arose whether even the householders could not dispense with the costly and complicated ritual. Buddha protested against those who were standing still in the letter and proclaimed that salvation was not external and legal but inward and spiritual.

The Upaniṣads advocated the principle of ahiṁsā or non-violence but not unreservedly. The Vedic outlook was so strongly entrenched that the Upaniṣads suffered Vedic institutions even if they were against the main spirit of their teaching. For example, the *Chāndogya Upaniṣad* declares that the aspirant after release should, among other things, 'never give pain to other creatures except at certain holy places,' i.e. during animal sacrifices.[65] But the slaughter of animals was in the highest degree offensive to Buddha[66] and he disallowed absolutely animal sacrifices.

65. Ahimsan sarvabhūtāny anyatra tīrthebhyaḥ, viii. 15.

66. See Kūṭadanta Sutta: Dīgha N., i. 127. Though Buddha insisted on a rigorous discipline for the monks, he did not interfere with the socioreligious practices of his disciples so long as they did not conflict with his central principles. He allowed the Brahmin Kūṭadanta to perform the sacrifices which did not involve the killing of animals. Kumāra Kassapa, an immediate disciple of Buddha, instructs Prince Pāyāsi that sacrifices which do not involve any cruelty are better than those which do. See *Pāyāsi Suttanta*: Dīgha N., ii. The highest sacrifice according to Buddha is love of humanity and moral life. See Chān. Up., iii. 16 and 17.

While the Upaniṣads tolerated, even if they did not encourage the caste rules, Buddha's scheme definitely undermined the institution of caste. He declared that individuals were higher or lower not according to their birth but according to their character.[67] While the Brahmins reserved the study of the sacred scriptures to the members of the three 'twiceborn' castes, Buddha abolished all such restrictions. Admitting the intellectual pre-eminence of the Brahmins, Buddha ranked along with them the Sramanas and opened the latter order to the Śūdras and the Caṇḍālas. Sunīta, the sweeper, was as readily taken into the fold as the high caste Brahmin.[68]

In spite of the reforms which he wished to introduce, Buddha lived and died in the belief that he was restoring the principles of the venerable Aryan faith. He did not think of himself as the founder of a new religion, though he was anxious to purify Brahmanical Hinduism and revivify the society round him. But the pioneers of progress are regarded in every age, with not unnatural suspicion, as the champions of revolt and rebellion. By putting spiritual brotherhood in place of hereditary priesthood, personal merit in place of distinctions of birth, logical reason in place of vedic revelation, moral life in place of ceremonial piety, and the perfected sage above the Vedic gods, Buddha provoked the wrath of the Hindu priest who regarded him as an anti-social force. What made Buddha and his followers unpardonable heretics in the eyes of the Brahmin priests is the social revolution which they preached. There is nothing in the doctrine of Buddha which cannot be reconciled with Hindu thought; but the conflict between a social system based on brahmanical supremacy and one which denied it is radical. In theological discussions, which are generally heated, every dissenter is an atheist. If one does not share our illusions, he is a heretic; if he adopts a different standard of morality, he is immoral. The protagonist of the Vedic sacrificial religion regarded Buddha as an enemy of the faith. When Buddha approached Bhāradvāja the Brahmin, as he was performing a sacrifice to the fire, the latter cried out, 'Stop there, O shaven-headed one, there O Samanaka, there thou of low caste.'[69] Hindu orthodoxy adopted a

67. *Agañña Suttanta*: Dīgha N., iii.; Saṁyutta N., ii. 138; Anguttara N., ii. 20.

68. *Kassapasīhanāda Sutta*; *Samannaphala Sutta*, 14; Aśoka's Inscriptions at Girnir and Sahabajgar. See also Vinaya Piṭaka, vol. ii., and *Madhurā Sutta*. Cp. 'The kṣatriya is the best of this folk who put their trust in lineage. But he who is perfect in wisdom and righteousness, he is the best among gods and men' (*Ambattha Sutta*).

69. Tatr'eva muṇḍaka, tatr'eva samanaka, tatr'eva vasalaka, tiṭṭhāhi.

similar attitude whenever there were protests against the Vedic religion. Maṇḍana Miśra rebuked Śaṁkara for subordinating Vedic piety to knowledge of the absolute.[70] Buddha's revolt is not against the metaphysics of the Upaniṣads but against Brahmanical Hinduism. The schism became wider as the followers of Buddha acquired the zeal characteristic of the professors of a new learning, and developed their doctrine in a way opposed to the growing tradition of the Vedānta. The negative view of Buddha's teaching is embodied in the *Kathāvattu* and the *Questions of King Milinda* as well as in the classics of the Hīnayāna and the Mahāyāna forms. No wonder the scholiasts of the Vedānta subject the different types of Buddhism to a severe criticism.

X

The four Buddhist schools profess to be loyal to the teaching of Buddha who discovered the elements of existence (dhammā), their causal connection, and the method to suppress their efficiency for ever. As against the Ājīvakas who denied the influence of the past on the present, since the past was dead and irrecoverably gone, Buddha affirmed that 'everything exists' though things were looked upon as combinations of forces (saṁskārasamūha). Buddha maintained the existence of all things in the interests of moral life. The Sarvāstivādins (the Vaibhāsikas and the Sautrāntikas) uphold a pluralistic realism. The nāmarūpa of the Upaniṣads was elaborated by the Buddhists into the elements of matter (rūpa) and the four mental factors (nāma) of perceptions, feelings dispositions and intellect. Sense-data are matter and the other four constitute the soul. Often the elements of existence are classified into the six receptive faculties (ṣaḍāyatana), the five senses and manas and their sixfold objects.[71] The objects of manas are non-sensuous and are of sixty-four kinds. Sometimes in addition to the five senses, manas and the sixfold objects, six modes of

70'. At that time, while Maṇḍana Miśra, having invited all the gods by the invocation of Sālagrāma, was washing his hand of the darbha grass, he saw the feet of Śaṁkarācārya inside the sanctified circle. On inspection of his person he knew him to be a saññyāsin and was in a moment ruffled with clamorous wrath and cried out, "Whence comes this shaven-headed man?"' (Kuto muṇḍi). Ānandagiri: *Śaṁkaravijaya*.

71. The elements are classified into skandhas, āyatanas and dhātus. See *Theragātha*, 1255.

consciousness are mentioned and we get the eighteen dhātus. Strictly speaking, there cannot be any distinction between internal and external or any real interaction between the separate elements, though popular usage indulges in these unauthorised conceptions. Both matter and mind are transformed into continuously flowing, discrete moments, of impenetrable stuff in the case of matter and of consciousness in the case of mind. These sense-data and elements of mind are regarded as obeying causal laws. But causation, with reference to momentary entities which simply appear and disappear but do not move or change, acquires a new meaning. It is only pratītyasamutpāda or dependent origination. One state springs into being after another. There is no question of one state producing another.

According to the theory of pluralistic realism, knowledge is nothing more than the compresence of consciousness with the object. As Professor Stcherbatsky puts it: 'A moment of colour (rūpa), a moment of the sense of vision matter (caksuḥ) and a moment of pure consciousness (citta) arising simultaneously, in close contiguity constitute what is called a sensation (sparśa) of colour.'[72] It means that the element of consciousness appears qualified by an object and supported by a sense organ. Consciousness does not apprehend the sense organ but only the object, since there is a special relation of co-ordination (sārūpya) between the two. Consciousness is said to apprehend even as a light is said to move. The *Abhidharmakośa* says: 'The light of a lamp is a common metaphorical designation for an uninterrupted production of a series of flashing flames. When this production changes its place, we say the light has moved. Similarly, consciousness is a conventional name for a chain of conscious moments. When it changes its place (i.e. appears in co-ordination with another objective element) we say that it apprehends that object.'[73] We have only a series of evanescent flashings of consciousness itself, but there is nothing that cognises. In the continuity of conscious moments, the previous moment is the cause of the succeeding one.

From this view it is but a step to the Vijñānavāda of the Yogācāras, which reduces all the elements into aspects of one receptacle consciousness (ālayavijñāna). Elements of existence (dharmas) are products of thought. Objects rise into consciousness as the result of our past experiences. The external world is the creation of our thought to which we give names and

72. Trayāṇām sannipātaḥ sparśah (*The Central Conception of Buddhism* p. 55).
73. IX: See Stcherbatsky, *The Central Conception of Buddhism*, p. 57.

ideas.[74] The theory of the everflowing stream of thought in which the preceding moment is the cause of the succeeding one, where the two are bound together by the relation of mere samanantaratva, gives place to the doctrine of a substantial universal consciousness (ālaya) of which the mental states are the modifications (pariṇāma). The conception of the degrees of unreality is a tacit recognition of an absolute reality. Individual ideas are unreal (niḥsvabhāva): firstly, because they are logical constructions (parikalpita) with no corresponding reality in the extra-mental world; secondly, because they are only contingently real (paratantra); and thirdly, because they are all merged in the one reality (pariniṣpanna) of the absolute (tathatā). The individual elements are not real in themselves, but have their reality in the absolute, which is of the nature of pure consciousness undifferentiated into subject and object (grāhya grāhaka rahita).[75] Since the absolute is immanent in the world, all that is necessary for the attainment of nirvāṇa is a change of outlook. The mystic power of the Yoga helps us to see the things of the world *sub specie aeternitatis.* Saṁsāra to the unregenerate is nirvāṇa to the regenerate. But the Yogācāra does not carefully discriminate between the individual and the universal consciousness. When he makes out that the distinctions of knower, known and knowledge are not real, but are due to a beginningless defilement of consciousness, when he compares the relation of particular conscious states to the universal consciousness to one of waves to the sea, when he admits the eternal reality of tathatā and regards it as the only uncompounded reality (asaṁskṛtadharma) and relegates all else to the region of relativity, when he reduces all dharmas to modes of one fundamental essence; he tacitly admits the reality of an absolute consciousness, though the subjectivistic tendency makes itself heard quite frequently. The Mādhyamikas subject the Yogācāra theory to a searching scrutiny. They contend that we cannot have any self-consciousness (svasamvitti), for a thing cannot act on itself. The finger cannot touch itself, nor can the knife cut itself. The Mādhyamikas view all the elements of existence as contingent on one another and so declare the world to be empty of reality or śūnya. Śūnya is also said to be the fundamental truth of all existence. Almost all students of Nāgārjuna's Mādhyamika metaphysics regard his

74. Nāmasaṁjñāvyavahāra. *Laṁkāvatāra Sūtra*, p. 85.

75. Advayalakṣaṇam vijñaptimātram. See Stcherbatsky, *The Conception of Buddhist Nirvāṇa*, pp. 32–33.

system as nihilistic.[76] In my account of it,[77] I made out that it was more positive than it was generally represented to be. I urged that Nāgārjuna believed in an ultimate reality, which was śūnya only in the sense that it was devoid of all empirical determinations. Let us try to determine whether Nāgārjuna's ultimate reality is or is not a stupendous void, an unmitigated negation.

XI

There is no doubt about Nāgārjuna's conception of the world as unreal or śūnya. We mean by real any entity which has a nature of its own (svabhāva), which is not produced by causes (akṛtaka), which is not dependent on anything else (paratra nirapekṣa).[78] Whatever is relative or dependent is unreal, śūnya (svabhāva-śūnya). The real is the independent uncaused being.[79] The world of experience is bound by the relations of subject and object, substance and attribute, actor and action, existence and non-existence, origination, duration and destruction, unity and plurality, whole and part, bondage and release, relations of time, relations of space; and Nāgārjuna examines every one of these relations and exposes their contradictions.[80] If non-contradiction is the test of reality, then the world of experience is not real. The world is neither pure being nor pure non-being. Pure being is not an existence or an item of the world process; pure non-being is not a valid concept, for, were it so, absolute nothingness will be an entity, and what is by definition the negation of all existence will become an existent. Nothing is not a thing. Existence is a becoming. Things of the world are not but always become. They ever supersede themselves. They are neither self-existent nor non-existent, since they are perceived and induce action and produce effects. *Lalitavistara* says: 'There is no object which is existent nor is there any which is non-existent. One who knows the chain of conditional existence passes beyond both.'[81] Nāgārjuna opens his work

76. Kern, *Manual*, p. 126; Jacobi: *A.O.J.*, xxxi., p. 1; Keith, *Buddhist Philosophy*, pp. 237, 239, 247, 261.

77. Pp. 643 ff.

78. M.K., xv. 2.

79. Aśūnyam ... apratītyasamutpannam. M. Vṛtti, 403.

80. Pp. 645 ff.

81. Na ca punar iha kaścid asti dharmaḥ
So' pi na vidyati yasya nāsti bhāvāḥ
Hetukriyāparaṁparā ya jāne
Tasya na bhotiha astināstibhāvāḥ—(Chap. xxv.)

with the statement that things are neither transient nor eternal, neither produced nor destroyed, neither same nor different, neither coming forth nor passing away.[82] There is no real production (samutpāda), but only conditioned (pratītya) relative, apparent production. There is no real destruction but only apparent destruction (pratītya-samuccheda); so with the rest. All things of the universe are conditioned and relative only. 'Śūnya' is the term used by Nāgārjuna to designate the conditioned character of the world.[83] If a thing were real and unconditioned, then it must be free from origin and destruction.[84] There are no objects in the world which are not subject to change and so the world is śūnya.

Nāgārjuna, as the upholder of the middle path, does not dismiss the world as mere illusion. His attack is directed against the theory of the self-existence of things, but does not in any way impair the conditioned existence of things. Candrakīrti, commenting on Nāgārjuna, says: 'Our argument that objects are not self-existent affects the reality of the universe for you who accept the doctrine of the self-existence of objects. The view that objects are not self-existent does not touch our theory of the conditioned existence of objects.'[85]

But it cannot be that Nāgārjuna treated the world as unreal and yet believed in no other reality. If all thought is falsification, there must be a real that is falsified. For, if there be no truth, then falsehood loses its meaning. There is no relative knowledge without absolute knowledge being immanent in it. There is nothing empirical which does not reveal the

82. Anirodham anutpādam anucchedam aśāśvatam
Anekārtham anānārtham anāgamam anirgamam.

83. Yaḥ pratītyasamutpādaḥ śūnyatām tām pravakṣyate.—M.K., xxiv.
Śūnyāḥ sarvadharmāḥ niḥsvabhāvayogona. *Prajñāpāramitā.*

84. Yady āśūnyam idam sarvam udayo nāsti na vyayaḥ.—M.K., xxiv.

85. Bhavatas tu svabhāvavādinaḥ, svabhāvasya bhāvānām vaidhuryāt sarvabhāvāpavādaḥ saṁbhāvyate; vayam tu pratītyotpannatvāt sarvabhāvānām svabhāvam evam nopalabhāmahe, tat kasyāpavādam kariṣyāmaḥ, M. Vṛtti, viii. There are passages which suggest the theory of absolute illusion. In xviii., Nāgārjuna compares the things of the world to dream-castles in the air and the like:

Kleṣāḥ karmāṇi dehāśca phalāni ca
Gandharvanagarākārā marīcisvapnasannibhāḥ.

Candrakīrti argues that they are characterless like these and not illusory: 'gandharvanagarākārādivan niḥsvabhāvā veditavyāḥ.' Candrakīrti insists that 'we are relativists, we are not negativists,' M. Vṛtti, 368.

transcendental. 'O Subhūti, all things have for their refuge śūnyatā, they do not alter that refuge.'[86] If things appear to be independent, such appearance is due to māyā.[87] 'O Sāriputra, things which do not exist, when they are affirmed as existing, are called avidyā.'[88] If we mistake the phenomenal world for the noumenal reality, it is a case of avidyā. But we cannot understand the transcendental reality except through the world of experience; and we cannot attain nirvāṇa except through the understanding of the ultimate reality.[89]

The aim of the Mādhyamika Śāstra is to teach the nature of nirvāṇa, which consists in the annulment of the whole world, and is of the nature of bliss.[90] Nirvāṇa which is the non-perception of things is the absolute truth.[91] It is identified with śūnyatā in the celebrated work *Śataka*.[92] Both nirvāṇa and śūnyatā are characterised in the same negative way. Nirvāṇa is neither existent nor non-existent, but is beyond both.[93] Śūnyatā is truth or 'tathatā which neither increases nor decreases.'[94] In the *Aṣṭasahasrīkāprajñāpāramitā*, śūnyatā is said to be profound. 'The word "profound," O Subhūti, is the synonym of that which has no cause, that which is beyond contemplation, that which is beyond conception, that which is not produced, that which is not born of non-existence, of resignation, of restraint, of extinction or of final journey.'[95] For Nāgārjuna, nirvāṇa, Buddha, śūnyatā are different names for the same reality. If nirvāṇa is interpreted as the cessation of the world, then it becomes a

86. Sūnyatāgatikā hi subhūte, sarvadharmāḥ, te tām gatim na vyativartante.

87. Dharmataiṣā sarvadharmāṇām māyādharmatām upādāya....

88. Yathā, sāriputra, na samvidyante tathā samvidyante evam avidyamānās tenocyante avidyeti.

89. Vyavahāram anāśritya paramārtho na deśyate
Paramārtham anāgamya nirvāṇam nādhigamyata iti.—M.K., xxiv.

90. Sarvaprapañcopaśamaśivalakṣaṇam nirvāṇam śāstrasya prayojanam, M. Vṛtti; see also Māṇḍūkya Up., 7 and 12. Cp. Candrakīrti: Bhāvābhāvāntardvayarahitatvāt sarvasvabhāvānutpattilakṣaṇā śūnyatā.—M. Vṛtti, xxiv.

91. Yo'nupalaṁbhaḥ sarvadharmāṇām sā prajñāpāramitety ucyate.

92. Śūnyatām eva nirvāṇam kevalam tad ihobhayam.—M. Vṛtti, xviii.

93. Na cābhāvopi nirvāṇam kuta evāsya bhāvatā
Bhāvābhāvaparāmarśakṣayo nirvāṇam ucyate,—*Ratnāvali*.

94. M.M. Haraprasād Śāstri says: 'There is in the midst of all these negative descriptions an inconceivable positive which is śūnya' (*Journal of the Buddhist Text Society*, vol. ii., pt. iii, p. vi).

95. xviii.

relative notion, something brought about by causes. To assume that the world exists before nirvāṇa and becomes non-existent after it, is an illogical conception. So Nāgārjuṇa insists that there is no real difference between the absolute and the phenomenal, nirvāṇa and saṁsāra. He says: 'Having regard to causes or conditions, we call this world a phenomenal one. This same world, when causes and conditions are disregarded, is called the absolute.'[96] When Nāgārjuna describes the ultimate reality as not created, not liable to destruction, not eternal, not passing away, he means that the real is opposed to all empirical characters. He describes his śūnyatā almost in the very words in which the nirguṇa Brahman is characterised in the Upaniṣads.[97] It is neither one nor multiple, neither existent nor non-existent.[98] Śūnya, the ultimate reality, cannot be comprehended by thought or described by words.[99]

Śāntideva says that absolute reality does not fall within the domain of intellect (buddhi) confined to the realm of relativity. The Mādhyamika denies that discursive thought can establish ultimate truth. The learned call śūnyatā the annulment of all conceptions; even those who look upon it as śūnyatā are said to be incapable of improvement.'[100] 'What description or knowledge can be given of an object that cannot be described by letters? Even this much—that it does not admit of representation by letters—is made by means of illusory attribution.'[101] In 'illusory attribution' we use a notion which is the closest approximation to the object studied but at once withdraw it since it is inadequate to its content.[102] To know śūnya is to know all; if we do not know it, we know nothing.[103] The unique undefinable (anirvacanīya) being is said to be the real of all reals (dharmāṇām dharmatā),

96. M.K., xxv. 9.

97. Kena, 3. 11; Bṛh., ii. 5. 19; iii. 8–8; Kaṭha, iii. 15; Īśā, 9–10; Muṇḍaka, i. 6; Mānd., 7.

98. Nāstiko durgatim yāti, sugatim yāti anāstikaḥ
Yathābhūtaparijñānam moksam advaya niśritā.—*Āryaratnāvali.*

One who holds it to be non-existent attains to misery while one who does not think so attains to happiness; but release is for those who have the true knowledge of reality which is neither existent nor non-existent.

99. *Bodhicaryāvatāra*, ix. 2.

100. Śūnyatā sarvadṛṣṭinām proktā niḥsaraṇam jinaih
Yeśām tu sūnyatādṛṣtis tān asādhyān vabhāṣire.—M.K., xiii.

101. Anakṣarasya dharmasya śṛutih kā deśanā ca kā
Śṛūyate yasya taccāpi samāropād anakṣara.—M. Vṛtti, xv.

102. See *Vedāntasāra*, p. 8 (Jacob's ed.).

103. M.K., xxiv.; cf. Bṛh. Up., ii. 4. 5. 7–9; iii. 2. 1; iv. 4. 21; v. 1. 1; Muṇḍaka, i. 3.

the essential thisness (idaṁtā), suchness (tathatā), the suchness of all existence (bhūtatathatā), the very matrix of the lord Buddha (tathāgatagarbha). It will be very difficult to account for Nāgārjuna's metaphysics and his insistence on devotion (bhakti) if we do not admit the absolutist implications of his doctrine of śūnya.[104]

XII

Much of the confusion is due to the ambiguous word 'śūnya.' It is applied to the world of experience as well as to the ultimate reality. The world of experience, built by the relations framed by intellect, is unintelligible. Consistently Nāgārjuna denies that he has any thesis of his own to defend, since every intellectual proof would be subject to the same weakness. If intellect is incapable of explaining experience, since it finds hopeless antinomies there, it cannot be expected to be more successful with regard to the ultimate reality. One is as mysterious as the other, and Nāgārjuna employs the same term 'śūnya' with reference to both. Truth is silence which is neither affirmation nor negation. In different senses, both the world of experience and ultimate reality defy description as existent or non-existent. If we take ultimate reality as true being, the world is not; if we take the being of the world as true being, ultimate reality is not. Both are śūnya though in different senses.

Towards the end of my discussion of Nāgārjuna's system, I suggested certain points of similarity between the Sūnyavāda and the Advaita Vedānta.[105] Both of them regard the world as subject to change and therefore unreal.[106] The real, which transcends all distinctions of experience and knowledge, is admitted by both;[107] only Nāgārjuna suggests it, but does not work it out in all its fullness, as the Advaita Vedānta does. The

104. Rudolf Otto says: 'What is true of the strange nothingness of our mystics holds good equally of the śūnyam and the śūnyatā, the void and emptiness of the Buddhist mystics. The void of the Eastern like the "nothing" of the Western mystic is a numinous ideogram of the "wholly other." Nothing can be said of it since it is "absolutely and intrinsically other than and opposite of everything that is and can be thought"' (*The Idea of the Holy*, E.T., p. 30).

105. Pp. 668–669.

106. Śaṁkara would endorse this passage:
Jarāmaraṇadharmeṣu sarvabhāveśu sarvadā
Tiṣṭhanti katame bhāvāḥ jarāmaraṇam vinā.—M.K., vii.

107. Candrakīrti's statement, sarvakalpanājālarahitajñānajñeyanivṛittisvabhāvam, sivam, paramārthasvabhāvam, is true to Śaṁkara's conception of release and reality. See also S.B., iii. 2. 17; B.G., xiii. 12.

doctrines of māyā and avidyā are taken up and developed considerably in the Advaita Vedānta. Virtue and vice are regarded in both as means to higher and lower stages in saṁsāra, while ultimate release remains entire and unaffected by these.[108] In giving a rational, as distinct from scriptural, foundation for the Advaita Vedānta, Gauḍapāda finds nothing so useful as the Mādhyamika theory. Many of his Kārikās remind us of Nāgārjuna's work.[109] Not without reason does Vācaspati look upon the upholders of Sūnyavāda as those of advanced thought (prakṛṣṭamati), while the pluralistic realists (Sarvastivādins) are said to be of inferior thought (hīnamati) and the Yogācāras of middling (madhyama) ability.[110]

108. Dharme ca satyadharme ca phalam tasya na vidyate, M.K. viii. Cp. Bṛh. Up., iv. 3. 21–22; Kaṭha, ii. 14.

109. Cp. Gauḍapāda's *Kārikā*, ii. 32; iv. 22; iv. 88.

110. *Bhāmatī*, ii. 2. 18.

Notes

CHAPTER I

Pages 6–7 [27].—God, according to Praśastapāda, is the creator of the universe. See *Padārthadharmasaṁgraha*, p. 48.

Page 11 [33], *n.* 9 [1].—*Bhāmatī*, i. 1. 1.

Page 21 [44].—For the use of the word 'darśana' in the sense of 'point of view' or 'philosophic opinion,' see Candrakīrti on Nāgārjuna's *Kārikā* (p. 75 of the St Petersburg edition), and the quotations from Bhartṛprapañca in the *Tīkā* on Sureśvara's *Bṛhadvārttika*, p. 890. See also Jacobi, Introduction to vol. 22 of S.B.E., p. xlv. I owe the reference to Professor Hiriyanna.

Pages 24–25 [48].—This view is called Śākhācandranyāya.

Pages 28–29 [52].—'It is not too much to say that in no literature is the moralising note so prominent. It is perhaps just owing to the universality of this mode of expression that there are so few works in Sanskrit dealing with morality exclusively' (Macdonell: *Comparative Religion*, p. 70).

Pages 33–34 [58].—'Sūtra period' is used here with special reference to the philosophical Sūtras and not the Vedic or Kalpa Sūtras. The period of the latter is said to be 500 BC to 200 BC.

CHAPTER II

Pages 39–40 [64].—The hymns included in the Ṛg-Veda, it is generally held, were composed in the north-west of India. See Macdonell: *Sanskrit Literature*, p. 40.

Pages 41–42 [66].—Arnold takes as the main criteria of the fivefold division, metre, language and vocabulary.

Pages 42–43 [67].—Regarding the age of the Veda, Professor Winternitz sums up the results of his investigations thus:

1. Buddhism and Jainism presuppose the whole of the Veda. If, as it is probable, the origin of the Jaina religion goes back to Pārśva, the predecessor of Mahāvīra, the Veda must have been completed and considered as the sacred texts of Brahmanism as early as the eighth century BC.
2. The hymns of the Ṛg-Veda are older than all the rest of Indian literature.
3. The origin and growth of the Ṛg-Veda-Saṁhitā requires a long time, several centuries.

4. The Ṛg-Veda-Saṁhitā is considerably older than the Atharva-Veda-Saṁhitā and the Yajur-Veda-Saṁhitā.
5. All the Saṁhitās are older than the Brāhmaṇas.
6. Both the Brāhmaṇas and the Upaniṣads need a long time for their development.
7. The close relationship between the language of the Vedic Saṁhitās on the one hand and Avesta and Old Persian on the other, does not allow us to date the beginning of the Vedic period back into a hoary age of many thousands to say nothing of millions of years BC.
8. On the other hand, the facts of political, religious and literary history require a period of at least a thousand years and probably more between the earliest hymns of the Ṛg-Veda and the latest parts of the old Upaniṣads and the rise of Buddhism.
9. It is not possible to give any definite date for the beginning of Vedic poetry. We do not know more for certain than that Vedic literature began at some unknown time in the past and extended up to the eighth century.
10. But it is more probable that this unknown time of the beginning of the Vedic literature was nearer 2500 or 2000 BC than to 1500 or 1200 BC.

(*Calcutta Review*, November 1923).

The recent finds at Harappa in the Punjab and Mohenjo Daro in Sind throw additional light on the antiquity of the Indian civilisation. We have now definite archaeological evidence to show that 5000 years ago, the peoples of Sind and the Punjab were living in well-built cities and had a relatively developed civilisation with a high standard of art and craftsmanship and a developed system of writing. The Punjab and Sind antiquities include 'houses and temples massively built of burnt brick and provided with well-constructed water conduits covered by marble slabs.' Besides a variety of potteries, both painted and plain, some fashioned by the hand and some turned on the wheel, toys and bangles of blue glass, paste and shell, we have a number of engraved and inscribed seals bearing inscriptions in a hitherto unknown pictographic script. Sir John Marshall, the Director General of Archaeology, writes that these discoveries 'have established once for all the existence on Indian soil in the third millennium BC of a civilisations as highly developed and seemingly as widespread as the Sumerian culture of Mesopotamia, with conclusive evidence of a close contact between the two.' Though it is too soon to say anything definite about the connection of India and Mesopotamia in the third millennium BC, these finds may perhaps furnish some clue to the Dravidian problem.

Pages 46–47 [72].—The word 'deva' is connected with the Latin *deus* and is referred to a root meaning 'to shine.' The *Nirukta* definition is late.

Pages 47–49 [73].—Yāska states in his *Nirukta* that many of the Vedic mantras admit of ādhibhautika (physical), ādhidaivika (religious) and ādhyātmika (spiritual) interpretations. Agni, for example, signifies fire on the physical plane, the priest god on the religious, and the great effulgence of God on the spiritual plane. When the natural forces were addressed, the devotee had in mind the underlying power and not the physical fact.

Page 79 [75], *n.* 16 [1].—The language spoken in the early Vedic period was a prior stage of what in a later age and probably in a different locality became Sanskrit (classical).

Pages 52–53 [78].—Ṛta is a conception that goes back to the Indo-Iranian period.

Pages 58–59 [85].—Indra was already known in the Indo-Iranian period. See Keith: *The Religion and Philosophy of the Veda*, vol. i, p. 133.

Pages 62–63 [89].—In the hymn to Vāk (x. 125), we find the conception of an immanent word, a force which dwells and operates in all things and in which unconsciously all men have their being.

Pages 71–72 [99].—In the R.V., where the interest is mainly cosmological, 'sat' means the world of objects or experience and 'asat' refers to the non-being or the primitive undifferentiated condition of things, which is the antecedent of the present world-order; cp. also *Tait. Up.*, ii. 7, where 'sat' or the world of name and form is said to be born of 'asat' or non-being.

Pages 73–74 [102].—In the Orphic cosmogony, the idea is found that in the beginning was the primeval water, from it arose an egg, and out of this proceeded the first creature, the god Phanes. See Nilsson: *A History of Greek Religion*, p. 73.

Pages 78–79 [107].—The ideas of iṣṭa (or what is given in sacrifice) and pūrta (or what is given as presents to the priests) (R.V., x. 14. 8) contain the germs of later ceremonialism. Iṣṭāpūrta is said to have a distinct substantial being with which we get united after death. It stands for the merit or demerit which we earn by our pious activities. The doctrine of karma is much influenced by this idea.

Page 80 [109].—Cp. Bloomfield: 'We have in connection with the ṛta a pretty complete system of ethics, a kind of "counsel of perfection"' (*The Religion of the Veda*, p. 126).

The sense of sin is not absent from the R.V.; cp. 'Loosen the bonds, O Varuṇa, that hold me, loosen the bonds, above, between and under.'

'So in the holy law may we, made sinless, belong to Aditi, O thou Āditya' (R.V., i. 24. 15; see also i. 31. 16; iv. 54. 3).

Pages 80–81 [110].—Cp. 'Thornless is the path for him who seeks the law' (R.V., i. 41). 'To him who keeps the law, whether old or young, thou givest happiness and energy that he may live well' (R.V., i. 91). See also R.V., iii. 59. 2.

CHAPTER III

Page 97[128]. *n.* 28 [1].—Strictly the root '*vid*' means 'to know.'

Pages 100–1 [131].—The older Vedic idea of ṛta relating to the order of the physical and the moral spheres becomes definitely transformed in the Brāhmaṇas into the concept of dharma which refers specially to the moral order of the world. It includes all those spheres which were later discriminated into ritual, code, law, custom and etiquette. Sometimes 'dharma' appears as a god. See *Śat. Brāh.*, xiii. 4. 3. 14.

Pages 104–5 [136].—See Keith: *Aitareya Brāhmana.*

CHAPTER IV

Page 113 [145].—Though we have spasmodic suggestions of the interest in the subject in earlier literature (see *Atharva Veda*, xviii. 44), it becomes dominant in the Upaniṣads.

Pages 130–31 [165].—Manas is bound to prāṇa. Cp. Prāṇa-bandhanam hi saumya manaḥ.

Pages 133–34 [168].—Śaṁkara takes 'ānandamaya' to be the jīva.

Page 134 [169].—The immanent conception of God also is found in the R.V. (see the hymns addressed to Aditi, i. 89. 10), but it becomes emphasised in the Upaniṣads.

Pages 150–51 [188] *n.* 139 [1]—Nāma and rūpa mean 'name' and 'corporeal form' in the Upaniṣads. See *Bṛh. Up.*, i. 6. 1–2; *Muṇḍaka Up.*, vi. 8; also Oldenberg's *Buddha*, pp. 445 ff.

Pages 180–81 [222].—Deussen thinks that in the earlier Upaniṣads only the three stages of the student, the householder and the anchorite are recognised, while those who know the truth are exalted above the āśramas. See *Philosophy of the Upaniṣads*, p. 368. *Jābāla Up.* mentions the four āśramas. See *Bṛh. Up.*, iv. 4. 10 and 22; *Chān. Up.*, ii. 23. 1; v. 10.

Pages 181–82 [223].—'There is current a rather ill-considered modern theory to the effect that the philosophers were not of the priestly caste but of the warrior caste, perhaps of non-indigenous origin; that even Buddha may have been of a foreign race. But there is little to support this theory and much that goes to disprove it. The germs of the philosophy of the Upaniṣads lie buried in the (priestly) *Atharva-Veda* and Brāhmaṇas, and it is from them that we have to derive the unsystematic philosophic utterances of the later sages in whose debates, however, the Rājas of the day probably took the condescending interest customary to cultured royalty and in which, when they took part, they were credited with victory' (Hopkins: *Ethics of India*).

Pages 186–87 [229], *n.* 240 [2].—Svayam eva rājate. Then it means he is self-luminous or self-dependent.

Pages 191–92 [234].—Dhātuprasāda is the expression used. *Kaṭha Up.*, ii. 20.

Pages 197–98 [241].—The term jīvanmukta is a later one, though the idea is contained in the Upaniṣads. Cp., e.g., *Kaṭha Up.*, vi. 14.

Page 220 [267].—See also Belvalkar and Ranade: *History of Indian Philosophy*, vol. ii; Keith: *The Religion and Philosophy of the Veda*, 2 vols.; and Ranade: *A Constructive Survey of Upaniṣadic Philosophy.*

CHAPTER V

Pages 225–26 [274].—Sānjaya's scepticism influenced considerably Buddha's attitude to metaphysics and the Jaina view of Saptabhaṅgī. Cp. 'If you ask me whether there is another world (atthi paraloko)—well, If I thought there were, I would say so. And I do not think it is thus or thus. And I do not think it is otherwise. And I do not deny it' (*Sacred Books of the Buddhists*, vol. ii, p. 75).

Pages 228–29 [278].—Bhāskara, in his commentary on *Brahma Sūtra* (iii. 3. 53), refers to the Sūtra of Bṛhaspati.

Pages 229–30 [279].—If Cārvāka is a proper name, it may be the name of a pupil of Bṛhaspati. It is often regarded as a common name. See Macdonell: *Sanskrit Literature*, p. 450.

Pages 233–34 [283].—Materialism is ranked with the Sāṁkhya and the Yoga in the *Arthaśāstra*. See i. 2.

CHAPTER VI

Pages 237–38 [288].—It is sometimes said that the Jains have ten Niryuktas as well as a number of Bhāṣyas.

Pages 242–43 [294].—Inductive truths are derived from anupapatti or the impossibility of conceiving the opposite. See *Prameyakamalamārtāṇḍa*, pp. 40, 50, 100–1.

Pages 243–44 [295].—The validity of knowledge *consists* in the faithful representation of objects, while it is *tested* by practical efficiency.

Pages 245–46 [297].—'Although all these (five stages) are in a way the same, they have different designations in virtue of being special phases. In some cases the succession is unobserved by reason of rapid origination' (*Pramāṇanayatattvālokālaṁkāra*, ii).

CHAPTER VII

Pages 287–88 [342].—Cp. K.J. Saunders: 'The great keynotes of our modern scientific thinking, causality and the unity of the universe, even if Gautama did not first formulate them, were popularised by him' (*Epochs in Buddhist History*, p. ix).

Page 288 [343].—The Tipiṭaka contains products of different ages. Whether or not the Canon of the Dharma and the Vinaya as found today were composed at the first Council, it is clear that the elders of the faith gathered together soon after the demise of Buddha and discussed questions of doctrine and discipline. We are on more certain ground with regard to the second Council at Vesali, dated a hundred years after the death of Buddha, which was aimed specifically at the repudiation of the ten errors which crept into the doctrine in the meantime. It may well be that the Canon was actually drawn up at the third Council of Pataliputra, presided over by Tissa, which met during Aśoka's time, and by then different sects developed on the basis of the master's teaching. Aśoka's edicts protest against the schismatic tendencies of his age. The Ceylonese tradition relates that the Canon composed at the third Council was carried to Ceylon by Mahinda, the pupil of Tissa and the younger brother or the son of Aśoka (according to another tradition), and committed to record under Vattagāmani. See Keith: *Buddhist Philosophy*, pp. 3, 13–32.

Pages 288–89 [344].—Professor Keith thinks that the *Abhidhamma Piṭaka* is the work of Vibhajyavādins. See *Buddhist Philosophy*, pp. 152–3.

Pages 290–91 [346].—Buddhaghoṣa wrote a commentary on the *Dīgha Nikāya* called *Sumaṅgalavilāsinī*.

Pages 296–97 [353].—See Śīlācāra, *Discourses of Gotama, the Buddha*, vol. ii, xxxv and xxxvi.

Page 297 [353], *n.* 18 [1].—See *Cūlasaccaka Sutta*, M.N. (35), i. 237.

Pages 297–98 [354].—We read from the *Jātakas* of cow sacrifices (i. 144) and even human sacrifices (iii. 314).

Pages 299–300 [356].—The *Jātakas* refer frequently to the degeneration of the Brahmin and his eagerness for money. In i. 77, the king's chaplain persuades a young Brahmin, who is opposed to the sacrifice, in these words: 'My son, this means money to us, a great deal of money.' Similarly, when the disciple of the royal priest protests against animal sacrifices, he is told: 'We shall have abundance of dainties to eat; only hold your peace' (iii. 314). The jackal in the *Srigala Jātaka* says, 'The Brahmins are full of greed for wealth' (i. 142; see also iv. 496).

Pages 302–3 [360], *n.* 27 [1].—M.N., i. 265.

Pages 304–5 [362].—Cp. the four truths of Buddhism with the division of medical topics into disease, origin of disease, health and healing. Y.B., ii. 15.

Pages 311–12 [370].—Though the idea of orderly development is contained in the Upaniṣads (see *Kaṭha*), the Buddhist formula of causality emphasises it.

Later Buddhist texts make the important distinction between causes generally (paccaya) and the cause proper (hetu), which is the real producer of the result, the other causes being conditions, coefficients or auxiliaries. The *Paṭṭhāna* classifies conditions under twenty-four heads. The power of one idea to affect another is called, in later Buddhism, satti or ability.

Pages 312–13 [371]., *n.* 55 [1]—See A.N., i. 286; S.N., ii. 25; D.N., ii. 198.

Page 313 [373].—*Mahāvagga*, i. 21; S.N., i. 133; iv. 157 and 399. It is difficult to say definitely when the theory of momentariness (kṣaṇikavāda) was formulated. *Kathāvattu* (viii. 8) seems to be familiar with it. *Ekacitta kṣaṇikā sabbe dhammā*. All things are momentary like mental states. Disappearance is the very essence of existence. Whatever exists perishes at the next moment. Everything comes out of nothing and vanishes into nothing. *Nyāyabindutīkā*, p. 68; see also Ratnakīrti's *Kṣaṇabhaṅgasiddhi.*

Pages 313–14 [374].—On the view of momentariness, causation is neither the evolution of the cause into the effect, nor the creation by the cause of an effect different from itself, but is the necessary succession of determined effects. No real causality can be attributed to the strictly momentary.

Kathāvattu (xvii. 3; xxi. 7 and 8) seems to admit the possibility of acts without fruits. See also xii. 2; xvii. i. In *Milinda*, the arhat is said to suffer pain over which he has no mastery (pp. 134 ff.). It expressly asserts chance (animitta); pp. 180 ff.

Page 316 [376], *n.* 61 [1].—*Proceedings of the Aristotelian Society*, 1919, p. 236.

Pages 319–20 [380].—The doctrine of pratītyasamutpāda or the formula of causation, which has for its first member avidyā (ignorance), lends support to the subjective view of the world.

Pages 320–21 [381].—The doctrine of perception suggested in the early literature (*Majjhima N.*, iii. 242) supports a realistic view of the world.

The Abhidhamma regards the four elements as underived matter and makes ether (ākāśa) a derived one (*Dhammasaṅgaṇi*, M.N., i. 423; ii. 17). We find sometimes mention of six real elements where space and consciousness are added to the ordinary four elements (see *Itivuttaka*, 44, 51 and 73).

Page 321 [382], *n.* 72 [1].—M.N., i. 426.

Page 323 [384], *n.* 77 [1].—See also *Mahanidāna Sutta*, D.N., ii. 66; M.N., i. 138, 300; S.N., iii. 66, iv. 34.

Pages 323–24 [385].—In the *Alagaddūpama Sutta* (M.N., i. 140), Buddha repudiates the pantheistic view which identifies the self with the world.

Pages 324–25 [386].—For the dialogue of Vacchagotta, see *Aggivacchagotta Sutta*, M.N., 72; i. 484–489. See Dahlke, *Buddhism and its Place in the Mental Life of Mankind*, pp. 37 ff.

Pages 325–26 [387].—The Vajjiputtakas adopt the view of pudgala or person over and above the impermanent factors of empiric individuality. They maintain that the person, though implicated in the elements of empiric individuality, is quite distinct from them, even as fire is neither the same as nor different from the burning stick, but is something more than the stick. M. Poussin writes: 'I cannot help thinking that the pudgalavāda is more in harmony with the duḥkhasatya and the law of karman than the nairātmyavāda' (J.R.A.S., 1901, p. 308). Vasubandhu, the Sautrāntika, objects to the view of an uncaused, eternal, changeless self, inactive and inefficient.

Mrs Rhys Davids summarises her views on this question thus: '(1) So far as we can trace it, the earliest teaching we call Buddhist *did not deny the very man, or self.* To see this, we must shed our own standpoint of the eighteenth century in force still with us; we must imagine the power of the word *ātman*, *attan* for an educated Indian of the seventh century BC, when invited by a religious teacher that he would do well to 'seek the *attan*.' Almost it was tantamount to bidding him 'seek God,' or, 'seek the Holy Spirit within yourselves.' This is said to have been one of the earliest addresses of the founder of Buddhism. Vinaya, i. 23 (*Mahāvagga*, 1. 14); *Buddhist Psychology*, pp. 28 ff. It is historically of deep significance. And it is supported by many passages in the four chief books (*Nikayas*) and the *Dhammapada*, where the subject is man's communing with and knowing *himself*—ways, too, of wording which are *not maintained in later teaching.*

'What was denied from the very first was that man, the spirit, the *attan*, could rightly be considered as either body or mind. Were he either or both, then as being things so weak and transient as either of these, he could not will-to-become (as will he did); he could not be chooser of his destiny. This is not to deny that the "man-in-man" is. It is to say: "Form not so wrong a notion of what you really are." But to have said, at that day in India, "You are neither the one nor the other, therefore you are not at all, you, that is, are just only a hundle of both," would have made the new gospel an absurdity, an insult on the intelligence of the hearer.

'(2) Yet even now the Southern Buddhist in Asia and the very latest writers on Buddhism in the West fail to discern the change which spread like a very canker over Buddhism in this matter.

'(3) Is there none who will vindicate this helper of men, noble and wise? Is there none who will understand that he who brings the new message, which we call a religion, to men is one who, whatever he did teach, did not teach certain things because he simply could not, being who he was, so teach. If we have what I have put forward above as a right perspective in contemplating the relation: Mandater of gospel; the mandate or gospel; the mandated (viewed as the two terms of the relation and the bond between them), then shall we be sure that the mandater, in appealing to the very "man-in-man," could not tell the mandated that this "he" was not real, was non-existent. We shall be sure that he would, on the contrary, strengthen man's belief in his reality by enlarging man's knowledge *about himself*. No less sure shall we be, that the mandater could not, in so enlarging man's knowledge, and thereby bringing about a new becoming, a fresh change in man, tell the mandated that there was, in man, that which was unchangeable.'—*Calcutta Review*, November 1927.

Page 325 [387], *n.* 84 [1].—M.N., i. 256.

Page 336 [399], *n.* 102 [3].—See D.N., ii. 62.

Pages 339–40 [403].—According to M.N., i. 190, three factors are involved in perception, objects, senses and the acts of attention.

Pages 340–41 [404].—In the *Dhammasaṅgaṇi*, citta includes the five forms of sense cognition, activity of mind and representative cognition, while zetasika covers the other three aggregates of feelings, perceptions and dispositions.

Pages 342–43 [406].—Buddhaghoṣa regards perception (saṁjñā), intelligence (vijñāna) and intuition (prajñā) as successive steps in a staircase comparable to the different reactions provoked by the sight of precious metals in a child who sees in them coloured objects, in a citizen who recognises their exchange value, and in an expert who knows all about their origin and development. See Buddhaghoṣa on M.N., i. 292.

We have no systematic account of the emotions in the Buddhist Canon. Lobha or attraction or appetite, doṣa or aversion, and moha or delusion are mentioned along with their opposites of alobha, adoṣa, and amoha, disinterestedness, amity and right knowledge. Feelings of friendship or love (metta), sympathy with suffering (karuṇa) and sympathy with happiness or joy (muditā) are also mentioned. The idea of continuity (saṁtati) is found in the Abhidhamma (*Dhammasaṅgaṇi*, 585, 643, 734; *Kathāvattu*, x. 1; xi. 6 and xxi. 4; *Abhidhammattasaṅgaha*, v. 12, 15 and 16). Experiences of objects leave behind their seeds or impressions in the consciousness-continuum, and in the fullness of time the seed ripens and rises into consciousness and we have recognition. This consciousness-series reaches its end only at liberation. This view of continuity is developed by the Sautrāntikas, who regard the person as equivalent to cittasaṁtāna.

Page 345 [409].—Though rebirth is new birth, there is, however, continuity between the consciousness which appears at birth and the consciousness at the time of death (*Milinda*, p. 47). This is why it is often urged that the last thought at the time of death has an essential influence on the form of rebirth.

Pages 345–46 [410].—The individual carries with him at every moment his future (*Milinda*, p. 101). Each moment of our life is charged with the satti or the force of the past, and the present impresses itself on all that follows, perfuming it, as it were, as the term vāsana indicates.

Pages 346–47 [411].—The first moment of the new life is called vijñāna, but it is the third member on the list. Its antecedents are the good and the bad dispositions sticking to it from the beginning. They are called saṁskāras or prenatal forces. Avidyā, the first member, represents the defiling character of ignorance.

Page 346 [411], *n.* 126 [1].—S.N., ii. 10.

Page 347 [411], *n.* 128 [3].—V. 388; A.N., i. 177.

Pages 349–50 [414].—While consciousness is said to pass from life to death, we are not sure whether it is visible in itself or is accompanied by a subtle body.

Page 349 [414], *n.* 131 [1].—D.N., ii. 63.

Page 350 [415].—For the different views about the chain of causation, see Keith: *Budd. Phil.*, pp. 105–111.

Page 352 [417], *n.* 138 [1].—*Dhammapada*, 60.

Pages 355–56 [421].—See *Śīlācāra: Discourses of Gotama, the Buddha*, vol. i, p. 41.

Page 356 [422].—*Milinda* (pp. 95, 117) refers to the doctrine that a man may transfer his merit to another instead of keeping it to himself.

Page 356–57 [423].—Intuition is intimately related to intelligence. See *Majjhima N.*, i. 292 ff.

Page 365 [432], *n.* 165 [4].—D.N., i. 124.

Page 370 [438].—'There is nothing to show that Buddha tried to abolish caste as a social institution. There was no reason why he should do so in so far as his teaching could be enforced that the true Brahmin was the virtuous Brahmin. And within the order, caste did disappear, and there are many instances of low-caste persons being admitted as monks' (E.J. Thomas, *The Life of Buddha*, 128; see also *Udāna*, v. 5). One of Buddha's early disciples is a barber who later became a leader in the Order. In the *Aggañña Suttanta* (D.N., iii. 80 ff.), the claims of the Brahmins to pre-eminence on the ground of birth are contemptuously set aside.

Pages 371–72 [440].—We, however, come across statements, though they are very few, that accidental happenings which do not apparently conform to the law of karma are possible. *Kathāvattu*, x ii. 3; xvi. 8; *Milinda*, pp. 135 ff., 180. These are really exceptions which prove the rule.

See *Majjhima N.*, ii. 104.

Pages 374–75 [443].—Early Buddhism admits the reality of invisible world systems each containing three regions or worlds, those of desire (kāma), of material form (rūpa) and the formless ones (arūpa). The first are the abodes of ghosts (pretas), of demons (asuras), of men and of gods. The second includes the brahmalokas, sixteen in number, distinguished according to the gods freed from desires, who abide there. Those who practice the four meditations and are freed from rebirth remain there until they attain nirvāṇa. The world without form is the dwelling of those who carry out the formless meditations.

Pages 376–77 [446].—The Vaibhāṣikas accept this intermediate state with a quasi-material transporting (ativāhika) body.

Pages 377–78 [447].—The beautiful poetry of the Thera and the Therī gāthas is inspired by ideas of the happiness of nirvāṇa, which is capable of attainment even in this life (see *Dīgha N.*, i. 84).

Pages 378–79 [448].—For Nāgasena there is temporal experience for the individuals who are reborn; for those freed from saṁsāra there is no temporal experience. Time belongs to the stuff of worldly life (see *Milinda*, pp. 50 ff.).

Pages 379–80 [449].—See M.N., i. 487; S.N., iv. 347; iii. 109. Cp. also *Patisambhidāmagga*, i. 143–5.

Pages 380–81 [450].—According to *Milinda* (p. 271), space and nirvāṇa last independently of all forms of causation.

Pages 381–82 [452].—See M.N. (63), i. 427–432.

Page 382 [453], *n.* 208 [1]—*Alagaddūpama Sutta*, M.N., i., 140–1.

Pages 384–85 [455].—In the cosmic evolution, men of great merit secure the rank of gods. Even the appearance of Brahmā with the delusion that he is self-created (svayambhū) is in accordance with this principle.

Page 385 [456], *n.* 214 [1].—See Lakshminarasu, *Essence of Buddhism*, pp. 261–2, 275–6.

Pages 393–94 [465].—See Pratt, *The Pilgrimage of Buddhism*, chap. v.

Pages 399–400 [472].—The Sāṁkhya conception of the constant process of nature is analogous to the Buddhist conception of the world as a perpetual becoming. In both, the law of causality governs the process. The stress on avidyā as the cause of all misery is common to the two systems.

Page 400 [473].—The ideas of the Yoga system had a powerful hold on early Buddhism. Ālārakālāma and Uddaka, two teachers of Buddha, were adepts in the practice of Yoga. It is quite possible and very probable that Buddha borrowed his ideas of the discipline of mind from the Yoga system, as the use of the words citta (thought), nirodha (suppression) suggests. The Yoga makes ignorance the cause of misery and regards it as a kleśa or defilement which is at the root of all others. The four stages of samādhi or concentration may have been the original of the Buddhist view of the four ordinary meditations (Y.S.I., 17). The four brahmavihāras of friendship, sympathy with sorrow, sympathy with happiness and indifference have also their parallel in the Yoga system (Y.S.I., 33). It is not difficult to trace the chain of causation to the Yoga philosophy (iv. 11). See also Stcherbatsky: *The Conception of Buddhist Nirvāna*, pp. 2 ff.

Page 402 [476].—See also Keith: *Buddhist Philosophy*.

CHAPTER VIII

Pages 405–6 [480].—The conception of 'trimūrti' is often regarded as of a much later date. See Hopkins: *The Great Epic*, pp. 46, 184. We can trace it, however, to the *Maitri Up.*, iv and v, though the part of the Upaniṣad in which it occurs is regarded as a late addition.

Pages 408–9 [483].—The passage in which Buddha is mentioned in the *Rāmāyaṇa* is said to be an interpolation.

Pages 414–15 [490].—In the first two stages of the development of the Epic, Viṣṇu with his Vedic ancestry, Nārāyaṇa, the cosmic god controlling the whole evolution of the universe, Vāsudeva, the saviour god, and Kṛṣṇa, the friend and comforter, meet and coalesce. See *Śānti P.*, 341. 20–6. 342. 129.

Page 416 [492], *n.* 46 [2].—'Āpo nārā iti proktā āpo vai narasūnavaḥ ayanam tasyatāḥ pūrvam tena nārāyaṇa smṛtaḥ.'

Pages 420–21 [496].—Dr Jha quotes an ingenious suggestion that 'the system (pañcarātra) is so called by reason of the fact that it was promulgated for the purpose of meeting the religious cravings of men during the five days the Vedas remained with the demon from whom they were rescued by Viṣṇu before the recreation of the world after pralaya' (*Hindustan Review*, January 1924, p. 219).

Page 428 [504], *n.* 99 [5].—Cakṣuḥ paṣyati rūpāṇi manasā na cakṣuṣā.

Page 428 [505], *n.* 103 [3].—Duḥkhād udvijate sarvas sarvasya sukham īpsitam.

Page 431 [508], *n.* 133 [10].—Pāpam karma kṛtam kiñcid yadi tasmin na dṛśyate,
Nrpate tasya putreśu pautreṣvapi ca naptṛṣu.

Pages 433–34 [511].—Time and nature are not peculiarly Buddhistic. They belong to the early naturalistic speculations as well. See *Atharva-Veda*, xix. 53, where time is deified.

CHAPTER IX

Page 452 [531], *n*.39 [1].—Ānandagiri, who refers to a Vṛttikāra twice in his *Ṭīkā*, S.B.G. (pp. 6 and 27 of the Ānandāśrama ed.), does not identify him with Bodhāyana.

Page 459 [538], *n*.60 [1].—See also R.V., x. 129.

Pages 462–63 [542].—Lālane tāḍane mātur nākāruṇyam yathā'rbhake
Tadvad eva maheśasya niyantur guṇadośayoh.

Pages 464–65 [544].—*Bhāgavata*, i. 3. 2. 8.

Page 474 [555] *n.* [115]—Bradley, *Appearance and Reality*, pp. 5–6.

Pages 483–84 [565].—'The worship of the Blessed One does not express itself in mere ecstasy. In it the whole of one's being is engaged. "He is of right purpose." In this rightness of purpose there is the guarantee of righteousness in deed' (McKenzie, *Hindu Ethics*, p. 131).

Pages 487–88 [569].—Cp. Nivṛttir api mūḍhasya pravṛttir upajāyate
Pravṛttir api dhīrasya nivṛtti-phalabhāginī.

Pages 490–91 [572].—See M.B., *Śānti P.*, 320. 36 and 38.

Page 494 [576].—See B.G., v. 23–5.

CHAPTER X

Pages 506–7 [590].—In the Mahāyāna, Buddha loses his human character and is endowed with superhuman powers. The *Jātakas* of the Hīnayāna give place to the Avadānas or the glorious achievements of Buddha and his followers.

Pages 507–8 [592].—In the *Mahāyānasaṁparigrahaśāstra*, Asaṅga enumerates seven points in which the Mahāyāna may be regarded as superior to the Śrāvakayāna. 'The Mahāyāna is comprehensive; whatever has been taught by Buddha, not by Śākyamuni in one life alone, is accepted; nay, more, as we have seen, whatever is well said, is to be deemed the word of a Buddha. Secondly, the Mahāyāna aims at general salvation, not at individual release, thus excelling in love for all created things. Thirdly, the Mahāyāna is intellectually wider in range than the Hīnayāna; the latter denies the reality of the self, the former goes so far as to deny all phenomenal reality whatever. Fourthly, the Mahāyāna inculcates spiritual energy; to seek swift release for oneself is not its aim as it is that of the Śrāvaka. Fifthly, the Mahāyāna is skilled in the manifold means (upāya) to lead men to salvation; it is unwearied in their varied application. Moreover, it leads to a far higher ideal; the adept aims to become not a mere saint but a Buddha in his complete perfection. Lastly, when an adept becomes a Buddha, he has the infinite power of manifesting himself throughout the universe in a body of bliss.' See Suzuki: *Mahāyāna Buddhism*, ch. ii.

Pages 509–10 [594].—Vasubandhu says that the transitoriness of existence and the eternity of nirvāṇa are both implied by the reality of the absolute.

Pages 512–13 [597].—In the Hīnayāna, the physical body of the Buddha is distinguished from the body of the law which each man has to realise for himself. Later in the *Divyāvadāna* (pp. 19 ff.; see *Dīgha N.*, iii. 84), we find the idea that the material body of the Buddha is the body, while his soul is the law. The true nature or soul of Buddha is the intuition (prajñā) or enlightenment (bodhi) attained by him. When expressed in metaphysical terms, it is the ultimate reality which underlies the phenomenal universe. While this reality belongs to every Buddha, each Buddha is said to have at the same time a dharmakāya of his own. The dharmakāya is identified with the Tathāgata, or primitive undifferentiated reality, or the womb of the Tathāgata, or the source of every individual being (*Laṁkāvatāra*, p. 80). Each Buddha is conceived as possessing a body of ineffable brilliance which is called saṁbhogakāya. The relation of saṁbhogakāya to dharmakāya is explained by Candrakīrti (*Mādhyamakāvatāra*, iii. 12). Those equipped with wisdom (jñāna), as the Buddhas, reach dharmakāya, while those equipped with merit (puṇya), as the Bodhisattvas, reach saṁbhogakāya. One cannot, however, be sure of this, since the Mahāyāna literature gives visible forms to Amitābha and Śākyamuni.

Page 512 [597] *n.*33 [1].—See *Sūtrālaṁkāra*, ix. 77, and *Kāraṇḍavyūha*. There is no absolute being possible even for a Buddha.

Page 513–14 [598].—'Those who worship the Bodhisattvas and read the *Mahāyāna Sūtras* are called the Mahāyānists (*I-Tsing*: Takakusu's E.T., p. 14).

The conception of law as the body of the Buddha is suggested in the Canon. The Sautrāntikas seem to accept a body of bliss, one of the three kāyas.

Pages 514–15 [599].—The conception of the absolute realising itself in Buddhas and Bodhisattvas is of great religious value. It shows how the absolute is co-operating with the individual to secure for him the bliss of deliverance.

Page 515 [600].—The radiant vijñāna transforms itself into active intellect and develops into the world of matter and consciousness.

Pages 515–16 [601].—See also *Mahāvastu*.

Pages 516–17 [602].—The Bodhisattva, out of compassion, is prepared to face the tortures of hell (*Bodhicaryāvatāra*, vi. 120; *Śikṣāsamuccaya*, p. 167). The sufferings of the Bodhisattvas are not the penalties of past crimes, but opportunities for the exercise of their perfections (*Bodhicaryāvatāra*, vi. 106). To the Bodhisattvas we owe homage and adoration. By confessing our sins to them we merit their forgiveness (ibid., vi. 119. 122. 124; cp. also *Śikṣāsamuccaya*, pp. 160 ff.). By the transfer of one's merit, one can please the Bodhisattvas (*Bodhicaryāvatāra* v. 85; *Śikṣāsamuccaya*, p. 127). Śāntideva is alive to the folly of the man who hands over his body to the wild beasts for food, when he could confer on others the precious gift of the knowledge of the true faith (*Śikṣāsamuccaya*, pp. 119 and 34 ff.; *Bodhicaryāvatāra*, v. 86 ff.; *Bodhisattvabhūmi*, i. ix). There is no disgust with life. The rigours of monasticism are relaxed, and the householder is regarded as being in a favourable position for the attainment of Buddhahood. See Suzuki: *Mahāyāna Buddhism*, chap. xii.

Pages 517–18 [603].—We cannot say how enlightenment arises. 'The ancient alone knoweth the incomprehensible faith of action in that he doth lead to release men, even when they have abandoned thought of enlightenment' (*Bodhicaryāvatāra*, iv. 27).

Page 519 [604], *n.* 52 [3].—Rāgadveṣamohakṣayāt parinirvāṇam.

Pages 519–20 [605].—*Vimalakīrti Sūtra* gives a positive account of nirvāṇa. It admits the possibility of the growth of insight in the midst of life with all its distractions. Nirvāṇa is saṁsāra, and we must try to attain nirvāṇa in and through life and not through abstention from its activities. According to Asaṇga's *Mahāyānasaṁparigrahaśāstra*, the Buddha, though free from attachment and defilement, is yet full of compassion for the departed souls who are to be rescued by him.

Page 524 [610].—See also K.J. Saunders, *Epochs in Buddhist History;* Sir Charles Eliot: *Hinduism and Buddhism*; J.B. Pratt, *The Pilgrimage of Buddhism.*

CHAPTER XI

Page 525, 611 *n.*1 [1].—See Aśoka's *Bhābrū edict* and *Divyāvadāna*, p. 272. In *Anguttara N.* (iv. 163), Buddha is compared to a granary whence men bring every good word. See Vincent Smith: *Aśoka*, p. 154.

Pages 526–27 [613].—On Sarvāstivāda or the view that everything exists, see Stcherbatsky's *The Central Conception of Buddhism.* Sarvāstivāda was an ancient school of Buddhism of which the Vaibhāṣika system is a continuation.

Page 527 [613], *n.*4 [1].—Dhamatrāta is the author of *Udānavarga* and *Saṁyuktābhidha-rmahṛdayaśāstra.* M.M. Haraprasād Śāstri says that 'Ārya-deva hails from Kañci' (*Indian Historical Quarterly*, 1925, p. 111).

Pages 528–29 [615].—The self or living being is not an ultimate fact, while the real elements (dharmas) are. Nairātmya or soullessness is the negative way of expressing the existence of ultimate reality (dharmatā); only what we call the soul is not that. Cp. Yaśomitra on *Abhidharmakośa*, ix. Pravacanadharmatā punar atra nairātmyam buddhānuśāsanī vā. Stcherbatsky says: 'Buddhism never denied the existence of a personality or a soul, in the empirical sense; it only maintained that it was no ultimate reality (not a dharma)' (see *The Central Conception of Buddhism*, pp. 25–26).

'The elements had four salient features: (1) they were not substance—this refers to all the seventy-five elements, whether eternal or impermanent; (2) they had no duration—this refers only to the seventy-two impermanent elements of phenomenal existence; (3) they were unrest—this refers only to one part of the latter class, that which roughly corresponds to the ordinary man as opposed to the purified condition of the elements of a saint (ārya); (4) and their unrest had its end in final deliverance. Speaking technically: (1) all dharmas are anātman, (2) all saṁskṛta dharmas are anitya, (3) all sāśrava dharmas are duḥkha, and (4) their nirvāṇa alone in śānta. An element is non-substantial, it is evanescent, it is in a beginningless state of commotion, and its final suppression is the only balm.'

Regarding the relation of the permanent elements to their manifestations, the *Vibhāṣa* seems to suggest four different views. Dharmatrāta maintains unity of substance (dravya) along with change in existence (bhāva). The essence remains unchanged while the existence alters as when milk changes into curds. This view seems to be influenced by the Sāṁkhya theory. Ghoṣa assumes that elements, though existent in the past, present and future, change their aspect (lakṣaṇa) at different times. This view is not generally accepted, as it implies the co-existence of the different aspects at the same time. Buddhadeva thinks that the past, the present and the future are contingent on one another, and the same entity may be described as past, present or future in accordance with its relation to the preceding or succeeding moment, even as a woman may be regarded as mother, wife or daughter. This view does not find acceptance, as it is said to involve a confusion of the three periods of time. Vasumitra advocates a change of condition (avasthā), i.e. of efficiency in the present and non-efficiency in the past and the future. When an entity has performed its function and has ceased to act, it is past; when it is producing it, it is present; when it has not yet produced it, it is future. There is real existence in all the three states. The past is real, for were it not so, it could not be the object of knowledge, nor could it determine the present. The Vaibhāṣikas generally accept the view of Vasumitra. The Vibhajyavādins adopt the view that the present elements and those among the past which have not yet produced their function are existent, while the future elements and those of the past which have produced their function are non-existent. See Stcherbatsky, *The Central Conception of Buddhism*, p. 46, and Appendix 1; Keith, *Budd. Phil.*, pp. 104–5.

Pages 529–30 [616].—The Sarvāstivāda holds that there are fourteen kinds of atoms answering to the five sense-organs, the five sense-objects and the four mahābhūtas. These atoms are not eternal like those of the Vaiśeṣikas or the Jainas. In consistency with the doctrine of momentariness (kṣaṇikavāda), they are said to spring into being from time to time and lapse into non-being. Even the paramāṇus, which are said to sustain the atoms, are not permanent, since they are subject to the fourfold process of birth, continuance, decay and destruction.

The Sarvāstivāda admits the existence of what is called the avijñaptirūpa or unmanifested matter. The Buddhist theory requires that every physical act, word or thought should have some corresponding result. Every act modifies the nature and position of the molecules. Even where it does not do so visibly, it must do so invisibly, for it is impossible that an action can have no result. While the Sarvāstivādins admitted the reality of avijñaptirūpa, they were not decided about its nature. Harivarman, in his *Sattvasiddhi*, makes out that it is neither physical nor mental and belongs to cittaviprayukta dharmas. As the Sarvāstivādins claim that all character is ultimately material, avijñaptirūpa is also a rūpa dharma.

Page 529 [616], *n.* 9 [1].—The Caitta dharmas are distinct from citta and not mere phases of it as in the Yogācāra. The later Sthaviravādins gave a relative unity to citta and caitasika dharmas where citta is compared to a sphere and caitasikas to sections of it. The caitasikas are elements out of which mental complexes are made. 'Just as the four mahābhūtas and the five sense-object atoms may combine in an infinite number of ways to form the complex external world around us, so may the various caitasikas be compounded in an infinite number of ways, ranging from the simple thoughts and desires of a child to the most abstruse metaphysical inference' (McGovern: *Buddhist Phil.*, p. 138). The caitasikas are broadly distinguished into (1) general mental properties which are neither meritorious nor demeritorious, (2) meritorious and (3) demeritorious. While the Sthaviravādins have only these three, the Sarvāstivādins and the Yogācāras add a fourth indeterminate.

Pages 530–31 [617].—See *Abhidharmakośa*, iv. 1b; also Stcherbatsky, *The Conception of Buddhist Nirvāṇa*, pp. 27–29.

Pages 531–32 [618].—'Pratisaṁkhyā means conscious deliberation and is a type of intelligence, since it deliberates upon each of the four noble truths. The attainment of cessation or nirodha by means of the power of deliberation is therefore called pratisaṁkhyānirodha, just as a cart pulled by bullocks is called a bullock-cart by the elimination of the middle term' (*Abhidharmakośa*, i. 3b; McGovern, *Buddhist Phil.*, p. 111).

The Sarvāstivādins 'make a difference between the essence and the manifestations of the dharmas. At the time of nirvāṇa, the manifestations have ceased for ever, and there will be no rebirth, but this essence remains. It is nevertheless a kind of entity where there is no consciousness' (Stcherbatsky, *The Central Conception of Buddhism*, p. 53).

See *Abhidharmakośa*, iii. 30. where a distinction is made between the perception of 'blue' and the judgment 'this is blue.'

Page 532 [619].—The *Abhidharmakośa* insists on the importance of volition (see iv). The accidental destruction of a human being when aiming at a pumpkin is no murder. This view is perhaps intended against the Jaina argument that a man who slays, however unwittingly, is guilty of murder, even as one who touches fire, however unknowingly, is burned. The *Abhidharmakośa* distinguishes the psychological from the physical effect of action. A volition leaves only an impression (vāsana) on the mental series, while the bodily acts produce something quasi-material, called by the scholastics, avijñapti, which persists and develops without any consciousness on the part of the individual. The mechanism of rebirth is more clearly conceived. The last consciousness of life determines the new birth to be achieved. Rebirth or consciousness of conception (pratisaṁdhivijñāna) is a continuation of the last consciousness before death. The last consciousness of the dying man creates for itself the necessary body out of unorganised matter.

Page 532 [619], *n.* 16 [1].—The three are one and the same thing, functioning in different ways. 'The Buddhists, at least the Sarvāstivādins and the Sthaviravādins, agree that there is only a difference in terminology, and that the thing spoken of is the same' (McGovern, *Buddhist Phil.*, p. 132.)

Pages 533–34 [621].—The Sautrāntikas dispute the Vaibhāṣika belief in the existence of permanent substances persisting through all time. They contend that, if the past is to be regarded as real on the ground that it exercises efficiency, it cannot be distinguished from the present. It is idle to argue that we cannot know non-existent entities. Entities which are actually non-efficient are also known. To distinguish between an entity and its efficiency is untenable, for it is difficult to know why an entity suddenly assumes active efficiency. The Sautrāntikas maintain that all entities are momentary, suddenly come into being, exist for a moment and pass out into non-existence. Their existence and efficiency are one. It follows that 'things' are mere names for certain momentary colours, tastes, etc., fictitiously unified under a label. The self is also a designation for a series of momentary psychic happenings which are in causal relation. Memory requires no self but only an earlier experience. It arises when the suitable conditions of attention, freedom from pain and the like are present. The last moment of the consciousness series determines the new life. It is not clear whether the seed of consciousness has any subtle matter accompanying it into a new body or not. See Keith: *Budd. Phil.*, p. 166.

'The Sautrāntikas are credited with three different views of the nature of the perception of an object. (1) All its characteristics are represented in thought form and so apprehended; (2) thought form is of the total actual presentation only, e.g. of variegated colour as such; (3) all aspects of the object are presented in thought, but it synthesises them in one view, e.g. the different colours are made one' (ibid., 162 n.).

Pages 534–35 [622].—According to the *Abhidharmakośa*, the phenomenon of knowledge is resolved into a simultaneous appearance of a number of elements. There is no question of contact, influence or interrelation. A movement of colour (rūpa), a movement of the visual sense (cakṣuḥ), a movement of pure consciousness (citta) arise simultaneously in close contiguity and constitute the sensation (sparśa) or colour. The element of consciousness always appears, supported by an object (viṣaya) and a receptive organ (indriya). The consciousness is said to grasp the object, since there is between consciousness and the object a special relation called sārūpya or co-ordination. The consciousness apprehends the colour and not the visual sense. As a matter of fact, what happens is evanescent flashings of consciousness. 'Consciousness apprehends in the way in which a light moves. The light of a lamp is a common metaphorical designation for an uninterrupted production of a series of flashing flames. When this production changes its place, we say that the light has moved. Similarly, consciousness is a conventional name for a chain of conscious moments. When it changes its place (i.e. appears in consideration with another objective element), we say that it apprehends that object' (*Abhidharmakośa*, ix; Stcherbatsky, p. 57).

Page 535 [622], *n.* 22 [1].—*Abhidhammatthasaṅgaha* gives the four causes as hetu which produces the thing, the ālambana or the support which produces the thought and its sequel, samanantara or the immediately contiguous cause which allows in the stream of thought the new presentation, and the adhipati, that on whose existence the other depends. See Keith, *Budd. Ph.*, b. 177.

Svalakṣaṇa means the bare particular.

Pages 535–36 [623].—The Sautrāntikas gave up the idea of self-consciousness, as the consciousness of the preceding moment by the succeeding consciousness not only lights the objects but lights itself, even as the lamp lights not only the room but itself. All consciousness is self-consciousness. For the Sautrāntikas, the perception of external things is only indirect. Things are known because consciousness takes, through the medium of the sense organism, the form of the object and is also conscious of itself. We recognise the externality of objects on account of third temporary and accidental character, which shows that they are not parts of consciousness itself.

Page 535 [623], *n.* 23 [1].—See also Ui: *The Vaiśeṣika Philosophy*, pp. 26–28.

Page 536 [623], *n.* 26 [4].—*Abhidharmakośavyākhyā*, vii.

Page 536 [624], *n.* 27 [1].—Keith assigns Dignāga to about AD 400. See his *Budd. Phil.*, p. 305.

Vasubandhu's *Vijñaptimātratātriṁśat kārikā* had nearly ten commentaries on it. Dharmapāla, the teacher of Sīlabhadra who was the teacher of Yuan Chwang, wrote *Vijñaptimātratāsiddhiśāstra*. He upholds subjective idealism in epistemology and refutes all realism.

Pages 536–37 [625].—To accept the view of Sarvāstivāda that the world is the result of the changing combination of the seventy-five unchanging elements is to go against the central truth of impermanence.

Pages 542–43 [631].—Objects arise in our consciousness as the result of our past experience. They seem to be given, while they are the creation of our thought. The external world is the product of our thought to which we give names and ideas (nāmasaṁjñāvyavahāra). See *Laṁkāvatāra sūtra*, p. 85.

Even the internal distinctions of subject, object and knowledge are not real. They are the results of the defilement of thought, though we cannot trace the beginning of this defilement. The Ālaya has no origin, duration or destruction. Particular intellectual movements stand to it as the waves to the sea.

Page 549 [639], *n.* 52 [1].—The Yogācāras admit eight kinds of vijñāna, the five answering to the five material sense-organs, the sixth manovijñāna of a more general character, exercising the functions of memory and judgment, the seventh kliṣṭamanovijñāna or literally soiled mind-consciousness. McGovern says regarding it: 'Whereas manovijñāna carries on the ordinary process of reasoning, it deals with ideas more or less as they come, without consciously or continuously distinguishing between that which appertains to the self and that which appears to the non-self. This continual distinction is the work of the seventh vijñāna, which, according to the Yogācāras, functions even when a man is asleep, or is otherwise unconscious. It is the basis of the constant tendency towards the ātmans theory, for it falsely considers the ālayavijñāna to be a real and permanent ego entity, although in reality it is in a constant state of flux' (*Buddhist Phil.*, p. 134). The same writer speaks of the triple function of the ālayavijñāna. 'The first we can call the positive, because it stores up the seeds of all other vijñānas. The second we can call the negative, because it receives the influence of all the other phenomenal vijñānas. The third is this vijñāna considered as the object of false belief, for the seventh vijñāna constantly considers that this ever-changing ālayavijñāna is an eternal ego entity' (p. 135). The Yogācāras are inclined to call the sixth vijñāna, the seventh manas and the eighth citta.

Page 550 [640], *n.* 53 [1].—See McGovern, *Buddhist Phil.*, p. 113.

Pages 553–54 [643].—Kern is of opinion that Buddhism is from the outset a system of idealistic nihilism. See M.N., i. 4, 134, 297 and 329; ii. 261; iii. 246.

Pages 563–64 [655].—When Nāgārjuna denies Buddha, it is the Hīnayāna view of Buddha conceived as the ultimate goal of the world's progress that he rejects and not the Buddha who is above all empirical determinations. See Candrakīrti's *M. Vṛtti*, 432 ff.

Page 570 [662].—The illusionist tendencies are found developed in Buddhapālita and Candrakīrti and in a manner in Śāntideva, while the more reasonable view is found in Bhavaviveka's exposition of Nāgārjuna's views.

Page 572 [664], *n.* 110 [2].—Cp. also.

Prabhāśūnyam manaśśūnyam buddhiśūnyam nirāmayam,
Sarvaśūnyam nirābhāsam samādhis tasya lakṣaṇam.

Pages 575–76 [668].—See Kern, *Manual of Indian Buddhism*, p. 126.

Page 576 [669].—See also Keith, *Buddhist Philosophy*. McGovern, *A Manual of Buddhist Philosophy*. Stcherbatsky: *The Central Conception of Buddhism; The Conception of Buddhist Nirvāṇa*; Pratt, *The Pilgrimage of Buddhism*, chap. xii.

Index